Expanded edition

THE COMPLETE CROSSWORD COMPANION

Jeremy Howard-Williams

Wordsworth Editions

Contents

Introduction

History

Playing with words has captured man's imagination since shortly after he learned to write; indeed, it has been an integral part of the art of calligraphy, as can be traced in the development of Coptic hieroglyphs in ancient Egypt. From a later period, the poet Samonicus, who lived during the second century A.D., has left a record of the use of the word Abracadabra as a charm against agues and fevers. Written on parchment in a triangular form, the amulet was then folded into a cross and hung round the sufferer's neck for nine days before being cast into a stream:

ABRACADABRA
BRACADABR
RACADAB
ACADA
CAD
A

It will be noted that it reads round the outside as well as across the top (and through the middle). Not surprisingly, the amulet was eventually found to be ineffective, so that the word came to imply contempt for useless mumbo-jumbo.

Simple squares, where across and down words read the same, have been around for at least the same length of time; in some cases, the square will also read backwards:

AMOR
MARO
ORAM
ROMA

The Crossword Proper

It was not until 1913, however, that one Arthur Wynne suggested to
the New York *Sunday World* that the paper should adopt a novel
form of diversion for its readers. The first true crossword was
diamond-shaped, and its inventor called it a *Word Cross*. The idea
took the better part of ten years to travel to England, but in August
1982, G. E. Cousins was to have a letter published in the *Daily
Telegraph*, wherein he commented on the diamond jubilee of the
crossword in the UK. It seems that in March 1922 he was a junior
reporter in august company, listening with some respect as his
superiors discussed the new craze. The judgement of his boss was
that it would be 'a nine days' wonder'. This somewhat sweeping
condemnation was supported by contemporary medical opinion,
which held that the dazzling patterns could eventually lead to
neuroses and eye trouble; it said nothing about brain fatigue.

Two years later, however, a book of crossword puzzles was
published, and the habit took a firm hold in this country. It is,
perhaps, interesting to look back at some of the clues and answers
from the novelty's first appearance in the *Daily Telegraph* (30 July
1925):

Traveller's haven (3)	INN
Beverage (4)	BEER
Consider (4)	DEEM
A people with unalterable laws (5)	MEDES
The germ of a building (4)	PLAN

The last two were about the only clues to go any further than a
dictionary definition. Since those days, the cult has developed to the
point where two distinct forms have emerged. The first of these
requires some etymology and a store of synonyms, together with a
grounding in general knowledge (or else a dictionary and a good
encyclopaedia); the second needs a more convoluted mind, where
homonyms are more important than synonyms, and where clues
have to be dissected, examined, twisted and even repunctuated. The
latter, more cryptic, form took a number of years to appear, and was
eventually developed by some of the more serious newspapers, while

the popular tabloids continued to pursue the more direct line, which became known as the 'quick' crossword. During the Second World War the Germans even turned the quick crossword into a weapon: in 1944 they literally fired it at Britain by means of the V1 flying bomb as a crude form of propaganda. (**He is your enemy too** (9) gave BOLSHEVIK; **This is the beginning of a German victory** (2) was VI. The black squares of the grid were in the shape VI.) Not many of them reached the general public.

In this *Companion* we are concerned with both forms. For the quick puzzler there are lists of synonyms for many of the more popular clue words, so that the book acts as a kind of thesaurus; there are also a lot of groups of words listed either alphabetically (where the number is small enough to allow easy reference), or else broken down into groups each containing 3, 4, 5, 6 etc letters. For instance, **ANTELOPE** is a word which often appears in clues, and there are over 40 breeds listed; there are 2 dozen words meaning **SALMON**; under **CASTLE** we find not only a dozen words connected with military architecture (bailey, motte, rampart etc), but also the names of more than 350 castles in the UK, broken down into groups of 3-lettered names, 4, 5, 6, up to 9 letters, and then those with 10 or more.

These classifications are, of course, also of use to the cryptic puzzler, but he or she is more likely to need help in lateral thinking. For instance **ARROW** not only lists synonyms, but also suggests that *bowman* might be a useful line of enquiry, under which we read of *fiddler* and *cellist*, each with its own entry; we also see that **ARROW** is a kind of *grass* (which has a couple of dozen entries of its own). Besides its connection with love, **COURTED** suggests the law courts (*judged*, *sued*) and *tennis* (which in turn lists the more popular venues, together with some terms from real tennis). Both **GOLD** and **SHOWER** refer the reader to *Danae* (who was visited by Zeus in a shower of gold when he fathered Perseus); incidentally **SHOWER** also gives *demonstrator* and *exhibitor* in case the puzzler should forget (and how about *anaesthetic* under **NUMBER**? Work it out). The Greek and Roman gods, so beloved of puzzle setters, receive full coverage.

The Art of the Setter

The Crossword Editor of *The Times* is on record (31 December 1981) as warning would-be solvers to distrust every word in a clue, because the puzzle setter's aim is to say one thing while meaning another.

Once the ruthless nature of the setter has been established, the solver is half-way towards success. The master-craftsman of the setting world is devious, inventive, clever, impudent, and extremely cunning, but always scrupulously fair (well, nearly always). An average cryptic clue will usually have two indications or pointers to its solution, both twisted and often deliberately mingled. If the attention of the solver can be directed on to a false trail, then the setter will consider that he has won a partial victory. To this end he will adopt many strategems but, in the final analysis, the solver should be able to tip his hat and say 'Oh, I see; well done', even if, once the answer is known, he or she adds 'What a nerve!'

Asterisks and Brackets

Before embarking on explanations and examples of different forms of cryptic clue and answer, it should be pointed out that the asterisk is used throughout this *Companion* to indicate where a letter has been omitted or two words joined to form one. Brackets in an answer show where a letter or word has been inserted. This is purely a mechanical aid to understanding how an answer is reached, and the solver should read such words as though the intruders were not there. Thus **It is forbidden to have a girl in a bed** (6) = B(ANN)ED, should be read as BANNED; in **The boy loses some time** (3) = TIM*, the asterisk should be ignored.

Anagrams
In the more esoteric puzzles, a clue will not be so brash as to say baldly *Anag*; the solver will be left to deduce, not only that an anagram is intended, but also which words form the letters to be shuffled. It is not too much to say that ten per cent of all adjectives, verbs and adverbs, and many nouns, can be interpreted as intending an anagram, even if the reasoning is sometimes rather cryptic.

Words such as 'stew', 'badly', 'twisted' and 'replaced' are fairly easy indicators, while 'grim', 'wry' and 'horrible' are, perhaps, less obvious. An example is: **Wrong vote blocks the decision** (4) = VETO; it will be seen that there are the requisite two indicators to the solution, which is reached by the anagram of **vote** (**wrongly** written) forming an answer meaning something which **blocks a decision**.

To help identify some of the many indications that letters should be shuffled, use of the word *Anag* in this *Companion* implies that an entry may intend this interpretation. It should be noted, however, that 'anagram' is taken to mean any rearrangement of letters, even if in their new form they do not make a proper word in themselves. Thus, **Escaping, the wayward nun is caught by the gang** (7) = R(UNN)ING; the word **nun** is reordered to UNN and placed in, or **caught by**, a synonym for **gang**, which is RING, to give the answer which means **escaping**. This may be termed a loose anagram of **nun** and is restricted to one which forms only part of the solution. **WAYWARD** would have *Anag* written after it if it were an entry in the *Companion*; we may take the word 'wrong' as another example, and a typical clue might read **The Redcap has gone wrong, and gets into hot water**. This could give the solution SP*ONGE, where SP stands for 'service policeman' (slang = **Redcap**) and ONGE is a loose anagram of **gone**; a sponge is often used in **hot water**. Note that **wrong** here could also refer to **Redcap**, whose anag might give us CARPED – but this does not conform with the second half of the clue which, to justify such an interpretation, would have to read something like **The Redcap has gone wrong and found fault**. See also **SCRAMBLED EGG** in the main text, which can give GGE as a cryptic answer. This, of course, is not a word in itself, but it might be used in the make-up of a solution, as in **The king's got scrambled egg covering the roe – quite properly sent back** = G*EOR*GE (GGE is **scrambled egg** and it is round, or **covering**, EOR which is **roe** backwards without any other alteration – **quite properly sent back**. The whole is the name of a **king**). The reader is referred to **Anag** in the main text for further information.

Hidden Word
There are plenty of underhand ways of showing that the answer is formed by letters which appear consecutively in the clue, even though they may form parts of two or more words in that clue.

'Holds', 'contains' and 'part of' are self-evident indications; 'betrays', 'we see', 'carries' and 'is evident' are less direct: **To go unceremoniously carries weight** (5) = O*UNCE.

Sometimes the clue has to be modified before the word can be made. **The best tray à la carte, without a good man, will yield treachery** (8) = BE*TRAY*A*L. This involves removing the letters **st** from the second word (so that it is without a saint, or **good man**) before running the next six letters on to it, to give (or **yield**) a synonym for **treachery**. See entry **Hidden word** for further discussion.

Punctuation

It is considered fair play to change punctuation of a clue so that a different meaning is conveyed. Thus, **Gad! Wall-joint gets the bird** (7) = GAD*WALL (which is a duck), because it should be read **Gad/wall joint, gets the bird**. Alternatively, **Thanks to the French, a sacked part of Old England** (6) should be read **Thanks (to the French), a; sacked part of old England**, which gives us MERCI*A.

A slightly more abstruse misuse of punctuation is shown by the clue **Forty-nine out for a duck** (3, 5). This should be read as **Forty. Nine out for a duck**, to give TWO SCORE (implying not only the quantity 40, but also that only two batsmen scored any runs from a cricket team of eleven, so that nine of them made nought). Note that there are still two pointers to the solution.

The reader should beware how punctuation is rearranged. Take an innocent short part-clue such as **I left in South Africa**. This can be read in four ways, depending where the comma is mentally placed (some of the results of this example are a bit unwieldy, but it should be remembered that this is a hypothetical example to demonstrate a principle).

1. **I, left in South Africa** requires the letter I to be written, followed by the letter L for **left** placed in an abbreviation for **South Africa** = I*S(L)A.
2. **I left, in South Africa** requires letters for I and **left** put into the abbreviation for **South Africa** = S(I*L)A.
3. **I left in, South Africa** requires the letter i to leave the word **in**, and to be followed by SA = N*SA.
4. **I left in south, Africa** requires the letters I and L to be placed in

an abbreviation for **south**, and followed by one for **Africa** = S(I*L)O*AF ('so' being an abbreviation for south, and 'Af' one for Africa).

See also the entry **Question Mark** in the main text.

Split Words

If the foregoing is enough to show that many switches can be played within a clue to give a wide range of interpretation, the following will demonstrate how the answer itself has sometimes to be read in different ways in order to satisfy both halves of the clue. **Play some role in dismantling** (4, 5) provides the usual two pointers, and from the first half we get TAKE A PART (4, 1, 4); if this is read as TAKE APART (4, 5), it becomes **dismantling**. Similarly, we may have **Piece on board or back all right** (4) to give ROOK, which is a castle on a chess board, and can also be read as **or back** (RO) plus **all right** (OK).

A word may also be split and then tampered with. **Influence me to replace the head of Victoria, say** (7) should be started with a close look at **say** which, in this case, means 'for instance'. Victoria is often given as an instance of a railway station, a queen or an empress; here 'me' or 'I' should replace her 'head' or first letter. ME*TATION, I*TATION, ME*UEEN and I*UEEN get us nowhere, but ME*MPRESS or I*MPRESS look better, for the latter rings the bell with a word which also means **influence**.

Pronunciation

Another weapon in the setter's armoury is brainwashing. If he can persuade the solver that a particular (wrong) meaning should be given to a clue, he will go happily on his way, satisfied that he has fairly misled his opponent (for be under no illusions – solver and setter are deadly enemies in this war of words). **Draw from this water-tower** (3) encourages a train of thought which conjures up a large tank of water on top of a pillar or column, with someone drawing water from it by means of a pipe with a tap. In fact, the water-tower refers to something which is water-borne and pulls or **tows**; the answer is TUG. Another common deception is use of the word 'flower', intended to make the solver think of daffodils and roses whereas, pronounced in a different way, it can also mean something which 'flows' – usually a river. Thus, **Flower of England** (4) is designed to conjure up the word ROSE, and the spectre of the setter will chortle with glee if this is written in; to be fair, the usual secondary clue should help identify the answer and, in this case, it might be **A single flower of England** (4), which would give A*RUN (referring to a single run at cricket, and to the river Arun).

Note how the mind is programmed to think along the wrong lines, and look for a pronunciation which is different from the obvious; be prepared for any word in the clue to have a meaning other than one which is associated with the obvious pronunciation. If **Sewer cover** comes into the clue, don't think immediately of drains and inspection pits, but consider the alternative pronunciation of **sewer** and a seamstress should come to mind; her **cover** might be a THIMBLE.

When we turn to words which are pronounced the same but spelled differently, a whole new range of possibilities is opened up. These have been indicated in the text of the *Companion* by abbreviating the words 'sounds like . . .' to 's/l . . .' and adding the word in question. Thus, the entry **SOURCE** (s/l *sauce*) will encourage the reader to branch off into thoughts of impudence or ketchup, if he or she is confronted by a clue which starts **Sound source of** . . .

Warning that such a meaning is intended may not be conveyed so obviously as this; the word 'hear' is often used for this purpose, so that we get **It's boring to hear you in a wild rage** (5) = A(U)GER, in which the letter U is heard as **you**, and is placed in a loose anagram (**wild**) of **rage**; the whole word means something which can be used for **boring** a hole.

Before we leave pronunciation, a few final words of warning are in order. Always keep your mind open to further deception (as you should do at all times): **Sounds like a sheep** = BLEATS or BAA; **Sound asleep** = SNORE or ZZ. **Sound** here is being used in onomatopoeic form to indicate the noise being suggested. Compare also: **Food said to raise a smile** (6) = CHEESE (in front of the portrait camera).

Homonyms

The *OED* tells us that a homonym is a word of the same form as another, but with a different sense. The setter is therefore faced with a similar pronunciation for the two meanings of the word he is using; if he wants to brainwash his opponent into thinking of the wrong one, he must resort to other means. If we read **Get rid of the batter and wash the dish** (5, 4), beware of being persuaded by the second part of the clue that the whole of it refers to cooking; **batter** here is another way of saying 'batsman' and refers to cricket, so that the solution is CLEAN BOWL (**get rid of**, or 'bowl out' the batsman; and **wash** or CLEAN the **dish** or BOWL).

The setter is also apt to invent his own cryptic homonyms (or, more likely, to use any of a series of conventionally accepted ones, such as have already been suggested, e.g. **bloomer** for FLOWER, **operator** for SURGEON, and so on). **Swiss banker** (5) might encourage the answer GNOME, being one of the celebrated financial wizards known as the gnomes of Zurich; but **banker** is more likely to mean 'river' (it flows between banks), so that the answer required is RHONE. A really nasty setter might give easy clues for the words which produce the intersecting O and E, thereby further encouraging GNOME, to the detriment of the answer which runs across the beginning of the word. The correct solution would depend on the secondary clue which, in this instance, could well bring in the word 'currency' – another cryptic homonym which seems to support the GNOME and his financial dealings but which, in this instance, is a second reference to a river (which has a 'current').

One final example under this heading will serve to reveal a further series of pitfalls which lie in wait for the unwary. The setter takes a word like 'distressed' and throws it into the clue somewhere. The tyro could be forgiven for seizing triumphantly on it with a cry of 'Anagram!' Indeed, a part-clue like **distressed hair-net** may intend an anagram (THE RAIN), but it is more likely to require a synonym for 'tress' (curl, hair, lock etc) to be removed from the word, leaving ****NET in this case. Many words starting 'de-' or 'dis-' can be used in this way, thus 'disrobed' can require the removal of a synonym for clothes, 'disgrace' takes away 'grace' or any of its alternatives, and so on.

Inversion

I term it an inversion where the word to be written into the grid is, in effect, the clue; the answer to this clue is given by the setter as the clue. This may sound complicated, but can quickly be explained by an example. Presented in the usual way, **Wild rose is hurt** (4) could expect SORE as an answer (being **rose** written **wildly** or in anagram form, and meaning **hurt**). But if the clue were to read **Sore, perhaps, for not being cultivated** (4, 4), we should get the answer WILD ROSE (an instance of **rose** written **wildly** could be **sore**, and the whole thing is **uncultivated**). Similarly **Cat ham** (3, 5) could become ACT BADLY (**act** written **badly** is **cat**, and to act badly is to 'ham' it up). Note that the words 'wild' and 'badly', each denoting an anagram, now appear in the answer.

A related example, which switches only part of the clue into the answer, is furnished by **The young cow plays into the hands of Alfred** (4). This requires C*ALF, because the second part of the clue can be turned into 'is caught at cricket by Alf', which would be written into the score-book as c. Alf.

If the words 'perhaps' or 'for instance' are included in the clue, the implication is that a quote or meaning from the answer has been given in the clue, and this can be used in a number of ways other than the one instanced above with the **wild rose** clue. **Immoral, perhaps, he might say paradoxically** (5) = PRUDE (because a prude might say 'I'm moral', and it would be paradoxical for a prude to be immoral); and see **IMPERFECT** in the entries. In a similar vein, **I, for instance, represent investment** (7) = CAPITAL, because the letter **I** as written in the clue is an **instance** of a capital letter; the answer also means money, or **investment**. See also example about **Victoria, say** under *Split Words* above.

Alphabet

There are, of course, literally hundreds of different ways of suggesting a single letter. Because the answer will form only part of the final solution, the pointer will be a part-clue and must, of necessity, be short and snappy if the whole clue is not to become long and unwieldy. In the following examples, I have given each clue a second indication (which is put in brackets); either may be used independently of the other, or they may be joined together.

A	First (across).	G	German (third degree).
B	A follower (is born).	H	Beethoven's fifth (is hot).
C	A hundred (Centigrade).	I	One (island).
D	Five hundred (died).	J	Judge (James the First)
E	Final score (for bridge player).	K	Cork tip (king).
		L	Second class (lake).
F	Feminine (mid-off).	M	A thousand (married).

N	Name (the ultimate sin).	U	Acceptable (you hear).
O	Love (a duck).	V	Five (against).
P	Quiet (president).	W	With (raw edge).
Q	Cue for sound (question).	X	Ten (wrong).
R	Royal (year end).	Y	Fourth of July (in
S	Stop-start (bender).		Yugoslavia).
T	Square (car).	Z	Last (model gauge).

Test Your Skill

If you have read this far, you should now be ready to try your hand at a few tests of varying complexity. The following represent examples of the more common cryptic clues, some of which have been taken from puzzles appearing in the more serious newspapers, some have been adapted, and some have been concocted specially.

1. A pinch added to tuck at a pinch (3).
2. Extremes of cold seize a blackguard (3).
3. Rotten starters of banquets and dinners (3).
4. Unmatched in the food department (3).
5. Crazy about you finally being asked into the garden (4).
6. Small mechanical device to alleviate child-bearing (4).
7. Dog food (4).
8. Pop wine (4).
9. The case for a sewer (4).
10. The way a land measure is brought out (4).
11. Spirit in which there's a profit (4).
12. Backroom for Othello, perhaps (4).
13. Doctor leaves the capital by boat (4).
14. Quiet time for bookmaker (4).
15. Country starting with a long Eisteddfod session (5).
16. Peach under the tree (5).
17. Can a sty hold such unpleasantness for a pig? (5).
18. Makes war pay (5).
19. Change for one pound in old money (5).
20. Some of one's energies misplaced in the Alps (5).
21. Not smiling at the back (5).
22. Conclude there's not much information you can give the Queen (5).

23. Feeling one's lost direction in Austen Abbey (5).
24. Vehicle transport with no French iron to convey (5).
25. Secure kind of delivery (6).
26. See the old fool dodder – not half – grabbing a sailor (6).
27. Getting through in a U-boat is magnificent (6).
28. Stick a suitable notice in the agony column (6).
29. Where one presents one's case in Calais (6).
30. Setting music is nothing, leaving out Beethoven's fifth (6).
31. Cut off-licence tax (6).
32. Greek island ways, they say (6).
33. Deny entry on Tyneside (6).
34. Second class ways in Norfolk (6).
35. Proverbially tearful, Misses Bo-Peep and Lockett? (6).
36. Gas about a Spanish region (6).
37. Reassure a number in solitary confinement (6).
38. Not the same appeal by the Royal Society (6).
39. Pious man, having the last word, makes a bit of a bloomer (6).
40. Begins to get sour on board (6).
41. A prisoner in the string section (7).
42. A thunderous immortal described by American men of letters (7).
43. Not free to wed? (7).
44. Whip a Chinese coin out in Mexico (7).
45. Tried putting a politician into a toboggan (7).
46. Bone found by archaeological research party (7).
47. Rush to get river payment from tenant (7).
48. A boat for every customer present (7).
49. Supporter on the blower in Italy (7).
50. Seconds out, in ten days from starting this find (7).
51. When forming path around pound this (7).
52. Simple but callous as the Cockney said (7).
53. Obscures setting of Indian city-figures (8).
54. A house, many springing up here (8).
55. We hear the French after self-satisfied duty-dodger (8).
56. Saving money eagerly for those who post bills (8).
57. Disregarding gold in mixed double gin (8).
58. Teddy's family goes on ahead in the army (8).
59. Happy-go-lucky, but it's said he wasn't so well off (8).
60. Enclosed, we turn on her and hit out (8).

61. Wild pig, dressed in its own fat and old port (8).
62. Billy's mad on mountain butter (4, 4).
63. Shows consideration for ladies, but not for his date (6, 2).
64. They form part of the family accounts (9).
65. Like a measure in a volume for stargazers (9).
66. Unknown partner is a shade before time (5, 4).
67. Suitable confection for a hen-party? (5, 4).
68. A stiff examination (4, 6).
69. Dogmatic French governor, legislator and party man (10).
70. He would stick up for his employer (10).
71. Some bounder going to seed? (6-4).
72. Traitor gets pass to unfinished test centre (12).
73. Tell it, for instance, much the same (6, 6).
74. Information broadcast from all directions getting round at home (4, 8).
75. He should provide relaxation, atmosphere and true cooking (12).

Answers to Test Clues

1. NIP. Not only does the answer mean **pinch**, but, when paired with **tuck** to give 'nip and tuck', means **at a pinch**. See also the entry **ACCOMPANYIST** in the main text.
2. C(A)D. The extremes of a word are often taken as the first and last letters. When they **seize**, or enfold, the letter **a**, the result means **blackguard**.
3. BAD. The answer is formed by the **starters**, or initials, of the second half of the clue; it means **rotten**.
4. ODD. Besides meaning **unmatched**, this word is hidden in the clue (fo*OD* D*epartment*).
5. MA(U)D. **Crazy** often implies an anagram, but not here; a synonym is MAD, which when placed **about you finally**, or about the final letter of **you** (U), gives the name of the young lady whom Tennyson asked to come **into the garden**.
6. PRAM. **Child-bearing** here means baby-carriage rather than childbirth. **Small** means abbreviation in this case, and the shortened version of perambulator gives the answer.
7. CHOW. A short snappy clue, where the solution responds to each

word individually, being a breed of **dog** as well as a slang for **food**.

8. HOCK. Here again the solution can mean either half of this short clue.

9. ETUI. No drain intended here, but a seamstress, whose hold-all provides the answer.

10. RO(A)D. A **way** or ROAD is formed by the letter A with ROD, or a **land measure**, outside it.

11. G(A)IN. **Spirit** can mean any one of elf, pixie, goblin or, as here, liquor (rum and gin are popular, because they are conveniently short words). GIN, **in which there's** A, means **profit**.

12. MOOR. Almost too easy, this one. **Perhaps** can mean anagram (as can 'for instance' or 'say') but they are all more likely to mean 'is an example of . . .' Shakespeare's character is an example of a MOOR, which is **backroom**, or room written backwards.

13. (mo)SCOW. If the **doctor**, or MO, **leaves the capital** (of Russia, as it happens), a form of **boat** remains.

14. P*AGE. This is a nice one, and I wish I had thought it up. P is the letter for pianissimo or **quiet** which, when added to AGE (or **time**), gives part of the make-up of a book.

15. WALES. **Eisteddfod** should be enough to give us the **country** we are seeking, and this is confirmed by the knowledge that it is formed by the letters **starting** the words which follow.

16. GRASS. The clue is designed to make the solver think of a fruit-tree; but the **peach** we want means 'betray', for which another slang word provides the answer.

17. N*A*STY. The clue **holds** the answer, which is thus a hidden word meaning **unpleasantness**.

18. WAGES. If a comma is mentally placed after **war**, each part of this clue points to the answer.

19. NOBLE. This **pound** is not one of currency but of weight, despite appearances. ONE LB (**one pound**) is **changed**, or put into anagram, to give the name of an old coin.

20. EIGER. This is an example of the kind of somewhat naughty clue which sometimes creeps in unfairly. Five letters (or **some**) of the word **energies** are put into anagram (**misplaced**) to give the solution.

21. STERN. Place a comma mentally after **smiling**, and each part of the clue then points independently to the solution.

22. INF*ER. An abbreviation (**not much**) for **information** is placed next to the royal cypher to give a word meaning deduce or **conclude**.

23. ANGER. Jane **Austen** wrote about Northanger Abbey. If a meaning for **direction** (north, in this case) is removed (or **lost**) the result is a **feeling**.

24. CAR(fer)RY. A **vehicle transport** here is a car ferry. If the **French** word for **iron** is removed, the result is CARRY which means **convey**.

25. RESCUE. The words **kind of** imply both anagram and synonym. In this case the anag is of **secure** and the synonym for **delivery**.

26. DO(TAR)D. The word **dodder** which has **not half** its letters is either DOD or DER; these are put round (**grabbing**) another word for **sailor**, and a process of elimination brings the answer which means **old fool**.

27. SU(PER)B. A mechanical make-up, of a word for **through** which is **getting in** a word for **U-boat** or submarine.

28. AD*HERE. The **agony column** might announce 'Place your small-ad here'; the whole means **stick**.

29. DOUANE. The cryptic part of this clue is provided by **presents one's case**, but here it concerns presenting a suit-case to the French Customs, not a court case to a judge.

30. NOT*ING. This should present no difficulty once **Beethoven's fifth** has been established as the letter H. Leaving this out of the word **nothing** provides the answer, which is a cryptic way of describing **setting music**, or composing.

31. EXCISE. Before the answer is attempted, the hyphen in this clue should be read as a dash. Each half then provides the answer separately.

32. RHODES. **Ways, they say** requires that the answer, when said aloud, should sound like **ways** or a synonym, 'roads' in this case.

33. NE*GATE. **Tyneside** is usually NE, much as 'home counties' or 'Kent' is SE. Add a synonym for **entry** to give an answer which means **deny**.

34. B*ROADS. If you got RHODES above, this one should present little problem; it is self-evident when the answer is split as shown.

35. LOSERS. A working acquaintance with proverbs and sayings is useful. Here, 'finders keepers, losers weepers' is the one which links the two young ladies in the clue, who lost respectively sheep and a pocket.

36. AR(A)GON. ARGON (**gas**) placed about A, giving a **Spanish region**.
37. SOL(A*C)E. **A number** can be any Roman single-letter figure (V, X, L, C, D or M; the last three may be clued as 'many'). Here the letters for a hundred (including the indefinite article) are **confined** in a word for **solitary**, all meaning **reassure**.
38. O*THE*RS. An **appeal** is often written as the exclamation O or OH; here it is written **by**, or next to, **the** and also (letters for) **Royal Society**. Put together, it means **not the same**.
39. ST*AMEN. A **pious man**, like a 'good man', is usually ST (being 'saint'). **The last word** can be either OMEGA or AMEN. The answer is **a bit of a bloomer** (i.e. part of a flower – which blooms).
40. S(TART)S. **Sour** can be 'acid' or, as here, TART which, when placed in letters for a boat (i.e. in a steam ship or **on board**), gives a word meaning **begins**.
41. CELLIST. Someone who inhabits a cell is a **prisoner**.
42. A*U(THOR)S. THOR was the Norse god of **thunder**; when **described** (surrounded) by a synonym for **American**, we get U(THOR)S. The clue starts with the indefinite article, and A should be put first, so that it all means **men of letters**.
43. ENGAGED. It is usually necessary to split a clue into two, and then find an answer which satisfies both parts. **Not free** suggests being sold rather than given away, or a prisoner, or restricted or occupied; **to wed** conjures up marriage, groom, church and fiancée. A question mark is often a hint from the setter that he is being devious; here it signals that the clue, in fact, means just the opposite. ENGAGED satisfies all the pointers.
44. YU(CAT)AN. Another word-split. **Whip** = CAT; **Chinese coin** = YUAN; when the latter is **out**, or outside of, the former, it all means a city **in Mexico**.
45. S(A*MP)LED. It all means **tried**. **A politician** (A*MP) is put into a SLED. Note the indefinite article is sometimes included in the answer and sometimes not.
46. SHIN*DIG. A simple joining of types of **bone** and **archaeological research** produces a synonym for **party**.
47. TO*R*RENT. TO **gets** the abbreviation for **river** and then **payment from tenant**, to form a word meaning **rush**. To be ethical, a clue should mean something as a sentence; it must be confessed that this one doesn't mean a lot.
48. SH(ALL)OP. In this case, **every customer present** requires slightly

more thought than we have needed so far: 'all who are in the shop'. Put together in the way shown, the answer means **a boat**.

49. LEG*HORN. Use of the slang word **blower** in the clue implies an equally slang word in the answer, which gives us a choice between 'phone' and 'horn' or possibly use of 'buzz' or 'bell'. A **supporter** is often a 'foot' or 'leg' (or a 'fan', but not in this instance). A process of selection produces the only combination which forms a place **in Italy**.

50. UNEARTH. **Seconds** can be 'secs' or, as here, the second letters of the appropriate words. This clue needs mentally repunctuating, by deleting the comma, putting a colon after **Seconds** and a full stop before **find**. The second letters of the phrase between these stops then form the answer, meaning **find** (as a verb, not the noun implied by the clue).

51. AS*PHA(L)T. **When** = AS, followed by anag of (**forming**) **path** placed **around** L (= **pound**).

52. ARTLESS. The answer means **Simple**. **Callous** = heartless, and the usual implication of **Cockney** is to drop an initial aitch; **said** means 'sounds like', so the first 'e' goes as well (**Cockney** can also mean rhyming slang, but not in this case.)

53. DI(AGRA)MS. **Setting** implies one word in another. In this clue we take DIMS for the word **obscures**; an **Indian city** (AGRA is often a safe bet) is **set** inside to produce a word meaning **figures**. Note that the hyphen should be read as a dash.

54. D*WELLING. **Many** is often a Roman letter meaning 100, 500 or 1,000 (C, D, or M). If things are **springing up** they are WELLING; when you get 500 of them, the answer means **a house**.

55. SMUGGLER. This is a good illustration of the use of pronunciation. **The French** is 'le'; **we hear** tells us that it is a question of 'sounds like . . .' Someone who is **self-satisfied** is 'smug', and this is also governed by **we hear** to give SMUGG. Put together, it means **duty-dodger**.

56. HOARDING. If a comma is mentally placed after **eagerly**, the answer responds directly to each part of the clue.

57. IGN(OR)ING. **Gold** is often either the chemical symbol AU or, as here, the heraldic OR (it can also imply an Olympic winner). The reader who has reached this far should need no explanation of **mixed double gin**.

58. BEARS*KIN. **Family** can be either KITH or KIN. **Teddy's family** is

now obvious. Put together, it goes on a head (not **ahead**) in **the army**.

59. HEED*LESS. **It's said** (or 'we hear') nearly always implies pronunciation in one form or another. Use of contractions in the clue implies an equal and opposite use of contractions in the answer. In this case, **not so well off** could be expressed as 'he had less'; this could be contracted to 'he'd less', which in turn could sound like HEED*LESS. This also means **happy-go-lucky**.

60. HER*EW*ITH. This one is built up literally through and through. **We turn** gives EW; **on her** means 'added to her' = HER*EW; **hit out** could mean place HIT outside the result, but this gives us nothing; or else add an anagram of **hit** = ITH. The word **enclosed** points towards the answer as a whole.

61. LAR(BOAR)D. **Wild pig** could either require a loose anagram of 'pig' or else be literal and mean BOAR. The comma needs to be mentally moved from after **pig** to after **fat**, so that **dressed in** = enclosed in; **its own fat** = LARD. The result is an old word for **port** (as opposed to starboard).

62. WILD GOAT. **Butter** often requires GOAT (one who butts), as opposed to margarine or fat of any kind. **Billy** is also a GOAT.

63. STANDS UP. This is more literal, but derives its cryptic meaning from interpretation of the answer rather than the clue. One who STANDS UP for ladies, gives up his seat **considerately**; if he STANDS UP **his date**, he fails to keep a tryst, and is thus not **considerate**.

64. RELATIONS. **Accounts** = narrations or RELATIONS; **family** = kith, kin or RELATIONS.

65. AS*T(ROD)OME. **A volume** is either a quantity, or a vol, a book or a tome; use of the word **measure** is designed to distract the solver towards the first of these. But this should be ignored, for we have TOME, which has ROD (a **measure**) in it, preceded by AS (**like** in the clue) to give something for **stargazers**.

66. BLIND DATE. A **shade** = BLIND (or awning), and it is placed **before** a word for **time**; the whole meaning **unknown partner**.

67. LAYER CAKE. Responds to both **confection** and **hen** (which lays).

68. POST MORTEM. This is an example of a single pointer to the solution. Given the licence of calling a dead body a **stiff**, it is a literal interpretation of the clue. It was quoted on BBC Radio 4 in February 1983 by logophile and inveterate puzzle setter Roger Squires as one of his favourite clues.

69. PERE*MP*TORY. Licence is also required here to render **French governor** as PERE by way of 'father' (for which **governor** is an archaic term). From there, addition of MP and TORY are short steps to a **dogmatic** answer.

70. BILLPOSTER. This requires two meanings for **stick up**.

71. TENNIS-BALL. **Bounder** means 'ball' as often as it means 'cad'. **Seed** refers here to tennis tournament handicapping.

72. COL*LABORATOR(y). A **pass** is often a COL; a **test centre** can be a LABORATORY which, if it is **unfinished**, loses its last letter(s), to complete the word for **traitor**.

73. LITTLE CHANGE. An example of the answer being partly a clue. **Tell it** is an **instance** of LITTLE being **changed**, or anagrammed.

74. NEWS BULLETIN. **All directions** indicates north, east, west and south (NEWS); **round** can be a BULLET; and **at home** = IN (i.e. not out). It all means **information broadcast**.

75. REST*AURA*TEUR. **Relaxation** = REST; **atmosphere** = AURA; **true cooking** = anag **true**. The whole clue also relates to the answer.

How to Use This Companion

The puzzle setter uses devious methods of saying one thing while meaning another, thereby hoping to distract the would-be solver's mind from the correct line of approach to a clue. This *Companion* uses different type-faces to encourage the reader into lateral thinking, and thus to avoid the traps with which most cryptic clues abound. The reader must usually expect to refer to a second entry, suggested either [by square brackets] as an associated idea, or else (*by italics*) as an alternative meaning with its own entry.

CAPITALS
Capitals are used for words which are either entries or answers.

BOLD CAPITALS. All main entries are in bold capital letters.

PLAIN CAPITALS. A word suitable as an answer to the entry against which it appears is in plain capital letters.

ITALIC CAPITALS. A word suitable as an answer, which is also an entry in its own right (having further possible answers with different connotations), is in italic capital letters.

SMALL CAPITALS. Answers to example clues within an explanation are printed in small capital letters. They are largely used to demonstrate clue construction, and therefore are not direct answers to the entry under which they appear.

ITALICS
Italic letters are used to show that the word concerned forms an entry elsewhere in the *Companion*, either as it stands, or else in allied form (thus *relative* appears as **RELATED** and **RELATION**, and *lovely* as **LOVE** and **LOVER**).

ITALIC CAPITALS. Since the letters are capitals, they show a possible answer to the entry against which they appear. Since they are italic, they also show that the word has an entry in its own right.

Italic lower case. Because the word is not in capital letters, it does not form a direct answer to the entry against which it appears. But its italic lettering shows that it has an entry in its own right, which could lead to a different train of thought and a possible answer.

BOLD LETTERING
Bold lettering is reserved for clue-words in one form or another.

BOLD CAPITALS. Bold capitals are used for main entries, which are normally words taken directly from the clue being examined.

Bold lower case. Bold lower case letters are used for example clues within an explanation. They are also used for sub-entries within an explanation, thus the entry **VICTORY** has a sub-entry **Goddesses**, giving the names of the Greek and Roman goddesses of victory.

Saying
The word *saying* in an entry means that there is an appropriate quotation or saying, with its derivation, listed alphabetically under S.

Order and Punctuation
Different meanings of a particular entry obey no hard and fast rule as to the order in which they appear in the explanation. In broad terms, abbreviations tend to come first, and the rest follow in alphabetical order. Commas divide words of similar meaning within an explanation; semi-colons make a bigger difference, perhaps between nouns and verbs of the same meaning. Colons introduce a list of words: breeds of dog, characters from Shakespeare, rivers of the world etc. An equals sign shows a direct link with the preceding word(s), thus **VICTORY** has **Goddesses: Gk** = NIKE; **Rom** = VICTORIA.

A full stop signifies that the meaning changes completely, thus **BOOT** has SHOE; WELLINGTON. DISMISS, FIRE, SACK. TRUNK (US). AVAIL. Where an entry has textual as well as one-word explanations, these are differentiated by use of 1, 2, 3 etc.

(   ) Round brackets enclose words which augment an explanation. When used in an answer to an example clue (which therefore has small capital letters), they reveal where a letter or letters have been inserted in the cryptic make-up of that answer, and they should be mentally dismissed when reading such a word. Thus, **All at sea, I'm in the hill** = T(IM)OR shows that the letters IM have been inserted in TOR, and it should be read as TIMOR.

[ ] Square brackets enclose words which suggest further avenues
       for possible investigation. The words are not answers in
       themselves, but are an encouragement to lateral thinking.

*   An asterisk shows where a word has been split, or else letters
       have been removed, to form a cryptic answer. Asterisks
       should be mentally ignored when reading the word concerned
       because, like round brackets, they are purely a mechanical
       method of showing how an answer has been reached. Thus, **A
       quiet time for the attendant** = P*AGE, shows that the letter P
       represents **quiet**, while AGE = **time** but, when read as PAGE,
       the word means **attendant**.

~   A tilde signifies repetition of the entry word, or of the word
       immediately preceding the sign itself; identification will be
       evident from the sense of the text.

Registered Trade Names

Many proprietary names and trade marks have passed into the
language as everyday terms. Where such words have been
knowingly included in this *Companion*, they have been
indicated by the symbol ®. Unwitting inclusion of further
unidentified trade marks does not imply that they have
necessarily acquired a general significance in the legal sense;
their omission is regretted, as is any wrong attribution which
may have been made. Corrections will be made in subsequent
reprints, if substantiated objections are made with adequate
notice.

Cross-Reference

If an entry fails to satisfy, don't give up! Any word in italics
has its own entry, so the reader should cross-refer. For
instance, when wanting to know Red Indian tribes, the reader
who looks up any one of those three words will find
AMERICAN INDIAN (in italics); the entry **AMERICAN
INDIAN** lists over 70 tribes. Equally, the entry **SHIP** gives
(among others) *BOAT*; the entry **BOAT** gives 80 different
types of ship or boat. *Cross-refer to words in italics.*

Abbreviations

The following abbreviations are used in this *Companion*. They are not necessarily such as may appear in clues or solutions, although inevitably some of them might do so.

A	Austria, ~n	C	Cambridge
abbr	abbreviated	Cam	Cambodia, ~n
aero	aeronautical	Can	Canada, ~ian
Af	Africa, ~n	Ch	China, ~ese
Afghan	Afghanistan	ch	church
A-Hung	Austro-Hungary, ~ian	chem	chemical
anag	anagram	CI	Channel Islands
anon	anonymous	coaln	coalition
Arab	Arab, ~ian, ~y	coll	collector
arch	archaic; architecture	comm	commercial
Arg	Argentina, ~ian	Cong	Congo, ~lese
A-Sax	Anglo-Saxon	Cons	Conservative
ass	assassinated	cook	cookery, ~ing
Aus	Australia, ~n	crypt	cryptic
av	aviation	Cz	Czechoslovakia, ~n
Bab	Babylon, ~ian	d	daughter; died
Belg	Belgium, ~ian	Dem	Democrat
bibl	biblical	div	divorced
bot	botanical	dn	down clue only
Br	Britain, ~ish		
br	brother	E	east
Braz	Brazil, ~ian	eccles	ecclesiastic, ~al
Bud	Buddha, ~ist	e.g.	for example
Bur	Burma, ~ese	Egy	Egypt, ~ian

elect	electrical	Jap	Japan, ~ese
Eng	England, ~ish	Jor	Jordan, ~ian
Eq	Equatorial	jun	junior
esp	especially		
Eur	Europe, ~an	k	killed
ex	dead, extinct, former		
		Lab	Labour
f	father	Lat	Latin
fem	female	leg	legal
fict	fictional	Lib	Liberal
fig	figurative	lit	literal, ~ly
Fin	Finland, ~nish		
Fr	France, French	m	mother of
		mar	married
Gab	Gabon	math	mathematics
Gam	Gambia	mech	mechanical
G and S	Gilbert & Sullivan	med	medical
geog	geographical	met	meteorological
Ger	German, ~y	Mex	Mexico, ~an
Gk	Greece, Greek	mil	military
gram	grammatical	Mong	Mongolia
		Mos	Moslem
h	husband	Moz	Mozambique
Heb	Hebrew	Ms	manuscript
herald	heraldry	mus	musical
Hind	Hindu, ~i	myth	mythology, ~ical
hist	historical		
HK	Hong Kong	N	north
Hung	Hungary, ~ian	naut	nautical
		Nig	Nigeria, ~n
i.e.	that is	NL	Netherlands, Dutch
Ind	India, ~n	Nor	Norse, Norway
int	international	NT	New Testament
Ire	Ireland, Irish	NZ	New Zealand
IOM	Isle of Man		
IS	Isles of Scilly	O	Oxford
Is	island	OE	Old English
Isr	Israel, ~i	ON	Old Norse
It	Italy, ~ian	opp	opposite

Ork	Orkneys	sis	sister
OT	Old Testament	sl	slang
		s/l	sounds like
Pak	Pakistan, ~i	Som	Somalia
parl	parliament, ~ary	Sp	Spain, Spanish
Pers	Persia, ~n	Swe	Sweden, ~ish
	Iran, ~ian	Swi	Switzerland, Swiss
Phoen	Phoenicia, ~n		
photo	photography, ~ic	Tanz	Tanzania
Pl	plural	tech	technical
Pol	Poland, ~ish	theat	theatrical
polit	political	trad	traditional
Port	Portugal, ~uese	trans	translate, ~ion
print	printing	Turk	Turkey, ~ish
		TV	television
q.v.	which see		
		UK	United Kingdom
Rep	Republic, ~an	US	United States of
rh sl	rhyming slang		America
rly	railway	USSR	Soviet Russia, ~n
Rom	Roman		
Rum	Romania, ~n	Venez	Venezuela, ~n
Russ	Russia, ~n	Viet	Vietnam, ~ese
S	south	W	west
s	son	w	wife
SA	South Africa, ~n	Wal	Wales, Welsh
Sax	Saxon		
Sc	Scotland, Scottish	Y	Yugoslavia, ~n
Scand	Scandinavia, ~n		
Shak	Shakespeare	Z	Zanzibar
Shet	Shetlands	Zam	Zambia, ~n
sig	signature	Zod	Zodiac
Sing	Singapore	zool	zoological

Mini-biographies

Fact

Alban
Antony
Archimedes
Attila
Boadicea
Caesar
Cato
Chaucer
Cleopatra
David, King
Hippocrates
Incitatus
King Arthur
Mohammed
Pompey
Ptolemy
Socrates
Terpander
Xerxes

Fiction

Acheron
Achilles
Actaeon
Adonis
Aeneas
Aeolus

Aesculapius
Agamemnon
Amphitrite
Andromeda
Anubis
Aphrodite
Apollo
Argonauts
Argus
Ariadne
Artemis
Artemisia
Asclepius
Astarte
Atalanta
Athene
Atlas
Augeas
Autolycus
Bacchus
Balder
Bellerophon
Cassandra
Castor
Cercyon
Charon
Chiron
Clytemnestra
Daedalus
Danae
Daphne

Diana
Dido
Doris
Echo
Electra
Eris
Eurydice
Frey
Freya
Frigg
Galahad
Galatea
Grundy, Solomon
Guinevere
Hebe
Hecate
Hector
Hecuba
Hel
Helen
Helle
Hera
Hercules
Hermes
Hero
Hippolyte
Holmes, Sherlock
Icarus
Janus
Jason
Juno

Jupiter
Kali
Lancelot
Leander
Loki
Maia
Mars
Medea
Medusa
Mercury
Midas
Minerva
Minos
Minotaur
Narcissus
Neptune
Nereus

Niobe
Nyx
Oedipus
Orestes
Orion
Orpheus
Pandora
Paris
Penelope
Periphites
Persephone
Perseus
Phaeton
Pluto
Priam
Procrustes
Prometheus

Pygmalion
Remus
Rhea
Sciron
Selene
Sisyphus
Tantalus
Terpsichore
Theseus
Thor
Typhon
Ulysses ·
Uranus
Woden
Xanthippe
Zeus

Authors' works

Andersen, Hans
Austen, Jane
Brontës, the
Chaucer, Geoffrey
Dickens, Charles
Gilbert, W.S.
    (G & S)
Grahame, Kenneth

Haggard, Rider
Kipling, Rudyard
Lear, Edward
Milne, A.A.
Orwell, George
Potter, Beatrix
Scott, Sir Walter

Shakespeare,
    William
Shaw, G.B.
Sullivan, see
    Gilbert
Swift, Jonathan
Wodehouse, P.G.

Heading Lists

African tribes
Aircraft
Airlines
Airports
Alice in Wonderland characters
American Indians
Andersen, Hans
Anniversaries
Antelopes
Apples
Architectural terms
Argonauts
Assemblies, nouns of
Austen, Jane, books
Aversions
Awards (theat)
Battles, air, land, sea
Bears
Bell-ringing, changes
Bells
Biblical towns
Birds
Birthstones
Boat types
Bones of the body
Bottle sizes
Brontës, the, books
Butterflies, see Lepidoptera
Capital cities
Card games
Car plates (countries)

Carriages
Castles in the UK
Cathedrals in the UK
Cats
Cattle
Ceramics
Chaucer characters
Cheeses
Chemical elements
Church dress
Churchmen
Clerks
Clowns, see Jesters
Clubs, London
Coins
Collectors
Colours
Comics
Commonwealth countries
Composers
Companies, City livery
Companions, celebrated
Constellations
Counties, see Divisions
Cricket grounds
Currencies
Dances
Deer
Deserts
Detectives
Dickens characters

Dinosaurs
Discoveries
Divisions of the UK
Doctors, celebrated
Dog breeds
Drinks
Ducks
Dwarfs
Eagles
Ear parts
Episcopal signatures
Explorers
Eye parts and disorders
Fairies
Fates
Fishes
Five towns
Flowers
Football teams and grounds
Forests
French Revolutionary calendar
Friars
Fruit
Gaols
Gates of London
Gems
Gilbert & Sullivan, see G and S
Gods
Goddesses
Grahame, Kenneth, characters
Grasses
Guards (mil)
Gulfs
Habitations
Haggard, Rider, books
Hats
Heraldic terms
Herbs
Hercules' labours
Holmes, Sherlock, cases
Horses
Hunchbacks
Indian States
Insects
Instruments (mus)
International units
Inventions
Islands of the UK
Japanese words
Jesters/clowns
Kipling, Rudyard, books
Knighthood, orders of
Knots
Lakes, principal
Landladies (fict)
Landlords (fict)
Law practitioners (fict)
Lear, Edward, books
Legislative assemblies
Lemurs
Lepidoptera
Liqueurs
Lizards
Lovers, celebrated
Lovers of . . . (-ophiles)
Maids (fict)
Male and female animals
Markets (London)
Materials
Measures
Military leaders
Milne, A.A., characters
Monarchies of the world
Monarchs of Eng/UK
Monkeys
Monsters
Moths, see Lepidoptera
Muses

Musical instruments, see
   Instruments (mus)
Music terms, see Tempo
Nicknames
Nine angelic orders
Nine worthies
Numbers, specific
Nurses, celebrated
Obsessions
Offspring
Organ parts (mus)
Orwell characters
Outlaws
Owls
Oxen
Palaces
Palms
Parasites
Parrots
Patron saints
Pears
Philosophers
Pigs
Pirates
Planets
Plants
Potter, Beatrix, books
Presidents of the USA
Prime Ministers of the UK
Prisoners
Prophets
Provinces of Canada
Public schools
Q without U
Rabbits
Racetracks, horses
Racetracks, motor cars
Red Indians, see American ~
Reference books

Religions
Rhyming slang
Rivers of the world
Robbers, celebrated
Roman place names, UK
Roman roads in England
Round table knights
Royal families
Rugby grounds
Sailors
Sails
Salmon
Sayings/quotations
Schoolmasters
Schools (fict)
Scott, Sir Walter, books
Seas
Seaweeds
Servants (fict)
Seven ages of man
Seven deadly sins
Seven hills
Seven sages
Seven seas
Seven wonders of the world
Shakespeare characters
Shakespeare plays
Sharks
Shaw, G.B., plays
Sheep
Shells (zool)
Shoes
Slaves
Snakes
Soldiers
Songs
Spacecraft
Space travellers
Spices

Stately homes
States of the USA
Stevenson, R.L., books
Stoics
Straits of the world
Street markets
Study of . . . (-ology)
Swift, Jonathan, books
Swiss cantons
Tarot cards
Taverns (fict)
Teeth, see Bones
Tempi (mus)
Ten commandments
Tennis venues
Thames bridges
Titans
Trees
Tribes (Roman Britain)
Tribes (World)

Twins, celebrated
Underworlds
Unions, initials
Universities
Unseen characters (fict)
Vegetables
Violin parts
Waterfalls
Weapons
Weights in boxing
Whales
Wild plants/weeds
Winds, local, celebrated
Winds, Gk and Rom
Wines
Wodehouse, P.G., books
Woodpeckers
World girdlers
Writers
Zodiac, signs of

This represents over 230 lists with a total number of interpretations which exceeds 10,000.

The Complete Crossword Companion

A (s/l *eh*). *ABOUT*. ACROSS. ADULTS ONLY, ADVISORY,
PARENTAL GUIDANCE (film *censorship*). ALPHA.
AREA. ARGON (*chem*). AUSTRIA (*car plate*). Austria, ~n.
BEST. KEY; NOTE.

AA ALCOHOLICS ANONYMOUS. ANTI-AIRCRAFT; FLAK.
AUTOMOBILE ASSOCIATION; CAR CLUB. *MILNE.*
FILM *CENSORSHIP*.

AB *SAILOR*. BACKWARD SCHOLAR (crypt). Heb month.

ABACK 1. BACKWARDS, BEHIND. DISCONCERTED,
SURPRISED. MOUNTED, RIDER. 2. Word/answer reversed,
e.g. **Little Trevor's taken aback and green** (4) = VERT.

ABBEY MONASTIC BUILDING; **celebrated:** BATTLE,
BUCKFAST, FOUNTAINS, FURNESS, GLASTONBURY,
KIRKSTALL, MELROSE, ROMSEY, TINTERN,
TITCHFIELD; [Abbess, Abbot]. NORTHANGER (*Austen*).

ABC ALPHABET [Reading]. RATING. *BROADCASTING
(Aus; US). REFERENCE WORK* (rly).

ABCDEFGHIJKLM A*TO*M (crypt).

ABEL (s/l *able*). s of *Adam*; *Adamson*, FIRST VICTIM, THIRD
PERSON; [Garden of Eden; murder].

ABERDEEN *UNIVERSITY*. **Episcopal sig** = ABERDON.
[Granite]. THE DONS (*football*).

ABERDON *Episcopal sig* of ABERDEEN.

ABET AID, *ASSIST*, EGG, ENCOURAGE, URGE; (**opp** =
hinder). A*WAGER (crypt).

ABIGAIL MAID (The Scornful Lady, Beaumont and Fletcher).
'FATHER'S DELIGHT'.

ABLE (s/l *abel*). ADROIT, CLEVER, SKILLED (**opp** = inept).

ABOARD ON BOARD, SHIPPED; hence put S*S round, e.g. **Very
French aboard leads to an accent** (6) = S*TRES*S. A*PLANK
(crypt).

ABOMINABLE SNOWMAN *MONSTER* (Himalayan), YETI; BIG-
FOOT (Can; US); BUNYIP (Aus); SASQUATCH (US);
YAMINSKAY (S Andes).

ABOUT 1. A, C, CA, RE. ON, NEAR, *ROUND*, TURN.
A*FIGHT (crypt). 2. Reverse word. 3. Put word round another,
e.g. **It's about the backward writer, and incompetent** (5) =
I*NEP*T.

ABROAD 1. FOREIGN. OUTDOORS; WIDELY. 2. Translate,
e.g. **I'm abroad** = JE or ICH etc.

ABSORB ENGROSS. BLOT, MOP UP (**Dn** = POM), SOAK.

ABSTAINER *AA*, *TT*. MUSLIM; RECHABITE; [drink, *pussyfoot*,
Johnson, *Turner*].

ABSTRACT ABSTRUSE, IDEALISTIC, DEDUCT,
DISENGAGE, REMOVE, SEPARATE; SUMMARY; [legal
evidence].

AC *ACCOUNT*, ~ANT, BILL, *SETTLEMENT*. ACROSS.
ACTINIUM (chem). AIRMAN. ALTERNATING
CURRENT, hence CURRENCY (crypt).

ACCENT PRONUNCIATION; STRESS. Such a mark: ACUTE
(´), *BREVE* (˘), *CEDILLA* (¸), *CIRCUMFLEX* (ˆ), *DIAERESIS*
(¨), *GRAVE* (`), *MACRON* (¯), *TILDE* (˜), UMLAUT (¨).

ACCEPTABLE U. PLEASING, TOLERABLE, WELCOME.

ACCOMPANYIST 1. APPENDAGE, ESCORT, SUPPORTER
(**opp** = loner). 2. Word which often goes with another, e.g. **Bill's
accompanyist** (3) = COO.

ACCOUNT AC. NARRATIVE, *REPORT*, STATEMENT,
STORY. CONSIDER, ESTIMATE; PROFIT, REGARD,
RECKONING. ALLOW, JUSTIFY. [money].

ACCOUNTANT CA, FCA. CASHIER. AUTHOR, *REPORTER*,
STORY-TELLER, *WRITER*; [Scheherazade].

ACCUMULATOR *COLLECTOR*, GATHERER. *BET*.
BATTERY, *CELL* (elect). COMPUTER, *MEMORY*,
RETRIEVAL *BANK*.

ACE I, MONAD, ONE. BEST, CHAMPION, EXPERT, TOP.
CARD, ONE CARD. SERVICE (*tennis*).

ACELDAMA BLOODSHED, SLAUGHTER (bibl).

ACHERON Gk myth s of *Ceres*. He was changed into a river across
which (with the *Styx*) *Charon* ferried the souls of the dead.

ACHILLES Gk myth s of Peleus and Thetis. Invulnerable except in

his heel, where he was killed in the war of *Troy* by an arrow shot
by *Paris*. His *horse* was Xanthus (*Shak*, T and C).

ACID BITING, SEVERE, SHARP, SOUR; [PH, silica] (**opp** =
alkali). *DRUG*, LSD (sl).

ACOLITE (s/l *acolyte*). BRIDGE PLAYER (crypt).

ACOLYTE (s/l *acolite*). ATTENDANT (eccles), BEGINNER,
CHURCHMAN.

ACT *DEED*, OPERATION; BEHAVE, PERFORM,
PORTRAY. LAW.

ACTAEON Gk myth hunter trained by *Chiron*. He spied on
Artemis (**Rom** = *Diana*) bathing, and was transformed into a *stag*
which was killed by his own dogs.

ACTION ACT, *DEED*, EVENT, EXERTION (**opp** = inertia).
ENGAGEMENT, FIGHTING, OPERATIONS (mil). LEGAL
PROCESS. MECHANISM, WORKS. INACTION, STRIKE.

ACTOR PERFORMER, PLAYER, THESPIAN; OLIVIER,
IRVING, TREE etc. [*stage*].

ACUTE CRITICAL. KEEN, POINTED, SHARP (**opp** = blunt).
HIGH, SHRILL. *ACCENT*.

AD (s/l *add*). ANNO DOMINI, NOWADAYS, YEAR . . .
ADVERT (~ISEMENT), HOARDING, NOTICE, POSTER.
TO.

ADAM FIRST FALLER, FIRST PERSON, FIRST GARDENER;
[Eden]. A*BARRIER; A*MARE (crypt). *ARCHITECT*,
CABINET MAKER [Fireplace]. *ISLAND*. SERVANT (*Shak*).

ADAMSON ABEL, CAIN, SETH (crypt).

ADD (s/l *ad*). SUM, TOT, TOTAL (**opp** = subtract). INCLUDE.

ADDER *SNAKE*, VIPER [*Wyvern*]. CALCULATOR,
COUNTER, TELLER; *SUMMER* (crypt).

ADDITIONALLY ADDED, SUPPLEMENTARY. Add to word.

ADDRESS HOME. POISE, PRESENCE (**opp** = gaucherie).
SPEAK TO, SPEECH, AIM AT, APPLY.

ADD UP CALCULATE, COMPUTE, SUM, TOTAL, TOT UP.
MAKE SENSE. DDA (dn).

ADJUST *Anag*. ADAPT, ARRANGE, *ORDER*.

ADMIT CONCEDE, CONFESS, OWN (**opp** = deny). ALLOW,
LET IN.

ADMIX ADD, MINGLE, STIR IN. YEAR 1009 (crypt – Lat).

ADONIS 1. PHEASANT'S EYE (*flower*). 2. Gk myth handsome youth loved by *Aphrodite* (**Rom** = Venus). After he was killed by a boar, he was allowed by the Gods to spend half of each year with her. The *flower* anemone sprang from his blood in the earth. [Good looks].

ADORN BEDECK, *DECK*, ORNAMENT.

ADRIFT *Anag* (e.g. **Gone adrift** = NEGO, ONGE etc). ILL-INFORMED, OUT OF ORDER, OUT OF TOUCH. DRIFTING, UNFASTENED [flotsam, jetsam, lagan].

ADVANCE GO FORWARD, GO ON (**opp** = retreat). FLOAT, LEND, LOAN, PAY ON ACCOUNT, RAISE A LOAN. PROMOTE, PROGRESS.

ADVERTISEMENT AD, PR. ANNOUNCEMENT, *NOTICE*, PUBLICITY.

AEGIS 1. COVER, DEFENCE, PROTECTION. 2. The shield of *Athene* and *Zeus*.

AENEAS Rom hero of *Troy*; founder of the Roman state. *Companion* = Achates. (*Shak*, T and C).

AEOLUS Gk myth king of Aeolia, god of the *winds*, which he kept shut up in a *cave* [harp, *instrument* (mus)].

AESCULAPIUS Rom equivalent of *ASCLEPIUS* (Gk), *god* of medicine [*Hippocrates*].

Af Africa.

A FRENCH UN, UNE.

AFRESH *Anag*. ANEW.

AFRICAN ASHANTI, BANTU, BERBER, BOER, HOTTENTOT, KIKUYU, MASAI, MOOR [Othello], TAUREG, XHOSA, ZOUAVE, ZULU etc. [*tribe*].

AFRICUS Rom myth SW *WIND* (**Gk** = LIPS).

AFTERTHOUGHT PS. ADDED; CODICIL. LATER CHILD.

AG *SILVER* (*chem*). LIMITED COMPANY (Ger).

AGAIN *Anag*. BESIDES, FURTHER, ONCE MORE, RE-. A*PROFIT (crypt).

AGAINST V, VS, VERSUS. ANTI, *CON* (**opp** = for, *pro*).

AGAMEMNON Gk myth hero, who led the Greeks to *Troy*. Quarrelled with *Achilles* over slave-girl Briseis. Killed by his unfaithful wife *Clytemnestra* on his return to Argos. Father of *Electra*. (*Shak*, T and C).

AGATE *GEM*, SEMI-PRECIOUS *STONE*, *CHALCEDONY*: CORNELIAN, ONYX, SCOTCH PEBBLE; *Birthstone* (June).

WRITER. A*BARRIER, AN*ENTRANCE, AN*OPENING, A*MOUTH (crypt).

AGENT FACTOR. A*GENTLEMAN (crypt). MOLE, SPY; **celebrated** (fact): NURSE EDITH CAVELL, ODETTE CHURCHILL, MATA HARI, VIOLETTE SZABO; (fiction): DICK BARTON, JAMES BOND, BULLDOG DRUMMOND, THE SAINT, SMILEY, SIMON TEMPLAR.

AGE GET ON, GROW OLD; **saying**. [Picture of Dorian Gray (Wilde)]. PERIOD (in hist order): *STONE*, EOLITHIC, PALAEOLITHIC, MESOLITHIC, NEOLITHIC, *COPPER*, *BRONZE, IRON*. **Pl** = *Seven* ~s (*Shak*).

A GERMAN EIN, EINE.

AGORAPHOBIA *Aversion* to open places.

AGREE CONCUR, CONFORM, CONSENT, GET ON (**opp** = dissent).

AHAB *SAILOR, WHALER* (Moby Dick, Herman Melville; *ship* = Pequod). Bibl *king*.

AHEAD ON. IN FRONT (**opp** = behind). A*HEAD (crypt).

AHEM COUGH, HESITATION. A*BORDER (crypt).

AI BEST, FIRST CLASS [*Lloyds*]. 3-TOED *SLOTH* (S Am). *Bibl town*.

AIM DESIGN, END, GOAL, INTENT, OBJECT, TARGET; DIRECT, POINT.

AIRBORNE FLYING (**opp** = *grounded*). PARA, RED BERET, RED DEVIL, SAS. [AWACS].

AIRCRAFT FLYING MACHINE: AEROPLANE, AIRPLANE (US), AIRSHIP, BALLOON, GLIDER, HANG-GLIDER, HOVERCRAFT, MICRO-LIGHT, UFO.

Celebrated (fighters)®:	**Celebrated (bombers)®:**
BEAUFIGHTER (UK)	*AVENGER* (US)
BUCCANEER (UK)	*BADGER* (USSR)
CAMEL (UK)	BEAR (USSR)
CORSAIR (US)	BOSTON (UK/US)
HARRIER (UK)	FLYING FORTRESS (US)
HAWK (UK)	GOTHA (Ger)
HELLCAT (US)	HALIFAX (UK)
HUNTER (UK)	HUSTLER (US)
HURRICANE (UK)	LANCASTER (UK)

LIGHTNING (UK)   LIBERATOR (UK/US)
MIG (USSR)   *LINCOLN* (UK)
MOSQUITO (UK)   *MOSQUITO* (UK)
MUSTANG (UK/US)   STIRLING (UK)
PHANTOM (UK/US)   SUPER FORTRESS (US)
PUP (UK)   VALIANT (UK)
SABRE (UK/US)   VICTOR (UK)
SPITFIRE (UK)   *VULCAN* (UK)
THUNDERBOLT (US)   *WELLINGTON* (UK)

AIRFIELD AERODROME, *AIRPORT*.

AIRLINE BREATHING TUBE, TRACHEA, WINDPIPE (all crypt). AIR SERVICE, CIVIL AIR-CARRIER; **celebrated (all ®):** AEROFLOT (USSR), BA (UK), BEA (ex-UK), BOAC (ex-UK), CAC (Ch), EL AL (Isr), IBERIA (Sp), KLM (NL), PAN-AM (US), QANTAS (Aus), SABENA (Belg), SAS (Scand), TAP (Port), TWA (US).

AIRMAN AC, FO, PO. BALLOONIST, FLYER, *PILOT*. *DAEDALUS*, *ICARUS* (myth). BARITONE, *BASS*, BUGLER, FLAUTIST, OBOIST, ORGANIST, *SINGER*, TENOR, TRUMPETER (crypt). SHOW-OFF, SWANKER.

AIRPORT NOSTRIL, MOUTH (crypt). AERODROME, AIRFIELD; **celebrated:**

Aberdeen, DYCE; **Amsterdam**, SCHIPOL; **Ayr**, PRESTWICK; **Azores**, SANTA MARIA; **Berlin**, SCHONEFELD, TEGEL, TEMPELHOF; **Birmingham**, ELMDON; **Blackpool**, SQUIRES GATE; **Boston**, LOGAN; **Bournemouth**, HURN; **Buenos Aires**, EZEIZA, JORGE NEWBERY; **Cardiff**, RHOOSE; **Chicago**, O'HARE; **Copenhagen**, KASTRUP; **Corfu**, KERKYRA; **Dallas**, FORT WORTH; **Frankfurt**, RHEIN MAIN; **Fiji**, NADI; **Geneva**, COINTRIN; **Hamburg**, FUHLSBUTTEL; **Hong Kong**, KAI TAK; **Isle of Man**, RONALDSWAY; **Leeds**, YEADON; **Limerick**, SHANNON; **Liverpool**, SPEKE; **London**, CROYDON (ex), GATWICK, HEATHROW, HOUNSLOW (ex), MAPLIN, NORTHOLT, STANSTED; **Lydd**, FERRYFIELD; **Malta**, VALETTA; **Marseilles**, MARIGNANE; **Melbourne**, TULLAMARINE; **Middlesbrough**, TEES-SIDE; **Minneapolis**, ST PAUL; **Montreal**, DORVAL, MIRABEL; **Moscow**, BYKOVO, DOMODEDOVO, SHEREMETYEVO,

VNUKOVO; **New York,** IDLEWILD, JFK, KENNEDY, LA
GUARDIA; **Oslo,** FORNEBU; **Paris,** DE GAULLE, LE
BOURGET, ORLY, ROISSY; **Peking,** BEIJING; **Rio de
Janeiro,** SANTOS DUMONT; **Rome,** CIAMPINO,
FIUMICINO, LEONARDO DA VINCI; **Rotterdam,**
WAALHAVEN; **Saigon,** TAN-SON-NHUT; **Seattle,** TACOMA;
Southampton, EASTLEIGH; **Stockholm,** ARLANDA,
BROMMA; **Sydney,** KINGSFORD SMITH; **Tel Aviv,** LOD;
Tokyo, NARITA; **Washington,** DULLES.

AL ALUMINIUM (chem). CAPONE, GANGSTER. ALBERT,
ALEC (abbr). ALABAMA (US *state*). ALBANIA (*car plate*).
ALBERTA (*province*, Can).

ALAS PITY! WOE! (Yorick, Hamlet, *Shak*). ALASKA (US *state*).

ALBAN 1. Roman soldier who was first Christian martyr in Britain,
AD 304; canonized. 2. *Episcopal sig* of ST ALBANS.

ALBATROSS *BIRD*, PETREL [Ill-omen]. Three under *par* on *golf
course*.

ALECTO One of the *FURIES*.

ALEXANDER BEETLE (*A.A. Milne*). THE GREAT
(Bucephalus, horse). FIELD MARSHAL. *MILITARY
LEADER*. [Antipater (Macedonia)].

ALGOPHILE *Lover* of pain.

ALGOPHOBIA *Aversion* to pain.

ALIAS OTHERWISE. NOM DE PLUME, PEN NAME.

ALIBI ELSEWHERE (**opp** = ibid) [**saying**]. EXCUSE [crime].

ALICE Girl's name, especially character by Lewis Carroll (Rev
Charles Lutwidge Dodgson) in '~ in Wonderland'; drawings by
John Tenniel; **other characters:** Dinah the *cat*, the White *Rabbit*,
Bill the *lizard* (curiouser and curiouser); Dodo, *Dory, Duck*,
Eaglet, Mouse (Caucus-race); Caterpillar (hookah, mushroom,
Father William); Dormouse, Mad Hatter, March Hare (tea-
party); King, Queen and Knave of *Hearts*, 1-10 of *Hearts*
(children), 2, 5 and 7 of *Spades* (*gardeners*), courtiers
(*Diamonds*), *soldiers* (*Clubs*), Duchess, Cheshire *Cat* (vanished
but for its smile), hedgehogs, flamingos and soldiers (respectively,
croquet balls, mallets and hoops; 'off with his head'); Mock
Turtle, Gryphon (arithmetic: ambition, distraction, uglification,
derision; mystery ancient and modern; sea-ography; drawling,

stretching and fainting in coils; laughing and grief; lobster quadrille, porpoise, snail, whiting). Also 'Through the Looking-Glass (and what Alice Found There)'; **other characters:** Red and White Kings, Queens and Knights; Dinah the *cat*; Tiger-Lily; Jabberwock, Tove, Borogrove, Mome Rath, Jubjub Bird, Bandersnatch, Tumtum Tree, Vorpal Sword, Tulgey Wood; Tweedledum, Tweedledee, Humpty Dumpty; Gnat, Goat, *Beetle*, Rocking-horse fly, *Walrus*, *Carpenter*, *Oysters*, *Lion*, Unicorn; Haigha, Hatta (*messengers*). **Inspiration** = Alice Liddell.

ALIGNMENT DRESSING, *ROW*.

ALIVE ACTIVE, BRISK, RESPONSIVE; SWITCHED ON, WORKING, LIVING, QUICK (**opp** = *dead*).

ALKALINITY PH (**opp** = acidity).

ALL 1. (s/l *awl*). WHOLE, WHOLLY (**opp** = none). BOTH SIDES, EACH, EVERYBODY. *SUM*, TOTAL (**opp** = *part*). ENTIRELY, QUITE. *HUNDRED*, C (crypt); A*FIFTY*FIFTY (crypt, hence A HALF). 2. Start antonym with O, e.g. **All female sign** (4) = OMEN.

ALLOCATED *Anag*. ALLOTTED, ASSIGNED, DEVOTED, PUT IN PLACE; APPORTIONED.

ALLOW ADMIT, CONCEDE (**opp** = deny). *LET*, PERMIT, TOLERATE (**opp** = *refuse*). ASSERT, CONSIDER. ADVANCE, GIVE.

ALLOY *Anag*. DEBASE, MIX, MODERATE.

ALMOST 1. NEARLY, NIGH. 2. Word less one or two letters, e.g. **Almost dinner on target** (5) = *INNER.

ALONE 1. EXCLUSIVELY, ONLY. APART, NOT WITH OTHERS, SOLO. 2. 'One is one and all alone' in *song*.

ALPH 1. Sacred Gk *river*. 2. First half of alphabet, i.e. A*TO*M.

ALPHA A, FIRST, GOOD. CHIEF STAR.

ALSO-RAN FAILURE, UNPLACED (**opp** = *first*, winner).

ALTERNATING *Anag*. CHOICE, OR. DEPUTY, SUBSTITUTE; INTERCHANGING.

~ **CURRENT** AC.

ALUMINIUM *AL (chem)*. LIGHT *ALLOY*.

ALWAYS EER, EVER, REPEATEDLY (**opp** = *never*). NESW or any *anag* (crypt).

AM Amplitude modulation (radio). ANTE MERIDIEM, MORNING. I EXIST. FIRST AID MAN (crypt).

A — M A*TO*M (crypt); hence *ALPH* (crypt).

AMAZON *RIVER*. *WOMAN WARRIOR*, HIPPOLYTE, PHILOSTRATE (MND, *Shak*).

AMERICAN INDIAN BRAVE, REDSKIN, TRIBESMAN (**opp** = paleface); HIAWATHA, MINIHAHA (Longfellow); POCAHONTAS [squaw, teepee, wigwam]; **celebrated:**

3-letters
FOX (N)
WEA (N)

4-letters
CREE (N)
CROW (N)
ERIE (N)
INCA (S)
MAYA (S)

5-letters
ADENA (N)
AZTEC (S)
CREEK (N)
HAIDA (N)
HURON (N)
MIAMI (N)
NAZCA (S)
OLMEC (Mex)
OMAHA (N)
PONCA (N)
SIOUX (N)

6-letters
APACHE (N)
APINAI (S)
ATOARA (S)
CAYUGA (N)[6]

DAKOTA (N)
LENAPE (N)
MICMAC (N)
MOHAVE (N)
MOHAWK (N)[6]
MOJAVE (N)
NOOTKA (N)
ONEIDA (N)[6]
OTTAWA (N)
PANARE (S)
PAWNEE (N)
SENECA (N)[6]
SIWASH (N)
TOLTEC (N)
TUPIAN (S)

7-letters
ARAPAHO(E) (N)
ARAUCAN (S)
CHIBCHA (S)
CHOCTAW (N)
FUEGIAN (S)
MOHICAN (N)
QUECHUA (S)
SHAWNEE (N)
TLINGIT (N)
WAIMIRI (S)
WYANDOT (N)

8-letters
ARAPAHO(E) (N)
ARIKAREE (N)
CHEROKEE (N)
CHEYENNE (N)
CHIBCHAN (S)
CHIPPEWA (N)
COMANCHE (N)
DELAWARE (N)
IROQUOIS (N)
MESQUITO (S)
ONONDAGA (N)[6]
PUEBLOAN (N)
QUICHUAN (S)
SEMINOLE (N)
SHOSHONE (N)

9+ letters
ALACALUFAN (S)
ALGONQUIAN (N)
ATHABASCAN (N)
BLACKFOOT (N)
CHICKASAW (N)
GUARANIAN (S)
HOOCHINOO (N)
MICCOSUKEE (N)
PATAGONIAN (S)
PUELCHEAN (S)
TUSCARORA (N)[6]

[6] = One of the Confederation of Six Nations.

AMETHYST *GEM*, PRECIOUS STONE; *Birthstone* (February). *COLOUR* (purple).

AMISS *Anag.* INAPPROPRIATE, OFFENCE, WRONG. A*GIRL, A*SPINSTER (crypt).

AMONG AMID, AMIDST. Hidden word.

AMOR = *CUPID*, Rom *god* of *LOVE*; (**Gk** = EROS).

AMP AMPERE (elect). A member (crypt).

AMPHITRITE Gk myth *Nereid* or Oceanid, goddess of the sea. The d of *Nereus*, mar to *Poseidon*, she was m of Triton.

AMPHITRYON In order to seduce ~'s wife Alcmena, *Zeus* gave a party in ~'s house in his absence. ~ returned home and claimed to be the *host* but, as Molière put it, he who gives the party is reckoned to be the host (the other is presumably the *servant*). In Gk myth, Alcmena subsequently gave birth to *Heracles*.

AN Article. IF (arch).

ANAESTHETIC *Drug*, DULLER, GAS, NEEDLE; NUMBER (crypt). [hospital, operation].

Anag ANAGRAM. ADJUST, ARRANGE, *ORDER*, RE-ORDER. About ten per cent of all clues are capable of being interpreted as intending an anagram. To give just a few examples from the first letter of the alphabet, of words which can be so interpreted: adrift, afresh, allocated, alloy, altered, alternate, amiss, angled, annoyed, anyway, arranged, awful, awkward. All those can be construed in another way (both 'construed' and 'in another way' are also candidates). In this *Companion*, the word 'anagram' is taken to mean any re-ordering of letters, even if they do not in themselves make a word – they may form only part of the final word. So, if a clue is troublesome, try looking for an anagram somewhere – and the word or words giving the letters may not necessarily be actually in the clue. Thus: **I cut a deep ditch arranged for defensive purposes** (9) gives: **I cut a moat** = AUTOMATIC. The anagram indicator may appear in the answer, i.e. **Ham for cat** = ACT BADLY.

ANAPAEST *FOOT*.

ANATOLE *FRANCE*.

ANDERSEN Hans Christian ~, Danish writer; **stories:** Emperor's New Clothes (*Nude*); Inchelina (Maja); Little Mermaid; *Nightingale* (clockwork); Princess and the Pea (*bed*); Red Shoes (*dancing*); Snowman (stove); Snow Queen; Tinderbox (*dogs*); Tin

Soldier (ballerina, steadfast); Ugly Duckling (*swan*); Wild Swans (Elisa).

AND NOT 1. NOR. 2. Add NOT before or after word, e.g. **Cold and not remarked** (7) = NOT*ICED.

ANDREW *PATRON SAINT* (Sc) [Apostle, Fisherman, 30 Nov].

ANDROMEDA 1. Gk myth heroine who was chained to a rock as sacrifice to a *monster* sent by the *Nereids*, who were angry at her beauty. *Perseus* turned the monster to stone by exhibiting the head of *Medusa*, and he then married Andromeda. 2. A *constellation* in N hemisphere.

ANGEL *BACKER. CAKE. COIN.* CHERUB, SAINT, ST **(saying)**. ITHURIEL (Paradise Lost, Milton). [*Nine* angelic orders]. *SHARK. WATERFALL.* **Pl** = HEIGHT (RAF sl).

ANGER DISPLEASURE, DISTEMPER, ENRAGE, HEAT, IRE, RILE, *TEMPER*, WRATH (**opp** = pleasure).

ANGLE ARRANGE, CONTRIVE. ASPECT, *BEARING*, POINT OF VIEW. *FISH. TRIBESMAN* (Eur).

ANGLOMANIA *Love* of English ways.

ANGLOPHOBIA *Aversion* to English ways.

ANNIVERSARY DATE (yearly return); CELEBRATION.

(1) *PAPER*	(14) *IVORY*
(2) *COTTON*	(15) *CRYSTAL*
(3) *FEATHER*	(20) *CHINA*
(4) *FLOWER*	(25) *SILVER*
(5) *WOOD*	(30) *PEARL*
(6) *CANDY*	(35) *CORAL*
(7) *WOOL* or *COPPER*	(40) *RUBY*
(8) *BRONZE*	(45) *SAPPHIRE*
(9) *POTTERY*	(50) *GOLD*
(10) *TIN*	(55) *EMERALD*
(11) *STEEL*	(60) *DIAMOND*
(12) *SILK*	(70) *PLATINUM*
(13) *LACE*	(75) *(DIAMOND)*

ANNO DOMINI AD, NOWADAYS. TO (if allied to 'shortly' or similar word indicating abbreviation to A.D.; crypt).

ANNOY *Anag.* GALL, HARASS, IRRITATE, MOLEST, RILE (**opp** = *please*).

ANNUAL *FLOWER*. YEARLY. *BOOK*, DIARY.
ANON *SOON*. ANONYMOUS, UNKNOWN.
ANT INSECT; EMMET; *WORKER*. ARE NOT, IF IT (arch).
ANTE (s/l *anti*). BEFORE, PRE. *BET*, STAKE, WAGER.
ANTELOPE Ruminant quadruped, like a *deer*; **breeds:**

ADDAX	GRYSBOK	PALLAH
AUDAX	HART	PRONGHORN
BLACKBUCK	HARTEBEEST	PYGARG (bibl)
BONGO	IMPALA	REEBOK
BUSHBUK	*INDIAN*	*ROYAL*
CHAMOIS	IZARD	SAIGA
CHIRU	KAAMA	SASIN
CHOUSINGHA	KLIPSPRINGER	SEROW
DIK-DIK	KOB	*SPRINGBOK*
DUIKER	KUDU	STEINBOK
ELAND	NILGAI	TAKIN
GAZELLE	NYALA	TARTARY
GEMSBOK	OKAPI	THAR
GNU	ORIBI	WILDEBEEST
GORAL	ORYX	

ANTE MERIDIEM *AM*, FORENOON, MORNING.
ANTEPENULTIMATE LAST BUT TWO, SECOND FROM
 LAST, CHI (Gr), X.
ANTHONY (s/l *Antony*). HOPE. PATRON OF SWINEHERDS.
 RUNT.
ANTI (s/l *ante*). AGAINST, VERSUS, V, VS (**opp** = *pro*).
ANTI-AIRCRAFT *AA*, FLAK. V-BOMBER (crypt).
ANTICIPATE 1. EXPECT, FORESTALL. 2. Come before in a
 word, e.g. **He anticipates the record to be of assistance** (4) =
 HE*LP.
ANTONY (s/l *Antony*). 1. MARK ~, lived B.C. 83-30. Ally of
 Caesar, mar (1) Fulvia, (2) Octavia, (3) Cleopatra (paramour).
 Triumvirate B.C. 43. Infatuated with Cleopatra, he forsook *Rome*
 and turned Egyptian. Beaten at sea by Octavian (his br-in-law) at
 Actium, he committed suicide in Alexandria. 2. ~ and Cleopatra
 (*Shak*).
ANUBIS Gk rendering of Egy *conductor* of souls to *Osiris*; it had a

hyena's head (sometimes jackal).

ANVIL BLOCK, SHAPE [*smith*]. BONE (*ear*). *INSTRUMENT* (mus).

ANYWAY *Anag.* IN ANY WAY, IN ANY CASE, AT ANY RATE, REGARDLESS.

AOC AIR OFFICER COMMANDING (mil).

AP ASSOCIATED PRESS; *PRESS, REPORTERS.* SON OF (Wal).

APE COPY, IMITATE, MIMIC, TAKE OFF. TAILLESS *MONKEY* (hence MONKE, crypt); **breeds:** BARBARY, CHIMPANZEE, GIBBON, GORILLA, MAGOT, ORANG-(O)UTANG.

APELIOTES Gk myth EAST *WIND* (**Rom** = SUBSOLANUS).

APHRODITE Gk *goddess* of LOVE (**Rom** = *VENUS*), d of *Zeus* and Dione; mar Hephaestus (**Rom** = *Vulcan*), and m of *Eros* by *Ares.* [*ASTARTE, FREYA, ISHTAR, ISIS*].

APOLLO 1. Gk *god* of beauty, music, prophecy, sun etc; s of *Zeus* and Leto, *twin* of *Artemis* and f of many gods, including *Asclepius.* **Rom** = *PHOEBUS.* 2. *SPACECRAFT.*

APOSTLE MESSENGER. **12 of Christ:** ANDREW, BARTHOLOMEW, JAMES, JAMES THE LESS, JOHN, JUDAS ISCARIOT, MATTHEW, PHILIP, SIMON PETER, SIMON THE CANAANITE, THADDEUS, THOMAS; **later:** BARNABAS, ST PAUL, MATTHIAS: also the 70 disciples. *Song.*

APPEAL ATTRACT, PLEASE. RETRIAL [judge]. ASK, BEG, IMPLORE, IMPORTUNE [umpire (cricket)]. HEY, HOY, O, OH.

APPEAR 1. MANIFEST (**opp** = *vanish*) [ghost]. SEEM. 2. Read as . . ., or include word mentioned, e.g. **It appears to me on reflection** (4) = IT*EM.

APPLE FRUIT; TREE (genus Malus) [*Adam, Atalanta, Heracles, Hesperides, Paris*]; **types:**

BRAMLEY'S SEEDLINGS, CAPE DELICIOUS, COX'S ORANGE PIPPIN, DISCOVERY, EGREMONT, ELLISON'S ORANGE, EPICURE, GEORGE CAVE, GOLDEN DELICIOUS, GOLDEN NOBLE, GRANNY SMITH, GRENADIER, HOWGATE WONDER, IDARED, JAMES

GRIEVE, KIDD'S ORANGE RED, LANE'S PRINCE
ALBERT, LAXTON'S FORTUNE, LORD DERBY, LORD
LAMBOURNE, MERTON KNAVE, NON PAREIL,
ORLEANS REINETTE, RUSSET, SPARTAN, ST
EDMUND'S RUSSET, SUNSET, WORCESTER
PEARMAIN. **Pl** = *STAIRS* (rh sl).

APPOINTMENT ASSIGNATION, *DATE*, *ENGAGEMENT*,
MEETING, TRYST. *DEGREE*, *OFFICE*, ORDINANCE,
POSITION, POSTING. EQUIPMENT, FITTING;
FURNISHING, OUTFIT (and pl).

APRIL (4th) MONTH, M, APR (Rom Aprilis, bud-opening);
(**birthstone** = *diamond*) [~ fool; ~ showers]. Girl's name.

APT APPROPRIATE, SUITABLE. CLEVER,
QUICK-WITTED. *TEND*. ADVANCED PASSENGER
TRAIN (rly).

AQUAMARINE *GEM*; *BERYL*. *COLOUR* (blue-green).

AQUILO Rom myth NE *WIND* (**Gk** = KAIKAS).

ARACHNE Gk myth d of Idmon, who was turned into a *spider*.

ARCH *BRIDGE*, SPAN, VAULT. *COY*, PERT, PLAYFUL,
SAUCY, *SHY*, *TEASING* (**opp** = *modest*). CHIEF,
SUPERIOR. ARCHAIC (abbr). ARCHITECTURE (abbr).

ARCHER 1. *BRIDGE*, SPAN, VAULT (crypt). *BOWMAN*,
TOXOPHILIST; **celebrated:** *CUPID*, DAN (radio), ROBIN
HOOD, WILLIAM TELL. 2. *Constellation* (Sagittarius); (9th)
sign of *Zodiac*.

ARCHIMEDES Gk mathematician (B.C. 287-212) who invented the
screw for pumping water (cochlea); also discovered the principle
of water displacement [eureka!], and the use of the lever.

ARCHITECT THE CREATOR, GOD. ACHIEVER,
SCHEMER. BUILDER, DESIGNER, PLANNER; **celebrated:**
ADAM, INIGO JONES, LUTYENS, SIR GILES GILBERT
SCOTT, WREN [si monumentum requiris, circumspice].

ARCHITECTURE BUILDING ART, ~ CONSTRUCTION,
~ LAYOUT, ~ SCIENCE (see *castle* for special fortification
terms); **styles:** Arenated, Byzantine, Decorated, Early English,
Eastern, Egyptian, Gothic, Grecian, Jacobean, Minoan, Norman,
Perpendicular, Pointed, Rectilinear, Renaissance, Romanesque,
Sumerian, Superimposed, Trabeated, Transitional; **Five Orders:**

Composite, Corinthian, Doric, Ionic, Tuscan. **Terms** (and see *Cathedral parts*):

4-letters
ARCH (cinquefoil, elliptical, gothic, horseshoe, ogee, norman, pointed, segmented, semi-circular, trefoil)
DADO (body of a pedestal)
JAMB (side of a chimney, door or window)
OGEE (round and hollow moulding; type of arch)
STOA (portico, roofed colonnade)

5-letters
AMBRY (niche)
GABLE (triangular upper part of wall)
NICHE (recess for statue, vessel or ornament)
OGIVE (gothic arch)
SHAFT (main part of column)
SOCLE (plinth)
TORUS (semi-circular moulding)

6-letters
ABACUS (upper part of capital)
ALMERY (niche)
ARCADE (series of arches [colonnade])
ASHLAR, -ER (hewn stone)
AUMBRY (niche)
AUMERY (niche)
COLUMN (vertical pillar comprising plinth, foot, base, dado, cornice and capital)
CORBEL (projecting frame support)
CUPOLA (ceiling of a dome)
FINIAL (pinnacle or spire ornament)
FLECHE (spire)
FRIEZE (relief band on entablature)
IMPOST (top of pillar)
LANCET (arch)
LIERNE (cross rib)
LINTEL (top of doorway)
METOPE (recess in frieze [*intaglio*])
PILLAR (vertical support or ornament)

PLINTH (projecting base of column)
SCREEN (partition)
SOFFIT (undersurface of arch or ceiling)
VOLUTE (spiral scroll)

7-letters
CAPITAL (head of column)
CORNICE (top of column)
ECHINUS (egg and anchor ornament)
ENTASIS (swelling column)
PORTICO (range of columns)
TRANSOM (horizontal bar in window)

8-letters
ABUTMENT (pier, wall of arch)
ASTRAGAL (beading)
ATLANTES (male supporting figures [Caryatides])
BUTTRESS (support)
GARGOYLE (grotesque animal forming water spout)
KEYSTONE (topmost voussoir)
PEDESTAL (base of column; specially, a whole Classical
  column)
PEDIMENT (triangular gable)
PILASTER (square supporting column)
TRIGLYPH (projection on frieze [*cameo*])
VOUSSOIR (tapered archstone)

9+ letters
ARCHITRAVE (ornamental door moulding)
BALUSTRADE (parapet)
COLONNADE (series of columns [arcade])
ENTABLATURE (superstructure across two columns)
CARYATIDES (female supporting figures [Atlantes])
STANCHION (vertical bar in window)
TRIFORIUM (gallery)

ARENA RING, SPHERE, ZONE.
ARE NOT AINT, ANT, ARENT.
ARES Gk *god* of WAR (**Rom** = *MARS*); s of *Zeus* and *Hera*.

Arg Argentina, ~ian.

ARGENT AG (*chem*); *SILVER* (*herald*). FRENCH MONEY (crypt).

ARGON A (*chem*); GAS (inert).

ARGONAUT CEPHALOPOD, NAUTILUS (zool). **Pl** = Gk myth adventurers who sailed in the Argo under *Jason* in search of the *golden fleece*: ADMETUS (mar Alcestis), AMPHIARUS (a *prophet*), CALAIS (s of *Boreas*), *CASTOR*, GLAUCUS (builder, but see *Argus*, and *steersman* of the Argo), *HERACLES*, MOPSUS (a *prophet*), NESTOR (a *sage*), *ORPHEUS* (a *singer*), PELEUS (f of *Achilles*), PHILAMON (a *poet*), *POLLUX*, *THESEUS*, TYDEUS (f of Diomedes), ZETES (s of *Boreas*).

ARGUS 1. Gk myth *god* with 100 eyes, set by *Hera* to watch *Io*. Stolen by *Hermes*, his eyes were placed on the peacock's tail. 2. *Ulysses'* dog (also ARGOS). 3. Some say builder of the Argo (but see *Argonaut*); s of Phrixus. 4. PHEASANT.

ARIADNE 1. Gk myth d of *Minos*, who mar *Dionysus*. Helped *Theseus* to escape from the *labyrinth* by means of a silken thread, and then went to Naxos. 2. A minor *PLANET*.

ARIEL (s/l aerial). SPRITE, *SPIRIT*. Character in Temp (*Shak*).

ARMOUR MAIL, PROTECTION (chain ~, plate ~); **parts:** ACTON (jacket), BEAVER (jaws), BREASTPLATE (breast), CUIRASS (body), CUISSE (thigh), GORGET (neck), GREAVE (shin), HABERGEON (coat), HAUBERK (coat), HELM (head), PANOPLY (suit), PAULDRON (shoulders), TASSET (hip), VAMBRACE (arm), VISOR (eyes). [chain ~, plate ~, *patron saint*].

ARMS (s/l alms). LIMBS, MEMBERS (*bone*). SLEEVES. BRANCHES. *WEAPONS*. *HERALDRY*.

ARMY 1. *SA*. *TA*. CORPS, HOST, *SOLDIERS* [~ and Navy *Club*/Stores; Fred Karno's ~; Salvation ~]. *KALI* (crypt). 2. Of the arm, e.g. **army cover** = SLEEVE; **army connections** = SHOULDERS.

AROUND 1. ABOUT. A*ROUND q.v. A*BULLET (crypt). 2. Reverse the word, e.g. **Idol to follow around** (3) = GOD.

ARRIVAL TIME ETA. BIRTHDAY (crypt).

ARRIVED CAME, HERE. MADE.

ARRIVES ARR. COMES. (**opp** = *leaves*).

ARROW *DART*, FLECHETTE, FLIGHT; *MISSILE*, *WEAPON* [*Bowman*]. *GRASS*. DIRECTION INDICATOR, POINTER, SIGNPOST. ~ ROOT.

ARSENIC AS (*chem*). POISON, SEMI-METALLIC ELEMENT. [Old Lace].

ARSON FIRE-RAISING, INCENDIARISM; LIGHT CRIME (Pyro-*mania*).

ARSONIST BLAZER, FIREMAN, PYRO-*MANIAC*.

ART 1. CRAFT, KNACK, SKILL. ARTICLE. ARE (arch). ARTHUR (abbr). PAINTING, SCULPTURE. 2. **Goddess: Gk** = *ATHENE*, **Rom** = MINERVA.

ARTEMIS 1. Gk virgin *goddess* of *nature* and *hunting* (**Rom** = *DIANA*); d of *Zeus* and Leto, and *twin* of *Apollo* [UPIS, HECATE, SELENE]. A minor *PLANET*.

ARTEMISIA Queen of Halicarnassus; mar Mausolus and built the *Mausoleum* as his tomb [*Daedalus*, *Minos*].

ARTICLE A, AN, ART, THE. ITEM, THING. CLAUSE, PARTICULAR. LITERARY PIECE, WRITING. **Pl** = APPRENTICESHIP.

ARTILLERY *RA*; GUNS, *WEAPONS*.

ARTIST (s/l *Artiste*). *RA*; *PAINTER*. CRAFTSMAN, DEVOTEE; THESPIAN.

ARTISTE (s/l *Artist*). DANCER, PERFORMER, SINGER, THESPIAN [*stage*].

ARTS MAN BA, MA.

AS *ARSENIC* (*chem*). ROMAN *COIN*. BECAUSE; LIKE. WHEN. FRENCH *ACE*.

AS AT QUA.

A-Sax Anglo-Saxon.

ASCENT 1. CLIMB, MOUNTING, RISE. 2. Word reads upwards (dn).

ASCLEPIUS Gk *god* of medicine, s of *Apollo*; mar Epione and f of *Hygieia*; killed by *Zeus* with a *thunderbolt*. His attribution is a staff with entwined winged serpent. *Hippocrates* was one of his supposed descendants (the Asclepidae) [*Oath*]. **Rom** = AESCULAPIUS.

ASP *SNAKE* [A and C, *Shak*]. AS SOON AS POSSIBLE.

ASPIRATION AMBITION, HOPE. Sound the letter H. BREATHING, VENTILATION.

ASS ASSASSINATED, ~ION. BURRO (US). DONKEY,
MOKE; NEDDY [mule]; **breed:** ONAGER; **male** = *JACK*,
female = *JENNY*; [hinny]. FOOL ABOUT. BACKSIDE (US).

ASSEMBLY DELIBERATIVE BODY, *LEGISLATIVE*
COUNCIL. FITTING TOGETHER, MANUFACTURING,
PRODUCTION. *MUSTER* (mil); CONCOURSE, *CROWD*,
GATHERING, MEETING; COLLECTION OF ANIMALS as:

Antelope	TROOP
Apes	SHREWDNESS
Badgers	CETE
Bees	SWARM
Card players	*SCHOOL*
Cats	CLOWDER
Cattle	*HERD*
Chickens	*FLOCK*
Choughs	CHATTERING
Clans	*GATHERING*
Crows	MURDER
Deer	*HERD*
Doves	*FLIGHT*
Draught animals	*TEAM*
Ducks	*FLIGHT*, PADDLING
Elephants	*HERD*
Finches	*CHARM*
Fish	*SCHOOL*, SHOAL
Foxes	SKULK
Geese (domestic)	*FLOCK*, GAGGLE
Geese (wild)	SKEIN
Goats	*FLOCK, HERD*
Grouse	*PACK*
Gulls	COLONY
Hares	*DOWN*
Hawks	*CAST*
Hens	BROOD
Herons	COLONY, SEDGE
Hounds	PACK
Hyenas	*PACK*
Jellyfish	SMUCK

Kine	DROVE
Kittens	KINDLE
Lapwings	*DESERT*
Larks	*BEVY, EXALTATION*
Leopards	LEPE
Lions	PRIDE
Mallards	*FLUSH*
Monkeys	TROOP
Nightingales	*WATCH*
Oxen	*TEAM*
Partridges	COVEY
Peacocks	*MUSTER*
Penguins	ROOKERY
Pheasants	NIDE, NYE
Pigs	*HERD*
Pigeons	*FLOCK*
Plovers	CONGREGATION
Porpoises	*SCHOOL*
Quails	*BEVY*
Rooks	BUILDING, *ROOKERY*
Seals	*ROOKERY*
Sheep	*FLOCK, HERD*
Snipe	*WISP*
Starlings	MURMURATION
Swans	*HERD, WEDGE*
Swine	*HERD, SOUNDER*
Teal	*SPRING*
Whales	*SCHOOL*
Witches	COVEN
Wolves	*PACK*
Woodcocks	*FALL*
Young *ducks*	*TEAM*
Bevy	*LARKS, QUAILS*
Brood	HENS
Building	*ROOKS*
Cast	HAWKS
Cete	*BADGERS*
Charm	FINCHES

Chattering	CHOUGHS
Clowder	*CATS*
Colony	GULLS, HERONS
Congregation	PLOVERS
Coven	*WITCHES*
Covey	PARTRIDGES
Desert	LAPWINGS
Down	HARES
Drove	KINE
Exaltation	*LARKS*
Fall	WOODCOCK
Flight	DOVES, *DUCKS*
Flock	*CHICKENS, GEESE, GOATS, PIGEONS, SHEEP*
Flush	MALLARDS
Gaggle	*GEESE*
Gathering	CLANS
Herd	CATTLE, *DEER, ELEPHANTS, GOATS, PIGS, SHEEP, SWANS, SWINE*
Kindle	KITTENS
Lepe	LEOPARDS
Murder	*CROWS*
Murmuration	STARLINGS
Muster	PEACOCKS
Nide	PHEASANTS
Nye	PHEASANTS
Pack	*GROUSE, HOUNDS*, HYENAS, *WOLVES*
Paddling	*DUCKS*
Pride	*LIONS*
Rookery	PENGUINS, *ROOKS*, SEALS
School	CARD PLAYERS, *FISH*, PORPOISES, *WHALES*
Sedge	HERONS
Shoal	*FISH*
Shrewdness	*APES*
Skein	*GEESE*
Skulk	*FOXES*

Smuck	JELLYFISH
Sounder	*SWINE*
Spring	TEAL
Swarm	BEES
Team	DRAUGHT ANIMALS, OXEN, YOUNG *DUCKS*
Troop	*ANTELOPES*, MONKEYS
Watch	NIGHTINGALES
Wedge	SWANS
Wisp	SNIPE

ASSESS ESTIMATE, VALUE. JENNY, SHE-MULE.

ASSIST *ABET*, AID, GUIDE, HELP. BE PRESENT, TAKE PART. MULETEER (crypt).

ASSOCIATION FRIENDSHIP. CONNECTION. CLUB, ORGANIZATION. [*Football*].

ASSUME POSIT, POSTULATE. DON, PUT ON. SIMULATE. ARROGANT. UNDERTAKE.

ASSUMPTION 1. ARROGANCE, SIMULATION, TAKING, UNDERTAKING. CLOTHING (crypt). 2. Reception of Virgin Mary in Heaven.

ASTARTE 1. MOLLUSC. 2. Phoen *goddess* of *LOVE*; **Gk** = *APHRODITE*; **Rom** = *VENUS*. 3. Heroine of Byron's poem 'Manfred'.

ASTRONOMY STARGAZING, STUDY OF THE HEAVENS. **Gk Muse** = *URANIA*.

ATALANTA Gk myth maiden who avoided mar by refusing suitors who could not beat her in a race; she killed the unsuccessful. Eventually Milanion (or Hippomenes) distracted her by dropping golden *apples* given him by *Aphrodite*, and he won.

ATE 1. CONSUMED. 2. Gk *goddess*, d of *Zeus*; personification of *RETRIBUTION*. 3. A minor *PLANET*.

ATHENE = PALLAS. Gk *goddess* of *ART*, *WAR*, and *WISDOM*; d of *Zeus*, her *shield* was called *Aegis*. **Rom** = *MINERVA*.

ATHENIAN ATTIC, GREEK [TIMON (*Shak*)].

ATHLETE *BLUE*; COMPETITOR; RUNNER.

AT HOME IN, NOT OUT (**opp** = *out*). COMFORTABLE.

ATLAS 1. MOUNTAIN RANGE. *BONE*, FIRST VERTEBRA. WORLD MAP. 2. Gk myth *TITAN*, who bore the universe on his shoulders; he was turned by *Perseus* into *stone* (and thus became the Atlas mountains). 3. *SPACECRAFT*.

ATOM 1. PARTICLE. SMALL PORTION/QUANTITY. 2. First half of alphabet (i.e. A*to*M) hence *ALPH* (crypt).

ATOMIC NUMBER 1 = HYDROGEN. **92** = URANIUM.

~ WEIGHT 1 = HYDROGEN. **238** = URANIUM.

ATTEMPT ENDEAVOUR, ESSAY, *GO, TRY, TURN*.

ATTENDANT AIDE DE CAMP, PAGE, *SECOND*, SERVANT; WAITING. CONCOMITANT.

ATTENTION HARK, HEED, *LIST*, LISTEN. ERECT, READY, SHUN. CARE, CONSIDERATION.

ATTIC LOFT, TOP ROOM. ATHENIAN, GREEK.

ATTILA King of the *Huns*. He sacked eastern Europe and extorted tribute from Emperor Theodorus. Advancing into *Gaul*, he was defeated in A.D. 451 near Châlons-sur-Marne. He died advancing on Rome two years later.

ATTRACT *DRAW*, PULL (**opp** = *repel*).

ATTRACTIVE ARRESTING, GOOD LOOKING, PRETTY, TAKING (**opp** = *ugly*); MAGNETIC.

AU *GOLD* (*chem*). TO THE FRENCH (crypt).

AUC AB URBE CONDITA (foundation of *Rome*).

AUGEAS Gk legendary king of Elis. Owned stables housing 3,000 oxen, which were cleansed by *Hercules* in one day, when he diverted two rivers for the purpose.

AUGUST IMPRESSIVE, MAJESTIC, NOBLE, VENERABLE. (8th) MONTH, M, AUG (Augustus *Caesar*); **birthstone** = *sardonyx*.

AUK SEABIRD; **breeds:** GUILLEMOT, GREAT ~ (ex), LITTLE ~, PUFFIN, RAZORBILL [cormorant, shag].

AUNT SALLY *SHY*.

AURAL (s/l *oral*). AUDITORY, BY *EAR*.

AURORA 1. Rom *goddess* of *DAWN* (**Gk** = EOS). She rose in the east at the end of night, and crossed the sky in a chariot drawn by two horses. 2. A minor *PLANET*.

Aus Australia, ~n; and *car plate*.

AUSTEN CHAMBERLAIN (polit). JANE, WRITER; **books:** Emma (Hartfield, Highbury; Emma Woodhouse, Mr Knightley, Frank Churchill); Mansfield Park (Northampton; Lady Bertram, Fanny Price); Northanger Abbey (Wiltshire; Morlands, Thorpes,

Tilneys); Persuasion (Kellynch Hall, Somerset; Sir Walter Elliot, Anne Elliot, Capt Wentworth); Pride and Prejudice, ex First Impressions (Longbourn, Netherfield Park, Herts; Elizabeth Bennet, Mr Darcy; Jane Bennet, Mr Bingley; Lydia Bennet, Mr Wickham); Sense and Sensibility (Norland Park, Barton Park, Sussex; Dashwoods, Ferrars, Lucy Steele); The Watsons (unfinished).

AUSTER Rom myth SOUTH *WIND* (**Gk** = NOTOS). AIRCRAFT.

AUSTRIA A; and *car plate*.

AUTHOR *ACCOUNTANT* (crypt). CRIME WRITER, DRAMATIST, NOVELIST, PLAYWRIGHT; ORIGINATOR. See *writers* for list.

AUTHORITY POWER, SAY-SO. EXPERT. *BOOK*.

AUTOLYCUS 1. Gk myth s of *Hermes*; a *robber* who could change all he touched, and so avoid detection. Trapped by *Sisyphus* who marked under the hooves of cattle. 2. Gk astronomer of 4th century B.C. 3. A salesman in the Winter's Tale (*Shak*); 'a snapper-up of unconsidered trifles'.

AUTOMATIC MECHANICAL, NECESSARY, SELF-ACTING, UNCONSCIOUS (**opp** = *contrived*). BREN, BROWNING, COLT, LUGER, STEN, *WEAPON*.

AUTOMATICALLY MECHANICALLY, UNCONSCIOUSLY. OF GUNS, ORDNANCE.

AV AUTHORIZED VERSION, BIBLE. AVIATION.

AVAILABLE DISPOSABLE, ON OFFER, UP FOR GRABS. APPROACHABLE.

AVE HAIL, WELCOME. ALOHA, FAREWELL. AVENUE.

AVENGER EXACTOR OF RETALIATION/RETRIBUTION/ SATISFACTION. *AIRCRAFT*.

AVER AFFIRM, ASSERT, DECLARE. PART MEANS (AVERage; crypt).

AVERAGE ESTIMATE, MEAN, ORDINARY, *PAR*. DAMAGE, LOSS.

AVERSION 1. ANTIPATHY, DISLIKE, FEAR, *HATRED*, PHOBIA (**opp** = *lover*), as:

Beards	POGONOPHOBIA
Dogs	CYNOPHOBIA

Enclosed spaces	CLAUSTROPHOBIA
English customs	ANGLOPHOBIA
Feet	PODOPHOBIA
Fire	PYROPHOBIA
Foreigners	XENOPHOBIA
French customs	GALLOPHOBIA
Heights	ACROPHOBIA
Horses	HIPPOPHOBIA
Open places	AGORAPHOBIA
Pain	ALGOPHOBIA
People/races	GENOPHOBIA
Poisons	TOXIPHOBIA
Russian customs	RUSSOPHOBIA
Spiders	ARACHNEPHOBIA
Strangers	XENOPHOBIA
Water	HYDROPHOBIA
Women	GYNOPHOBIA

2. AN*ACCOUNT, A*BOOK, A*TRANSLATION; A*TURNING (crypt).

AWARD ASSIGN, GRANT, PAYMENT, PENALTY. JUDICIAL DECISION. *HONOUR*, *PRIZE*, TROPHY (theat) most ®: BAFTA (Br film, TV), CEZAR (Fr *Oscar*), *EMMY* (US TV), GOLDEN PALM (Cannes film), GOLDEN ROOSTER (Ch film), GOLDEN ROSE (Montreux film), GRAMMY (US popular music), IVOR NOVELLO (US music), OLIVIER (ex SWET, UK West End theat), *OSCAR* (US film), STELLA (UK film), TONY (US stage).

AWFUL *Anag.* IMPRESSIVE, NOTABLE. *BAD*; FRIGHTENING.

AWKWARD *Anag.* BUNGLING, CALLOW, CLUMSY; EMBARRASSED, *SHY*.

AWL (s/l *all*). AUGER, *DRILL*.

AZURE *BLUE* (herald). CLOUDLESS, SERENE.

B BARON. BEFORE. BELGIUM (*car plate*). BETA. BLACK. BORN. BORON (*chem*). BOWLED. KEY, NOTE. SECOND CLASS.

b born.

BA ARTMAN; BACHELOR OF ARTS. BARIUM (*chem*).

BAAL Chief *god*; *god* of *SUN* (Phoen). FALSE *GOD*.

Bab Babylonia, ~n.

BACCHUS (s/l back us). Rom *god* of *WINE* and *FERTILITY*; also IACCHUS. mar *Ariadne* and was worshipped in drunken orgies (**Gk** = DIONYSUS) [*drink*].

BACHELOR BA, MB. UNMARRIED [*Lear*].

~ OF ARTS BA.

~ OF MEDICINE MB.

BACK 1. BET ON, WAGER. SECOND, SUPPORT. GO BACK, REVERSE. RIVER (Can). **Pl** = *GROUNDS* (C). 2. Reads backwards, e.g. **Backward** = DRAW; **Back seat** = DEB (crypt).

BACKED WAGERED. SUPPORTED. REVERSED, WENT ASTERN. MOUNTED, RIDING, SADDLED [*horse*] (crypt). DE (crypt).

BACKER BETTER, PUNTER. SECOND, SUPPORTER; *ANGEL*. LORD CHANCELLOR (ceremonial). RE (crypt).

BACKWARD 1. ASTERN, REARWARD. UNDEVELOPED. *DRAW* (crypt). 2. Word reversed, e.g. **Backward scholar** = AB.

BACKWATER CUL DE SAC, DEAD END, STAGNATION POINT. WAKE, WASH. RETAW, OOH (H_2O backwards, crypt – but *chem* inaccurate).

BAD(LY) *Anag*. AWFUL. COUNTERFEIT, DEFICIENT, DUD, FOUL, INFERIOR, NO GOOD, ROTTEN, UNPLEASANT, WORTHLESS (**opp** = *good*, *well*).

BADGER WORRY, *TEASE*. ANIMAL [*assembly* (cete); *habitation* (sett)]. SHAVING BRUSH. *AIRCRAFT* (USSR). *ISLAND*.

BAD PRESS CRITICISM, POOR PUBLICITY. *RAG*. SPERS etc (*anag*).

BAFFLED *Anag*. FRUSTRATED, PERPLEXED. DAMPED, SILENCED.

BAG *BOOK*, DEMAND, RESERVE. KILL. CASE; *SACK*. **Pl** = *BAGGAGE*. TROUSERS; PANTS (US).

BAGGAGE BAGS, CASE, EQUIPMENT, GEAR, GRIP, KIT, LUGGAGE, *TRAPS*, TRUNK. HUSSY, JADE, MINX, SAUCY PIECE.

BAGPIPE INSTRUMENT (mus; Ire, Sc); MUSETTE (Fr); **parts:**
bag, bellows, blowpipe, bourdon, chanter, drone.

BAIL (s/l *bale*). SECURITY, SURETY. LIBERATE,
RELEASE. CASTLE WALL. WICKET TOP (cricket).
HOOP HANDLE. ACCOST, BUTTONHOLE (Aus). PUMP
OUT, SCOOP OUT (and *BALE*; naut). [parachute].

BALDER 1. LESS HAIR, SMOOTHER [Brynner; coot; Elisha;
Kojak]. 2. *God* of *SUN* (Nor), s of *Odin* and *Frigg(a)*, m
Nanna; slain by his blind br, who unwittingly used a poisoned
mistletoe dart supplied by *Loki*.

BALE (s/l *bail*). DESTRUCTION, EVIL, MISERY, PAIN,
WOE. PACK, WRAP. *MEASURE* (paper). PUMP OUT,
SCOOP OUT (and *BAIL*; naut). [parachute].

BALL (s/l *bawl*). *DANCE*. PILL; BEAMER, BOUNCER,
DELIVERY, FULL TOSS, LEG BREAK, LONG HOP, OFF
BREAK, YORKER; BOUNDER (crypt). [baseball, billiards,
cricket, *football*, hockey, *rugby*, *snooker*, *squash*, *tennis*].

~ OF CHALK WALK (*rh sl*).

BAN *BAR*, FORBID, VETO.

BAND (s/l *banned*). BOND, STRIP, TIE. CARTEL, CLIQUE,
COTERIE, GANG. HOOP, LOOP, STREAK, STRIPE,
ORCHESTRA, *PLAYERS*.

BANG DIN, EXPLOSION, NOISE. *FIRE*, *SHOOT*. BUMP,
KNOCK. CURL, FRINGE.

BANGER AUTOMATIC, *GUN*, *REVOLVER*, *ROCKET*,
SHELL. FIRECRACKER, *FIREWORK*; *REPORTER* (crypt).
CAR, OLD CROCK (sl). SAUSAGE (sl).

BANK EDGE, *LEAN*, *TILT*. RIVERSIDE, SLOPE; BUND.
PANEL, *ROW*. RELY ON. MONEY BOX, SAFE DEPOSIT;
LODGE (Barclays, *Lloyds*, Midland, Nat-West). MUD ~,
SAND ~ (naut). **Pl** = *STRAIT*.

~ CHARGES INTEREST, COMMISSION. FERRY TOLL,
RIVER TOLL (crypt).

BANKER CASHIER. ROTHSCHILD. DEALER (cards).
AILERON (aero). *RIVER* (crypt) e.g. **London banker** =
THAMES. [football pools].

BANNED (s/l *band*). FORBIDDEN, TABOO, TABU (**opp** =
allowed).

BAR (s/l baa). BISTRO, DIVE, INN, *PUB*, SNUG, *TAVERN*;

COUNTER [*drink*]. REST (mus). ESTOP, OBJECT, PREVENT, SHUT, *STOP*. BAN, FORBID, VETO. GRILLE, GRATING. LEVER. EXCEPT, SAVE. SANDBANK. **Pl** = PRISON.

BARABBAS *Robber* released by Pilate instead of Jesus.

BARGE CHARGE, LURCH, PUSH, SHOVE. *BOAT*: CANAL BOAT, FREIGHTER, HOY, THAMES, WHERRY; HOUSEBOAT; STATE CRAFT.

BARIUM BA (*chem*). METAL.

BARK (s/l barque). HOWL, YAP. RIND, SKIN. ABRADE, GRAZE. *CRY*, *HAWK*, PEDDLE, TOUT. *BOAT*, CLIPPER, SAILING SHIP.

BARKER CRIER, PEDLAR, TOUT. *DOG*. [Actor's benevolent fund].

BARMAID 1. SERVING WENCH, HOSTESS. ALTO, CONTRALTO, SOPRANO (crypt). 2. Gk myth *HEBE*, cupbearer to the *gods* (**Rom** = JUVENTAS).

BARMAN *HOST*, INNKEEPER, *LANDLORD*, PUBLICAN [*Ganymede*]. MUSICIAN (crypt).

BARNET Place (UK). HAIR (*rh sl*).

BARON B. LORD. [Richthofen; Rothschild]. MERCHANT. *JOINT* (meat).

BARONET BT, BART, KT; KNIGHT; SIR.

BARREL CASK, *MEASURE* (beer). CYLINDER, DRUM (capstan, winch). GUN PART.

BARRIE JM, *WRITER* [Peter Pan; **characters:** *Crocodile*, *Darlings*, Capt *Hook*, Lost boys, Nana, *Peter*, *Smee*, Tiger-Lily, Tinkerbell, *Wendy*; Never-Never Land].

BARRIER *FENCE*, *GATE*, RAILING; BOUNDARY, OBSTACLE. DAM. *LISTS*, PALISADE (jousting). DIVIDER; *NET* (tennis).

BART BARONET. BARTHOLOMEW. *PIRATE*.

BASE (s/l *bass*). BOTTOM (**opp** = *top*); FOUNDATION, GROUNDWORK, PRINCIPLE. ARMY CAMP, SUPPORT AREA. ESTABLISH. RELY. *COWARDLY*, DESPICABLE, LOW, *MEAN*, MENIAL.

BASEBALL FOOTBALL GROUND (Derby County). GAME (**originator:** Cartwright) [Joe di Maggio, Babe Ruth, rounders, softball]; **celebrated teams (US):** Boston Red Sox, Brooklyn

Dodgers, Chicago Cubs, Knickerbockers, New York Giants, New York Yankees, Phillies; **venue:** Houston Astrodome.

BASHFUL COY, DIFFIDENT, *MODEST*, SHEEPISH, *SHY* (**opp** = arrogant). *DWARF* (Snow White).

BASIC EDUCATION RRR (crypt).

BASS (s/l *base*). DEEP-SOUNDING, LOW (**opp** = alto). *FISH*, PERCH, SEA-DACE, SEA-WOLF. *STRAIT*. *BEER*®, *DRINK*. FIBRE, LIME-BARK, TIER [*raffia*].

BAT 1. IMPLEMENT; RACKET, RACQUET. *STRIKE*; BATSMAN. PACE, *RATE*, WINK. BINGE, SPREE.
2. Nocturnal flying mammal: Barbastelle, Bechstein's ~, Daubenton's ~, Flittermouse, Flying Fox, Fruit ~, Horseshoe ~, Kalong (largest), Pipistrelle, Vampire. 3. BAGGAGE (arch mil). **Pl** = CRAZY, *MAD*.

BATTALION BN, MEN, *SOLDIERS*, TROOPS.

BATTER BEAT, BREAK, BRUISE, HAMMER, HIT, *STRIKE*. COOKING MIX. PLAYER AT BAT (*baseball, cricket*).

BATTERY ASSAULT, BEATING. *GUNS* (crypt). *ACCUMULATOR*, PILE. COOP, HENHOUSE. INNING(S) (*baseball, cricket*; crypt).

BATTING WINKING. AT STRIKE, *IN*, STRIKING (*baseball, cricket*).

BATTLE STRUGGLE. ARGUMENT. TOWN. *FIGHT, WAR*: **celebrated:**

Air	PLOESTI
ATLANTIC	RUHR
BERLIN	SCHWEINFURT
BLITZ	TARANTO
BRITAIN	
CORAL SEA	**Sea**
GUERNICA	ARMADA
LEYTE GULF	ATLANTIC
LONDON	CAPE ST VINCENT
MALTA	COPENHAGEN
MATAPAN	CORAL SEA
MIDWAY	FALKLANDS
MOHNE DAM	GUADALCANAL
PEARL HARBOR	JUTLAND

LEYTE GULF
MATAPAN
MIDWAY
NILE
PEARL HARBOR
RIVER PLATE
SALAMIS
TARANTO
TRAFALGAR

Nelson
BASTIA (siege)
CALVI (lost eye)
COPENHAGEN
 ('I see no signal')
CAPE ST VINCENT
NILE (Aboukir Bay)
TENERIFE (lost arm)
TOULON
TRAFALGAR (death)

Land
ALAMEIN
ANZIO
ARDENNES
ARNHEM
AUSTERLITZ
BALACLAVA
BORODINO
BULGE
BULL RUN
BURMA
CASSINO
CORUNNA
CRETE
DIEN BIEN PHU
DIEPPE
DUNKIRK
FALKLANDS

FLANDERS
GALLIPOLI
GETTYSBURG
HASTINGS
IWO-JIMA
JENA
LITTLE BIG HORN
MARNE
MONS
OKINAWA
SHILOH
SOMME
STALINGRAD
TOBRUK
VERDUN
VIMY RIDGE
WATERLOO
YPRES

Civil War
ADWALTON MOOR
CHALGROVE FIELD
CROPREDY BRIDGE
DUNBAR
EDGE HILL (first)
GAINSBOROUGH
LANSDOWN
LOSTWITHIEL
MARSTON MOOR
NASEBY (last)
NEWBURY
PRESTON
ROUNDWAY DOWN
SELBY
TURNHAM GREEN
WINNINGTON BRIDGE
WORCESTER (final)

Alfred the Great	Wars of the Roses
ALDERSHOT	BARNET
ASHDOWN (first)	BOSWORTH FIELD (last)
BENFLEET (last)	EDGECOT
CHICHESTER	HEDGLEY MOOR
CHIPPENHAM	HEXHAM
EDDINGTON (Ethandun)	LOSECOAT FIELD
EXETER	MORTIMER'S CROSS
LONDON	ST ALBANS (first)
RIVER STOUR	TEWKESBURY
ROCHESTER	TOWTON
WAREHAM	WAKEFIELD

BATTLESHIP HMS, USS. DREADNOUGHT. CAPITAL SHIP, IRONCLAD. SHIP OF THE LINE. *WEAPON*.

BATTLE ZONE ARENA, FIELD, FRONT, *THEATRE*, WAR ZONE.

BAWL (s/l *ball*). CRY, HOWL, SHOUT, WAIL. REPRIMAND.

BAY (s/l *Bey*). BARK, HOWL [*dog, hound*]. *LAUREL TREE*. *HERB*. *HORSE*. BIGHT, *GULF*, INLET. RECESS, *SIDELINE*. BROWN *COLOUR*.

BB BOYS BRIGADE, CADETS. BARDOT (theat).

BBC BROADCASTING, RADIO, TV. AUNTIE.

BC BEFORE CHRIST. BRITISH COLUMBIA (*Province*, Can).

BDS DENTIST.

BEACHCOMBER LONGSHOREMAN, SCAVENGER, VAGRANT. *WAVE*. HUMORIST.

BEAK *BILL*, NEB (Sc), PECKER (mandible). *MASTER*, TEACHER (sl).

BEAKER BRONZE *AGE* FOLK, PRIMITIVE MAN. EWER, JAR, JUG, POT, URN. *BIRD*, HEN, LAYER (crypt).

BEAM LIGHT, RAY, SHAFT, SPOT. SMILE. JOIST, RAFTER, *SUMMER*, *TIMBER*.

BEAR (s/l bare). ANIMAL; URSA, URSUS; BRUIN; **breeds:** BLACK, BROWN, BRUANG, GIANT PANDA, GRIZZLY, HIMALAYAN, HONEY, KOALA, KODIAK, POLAR, *SLOTH*, SPECTACLED, SUN [**Offspring** = cub]; **celebrated:** BALOO, BOOBOO, MARY PLAIN, PADDINGTON, POOH, RUPERT, THREE BEARS (Goldilocks), YOGI. *AIRCRAFT*

(USSR). CARRY, GIVE BIRTH. ENDURE, SUPPORT.
OVERLOOK, SUBTEND. *ISLAND. CONSTELLATION.*
SPECULATOR (*comm*; **opp** = *bull*). **Pl** = *Football team* (US).

BEARD *BEAVER.* BRISTLES, GROWTH. AWN, EAR
(wheat). DEFY.

BEARER *BED.* CARRIER, *MESSENGER. MOTHER* (crypt).

BEARING 1. E, N, S, W (or NE, SW etc); HEADING. AIR,
APPEARANCE, ASPECT, *CARRIAGE, LOOK*, MIEN;
PORT, PORTAGE. ACCOUCHEMENT, CHILDBIRTH,
LYING IN (crypt). BALL-RACE, ROLLER. LEANING,
PUSHING, RELATION, REFERENCE. CHARGE, DEVICE
(*herald*). 2. Word attached to or 'bearing' another, e.g. **Harsh
south wind bearing east** (7) = AUSTER*E.

BEAT BEST, CHASTISE, LATHER, LICK, OVERCOME,
WORST; SLIPPER, *TAN*, THRASH, WHIP (**opp** = *lose*).
WHISK (cook). PULSE, RHYTHM. PERPLEX. DEFORM,
SHAPE (metal). CLOSE-HAUL, WORK TO WINDWARD
(naut).

BEATER (s/l *beta*). CONQUEROR, *VICTOR*. GAME ROUSER
(shooting). CARPET DUSTER. MIXER, WHIPPER,
WHISK. HEART, PULSATOR. TANNER. DRUMMER
(crypt).

BEAT UP COSH, MUG [GBH]. TAEB (dn).

BEAUTY 1. PULCHRITUDE, GOOD LOOKS; **saying**. 2. **Gods:
Gk and Rom** = *APOLLO*; **goddesses: Gk** = *APHRODITE*, **Rom**
= *VENUS*. [*Adonis, Aphrodite, Apollo, Helen, Paris, Venus* (de
Milo)].

BEAUTY SPOT FACE-PATCH. DELL, PANORAMA, VISTA.

BEAVER *BEARD*. FUR. RODENT (*habitation*). WORK AT.
FACEGUARD, VISOR [*armour*].

BECAUSE AS, FOR, SINCE.

BECK *BROOK, RIVER*, STREAM. CALL, NOD, SIGNAL.

BECOME TURN INTO. BEFIT, FLATTER, *SUIT*.

BED COUCH, DIVAN, *LITTER*, MATTRESS [*Hans Andersen.
Procrustes*]. BASE, FOUNDATION, *SEAT*, STRATUM.
PLANT. PLOT. SEABOTTOM.

BEDDING BEDCLOTHES, BEDLINEN, DUVET; TUCKING
UP. GARDENING (crypt).

BEE (s/l *B, be*). *INSECT*; (BUSY) WORKER; COMBER (crypt);

assembly = swarm. 'DEBORAH' [*Potter*. Queen ~. **companions** = birds, knees].

BEER (s/l *bier*). ALE, *BASS*®, BITTER, *DRINK*, LAGER, MILD, OCTOBER. MUG, PINT (*measure*) [~ and skittles]. PIG'S EAR (*rh sl*).

BEES AND *MONEY* (*rh sl*).

BEETLE *INSECT* (coleoptera) [*study*]; **breeds:** CRUSHER, *DOR*, RAM; **celebrated:** ALEXANDER (*Milne*), Through the Looking Glass (*Alice*). ASTIGMATIC. DICE GAME. OVERHANGING, PROJECTING; SCOWLING, SHAGGY. SCURRY. VOLKSWAGEN.

BEFORE ANTE, B, PRE (**opp** = after).

~ CHRIST BC.

BEGETTER WH (Shakespeare). *FATHER*, SIRE.

BEGGAR MENDICANT [*friar, patron saint*]. BREAK; EXHAUST.

BEGINNER 1. L; DEB, LEARNER, TYRO. *STARTER*. **Pl** = opening actors of new scene (theat). 2. Use first letter of word concerned, e.g. **Circus beginner** = C.

BEHEAD 1. DECAPITATE, EXECUTE, GUILLOTINE. 2. Omit first letter, e.g. **Behead them on the edge** (3) = (*) HEM.

BEHIND TIME 1. *LATE*. 2. Word after synonym for time, e.g. **Under age or behind time** (5) = MIN*OR.

Belg Belgium, ~ian.

BELGIUM B (*car plate*).

BELL (s/l belle). DINGALING, DING-DONG, *RINGER*; *INSTRUMENT* (mus) [campanology: ANGELUS, SANCTUS, Quasimodo (Dumas)]; **celebrated:** BIG BEN (Westminster), BOOM (RAF ch), CZAR KOLOKOL (Moscow), GREAT TOM (Oxford), ST PAUL (St Paul's). INVENTOR (Alexander Graham ~, telephone). WRITER (Brontë); [*Holmes*]. **Pl** = TIME (naut watchkeeping).

BELLEROPHON 1. Gk myth hero who rode *Pegasus* and slew the *monster Chimaera*. 2. Br warship which took Napoleon's surrender.

BELLOWS MAKER BULL, *COW*, OX; *LOWER* (crypt). FLUTE, (*Shak* MND).·

BELL RINGING CAMPANOLOGY; **changes:** Bob Major, Bob Maximus, Bob Minor, Bob Royal, Bob Triple, Grandsire Triple,

Great Tom, Nine Tailors, Oxford Treble Bob, Treble Bob, Yorkshire Surprise Major [Quasimodo].

BELONG *FIT*, GO WITH, *SUIT*. OWNED BY. PROCRASTINATE, TARRY (crypt).

BEM BRITISH EMPIRE MEDAL: *DECORATION*, *MEDAL*.

BEND *S*; *U*; CURVE. *BOW*, STOOP, SUBMIT. APPLY (to task). *KNOT*. PERVERT. SPREE. STRIPE (*herald*) [dexter; sinister (bastardy)]. **Pl** = Decompression sickness (astronauts, divers).

BENDER BINGE, SPREE. STOOP. PERVERTER. HINGE, JOINT; ELBOW, KNEE, KNUCKLE (crypt). *S*, *U* (crypt).

BENT *BOWED*, CRANKED, CURVED, OUT OF TRUE, TWISTED (**opp** = straight). DISHONEST.

BERMUDA *TRIANGLE*. **Pl** = *SHORTS*.

BERRY DOLLAR (US), POUND (sl). FRUIT (without stone); also HIP, HAW, SLOE. [Dornford Yates).

BERYL *GEM*, PRECIOUS STONE; AQUAMARINE, EMERALD (blue, green, white, yellow). GREY, REID (theat).

BESIDES *AGAIN*, AS WELL, ELSE, MOREOVER, OTHERWISE. ALONGSIDE.

BE SORRY APOLOGIZE, CARE, MOPE, REGRET.

BEST A, AI, *ACE*, NO*I; CHOICE, FIRST RATE, TOPS (**opp** = *worst*). *BEAT*; WORST.

BET ANTE, STAKE. GAMBLE, PUNT, RISK, SPECULATE, WAGER; **types:** *ACCUMULATOR*, DOUBLE, HEINZ, TREBLE, TRI-CAST, YANKEE.

BETA (s/l *beater*). B, *SECOND* (LETTER). ELECTRON.

BETRAY(ER) GIVE AWAY, *GRASS*, INFORM, NARK, PEACH, *SHOP*, SING, SNEAK, SPLIT, SQUEAL, STOOL PIGEON, TELL-TALE(S).

BETTER IMPROVED, SUPERIOR. GAMBLER, PUNTER, SPECULATOR; LAYER (crypt).

BETTING ODDS, SP. GAMBLING (and see *bet*).

BEVY *ASSEMBLY*, COMPANY (of beauty, ladies, *larks*, *quails*).

BEY (s/l *bay*). GOVERNOR, OFFICIAL (*Turk*).

BIBLE AV, RV; NT, OT. BOOK OF BOOKS. LAST WORD, MANUAL. [~ *King*].

BIBLICAL TOWN AERE, *AI*, APHEK, BETHEL, CANA, DAN, *DOR*, ENDOR, GATH, GAZA, GEBA, JAHAZ, JERICHO,

NAIN, NEVE, NOB, SIDON, *TYRE*, UR, ZIPH.

BIBLIOMANIA *Obsession* with books.

BIBLIOPHILE *Lover* of books.

BIER (s/l *beer*). FUNERAL LITTER, HEARSE, LAST TRIP/VEHICLE.

BIG OS, LARGE (**opp** = little, small); TIDY (sl). BOASTFUL.

BIG-GAME BEASTS, WILD ANIMALS. CHAMPIONSHIP, FINAL, MATCH, TEST (crypt).

BIGHT (s/l *bite*, byte). *BAY*, *GULF*, INLET. COIL, LOOP (naut).

BIKE RACE *TT* [Isle of Man]. TOUR DE FRANCE.

BILL *AC*, *ACCOUNT*, *CHECK*, INVOICE, *NOTE*, RECKONING, *SETTLEMENT*, TAB. BANKNOTE. POSTER; ANNOUNCE. *MEASURE* (parl). HALBERD, *PIKE*, *WEAPON*. WILLIAM, WM [Old ~ (Bairnsfather)]. *BEAK*; PECK [~ and coo]. *LIZARD* (*Alice*). **Pl** = *Football team* (US).

BILLYCOCK BOWLER *HAT*.

BIRD *GIRL*, YOUNG WOMAN (sl). RASPBERRY (sl). PRISON SENTENCE, *TIME* (sl). *WRITER*. FEATHERED VERTEBRATE; BEAKER, DICKY, LAYER [Audubon, *Male & female, offspring, study*]; **companions** = bees; **breeds** (under 9-letters):

2-letters	MOA (ex)	4-letters
KA	*NUN*	BAYA
OO	*OWL*	BUBO
	PAU	CIRL
3-letters	*PEN*	COCK
AUK (ex)	*PIE*	COOT
COB	POE	CRAX
ELK	ROC (myth)	*CROW*
EMU	ROK (myth)	DODO (ex)
ERN	RUC (myth)	*DOVE*
HEN	*TIT*	*DUCK*
JAY	TUI	ERNE
KAE	WRY	EYAS
KEA		FOWL
MAO		GAWK

Bird

GOWK
GUAN
GULL
HAWK
HERN (arch)
IBIS
KAGU
KAKA
KITE
KIWI
KNOT
KOEL
LARK
LOON
LORY
MINA
MYNA
NIAS
NYAS
PAUW
PAVO
PERN
PICA
PIET
POLL
RAIL
RHEA
ROOK
RUFF
RYPE
SHAG
SKUA
SMEE
SMEW
SWAN
TAHA
TEAL
TERN
TODY

URIA
WEKA
WREN
XEMA
YAUP
YITE
YOIT
YUNX
ZATI

5-letters

AGAMI
AMSEL
ANNET
ARGUS
BIDDY
BOOBY
BOWET
BRENT
BUCCO
CAPON
CHICK
CLAIK
COLIN
CRAKE
CRANE
CURRE
DAKER
DIVER
DUNNE
EAGLE
EGRET
EIDER
FINCH
FRANK
GLEDE
GOOSE
GREBE
HERON

HOBBY
HOMER
IMBER
JAGER
JUNCO
LAYER
LOXIA
LYRIE
MACAW
MADGE
MAVIS
MERLE
MOLLY
MONAL
MURRE
MYNAH
NANDU
NODDY
ORNIS
ORTYX
OUSEL
OUZEL
PAAUW
PEWIT
PICUS
PIPIT
POKER
POLLY
POULT
PURRE
QUAIL
RALPH
RAVEN
REEVE
ROBIN
RODGE
RUDGE
RYPER
SAKER

SALLY
SCAUP
SCOBY
SCOPS
SCOUT
SCULL
SENEX
SERIN
SITTA
SKITE
SNIPE
STILT
STINT
STORK
STRIX
SWIFT
TARIN
TEREK
TIDDY
TOPAU
TOPET
TWITE
URILE
URUBU
VEERY
WADER
WHAUP
WHILK
WONGA
YACOU

6-letters
AIGLET
ANANAS
ANCONA
ARGALA
AVOCET
BOWESS
BULBUL

CANARY
CHOUGH
CONDOR
CORBIE
CORVUS
CUCKOO
CULVER
CURLEW
CUSHAT
CYGNET
DARTER
DIPPER
DRONGO
DUNLIN
EAGLET
FALCON
FULMAR
GANDER
GANNET
GENTOO
GODWIT
GRAKLE
GROUSE
GUINEA
HOOPOE
HOOPOO
JABIRU
JACANA
JERKIN
KELTIS
KONDOR
LANNER
LINNET
LORIOT
MAGPIE
MARROT
MARTIN
MERLIN
MERULA

MISSEL
MISTLE
MOPOKE
MOT-MOT
NANDOO
NESTOR
NICKER
ORIOLE
OSPREY
OUZLEM (myth)
OXBIRD
PARROT
PARSON
PASTOR
PAVONE (arch)
PEAHEN
PEEWIT
PETREL
PHENIX (myth)
PHOEBE
PIGEON
PLOVER
POUTER
PUFFIN
PULLET
QUEEST
QUELEA
QUEZAL
RAPTOR
REDCAP
RUDDOC
SCOTER
SEAHEN
SEAMEW
SERULA
SHRIKE
SICSAC
SIMBIL
SISKIN

SOLAND
SPARVE
SULTAN
SURREY
TATLER
TERCEL
TEWHIT
THRUSH
TOM-TIT
TOUCAN
TROGON
TURBIT
TURKEY
TURNER
TYSTIE
WEAVER
WIGEON
WILLET
WITWAL
XENOPS
YAFFLE
YAFFIL
YUCKER
ZICSAC
ZOO-ZOO

7-letters
AWL-BIRD
BEE-BIRD
BITTERN
BLUE-CAP
BLUE-JAY
BLUE-TIT
BUNTING
BUSHTIT
BUSTARD
BUTCHER
BUZZARD
CHICKEN

COAL-TIT
COLIBRI
COW-BIRD
CREEPER
DIDIDAE
DOTTREL
DUNNOCK
FEN-DUCK
FERN-OWL
FLUSHER
GADWALL
GOBBLER
GORCOCK
GOSHAWK
GRAY-LAG
GRAY-OWL
GREY-HEN
GREY-LAG
HALCYON (myth)
HARRIER
HAWK-OWL
HICKWAY
JACAMAR
JACKDAW
KESTREL
LAPWING
LAVROCK
MALLARD
MARABOU
MAY-BIRD
MOORHEN
ORTOLAN
OSTRICH
OVEN-TIT
PEACOCK
PELICAN
PENGUIN
PETEREL
PHAETON

PHOENIX (myth)
PINNOCK
PINTADO
PINTAIL
POCHARD
POULTRY
QUABIRD
RADDOCK
RATITAE
REDPOLL
REDTAIL
REDWING
ROOSTER
ROSELLA
ROYSTON
RUDDOCK
SAWBILL
SAWWHET
SCOOPER
SEA-CROW
SEA-DOVE
SEA-DUCK
SEAGULL
SEA-HAWK
SKIMMER
SKYLARK
SNOW-OWL
SPARROW
SUNBIRD
SWALLOW
TANAGER
TARROCK
TIERCEL
TITLARK
TOURACO
TUMBLER
VULTURE
WAGTAIL
WARBLER

WAXWING

WHOOPER

WIDGEON

WILLOCK

WIMBREL

WOOD-OWL

WRYBILL

WRYNECK

WYANDOT

YELDRIN

8-letters

ACCENTOR

ADJUTANT

ALCATRAS

AMADAVAT

BARNACLE

BEE-EATER

BELL-BIRD

BLACKCAP

BLUEBIRD

BOATBILL

BOBOLINK

CURASSOW

DABCHICK

DINORNIS

DOTTEREL

DUCKLING

DUN-DIVER

EAGLE-OWL

FALCONET

FENGOOSE

FIRETAIL

FISH-HAWK

FLAMINGO

FORKTAIL

HACKBOLT

HAWFINCH

HEATH-HEN

HORNBILL

LANDRAIL

LANNERET

LINGBIRD

LOVEBIRD

LYRE-BIRD

MARABOUT

MARSH-HEN

MARSH-TIT

MIRE-CROW

MOORCOCK

MOREPORK

NESTLING

NUTHATCH

OVEN-BIRD

OX-PECKER

PARAKEET

PARAQUET

PAROQUET

PENELOPE

PHEASANT

PHILOMER

PICKEREL

PUFF-BIRD

RAINBIRD

REDSHANK

REEDBIRD

REEDLING

RICE-BIRD

RING-BILL

RING-DOVE

RINGTAIL

ROCKDOVE

RUBECULA

SAND-BIRD

SAND-COCK

SAND-LARK

SARCELLE

SARDELLE

SCREAMER

SEA-EAGLE

SEA-QUAIL

SEA-RAVEN

SEDGE-HEN

SHELDUCK

SHOEBILL

SNOWBIRD

SONGBIRD

SONGSTER

STARLING

THRESHER

THROSTLE

TITMOUSE

TITTEREL

WATER-HEN

WHEATEAR

WHIMBREL

WHINCHAT

WILDFOWL

WOODCOCK

WOODLARK

WRANNOCK

XANTHURA

YELDRING

YELDROCK

ZOPILOTE

BIRDIE One under par on a *golf-course*, hence PAR*I or PAR*ONE (dn). [camera].

BIRTHSTONE Jan = *GARNET*; **Feb** = *AMETHYST*;

Mar = *BLOODSTONE*; **Apr** = *DIAMOND*; **May** = *EMERALD*;
Jun = *AGATE*; **Jul** = *CORNELIAN*; **Aug** = *SARDONYX*;
Sep = *CHRYSOLITE*; **Oct** = *OPAL*; **Nov** = *TOPAZ*;
Dec = *TURQUOISE*.

BISHOP *CHURCHMAN*, CLERGYMAN [*episcopal sig*; *see*]; RR,
Rt Rev. CHESSPIECE, *ROOK*. *Military leader* (air).

BIT *BORE*, CUTTING IRON, *HEAD*, PIECE. CHEWED,
GRIPPED, NIPPED. BRIDLE, HACKAMORE, SNAFFLE
(*harness*). MORSEL. SOMEWHAT. CONTRIBUTION.
BINARY DIGIT, COMPUTER INFORMATION.

BITCH *FEMALE* DOG/FOX/OTTER/WOLF. MALICIOUS
WOMAN, TERMAGANT, *VIXEN*. GRUMBLE, MUDDLE.

BITE (s/l *bight*, byte). CHEW, NIP; FOOD, MEAL. BORROW,
EXTORT. STING. GRIP. INFECT.

BL BRITISH LEGION. BRITISH LEYLAND.

BLACK B; *COLOUR*; DARK; SABLE (*herald*); [~ Rod, Garter].
SEA. SNOOKER BALL (score 7).

BLACKBIRD SONGBIRD (turdus merula; thrush family); MERLE
(arch Sc) [24 ~s baked in a pie]. NEGRO SLAVE.
SPY-PLANE (US mil).

BLACKFRIARS DOMINICANS, PREACHING *FRIARS*.
THAMES BRIDGE.

BLACKSMITH FARRIER, FORGER, METAL-WORKER
[*Company* (livery)]; **celebrated:** JAMES BURTON (Kingsley),
JOE GARGERY (Great Expectations, Dickens), THE
VILLAGE ~ (Longfellow).

BLADE LEAF. CHISEL, KNIFE, SWORD. DASHING
FELLOW. Part of bat, oar, paddle wheel, propeller, spade,
turbine.

BLAZE BRIGHT FLAME, BURN, *FIRE*. *COLOUR*, EMIT
LIGHT. PROCLAIM. MARK ON HORSE; SLASH A TREE.

BLAZER COLOURED JACKET, SCHOOL COAT. ARSONIST;
FIREMAN (crypt).

BLEND(ED) *Anag*. *ADMIX*, AMALGAM, MIX, MIXTURE.

BLEW (s/l *blue*). WAFTED. BURST. SPENT,
SQUANDERED.

BLIND RASH, RECKLESS, UNSWERVING. CONCEALED,
DEAD-END, PLAIN, WALLED-UP. DAZZLE, DECEIVE.
ANOPTIC, SIGHTLESS, UNSEEING [King of Bohemia.

Oedipus. Pew (*Stevenson*). Bat, mole, owl]. AWNING,
CURTAIN, SCREEN, SHUTTER, SUNSHADE. DUMMY,
MASK, PRETEXT, SMOKE-SCREEN, STALKING-HORSE,
SUBTERFUGE, VEIL. DRUNK (sl).

BLONDEL MINSTREL [*Lionheart*, ransom, Richard].

BLOODSTONE *GEM*, SEMI-PRECIOUS STONE,
CHALCEDONY (green/red). *Birthstone* (Mar).

BLOODSUCKER LEECH, *MOSQUITO*, *TICK*, VAMPIRE.
GOLD-DIGGER (sl).

BLOOMER BLUNDER, ERROR, MISTAKE. FLOWER
(crypt). **Pl** = *DRAWERS*, KNICKERS, UNDERWEAR.

BLOOMING FLOWERING, *OUT*. DASHED, WRETCHED.

BLOW PANT, PUFF, VENT, *WIND*. EXPLODE, PUNCTURE.
BREAK, FUSE, MELT. *BETRAY*. FLY'S EGGS. HIT,
KNOCK, ONER, *SMACK*. DISASTER, SHOCK. SPEND,
SQUANDER. *COMPOSER*.

BLOWER *WIND*. ENGINE, PUFFER, STEAM-TRAIN.
SUPERCHARGER (sl). TELEPHONE (sl).

BLOW-OUT PUNCTURE; FUSED. VOLCANO (crypt).
MEAL. *Anag* 'blow'.

BLUE (s/l *blew*). *COLOUR*, AZURE (*herald*), INDIGO (anil,
woad). SNOOKER BALL (score 5). COLD, DEPRESSED,
DISCONSOLATE, DISPIRITED, DOWN, LOW. BRUISED.
FEAR. INDECENT, SALTY. LEARNED. *GRASS*.
OXFORD or *CAMBRIDGE ATHLETE* or *PLAYER*.
SPEND. **Pl** = DEPRESSION, DUMPS. HORSEGUARDS,
HOUSEHOLD CAVALRY. UNIVERSITY TEAM (O and C).

BLUSH *COLOUR*, FLUSH, REDDEN. GLANCE, GLIMPSE.

BM BRITISH MUSEUM.

BMA BRITISH MEDICAL ASSOCIATION.

B MUS MUSICIAN.

BN BATTALION, *SOLDIERS*, TROOPS.

BO BODY ODOUR [perspiration, sweat]. Sacred tree of Buddha.

BOADICEA BOUDICCA. Queen of the *Iceni*, she withstood the
Romans, defeating them at Camulodunum (*Colchester*) and
London, where she slew 50,000. Was finally defeated by
Suetonius Paulinus, and committed suicide in A.D. 61.

BOAR (s/l *bore*). *MALE PIG*/GUINEA-PIG. [Labour of
Heracles].

82   *Board*

BOARD (s/l *bored*). *FOOD*, KEEP, MEALS; *TABLE*. PLANK,
SLAB. COVER OVER. EMBARK, GET ABOARD/ON.
SHIP'S SIDE, TACK. *DIRECTORS*.

BOARD, ON 1. EMBARKED. 2. Word with S . . . S round it, e.g.
I go on board to find my little sister (3) = S*I*S. 3. Game played
on a board: CHECKERS, CHESS, DRAFTS, DRAUGHTS,
LUDO etc. 4. AT TABLE, DINING.

BOAT ARGO(SY), PACKET, SHIP, SS, *VESSEL*; **types:**

3-letters	*BARGE*	PACKET
ARK	CANOE	RANDAN
CAT	DANDY	ROWING
COB	E-BOAT (mil)	SAMPAN
FLY	*FUNNY*	SETTEE
GIG	*KETCH*	SURFER
HOY	*LINER*	TARTAN
MTB (mil)	PARDO	TENDER
TUG	PRAAM	VESSEL
	PRAHU	*WHALER*
4-letters	SKIFF	WHERRY
BARK	SLOOP	
BRIG	*SMACK*	**7-letters**
BUSS	U-BOAT (mil)	BEAN-COD
DORY	XEBEC	BUGALET
JUNK	YACHT	CARRIER (mil)
KOFF		CHAMPAN
PINK	**6-letters**	*CLIPPER*
PRAM	ARGOSY	CORACLE
PRAU	BARQUE	CRUISER (mil)
PROA	BIREME	FELUCCA
PUNT	CUTTER	FRIGATE (mil)
SCOW	DINGHY	GALLEAS (mil)
SHIP	DOGGER	GALLEON
SKIP	GALLEY	GALLIOT
SNOW	*HOOKER*	HOUARIO
YAWL	HOWKER	LYMPHAD (*herald*)
	LAUNCH	POLACRE
5-letters	LORCHA	SHALLOP
BALSA	LUGGER	TRIREME

8+ letters	DESTROYER (mil)	SUBMARINE (mil)
BATTLESHIP (mil)	HERRINGBUSS	TRIMARAN
CARACORE	OTAHEITE	WINDSURFER ®
CATAMARAN	PERIAGUA	
CORACORE	*SCHOONER*	

BOAT-GIRL FLORA (MacDonald). STEWARDESS. WAVE
(US), WREN, WRNS.

BOB S, SHILLING, VP, XIID. HAIRSTYLE, PAGEBOY,
TASSEL. SLED, SLEDGE, SLEIGH. BOUNCE, CURTSEY,
DANCE, *DUCK*, JERK, WEAVE. PLUMB, WEIGHT.
CHANGE (*bell ringing*). ETONIAN (**dry** ~ = cricketer, **wet** ~
= rower).

BOBBY ROBERT. *POLICEMAN* (*Peel*). *CALF*.

BOFFIN 1. BACKROOM BOY, SCIENTIST (sl). 2.
NICODEMUS ~ (*Dickens* character, Our Mutual Friend;
dustman who became rich).

BOGEY BUGBEAR. GOBLIN, *SPIRIT*. PAR (golf).

BOIL *Anag*. BUBBLE, SEETHE, STEW, UNDULATE (all of
which also mean *anag*). GATHERING, TUMOUR (med).

BOMBER *AIRCRAFT*.

BONDED DUTY-FREE, EX-CUSTOMS, SCOT-FREE,
TAX-FREE. GLUED, SEALED, TIED UP. [Ian Fleming;
007].

BONE *ROB*, *STEAL* (sl). FILLET. STIFFEN. HARD TISSUE,
DENTINE, IVORY, WHALEBONE [scrimshaw, *study*]. ~s of
the body: **head:** CRANIUM (skull) [antrum, sinus],
ALVEOLUS, MANDIBLE, MAXILLA (jaw); BICUSPID,
CANINE, EYETOOTH, INCISOR, MILKTOOTH, MOLAR,
PREMOLAR, WISDOM TOOTH (teeth); **neck:** *ATLAS*, AXIS;
shoulder: CLAVICLE (collar ~), CORACOID, SCAPULA
(shoulderblade); **spine:** COCCYX, SACRUM, VERTEBRA
[cervical, thoracic, lumbar]; **arm:** HUMERUS (upper), ELBOW,
RADIUS, ULNA (forearm); **hand:** CARPUS (wrist),
METACARPUS, *PHALANX* (finger), TRAPEZIUM; **chest:**
RIB, STERNUM (breastbone); **hip:** ILIUM, PELVIS,
SACRUM; **leg:** FEMUR (thigh), PATELLA (kneecap),
FIBULA, TIBIA (shin) [Pott's fracture]; **foot:** TALUS (ankle),
CALCANEUM (heel), *PHALANX* (toe), METATARSUS,

TARSUS; [calcium, marrow, necrosis, ossify]. **Pl =** SKELETON. ESSENTIALS, FRAMEWORK. CASTANETS, *INSTRUMENT* (mus).

BOOK ENTER, LIST, LOG. BAG, *ENGAGE*, RESERVE. BETTING. *ANNUAL*, EDITION, ISSUE, PUBLICATION, VOL(UME), TOME. BIBLE. [*measure* (paper size)].

BOOKED ENTERED, LISTED, LOGGED. BAGGED, ENGAGED, RESERVED. BOUND, ISSUED, PUBLISHED, WRITTEN ABOUT (crypt).

BOOKLET BK, ED, VO, VOL.

BOOKMAKER AUTHOR, COMPILER, EDITOR, PAGE(S), PUBLISHER, *WRITER* (all crypt). [*patron saint*]. BETTING MAN, BOOKIE [*racetrack*, tote].

BOOT *SHOE*; *WELLINGTON*. *DISMISS*, *FIRE*, *SACK*. TRUNK (US). AVAIL.

BORACIC LINT BROKE, SKINT (*rh sl*).

BORE (s/l *boar*). MINE, WELL. AUGER, AWL, DRILL; *MISER*. CALIBRE. EAGRE, (TIDAL) *WAVE*. TIRE (**opp** = *enchant*). BEGAT.

BOREAS Gk myth NORTH *WIND*.

BORED (s/l *board*). DRILLED. RIFLED. *TIRED*.

BORING DRILLING. ENNUI, TEDIOUS, TIRING; *DRY*, DULL.

BORN (s/l *borne*, *bourn*). B, NE, NEE. DESTINED. *NATIVE*, ORIGINATED.

BORNE (s/l *born*, *bourn*). *CARRIED*. NARROW MINDED.

BORON B (*chem*).

BOSIE LORD *ALFRED* DOUGLAS. *CHINAMAN* (Bosanquet, *cricket*).

BOSPHORUS STRAIT; OX-FORD [*Io*].

BOSS EMPLOYER, FOREMAN, MANAGER, OVERMAN, OVERSEER; M (Bond's ~). KNOB, STUD.

BOTHER CONFOUND, DAMN, DRAT. ADO, FUSS, TODO. IRRITATE, *NETTLE*, WORRY.

BOTH SIDES 1. EW, LR (crypt). 2. Word at start and end, e.g. **One on both sides** (5) = ON*I*ON.

BOTTLE RESTRAIN, STOP UP (hence POTS, dn) (**opp** = decant; release). ELAN, NERVE. *ISLAND*. CONTAINER, *MEASURE*, VIAL; **types:** *SPLIT* (¼ bot), HALF-BOTTLE,

BOTTLE (80 cl), MAGNUM (2 bots), JEROBOAM (4 bots),
REHOBOAM (6 bots), METHUSELAH (8 bots),
SALMANAZAR (12 bots), BALTHAZAR (16 bots),
NEBUCHADNEZZAR (20 bots); DEMIJOHN. CARAFE.
[ten green ~s].

BOUDICCA *BOADICEA*.

BOUGH (s/l *bow*). BRANCH, STEM.

BOUND BOUNCE, JUMP, LEAP, RECOIL, SPRING. TIED,
LIMIT(ED). *BOOK*, PUBLISHED (crypt). CERTAIN,
DESTINED, SURE.

BOUNDARY BARRIER, EDGE, LIMIT, PALE; MARCH.
TRAMPOLINE (crypt). **Rom god** = TERMINUS.

BOUNDED DELINEATED, EDGED, LIMITED. JUMPED,
LEAPED, SPRANG. TIED UP.

BOUNDER *HOPPER*, *JUMPER*; *CRICKET*, FROG, GOAT,
GRASSHOPPER, KANGAROO (all crypt). CAD. *BALL*
(crypt).

BOURN (s/l *born*, *borne*). *BROOK*. GOAL, LIMIT.

BOVINE COWLIKE, OX-LIKE, STUPID.

BOW (s/l *bough*). NOD, OBEISANCE, SALUTE, SUBMIT.
FRONT, STEM (naut); ROWER. SLIPKNOT. *ARCH*,
CURVE. LONGBOW, *WEAPON* [*Ulysses*]. RAINBOW.
PLAY *FIDDLE*/VIOLIN etc.

BOWED *ARCHED*, BENT, CURVED, HUNCHED. NODDED,
SALUTED. FIDDLED, PLAYED (crypt). SHOT ARROW
(archery, crypt).

BOWER *CELLIST*, FIDDLER, VIOLINIST (crypt). ARCHER,
ROBIN HOOD, WILLIAM TELL (crypt). ARBOUR.
CONSENTER, NODDER, SUBMITTER; COURTIER,
LACKEY, USHER. ANCHOR. *CARD* (euchre, knave).

BOWERY 1. OBEISANCE (crypt). ARBOUR. 2. District of New
York.

BOWL BASIN, DISH. DELIVER, TAKE OVER (*cricket*).
TRUNDLE. BIASED BALL, JACK, WOOD [bowls, skittles].

BOWLED B, DELIVERED, SENT DOWN (*cricket*). SALAD
(crypt).

BOWLER CRICKETER, DELIVERY MAN, PITCHER.
DRAKE (crypt). BILLYCOCK, *HAT*. POTTER.

BOWMAN ARCHER; CUPID, ROBIN HOOD, WILLIAM

TELL. *CELLIST*, *FIDDLER*, VIOLINIST (crypt).

BOX *FIGHT*, *SPAR* [pugilism]. CARTON, CASE. TELLY, TV. *TREE*. *MEASURE* (fish). *PLANT*.

BOXER *FIGHTER*, PUGILIST; *POLLUX*. *HORSE* (Animal Farm, *Orwell*). CASE-MAKER, PACKER. CHINAMAN. LETTER-SENDER/POSTER (crypt). SENTRY (crypt).

BOY 1. KID, LAD, NIPPER. DICK, ED, JACK, SAM, TOM etc. 2. Three lily-white ~, in *song*. [~ **and girl** = pigeon pair].

~s BRIGADE BB, CADETS.

BR BRAZIL (*car plate*). *BRIDGE*. BRITISH *RAIL*. *BROTHER*.

Br Britain, ~ish. Brother.

BRAG BOAST, SHOW OFF (**opp** = *modest*). *CARD GAME*.

BRAHMA Principal Indian *god*.

BRAKE (s/l *break*). BROKE (OE). BRACKEN, BRUSHWOOD. SKID, SLIPPER (tech); CHECK, CRUSH, RETARD. *CARRIAGE*, ESTATE CAR, WAGON.

BRAND BURN, CHAR. MARK, STIGMA. LABEL, TRADEMARK; HOT IRON. SWORD. BLIGHT.

BRASS 1. *MONEY*. BUGLE, TROMBONE, TRUMPET, TUBA etc. STAFF OFFICERS. 2. Copper/Zinc alloy, hence CU*ZN.

BRAVE FACE UP TO; BOLD, FEARLESS; **saying**. *AMERICAN INDIAN* (**opp** = paleface).

BREAD CRUST, *LOAF*, ROLL; DOUGH; **saying**. *MONEY* (sl).

BREAK (s/l *brake*). *Anag*. BUST, *CRACK*, FRACTURE, SEPARATE, SHATTER, SNAP. GAP, INTERVAL. ESCAPE; *EXHAUST*. TAME.

BREAKER KEG. *COMBER*, SURF, *WAVE*. CRACKSMAN, *ROBBER*. CB ENTHUSIAST (radio, sl).

BREAKING Word in another, e.g. **We are breaking the collection, Honey** (5) = S*WE*ET.

BREAKPOINT CRUNCH. PUBERTY (crypt).

BREATHER *REST*. *GILL*, MOUTH, *NOSE*, WEASAND, WINDPIPE; **saying**. VENT.

BREED RAISE, REAR. RACE, STOCK, TYPE.

BREEDING GROUND ATOMIC/NUCLEAR REACTOR (crypt). INCUBATOR, NURSERY, STOCK/STUD FARM.

BREVE *NOTE*. *ACCENT* (˘ = short). AUTHORITY, *LETTER* (papal, royal).

BREW *Anag.* CONCOCT, INFUSE. MAKE BEER/TEA
[*Company* (livery)]. FESTER.

BRIBE GREASE, OIL (palm); PALM-OIL (crypt). INDUCE,
SQUARE.

BRIDGE BR. ARCH, ARCHER, SPAN(NER) (crypt); RIALTO,
THAMES. CONNING TOWER/DECK. *CARD GAME*,
TRUMPERY (auction, contract) [Acol, Blackwood]. LOAN.
REST (snooker). **Pl** = *WRITER*.

~ GAME *CARDS*. TRUMPERY (crypt). POOHSTICKS (A.A.
Milne).

BRIDGEHEAD INROAD, SALIENT. CARD BUFF (Acolite;
crypt).

BRIDGE PLAYER E, N, S or W; EAST, NORTH, SOUTH,
WEST; BRIDGER, WE, THEY.

BRIDGER *BRIDGE PLAYER* (crypt). CAPTAIN,
NAVIGATOR (crypt). HORATIO (crypt).

BRIDGING TEAM RE, SAPPERS. BRIDGE PLAYERS, EW,
NS, WE/THEY (crypt). APPEASERS, CONCILIATORS,
ACAS (crypt).

BRIG BRASSHAT, BRIGADIER, SOLDIER. *BOAT*. *GAOL*
(naut). BRIDGE (Sc).

BRISTOL BREAST (*rh sl*). *UNIVERSITY*.

BRITISH LEGION BL.

~ LEYLAND BL.

~ MUSEUM BM.

~ RAIL BR, RLY, RY, LINES.

BROADCAST SCATTER, SOW. AIR(ING), RADIATE,
TRANSMIT; BBC, IBA, ITA, ITV (UK); ABC, CBS, NBC
(US).

BROKE BANKRUPT, INSOLVENT, PENNILESS, RUINED;
BORACIC LINT (*rh sl*) **opp** = *rich*. DID *BREAK*, BUST.
[Evans].

BROKEN *Anag* e.g. **Heartbroken** (5) = HATER. WAS BROKE.
SNAPPED. TAMED.

BROKEN FUSE BLOWN OUT, FUSED. Anag 'fuse' i.e. FUES.

BRONTË 1. *WRITER*; ANNE ~ = Acton Bell (Agnes Grey;
Tenant of Wildfell Hall). CHARLOTTE ~ = Mrs Nicholls =
Currer Bell (Jane Eyre; The Professor; Shirley; Villette; Land of
Angria). EMILY ~ = Ellis Bell (Wuthering Heights; Land of

Gondal).   PATRICK BRANWELL ~.   2. Lord Nelson and ~
(*military leader*; Emma Hamilton).   3. Gk myth THUNDER
[blacksmith].   **Pl** = CYCLOP.

BRONZE 1. *AGE*.   THIRD PRIZE.   *Anniversary* (8th).   2.
Copper/Tin alloy, hence CU*SN.

BROOK BECK, *BOURN*, BURN, CREEK, RILL, *RIVER*,
RIVULET, STREAM.   TOLERATE.

BROTHER BR, *SIB*.   *FRIAR*, *MONK*.   ASSOCIATE, EQUAL.
[Jonathan].   **Pl** = TUC.

BROTHERHOOD ASSOCIATION, FRATERNITY.   COWL
(crypt).

BROWN ROAST; *TAN*.   *COLOUR*.   *SNOOKER* BALL (score
4).   FATHER ~ (*Chesterton*).   Lancelot 'Capability' ~
(*gardener*).   TOM.   SHOOT HAPHAZARDLY (hence HOOTS
etc).   [Queen Victoria].   **Pl** = *Football team* (US).

BROWNE *SAM* (belt).

BROWNIE GOBLIN.   YOUNG GUIDE.   CAMERA®.

BROWNING AUTOMATIC, *WEAPON*®.   DYE, TANNING.
FIRING WILDLY.   GRAVY.   *WRITER*.

BRS BRITISH ROAD SERVICES.   Pl of BR.

BRUNHILDA (BRUNNHILDE) 1. Nor myth Chief of the *Valkyries*.
2. A minor *PLANET*.

BRUTUS *CONSPIRATOR* [honourable; Caesar, (*Shak*)].

Brz Brazil, ~ian.

BT BARONET.

BTU BRITISH THERMAL UNIT (heat).

BUCCANEER *PIRATE*.   *AIRCRAFT*.

BUCEPHALUS ALEXANDER'S HORSE.

BUCK *DOLLAR*.   JUMP, THROW.   DANDY, FOP.   CART.
SAW-HORSE.   PEARL (films).   *WRITER*.   *Male* deer, hare etc.

BUFF ENTHUSIAST.   POLISH.   NUDE, SKIN.   COLOUR.   **Pl**
= EAST KENT REGIMENT.   ['Steady the ~s' (*Kipling*)].

BUG BEETLE, PARASITE.   EAVESDROPPER, LISTENER,
TRANSMITTER.   RIVER (Pol).

BUILD *Anag*.   CONSTRUCT, COMPOSE, MAKE.
PROPORTIONS, SHAPE.

BULL 1. ROT, RUBBISH.   CENTRE, GOLD (archery).   DECK
GAME.   PAPAL EDICT.   DRINK.   PRICE RAISER (**opp** =
bear).   TAURUS; *male* cow, elephant etc; SIRE.   2. Gk myth

EUROPA [*Minos*. Seventh labour of *Hercules*]. 3. *Constellation* (Taurus); sign of *Zodiac* (2nd).

~ **AND COW** *ROW* (*rh sl*).

BULLETHOLE BARREL, CHAMBER, RIFLING (all crypt).

BULLSEYE CENTRE, *GOLD* [inner, magpie, outer]. LANTERN. *COMIC*. CANDY, GOBSTOPPER, SWEET. *DOG* (Bill Sikes).

BULLY BRAVO! EXCELLENT! FIRST RATE! CORNED BEEF. START (hockey). OPPRESSOR, THUG, TYRANT; **celebrated:** CERCYON (myth), FRONT DE BOEUF (Ivanhoe, Scott), JOSIAH BOUNDERBY (Hard Times, *Dickens*), SIR JOHN CHESTER (Barnaby Rudge, *Dickens*), LEGREE (Uncle Tom's Cabin, Harriet Beecher *Stowe*).

BUN HAIRPIECE; UPBRAIDED (crypt). BREAD ROLL: BATH, CHELSEA, CURRANT, HOT CROSS etc.

BUND *BANK*; QUAY.

BUNTER SCHOOLBOY, OWL OF THE REMOVE (*Greyfriars* School, Richards). *SERVANT* (to Lord Peter Wimsey, Dorothy L. Sayers).

BUNTING *BIRD*. *FLAG*, WORSTED (*material*).

BURDEN LOAD, OPPRESS, SADDLE; OBLIGATION, LIABILITY, PASSENGER. TONNAGE. CHORUS, REFRAIN, THEME.

BURGLAR *ROBBER*, THIEF, YEGG.

BURLAP CANVAS, JUTE, *MATERIAL*.

BURLINGTON HOUSE RA, (ROYAL) ACADEMY [*painters*].

BURN *BROOK*. BLISTER, SORE; *BLAZE*, *CHAR*, CONSUME, *FIRE*, PARCH, SCORCH, TAN. **Pl** = RABBIE, POET (Sc).

BURRO (s/l *burrow*). *DONKEY*.

BURROW (s/l *burro*). MINE. RABBIT WARREN/*HABITATION*. ISLAND (Eng).

BUSH SHRUB; FOREST, WOODLAND. HAIR. *PIG*. LINING, SLEEVE, WASHER. RIVER (Ire).

BUSINESS *CO*, FIRM, TRADE. AFFAIR, CONCERN, DUTY, OCCUPATION, TASK. AGENDA.

BUT (s/l *butt*, *butte*). EXCEPT, HOWEVER, ONLY. WITHOUT. YET. *UTTER*.

BUTCHER MEAT TRADER [*Company* (livery)].

SLAUGHTER. CUMBERLAND. *BIRD*. **Pl** = *LOOK* (*rh sl*).

BUTT (s/l *but, butte*). CASK, KEG, *MEASURE*. AIM, OBJECT, RANGE, STAND (shooting). HANDLE; ABUT(MENT). *FISH*: FLATFISH, PLAICE, SOLE. STUB, TREE TRUNK. CUE (snooker). NUDGE (with head).

BUTTE (s/l *but, butt*). *HILL*.

BUTTER FAT. ADULATE, PRAISE. GUNNEL (*fish*). GOAT (crypt, nudge). LANDLORD (crypt, cask). MARKSMAN (crypt, range). SNOOKER PLAYER (crypt, cue). SMOKER (crypt, stub).

BUTTERFLY *LEPIDOPTERA*; **coll** = LEPIDOPTERIST. MADAM ~ (Puccini; Nagasaki; Cho Cho San, Lt *Pinkerton*).

BUTTER UP FLATTER, PRAISE. RETTUB (dn, crypt).

BUZZ BOMB DOODLEBUG, FLYING BOMB, V1 [revenge].

BY (s/l *bye*). *NEAR*, NEXT, PER, THROUGH. SECONDARY, SIDE. SECRET. FATHERED/SIRED BY . . .

BYE (s/l *by*). *PASS*. *EXTRA* (cricket). INCIDENTAL. SIDE. SECRET.

BYE-BYE *FAREWELL*. **Pl** = SLEEP.

BYGONE ANTIQUE. PAST.

C *CAMBRIDGE*. CARBON (*chem*). *CAUGHT*. CELSIUS, CENTIGRADE. CHAPTER. CIRCA. *CLUB*. COLD. CONSERVATIVE. CUBA (*car plate*). ABOUT. *KEY*; *NOTE*. 100, ONE HUNDRED; MANY. SQ NO (10 × 10 = 100 = C).

CA ABOUT, CIRCA. CHARTERED ACCOUNTANT. CALIFORNIA (US *state*).

CABINET MAKER PRIME MINISTER, PM. ADAM, CHANNON, CHIPPENDALE, HEPPELWHITE, *KENT*, SHERATON.

CABLE WIRE; MESSAGE, TELEGRAM. 200 YARDS, CCYD, *MEASURE* (naut).

CACUS Rom myth s of *Vulcan*, who *robbed Hercules* of some of his cattle and was slain.

CAD *BOUNDER*, BRUTE, LOUT, SCOUNDREL, *SWINE*.

CADETS ATC, *BB*, JTC, OTC; BOYS BRIGADE, SCOUTS. YOUNGER SONS.

CADMIUM CD (*chem*). *COLOUR* (orange).

CAESAR AUTOCRAT, CZAR, DICTATOR, EMPEROR,
KAISER, TSAR; **celebrated:** AUGUSTUS, CALIGULA,
CLAUDIUS, NERO or, specifically, GAIUS JULIUS, B.C. 102-
44. s of Caesar and Aurelia; mar (1) Cossutia (div,
unconsummated), (2) Cornelia, d of Cinna (died; one d: Julia),
(3) Pompeia, d of Pompeius Rufus (div for adultery), and (4)
Calpurnia, d of Piso. Brilliant general, orator and writer, he was
ass Ides (15) Mar B.C. 44 by *conspiracy* of Brutus, Casca, Cassius
etc. [Invasion of Britain, Rubicon (crossed to Italy and civil war),
veni, vidi, vici (Pharnaces at Zela), leap year (introduced), *July*,
Cleopatra (one s: Caesarion), Mark *Antony*, *Pompey*, et tu Brute!
Conspirators. Shak (A and C; Caesar)].

CAIN (s/l *cane*). ADAMSON, FIRST BORN, FIRST ISSUE
[murderer].

~ & ABEL *TABLE* (*rh sl*).

CAKE SWEETBREAD; **celebrated:** *Angel,* banana, cherry,
chocolate, *Christmas*, coffee, Dundee, éclair, *fairy*, gateau,
Madeira, marble, plum, *Sally Lunn*, seed etc. OATBREAD
(Sc). CONGLOMERATE, WAD. *COAT, COVER.*
BENEFITS, NATIONAL OUTPUT, PROFITS.

CALCULATOR ABACUS, *ADDER*, COMPUTER, *SUMMER.*
GOLD DIGGER.

CALENDAR (s/l calender). CHRONOLOGICAL LIST, DATING
SYSTEM, DIARY (*French Revolution*; Julius *Caesar*). *LIST*,
REGISTER, SCHEDULE, *TABLE.*

CALF BACK OF LEG, LEG MUSCLE. SMALL ICEBERG.
ISLAND. Offspring of *cow, elephant*, walrus, *whale*; BOBBY.

CALL 1. PHONE, *RING*, TELEPHONE; *PAGE*, SHOUT: HI,
HEY, HO etc. BECK, SIGNAL. 2. *Pronounce* as . . . sound
like.

~ GIRL TELEPHONIST. PROSTITUTE.

CALLIOPE One of the nine Gk *MUSES* (epic *poetry*).

CALL SYSTEM DIAL, PAGING, PUBLIC ADDRESS, STD,
TANNOY®.

CAMBRIDGE C, CANTAB; LIGHT BLUES; *UNIVERSITY*
[cantabrigian]. DUROLIPONS (*Roman*).

CAMEL RUMINANT; SHIP OF THE DESERT [*llama*]; **breeds:**
ARABIAN, DOOD, DROMEDARY (one hump), BACTRIAN

(two humps). *COLOUR* (fawn). SPONSON. *AIRCRAFT* (fighter). RIVER (Eng).

CAMELOT Site of *King Arthur's* court: CADBURY CASTLE, CAMELFORD or TINTAGEL [round table].

CAMEO BROOCH, RELIEF WORK (**opp** = intaglio). THUMB-NAIL SKETCH.

CAMP *BASE* (mil), FORT, SETTLEMENT; CASTRA (Rom). TENTS (gipsies, guides, holiday-makers, scouts etc); LODGE. ADHERENTS, FOLLOWERS. DAVID (US). AFFECTED, BIZARRE, DRAG, EFFEMINATE, EXAGGERATED, HOMOSEXUAL, TRANSVESTITE.

CAMPTOWN *RACETRACK*. ALDERSHOT, CHESTER, LARKHILL, TIDWORTH. [*Roman place name*].

CAN *TIN*; PRESERVE. IS ABLE. *GAOL* (sl). RIVER (Eng). **Pl** = HEADPHONES (sl).

Can Canada, ~ian.

CANADA CDN (*car plate*). [Canuck. Maple leaves].

CANARD *HOAX*. *DUCK* (Fr). CONTROL SURFACE (aero).

CANDY SWEETMEAT; CRYSTALLIZE, PRESERVE. *Anniversay* (6th). GIRL.

CANE (s/l *Cain*). *BEAT*, CHASTISE, *TAN*, THRASH; BIRCH, ROD, *SWITCH*, MALACCA, STICK. SUGAR.

CANNED DRUNK (sl). PRESERVED; TINNED, hence word in 'can' or 'tin', e.g. **Skirt canned Egyptian god** (5) = T*RA*IN.

CANNON (s/l *canon*). GUN, ORDNANCE, PIECE, *WEAPON*; RA. COLLIDE, STRIKE; KISS (billiards).

CANON (s/l *cannon*). CHURCH DECREE, PAPAL LAW; CRITERION, PRINCIPLE. CATHEDRAL OFFICIAL, *CHURCHMAN*.

CANT CANNOT, UNABLE (**opp** = *may*). CATCH PHRASE, JARGON; HYPOCRISY. BEVEL, SLOPE, *TILT*; *LEAN*, SLEW, SWING, *TIP*. CANTICLES.

CANTAB Of C University.

CANTABRIGIAN Member of C or of Harvard University.

CANTERBURY 1. MUSIC HOLDER (furniture). *UNIVERSITY* (NZ). DUROVERNUM (*Rom*). 2. **Episcopal sig** = CANTUAR. 3. ~ Tales (*Chaucer*).

CANTON DIVISION ON SHIELD (*herald*). SUB-DIVISION OF COUNTRY (esp *Swiss*). TOWN (Ch).

CAP *HAT*, HEADGEAR. CAPITAL. CHAPTER. COMMON
AGRICULTURAL POLICY (European farming). COVER, TOP.

CAPE HEADLAND, NESS, *POINT*, PROMONTORY. CLOAK,
TALMA, TIPPET. APPLE.

CAPER FRISK, LARK, LEAP. *SPICE*. BOER, S AFRICAN
(crypt).

CAPITAL AI, FIRST RATE; VITAL. CORNICE (*architecture*).
CHIEF, HEAD, LEADING, IMPORTANT, PRINCIPAL.
UC, UPPER CASE (**opp** = lower case). First letter, first city,
seat of government e.g:

Country	Capital
Abyssinia (now Ethiopia)	ADDIS ABABA
Aden (now S Yemen)	ADEN
Afghanistan	KABUL
Albania	TIRANA
Algeria	EL DJEZAIR
	(was ALGIERS)
Andorra	LA VIEJA
Angola	LUANDA
(was Port W Africa)	
Antigua Is	ST JOHN'S
Argentina	BUENOS AIRES
Ascension Is	GEORGETOWN
Australia	CANBERRA
Austria	VIENNA
Bahamas	NASSAU
Bahrain	MANAMAH
Balearic Is	PALMA
Bangladesh	DACCA
Barbados	BRIDGETOWN
Basutoland (now Lesotho)	MASERU
Bechuanaland (now Botswana)	MAFEKING
Belgian Congo (now Zaire)	LEOPOLDVILLE
Belgium	BRUSSELS
Belize (was Br Honduras)	BELMOPAN
Benin (was part Fr W Africa, then Dahomey)	PORTO NOVO

Bermuda	HAMILTON
Bhutan	THIMBU
Bolivia	SUCRE
Botswana (was Bechuanaland)	GABORONE
Burkina Faso (was Upper Volta)	OUAGADOUGOU
Brazil	BRASILIA (was RIO DE JANEIRO)
Br Honduras (now Belize)	BELIZE
Cambodia (was part Fr Indo-China, now Kampuchea)	PHNOM PENH
Cameroon	YAOUNDE
Canada	OTTAWA
Canary Is	LAS PALMAS
Cape Verde Is	SAO THIAGO
Central African Republic (was part Fr Eq Africa)	BANGUI
Ceylon (now Sri Lanka)	COLOMBO
Chad (was part Fr Eq Africa)	NDJAMENE (was FORT LAMY)
Chile	SANTIAGO
China	PEKING (BEIJING)
Colombia	BOGOTA
Corsica	AJACCIO
Costa Rica	SAN JOSE
Crete	CANEA
Cuba	HAVANA
Cyclades Is	HERMOUPOLIS
Cyprus	NICOSIA
Czechoslovakia	PRAGUE
Dahomey (now Benin)	PORTO NOVO
Denmark	COPENHAGEN
Djibouti (was Fr Somaliland)	DJIBOUTI
Dominica Is	ROSEAU
Dominican Republic	SANTO DOMINGO
Dutch East Indies (now Indonesia)	BATAVIA (now JAKARTA)

Dutch Guiana (now Surinam) PARAMARIBO

Ecuador	QUITO
Egypt	CAIRO (was MEMPHIS)
Eire	DUBLIN
Elba Is	PORTO FERRAIO
El Salvador	SAN SALVADOR
England	LONDON
Eq Guinea (was Sp Guinea)	MALABO (was SANTA ISABEL)

Eritrea (now part Ethiopia) ASMARA
Est(h)onia TALLINN
Ethiopia (was Abyssinia) ADDIS ABABA

Faeroe Is THORSHAVN
Falkland Is PORT STANLEY
Fiji Is SUVA
Finland HELSINKI
Formosa (now Taiwan) TAIPEH
France PARIS
Fr Eq Africa (now Cameroon, Central Af Republic, Chad, Congo and Gabon) BRAZZAVILLE

Fr Guiana CAYENNE
Fr Indo-China (now Cambodia, Laos and Vietnam) SAIGON (now HO CHI MINH CITY)
Fr Somaliland (now Djibouti) JIBUTI
Fr W Africa (now Benin, Guinea, Ivory Coast, Mauritania and Senegal) DAKAR
Friendly Is (Tonga) NUKUALOFA or TONJOTABU

Gabon (was part Fr Eq Africa) LIBREVILLE
Gambia BANJUL (was BATHURST)

Germany, East BERLIN
Germany, West BONN
Ghana ACCRA

Granada (ancient kingdom)	GRANADA
Greece	ATHENS
Greenland	GODTHAB
Grenada Is	ST GEORGE'S
Guadeloupe	BASSE-TERRE
Guatemala	GUATEMALA
Guinea (was part Fr W Africa)	CONAKRY
Guinea Bissau (was Port Guinea)	BISSAU
Guyana	GEORGETOWN
Haiti	PORT AU PRINCE
Holland	THE HAGUE
Honduras	TEGUCIGALPA
Hong Kong	VICTORIA
Hungary	BUDAPEST
Iceland	REYKJAVIK
India	DELHI
Indonesia (was NL E Indies)	JAKARTA (was BATAVIA)
Iran (was Persia)	TEH(E)RAN
Iraq (was Mesopotamia)	BAGHDAD
Ireland, North	BELFAST
Ireland, Rep of	DUBLIN
Israel (disputed)	JERUSALEM
Italy	ROME
Ivory Coast (was part Fr W Africa)	ABIDJAN
Jamaica	KINGSTON
Japan	TOKYO (was YEDDO)
Jordan	AMMAN
Kampuchea (was Cambodia)	PHNOM PENH
Kenya	NAIROBI
Kiribati (was Gilbert Is)	JARAWA
Korea, North	PYONGYANG
Korea, South	SEOUL
Kuwait	KUWAIT

Laos (was part Fr Indo-China)	VIENTIANE
Latvia	RIGA
Lebanon	BEIRUT
Leeward Is	ST JOHN
Lesotho (was Basutoland)	MASERU
Liberia	MONROVIA
Libya	TRIPOLI
Liechtenstein	VADUZ
Lithuania	VILNA
Luxembourg	LUXEMBOURG
Madagascar (now Malagasy Rep)	ANTANANARIVO
Malagasy Rep (was Madagascar)	TANANARIVE
Malawi (was Nyasaland)	LILONGWE
Malaysia (was Fed Malay States)	KUALA LUMPUR
Malta	VALETTA
Manoa (myth)	EL DORADO (myth)
Martinique Is	FORT DE FRANCE
Mauritania (was part Fr West Africa)	NOUAKCHOTT
Mauritius	PORT LOUIS
Mesopotamia (now Iraq)	BAGHDAD
Mexico	MEXICO CITY
Moçambique (was Port E Africa)	MAPUTO (was LOURENÇO MARQUES)
Monaco	MONACO
Mongolia	ULAN BATOR (was URGA)
Montenegro	CETINJE
Morocco	RABAT
Muscat & Oman (was Oman)	MUSCAT
Namibia (was S W Africa)	WINDHOEK
Nepal	KAT(H)MANDU
Netherlands	THE HAGUE
New Zealand	WELLINGTON
Nicaragua	MANAGUA
Niger (was part Fr W Africa)	NIAMEY

Nigeria	ABOUGA (was LAGOS)
North Vietnam	HANOI
Norway	OSLO
Nyasaland (now Malawi)	ZOMBA
Oman (was Muscat & Oman)	MUSCAT
Pakistan	ISLAMABAD (was KARACHI)
Palestine (disputed)	JERUSALEM
Panama	PANAMA
Papua New Guinea	PORT MORESBY
Paraguay	ASUNCION
Patagonia (now Argentina & Chile)	PUNTA ARENAS
Persia (now Iran)	TEH(E)RAN
Peru	LIMA
Philippines	QUEZON CITY
Poland	WARSAW (was CRACOW)
Portugal	LISBON
Port E Africa (now Moçambique)	LOURENÇO MARQUES
Port Guinea (now Guinea Bissau)	BISSAU (was BOLAMA)
Port W Africa (now Angola)	LUANDA
Puerto Rico	SAN JUAN
Qatar	DOHA
Rhodesia (now Zambia and Zimbabwe)	SALISBURY
Romania	BUCHAREST
Russia	MOSCOW
Rwanda	KIGALI
Sabah	KOTA KINABALU
St Helena Is	JAMESTOWN
St Kitts-Nevis Is	BASSETERRE
St Lucia Is	CASTRIES
St Vincent Is	KINGSTOWN

Samoa	PAGO PAGO
San Marino	SAN MARINO
Sarawak	KUCHING
Sardinia	CAGLIARI
Saudi Arabia	RIYADH (was MECCA)
Scotland	EDINBURGH
Senegal (was part Fr W Africa)	DAKAR
Seychelles	VICTORIA
Siam (now Thailand)	BANGKOK
Sicily	PALERMO
Sierra Leone	FREETOWN
Sikkim (now part India)	GANGTOK
Singapore Is	SINGAPORE
Solomon Is	HONIARA
Somali (was Br and It East Africa)	MOGADISHU
Somaliland, Br (now part Somali)	HARGEISA
Somaliland, Fr (now Djibouti)	JIBUTI
Somaliland, It (now part Somali)	MOGADISHU
South Africa	PRETORIA
South Yemen (was Aden Protectorate)	MADINAT ASH SHAB
Spain	MADRID
Sp Guinea (now Eq Guinea)	SANTA ISABEL
Sp Sahara (now Saharan Arab Dem Rep)	VILLA CISNEROS
Sri Lanka (was Ceylon)	COLOMBO
Sudan	KHARTOUM
Surinam (was NL Guiana)	PARAMARIBO
Swaziland	MBABANE
Sweden	STOCKHOLM
Switzerland	BERNE
Syria	DAMASCUS
Taiwan (was Formosa)	TAIPEH
Tanganyika (now Tanzania)	DAR ES SALAAM
Tanzania (was Tanganyika)	DODOMA
Thailand (was Siam)	BANGKOK
Tibet	LHASA

Togo	LOME
Tonga (Friendly Is)	NUKUALOFA or TONJOTABU
Transylvania (was part Hungary, now part Romania)	CLUJ
Trinidad & Tobago	PORT OF SPAIN
Tristan da Cunha	EDINBURGH
Tunisia	TUNIS
Turkey	ANKARA
Tuvalu (was Ellice Is)	FUNAFUTI
Uganda	KAMPALA
Upper Volta	OUAGADOUGOU
Uruguay	MONTEVIDEO
USA	WASHINGTON
USSR	MOSCOW
Utopia (fict)	AMAUROTE (fict)
Vanuatu (was Espiritu Santo)	VILA
Venezuela	CARACAS
Vietnam (was part Fr Indo-China)	HANOI
Virgin Is, Br	ROADTOWN
Virgin Is, US	CHARLOTTE AMALIE
Wales	CARDIFF
West Irian (was NL New Guinea/Irian Jaya)	JAYAPURA
Windward Is	ST GEORGE
Yemen, North	SANA
Yemen, South (was Aden Protectorate)	MADINAT ASH SHAB (Aden)
Yugoslavia	BELGRADE
Zaire (was Belgian Congo)	KINSHASA
Zambia (was N Rhodesia)	LUSAKA
Zimbabwe (was S Rhodesia)	HARARE

CAPPED (s/l *capt*). CHOSEN, PICKED, SELECTED; awarded

cap/colours for club/county/country. COVERED,
PROTECTED, SHEATHED. FOLLOWED/IMPROVED
(story, yarn).

CAPT (s/l *capped*). CAPTAIN, *OFFICER*. HEAD BOY/GIRL,
LEADER, MASTER; **celebrated:** Jehu, Joab, Naaman (bibl).

CAPTURE *CATCH*, *COP*, *TRAPPED*; TAKING.

CAR AUTO, VEHICLE; **types (all ®):** AUSTIN, BENTLEY, *BL*,
BUICK, CADILLAC, CHEVROLET, *DODGE*, FIAT, *FORD*,
GENERAL MOTORS, MERCEDES, *MG*, *MINI*, MODEL T,
MORRIS, ROLLS, ROVER, SUNBEAM, *T*, TRIUMPH,
VAUXHALL, VOLKSWAGEN etc. *CARRIAGE*, CHARIOT,
NACELLE, GONDOLA (aero).

CARBON C (*chem*).

CAR CLUB *AA*, RAC.

CARD CAUTION, *CASE*, CHARACTER, WAG. CARDINAL.
TAROT; CLUB, DIAMOND, HEART, SPADE; TRUMP;
(*Alice*); **coll** = cartophilist; **games:**

3-letters	6-letters	KLONDYKE
GIN	*BRIDGE*	PATIENCE
NAP	ECARTE	PINOCHLE
	EUCHRE	
4-letters	FAN-TAN	9+ letters
BRAG	PIQUET	AUNT AGATHA
CRIB	RED DOG	BEGGAR-MY-
GRAB	*SPIDER*	NEIGHBOUR
FARO		BLACKJACK
SKAT	7-letters	FOUR SEASONS
SNAP	BEZIQUE	GERMAN FLEET
SOLO	CANASTA	HAPPY FAMILIES
STOP	CARLTON	MISS MILLIGAN
	THE STAR	ONE FOUNDATION
	STREETS	RACING DEMON
5-letters		THE REGIMENT
BUNKO	8-letters	ROUGE ET NOIR
DEMON	BACCARAT	TRENTE ET
OMBRE	CANFIELD	QUARANTE
POKER	THE CLOCK	TWENTY-ONE
RUMMY	CRIBBAGE	VINGT-ET-UN
WHIST	GIN RUMMY	

CARDIGAN *JERSEY*, PULLOVER, SWEATER, WOOLLY. EARL (Balaclava). *CASTLE*.

CARDINAL FUNDAMENTAL, IMPORTANT. *CHURCHMAN* [eminence, HE]. SONGBIRD (US). CLOAK. E, N, S, W (naut).

CARE ATTENTION, CAUTION, PAINS, TROUBLE. *CHARGE*, LOOK AFTER, PROTECT(ION). ANXIETY, WORRY; CONCERN, REGARD, *SORROW*. AFFECTION, LIKING, *LOVE*.

CARMELITE MENDICANT *FRIAR*, WHITE *FRIAR* [Berthold].

CARNATION *FLOWER*. BUTTONHOLE. MOTOR-RACE (crypt).

CARP *FISH*, *ID*, *ROACH*. CRITICIZE, FIND FAULT [captious].

CARPENTER CABINET-MAKER, JOINER, WOODWORKER [*Company* (livery)]; **celebrated:** ADAM BEDE (Eliot), QUINCE, SNUG (MND), MUDDLE (Marryat); [*Alice*; *Chaucer*].

CARPET DRUGGET, PILE, RUG [Axminster, Persian, Wilton]. REPRIMAND, REPROVE, *ROCKET*, TELL OFF (sl).

CAR PLATE REGISTRATION. **International identification:**

Country	Letters	Country	Letters
Albania	AL	Denmark	DK
Alderney	GBA	Egypt	ET
Algeria	DZ	Finland	SF
Argentina	RA	France	F
Australia	AUS	Germany, East	DDR
Austria	A	Germany, West	D
Bahamas	BS	Great Britain	GB
Belgium	B	Guernsey	GBG
Brazil	BR	Hong Kong	HK
Bulgaria	BG	Hungary	H
Canada	CDN	Iceland	IS
Colombia	CO	India	IND
Costa Rica	CR	Iran	IR
Cuba	C	Ireland	IRL
Cyprus	CY	Isle of Man	GBM
Czechoslovakia	CS	Israel	IL

Italy	I	**Romania**	R
Jamaica	JA	**South Africa**	ZA
Japan	J	**Spain**	E
Jersey	GBJ	**Sweden**	S
Luxembourg	L	**Switzerland**	CH
Malta	M	**Turkey**	TR
Morocco	MA	**UK**	GB
Monaco	MC	**USA**	USA
Netherlands	NL	**USSR**	SU
New Zealand	NZ	**Vatican City**	V
Norway	N	**Vietnam**	VN
Panama	PA	**Yugoslavia**	YU
Peru	PE	**Zaire**	ZR
Poland	PL	**Zambia**	Z
Portugal	P		

CARRIAGE *DELIVERY*, FREIGHT. *BEARING*, GAIT. PRAM, PUSH-CHAIR. HORSE-DRAWN VEHICLE; **types:**

3-letters
CAB
FLY
GIG

4-letters
DRAY
SHAY
TRAP

5-letters
BRAKE
BUGGY
COACH
GARRY
STAGE
SULKY
TONGA

6-letters
BERLIN
CALASH
CHAISE
HANSOM
JINGLE
LANDAU
RANDEM
SURREY
SPIDER
TANDEM
TROIKA
WHISKY

7-letters
CHARIOT
DROSHKY
GROWLER
HACKERY
HACKNEY

PHAETON
RATTLER
TILBURY
VIS-A-VIS

8-letters
BAROUCHE
BROUGHAM
CARRIOLE
CLARENCE
CURRICLE
DEARBORN
QUADRIGA
SOCIABLE
STANHOPE
VICTORIA

9+ letters
BONESHAKER
CABRIOLET

DILIGENCE   LANDAULET   STAGE COACH
FOUR-IN-HAND   OPPENHEIMER   WAGONETTE
KITTEREEN   POST-CHAISE

CARRY *BEAR*, SUPPORT, TOTE. BE PREGNANT.
~ ON CONTINUE. FLIRT. EMBARK, LOAD.
CASE *BAGGAGE*, BOX, GRIP. COVER, ENCLOSE. CAUSE, EVENT, SUIT (leg). CIRCUMSTANCE, INSTANCE, POSITION. CONDITION (med). NOUN FORM (gram): ABLATIVE, ACCUSATIVE, DATIVE, NOMINATIVE, POSSESSIVE. UPPER/LOWER TYPEFACE. *CARD*, CAUTION, *CHARACTER*, COMEDIAN, *COMIC*, RIGHT ONE, WAG.
CASH *MONEY*, READY; *COIN* (Ch and Ind); CENT, DOLLAR, PENNY, POUND etc [*currencies*]. DRAW OUT, PLAY WINNER (cards).
CASHIER ACCOUNTANT, BANK CLERK, TELLER. DISCHARGE, DISMISS (mil).
CASSANDRA 1. Gk myth d of *Priam* and *Hecuba*. *Apollo* gave her the ability to prophesy, but always unheeded. She was killed by *Clytemnestra*. [T and C (*Shak*)]. 2. A minor *PLANET*.
CASSOWARY Flightless bird (Aus) [Dinornis (ex, NZ), Emu, Moa, Nandoo, Ostrich].
CAST (s/l *caste*). PITCH, *SHED*, *SHY*, THROW. *FORM*, FOUND, MOLD (US), MOULD, SHAPE. ACTORS, DRAMATIS PERSONAE, PLAYERS, THESPIANS. WORM MOUND. TWIST; SQUINT. SHADE, TINGE. QUALITY, TYPE. *Assembly* of hawks.
CASTE (s/l *cast*). CLASS (Hind).
CASTLE *CHESSPIECE*, *ROOK*. FORT(RESS), STRONGHOLD [**architecture**: bailey (courtyard), ballistraria (arrow slot), barbican (outwork), bartizan (overhanging turret), bastion (rampart), battlement (indented parapet), crenel (embrasure), donjon (keep), drawbridge (lifting access), embrasure (battlement niche), keep (inner fort), merlon (battlement upright), moat (ditch), motte (fortified mound), oilette (missile slot), parapet (low projecting wall), portcullis (drop gate), postern (private entrance), rampart (defensive wall), turret (tower)]. **Examples in UK:**

3-letters
HAY (Wal)
MAY (Sc)
MEY (Sc)
MOY (Sc)
ODO (Wal)
OER (Sc)
RED (Sc)

4-letters
ACRE (Eng)
BERE (Wal)
DEAL (Eng)
DOON (Sc)
DOTE (Eng)
DRUM (Sc)
DUNS (Sc)
FAST (Eng)
HOLT (Wal)
LEOD (Sc)
MAOL (Sc)
MAUD (Sc)
PIEL (Eng)
POOL (Wal)
RABY (Eng)
RAIT (Sc)
RING (Eng)
ROCH (Wal)
STAR (Wal)
UDNY (Sc)
YORK (Eng)

5-letters
BLAIR (Sc)
BORVE (Sc)
BOYNE (Sc)
BURGH (Eng)
CAREW (Wal)
CHIRK (Wal)

CLARE (Eng)
COITY (Eng)
CORFE (Eng)
COWES (Eng)
CROFT (Eng)
CUTRA (Ire)
DONNE (Sc)
DOVER (Eng)
DROGO (Eng)
DUART (Sc)
ELCHO (Sc)
EWLOE (Wal)
FLINT (Wal)
FYVIE (Sc)
GYLEN (Sc)
HAWEN (Ire)
HEVER (Eng)
HURST (Eng)
KEISS (Sc)
KELDY (Eng)
KNOCK (Sc)
LEEDS (Eng)
LEWES (Eng)
LYMNE (Eng)
MYLOR (Eng)
POWIS (Wal)
RIBER (Eng)
SWEEN (Sc)
TENBY (Wal)

6-letters
ABOYNE (Sc)
AIRLIE (Sc)
AUCHEN (Sc)
BODIAM (Eng)
BOLTON (Eng)
BROUGH (Eng)
BUILTH (Wal)
CAWDOR (Sc)

CONWAY (Wal)
CORNET (CI)
DUDLEY (Eng)
DUFFUS (Eng)
DUNDEE (Sc)
DUNURE (Sc)
DURHAM (Eng)
EDZELL (Sc)
FLOORS (Sc)
FORTER (Sc)
FRASER (Sc)
GLAMIS (Sc)
GORDON (Sc)
GWRYCH (Wal)
GWYDIR (Wal)
HAILES (Sc)
HODDOM (Sc)
HOWARD (Eng)
HUNTLY (Sc)
KENDAL (Eng)
LUDLOW (Eng)
MAIDEN (Eng)
MIDMAR (Sc)
MILLOM (Eng)
MORTON (Sc)
NEWARK (Eng)
NUNNEY (Eng)
OGMORE (Wal)
OXFORD (Eng)
PICTON (Wal)
RAGLAN (Eng)
RAHEEN (Ire)
ROWTON (Eng)
SPYNIE (Sc)
STRAME (Sc)
WALMER (Eng)
WALTON (Eng)
YESTER (Sc)

7-letters
ADAMANT (*G and S*)
AFFLECK (Sc)
ALNWICK (Eng)
APPLEBY (Eng)
ARDROSS (Sc)
ARUNDEL (Eng)
BALLOCH (Sc)
BARHOLM (Sc)
BEESTON (Eng)
BELVOIR (Eng)
BLARNEY (Ire)
BRAEMAR (Sc)
BRAMBER (Eng)
BRATTON (Eng)
BRODICK (Sc)
CADBURY (Eng)
CAISTER (Eng)
CARDIFF (Wal)
CHESTER (Eng)
COOLING (Eng)
COWDRAY (Eng)
CRATHES (Sc)
DENBIGH (Wal)
DOUGLAS (Sc)
DUNLUCE (Ire)
DUNSKEY (Sc)
DUNSTER (Eng)
DUNTULM (Sc)
DYNEVOR (Wal)
FINAVON (Sc)
GUTHRIE (Sc)
HARLECH (Wal)
HUNTLEY (Sc)
KANTURK (Ire)
KENNEDY (Sc)
KIELDER (Eng)
KILMORY (Sc)
KINKELL (Sc)

LOCHNAW (Sc)
LOWTHER (Sc)
MINGARY (Sc)
NAWORTH (Eng)
NEWPORT (Wal)
NORWICH (Eng)
PENRHYN (Wal)
PENRICE (Wal)
PENRITH (Eng)
RATTRAY (Sc)
RUTHVEN (Sc)
SADDELL (Sc)
ST DENIS (Wal)
ST MAWES (Eng)
SEAGATE (Sc)
SIZERGH (Eng)
SKIPTON (Eng)
STALKER (Sc)
SUDELEY (Eng)
SWANSEA (Wal)
TAUNTON (Eng)
THREAVE (Sc)
TILBURY (Eng)
UISDEIN (Sc)
WARWICK (Eng)
WIGMORE (Eng)
WINDSOR (Eng)
WRESSLE (Eng)

8-letters
ABERDOUR (Sc)
AMBERLEY (Eng)
ARDMADDY (Sc)
BALMORAL (Sc)
BALVENIE (Sc)
BAMBURGH (Eng)
BERKELEY (Eng)
BROUGHAM (Eng)
BRUCKLEY (Sc)

BURLEIGH (Sc)
CAMPBELL (Sc)
CARDIGAN (Wal)
CARLISLE (Eng)
CARSLUTH (Sc)
CHEPSTOW (Wal)
CIGERRAN (Wal)
CORGARFF (Sc)
CRAWFORD (Sc)
CRICHTON (Sc)
DARNAWAY (Sc)
DELGATIE (Sc)
DIRLETON (Sc)
DOUBTING
   (Pilgrim's Progress)
DRYSLWYN (Wal)
DRUMMOND (Sc)
DUNOTTAR (Sc)
DUNTRUNE (Sc)
DUNVEGAN (Sc)
FINLARIG (Eng)
GOODRICH (Eng)
HELMSLEY (Eng)
HERTFORD (Eng)
KIDWELLY (Wal)
KILCHURN (Sc)
LANGWELL (Sc)
MAXSTOKE (Eng)
MOUNTJOY (Ire)
MUCHALLS (Sc)
NEIDPATH (Sc)
NOTTLAND (Sc)
PEMBROKE (Wal)
PEVENSEY (Eng)
PITCAPLE (Sc)
PITSLIGO (Sc)
PITTULIE (Sc)
PLYMOUTH (Eng)
RHUDDLAN (Wal)

RICHMOND (Eng)
ROTHESAY (Sc)
ST DONATS (Wal)
SANDWICH (Eng)
SOUTHSEA (Eng)
STIRLING (Sc)
STOKESAY (Eng)
STORMONT (Ire)
SYCHARTH (Wal)
TAMWORTH (Eng)
THETFORD (Eng)
TINTAGEL (Eng)
URQUHART (Sc)
WALWORTH (Eng)
YARNBURY (Eng)

9-letters
ALLINGTON (Eng)
BEAUMARIS (Wal)
BLACKNESS (Sc)
BORTHWICK (Sc)
CARDONESS (Sc)
CARLSWITH (Sc)
CAULFIELD (Ire)
CILGERRAN (Wal)
CLAYPOTTS (Sc)
CLITHEROE (Eng)
COMLONGON (Sc)
CRAIGNISH (Sc)
CRICCIETH (Wal)
CROOKSTON (Sc)
DALHOUSIE (Sc)
DALNAGLAR (Sc)
DINAS BRAN (Wal)
DONNAMORE (Ire)
DRUMMINOR (Sc)
DUMBARTON (Sc)
DUNDONALD (Sc)
EARLSHALL (Sc)

EAST COWES (Eng)
EDINBURGH (Sc)
FINDLATER (Sc)
FINDOCHTEY (Sc)
GLASCLUNE (Sc)
GREYSTOKE (Eng)
HAVERFORD (Wal)
HEDINGHAM (Eng)
HERMITAGE (Sc)
KIESSIMUL (Sc)
KILDRUMMY (Sc)
KILKERRAN (Sc)
KILLOCHAN (Sc)
KILRACOCK (Sc)
KIMBOLTON (Eng)
LANCASTER (Eng)
MANORBIER (Wal)
MIDDLEHAM (Eng)
MUNCASTER (Eng)
NEWCASTLE (Eng)
OLD SLAINS (Sc)
PEMBRIDGE (Eng)
PENDENNIS (Eng)
PICKERING (Eng)
POWDERHAM (Eng)
RESTORMEL (Eng)
ROCHESTER (Eng)
ST ANDREWS (Sc)
SAN SIMEON (US)
SCALLOWAY (Sc)
SKENFRITH (Wal)
TANTALLON (Sc)
TREGENNIS (Eng)
ULZIESIDE (Sc)
WARKWORTH (Eng)

10+ letters
ABERYSTWYTH (Wal)
ARMATHWAITE (Eng)

ASHBY DE LA ZOUCH (Eng)
AUCHINDOWN (Sc)
AUGHENTAINE (Ire)
BERRY POMEROY (Eng)
CAERLAVEROCK (Sc)
CAERNARFON (Wal)
CAERPHILLY (Wal)
CARISBROOKE (Eng)
CARMARTHEN (Wal)
CARNASSERIE (Sc)
CARREG CENNEN (Wal)
CASTELL Y BERE (Wal)
CASTLECRAIG (Sc)
CHILLINGHAM (Eng)
CHRISTCHURCH (Eng)
COCKERMOUTH (Eng)
COLCHESTER (Eng)
CONISBROUGH (Eng)
CRAIGIEVAR (Sc)
CRAIGNETHAN (Sc)
DOLWYDDELAN (Wal)
DONNINGTON (Eng)
DUNSTANBURGH (Eng)
EILEAN DONNAN (Sc)
FORT GEORGE (Sc)
FORT WILLIAM (Sc)
FOTHERINGHAY (Eng)
FRAMLINGHAM (Eng)
FRAOCH EILEAN (Sc)

HARRY AVERY'S (Ire)
HERSTMONCEUX (Eng)
INVERALLOCHY (Sc)
INVERLOCHY (Sc)
KAIM OF MATHERS (Sc)
KENILWORTH (Eng)
KINLOCHALINE (Sc)
KIRKCUDBRIGHT (Sc)
LAUNCESTON (Eng)
LINDISFARNE (Eng)
LINLITHGOW (Sc)
LLANSTEPHAN (Wal)
LOCHINDORE (Sc)
LOUGH CUTRA (Ire)
OKEHAMPTON (Eng)
PAINSCASTLE (Wal)
PONTEFRACT (Eng)
POR(T)CHESTER (Eng)
PORTSMOUTH (Eng)
RAVENSBURGH (Eng)
RAVENSCRAIG (Sc)
ROCKINGHAM (Eng)
ST BRIAVELS (Eng)
SCARBOROUGH (Eng)
SMAITHAM TOWER (Sc)
SUTHERLAND (Eng)
TATTERSHALL (Eng)
TOWER OF LONDON (Eng)
WINCHESTER (Eng)

[~s in the Downs = DEAL, *SANDWICH*, WALMER].

CASTOR (s/l caster). 1. (SWIVEL) WHEEL. BEAVER EXTRACT. OIL. *HAT* (sl). 2. Gk myth *twin* of *Pollux*. A horse tamer and patron of seamen. One of the *ARGONAUTS*. With Pollux, two stars: Dioscuri.

CAT 1. RAISE/WEIGH ANCHOR (naut). BURGLAR, *ROBBER*. JAZZ ENTHUSIAST. LASH, SCOURGE, *WHIP*, [~ o' nine tails]. *FAMILIAR*, GRIMALKIN [*witch*]. MALICIOUS WOMAN. VOMIT (sl). 2. Feline animal.

KITTY, MOGGIE, PUSS(Y), TOM; MARMALADE, TABBY,
TORTOISESHELL [T.S. Eliot; *Freya*; *Lear*; 9 lives]; **breeds:**
ABYSSINIAN (swims), AFGHAN, BLOTCHED, BLUE
RUSSIAN, BURMESE, CHARTREUSE, KILKENNY
(fighting), MALTESE, MANX (tailless), PERSIAN, SIAMESE;
male = TOM, **female** = QUEEN, **offspring** = KITTEN;
~ **family:** BOBCAT, CARACAL, CHEETAH, CIVET,
COUGAR, EYRA, GENET, JAGUAR, (SNOW) LEOPARD,
LION, *LYNX*, MARGAY, NANDINE, OCELOT, *OUNCE*,
PUMA, RASSE, SERVAL, *TIGER*, TIGON [feral; *weasel*];
celebrated: BAGHEERA (*Kipling*), CHESHIRE (*Alice*),
DINAH (*Alice*), FELIX (Sullivan cartoon), MITTENS,
MOPPET (*Potter*), ORLANDO (Marmalade ~), SHERE
KHAN (*Kipling*), SILVESTER (Tweetie Pie cartoon), SIMKIN
(*Potter*). TABITHA TWITCHIT (Beatrix *Potter*), ~ that walked
by himself (Just So Stories, Kipling), TOM (~ and Jerry
cartoon), TOM KITTEN (Beatrix *Potter*) and, all from T.S.
Eliot: BUSTOPHER JONES (~ about Town, *club*), OLD
DEUTERONOMY (*long life*), GROWLTIGER (bargee,
GRIDDLEBONE), GUS (theatre), JELLICLE ~s (*dancing*),
JENNYANYDOTS (Gumbie), MACAVITY (criminal, *unseen*),
MR MISTOFFELEES (conjuror), MORGAN (*pirate*,
commissionaire), MUNGOJERRIE and RUMPLETEAZER
(*robbers*), RUMPUSCAT (fierce), RUM TUM TUGGER
(curious), SKIMBLESHANKS (*railway*). [Dick Whittington;
Puss in Boots].

CATCH ARREST, CAPTURE, LAND, SNARE, *TRAP*.
INCUR, RECEIVE. AIR, DITTY, *SONG*. HIT. BAG
(fishing, shooting). DISMISS (*cricket*). COUP, GOOD
MATCH.

CATHAY CHINA (arch).

CATHEDRAL CHURCH (diocesan) [*bishop*; *episcopal sig*; *see*]
Parts: aisle, altar, aumbry, chancel, chapterhouse, choirschool,
clerestory, crypt, faldstool, Lady chapel, lectern, lich/lych
(corpse) gate, muniment room, nave, organ loft, presbytery,
reredos, rood screen, sanctuary, side chapel, tabernacle,
triforium, vestry. **Celebrated:** Aberdeen, Bath, Bristol,
Canterbury, Chester, Chichester, Coventry, Durham, Edinburgh,
Ely, Exeter, Glasgow, Gloucester, Guildford, Lichfield, Lincoln,

Norwich, Oxford, Peterborough, Rochester, St Albans, St Pauls, Salisbury, Tewkesbury, Truro, Wells, Winchester, Worcester, York Minster.

CATO 1. Rom statesman/general (234-149 B.C.). Consul and *censor*, he disliked Carthage. 2. Descendant of (1), lived 95-46 B.C., and was enemy of *Caesar*. 3. ~ Street, the site of an unsuccessful plot to murder Castlereagh in 1820.

CATTLE COW(S), KINE, LIVESTOCK, NEAT, *OX(EN)*, STOCK; LOWER (crypt); **assembly** = herd, **male** = BULL, **female** = *COW*, **offspring** = *CALF*; **breeds:** ABERDEEN ANGUS, AYRSHIRE, CHAROLAIS, *DEXTER*, FRIESIAN, *GUERNSEY*, HEREFORD, HIGHLAND, *JERSEY*, KERRY, REDPOLL, SHORTHORN, SOUTH DEVON, WELSH BLACK.

CAUCASIAN *WHITE*.

CAUGHT (s/l *court*). C, CT, DISMISSED (*cricket*). SNAGGED, SNARED, TRAPPED.

CAURUS Rom myth NW *WIND* (**Gk** = SKIRON).

CAUTION PRUDENCE; WARNING. *CASE*, CHARACTER, WAG.

CAVE CELLAR, ROCK DWELLING, POTHOLE [*Aeolus*; *study*]. *FORE*, LOOK-OUT (Lat). COLLAPSE, SUBSIDE.

CAVEMAN *HERMIT*, TROGLODYTE; CELLIST (crypt). LOOK-OUT, SENTRY (crypt).

CB COMPANION (Order of the Bath), *ORDER*.

CBE COMPANION (Order of the Br Empire), *MEDAL*.

CBI BOSSES, EMPLOYERS (Confederation of Br Industry).

CBS *BROADCASTING* (US).

CC CUBIC CENTIMETRES. TWO HUNDRED.

CD CADMIUM (chem). CIVIL DEFENCE. CORPS DIPLOMATIQUE.

CDR COMMANDER, OFFICER.

CE CHURCH (OF ENGLAND). CIVIL ENGINEER.

CEASEFIRE Stop shooting, hence CUT (crypt).

CEDILLA *ACCENT* (ç = sibilant).

CELEBRATED EXTOLLED, FAMOUS, PRAISED, WELL-KNOWN, HONOURED, OBSERVED, OFFICIATED, PERFORMED, SUNG.

CELEBRITY BIG-WIG, *LION*, *STAR*, VIP.

CELLIST *BOWMAN* (crypt); FIDDLER. CAVEDWELLER, *HERMIT*, PRISONER, RECLUSE (crypt). *GAOLER*, JAILER, WARDER (crypt).

CELSIUS C (centigrade temperature).

CENSORSHIP CUTTING, FAULT-FINDING, PRUNING, SCREENING [*Cato*]; **film categories:** A (adults only; advisory), AA (over 15, was over 14), G (general audience – US), H (horrific; over 16), PG (parental guidance), R (clubs; and restricted – US), U (universal), X (sexy – over 18).

CENT (s/l *scent*, sent). CENTURY, *COIN*.

CENTAUR 1. Myth horse with human head (thus H*ORSE or, with man's head, M*ORSE); *CHIRON*. 2. *CONSTELLATION*.

CENTIGRADE C [Celsius; temperature].

CENTRE MIDDLE. Centre of word or phrase, e.g. **Civic centre** = v, or **Town centre** = ow (crypt).

CERAMICS *CHINA*, EARTHENWARE, PORCELAIN, POTTERY; **types:**

BOW	LOWESTOFT
BRISTOL	MASON
CAUGHLEY®	MEISSEN (Ger)
CHELSEA	MING (Ch)
COALPORT®	MINTON®
COPELAND®	NEW HALL
DAVENPORT	ROCKINGHAM
DELFT (NL)	SEVRES (Fr)
DERBY	SPODE®
DOULTON®	STAFFORDSHIRE
DRESDEN (Ger)	TANG (Ch)
DUX	*WORCESTER*

CERBERUS Gk myth three-headed dog, guarding *Hades* on the banks of the *Styx*.

CERCYON Gk myth *bully*, who wrestled strangers to death; k by *Theseus*.

CERES 1. Rom goddess of *NATURE*; EARTH MOTHER; m of *Acheron*. **Gk** = *DEMETER*. 2. Largest of the minor *PLANETS*, with orbit between *Mars* and *Jupiter*.

CERTAIN *BOUND*, SPECIFIC, SURE.

CESTR *Episcopal sig* of *CHESTER*.

CETACEA AQUATIC MAMMAL: *DOLPHIN, PORPOISE, WHALE*.

CEZAR *AWARD*® (films, Fr).

CF COMPARE. CONFER. CARRY FORWARD (comm).

CH CHAPTER. CHILD. CHINA. CHURCH. (*COMPANION* OF) HONOUR. SWITZERLAND (*car plate*).

Ch China, ~ese.

CHAFF BADINAGE, BANTER, *TEASING*. HUSKS. ANTI-RADAR FOIL; WINDOW (code name).

CHAIRED CONTROLLED, TOOK THE CHAIR. CARRIED SHOULDER-HIGH. SEATED, UPHOLSTERED (crypt).

CHAIRMAN *MC*, PRESIDENT. SEDAN-BEARER (arch). Cabinet/furniture maker, upholsterer (crypt) e.g. ADAM, CHIPPENDALE, HEPPLEWHITE, SHERATON.

CHALCEDONY *GEM*, SEMI-PRECIOUS STONE; *AGATE, BLOODSTONE*, CHRYSOPRASE, *CORNELIAN, ONYX, SARD*, SARDONYX.

CHAMPION ACE, RECORD HOLDER. *COMIC*. WONDER *HORSE*.

CHANGE *Anag*. 1. ALTER, EXCHANGE, SUBSTITUTE, SWITCH, VARIETY. REDRESS (crypt). LOOSE COINS, MONEY: CENTS, PENCE etc. 2. Appearing as part of the answer, *anags* its fellow word, e.g. **Rove, for instance, the switch** (10) = CHANGEOVER.

CHANGE SIDES 1. CROSS THE FLOOR, DEFECT, SWITCH ALLEGIANCE, TURNCOAT. 2. *Anag* of 'sides' e.g. SISED, DISES etc (crypt).

CHAOS 1. CONFUSION, PANDEMONIUM, UPROAR (**opp** = *order*). FORMLESS SPACE, PRIMORDIAL DEEP, VOID. 2. Gk *goddess* of vacant space which existed before the Creation, m of Erebus and *Nyx*, and the oldest of the gods.

CHAPERONE DUENNA; GUARD OF HONOUR, NEAR MISS (crypt).

CHAPMAN COMMERCIAL TRAVELLER, DRUMMER, PEDLAR, *REP. WRITER*. COWBOY (crypt).

CHAPTER C, CH. ACT, STATUTE. ORDER. SECTION.

CHAR BURN, SCORCH. CLEAN(ER), DAILY, DO, DOMESTIC, MRS MOPP, TREASURE,

WASHER-WOMAN. TEA (sl). *FISH*, TROUT.

CHARACTER IDENTITY, PERSONALITY, TRAIT; TYPE (*study*). ATTRIBUTE, PROPERTY, QUALITY. LETTERS. *CASE*, COMEDIAN.

CHARGE CARE; *MINOR*, *WARD*. ASSAULT, ATTACK, ONSLAUGHT, RUSH. BOOST, ENERGIZE, REVITALIZE. PAYMENT, PRICE.

CHARIOT HORSE-DRAWN *CARRIAGE*, QUADRIGA (mil) [*Aurora*, *Boadicea*, Elijah, *Freya*, *Jehu*, *Phaeton*; *constellation*]. (*tarot*).

CHARM ATTRACTION, BEWITCH, DELIGHT, ENTICE, *ENTRANCE*, FASCINATE; **saying**. *GRACE*, IT, *SA*. AMULET, FETISH, MASCOT, TALISMAN; CANTRIP, INCANTATION, SPELL. *Assembly* of FINCHES.

CHARON Gk myth s of Erebus and *Nyx*. FERRYMAN of the dead over the rivers *Acheron* and *Styx* [*Cocytus*, *Lethe*], past the dog *Cerberus*; his fee was the Obolus.

CHART DIRECT, *PLOT*, RECORD. MAP, PLAN, SEA-MAP. Pl = RATING [top ten etc].

CHARTER *DEED*, GRANT. HIRE. *RIGHTS*. NAVIGATOR (crypt).

CHARY *SHY*, WARY.

CHARYBDIS A whirlpool which, with the rock *Scylla*, formed a hazard to seafarers in the Straits of Messina; now called Galofaro.

CHAUCER GEOFFREY (c 1340-1400); s of Agnes and John ~ vintner, mar Philippa and f of Lewis. *Page* to wife of Edward III's son and a court diplomat. Father of English poetry. **His works include:** Consolations of Philosophy (trans of treatise on the astrolabe), Romance of the Rose (trans), The Book of the Duchess, The House of Fame, The Legend of Good Women, The Parliament of Fowls, Troilus and Cressida, and The Canterbury Tales with its Prologue, whose **characters** assembled at the Tabard Inn, Southwark, **include:** the Canon's Yeoman, the *Cook*, the *Doctor* of Medicine (Physician), the Franklin, the *Friar* (a Limiter), *Host* (Harry Bailey), the *Knight*, the Lady Prioress (Madam Eglantine), the Manciple, Milibeus, the Merchant, the Miller (a *wrestler*), the *Monk*, the *Nun's* Priest, the Pardoner, the *Parson* and his br the Ploughman, the *Reeve*, the *Scholar* (Clerk), the Sea Captain, *Sailor* or Shipman (his boat, the Magdalen), the

Second *Nun*, the *Sergeant-at-Law* (Man of Law), Sir *Topaz*, the Squire (s of the Knight), the Summoner and the Wife of Bath (gap-toothed); also travelling, but without a recorded tale, were the *Carpenter*, the Dyer, the Haberdasher, the Ploughman, the Tapestry Maker, the *Weaver* and the Yeoman.

CHCH CHRISTCHURCH.

CHE GUEVARA, REVOLUTIONARY.

CHEAT CON, COZEN, DECEIVE(R), FIDDLE, FRAUD, SWINDLE(R), TRICK(STER).

CHECK DAM, HOLD IN, STEM. CONTROL, MAKE SURE. DRAFT, CHEQUE, LETTER OF CREDIT (US).

CHEESE MALLOW FRUIT. SKITTLES DISC. VIP (sl). Decorative coil of rope (naut). [camera, smile]. PRESSED CURDS;

types (all ®):	**8+ letters**
under 8 letters	BRICKBAT
BLUE	CAMEMBERT
BOURSIN	CHESHIRE
BRIE	COTSWOLD
CHEDDAR	GAMBOZOLA
COTTAGE	GLOUCESTER
CREAM	GORGONZOLA
DUTCH	JARLSBERG
EDAM	LYMESWOLD
GOUDA	PARMESAN
GRUYERE	PECORINO
MYCELLA	PORT SALUT
SAGE	ROQUEFORT
STILTON	TILSITER
SWISS	WENSLEYDALE
	WESTMINSTER BLUE

Chem Chemistry.

CHEMICAL ELEMENT BASIC SUBSTANCE, IRRESOLVABLE; e.g:

Actinium	$= AC$	Argon	$= A$
Aluminium	$= AL$	Arsenic	$= AS$

Barium	= *BA*	Neon	= NE
Boron	= *B*	Nickel	= *NI*
Cadmium	= *CD*	Nitrogen	= *N*
Carbon	= *C*	Oxygen	= *O*
Chromium	= *CR*	Palladium	= *PD*
Cobalt	= *CO*	Phosphorus	= *P*
Copper	= *CU*	Platinum	= *PT*
Fluorine	= *F*	Potassium	= *K*
Gold	= AU	Silicon	= *SI*
Helium	= *HE*	Silver	= *AG*
Hydrogen	= *H*	Sodium	= *NA*
Iodine	= *I*	Sulphur	= *S*
Iridium	= IR	Tin	= SN
Iron	= FE	Titanium	= TI
Krypton	= KR	Uranium	= *U*
Lead	= PB	Wolfram	= *W*
Magnesium	= *MG*	Xenon	= XE
Mercury	= HG	Zinc	= ZN

A	= ARGON	K	= POTASSIUM
AC	= ACTINIUM	KR	= KRYPTON
AG	= *SILVER*	MG	= MAGNESIUM
AL	= ALUMINIUM	N	= NITROGEN
AS	= ARSENIC	NA	= *SODIUM*
AU	= *GOLD*	NE	= NEON
B	= BORON	NI	= *NICKEL*
BA	= BARIUM	O	= OXYGEN
C	= CARBON	P	= PHOSPHORUS
CD	= CADMIUM	PB	= *LEAD*
CO	= COBALT	PD	= PALLADIUM
CR	= CHROMIUM	PT	= *PLATINUM*
CU	= *COPPER*	S	= SULPHUR
F	= FLUORINE	SI	= SILICON
FE	= *IRON*	SN	= *TIN*
H	= HYDROGEN	TI	= TITANIUM
HE	= HELIUM	U	= URANIUM
HG	= *MERCURY*	W	= WOLFRAM
I	= IODINE	XE	= XENON
IR	= IRIDIUM	ZN	= ZINC

CHEMIST DISPENSER. MPS.

CHESSPIECE BISHOP, *CASTLE*, *KING*, *KNIGHT*, PAWN, *QUEEN*, *ROOK*. BOARDMAN (crypt).

CHESTER 1. DEVA (*Rom*). *CASTLE*. *RACETRACK* (horses). 2. **Episcopal sig** = CESTR. 3. *Herald*.

CHESTERTON Gilbert Keith, *writer*; **books:** The *Club* of *Queer* Trades, *Father Brown detective* stories, The Man who was *Thursday*, The *Napoleon* of Notting Hill.

CHIC A LA MODE, FASHIONABLE, IN, SMART.

CHICHESTER 1. *WORLD-GIRDLER*. NOVIOMAGUS (*Rom*). 2. **Episcopal sig** = CICESTR.

CHICKEN AFRAID. YOUNG WOMAN. BIDDY, HEN, POULTRY (*male* and *female*).

CHIEF GOD **Gk** = *ZEUS*, **Rom** = JOVE, *JUPITER*, **A-Sax** = *WODEN*, **Bab** = ANU, BEL/BELUS, **Ch** = XANGTI, **Egy** = *OSIRIS*, TEMU, **Ind** = BRAHMA, SHIVA, **Nor** = *ODIN*, **Phoen** = *BAAL*.

CHIEF GODDESS **Gk** = *HERA*, **Rom** = *JUNO*, **Egy** = *ISIS*, **Ind** = *DEVI*, **Bab** = BELIT/BELTIS.

CHILD 1. CH, ISSUE. TOT. Human *offspring*. [*Dickens*; *patron saint*]. 2. Monday's ~ is fair of face; Tuesday's ~ is full of *grace*; Wednesday's ~ is full of woe; Thursday's ~ has far to go; Friday's ~ is *loving* and giving; Saturday's ~ works hard for its living; but the ~ that is born on a Sabbath day is bonny and blithe, and *good* and gay.

CHILDBIRTH 1. BEARING, DELIVERY, LABOUR. 2. **Goddess: Gk** = *HERA*, **Rom** = JUNO.

CHIMAERA Gk myth firebreathing *MONSTER* (front lion, middle goat, back dragon), slain by *Bellerophon*. VOLCANO. [*Typhon*].

CHINA Ch. CATHAY [mandarins, *study*]. *CERAMICS*; DISHES, PLATES, SERVICE. 20th *anniversary*.

CHINAMAN *BOXER*, CHINK, MANDARIN. *BOSIE*, GOOGLY (*cricket*).

CHIRON 1. Gk myth wise CENTAUR, teacher of *Achilles*, Diomedes and *Jason* in gymnastics, hunting, medicine, music and prophecy. 2. A minor *PLANET* orbiting the *Sun* between *Saturn* and *Venus*.

CHLORIS Gk *goddess* of *FLOWERS*. **Rom** = *FLORA*.

CHOICE PREFERENCE, SELECTION. APPROPRIATE,

ELITE, EXQUISITE, *FLOWER*, SELECT. ALTERNATIVE
[Devil and deep blue sea; Hobson's ~; Scylla and *Charybdis*].
CHOPSTICKS CLEAVE/SPLIT FIREWOOD. PIANO TUNE.
EATING TOOLS (Ch).
CHORIAMB *FOOT*.
CHRISTCHURCH CHCH. (*University*) COLLEGE. *CASTLE*.
CHRISTMAS NATIVITY. PRESENT DAY (crypt) [Santa Claus].
~ box, ~ cake, ~ card, ~ present, ~ stocking, ~ tree, ~ *song*:

    (12) *Lords* a-leaping   (6) *Geese* a-laying
    (11) Ladies *dancing*   (5) Golden *rings*
    (10) *Pipers* piping   (4) Calling *birds*
    (9) *Drummers* drumming   (3) French *hens*
    (8) *Maids* a-milking   (2) Turtle *doves*
    (7) Swans a-swimming   A *partridge* in a pear-tree.

CHRISTOPHER *KIT*, TRAVELLER. *PATRON SAINT*
(wayfarers).
CHROMATIC INTERVAL, SCALE (mus).
BRIGHT-COLOURED.
CHROMIUM CR (*chem*).
CHRYSOBERYL *GEM* (green/yellow).
CHRYSOLITE *GEM*, PRECIOUS STONE; OLIVINE,
PERIDOT. *Birthstone* (September).
CHRYSOPRASE *GEM*, SEMI-PRECIOUS STONE;
CHALCEDONY (green).
CHURCH CH. CE, RC. HOUSE OF WORSHIP.
ESTABLISHMENT.
CHURCH DRESS **Headgear:** BIRETTA (RC), CALOT(T)E (RC),
HOOD (friar), MITRE (abbot, bishop), SHOVEL HAT
(clergy), TIARA (pope). **Vestments:** ALB (clergy), AMICE
(shoulders), APRON (bishop), CANONICALS (clergy),
CASSOCK (clergy), CHASUBLE (clergy), CHIMERE (bishop),
COPE (processional cloak), DALMATIC (bishop, deacon),
EPHOD (Jewish), MANIPLE (eucharistic napkin), MORSE
(cope fastening), ORPHREY (embroidered scarf), ROCHET
(surplice), SCAPULAR, ~Y (monk), SOUTANE (RC), STOLE
(scarf), SURPLICE (clergy), TIPPET (cloth band), TUNICLE
(bishop), VEXILLUM (crosier cloth).

CHURCHMAN WREN (crypt). CLERGY, DD, *FATHER*, PRELATE, PRIEST, REVEREND, RR, e.g.:

4-letters
ABBE (RC)
CURE (RC)
DEAN
GURU (Ind)
IMAM (Mos)
LAMA (Bud)
MONK
POPE (Gk; RC)
YOGI (Ind)

5-letters
ABBOT
CANON
DRUID (Wal)
FAKIR (Mos)
FRIAR
HADJI (Mos)
MUFTI (Mos)
PADRE
PRIOR
VICAR

6-letters
BEADLE
BISHOP
CLERIC
CURATE
DEACON
MULLAH (Mos)
PARSON
PASTOR

RECTOR
SCRIBE (Heb)
SEXTON
VERGER

7-letters
ACOLYTE
BRAHMIN (Ind)
BROTHER
MUEZZIN (Mos)
PONTIFF (RC)
PRELATE
PRIMATE

8+ letters
ARCHBISHOP
ARCHDEACON
AYATOLLAH (Mos)
CARDINAL (RC)
CHAPLAIN
CHURCHWARDEN
ECCLESIASTIC
GODBOTHERER (sl)
METROPOLITAN (Gk)
MINISTER
MISSIONARY
PATRIARCH (Gk)
PREBENDARY
PRECENTOR
PRESBYTER
SKYPILOT (sl)

CHURCHWOMAN ABBESS, CANONESS, MOTHER SUPERIOR, NOVICE, NUN, POSTULANT, PRIORESS, *SISTER*.

CI CHANNEL ISLANDS. CIRRUS. (Order of the) CROWN OF
INDIA.

CIA CENTRAL INTELLIGENCE AGENCY.

CICERO 1. DRUM *HORSE*. 2. ORATOR, B.C. 104-43; mar (1)
Terentia (one d Tullia, one s Marcus), (2) Publilia. Ass by Mark
Antony B.C. 43. Writings include: De Oratore, De Republica, De
Legibus, De Officiis, De Finibus etc.

CICESTR *Episcopal sig* of CHICHESTER.

CINQUE PORTS DOVER, HASTINGS, HYTHE, ROMNEY,
SANDWICH (+ *RYE* and *WINCHESTER*) [Lord Warden.
Walmer *Castle*]. Vessel (*Crusoe*).

CIPANGU *JAPAN*.

CIRCA *ABOUT, C, CA*.

CIRCLE O, *RING*, ROUNDEL, *ZERO* [*Pi*].

CIRCUMFLEX BENDING, CURVED. *ACCENT* (ˆ).

CIRCUMNAVIGATORS EXPLORERS, *WORLD-GIRDLERS*.

CIRRUS *CI, CLOUD*, MACKEREL SKY.

CISTERCIAN *MONK*; BENEDICTINE, *TRAPPIST*.

CIVIL SERVICE CS (**Unions** = NALGO, NUPE). REGISTRY
OFFICE WEDDING (crypt). POLITE WAITER (crypt).

CLASS *FORM, REMOVE*, SCHOOL. TYPE, RANK. STYLE,
TONE, *U* (and crypt, e.g. **Quietly classy** = U*P).

CLASSED DESIGNATED, RANKED, REGISTERED. AT
SCHOOL, IN FORM, LEARNING (crypt).

CLAUSTROPHOBIA *Aversion* to enclosed spaces.

CLEAN SHEET FRESH START. UNWRITTEN, VIRGIN
PAPER. NEW BEDLINEN.

CLEF BASS, TREBLE; *KEY*.

CLEOPATRA 1. QUEEN OF EGYPT (B.C. 68-30); d of *Ptolemy*
Anletes, mar her br Ptolemy; was lover (1) Julius *Caesar* (one s,
Caesarion) and (2) *Antony*. Caused Antony to lose the sea battle
of Actium by withdrawing her fleet, then spread the rumour that
she had died. Antony stabbed himself, whereupon she also killed
herself, with an asp [beauty; snake]. 2. Minor *PLANET*. 3.
Shak (A and C). *Shaw* (Caesar and ~).

CLERGY *CHURCHMEN*.

CLERK CLERGYMAN, LAY OFFICER (~ of Oxenford,
Chaucer). HOTEL/SHOP ASSISTANT (US). AGENT,
COURT OFFICIAL, RECORDER. OVERSEER.

BANK/OFFICE WORKER; **celebrated:** BOB CRATCHIT (Scrooge's in Christmas Carol); URIAH HEEP ('umble to Wickfield in David Copperfield); TIM LINKINWATER (Cheerybles' in Nicholas Nickleby); NEWMAN NOGGS (Ralph Nickleby's in Nicholas Nickleby); JOHN WEMMICK (Jaggers' in Great Expectations).

CLIFFHANGER TENSE SITUATION, THRILLER. NEST (crypt). ROCKY PLANT e.g. IVY, MESA VERDE, SAMPHIRE (crypt).

CLIMBER ALPINIST, MOUNTAINEER. IVY, *PLANT*, LIANA, MESA VERDE, SAMPHIRE, STEPHANOTIS. SOCIAL SNOB, PUSHER.

CLIMBING 1. MOUNTAINEERING, MOUNTING, SCALING. PUSHING. 2. Word reads upwards (dn) e.g. **Climbing weed** = DEEW (crypt, dn).

CLIMBING FRAME LADDER (crypt). EMARF (dn, crypt).

CLINK *GAOL* (sl). CLANK, *RING*.

CLIO One of the nine Gk *MUSES* (myth).

CLIPJOINT DIVE, NIGHTCLUB, SPEAKEASY. STAPLE, PAPER-CLIP (crypt). BARBERSHOP, HAIRDRESSER (crypt).

CLIPPER *BOAT*, SAILING SHIP. SCISSORS, SHEARS, SNIPPERS; HEDGE-TRIMMER. BARBER (crypt).

CLOAK CONCEAL. DISGUISE, MASK. GARMENT; CLOKE (arch); **types:** BURNOUS (Arab), DOLMAN (Turk), KIRTLE (arch), PALETOT (19th cent), PALLIUM (Gk), *TABARD* (herald, knight), TOGA (Rom). [~ and dagger].

CLOCK TIME-KEEPER, TIME-PIECE, *WATCH*; TICKER; GRANDFATHER [*Company* (livery); Knibb, Tompion]. FACE (sl).

CLOSE *NEAR*, NIGH. MEAN, MISERLY, NIGGARDLY, STINGY, TIGHT. *END*, FINISH; SHUT. PRIVATE, QUIET [oyster]. MUGGY, OPPRESSIVE, *SULTRY*, WARM (**opp** = *cold*). COURTYARD, QUAD.

CLOTH FABRIC, *MATERIAL*, RAG [*Company* (livery); *measure*]. DUSTER. *CLERGY*.

CLOTHES CLOBBER, *DRESS(ES)*, DUDS, GEAR, GLAD RAGS, RIG. BEDECKS. [Hans *Andersen*].

CLOUD BEFOG, OBFUSCATE. WATER-VAPOUR e.g. *CI*,

CIRRUS, CU, CUMULUS, NIMBUS, STRATUS.

CLOWN RUSTIC (arch). *FOOL, JESTER* (q.v.); PAGLIACCIO, RIGOLETTO (Verdi; *hunchback*).

CLUB 1. COSH, CUDGEL, NIGHTSTICK, TRUNCHEON, *WEAPON* [*Periphites*]. GOLF STICK; **types:** BLASTER, BRASSIE, CLEEK, *DRIVER, IRON*, MASHIE, NIBLICK, *PUTTER*, SANDWEDGE, *SPOON, WEDGE, WOOD*. **Pl =** *CARDS, SUIT*; SOLDIERS (*Alice*). 2. C; ASSOCIATION, SOCIETY [*Cat; Chesterton*]; **celebrated London** ~s:

Alpine	Junior Naval & Military
Army & Navy (the Rag)	Junior Carlton
Athenaeum	Lyceum
Bachelors	Marlborough
Badminton	National Sporting
Bath	Naval & Military (In and Out)
Bellona (Sayers)	Portland
Boodle's	Pratt's
Brooks's	Public Schools
Buck's	Reform
Carlton	Royal Air Force
Cavalry	Royal Automobile
Cavendish	Royal Thames Yacht
Conservative	St James's
Constitutional	Savage
Diogenes (*Holmes*)	Savile
Drones (*Wodehouse*)	Travellers'
Eccentric	United Services
Garrick	White's
Guards	

CLUBLAND ST JAMES. GOLF COURSE (crypt).

CLUBMAN ROTARIAN. GOLFER (crypt). COSHER, THUG [*Periphites*].

CLYTEMNESTRA 1. Gk myth sis of *Castor, Pollux* and *twin* of *Helen*; mar *Agamemnon* (one s Orestes, two d *Electra* and Iphigenia); k by her s Orestes for adultery with Aegisthus while Agamemnon was fighting at *Troy*. 2. A minor *PLANET*.

CO CARE OF. COBALT (*chem*). (COMMANDING)

OFFICER. COLORADO (US *state*). COLOMBIA (*car plate*). *COMPANY*, FIRM.

COACH BUS, *CARRIAGE*, CHARABANC, TRANSPORT. CRAMMER, INSTRUCT(OR), TEACH(ER), TRAIN(ER), TUTOR.

COATED 1. CAKED. PAINTED. DRESSED (crypt). 2. Word outside another e.g. **Beaten egg is sent back coated with mud** (6) = MU*GGE*D.

COATING COVERAGE, LAYER. JACKET, OVERCOAT, REEFER.

COB *BOAT*. BREAD, LOAF. CLAY BRICK. COAL. *HORSE*. NUT. SWAN (*male*).

COBALT CO (*chem*).

COBBLER CORDWAINER, SHOEMAKER, SNOB [*last*, Manette (*Dickens*)]. *DRINK*. **Pl** = BALLS (*rh sl*). NORTHAMPTON (*football* team).

COCAINE *DRUG*, SNOW; NUMBER (crypt). [*Holmes*].

COCKTAIL *Anag. DRINK*: JOHN COLLINS, HIGHBALL, MARTINI®, SCREWDRIVER, SIDECAR etc. AMALGAM, MIX(TURE). FEATHER (crypt). K (crypt).

COCYTUS Gk myth tributary of the river *Acheron* [*Underworld*].

COD *FISH*. CASH ON DELIVERY.

CODE LAWS, RULES, STATUTES. ETHIC, STANDARD. CRYPTOGRAM, CYPHER (mil). *MORSE*, SEMAPHORE, W/T. STD.

COIGN (s/l *coin*). CORNER, VANTAGE POINT.

COIN (s/l *coign*). INVENT, MAKE; UTTER. Put CO* in word (crypt), e.g. **Coin sop ladle** (5) = S*CO*OP; **vague inherent coin** (5) = IN*CO*HERENT. MONEY, SPECIE, SMALL CHANGE (hence MALLS; crypt); C, D, P, S. **Types (OE gold)**: JOANNES (36s 0d), MOIDORE (27s 0d), JACOBUS (25s 0d), CAROLUS (23s 0d), *GUINEA* (21s 0d), *MARK* (13s 4d), *ANGEL* (10s 0d), NOBLE (6s 8d), *DOLLAR* (4s 6d); **(OE silver)**: *TESTER* (6d), GROAT (4d). **Old Scots:** BODLE (2d), PLACK or GROAT (4d), BAWBEE (6d), SHILLING (12d), *POUND* (20s), MERK (13s 4d). **Others:**

2-letters	3-letters
AS (Rom)	*BOB* (UK)

ECU (Fr)
SOU (Fr)

4-letters
CASH (Ch, Ind)
CENT (US etc)
DIME (US)
MARK (Eng, Fin, Ger)
MITE (bibl)
PEAG (Ind)
REAL (Sp)

5-letters
CROWN (Eng, Scand)
DUCAT (Eur)
FRANC (Fr)
FRANK (Eur)
PENNY (UK)
ROYAL (Eng)

6-letters
GUINEA (UK)

NICKEL (US)
PESETA (Sp)
ROUBLE (USSR)
SHEKEL (Hebr)
STATER (Gk)
STIVER (sl)
TALENT (bibl)
TANNER (UK)
TESTER (Eng)
ZECHIN (Hebr)

7+ letters
DENARIUS (Rom)
DOUBLOON (Sp)
FARTHING (UK)
KRUGERRAND (SA)
MARAVEDI (Sp)
PRINDLE
QUARTER (US)
SOLIDUS (Rom)
SOVEREIGN (UK)

Coll = numismatist. And see *currency*.
COL *COLONEL*, *SOLDIER*. *COLUMN*. *DEPRESSION*,
LOW. *DEFILE*, *PASS*, *SADDLE*.
COLCHESTER 1. *CASTLE*. NATIVE, *OYSTER* [Whitstable].
2. Scene of battle by *Boadicea*. CAMULODUNUM (Rom).
COLD C, CHILLY, NIPPY, FRIGID, ICY (**opp** = *close*, *heat*).
CORYZA, SNIFFLES [catarrh].
COLLECTION ACCUMULATION, *ASSEMBLY*, GATHERING,
GROUP. CALLING FOR, FETCHING; REMOVAL (postal)
[*COD*]. OFFERING [eccles]. CONCENTRATION,
RECOVERING (senses).
COLLECTOR *ACCUMULATOR*, ASSEMBLER, GATHERER,
MAGPIE (sl); HOBBYIST:

Books   = BIBLIOPHILE
Butterflies   = *LEPIDOPTERIST*

Cards	= CARTOPHILIST
Coins	= NUMISMATIST
Insects	= ENTOMOLOGIST
Matchbox labels	= PHILLUMENIST
Medals	= NUMISMATIST
Moths	= LEPIDOPTERIST
Shells	= CONCHOLOGIST
Stamps	= PHILATELIST

COLLEGE *ETON*. [*universities*].

COLONEL (s/l *kernel*). CO, *COL*, OFFICER; REGIMENTED (crypt).

COLOUR INFLUENCE; INTEREST. BLUSH, FLUSH, REDDEN. PAINT; HUE e.g.:

Blacks
COAL
DUSKY
EBON(Y)
JET(TY)
PITCH
SABLE (*herald*)
SOOT
SWART

Blues
AQUAMARINE
AZURE (*herald*)
BERYL
BICE
CAMBRIDGE
CERULEAN
COBALT
ELECTRIC
INDIGO
LAPIS LAZULI
NAVY
OXFORD
PERSE

ROYAL
SAPPHIRE
SEA
SKY
SMALT
TURQUOISE
ULTRAMARINE
WATCHET

Browns
AUBURN
BAY
BISTRE
CAMEL
ECRU
FAWN
HAZEL
HENNA
KHAKI
OCHRE
PUCE
RUSSET
SEPIA
SORREL

TAN
TAWNY
TENNY (*herald*)
VANDYKE

Greens
BERYL
BICE
EMERALD
JADE
OLIVE
RESEDA
TURQUOISE
VERDIGRIS
VERT (*herald*)

Oranges
BRASS
CADMIUM
COPPER
FLAME
OCHRE

Purples
AMETHYST
INDIGO
LAVENDER
LILAC
MAUVE
PLUM
PUCE
PURPURE (*herald*)
VIOLET

Reds
BURGUNDY
CARMINE
CERISE

CINNABAR
CRIMSON
GULES (*herald*)
MAGENTA
MINIUM
MODENA
PILLAR-BOX
RUBY
RUST
SCARLET
VERMILION

Whites
BLANCH
BLEACH
CHALKY
CREAMY
IVORY
LILY
MILK
PEARL

Yellows
AMBER
AUREATE
BUFF
CREAM
FALLOW
GAMBOGE
GILDED
GILT
GOLD
LEMON
PRIMROSE
SAFFRON
SULPHUR
TOPAZ
XANTHIC

Heraldic colours: black = *SABLE*, blue = *AZURE*, brown = TENNE/TENNY, green = VERT, gold = OR, purple = PURPURE, red = GULES, silver = ARGENT. **Primary colours:** *GREEN*, *RED*, VIOLET. **Primary colours (painting):** *BLUE*, *RED*, *YELLOW*. **Rainbow colours** (from outside to in): *RED*, *ORANGE*, *YELLOW*, *GREEN*, *BLUE*, INDIGO, VIOLET.

COLT 1. GREENHORN, TYRO. AUTOMATIC, *WEAPON*®. 2. *Offspring* of camel or horse. **Pl** = JUNIOR TEAM. *Football team* (US).

COLUMN COL. FILE, TROOPS. VERTICAL CYLINDER/DIVISION/JET, PILLAR. ARTICLE, REPORTING.

COMBER BREAKER, FOAM, SURF, WAVE. HAIRDRESSER (crypt) [curry ~]. *BEE* (crypt). FISH.

COMEBACK 1. ENCORE, RETURN, REVIVAL. EMOC (crypt). 2. Word written backwards, e.g. **Elba's comeback looks gloomy** (5) = SABLE.

COMEDOWN ANTICLIMAX. ALIGHT, *LAND* (crypt).

COMET 1. TAILED STAR, SUN SATELLITE (Biela, Ericke, Halley). AIRCRAFT. *REINDEER*. 2. First Br passenger (paddle) steamer.

COMIC AMUSING, BURLESQUE, FACETIOUS, *FUNNY*, HUMOROUS, LAUGHABLE, RIDICULOUS, RISIBLE, WITTY; *CASE*, COMEDIAN. Children's periodical, **names** (all ®): BEANO, BOP, BOY'S OWN PAPER, *BULLSEYE*, *CHAMPION*, *DANDY*, *EAGLE*, HOTSPUR, MAGNET, TIGER TIM, *WIZARD*.

COMING TO One word precedes another, e.g. **Commie coming to see** . . . (3, 4) = RED SPOT.

COMMANDER AOC, CINC, FOC, GOC (mil), [SEAC]. WOODEN MALLET.

COMMANDING DIGNIFIED, IMPRESSIVE. OVERLOOKING. CO, *COMMANDER*, IC, IN CHARGE.

COMMANDMENT DIVINE COMMAND, *TEN* ~s (q.v.) [Moses, Mt Sinai]. Ten in *song*.

COMMON PUBLIC, SHARED. VILLAGE GREEN. ORDINARY, USUAL. INFERIOR, NON-U, VULGAR (**opp** = *U*). NOUS, SENSE (sl). **Pl** = FOOD, RATIONS. *HOUSE*,

LEGISLATIVE ASSEMBLY.

COMMONLY 1. SLANG, VULGARLY. REGULARLY, USUALLY. 2. Employ slang for word(s) in clue, e.g. **Son is not commonly a good man** (5) = S*AINT.

COMMONSENSE NOUS.

COMMONWEALTH GOVERNMENT (Cromwell). STATE. **British members:** Australia, Bahamas, Bangladesh, Barbados, Bermuda (colony), Botswana, Brunei, Canada, Cyprus, East Caribbean States, Fiji, Gambia, Ghana, Grenada, Guyana, India, Jamaica, Kenya, Lesotho, Malawi, Malaysia, Malta, Mauritius, Nauru, New Zealand, Nigeria, Papua New Guinea, Sierra Leone, Singapore, Sri Lanka, Swaziland, Tanzania, Tonga, Trinidad and Tobago, Uganda, United Kingdom, Western Samoa, Zambia.

COMMUNIST COMMIE, RED, *TROT*; IVAN.

COMMUNITY BODY, FELLOWSHIP. EEC (Treaty of Rome).

COMPANION 1. DECKHOUSE, HATCHWAY, hence ACCESS STEPS (naut). ASSOCIATE, BROTHER IN ARMS, FELLOW, FRIEND, *MATE*, OPPO (sl), PAL. AU PAIR, HOUSEKEEPER, LIVER-IN. *REFERENCE WORK. CH* (crypt). 2. Word commonly associated with another (crypt), e.g. **Bill's** ~ = COO; **Cop's** ~ = PROP; **Jeff's** ~ = MUTT; **celebrated** ~ s: AENEAS/ACHATES, BIRDS/BEES, BOSWELL/JOHNSON, CASTOR/POLLUX, DAMON/PHINTIAS (not Pythias), DANTE/BEATRICE, DARBY/JOAN, DAVID/JONATHAN, EURALUS/NISUS, FORTNUM/MASON, GIN/TONIC, MASON/DIXON, MOHAMMED/MOUNTAIN, ORESTES/PYLADES, PETRARCH/LAURA, PUNCH/JUDY, ROLAND/OLIVER, ROMEO/JULIET, SOHRAB/RUSTAM (-EM, -UM), SNAKES/LADDERS, SWAN/EDGAR, WHISKY/SODA or SPLASH, WILL/WAY (see also *inspiration* and *lovers*).

COMPANY *ASSEMBLY*, *COMPANIONS*, GUESTS, *PARTY*, VISITORS. ACTORS, CAST [touring ~]. CREW (naut). BODY OF MEN, *SOLDIERS*, TROOPS. BUSINESS, *CO*, CONCERN, CORPORATION, *COY*, *FIRM*, GUILD, PLC; **City livery** ~s:

APOTHECARIES	BARBERS
BAKERS	BASKET MAKERS

BLACKSMITHS
BREWERS
BUTCHERS
CARPENTERS
CLOCKMAKERS
CLOTHWORKERS
COACH & COACH HARNESS MAKERS
COOPERS
CORDWAINERS
CURRIERS
CUTLERS
DISTILLERS
DRAPERS
DYERS
FANMAKERS
FARRIERS
FELTMAKERS
FISHMONGERS
FLETCHERS
FOUNDERS or COPPERSMITHS
FRAMEWORK KNITTERS or STOCKING WEAVERS
FRUITERERS
GIRDLERS
GLASS SELLERS
GLAZIERS
GOLD & SILVER WYRE DRAWERS
GOLDSMITHS
GROCERS
HABERDASHERS
INNHOLDERS
IRONMONGERS
LEATHER SELLERS
MASONS
MERCERS
MERCHANT TAYLORS
PAINTERS or PAINTER STAINERS
PATTEN MAKERS
PEWTERERS
PLAISTERERS or PARGETTORS

PLAYING CARD MAKERS
PLUMBERS
POULTERS
SADDLERS
SALTERS
SCRIVENERS
SHIPWRIGHTS
SKINNERS
SPECTACLE MAKERS
STATIONERS
TALLOW CHANDLERS
TIN PLATE WORKERS
TURNERS
TYLERS & BRICKLAYERS
VINTNERS
WAX CHANDLERS
WEAVERS
WHEELWRIGHTS

COMPARE (s/l compère). *CF*, LIKEN. *MEASURE*.
COMPASS *BOUNDARY*, CIRCUMFERENCE, LIMIT;
EXTENT, RANGE, SCOPE. LODESTONE, PELORUS
(naut). INSTRUMENT, SCRIBER [dividers].
COMPLAINT AILMENT: CHICKENPOX, DIPHTHERIA,
FEVER, MALARIA, MEASLES, MUMPS, POX, TYPHOID
etc. ACCUSATION, CASE, GRIEVANCE.
COMPOSED OF *Anag.* COMPRISING, MADE OF.
COMPOSER CONSTRUCTOR. PEACE-MAKER, *SETTLER*.
ARRANGER, MUSICAL AUTHOR; **celebrated:**

3-letters
BAX, Sir Arnold Edward
  Trevor (Eng)
CUI, Cesar (Fr/USSR)
IVE, Simon (Eng)
MAW, Nicholas (Eng)

4-letters
ARNE, Thomas Augustine
  (Eng)

BACH, Johann Sebastian
  (Ger)
BERG, Alban (A)
BLOW, John (Eng)
BYRD, William (Eng)
IVES, Charles (US)
KERN, Jerome (US)
NERI, St Philip (It)
ORFF, Carl (Ger)

PERI, Jacopo (It)
WOLF, Hugo (A)

5-letters
BIZET, Georges (Fr)
BLISS, Sir Arthur (Eng)
CESTI, Marcantonio (It)
ELGAR, Sir Edward (Eng)
GLUCK, Christoph von
  (Ger)
GRIEG, Edvard Hagerup
  (Nor)
GROFE, Ferdie (US)
HAYDN, Franz Joseph
  (A)
HOLST, Gustav (Eng)
LISZT, Franz (Hung)
RAVEL, Maurice (Fr)
SOUSA, John Philip (US)
VERDI, Giuseppe (It)
WEBER, Carl Maria von
  (Ger)
WEILL, Kurt (Ger/US)

6-letters
ARNOLD, Matthew (Eng)
BARTOK, Bela (Hung)
BERLIN, Irving (Israel
  Baline) (USSR/US)
BOULEZ, Pierre (Fr)
BRAHMS, Johannes (Ger)
CHOPIN, Frederic
  François (Pol)
COWARD, Sir Noel (Eng)
DELIUS, Frederick (Eng)
DVORAK, Antonin (Cz)
FLOTOW, Friedrich von
  (Ger)

FRANCK, Cesar Auguste
  (Belg)
GLINKA, Michael (USSR)
GOUNOD, Charles (Fr)
LERNER, Alan (US)
HANDEL, George Fredk
  (Ger/Eng)
LANNER, Joseph Franz
  Karl (A)
LENNON, John (Eng)
MAHLER, Gustav (A)
MOZART, Wolfgang
  Amadeus (A)
PORTER, Cole (US)
RIDLEY, Arnold (Eng)
SEARLE, Humphrey (Eng)
STRAUS, Oscar (A)
WAGNER, Richard (Ger)
WALTON, Sir Wm Turner
  (Eng)

7-letters
ARENSKY, Anton (USSR)
BELLINI, Vicenzo (It)
BERLIOZ, Hector (Fr)
BORODIN, Alexander
  (USSR)
BRITTEN, Edward
  Benjamin (Eng)
COPLAND, Aaron (US)
DEBUSSY, Claude Achille
  (Fr)
GIBBONS, Orlando (Eng)
IRELAND, John (Eng)
JANACEK, Leos (A/Cz)
LAMBERT, Constant
  (Eng)
LUTYENS, Elizabeth
  (Eng)

NOVELLO, Ivor (Eng)
POULENC, Francis (Fr)
PUCCINI, Giacomo (It)
PURCELL, Henry (Eng)
ROSSINI, Gioacchino
  Antonio (It)
SMETANA, Bedrich (Cz)
STAINER, John (Eng)
STRAUSS, Eduard (A)
STRAUSS, Johann I, II &
  III (A)
STRAUSS, Joseph (A)
STRAUSS, Richard (Ger)
TIPPETT, Sir Michael
  (Eng)
VIVALDI, Antonio (It)

8-letters
BENEDICT, Julius (Ger)
BRUCKNER, Anton (A)
CLEMENTI, Muzio (It)
COUPERIN, François (Fr)
KREISLER, Fritz (A)
MASSENET, Jules Emile
  (Fr)
SCHUBERT, Franz Peter
  (A)
SCHUMANN, Robert
  Alexander (Ger)
SIBELIUS, Jean (Fin)
SKRYABIN (SCRIABIN),
  Alexander (USSR)
SPONTINI, Gasparo Luigi
  (It)
SULLIVAN, Sir Arthur
  Seymour (Eng)
WHITEMAN, Paul (US)
ZARENSKI (Pol)

9+ letters
BEETHOVEN, Ludwig
  van (Ger)
DONIZETTI, Gaetano (It)
GRUENBERG, Louis
  (USSR/US)
HUMPERDINCK,
  Engelbert (Ger)
LLOYD-WEBBER,
  Andrew (Eng)
McCARTNEY, Paul (Eng)
MENDELSSOHN, Felix
  (Ger)
MEYERBEER, Giacomo
  (Ger)
MONTEVERDI, Claudio (It)
MUSSORGSKY, Modeste
  (USSR)
OFFENBACH, Jacques (Ger/Fr)
PROKOFIEV, Sergei
  (USSR)
RACHMANINOV, Sergei
  (USSR/US)
RIMSKY-KORSAKOV,
  Nikolai (USSR)
SAINT-SAENS, Charles
  Camille (Fr)
SCARLATTI, Alessandro
  (It)
SCARLATTI, Domenico
  (It)
SCHO(E)NBERG, Arnold
  (A)
SHOSTAKOVICH, Dmitri
  (USSR)
STOCKHAUSEN,
  Karlheinz (Ger)
STRAVINSKY, Igor
  (USSR)

TCHAIKOVSKY, Peter
Ilyich (USSR)

VAUGHAN WILLIAMS,
Ralph (Eng)
XANARCHIS (Gk)

COMPUTER CALCULATOR, MICRO-PROCESSOR [bits, bytes, ERNIE, memory, retrieval bank, VDU].

CON CHEAT, DIDDLE, *DO*. *AGAINST* (**opp** = *pro*). *LOOK*, *STUDY*. NAVIGATE, PILOT, *SAIL*, *STEER*.

CONCEAL Hidden word. *HIDE*, *SCREEN*, SECRETE.

CONCERN WORRY. *FIRM, COMPANY*. AFFECT.

CONCERNING *ABOUT*, ANENT, *OVER*, RE.

CONCERTINA ACCORDION; PRESS-BOX (crypt). COLLAPSE, COMPRESS, *FOLD*, PLEAT.

CONCLUSION 1. DECISION, REALIZATION. *END*. 2. Last letter of word concerned, e.g. **Bob's conclusion is encored** (3) = B*IS.

CONDITION *STATE*. *TERM*.

CONDUCTOR MAESTRO, MD (mus). GUARD, TICKET COLLECTOR. DRAGOMAN, GUIDE; *SHOWMAN* (crypt). *EARTH* (elect). **Myth:** *ANUBIS, CHARON*.

CONFINING 1. BORDERING, ENCLOSING, LIMITING, RESTRICTING; *GAOLING*. BEDDING, LABOURING [childbirth]. 2. Word round another, e.g. **He's confining publicity, and it's Hell** (5) = H*AD*ES.

CONFUSED *Anag.* BEWILDERED, MUDDLED.

CONNECTION 1. AFFILIATION, ASSOCIATION; DEALINGS. JOINERY, UNITY (crypt). TRANSFER (rly). EARTH, ON MAINS (elect). 2. Join two words, e.g. **See the connection bubble up** (4) = SEE*THE = BOIL.

CONQUEROR *VICTOR*, VIC. WILLIAM.

Cons Conservative.

CONSCIENTIOUS PUNCTILIOUS, SCRUPULOUS, THOROUGH. HAMLET (crypt).

CONSPIRATOR PLOTTER; **celebrated:** MARCUS BRUTUS, DECIUS BRUTUS, CASCA, CASSIUS, METELLUS CIMBER, CINNA, LIGARIUS, TREBONIUS (*Shak*, Caesar); GUY FAWKES.

CONSTABLE ARTIST, *PAINTER*, RA. *POLICEMAN*. HEAD OF HOUSEHOLD (hence H, crypt), MAJOR DOMO,

SENESCHAL; **celebrated** (all *Shak*): DULL (LLL), ELBOW (Meas for Meas), MALVOLIO (12th Night), VERGES and DOGBERRY (Much Ado).

CONSTELLATION STAR CLUSTER/GROUP/OUTLINE; **celebrated:**

3-letters
ARA
LEO (Zod) (lion)

4-letters
CRUX (southern cross)
GRUS
LYRA (lyre)

5-letters
ARIES (Zod) (ram)
CETUS (sea monster)
DRACO (dragon)
HYDRA
INDUS
LEPUS
LIBRA (Zod) (scales)
LUPUS (wolf)
MUSCA
ORION (hunter)
VIRGO (Zod) (virgin)

6-letters
AQUILA (eagle)
AURIGA (charioteer)
BOOTES (herdsman)
CANCER (Zod) (crab)
CARINA (keel)
CORVUS (crow)
CRATER
CYGNUS (swan)
DORADO
FORNAX

GEMINI (Zod) (twins)
HYDRUS
PISCES (Zod) (fishes)
PUPPIS
TAURUS (Zod) (bull)
TUCANA

7-letters
CEPHEUS (myth king)
COLUMBA (dove)
PEGASUS (winged horse)
PERSEUS
PHOENIX
SCORPIO (Zod) (scorpion)
SERPENS (serpent)

8+ letters
ANDROMEDA
AQUARIUS (Zod)
 (water carrier)
CANES VENATICI
CANIS MAJOR (great dog)
CANIS MINOR (little dog)
CAPRICORNUS (Zod)
 (sea-goat)
CASSIOPOEIA (myth queen)
CENTAURUS
CORONA BOREALIS
 (northern crown)
DELPHINUS (dolphin)
ERIDANUS
HERCULES
OPHIUCHUS (serpent bearer)

PISCIS AUSTRALIS
SAGITTARIUS (Zod) (archer)
TRIANGULUM

TRIANGULUM AUSTRALE
URSA MAJOR (great bear)
URSA MINOR (little bear)

CONSUMER DRINKER, EATER; PURCHASER, USER. SPENDER, WASTER. MOUTH (crypt).

CONTAINS 1. HOLDS, KEEPS IN. 2. Hidden word; one word in another.

CONTEND CLAIM, MAINTAIN. VIE, WAR.

CONTINENT LAND MASS: PANGAEA (pre-hist supercontinent); GONDWANA, LAURASIA (first split); AFRICA, AMERICA, ANTARCTICA, ASIA, AUSTRALASIA, EUROPE. CHASTE, CONTROLLED, TEMPERATE.

CONTINUOUS 1. ENDLESS, UNBROKEN, UNENDING, UNINTERRUPTED. 2. Join two or more words in clue, e.g. **Heat her continuously for another girl** (5) = HEAT*HER = ERICA.

CONTRACT AGREEMENT. JOB. SHORTEN, SHRINK, TIGHTEN. *BRIDGE* (cards).

CONTRIVED *Anag.* FABRICATED, INVENTED. MANAGED (**opp** = *automatic*).

CONTROL (GEAR) LEVER, THROTTLE, JOY-STICK, RUDDER; *REIN*. DIRECT, MONITOR, ORGANIZE. DISCIPLINE. [AWACS (av)].

CONVERSE 1. CHAT, SPEAK WITH, TALK. OPPOSITE. 2. Word reversed, e.g. **Rat's converse shines brightly** (4) = STAR.

CONVICT ADJUDGE, DECLARE GUILTY [belief, convince, persuade]. CRIMINAL, *GAOL*-BIRD, LAG, *PRISONER*; (**celebrated**): Magwitch (Great Expectations, *Dickens*).

COOK *Anag.* CHEF, GALLEY SLAVE; MRS BEETON, BETTY CROCKER, FANNY FARMER (books); KITCHENER (crypt). CONCOCT, PREPARE FOOD (**saying**). BAKE, BOIL, FRY, GRILL, ROAST, SEETHE. *FIDDLE*, FIX. *STRAIT*. *EXPLORER*. *Chaucer* character.

COOKED *Anag.* DONE (**opp** = *raw*). *FIDDLED*, FIXED, FORGED.

COOKER BURNER, GRILL, HOB, OVEN, STOVE. VOLCANO (crypt). FORGER (crypt). And see *Cook*.

COOLER *GAOL* (sl). AIR CONDITIONER, *BREEZE*, DRAFT,

DRAUGHT, *FAN*, JALOUSIE, SHADE; LESS HOT, NOT SO
HOT (**opp** = *warmer*). DEEP FREEZE, FRIDGE.
COP *POLICEMAN*. ATTRACT, CAPTURE. HA'PENNY
(crypt: half cop*per). SPOOL [prop and ~].
COPPER CU (*chem*). *POLICEMAN*. PENNY, D.
WASH-BOILER. *COLOUR* (orange). *AGE*. *Anniversary*
(7th). **Pl** = CHANGE.
COPY CARBON, CRIB (sl), DOUBLE, DUPLICATE,
IMITATION, REPRODUCTION, RINGER; FACSIMILE (any
craftsman), REPLICA (original craftsman); TRANSCRIBE.
ADVERTISING TEXT; PRINTER'S TEXT.
CORA *PERSEPHONE*.
CORAL Calcareous secretion of marine polyps; REEF. COLOUR
(pink). LOBSTER ROE. *SEA* [*battle*]. *SNAKE*. *Anniversary*
(35th).
CORALLINE *SEAWEED*. CORAL-RED.
CORDIAL FRIENDLY. *DRINK*.
CORE (s/l caw). 1. CENTRE, KERNEL, MIDDLE. 2. Use
middle letter(s), e.g. **Apple core** = P.
CORNELIAN *GEM*, SEMI-PRECIOUS STONE,
CHALCEDONY: AGATE (red). *Birthstone* (July).
CORNWALL SW.
CORPORAL CPL, NCO; **celebrated:** HITLER, NAPOLEON,
NYM (*Shak*), TRIM (Tristram Shandy, Sterne). BODILY.
CLOTH, *MATERIAL* (eccles).
CORPORATION TOWN COUNCIL. FATNESS, OBESITY.
CORSAIR *AIRCRAFT*. *PIRATE*.
CORYBANTES PRIESTS of *Cybele*, frenzied and noisy dancers.
COS BECAUSE (sl). COSINE. *ISLAND*. LETTUCE.
COSH MUG; CUDGEL, CLUB, *WEAPON*; NIGHTCLUB
(crypt).
COTTON CLOTH, *MATERIAL*, THREAD. ADMIRE, LIKE,
TAKE TO, UNDERSTAND. 2nd *anniversary*.
COUGH *HAWK*, *HEM*. CONFESS (sl). PAY-UP (sl).
COULD BE *Anag*. MAYBE.
COUNT (E)NUMERATE, *NUMBER*, RECKON, *TELL*, *TOT*.
EARL; *DRACULA*.
COUNTER AGAINST, OPPOSITE; CONTRADICT, OPPOSE,
RIPOSTE. DUPLICATE. CHIP, TALLY, TOKEN.

ADDER, CALCULATOR, CASHIER, COMPUTER,
SUMMER (crypt), TELLER. BAR, TABLE. HORSE'S
NECK. SHIP'S STERN. SHOE'S HEEL. SKATING
FIGURE.
COUNTRY FATHERLAND, LAND, MOTHERLAND,
NATION, REGION, TERRITORY. RURAL AREA. And
see *capital cities*.
~ HOUSE MANSION, PLACE, SEAT, *STATELY HOME*.
COUNTY 1. ARISTOCRATIC, LAH-DI-DAH, *U*,
WELL-BRED. CO. 2. ~ of the UK, see *DIVISION*.
COURSE E, N, S, W, NE, SE etc. DIRECTION, LINE.
RACETRACK; *LINKS*. CURRENT, RIVER BED.
PURSUE, RUN. *SAIL*. LECTURE SERIES. CAREER.
LAYER, STRATUM. *MEAL*: AFTERS, DESSERT, ENTREE,
ENTREMETS, HORS D'OEUVRE, MEAT, PUDDING,
SAVOURY, SOUP, *STARTER*, SWEET.
COURT (s/l *caught*). WOO. HALL OF JUSTICE, TRIBUNAL.
PLAYING AREA (squash, *tennis* etc). ROYAL
ENTOURAGE. CT, QUAD(RANGLE), YARD.
COURTED WOOED. JUDGED, SUED (crypt). WIMBLEDON,
TENNIS VENUE (crypt).
COURT EXPERT BARRISTER, JUDGE, *LAW
PRACTITIONER*, LAWYER. SEED (tennis, crypt).
COURTING WOOING. ACTION, DEFENDING, PLEADING,
PROSECUTING, SUITING (crypt). SERVING, *TENNIS*
(crypt). ROYAL HOUSEHOLD (crypt).
COVEN *Assembly* of *witches*.
COVER 1. ALTER EGO, DISGUISE, NOM DE PLUME,
PSEUDONYM. ASSURANCE, INSURANCE. CAP, COWL,
HAT, HOOD, LID. *CLOAK*, DRESS, SHROUD.
ENVELOPE, WRAP(PING). FRONT PAGE, JACKET.
CRICKETER, FIELDER. 2. Enclose word in another, e.g. **He
covers the order to get a house** (4) = H*OM*E.
COVERING LID, CAP, *HAT*. *DRESSING*.
COVER STORY BLUFF, FALSE BACKGROUND, LIE.
LEADER, LEADING ARTICLE (crypt).
COVER UP DRESS. CONCEAL(MENT). REVOC (dn).
COVEY *Assembly* of partridges.
COW DOMINATE. *CASTLE* (arch). *CATTLE*, KINE, NEAT,

STEER; LOWER (crypt); *female* cattle, walrus etc (**offspring** = calf, **yak/cow** = dzho, dzo).

COWARDLY 1. AFRAID, FRIGHTENED, SCARED, YELLOW (**saying**); [Bob Acres (The Rivals, Sheridan); Bardolph, Nym, Pistol (H.v., Merry Wives); Capt Bobadil (Ben Jonson); Braggadochio (Faerie Queen, Spenser); lion (Wizard of Oz)].
2. Written by Noel Coward (crypt).

COWBOY GAUCHO, HERDSMAN, VAQUERO; STEERSMAN (crypt); **celebrated:** GENE AUTRY (singing), HOPALONG CASSIDY, WILLIAM S. HART, TOM MIX, AUDIE MURPHY, ROY ROGERS (horse Trigger), JOHN WAYNE. [Wells Fargo; *outlaw*]. CHAPMAN (crypt).
Pl = *football* team (US).

COY *ARCH*, BASHFUL, DIFFIDENT, *SHY*; **saying**. COMPANY.

CPL *CORPORAL*.

CR CHROMIUM (*chem*). COSTA RICA (*car plate*). CREDIT.

CRAB 1. CRITICIZE, SPOIL. *APPLE*. SOUR PERSON. HOIST, LIFT (mech). GO/WALK SIDEWAYS. CRUSTACEAN (Brachyura). 2. *Constellation* (Cancer); (4th) sign of *Zodiac*.

CRACKED *Anag.* BROKEN, CHIPPED, *SPLIT*, BEATEN, OVERCOME. *CRAZY*.

CRANE DERRICK, HOIST, JIB. CAMERA PLATFORM, DOLLY. *BIRD*. PEER, STRETCH.

CRAZY *Anag.* CRACKED, DERANGED, LUNATIC, MAD. RANDOM, SCATTERED (paving).

CREATOR 1. FABRICATOR, MAKER, MANUFACTURER, ORIGINATOR, PRODUCER. FUSSPOT, GRUMBLER. 2. **Gods: Gk** = ZEUS, **Rom** = JOVE, *JUPITER*, **A-Sax** = *WODEN*, **Bab** = BEL/BELUS, **Egy** = *OSIRIS*, TEMU, **Ind** = BRAHMA, SHIVA, **Nor** = *ODIN*, **Phoen** = *BAAL*.

CREDIT CR. BALANCE. *TICK*. ASCRIBE, BELIEF, BELIEVE, TRUST; ACKNOWLEDGEMENT; MERIT, REPUTATION.

CREEK *RIVER*. *AMERICAN INDIAN*.

CREEP CRAWL, *INCH*; INSINUATE, SNEAK. TOADY. LOW ARCH. MOVEMENT. **Pl** = SHIVERS (fear).

CREEPER *BIRD*. IVY, CLIMBING PLANT. *INSECT*.

CRESTA RACE, *RUN* [toboggan].

CREW EIGHT, EQUIPE, FOUR, *TEAM*. DECKHAND, *MAN*, *SAILOR*. BOASTED, EXULTED.

CRIB *CHEAT*, COPY, EMULATE. COT, CRADLE. *CARD GAME*.

CRICKET BAT AND BALL, *GAME*. *INSECT*. [~ on the Hearth (*Dickens*)].

CRICKETER PLAYER (FLANNELLED FOOL), DRY-*BOB*; TESTER (crypt). *BATSMAN*: BAT, OPENER, INNER (crypt), INSIDER (crypt); *FIELDER*: *BOWLER*, CATCHER, *COVER*, FINE-LEG, GULLY, KEEPER, LONG-OFF, LONG-ON, LONG-STOP, MID-OFF, MID-ON, MID-WICKET, OUTSIDER (crypt), *POINT*, SHORT-LEG, SILLY-POINT, SLIP, THIRD-MAN; **celebrated:** GRACE, W.G.

CRICKET GROUND PLAYING FIELD, TEST ZONE, TESTING GROUND; **celebrated:** EDGBASTON (Birmingham), FENNERS (C), GRACE ROAD (Leicester), THE HILL (Sydney), HEADINGLEY (Leeds), LORD'S (MCC), OLD TRAFFORD (Manchester), THE OUTER (Melbourne), THE OVAL (Adelaide, Kennington), THE PARKS (O), TRENT BRIDGE (Nottingham), WACA (Perth), WOOLONGABBA (Brisbane).

CRIPPLED *Anag*. DEFORMED, *GAME*, HALT, *LAME*. [*patron saint*].

CROCODILE REPTILE (saurian): ALLIGATOR (Amer, Ch), CAYMAN (S Amer), GHARIAL (Ind), MUGGER (Ind) [~ tears]. Schoolchildren in line.

CROESUS KING OF LYDIA, RICH MAN [Dives, *Midas*].

CRONOS Gk *god* of AGRICULTURE (**Rom** = *SATURN*).

CROONER BING; *SINGER*.

CROSS 1. X; CRUCIFIX, MARK, ROOD, SALTIRE. ANGRY, ANNOYED, MAD. FRUSTRATE, THWART. HALF-CASTE, HYBRID. 2. *Constellation* (Crux).

CROSSBOW-MAN *CELLIST*, FIDDLER, VIOLINIST (crypt). *ARCHER* [*weapon*].

CROSS DECISION ELECTION, VOTE (crypt).

CROSSING *BRIDGE*, FERRY, *FORD*, TRAVERSING. BELISHA, PELICAN, ZEBRA. KISS (crypt). VOTING, POLL (crypt).

CROSSPATCH GROUCH, GRUMPY PERSON, SCOLD.
 PEDESTRIAN *CROSSING* (crypt).
CROSSWORD PUZZLE. ~ **solver** = cruciverbalist; **lover of** ~ =
 cruciverbophile; **aversion to** ~ = cruciverbophobia (myth).
 Pl = ARGUMENT. *ROW* (crypt).
CROW *BIRD* (corvidae): CARRION ~, CHOUGH, DRONGO,
 GREY, HOODED ~, JACKDAW, JAY, MAGPIE, RAVEN,
 ROOK, ROYSTON ~ (*assembly, constellation*). BUTTERFLY
 (*lepidoptera*). *CRY*, EXULT, TRIUMPH (past tense = *crew*).
 AMERICAN INDIAN.
CROWD ATTENDANCE, AUDIENCE, *GATE*, SPECTATORS;
 celebrated: THE HILL (Sydney cricket), THE KOP (Liverpool
 football), THE *OUTER* (Melbourne cricket), THE SHED
 (Chelsea football), THE TAVERN (Lord's cricket).
CROWN 1. CORONET, DIADEM; **saying;** 'STEPHEN'.
 WREATH. *COIN*. TOP (of anchor/arch/head/hill). CAP,
 PROTECTION. 2. *Constellation* (Corona Borealis).
CRUSE (s/l *crews*, cruise). BOWL, VESSEL [widow].
CRUSOE Robinson ~. Book by Defoe based on adventures of
 Alexander Selkirk, stranded from the galley *Cinque Ports* on Juan
 Fernandez island, 1704-9.
CRY *CALL*, EXCLAIM, SHOUT, YELL, YELP: HI, OUCH,
 OW [~ Wolf]. APPEAL, ENTREATY. RUMOUR.
 BEWAIL, BLUB, *GREET*, *KEEN*, LAMENT, SHED TEARS,
 WAIL, WEEP [**saying;** *Niobe, Ruth*]. *BARK*, *HAWK*,
 PEDDLE, TOUT.
CRYSTAL MINERAL. GLASS. *PALACE*. *BALL* [forecasting,
 prophecy; clarity]. *Anniversary* (15th).
CS *CIVIL SERVICE*.
CT *CAUGHT*. *COURT*.
CU *COPPER* (*chem*). CUBE, ~ IC. CUMULUS.
CUB YOUNG SCOUT. YOUNG REPORTER. *OFFSPRING*
 (bear, etc).
CUBE CU. BOX. EIGHT (crypt).
CUBIST PAINTER. DICE PLAYER (crypt).
CUDGEL CLUB, STICK, *WEAPON*. RACK, WORRY (brains).
CUER (s/l *queuer*). BILLIARD/POOL/SNOOKER PLAYER.
CULTURE CIVILIZATION [*study*]. FARMING, TILLING
 (crypt).

CUMBERLAND A *division* of England. *BUTCHER* (mil).
CUMBRIA NW.
CUPBEARER 1. CHAMPION, TROPHY WINNER. 2. WINE-SERVER; NEHEMIAH (to King Artaxerxes). **Gk god** = GANYMEDE; **Gk goddess** = *HEBE*, **Rom** = *JUVENTAS*.
CUPID Rom *god* of *LOVE*; also AMOR (**Gk** = EROS). Son of *Venus* and *Jupiter*; an archer. 2. *REINDEER*.
CURE HEAL, MEND; REMEDY, RESTORATIVE TREATMENT [*spa*]. *DRY*, HARDEN, MATURE, PRESERVE, SMOKE. *CHURCHMAN*, PRIEST (Fr).
CURRANT (s/l *current*). RIBES; DRIED GRAPE. FRUIT (black~, red~, white~).
CURRENCY FLUENCY, REPUTATION. RIVER, WATERFLOW (crypt). AC, DC, ELECTRICITY (crypt). COINAGE, **celebrated** (worldwide):

Country	Currency
Albania	LEK
Algeria	DINAR
American Ind	WAMPUM
Argentina	PESO
Australia	DOLLAR
Austria	SCHILLING
Belgium	FRANC
Bolivia	PESO
Brazil	CRUZEIRO
Bulgaria	LEV
Burma	KYAT
Canada	DOLLAR
Chile	PESO
China	YUAN
Colombia	PESO
Costa Rica	COLON
Cuba	PESO
Czechoslovakia	KORUNA
Denmark	KRONE
Ecuador	SUCRE
Egypt	*POUND*
El Salvador	COLON

Currency

Ethiopia	DOLLAR
Finland	MARKKA
France	FRANC
Germany, E.	MARK
Germany, W.	DEUTSCHMARK
Greece	DRACHMA
Guatemala	QUETZAL
Hungary	FORINT
Iceland	KRONA
India	RUPEE
Iran	RIAL
Iraq	DINAR
Ireland	PUNT
Israel	SHEKEL
Italy	LIRA
Japan	YEN
Kenya	*SHILLING*
Lebanon	*POUND*
Libya	DINAR
Mexico	PESO
Netherlands	GUILDER
New Zealand	DOLLAR
Nigeria	NAIRE
Norway	KRONE
Pakistan	RUPEE
Peru	SOL
Poland	ZLOTY
Portugal	ESCUDO
Rumania	LEU
Russia	ROUBLE
South Africa	RAND
Spain	PESETA
Sweden	KRONA
Switzerland	FRANC
Syria	*POUND*
Thailand	BAHT
Tunisia	DINAR
Turkey	LIRA
UK	*POUND*

USA	DOLLAR
USSR	ROUBLE
Uruguay	PESO
Venezuela	BOLIVAR
Vietnam	DONG
Yemen	RIYAL
Yugoslavia	DINAR

Currency	**Country**
Baht	THAILAND
Bolivar	VENEZUELA
Colon	COSTA RICA, EL SALVADOR
Cruzeiro	BRAZIL
Deutschmark	WEST GERMANY
Dinar	ALGERIA, IRAQ, LIBYA, TUNISIA, YUGOSLAVIA
Dollar	AUSTRALIA, CANADA, ETHIOPIA, NEW ZEALAND, USA
Dong	VIETNAM
Drachma	GREECE
Escudo	PORTUGAL
Forint	HUNGARY
Franc	BELGIUM, FRANCE, SWITZERLAND
Guilder	NETHERLANDS
Koruna	CZECHOSLOVAKIA
Krona	ICELAND, SWEDEN
Krone	DENMARK, NORWAY
Kyat	BURMA
Lek	ALBANIA
Leu	RUMANIA
Lev	BULGARIA
Lira	ITALY, TURKEY
Mark	EAST GERMANY
Markka	FINLAND
Naire	NIGERIA
Peseta	SPAIN
Peso	ARGENTINA, BOLIVIA, CHILE, COLOMBIA, CUBA, MEXICO, URUGUAY

Pound	EGYPT, LEBANON, SYRIA, UK
Punt	EIRE, *IRELAND*
Quetzal	GUATEMALA
Rand	SOUTH AFRICA
Rial	IRAN
Riyal	YEMEN
Rouble	USSR
Rupee	INDIA, PAKISTAN
Schilling	AUSTRIA
Shekel	ISRAEL
Shilling	KENYA
Sol	PERU
Sucre	ECUADOR
Wampum	N. *AMERICAN INDIAN*
Yen	JAPAN
Yuan	*CHINA*
Zloty	POLAND

CURRENT (s/l *currant*). EXISTING. COURSE, FLUID, RUNNING, STREAM, TIDE, UNDERTOW [river]. AMP, ELECTRICITY; AC, DC.

CURTAIL 1. DOCK, SHORTEN. 2. Omit last letter, e.g. **Some curtailed party** (4) = PART.

CURTAIN BARRIER, DRAPE, SCREEN. **Pl** = TAPS (theat). *DEATH*, FINISH, THE END.

CUSTOM HABIT, PRACTICE, PRAXIS, TRADITION, USAGE, USE, WONT; **saying.** **Pl** = DUTY, PREVENTIVE MEN, LEVY [*smuggle*, *tax*]. MORES [O tempora, O mores! (Cicero)].

CUT 1. LANCE, PARE, SEVER, SLICE. STOP FILMING. EDIT(ED); CENSORED. IGNORE, *OMIT*, SEND TO COVENTRY, SHUN, SNUB. STROKE (*cricket*). 2. Shortened form of . . . e.g. **Defence cut** (3) = DEF.

~ DOWN CHOP(PED), FELL(ED). REDUCE(D).

~ UP *Anag.* CHOP(PED), FELL(ED), SLICE(D). DISTRESSED, HURT, PAINED. TUC (dn).

CWT HUNDREDWEIGHT, *MEASURE*.

CYBELE 1. RHEA. Gk *goddess* of *FERTILITY*, whose priests were the *Corybantes* (**Rom** = CERES). 2. A minor *PLANET*.

CYCLOPES Gk myth one-eyed *monsters*: ACAMUS, ARGES, BRONTES, POLYPHEMUS, PYRACMON, STEROPES.
CYNOPHILE *Lover of dogs*.
CYNOPHOBIA *Aversion to dogs*.
Cz Czechoslovakia.

D DAUGHTER. DAY. DELTA. DENARIUS. DEUTERIUM, (*chem*). *DIED*. *DIRECTOR*, ~ED. *DOWN*. GERMANY (*car plate*). *KEY*; *NOTE*. PENNY. 500.
d daughter. died.
DACTYL 1. FOOT (‒ᵕᵕ). FINGER. 2. **Pl** = GIANTS [discovered *iron*; served *Rhea*].
DAD *FATHER*. FIRST IN DIVINITY (crypt: D*A*D).
DAEDALUS Gk myth sculptor, who built the labyrinth to house the *Minotaur* at Cnossos in Crete for King *Minos*. Imprisoned, he made wings for himself and Icarus (his s) and flew to Sicily; the wax securing Icarus' wings melted, and he fell into the sea and was drowned.
DAILY *CHAR*. EACH DAY. JOURNAL, *NEWSPAPER*, PAPER, QUOTIDIAN; EXPRESS, MAIL, MIRROR, OBSERVER, SUN, TELEGRAPH, TIMES etc (all ®).
~ LEADER D (crypt). ED, EDITOR. COVER STORY.
~ WORKER (NEWS)PAPER. HAND. *CHAR*.
DAMAGE(D) *Anag*. RUIN(ED), SPOIL(ED).
   Pl = COMPENSATION.
DANAE 1. Gk myth *goddess* of *FERTILITY*. m of *Perseus* by *Zeus*, who came to her in a *shower* of gold. **Rom** = *CERES*, *DIANA*. 2. A minor *PLANET*.
DANCE *BALL*, *BOB*, CAPER, *FOOT*, HOP, JIVE, *MEASURE*, PAS, *SET*, *STEP*, TOE. [*cat*; Hans *Andersen*]. **Gk goddess** = TERPSICHORE (*Muse*) [*Corybantes*]. **Celebrated:**

3-letters	CLOG	ROCK
JIG	FOLK	SHAG
PAS	GO-GO	
	HAKA	5-letters
4-letters	HULA	BELLY
BARN	*REEL*	CONGA

FLING
GALOP
GIGUE
LIMBO
MAMBA
PAVAN
POLKA
RUMBA
SAMBA
SWORD
TANGO
TWIST
VOLTA
WALTZ

6-letters
BALLET
BOLERO
CHA-CHA
FLORAL
MINUET
MORRIS
PAVANE
RHUMBA
SHIMMY
SQUARE

7-letters
CZARDAS
FOXTROT
GAVOTTE
HOE-DOWN

LANCERS
MAZURKA
MUSETTE
ONE-STEP
TWO-STEP

8-letters
BIG APPLE
COTILLON
FANDANGO
FOURSOME
GALLIARD
HORNPIPE
HULA-HULA
RIGADOON
SARABAND

9+ letters
ALLEMANDE
BLACK BOTTOM
CHARLESTON
CORROBOREE
EIGHTSOME
FARANDOLE
POLONAISE
ROCK 'N' ROLL
QUADRILLE
QUICKSTEP
STRATHSPEY
SCHOTTISCHE
TARANTELLA
TURKEY-TROT

~ **CENTRE** BALLET SCHOOL. MAYPOLE (crypt). N. (crypt).
DANDY BLOOD, FOP, *RIP. GOOD*, EXCELLENT, FINE.
  COMIC.
DAPHNE 1. Gk myth d of a river god, she was changed into a laurel
  tree to escape the pursuit of *Apollo*, and it became his favourite
  tree. 2. A minor *PLANET*. 3. Flowering shrub.

DARBY (s/l *Derby*). Husband of *Joan*. **Pl** = HANDCUFFS.

DARDANELLES HELLESPONT [*Helle.* Gallipoli].

DARKNESS GLOOM, NIGHT, OBSCURITY, STARLESSNESS; WICKEDNESS. **Egy god** = *SET*; **Gk goddess** = *HECATE*.

DARLING ACUSHLA (Ire), DEAREST, FAVOURITE, *PET*, SWEETHEART. *GRACE* ~ (lighthouse-keeper's d; rescuer). *WENDY* (Peter Pan). RIVER (Aus).

DART *DASH. ARROW*, FLECHETTE. GUSSET (seam). *RIVER.*

DASH *DART*, FALL. ADVANCE, MOVE, ONSET, RUSH, SPEED; *WHIP.* BOTTLE (sl), DRIVE, ELAN. CONFOUND, DAUNT, DISCOURAGE, FRUSTRATE, SHATTER. *CAST*, FLING, HURL, KNOCK, THROW, THRUST. DILUTE, DROP, INFUSION, SPLASH, *SPOT.* DAMN, DARN (swear). SCRIBBLE. PARENTHESIS; MACRON, TILDE (accentˉ). LONG SIGN (morse; **opp** = *dot*).

DATA GEN, INFORMATION, PARAMETER, QUANTITY (math), TABLE [problem].

DATE ESTABLISHED PERIOD; *TIME*, IDES, NONES (Rom). *APPOINTMENT*, MEETING, TRYST; ESCORT, TAKE OUT. *PALM*-BERRY, *PHOENIX*, ~ FRUIT; *TREE.*

DATED AG(E)ING, OLD-FASHIONED, *SQUARE. FRANKED, STAMPED.* ESCORTED, SQUIRED, TAKEN OUT, TOOK OUT.

DAUGHTER D; *OFFSPRING*, PROGENY (fem); GIRL.

DAVID 1. KING OF JUDAH, s of Jesse and f of Absalom; ARMOUR-BEARER, HARPIST, SHEPHERD [Goliath, Jonathan, Saul]. 2. PATRON SAINT (Wal), s of Non, uncle of *King Arthur* [1 March]. 3. KING OF SCOTLAND, s of Robert Bruce. 4. 'BELOVED'.

DAVIDSON ABSALOM.

DAWN 1. AUBADE, MORNING, SUNRISE. COME TO, REALIZE. 2. **Goddess: Gk** = EOS, **Rom** = AURORA.

DAY D. *SUNDAY, MONDAY, TUES* etc; S, M, T etc (**opp** = *night*). DAYLIGHT. DATE, PERIOD. VICTORY. [Policeman ~ (*Kipling*)].

DB DECIBEL (noise).

DC DIRECT CURRENT; *CURRENCY* (crypt, elect). DISTRICT COMMISSIONER. DISTRICT OF COLUMBIA.

DD DIVINE, DOCTOR OF DIVINITY; *CHURCHMAN*. DAUGHTERS.

DDR EAST GERMANY (and *car plate*).

DEAD D, DEFUNCT, EX, EXPIRED, LATE, PASSED ON/OVER (**opp** = live). FINISHED, OVER. UNCHARGED. *SEA*.

DEAR (s/l *deer*). *DARLING*, DUCK, HONEY, LIEF, *LOVE*, LUV, SWEETIE. A LOT, COSTLY, EXPENSIVE, PRICEY.

DEATH 1. EXPIRATION, FATHER TIME, FINIS, REAPER, THE END; [*Charon*]. **saying**. 13 (*tarot*). 2. **God: Gk** = THANATOS, **Rom** = MORS, **Egy** = ANUBIS/OSIRIS, **Ind** = SHIVA.

DEB L, BEGINNER, DEBUTANTE, TYRO[come out]. BACK SEAT (crypt).

DEBT IN THE RED, IOU, MARKER [bankruptcy]. See *IN* ~ (2).

DEBTOR BANKRUPT, *DR*, OWER.

DEC DECLARED, INNINGS CLOSED. DECEASED. *DECEMBER*.

DECEMBER (12th) MONTH, M, DEC (Rom 10th month, until Julius *Caesar* reorganized the calendar). **Birthstone** = Turquoise.

DECIBEL DB, NOISE-LEVEL.

DECK ADORN, BEDECK, DRESS, GARLAND, ORNAMENT. *BRIDGE*, LEVEL (naut). GROUND (sl). PACK (*cards*).

DECLARE AFFIRM, ASSERT, *AVER*, SAY, STATE. CLOSE INNINGS, DEC (*cricket*).

DECLINE *REFUSE*, REJECT. DESCENT, DOWNWARD PATH/SLOPE, SETTING, STEP DOWN. DECAY, DROOP, FALL (OFF). INFLECT (gram).

DECORATION *MEDAL*: VC, GC, DSO, GM, DSC, MC, DFC, DCM, MM, DFM etc. ADORNMENT, APPEARANCE, PAINTWORK; FILIGREE.

DECREASE DIMINISH, LESSEN. *IRON*, PRESS (crypt).

DEED ACT, FACT, PERFORMANCE. CHARTER, DISPOSITION, INSTRUMENT, PROOF OF TITLE.

DEER (s/l *dear*). RUMINANT QUADRUPED (Cervidae); **breeds:** AXIS, BARKING, CARIBOU, CHITAL, ELK, FALLOW, HIND, MOOSE, MUNTJAK, MUSK, *RED*, *REINDEER*, ROE, RUSA, SAMBUR, SIKA, *SKIPPER*, WAPITI.

Assembly = herd; **male** = *buck*, hart, *stag*; **female** = doe, hind;
offspring = *fawn* [*antelope*, Bambi, *goat*, venison].

DEERSTALKER GHILLIE, KEEPER. *HAT* [*Holmes*].

DEFEAT BEAT, OVERCOME, WORST.

DEFECT FAULT, FLAW. ABANDON, CHANGE SIDES, CROSS THE FLOOR, RENEGE, SWITCH ALLEGIANCE, TURNCOAT.

DEFILE GORGE, PASS. MARCH IN FILE. BEFOUL, CORRUPT, DESECRATE, PROFANE, RUIN, SPOIL.

DEFORMED *Anag*. *CRIPPLED*. MISSHAPEN, TWISTED.

DEGREE GRADE, LEVEL, SCALE, STANDARD, STEP [hot, cold]. ANGLE, MEASUREMENT (naut; math) [latitude, longitude]. CLASS, CONDITION, PROFICIENCY, RANK, STATUS; BA, MA [*university*].

DEL DELINEAVIT, DREW. LED BACK (crypt).

DELETED 1. ERASED, REMOVED. 2. Delete letter 'd' from clue, e.g. **Drink deleted is iced** (4) = *RINK.

DELIBERATE EXPRESS, ON PURPOSE, PURPOSEFUL, STUDIED. CONSIDER, DISCUSS. IMPRISON (crypt).

DELIVERY *BALL*. *CARRIAGE*, FREIGHT. *CHILDBIRTH*. *POST*. TRANSFER. RESCUE, SALVATION. *SPEECH*.

~ **MAN** *BOWLER*, *PITCHER*. ROUNDSMAN. TRADESMAN. DOCTOR, MALE NURSE (crypt).

DELPHI Town in Phocis on Parnassus, with *Oracle*; now Kastri.

DELTA D; 4th Gk letter. RIVER MOUTH.

Dem Democrat [elephant].

DEMAND ASK, REQUEST. MARKET.

DEMETER Gk *goddess* of NATURE. Her d *Persephone* (Proserpine) by *Zeus* was seized by *Pluto*, and *Hermes* brought her back. **Rom** = *CERES*.

DEMIJOHN LARGE *BOTTLE*.

DEMOCRAT PARTY (polit; anti-Rep) [elephant].

DEMON CRUEL BEING, GHOUL. AFREET, AFRIT (Mos), EVIL *SPIRIT*. *CARD GAME*.

DEMONSTRATE PROVE, SHOW. PARADE, RALLY.

DEN STUDY, WORKROOM. *HABITATION*, LAIR. DENIER (cloth count).

DENARIUS D, COIN (penny). [L, S, D].

DENMARK DK (*car plate*). *STRAIT*. [*Hamlet*].

DENTIST BDS, *DRAWER*, EXTRACTOR, ORTHODONTIST, PULLER; FANG-PRANGER (sl). PANEL-BEATER (crypt).

DEPARTED GONE, *LEFT*, WENT. *DEAD*, EX, LATE.

DEPLOYED 1. *Anag.* ARRANGED, SET OUT. 2. Remove letters PLOY from word(s).

DEPOSIT *LODGE*, ASH, SILT.

DEPRESSION *BLUES*, DUMPS. DENT, DIP, HOLLOW; GLEN, VALE, VALLEY. *COL*, CYCLONE, *LOW* (met).

DERANGED *Anag.* *CRAZY*. DISTURBED.

DERBY (s/l *Darby*). BOWLER, *HAT*. CLASSIC. LORD. *CERAMICS®*. CITY (Baseball ground, *football*).

DESCRIBE 1. ABOUT, ANENT, RE. *DRAW*, ENCIRCLE, MARK OUT. EXPLAIN, QUALIFY, RECITE DETAILS OF. 2. Word round another, e.g. **On foot, she describes a circle (4)** = SH*O*E.

DESERT (s/l *dessert*). 1. *LEAVE*, RAT, RUNAWAY [turncoat]. ASSEMBLY OF LAPWINGS. (SANDY) WASTELAND; **celebrated:** ARABIAN (Af), ANATOLIAN (Turk), AN NAFUD (Arab), ATACAMA (Chile), BARREN (Pers), BLACK SAND (USSR), COLORADO (US), DEATH VALLEY (US), EASTERN (Af), GOBI (Ch), GIBSON (Aus), GILA (US), GREAT SANDY (Arab; Aus), GREAT SALT (Pers; US), GREAT VICTORIAN (Aus), KALAHARI (Af), KARA (USSR), KAVIR (Pers), KYZYL (USSR), LIBYAN (Af), LUT (Pers), MARGO (Afghan), MOHAVE (US), MONGOLIAN (Ch), NAFUD (Arab), NAMIB (Af), NAZCA (Peru), NEGEV (Israel), NUBIAN (Af), QARA QUM (USSR), SAHARA (Af), SHAMIYA (Arab), SINAI (Egy), SYRIAN (Arab), TAKLA MAKAN (Ch), THAR (Ind), ZIRREH (Afghan). **Pl** = *FATE*, MERITS, REWARDS. 2. Remove letter(s) indicated, e.g. **Trust gunners to desert rarely (4)** = **RELY.

DESIGN AIM, END, INTENT. DRAWING, PLAN, PATTERN [archit].

DESIRE LONGING, WISH, *MANIA*.

DESSERT (s/l *desert*). AFTERS, PUDDING, SWEET: *COURSE* (FRUIT, NUTS).

DESTROY *Anag.* ANNIHILATE, *BREAK*, CRUSH, FINISH.

DETAIL 1. ITEMIZE, ORDER, TELL OFF, LIST. MINOR

PARTICULAR. DETACHMENT (mil). DOCK (crypt).

2. Remove last letter(s), e.g. **Fine detail at the end** (3) = FIN*.

DETECTIVE *POLICEMAN*; DICK, FBI, G-MAN, GUMSHOE (sl), INVESTIGATOR, PRIVATE EYE, SCOTLAND YARD, TEC [*AGENT*]. **Pl** = YARDMEN (crypt). **Celebrated** (fiction):

BERGERAC	(TV)
FATHER BROWN	(*Chesterton*)
BUCKET	(*Dickens*)
FRANK CANNON	(TV)
NICK CARTER	(Hammett)
LEMMY CAUTION	(Films)
CHARLIE CHAN	(Films; Biggers)
COLUMBO	(TV)
GREGSON	(*Holmes*)
INSP FRENCH	(Allingham)
HARRY O	(TV)
HART & HART	(TV)
KOJAK	(TV; Mann)
LESTRADE	(*Holmes*)
MAIGRET	(Simenon)
PHILIP MARLOW	(Chandler)
MISS MARPLE	(Christie)
PERRY MASON	(Gardner)
McCLOUD	(TV)
McMILLAN & WIFE	(TV)
HERCULE POIROT	(Christie)
EDDIE SHOESTRING	(TV)
SAM SPADE	(Hammett)
SHERLOCK *HOLMES*	(Conan Doyle)
TENAFLY	(TV)
LORD PETER WIMSEY	(Sayers)

Pl = FBI, *Pinkerton* Agency, Scotland Yard.

DETOUR *Anag.* 1. DEVIATION, DIGRESSION. 2. Remove letters TOUR (or synonym) from clue, e.g. **Detour along the coast is a fiddle** (3) = CON****.

DEUTERIUM D (*chem*); HYDROGEN ISOTOPE.

DEVELOP *Anag.* PROCESS, TREAT (photo). REVEAL,

UNFOLD; ELABORATE. CONVERT LAND. PROGRESS.

DEVI Chief Ind *goddess*, wife of Shiva.

DEVIL DEMON, EVIL, IMP, TEMPTER (**saying**); ABADDON
(Hebr), APOLLYON (bibl), BELIAL (Hebr), DEUCE,
DICKENS, DIS, HADES (Gk), LUCIFER (Lat),
MEPHISTOPHELES (Ger), (OLD) NICK, OLD *SCRATCH*,
PLUTO, SATAN (bibl, lit = accuser). 15 (*tarot*). ERRAND
BOY (printer's); JUNIOR (leg); RESEARCH, SORT.

DEVISE 1. CONTRIVE, INVENT, PLAN, PLOT, SCHEME.
ASSIGN, BEQUEATH, WILL [testament, testify]. 2. Remove
letters 'vise' from word or sentence, e.g. **Derv is eating devised for
removal of household tariffs** (8) = DER****ATING.

DEVOUT PI, PIOUS, RELIGIOUS, REVERENTIAL.
EARNEST, GENUINE, HEARTY.

DEXTER RIGHT (*herald*). *CATTLE* (Ire).

DEXTERITY ADROITNESS. ON THE RIGHT,
RIGHT-HANDEDNESS.

DEXTEROUS ADROIT, HANDY, SKILFUL.
RIGHT-HANDED.

DG DEI GRATIE, BY GOD'S GRACE. DIRECTOR
GENERAL.

DI *DIANA*. DOUBLE . . .

DIA DIAMETER. ACROSS . . ., APART . . ., THROUGH . . .

DIAERESIS *ACCENT* (ë pronounced separately), UMLAUT.

DIAL FACE (sl). CALL, RING [STD]. INSTRUMENT.

DIAMOND *GEM*, PRECIOUS STONE: RHINESTONE;
CARBON, ICE (sl), ROCKS (sl) [girl's best friend]. *DOG*
(Newton). LOZENGE, RHOMB. BASEBALL FIELD (US).
Anniversary (60th or 75th). *Birthstone* (April). **Pl** = SUIT
(*cards*). COURTIERS (*Alice*).

DIANA 1. DELIA, DI; HORSEWOMAN, HUNTRESS. 2. Rom
goddess of HUNTING, MOON and FERTILITY; d of *Jupiter*;
her temple at Ephesus was one of the *Seven Wonders of the
World*. **Gk** = *ARTEMIS/HECATE*. [*Actaeon; Shak*].

DIARIST LOGGER, RECORDER [Evelyn, Pepys].

DICE Pl of DIE: BONES, CRAPS, CHECKER (US),
CHEQUER, CHOP INTO CUBES.

DICER CRAPS PLAYER/SHOOTER [sharpshooter].
CHOPPER, CUBIST (crypt).

DICKENS 1. *DEVIL*, DEUCE. 2. Charles (John Huffam), writer
1812-70; mar Catherine Hogarth 1836, separated 1858. BOZ,
QUIZ. **Illustrators:** Hablot Knight Browne (Phiz), George
Cruickshank. **Novels:** Barnaby Rudge (against a background of
the Gordon Riots, family enmity is transcended by the love of
Edwin Chester for Emma Haredale. Barnaby Rudge and his pet
raven *Grip* carry messages); Bleak House (Richard Carstone
secretly weds his cousin Ada Clare while they are wards of John
Jarndyce. Esther Summerson is shown to be the love child of
Lady Dedlock. The *lawyers* devour the fortune in the endless case
in Chancery of Jarndyce v Jarndyce); The Christmas Books (a
series dealing with Christmas and, often, the supernatural: The
Battle of Life, The Chimes, A Christmas Carol, The *Cricket* on
the Hearth, and The Haunted Man); Dombey & Son, Dealings
With the Firm of (Paul ~ is a cold egoist who puts his business
standing before all else. His s Paul dies and d Florence is
estranged. She eventually mar Walter Gray and forgives her f);
Great Expectations (*recluse* Miss Havisham, who was jilted on
her wedding day, lets Pip – Philip Pirrip – believe that he owes his
fortune to her, but it comes from the *convict* Magwitch, whom he
helped at one time. Estella, whom he loves vainly, is shown to be
Magwitch's d, brought up by Miss Havisham to spurn men); Hard
Times, For these Times (Josiah Bounderby, a self-made oafish
banker, mar young Louisa Gradgrind who, with her br Tom, has
been raised by her f in Coketown to acknowledge hard facts.
Strife and strikes occur among the workers, and Tom is shown to
be a thief; Louisa runs back to her f); Little Dorrit (Amy Dorrit,
d of William ~, spends her childhood unsullied by the corrosive
atmosphere of the Marshalsea debtors' *prison*. Father and
daughter inherit money and are released, while their friend
Arthur Clenham is sentenced in his turn. Intrigue and theft form
a damning social comment on complacent bureaucracy); Martin
Chuzzlewit (young Martin ~ is sacked at his grandfather's behest
by Pecksniff, and seeks his fortune in America. He returns to
make peace with the old man; his uncle Jonas ~ commits murder
and suicide. Sarah Gamp, coarse midwife and *nurse* 'dispoged' to
gin, converses with her non-existent and *unseen* friend Mrs
Harris); The Mystery of Edwin Drood (Edwin ~ breaks off
betrothal to Rosa Bud, ward of Mr Grewgious and music pupil of

John Jasper, who lusts after her. Neville Landless has to flee
when Edwin disappears, and the odious Jasper fosters the
suspicion which falls on him. The novel is unfinished); Nicholas
Nickleby (Ralph ~ places his nephew Nicholas with Wackford
Squeers, *schoolmaster* of Dotheboys Hall; and his niece Kate with
Madame Mantalini, a dressmaker. Squeers ill-treats all his boys,
especially Smike, who dies and turns out to have been Ralph ~'s
s. All is eventually put right by the *twin* bros Cheeryble); The Old
Curiosity Shop (Nell Trant's grandfather is proprietor of the shop,
and he gets into debt to Daniel Quilp, an evil *dwarf* with designs
on Little Nell. They have to flee when the grandfather cannot
pay. Quilp victimises several people who try to help, and
eventually all three die); Oliver Twist, or The Parish Boy's
Progress (Oliver ~ grows up in the workhouse. He runs away and
is picked up by Jack Dawkins (twice) who is one of Fagin's young
thieves and known as the Artful Dodger. Bill Sikes murders
Nancy when she tries to help Oliver, whose genteel background is
finally revealed by Mr Brownlow); Our Mutual Friend (the body
of John Harmon is found in the Thames, and papers show that his
fortune should go to Nicodemus *Boffin*, a dustman. Mistaken
identity, blackmail and greed abound along the river, as Bella
Wilfer rejects intrigue and is united with the real John Harmon.
The deformed Jenny Wren has to work as a doll's dressmaker to
keep her drunken f); The Pickwick Papers, or the Posthumous
Papers of the Pickwick Club (adventures of the four members of
the Corresponding Society of the Pickwick Club: Samuel
Pickwick, Augustus Snodgrass, Tracy Tupman and Nathaniel
Winkle. Mr Pickwick, supported by his manservant Samuel
Weller, also has to fight a breach of promise case brought by Mrs
Bardell); A Tale of Two Cities (Dr Manette is released from the
Bastille after 18 years; his d Lucie mar Charles Darnay, nephew
of the Marquis de St Evremonde. Sidney Carton adores Lucie and
eventually substitutes himself for her jailed husband, and goes to
the guillotine in his stead: 'It is a far, far better thing . . . than I
have ever done'). **Characters:** Artful Dodger (*robber*; Oliver
Twist); Bagstock, Major (JB, Josh, Old Joe; Dombey and Son);
Bardell, Mrs (Pickwick Papers); Barkis (a carrier; '~ is willin''';
David Copperfield); *Boffin*, Nicodemus (Our Mutual Friend);
Brass, Sampson & Sally (solicitors; Old Curiosity Shop);

Brownlow, Mr (Oliver Twist); Bucket (*detective*; Bleak House);
Bumble (petty official; Oliver Twist); Buzfuz, Serjeant (advocate,
Pickwick Papers); Carker, James (office manager; Dombey and
Son); Carton, Sidney (Tale of Two Cities); Cheeryble bros
(*twins*; Nicholas Nickleby); Codlin & Short (travelling showmen;
Old Curiosity Shop); Copperfield, David (Trot, ~), Corney, Mrs
(workhouse matron; Oliver Twist); Cratchit (*clerk*; Christmas
Carol); Cuttle, Capt (*sailor*; Dombey and Son); Dodson and Fogg
(*lawyers*; Pickwick Papers); Fagin (*robber*; Oliver Twist); Fang
(*magistrate*; Oliver Twist); Fips (legal agent; Martin Chuzzlewit);
Flite, Miss (pesters Chancery; Bleak House); Gamp, Sarah
(*nurse*; Martin Chuzzlewit); Gargery, Joe (*blacksmith*; Great
Expectations); Gradgrind (*schoolmaster*, 'facts', Hard Times);
Grimwig ('eat my head'; Oliver Twist); Guster (*maid*; Bleak
House); Havisham, Miss (*recluse*; Great Expectations); Heep,
Uriah ('umble lawyer's *clerk*; David Copperfield); Jaggers
(advocate; Great Expectations); Jingle, Alfred (swindling actor;
Pickwick Papers); Jo (poor outcast; Bleak House); Jorkins
(*lawyer*; David Copperfield); Jupe (*jester*, Hard Times); Krook
(rag and boneman; Bleak House); La Creevy, Miss (talkative
painter; Nicholas Nickleby); Little Dorrit (*child* of Marshalsea
debtors' prison; Little Dorrit); Little Em'ly (vain; David
Copperfield); Little Nell (tragic death; Old Curiosity Shop);
Mantalini (milliner; Nicholas Nickleby); Marchioness, the
(*nursed* and mar Dick Swiveller; Old Curiosity Shop); Micawber
('something will turn up'; David Copperfield); Miggs, Miss (*maid*;
Barnaby Rudge); Mould (*undertaker*; Martin Chuzzlewit);
Moucher, Miss (*hairdresser*; David Copperfield); Nancy
(murdered by Sikes; Oliver Twist); Nipper, Susan (Dombey and
Son); Noggs, Newman (*clerk*; Nicholas Nickleby); Omer
(*undertaker*; David Copperfield); Pecksniff, Seth (hypocrite;
Martin Chuzzlewit); Peggotty, Clara (*maid* who mar Barkis;
David Copperfield); Pickwick, Samuel (benevolence; ~ Papers);
Pinch, Tom (drudge; Martin Chuzzlewit); Pip (mar Gargery's sis;
Great Expectations); Pipchin, Mrs (*landlady*; Dombey and Son);
Plummer, Caleb (*toymaker*; Cricket on the Hearth); Prig, Betsy
(*nurse*; Martin Chuzzlewit); Quilp (*dwarf*; Old Curiosity Shop);
Sawyer, Bob (surgeon; Pickwick Papers); Scrooge, Ebenezer
(converted miserly killjoy; Christmas Carol); Sikes, Bill

(murdering *robber*; Oliver Twist); Sleary (circus owner; Hard
Times); Smike (son of Ralph Nickleby; Nicholas Nickleby);
Snagsby (Peffer and ~, law stationers; Bleak House); Snodgrass,
Augustus (Pickwick Papers); Spenlow, Dora (child wife of D
Copperfield); Spenlow & Jorkins (*lawyers*; David Copperfield);
Squeers (*schoolmaster*, Dotheboys Hall; Nicholas Nickleby);
Swiveller, Dick (debtor; Old Curiosity Shop); Tapley, Mark
(cheerful *servant*, Martin Chuzzlewit); Tiny Tim (lame boy;
Christmas Carol); Toots, Mr P ('It's of no consequence'; Dombey
and Son); Traddles, Thomas (sad boy at Salem House; David
Copperfield); Trotter, Job (Jingle's *servant*; Pickwick Papers);
Trotwood, Betsy ('Janet! Donkeys!'; David Copperfield);
Tulkinghorn, Mr (*lawyer*; Bleak House); Tupman, Mr Tracy
(lady's man; Pickwick Papers); Twist, Oliver ('more please';
Oliver Twist); Varden, Dolly (locksmith's daughter; Barnaby
Rudge); Verisopht, Lord (spineless sycophant; Nicholas
Nickleby); Weller, Sam (Pickwick's *servant*; Pickwick Papers);
Wemmick, John (*clerk* to Jaggers; Great Expectations);
Wickfield, Agnes (*lawyer's* d, mar David Copperfield); Wilfer
(*clerk*; Our Mutual Friend); Winkle (Pickwick Papers); Wren,
Jenny (deformed child; Our Mutual Friend).

DICKY *Anag.* RICHARD, BOY. ILL, SHAKY, UNSOUND,
UNWELL. BIRD. DONKEY. SHIRTFRONT.
BACKSEAT. RUMBLE-SEAT.

DICTIONARY LEXICON, WORD-BOOK; CHAMBERS®,
OED®, WEBSTER®; DR JOHNSON; [encyclop(a)edia,
thesaurus].

DIDO 1. ANTIC, CAPER, PRANK. DID NOTHING (crypt).
2. Princess of Tyre, sis of *Pygmalion*. Real name ELISSA (not
Astarte). Founded Carthage. Stabbed herself on a funeral pyre
rather than marry Iarbas [*Aeneas*]. 3. A minor *PLANET*.

DIED (s/l *dyed*). D, EXPIRED, OBIIT, *OSP* (without issue),
PEGGED OUT. **Saying**.

DIET BANT, SLIM; REGIME. *LEGISLATIVE ASSEMBLY*.

DIFFERENTLY *Anag.* DISSIMILARLY, DISTINCTLY.

DIFFIDENT MODEST, RETIRING, SHY, UNCONFIDENT.

DIG EXCAVATE, FORK OVER, UNEARTH. APPROVE,
UNDERSTAND (sl). **Pl** = LODGINGS.

DIGEST ASSIMILATE. ABSTRACT, PRECIS, RESUME,

SUMMARY, SYNOPSIS. HEAT (*chem*). ENDURE.

DIGGER MINER, PITMAN. EXCAVATOR. AUSTRALIAN.

DILIGENCE INDUSTRY, PERSISTENCE. *CARRIAGE*.

DIN *ROW*. DRUM (into), REPEAT. German standard (photo).

DINNER LUNCH, MEAL, SUPPER. NOISE-MAKER. PERCUSSIONIST (crypt).

DINOSAUR REPTILE (ex); **herbivores:** ATLANTOSAURUS, BRONTOSAURUS, CETIOSAURUS, DIPLODOCUS, GUANODON, STEGOSAURUS, TRICERATOPS; **carnivores:** MEGALOSAURUS, TYRANNOSAURUS.

DIOGENES 1. Gk cynic *PHILOSOPHER* who lived in a *tub*. 2. London Club of Mycroft *Holmes*.

DIONYSUS Gk equivalent of *BACCHUS*.

DIPLOMATIC CORPS CD [Court of St James].

DIRAE *FURIES*.

DIRECT *CONTROL*, INSTRUCT, ORGANIZE. ROUTE, STEER. STRAIGHT.

DIRECTION E, N, S, W, NE, SE etc; ROUTE, WAY. *CONTROL*, INSTRUCTION.

DIRECTOR ARROW, SIGN, SIGNBOARD. RUDDER, STEERING. CONTROLLER, MANAGER; **Pl** = BOARD.

DIS = *PLUTO*. Rom *god* of the *Underworld* (**Gk** = *HADES*).

DISARMING DEFUSING. DISBANDING, DEPRIVING OF WEAPONS. PACIFYING. AMPUTATING [Venus de Milo].

DISCHARGE BOOT, CASHIER, CANCEL, DISMISS, FIRE, RELEASE, SACK. CARRY OUT, PERFORM. LIQUIDATE, *PAY*. *SHOOT*. ASSOIL, UNLOAD.

DISCIPLE FOLLOWER (especially the 12 *apostles*).

DISCOVERER *EXPLORER*; INVENTOR. DISCLOSER, EXHIBITOR, FINDER. BETRAYER (arch). *SPACECRAFT*.

DISCOVERY 1. DISCLOSURE, REVEALING; *INVENTION*; **celebrated:** DISPLACEMENT, LEVER (3rd cent B.C. *Archimedes*); BLOOD CIRCULATION (1628 Harvey); GRAVITY (1689 Newton); VACCINATION (1798 Jenner); ELECTRICAL INDUCTION (1830 Faraday); ANTISEPSIS (1864 Lister); INOCULATION (1886 Pasteur); ELECTRON (1897 Thomson); RADIUM (1903 Curies); RELATIVITY (1905 Einstein); NUCLEAR PHYSICS (1913 Rutherford and Bohr); PENICILLIN (1928 Fleming); NEUTRON (1932 Chadwick).

2. SHIP (Baffin, Cook, Scott; *explorers*).

DISPLEASURE *ANGER*, DISAPPROVE, DISSATISFACTION.
HUNTING (crypt).

DISTEMPER *ANGER*, DERANGE, UPSET; DISORDER.
DISEASE (dogs). WALL PAINT.

DISTRESS *Anag.* 1. ANGUISH, PAIN, SORROW, STRAITS,
VEX. MAYDAY, SOS. BREATHLESSNESS,
EXHAUST(ION). CUT HAIR, SHEAR, SCALP (crypt). 2.
Remove synonym for hair from clue, e.g. **Distressed warlock in a
fight** (3) = WAR****.

DISTRIBUTION *Anag.* APPORTIONMENT, ARRANGEMENT,
CLASSIFICATION, DISPERSAL, SCATTER, SHARING.

DISTRICT AREA, COUNTY, CANTON, *DIVISION*, REGION,
SHIRE, STATE, TERRITORY, TRACT, *WARD*.

DITTO *DO*, DUPLICATE, SAME [*copy*].

div divorced.

DIVERSION *Anag.* DETOUR, DEVIATION. DISTRACTION,
FEINT. *GAME*, PASTIME.

DIVES RICH MAN [Croesus, *Midas*].

DIVIDER SEPARATOR, SCREEN; NET (tennis, crypt). **Pl =**
COMPASSES.

DIVINE DD, *CHURCHMAN*, PRIEST. GODLIKE;
BEAUTIFUL, DELIGHTFUL, EXCELLENT, GIFTED.
CONJECTURE, FORESEE, GUESS, PREDICT.

DIVISION DISTRIBUTION, SHARING. DISAGREEMENT,
DISCORD, SEVERANCE. CLASSIFICATION, GRADE.
FUNCTION, PROCESS (math). NET (tennis). VOTE (polit).
BOUNDARY, *DISTRICT*, PARISH, PART, SECTION, SEE,
ZONE; **specifically** COUNTY, REGION, SHIRE; ~ **of England:**

AVON	
BEDFORDSHIRE	BEDS
BERKSHIRE	BERKS
BUCKINGHAMSHIRE	BUCKS
CAMBRIDGESHIRE	CAMBS
CHESHIRE	CHES
CLEVELAND	CLEV
CORNWALL	
CUMBERLAND (ex)	CUMB

CUMBRIA	CUMB
DERBYSHIRE	DERBYS
DEVONSHIRE	DEVON
DORSETSHIRE	DORSET
DURHAM	DUR
ESSEX	ESX
GLOUCESTERSHIRE	GLOS
GREATER LONDON	
GREATER MANCHESTER	
HAMPSHIRE	HANTS
HEREFORD (ex)	
HEREFORD & WORCESTER	H & W
HERTFORDSHIRE	HERTS
HUMBERSIDE	
HUNTINGDONSHIRE (ex)	HUNTS
ISLE OF WIGHT	IOW
KENT	
LANCASHIRE	LANCS
LEICESTERSHIRE	LEICS
LINCOLNSHIRE	LINCS
LONDON (ex)	
MERSEYSIDE	MERS
MIDDLESEX (ex)	MIDDX
NORFOLK	
NORTHAMPTONSHIRE	NORTHANTS
NORTHUMBERLAND	
NOTTINGHAMSHIRE	NOTTS
OXFORDSHIRE	OXON
RUTLAND (ex)	
SHROPSHIRE	SALOP
SOMERSET	SOM
STAFFORDSHIRE	STAFFS
SUFFOLK	
SURREY	
SUSSEX (E & W)	E/W SSX
TYNE & WEAR	T & W
WARWICKSHIRE	WARKS
WEST MIDLANDS	W MIDS
WESTMORLAND (ex)	

WILTSHIRE	WILTS
WORCESTERSHIRE (ex)	WORCS
YORKSHIRE (N, S & W)	N/S/W YORKS

Subdivisions: hundred (all counties pre-Conquest), lathes (Kent), rapes (Sussex), ridings (Yorks), wapentakes (Lincs, Notts, Yorks), wards (Cumb, Dur, Northumberland, Westmorland).

~ of Scotland
(Regions & Island Areas)
BORDER
CENTRAL
DUMFRIES & GALLOWAY
FIFE
GRAMPIAN
HIGHLAND
LOTHIAN
ORKNEY
SHETLAND
STRATHCLYDE
TAYSIDE
WESTERN ISLES
KIRKCUDBRIGHTSHIRE
LANARKSHIRE
MIDLOTHIAN
MORAYSHIRE
NAIRN
PEEBLES
PERTHSHIRE
RENFREWSHIRE
ROSS & CROMARTY
ROXBURGH
SELKIRK
STIRLINGSHIRE
SUTHERLAND
WEST LOTHIAN
WIGTOWN

(ex Counties of Scotland)
ABERDEENSHIRE
ANGUS
ARGYLLSHIRE
BANFF
BERWICKSHIRE
CAITHNESS
CLACKMANNANSHIRE
DUNBARTONSHIRE
DUMFRIESSHIRE
EAST LOTHIAN
FIFESHIRE
INVERNESS-SHIRE
KINCARDINE
KINROSS

~ of Wales
(Counties)
CLWYD
DYFED
GLAMORGAN, MID/SOUTH/WEST
GWENT
GWYNEDD
POWYS

(ex Counties of Wales)
ANGLESEY
BRECKNOCK
CAERNARVON
CARDIGAN

CARMARTHEN
DENBIGH
FLINT
GLAMORGAN
MERIONETH
MONMOUTH
MONTGOMERY
PEMBROKE
RADNOR

~ **of Northern Ireland**
(Counties)
ANTRIM
ARMAGH
BELFAST
DOWN
FERMANAGH
LONDONDERRY
TYRONE

~ **of Eire**
(Counties)
CARLOW
CAVAN
CLARE
CONNAUGHT
CORK
DONEGAL (Tirconnel)
  ex ULSTER

DUBLIN
GALWAY
KERRY
KILDARE
KILKENNY
KING'S COUNTY
  (now OFFALY)
LAOIS (LEIX)
  (ex QUEEN'S COUNTY)
LEINSTER
LEITRIM
LIMERICK
LONGFORD
LOUTH
MAYO
MEATH
MONAGHAN
MUNSTER
OFFALY
  (ex KING'S COUNTY)
QUEEN'S COUNTY
  (now LAOIS)
ROSCOMMON
SLIGO
TIPPERARY
WATERFORD
WESTMEATH
WEXFORD
WICKLOW

DIY HOME HELP, SELF-HELP [handyman].
dn Down clues only.
DNA GENES. AND BACK (crypt).
DO ACCOMPLISH, ACHIEVE, ACT, CARRY OUT, EXECUTE, PERFORM, REALIZE, *SHIFT*. *PLAY* (theat). CELEBRATION, FESTIVITY, FIESTA, JOLLIFICATION, PARTY, RECEPTION, TREAT. DITTO. *CHAR*, CLEAN. KILL. CHEAT, CON, COZEN, DEFRAUD, DIDDLE, SWINDLE, TRICK. NOTE (mus; also DOH).

Pl = *DEER*, HARES (*fem*).

DOC (s/l *dock*). DOCTOR. *DWARF* (Snow White).

DOCH AN DORIS STIRRUP CUP (drink at the door).

DOCK (s/l *doc*). CURTAIL, CUT, LESSEN, LOP. BASIN, JETTY, QUAY, TERMINAL, WHARF. WEED. CRUPPER. ENCLOSURE (leg).

DOCTOR ADULTERATE, FIDDLE, FIX. *WIND* (cricket). DD (eccles); DR, GP, MB, MD, MO (med) [*patron saint*, vet]; B MUS (mus); **celebrated:** CAIUS (*Shak*); *GRACE* (*cricketer*); GULLIVER (*Swift*); HAKIM (Saladin disguised, Talisman, Scott); JEKYLL (*Hyde*); JOHNSON (dict); LIVINGSTONE (explorer); MANETTE (*Dickens*); NO (Bond); STRANGELOVE (film); WATSON (*Holmes*); WHO (TV); *Chaucer* character.

DODGE AVOID, *DUCK*, ELUDE, SHUFFLE. ARTIFICE, EXPEDIENT, *SHIFT*, TRICK. RACKET. CAR®. CITY (US).

DOE JOHN (average man). DEER (*fem*), HARE (*fem*).

Pl = ACTS, PERFORMS (see *DO*).

DOG 1. FOLLOW, PURSUE, TAIL, TRACK. LOCK; BAR, GRIP, PAWL. **Pl** = *ISLAND*. 2. *Male* canine (**fem** = bitch; **offspring** = puppy); **breeds:**

Hounds	Terriers
AFGHAN	AIREDALE
BASSET	BEDLINGTON
BEAGLE	BULL TERRIER
BLOODHOUND	CAIRN
BORZOI	DANDIE DINMONT
DACHSHUND	FOX TERRIER
DEERHOUND	IRISH TERRIER
ELKHOUND	KERRY BLUE
FOXHOUND	SCOTTISH TERRIER
GREYHOUND	SEALYHAM
HARRIER	SKYE TERRIER
IRISH WOLFHOUND	STAFFORDSHIRE
OTTERHOUND	TERRIER
SALUKI	WELSH TERRIER
WHIPPET	

Non-sporting
ALSATIAN
BOSTON
BOXER
BULLDOG
BULL MASTIFF
CHOW
COLLIE
CORGIE
DALMATIAN
DOBERMAN PINSCHER
GREAT DANE
MASTIFF
NEWFOUNDLAND
POODLE
PYRENEAN
  MOUNTAIN DOG
ST BERNARD
SAMOYED
SCHNAUZER
SHEEPDOG

Gundogs
CLUMBER SPANIEL
COCKER
LABRADOR
POINTER
RETREIVER
SETTER
SPANIEL
SPRINGER
WEIMARANER

Toy
CHIHUAHUA
GRIFFON
KING CHARLES SPANIEL
PAPILLON
PEKIN(G)ESE
POMERANIAN
PUG
SPITZ
TOY POODLE
YORKSHIRE TERRIER

Celebrated: ARGUS (*Ulysses*); ASTA (Thin Man); BLUEBELL, JESSIE, PITCHER (Animal Farm, *Orwell*), *BULLSEYE* (Oliver Twist), CAVALL (King Arthur), *CERBERUS* (*Charon*), DIAMOND (Sir Isaac Newton), DIGBY (Biggest in world), DOG OF FO (Ch lion dog), *FIDO* (acronym), FLUSH (Barretts of Wimpole Street), FURY (*Alice*), HOUND OF THE BASKERVILLES (Sherlock *Holmes*), KEP (*Potter*), LAIKA (First *space traveller*), LASSIE (films), MICK THE MILLER (greyhound), MONTMORENCY (*Three* Men in a Boat, Jerome), NANA (Peter Pan), NIPPER (HMV/RCA/Victor), OWD BOB (Edinburgh), PILOT (Jane Eyre, C. *Brontë*), *PLUTO* (acronym and Disney), RIN-TIN-TIN (films), SIRIUS (Dogstar), SNOOPY (Peanuts), TIMMY (Famous Five), TOBY (Punch & Judy), TRAY (Struwwelpeter). *Constellations*. [Hans *Andersen*].

DOLE GRIEF, MISERY, DISTRIBUTION, UNEMPLOYMENT

BENEFIT/PAY, JAM ROLL (*rh sl*) [job centre].

DOLLAR (s/l *dolour*). *BUCK, COIN, CURRENCY,* GREENBACK, MONEY, S.

DOLOUR (s/l *dollar*). GRIEF (**opp** = *joy*).

DOLPHIN *CETACEAN* MAMMAL, GRAMPUS; BOTTLE-NOSE, WHITE-BACKED, WHITE-SIDED; KILLER *WHALE* [Pelorus Jack]; *Constellation.* BEACON, STAKE (naut). **Pl** = *FOOTBALL* TEAM (US).

DOMESTIC *CHAR.* HOMELOVING. HOME MADE, *NATIVE*; TAME.

DOMINICANS BLACKFRIARS, PREACHING *FRIARS.*

DON FELLOW, TUTOR. NOBLEMAN (Sp). ASSUME, PUT ON. BRADMAN (*cricket*). RIVER (Eng; Sc; USSR). **Pl** = ABERDEEN; WIMBLEDON (both *football* teams).

DONE (s/l dun). *Anag.* ACCEPTABLE, MANNERS, U. COMPLETED, *ENDED*, FINISHED. TIRED. COOKED (**opp** = *raw*).

DONKEY *ASS*, BURRO (US), MOKE; NEDDY. [Republican, hinny, *mule*] **breed:** ONAGER; [*male/female*]. EEYORE (*Milne*). DULLARD, FOOL. **Pl** = [Trotwood, *Dickens*].

DOODLEBUG BUZZBOMB, DIVER (code name), FLYING BOMB, VI; *MISSILE.*

DOORWAY 1. ENTRANCE, OPENING. 2. **God: Gk** = HORUS, **Rom** = JANUS, **Egy** = HOR, SET. 3. Five *symbols* at ~ in *song.*

DOPE *DRUG. INFORMATION.*

DOPEY DRUGGED, SLEEPY. *DWARF* (Snow White).

DOR (s/l door). *BEETLE.* TOWN (*bibl*).

DORADO FISH. EL ~ (*lost city* of gold). *Constellation.*

DORIS 1. GIRL. ORDER (Gk archit). [*Doch an* ~]. 2. Gk myth d of Oceanus and Tethys; mar her br *Nereus* and m of the Nereides, hence the SEA. Also a country in Greece.

DORY *BOAT. FISH. Alice* character.

DOT *MARK*, SPECK, SPOT. DECIMAL POINT. DOWRY. HIT, STRIKE (sl). SHORT SIGN (*morse*; **opp** = *dash*).

DOUBLE 1. DEAD SPIT, DOPPELGANGER, LOOKALIKE, IMAGE, *TWIN*. TWOFOLD, TWICE. RUN. ROUND, TURN; FOLD, LOOP. 2. Repeat any following letter(s), e.g. **Doubles** = ss.

DOUBLET BODYGARMENT, LEOTARD. TT (crypt).

DOUBLETON TWO *CARDS*. 200. CC (crypt).

DOVE *BIRD*, PIGEON (*Constellation*). PEACELOVER (**opp** = *hawk*). HOLY SPIRIT. DIVED. 'JEMIMA'. RIVER (Eng).

DOWN *D*, DN. FROM ABOVE; ALIGHTED. FEATHERS, FLUFF, PLUMAGE. *BLUE*, DEPRESSED, DISPIRITED, LOW. HILLS, OPEN LAND. *DRINK*, SWALLOW. *Assembly* of hares. **Pl** = SEA (N Dover Straits) [**castles in the ~s** = Deal, *Sandwich*, Walmer].

DP DISPLACED PERSON; hence PRONES, SPERON etc (anag).

DR *DEBTOR*. *DOCTOR*. DRACHM (*measure*). DESPATCH RIDER (mil).

DRACULA Blood-sucking *monster* from Bram Stoker's novel, based on Prince Vlad of Wallachia in Rumania.

DRAGOMAN *CONDUCTOR*, GUIDE, INTERPRETER.

DRAGON BAT, CRONE, SCOLD, *SHREW*, TERMAGENT. *MONSTER*, WYVERN (*Constellation*; *herald*). CONTINUE, DRAW OUT, PROLONG (all crypt). [~ fly, *insect*].

DRAIN 1. DRAW OFF, EBB, *EMPTY*; TRICKLE. *DRINK*. CONDUIT, PIPE, TUBE (med); *SEWER*. DEMAND, EXPENDITURE, WITHDRAWAL; SAP. 2. Waterloo & City Line (sl; rly). 3. Put letters DRA in word(s), e.g. **Drain UN ft for rehash** (7) = UN*DRA*FT.

DRAKE *DUCK* (*male*) [*Potter*]. *MILITARY LEADER*, PIRATE; *BOWLER* (crypt) [Armada (*battle*)]. MAYFLY. **Pl** = ISLAND.

DRAMA PLAY. [Aeschylus, Euripides, Sophocles; *Shakespeare*].

DRAW DESIGN, DEPICT, PEN, SKETCH [artist]. ATTRACT(ION), EXTRACT, MOVE, PULL, TOW, TUG. SHARE, TIE. ELONGATE. LOTTERY.

DRAWBACK CON, DISADVANTAGE (**opp** = *pro*). DEDUCTION, REMITTED TAX. WARD (crypt).

DRAWER ARTIST, RA. DENTIST (crypt). PUBLICAN, TAPSTER. *TOWER*, TUG. SLIDING RECEPTACLE (furniture). **Pl** = BLOOMERS, KNICKERS, PANTIES.

DRAY *CARRIAGE*, CART. *Habitation* (squirrels).

DREAM 1. BROWN STUDY, FANCY, REVERIE, VISION; **saying**. BEAUTY. 2. **God: Rom** = MORPHEUS, **Egy** = SERAPIS, **Gk** = HERMES.

166   *Dress*

DRESS *Anag.* BANDAGE. BEDECK, BEFLAG, *COVER*, *DECK*; GARNISH, PIPE. CLOTHE (**opp** = *strip*); ATTIRE, FROCK, HABIT, OUTFIT, RIG, ROBE [*suit*]. ALIGN, RANGE, SIZE. PREPARE (cook).

DRESSING CLOTHING, COVERING, DONNING (CLOTHES), ROBING. ALIGNMENT, *ROW* (mil). MAYONNAISE. BANDAGE, PLASTER.

DREW DEL, DELINEAVIT, SKETCHED. ATTRACTED, PULLED. SHARED, TIED.

DRIER AIRER, SPINNER, TOWEL; LESS WET. OAST HOUSE.

DRILL COACH, PARADE; *TRAIN*. AUGER, AWL, *BORE*, GIMLET. BABOON, *MONKEY*. CLOTH, *MATERIAL*. FURROW, ROW.

DRINK DITCH, OGGIN, SEA (all sl). ABSORB, DRAIN, LAP, QUAFF, SIP, SWALLOW, TOPE; (CUP/GLASS OF) LIQUID, LIQUOR; **saying. Types** (many ®):

3-letters	COCOA	*SCOTCH*
ALE	*HOOCH*	SHERRY
GIN	LAGER	*SPIRIT*
POP	NEGUS	*SQUASH*
RUM	PIMMS®	WHISKY
RYE	SIROP	
TEA	*SLING*	**7-letters**
	TONIC	BOURBON
4-letters	VODKA	CAMPARI®
BEER		CINZANO®
COLA	**6-letters**	*COBBLER*
FLIP	BITTER	COLLINS
MEAD	BRANDY	*CORDIAL*
MILD	COFFEE	CURAÇAO
OUZO	COGNAC	*LIQUEUR*
PORT	EGG-NOG	MADEIRA
SODA	GENEVA	MARTINI®
WINE	KIRSCH	MINERAL
	KÜMMEL®	SHERBET
5-letters	*PORTER*	STENGAH
BUMBO	RED-EYE	STINGER

WHISKEY	LEMONADE	SLUG
	LIMEJUICE	FIFTH
8+ letters	MANHATTAN	*GLASS*
ABSINTHE	OLD FASHIONED	SNORT
BENEDICTINE®	ORANGEADE	FINGER
CHOCOLATE	SCREWDRIVER	NOGGIN
COCKTAIL	SUNDOWNER	SPLASH
COINTREAU®	TIA MARIA®	TIPPLE
DRAMBUIE®	TOM COLLINS	*DOCH & DORIS*
DUBONNET®	WHITE LADY	NIGHTCAP
GINGER		ONE FOR
ALE/BEER	**Measures**	THE ROAD
GRAND MARNIER	CUP	OTHER HALF
HIGHBALL	NIP	QUICKIE
HOLLANDS	DRAM	QUICK ONE
HORSE'S NECK	PINT	STIRRUP-CUP
JOHN COLLINS	SHOT	

DRIVE ENTHUSIASM, GO, IMPULSE. CONDUCT, STEER; OUTING. HIT, TEE OFF; STROKE (*cricket*, *golf*). FORCE, IMPEL. ENTRANCE, PRIVATE ROAD.

DRIVER 1. *CLUB*, WOOD (**opp** = iron); GOLFER. CHAUFFEUR, CAR-MAN, L. MARTINET. RAILWAYMAN. COWBOY, HERDSMAN (drover). 2. **Celebrated:** *FREYA*, *PHAETON* (myth), TOAD (*Grahame*), JEHU (bibl).

DROP 1. LET FALL, RELEASE. FALL, LOWER. OMIT, *SHED*. EARRING, PENDANT. CASCADE, SPLASH, WATERFALL. LOZENGE, SWEET. PARACHUTE. 2. Leave off letter/word, e.g. **Alfred drops the gangster and is a different man** (4) = **FRED.

DROP-OUT 1. HIPPIE, LAYABOUT. HERMIT, MONK, RECLUSE. PARACHUTIST (crypt). 2. Leave out letter concerned, e.g. **Alice, a drop-out, evinces parasites** (4) = *LICE.

DRUG ANAESTHETIC. MEDICAMENT. HALLUCINOGEN, NARCOTIC, OPIATE, STIMULANT; **types:** BHANG, CANNABIS, COCAINE, DOPE, GRASS, HASHISH, HEMP, HERB, HEROIN, LSD, MARIJUANA, POT, SNOW, SPEED, WEED [gone, high, mainline, spaced-out, trip]. UNSALEABLE.

DRUM TUB, VAT, BARREL, CYLINDER, SHAFT. BEAT, RESONATE, SUMMON, TAP, THRUM, THUMP. DRIVE, INJECT, PLAY. *INSTRUMENT* (mus), TRAP. MOUND. VOID.

DRUMMER 1. BANDSMAN; BEATER, SKINNER, TAPPER. CHAPMAN, COMMERCIAL TRAVELLER, PEDLAR, REP. *BIRD*, BITTERN, SNIPE. *FISH*. TEAPARTY. *EAR* (crypt). 2. Ninth day of *Christmas* in *song*.

DRUNK CONSUMED, DOWNED, SWALLOWED. HIGH, INEBRIATED, LIT, SMASHED, SOUSED, TIDDLY, TIGHT (**opp** = sober; *abstainer*).

DRY ARID, PARCHED, THIRSTY. MILKLESS, TT, WATERLESS. ALCOHOL-FREE. BARE, BITTER, COLD, IMPASSIVE, MEAGRE, SOLID, STERILE. SEC (Fr). CURE, SMOKE. SUNNY. DRAIN, SPIN, TOWEL, WIPE.

DUCK O, LOVE, NIL, NOUGHT, NO SCORE, ZERO. *BOB*, CURTSEY. *DODGE*. *DEAR*, LUV. CANVAS. Pl = PANTS, SHORTS, TROUSERS. [~s and drakes; ricochet, skim. Bombay ~ (fish)]. *BIRD* of genus Anatidae; **breeds:**

AYLESBURY	*MANDARIN*
CANVAS BACKED	MERGANSER
EIDER	SCAUP
GADWALL	SCOTER
GOLDENEYE	SHELDRAKE
MALLARD	SHOVELLER
MUSCOVY	*SMEE*
PINTADO	SMEW
PINTAIL	TEAL
POCHARD	WI(D)GEON

[**assembly** = flight, flock; **male** = *drake*; **female** = duck; **offspring** = duckling]. **Celebrated:** DAFFY, DONALD (cartoon film), JEMIMA PUDDLEDUCK (Beatrix *Potter*), *Alice* character. [Hans *Andersen*; *Lear*].

DUD BAD, DEFECTIVE. BAD CHEQUE. Pl = *CLOTHES*.

DUN (s/l *done*). IMPORTUNE, PESTER. GREY-BROWN (*colour*).

DUNELM *Episcopal sig* of DURHAM.

DURHAM 1. *CASTLE. GAOL. UNIVERSITY.* 2. **Episcopal sig** = DUNELM.

DUSTMAN REFUSE COLLECTOR: NICODEMUS *BOFFIN* (Our Mutual Friend, *Dickens*), ALFRED DOOLITTLE (Pygmalion, G.B. *Shaw*). SANDMAN.

DUTCH SHARING PAYMENT. *WIFE. CHEESE. HOLLAND*, NETHERLANDS. [courage].

DV DEO VOLENTE, GOD WILLING.

DWARF OVERAWE, TOWER OVER. MINI(ATURE), PUNY, STUNTED; ELF, GNOME, MIDGET, PYGMY, RUNT, TROLL (**opp** = *giant*); **celebrated:** ALBERICH, MIME (Wagner's Ring [Nibelheim]); BASHFUL, DOC, DOPEY, GRUMPY, HAPPY, SLEEPY, SNEEZY (Snow White); SIR GEOFFREY HUDSON (Scott); MISS MOWCHER (David Copperfield, *Dickens*); MUNCHKIN (Wizard of Oz, Frank Baum); QUILP (Old Curiosity Shop, *Dickens*); RUMPELSTILTSKIN (Grimm); TOM THUMB (US and Perrault); VAMANA (Hindu incarnation).

DYED (s/l *died*). COLOURED, TINTED (blue rinse, highlights, peroxide).

E 1. *EAST. ENERGY.* ENGLISH. *BRIDGE PLAYER. KEY; NOTE.* POINT. SPAIN (*car plate*). 2. Second class at *Lloyds*.

EA EACH. EAST AFRICA. EAST ANGLIA.

EAGLE 1. *BIRD* (**habitation** = eyrie; **offspring** = eaglet); **breeds:** bald ~, crowned ~, erne, golden ~, hawk ~, sea ~, white-tailed ~ [~ owl]. ENSIGN, *STANDARD. ISLAND. COMIC.* $10. LINEAGE (crypt: L*IN*EAG()E. **Pl** = *Football team* (US). 2. Two under par on *golf course*. 3. *Constellation*.

EAR HEAD, SPIKE (corn). HANDLE, LUG. ATTENTION, LISTENING; APPRECIATION. HEARING ORGAN; **parts, inner:** cochlea, labyrinth; **middle:** anvil, eustachian tube, incus, malleus (hammer), ossicle, syrinx, tympanum (eardrum, membrane), vestibule; **outer:** concha, helix, pinna, scapha; **disorders:** barotrauma, deafness, mastoiditis, Menière's, otitis media [cauliflower ~].

EARLY 1. BEFORE TIME, PREMATURE (**opp** = *late*); FORWARD. ARISTOCRATIC (crypt). 2. Use first letter(s), e.g. **Early afternoon** = A or AF; or, more cryptically, **Early speech** = DIAL(ect).

EARTH 1. LAND, MOULD, SOIL (Fuller's). WORLD, PLANET [*study*]; **saying**. HABITATION (*badger*, *fox*). CONDUCTOR, CONNECTION, GROUND (elect). 2. **Goddess: Gk** = *CERES*, GAEA/GE; **Rom** = LUA, MAIA, TELLUS, TERRA.

EARTHQUAKE *QUAKER*, TREMBLER [epicentre; Richter; seismograph]; GROUNDRENT (crypt). HARTE, HEART, RATHE etc (anag; crypt).

EASE (s/l eee). FACILITY. RELIEVE, LOOSEN, SLACKEN. REST.

EASTERN OFFICIAL BEY, CADI, DEWAN, NABOB, NAWAB, SAHIB, SATRAP, SULTAN, TUAN [*Turkish official*].

EAST KENT SE. **Pl** = BUFFS (mil).

EASY FACILE, SIMPLE. SITTER. [Midshipman ~].

EAT OUT BARBECUE, PICNIC [al fresco]. ATE, TEA (anag; crypt).

EAVESDROPPER BUG, LISTENER. ICICLE (crypt).

EBB DRAIN. DECLINE, DECAY. FLOW BACK, hence WOLF (crypt). RECEDE.

EBBTIDE DRAIN. DECLINE, DECAY. OUTFLOW (hence WOLF: crypt); EDIT (crypt).

EBOR *Episcopal sig* of *YORK*. RETIRING GOWN (crypt).

EC EAST CENTRAL, EAST END; CITY.

ECCENTRIC *Anag.* IRREGULAR, *ODD*, OFF-BEAT, WHIMSICAL. OFF-CENTRE, CAM. *CARD*.

Eccles Ecclesiastic. *Church*.

ECHO 1. *COPY*, IMITATION, REPEAT, REPETITION, RESOUND. *SPACECRAFT*. 2. Gk myth mountain *nymph*, made speechless by *Hera*, so that she could only repeat the last word of others. Loved *Narcissus* vainly, and pined away. 3. A minor *PLANET*.

ECONOMIZE BE FRUGAL, DO WITHOUT (hence D.....O; crypt, e.g. **Do without one race, all the same** (5) = D*ITT*O). SAVE, SPARE. USELESS (crypt).

EDENBURG *Episcopal sig* of EDINBURGH.

EDINBURGH *Capital* of Scotland. *CASTLE*. **Episcopal sig** =
EDENBURG. *RACETRACK* (horses). *UNIVERSITY*.

EDIT *Anag*. ARRANGE, CUT; COOK, GARBLE.
PREPARE (MS). EBBTIDE (crypt).

EDITION VERSION. BOOK, TOME, VOLUME.

EDMUND IRONSIDE. ED.

EDWARD ED, NED, TED. BEAR (*Milne*). LEAR. R.
POTATO. HYDE [Henry Jekyll; R.L. Stevenson].

EEC (COMMON) MARKET, COMMUNITY, EUROPE (treaty
of Rome).

EEL FISH [**offspring** = elver; slippery].

EFGHIJKLMN *ETON* (crypt).

EG EXEMPLA GRATIA, FOR EXAMPLE/INSTANCE.

EGG ENCOURAGE, EXHORT, SPUR, STIMULATE, *URGE*.
OVUM; O. BOMB. PERSON (sl). *ZERO*. **Pl** = OO, OVA,
ROE, SPAWN.

EGGER *MOTH*. SPUR, STIMULATOR. HEN (crypt).

EGYPTIAN GOD *ANUBIS*, HOR, MAAT, *OSIRIS*, *RA*, SEB,
SERAPIS, *SET*, *TEMU*.

EIGHT 1. See *number*. OCTAD, VIII. BLUE, ROWING
CREW; **Reserve ~s**: GOLDIE (C), *ISIS* (O). 2. Bold *rangers*
(*song*). *Maids* a-milking (*Christmas* song). [Pieces of ~ (parrot,
Treasure Island, *Stevenson*].

ELBOW HINGE (crypt); JOINT. NUDGE, PUSH. *Shak*
character (M for M).

EL DORADO *Lost city* of gold. **Capital** = Manoa.

ELECTRA 1. Gk myth d of *Agamemnon*, sis of Iphigenia and
Orestes, with whom she avenged the murder of her f by her m.
2. A minor *PLANET*. 3. Complex of d on f (**opp** = *Oedipus*).

ELECTRICITY AC, AMPS, DC, VOLTS; CURRENCY (crypt)
[BEAB].

ELEGANT CHIC, *FASHIONABLE*, IN, MODISH, STYLISH.

ELEMENT 1. AIR, *EARTH*, *FIRE*, *WATER*. COMPONENT,
FACTOR, RUDIMENT. RESISTANCE WIRE. 2. Hidden
word, e.g. **An element of beach air is relaxing** = CH*AIR.

ELEPHANT PACHYDERM [Democrat; roc]; **celebrated**: BABAR,
CELESTE, DUMBO, HEFFALUMP, JUMBO, KALAWAG,
NELLIE [**assembly** = herd, **female** = *cow*, **male** = *bull*, **offspring**

= *calf*]. MEASURE (paper).

ELEVEN 1. See *number*. HENDECA, II, IX; SIDE, SQUAD,
TEAM. IMPAIRED (crypt). **Pl** = SNACK. 2. Went to *Heaven*
(*song*). Ladies *dancing* (*Christmas* song).

ELIA ESSAYIST; LAMB; *WRITER*. **Pl** = ELIJAH, PROPHET.

ELIMINATE 1. DEFEAT. REMOVE, GET RID OF. 2. Remove
word(s)/letter(s) indicated, e.g. **A to-do*to eliminate*to-do** (3)
= A*DO.

ELISSA *DIDO*.

ELL LENGTH, *MEASURE* (cloth).

ELYSIUM 1. ELYSIAN FIELDS, *HEAVEN*. 2. Gk myth place
where souls of the good dwelt after death [*Valhalla*].

EM THEM (abbr). GAUGE (model rly). *MEASURE* (printing).
Pl = RIVER (Ger).

EMBARRASSED *Anag*. ASHAMED, AWKWARD;
PERPLEXED. COMPLICATED. ENCUMBERED,
IMPEDED.

EMBRACE 1. CLASP, COMPRISE, ENCLOSE, HUG,
INCLUDE. ACCEPT, TAKE IN. 2. Hidden word; word
contains another, e.g. **He embraces a foreign engineer and swings
for it** (5) = H*ING*E.

EMERALD 1. GEM; BERYL. GREEN. 2. *Anniversary* (55th).
Birthstone (May).

EMINENCE *HILL*, MOUND, MOUNT, TOR. *CARDINAL*, HE.

~ **GRISE** RICHELIEU'S SECRETARY (PERE JOSEPH).
MANIPULATOR, *UNSEEN* INFLUENCE; ROYAL
ENGINEER (crypt).

EMIT GIVE OUT, ISSUE, SEND FORTH, TRANSMIT. TIME
OUT, TIME-WARP, WRONG ITEM (anags; crypt).

EMMY *AWARD* (TV).

EMPLOY 1. USE. OCCUPY. HIRE. 2. Hidden word, e.g. **Mad
American employs a gardener** (4) = AD*AM.

EMPTY 1. HOLLOW, VACANT, VACATE. 2. Remove middle
letter(s) from word, e.g. **Empty threat** (4) = TH**AT. 3. Insert O
in word, e.g. **Empty cup** (4) = C*O*UP.

EMU FLIGHTLESS *BIRD* (Aus) [cassowary, dinornis (ex, NZ),
moa, nandoo, ostrich].

EN 1. Put word in another, e.g. **Enlist Z** (5) = LIS*Z*T.
2. *MEASURE* (printing).

ENCHANT CHARM, DELIGHT, *ENTRANCE*, SPELLBIND, TRANSPORT (**opp** = *bore*).

ENCOMPASS CONTAIN, SURROUND. NORTH ORIENTATE; relate to magnetic compass, e.g. **Tidings encompassed** (4) = NEWS.

ENCOURAGE ABET, AID, EGG, *URGE*. GO.

END 1. *AIM*, DESIGN, GOAL, PURPOSE. *CLOSE*, CONCLUSION, FINISH (**opp** = *start*). SESSION (bowls). 2. Last letter of word, e.g. **Southend** = H. **Pl** = letters at each end of word(s), e.g. **Dead ends** = D**D.

ENDANGER JEOPARDIZE, PUT AT RISK. MAKE PEACE, MAKE UP (crypt).

ENDING 1. CLOSURE. 2. Last letter (see *END* above).

ENDLESS 1. CEASELESS, PERPETUAL, UNCEASING. CIRCLE, RING, O. AIMLESS, POINTLESS; TIPOFF (crypt). 2. No first (or last) letter, e.g. **Endless hate** (3) = HAT.

ENERGY FORCE, POTENTIAL, POWER, VIGOUR. E, ERG, ERGON.

ENG ENGLISH [*patron saint*].

Eng England, English. Engineer.

ENGAGED AFFIANCED, BETROTHED, MATCHED, PROMISED. *BOOKED*, BUSY, OCCUPIED, RESERVED, TIED UP (**opp** = *free*). HIRED, TOOK ON.

ENGAGEMENT AFFRAY, *BATTLE*, SKIRMISH. BETROTHAL, MATCH. OCCUPATION. APPOINTMENT, DATE.

ENGINE MACHINERY, POWER SOURCE; INSTRUMENT, MEANS. WAR MACHINE; CATAPULTA, TESTUDO (Rom).

ENGINEER ARRANGE, CONTRIVE, FIX, MANAGE, ORGANIZE. CE, DESIGNER (mech), ENG. WORKER (elect, mech [**union** = AUEW], rly [**unions** = ASLEF, NUR]). BRIDGEBUILDER. RE, SAPPER.

ENGLISH E, ENG. SIDE, SPIN (ballgames – US).

ENGROSS ABSORB, ENRAPTURE, OCCUPY. DRAW UP, EXPRESS, PREPARE (leg). CORNER, MONOPOLIZE (arch).

ENIGMATIC *Anag.* BEWILDERING, PERPLEXING, PUZZLING.

ENLARGE EXPAND, EXPATIATE. DILATE, MAGNIFY. FREE, LIBERATE (arch).

ENLIST 1. ENGAGE, ENROL(L), JOIN COLOURS. 2. Word contained in another, especially in 'list' or 'roster', e.g. **Enlist one to revel** (7) = RO*I*STER.

ENOUGH AMPLE, ENOW, SUFFICIENT.

ENTER GO IN (**opp** = *leave*). LOG, *RECORD*, WRITE. BIND (contract, treaty). JOIN (church, forces; **opp** = *desert*).

ENTHUSIAST *FAN*.

ENTITLED 1. CALLED. ALLOWED, PERMITTED, RIGHTFUL. 2. With a title, e.g. Count, Dame, Sir etc.

ENTRANCE *DOOR(WAY)*, GATE, PASSAGE. ARRIVAL, ENTRY. ADMISSION FEE. *ENCHANT*.

ENVIRONMENT 1. MILIEU, SURROUNDINGS. 2. Word round another, e.g. **Or the environment** = O*THE*R (or TH*OR*E).

EOLITHIC *AGE*.

EOS 1. Gk *goddess* of DAWN (**Rom** = AURORA). 2. A minor *PLANET*.

EPISCOPAL SIGNATURE Initials or name of bishop, followed by archaic name for his see, e.g.

ABERDON	(Aberdeen)
ALBAN	(St Albans)
CANTUAR	(Canterbury)
CESTR	(Chester)
CICESTR	(Chichester)
DUNELM	(Durham)
EBOR	(York)
EDENBURG	(Edinburgh)
EXON	(Exeter)
NORVIC	(Norwich)
OXON	(Oxford)
PETRIBURG	(Peterborough)
ROFFEN	(Rochester)
SARUM	(Salisbury)
TRURON	(Truro)
VIGORN	(Worcester)
WINTON	(Winchester)

Eq Equatorial. Equals.

EQUAL EVEN, LEVEL, LIKE, PAR, SAME; MATCH. PEER; BROTHER.

~ **WINNER** *TIER*; DEAD-HEATER; DRAWER (crypt).

ERASED 1. DELETED, ERADICATED, REMOVED, RUBBED OUT. 2. Delete D from clue, e.g. **Draft erased is logged** (4) = *RAFT.

ERATO 1. Gk myth; one of the nine *Muses* (Love songs and erotic *poetry*). 2. A minor *PLANET*.

ERG ENERGY UNIT [dyne]. SAHARA DUNES [*desert*].

ERIC LITTLE BY LITTLE. (THE) RED.

ERICA *HEATH(ER)*. GIRL.

ERIE (s/l eyrie). *AMERICAN INDIAN. LAKE*.

ERINYES *FURIES*.

ERIS Gk *goddess* of DISCORD, sis of *Ares* (**Rom** = DISCORDIA). Angry at not being invited to the wedding of Peleus and Thetis, she threw among the guests a golden *apple* inscribed 'To the fairest'. *Aphrodite*, *Athene* and *Hera* all claimed it, and the judgement of *Paris* was that it be awarded to Aphrodite; this indirectly caused the Siege of *Troy*.

ERMINE STOAT [weasel]. FUR [judges, peers, *herald*].

EROS Gk *god* of *LOVE* (**Rom** = AMOR, CUPID), depicted as an *archer* [Piccadilly Circus].

ERRATIC *Anag.* WAYWARD, WILD; **saying**. *ODD*. IRREGULAR, UNCERTAIN.

ERROR *BLOOMER*, BISH, DEVIATION, FAULT, INFRINGEMENT, MISTAKE, SIN, WRONG.

ERUPTION *Anag.* BREAK-OUT, BURST, OUTBREAK; RASH.

ESCAPOLOGIST HOUDINI. JACK SHEPHERD. ESCAPER.

ESSAY (s/l s,a). ATTEMPT, EFFORT, TEST, TRY. ARTICLE. COMPOSITION.

ESSAYIST TRIER. *WRITER*: ELIA, LAMB.

ESTABLISHMENT AUTHORITY, ORGANIZATION, THEY [Civil Service (**union** = NALGO)]. GROUP, SET, SETTLEMENT, STAFF, VERIFICATION; AUTHORIZED HOLDING/MANNING. THE CHURCH.

ESTATE CLASS, ORDER. CONDITION. LAND, PROPERTY. VEHICLE (hatchback, shooting brake). [*three* ~s; fourth ~].

ETA ARRIVAL TIME, EXPECTED TIME OF ARRIVAL (**opp** = ETD).

ET AL AND OTHERS.

ETC ETCETERA, AND SO ON.

ETERNAL FLOWER ASPHODEL. ARTESIAN WELL, SPRING (crypt).

ETHIOPIAN KING RA.

ETON 1. COLLEGE, *PUBLIC SCHOOL*. E — N (crypt). 2. Returned note (crypt).

EUMINIDES *FURIES*.

EUROPA Gk myth d of Agenor and m of *Minos* by *Zeus* (who took the form of a bull). 2. A satellite of the *planet* Jupiter.

EUROPE EEC [Common Market. Treaty of Rome]. *CONTINENT*.

EUROS Gk myth SE *WIND* (**Rom** = VOLTURNUS).

EURYDICE 1. Gk myth d of *Nereus* and *Doris*, who mar *Orpheus*. When she died of a snake bite, Orpheus brought her back from *Hades* by magic, but lost her again by *looking back* for her. 2. A minor *PLANET*.

EUTERPE 1. Gk myth; one of the nine *Muses* (lyric *poetry*). 2. A minor *PLANET*.

EVA EXTRA-VEHICULAR ACTIVITY, SPACE-WALK. GIRL, SPACE-GIRL. PERON. 'LIFE'.

EVE (s/l eave). 1. EVENING, VIGIL. *ISLAND*. 'LIFE'. 2. Mother of Cain, Abel and Seth; wife of Adam. FIRST LADY, SECOND PERSON [apple; Eden; rib].

EVELYN DIARIST. JOHN; *WRITER* [Pepys].

EVEN LEVEL, *SMOOTH*, UNIFORM. NOT ODD. *JUST*, QUITE, SIMPLY, STILL. EVENING. EQUABLE, UNRUFFLED. BALANCED, EQUAL. **Pl** = EQUAL STAKES [odds]. *IRONS*, SMOOTHS (crypt).

EVENING *PM*. IRONING, SMOOTHING (crypt).

EVER ALWAYS, EER. STILL.

EVERGREEN BAY, CEDAR, FIR, LARCH, LAUREL etc.

EVERLASTING ENDLESS, ETERNAL, NEVERENDING.

EVERMORE ALWAYS. NEVERTHELESS (crypt).

EWE (s/l you, *U*). *SHEEP* (fem). *ISLAND*.

EWER CROCK, JUG, PITCHER, POT, URN, *VESSEL*. SHEPHERD (crypt).

EX (s/l X). *DEAD*, LATE, FORMER. OUT OF, *OUTSIDE*, WITHOUT.

Ex No longer extant.

EXALTATION 1. ELATION, *ENCHANTMENT*, RAPTURE, REJOICING. 2. *Assembly* (larks).

EXAM GREATS (O), LITTLE-GO (C); ORAL, VIVA VOCE, WRITTEN TEST [sit]. REGARD.

EXCELLENT AI, FIRST CLASS, PREEMINENT, VERY GOOD.

EXCEPT *BUT*, NOT INCLUDING; UNLESS. EXCLUDE, LEAVE OUT.

EXCERPT 1. EXTRACT, QUOTE. 2. Hidden word, e.g. **An excerpt from Milton's 'Il Penseroso' is throaty stuff** (6) = TONS*IL.

EXCHANGE *Anag.* CHANGE, INTERCHANGE, SWAP, SWOP, SWITCH. CURRENCY, MONEY CHANGING. BOURSE (Fr), COUNTING HOUSE; COMMERCIAL TRANSACTIONS. PBX, SWITCHBOARD, TELEPHONE CENTRE.

EXCLUSIVENESS 1. HIGH-CLASS. SELECTIVITY. 2. Delete NESS from clue, e.g. **Exclusiveness makes the prince's address exalted** (4) = HIGH(ness).

EXECUTE CARRY OUT, *DO*, PERFORM. VALIDATE. ASSASSINATE, BEHEAD, DECAPITATE, DISPATCH, EXTERMINATE, FINISH, GAS, GUILLOTINE, *HANG*, KILL, MURDER, PUT TO DEATH, SHOOT, SLAUGHTER, SLAY, WASTE, *TOP*.

EXERCISE PE, PT; DRILL, EXERTION, TRAINING (gym). PERPLEX, WORRY. DISCHARGE (duty). EMPLOYMENT, PRACTICE. TASK. COMPOSITION. MANOEUVRE (mil).

EXETER 1. ISCA DUMNUNIORUM (*Roman town*). *UNIVERSITY*; *UNIVERSITY COLLEGE*. 2. **Episcopal sig** = EXON.

EXHAUST FATIGUE, TIRE; BEGGAR, FINISH. OUTLET, PORT (tech).

EXHORT *URGE*.

EXIST AM, ARE, BE.

EXON *Episcopal sig* of EXETER.

EXPEL 1. CAST AWAY/OUT, EJECT, TURN OUT. 2. Remove

letter(s) indicated, e.g. **I am expelled from Sofia for a rest** (4) = SOF*A.

EXPERIENCED ACQUAINTED; FELT, UNDERWENT. SKILLED, TRIED (**opp** = *green*, tyro).

EXPERT *ACE*, PRO(FESSIONAL) (**opp** = *learner*). ABLE, CAPABLE. (**opp** = *fool*).

EXPLORER EXAMINER, INVESTIGATOR. *SPACECRAFT*, *SPACE TRAVELLER*. *DISCOVERER*, TRAVELLER; **celebrated:** AMUNDSEN ('Gjoa', 'Maud'), BYRD (North Pole), CABOT ('Mathew'), COLUMBUS ('Nina', 'Pinta', 'Santa Maria'), *COOK* ('Discovery', 'Endeavour', 'Resolution'), DARWIN ('Beagle'), DRAKE ('Pelican', 'Golden Hind'), FROBISHER ('Gabriel'), HILARY (Everest), HUNT (Everest, South Pole), *MAGELLAN* ('Trinidad', 'Vittoria'), NANSEN ('Fram'), SCOTT ('Discovery', 'Terra Nova'), SHACKLETON ('Endurance'), VASCO DA GAMA (Cathay).

EXPLOSION *Anag.* BURST, OUTBREAK. BANG, LOUD NOISE.

EXPRESS FORMULATE, SAY, STATE. EXPEDITE, FAST, SPEEDY. NEWSPAPER®. TRAIN (rly).

EXTRA ODD, OVER, SPARE, SUPERNUMERARY; EXCESS; FURTHER. GRACE NOTE (mus). BIT PLAYER, CROWD (film). PS. BYE, LEG BYE, NO BALL, RUN, WIDE (cricket).

EXTRACTOR DRAWER, PULLER. FAN, VENTILATOR. COPIER (crypt). DENTIST (crypt).

EXTRA LARGE OS, OUTSIZE, X.

EXTREME 1. FARTHEST, FURTHEST, OUTERMOST, UTTERMOST. SEVERE, STRINGENT. 2. **Pl** = use letters/words at each end, e.g. **Extremes of valour** = VR.

EXTREMELY 1. HIGHLY; SEVERELY, VERY. 2. Use letters/words at each end, e.g. **Extremely kind** = KD.

EYE (s/l Aye, I). EXAMINE, INSPECT, LOOK, REGARD. SIGHT. OPTIC; **parts:** *ball*, cornea, *iris*, lens, orbit, *pupil*, retina, rods, sclerotic, white; **disorders:** astigmatism, blindness, cast, cataract, conjunctivitis, glaucoma, iritis, myopia, myosin, myosis, myotic, nystagmus, squint, stye, tunnel vision.

EYESORE FRIGHT, HIDEOSITY, UGLY, OBJECT. *EYE DISORDER* (crypt).

F FAHRENHEIT. *FELLOW*. *FEMININE*. FLUORINE (chem). FOLIO, PAGE. FORTE. FRANCE (*car plate*). FRENCH. FRIDAY. *KEY*; *NOTE*. *LOUD*.

FA NOTE (mus; also FAH). FANNY ADAMS, NOTHING (sl). FOOTBALL ASSOCIATION.

FABRIC *MATERIAL* (felt, knit or weave). TEXTURE, TISSUE. BUILDING, EDIFICE, FRAME, STRUCTURE.

FACE CLOCK, DIAL, *MUG*, *PAN*, VISAGE. CONFRONT, OPPOSE; LOOK TOWARDS. *OBVERSE* (**opp** = *reverse*).

FACTOR AGENT. ELEMENT.

FACTORY MILL, *PLANT*, WORKS.

FACULTY APTITUDE, COMPETENCE. AUTHORIZATION, LICENCE. ART, SCIENCE; TEACHING STAFF.

FAHRENHEIT F.

FAIL BREAK. FLUNK, PIP, PLOUGH, PLOW (US).

FAIR (s/l *fare*). EVEN HANDED, UNBIASED. BLOND(E). *ISLAND*. *STRAWBERRY*, *WIDDICOMBE*. BEAUTIFUL [Monday's *child*]; **saying**.

FAIRY HOMO, QUEER; CAMP, GAY. (HOB)GOBLIN, IMP, SPRITE; **celebrated:** TITANIA (queen), OBERON (king), COBWEB, MOTH, MUSTARDSEED, PEASBLOSSOM, and PUCK/ROBIN GOODFELLOW (all MND), ARIEL (Tempest), TINKERBELL (Peter Pan). [*Barrie*, Grimm; Iolanthe (*G & S*). MND (*Shak*)].

FALL CROPPER, *DECLINE*, DESCEND, DROP, SLIP. WATERFALL. RAIN. ROPE (naut). AUTUMN, *SEASON* (US). *Assembly* (woodcock).

~ **OUT** HAPPEN. DISAGREE. NUCLEAR DEBRIS/DUST; SIDE-EFFECTS. DISMISS, LEAVE RANKS (mil).

FALSE *Anag*. ARTIFICIAL, COUNTERFEIT, DECEITFUL, DUMMY, FICTITIOUS, FRAUDULENT, ILLEGAL, PHON(E)Y, SHAM, SPURIOUS, WRONG (**opp** = correct). UNFAITHFUL (**opp** = *true*).

~ **REPORT** CANARD, HOAX, LIE. PORTER, PERROT etc (anag, crypt).

FAMILIAR COMMON, CURRENT, FRIENDLY, INTIMATE, USUAL, WELL-KNOWN. CASUAL, INFORMAL, UNCEREMONIOUS. *CAT*, DEMON, *SPIRIT* (*witch*). SECRETARY, SERVANT (of pope, RC *bishop*).

FAMILY CHILDREN, DESCENDANTS, HOUSE, KIN, KITH, LINEAGE. COMMON STOCK, GENUS, RACE.

FAMOUS FIVE ANNE, DICK, GEORGE, JULIAN, TIMMY (dog) [Enid Blyton]. JOHNNIE BULL, BOB CHERRY, FRANK NUGENT, RAM JAM SINGH, HARRY WHARTON [*Bunter*, Greyfriars] (Frank Richards).

FAN WAFT, WINNOW; *COOLER*. PROPELLER (av), SCREW (naut). *SAIL* (windmill). SPREAD OUT. ADMIRER, ENTHUSIAST, FOLLOWER, SUPPORTER.

FANG 1. *TOOTH* (dog, snake, wolf). PRONG. 2. Character in *Dickens* and *Shak*.

FANNY ADAMS FA, NOTHING (murder victim). CANNED MEAT (naut).

FARE (s/l *fair*). *FOOD*. *PASSAGE* MONEY. *GO*, JOURNEY, TRAVEL. HAPPEN, TURN OUT.

FAREWELL ALOHA, AVE, BYE BYE, GOODBYE, TA-TA, VALE (**opp** = *greeting*).

FARM HOLDING, RANCH; CULTIVATE, TILL [*husbandry*]. HIRE OUT, SPREAD.

FARO (s/l pharaoh). *CARD GAME*.

FAR SIDE 1. BEYOND. 2. Second part of word, e.g. **Far side of the Moon** = ON.

FASHION MODE, TON, HAUTE COUTURE. CONSTRUCT, MAKE, *SHAPE*.

FASHIONABLE A LA MODE, CHIC, *IN*, IN THE SWIM, MODISH, NEAT, SMART, UNSQUARE. MALLEABLE, WORKABLE.

FAST *FLEET*, QUICK, SPEEDY. ABSTAIN, *LENT*; RAMADAN (Mos). *FIRM*, *SET*. *CASTLE*.

FATE 1. DESERTS, DESTINY, LOT; KISMET. PREORDAIN. 2. **Pl** = *GODS*, WEIRD SISTERS. Three *goddesses* of DESTINY: **Gk** = MORAI: CLOTHO (thread of life), LACHESIS (quality and length), ATROPOS (severance); **Rom** = PARCAE; **Nor** = NORN.

FATHEAD CLOT, DUNCE, FOOL. F (crypt).

FATHER (s/l farther). ABBOT, *CHURCHMAN*, FR, *FRIAR*. DAD, GENERATOR, GOVERNOR, GUVNOR, OLD MAN, PA, PATER (FAMILIAS), POP; PROCREATE, SIRE, SPAWN (~**'s delight** = *Abigail*). [~ Brown, *Chesterton*; Old ~

William (*Alice*); Old ~ Thames; ~ Time].

FATHERLAND *COUNTRY. GERMANY.*

FAUN (s/l *fawn*). Rom eq of Gk *SATYR.*

FAUNUS Rom *god* of *herds*; s of Picus. Also INUUS, LUPERCUS. **Gk** = *PAN.*

FAVONIUS Rom myth WEST *WIND* (**Gk** = ZEPHYRUS).

FAVOUR BOON, *GRACE*, KINDNESS. PREFER. BUTTONHOLE, ROSETTE.

FAVOURITE PET, PREFERRED (**opp** = bête noire). MISTRESS.

FAWN (s/l *faun*). CRINGE, GROVEL; LICK-SPITTLE, TOADY, SYCOPHANT. *COLOUR* (PALE BROWN). *OFFSPRING* (DEER).

FBI *DETECTIVES*, FEDS, G-MEN.

FDR ROOSEVELT. WEST GERMANY.

FE *IRON* (*chem*). *SMITH* (Lord Birkenhead).

FEAR ALARM, APPREHENSION, *AVERSION*, DREAD, FRIGHT, PANIC, PHOBIA, SHRINK, TERROR. COWARDICE, FRIGHT, FUNK [yellow].

FEATHER 1. DOWN, PLUME, QUILL. 2. *Anniversary* (3rd).

FEATURE PORTRAY, *STAR*. LANDMARK. CHIN, EAR, EYE, MOUTH, NOSE etc.

FEBRUARY (2nd) MONTH, M, FEB (Lat februar = purification feast). **Birthstone** = *Amethyst.*

FED UP GORGED, SATED. BORED, BROWNED OFF, TIRED (**opp** = *enchanted*). DEF (dn; crypt).

FEET 1. Pl of *FOOT*; *MEASURE*. 2. Metric rhythm or scanning of verse; see *FOOT.*

FELL COLLAPSED, TRIPPED. AXE, CUT DOWN. HIDE, *SKIN. HILL*, MOUNTAIN. FIERCE, RUTHLESS.

FELLOW F. CHAP, COVE, DON, GENT, GUY, HE, MAN. CO-, PEER.

~ TRAVELLER COMMIE, RED. BACK-SEAT DRIVER, CREW MEMBER, OBSERVER (av), NAVIGATOR (av), PILLION PASSENGER.

FEMALE FEMININE, (CHILD)BEARER. GIRL, WOMAN. For animal genders, see *Male and Female.*

FEMININE F. FEMALE, WOMANLY.

FENCE BANK, BULWARK, ENCLOSE, FORTIFY, HEDGE,

PALISADE, PROTECT, RAILING, SCREEN, SHIELD, WALL. GAUGE, GUARD, GUIDE (mech). RECEIVER [*robber*]. PARRY, WORD PLAY. SWORDPLAY [lunge, parry, riposte; prime, seconde, tierce, quart, quinte, sixte, septime, octave].

FENCER DUELLIST, SWORDSMAN. STEEPLECHASER (crypt). BOUNDARY LAYER, FRONTIERSMAN (crypt).

FERRET SCOUT-CAR (mil). HUNT, SEARCH (hence DETECTIVE). *WEASEL* (fem = gill).

FERRY CONVEY, CROSS, TRANSPORT. TENDER, WORKBOAT. [*Acheron, Anubis, Charon, Lethe, Styx*].

FERTILITY 1. ABUNDANCE, FECUNDITY, FRUITFULNESS. 2. **Gods: Gk** = *DIONYSUS*, HYMEN; **Rom** = *BACCHUS*, GENIUS, LIBER; **Egy** = OSIRIS; **Ind** = KRISHNA; **Nor** = *FREY*. **Goddesses: Gk** = CYBELE, *DANAE*, RHEA; **Rom** = *CERES, DIANA*, OPS; FRIGG (**Nor**); BELIT, INNIN, ISHTAR (**Bab**); ATERGATIS (**Syrian**); EOSTRE (**A-Sax**; easter).

FF FOLIOS, PAGES. FORTISSIMO, VERY LOUD.

FIDDLE BOW, PLAY, SCRAPE, VIOLIN. FIDGET. ARRANGE, *CHEAT*, COOK, FIX, MANIPULATE.

FIDO *DOG*. Acronym (Fog Investigation Dispersal Operation, av).

FIELDING CAMPAIGNING. GRAZING, PLOUGHING (crypt). *WRITER*. AREA, PANORAMA, SPHERE. BOWLING, NOT IN (*cricket*). [Bow Street *Policeman*].

FIELDSMAN CATCHER, *CRICKETER*; OUTSIDER (crypt). [MCC]. FARMER, SHEPHERD (crypt). GATHERER. SCARECROW (crypt).

FIFTEEN See *number*. XV, SIDE, TEAM [rugby].

FIFTH 1. AMENDMENT. *DRINK, MEASURE*. VTH. G (Mus). 2. Beethoven's ∼ = H (crypt).

∼ **MAN** GUY FAWKES (crypt) [Robert Catesby, Thomas Percy, Gunpowder Plot].

FIFTY See *number*. *L*. HALF TON.

FIGHT *BATTLE*, COMBAT, DING DONG, QUARREL, SCRAP, SCRIMMAGE, SET-TO, WAR (**saying**).

FIGHTER COMBATANT, WARRIOR. *AIRCRAFT*; *WEAPON*. *BOXER*, PUGILIST.

FIGURE THINK, WORK OUT. INTEGER. CONE,
TRIANGLE etc. APPEAR, FEATURE. *FORM*, LINE,
SHAPE [vital statistics]. PERSON. DIAGRAM, DRAWING,
ILLUSTRATION; IMAGE LIKENESS, REPRESENTATION.
EMBLEM, SIMILE, TYPE.

FILLING REPLENISHMENT, TOP-UP. APPLE, FRUIT, JAM,
MINCE, PUREE etc (cook). STOPPING (dental).
SATISFYING. OCCUPYING.

FILM COATING, *LAYER*, MEMBRANE, PLATE, SKIN.
MOVIE; *SHOOT*. CASSETTE, REEL (photo). **Pl** =
CINEMA, FLICKS.

~ **CATEGORY** A, AA, G (US), H, PG, R, U, X [*censorship*].

~ **PART** REEL. ROLE, STAR. FI, FIL, ILM etc (crypt).

FIN FINLAND. FRENCH FINISH (crypt).

FINAL 1. *LAST*, ULTIMATE, Z, OMEGA. CONCLUSIVE,
DEFINITE. LATEST EDITION/NEWS. **Pl** = LAST EXAMS,
DECIDER (games). 2. Use last letter of word indicated, e.g.
Final destination = N; **Your final . . .** = R.

FINALE 1. CONCLUSION, *END*, ENDING. 2. Add letter E at
end of word indicated, e.g. **Artist finale** (7) = ARTISTE.

FINCH BIRD (**assembly** = *charm*).

FINISH (s/l Finnish). 1. CEASE, COMPLETE, *END* (**opp** =
start). ANNIHILATE, DESTROY, DISPATCH, KILL,
OVERCOME. PERFECT; POLISH, SHEEN. 2. Last letter(s)
of word, e.g. **Quick finish** = K.

FIRE 1. BLAZE, BRAND, FLAME, INFERNO (**saying**).
LIGHT. BOOT, *DISCHARGE*, DISMISS, SACK. SHOOT.
BAKE, GLAZE. 2. **Gods: Gk** = HEPHAESTUS; **Rom** =
VULCAN; **Nor** = *LOKI*.

FIREMAN ARSONIST, BLAZER. EXTINGUISHER.
GUNNER, MARKSMAN, RA, SNIPER [*patron saint*].
FOOTPLATE-MAN (**Union** = ASLEF, NUR).

FIRE-RAISER ARSONIST. MATCH. ERIF (dn; crypt).

FIREWORK *BANGER*, ROCKET, SQUIB, WHIZZBANG;
Pl = *ROW*, RUCTION. CHARCOAL BURNING (crypt).
GUNNERY (crypt).

FIRM COMPACT, FIXED, RIGID, *SET*, SOLID, *SOUND*,
STABLE, *STAUNCH*, STEADY. BUSINESS, CO, LTD, PLC,
WORKS. SIGNATURE, STYLE. CONSTANT, RESOLUTE,

STEADFAST, UNFLINCHING. 'CONSTANTINE'.

FIRST 1. A, I, IST, NO I. ALPHA, BEFORE(HAND). EARLIEST, FOREMOST, LEADING, PRIME, PRIMUS, TOP, WINNER. GOLD MEDALLIST. 2. Use first letters of word(s) indicated, e.g. **First-aid man** = AM; **First of all prehensiles everywhere** (3) = APE. 3. Put letter or word in front, e.g. **Try at first to give evidence** (6) = AT*TEST.

~ **BORN** B. CAIN. ELDEST [Herod].

~ **CLASS** C. AI. KINDERGARTEN, NURSERY SCHOOL (crypt).

~ **FALLER** F. *ADAM*.

~ **ISSUE** I. CAIN. ELDEST.

~ **LADY** L. EVE. PRESIDENT'S WIFE (US). *PANDORA*.

~ **OFFENDER** EVE.

~ **OF MONTH** M. J, JAN, JANI; F, FEB, FEBI etc.

~ **PERSON** P. *ADAM*. I, WE.

FISH 1. LOOK FOR (compliment). JOIN/MEND A SPAR (naut). 2. ANGLE, CATCH; TRAWL, TROLL. COLD-BLOODED MARINE ANIMAL; BOMBAY DUCK; **assembly** = school, shoal; **offspring** = fry; **types:**

2-letters	4-letters	ESOX
ID	AMIA	FAAP
	BASS	GEDD
3-letters	BIRT	GOBY
BIB	BLAY	HUSS
COD	BLEY	KELT
DAB	BRET	KETA
DAR	BRIT	LING
DOG	BURT	LIPP
EEL	BUTT	LOMP
EFY	*CARP*	LUCE
GAR	CHAD	LUMP
GED	CHAR	OPAH
IDE	CHUB	(ORCA)
(ORC)	CLAM	ORFE
RAY	CUSK	PARR
TAI	DACE	*PIKE*
	DORY	*POUT*

RUDD
RUFF
SCUP
SEER
SHAD
SOLE
TOPE
TUNA

5-letters
ABLEN
ABLET
ALLIS
ALOSE
ANGEL
ASKER
BANNY
BASSE
BERYX
BINNY
BLEAK
BLECK
(BOOPS)
BREAM
BRILL
CAPON
CHARR
CISCO
CNIDA
COLEY
DOREE
DORSE
ELOPS
ELVER
FLECK
GIBEL
GUPPY
JULIS
KNOUD

LOACH
LOCHE
LOGGE
LYTHE
MANTA
MARAY
MORAY
MUGIL
MURAY
MURRY
MYXON
POGGE
PERCH
PORGY
PRAWN
PRILL
QUARL
ROACH
ROKER
SARDA
SAURY
SCROD
SEPIA
SEWEN
SEWIN
SHARK
SKATE
SKEET
SMELT
SMOLT
SMOUT
SNOEK
SNOOK
SOLEN
SPRAG
SPRAT
SPROD
SQUID
SUDAK

SWORD
TENCH
TOGUE
TORSK
TROUT
TUNNY
TWAIT
UMBRE
(*WHALE*)

6-letters
ACEDIA
ALEVIN
ALLICE
ANABAS
BAGGIT
BARBEL
BELONE
BELUGA
BLENNY
BONITO
BOUNCE
BOWFIN
BRAIZE
BRASSE
BUCKIE
BURBOT
CAPLIN
CARANX
CARVEL
CEPOLA
CLIONE
CLUPEA
COCKLE
CONGER
CUTTLE
CYPRIS
DENTEX
DERBIO

DIODON	(NARWAL)	SEA-CAT
DIPNOI	NERITE	SEA-COW
DOCTOR	OSTREA	SEA-DOG
DORADO	*OYSTER*	SEA-EEL
(DUGONG)	PARTAN	SEA-EGG
ELLECK	PECTEN	SEA-FOX
FINNAN	PETREL	SEA-HOG
FINNER	PHINOC	SEA-ORB
FINNOC	PHOLAS	SEA-OWL
GARDON	PLAICE	SEA-PAD
GERVIE	PLAISE	SEA-PIG
GILPIN	POLLAN	SEA-RAT
GORAMY	PORGIE	SEPHEN
GRILSE	POULPE	SHANNY
GUNNEL	PUFFER	SHIPOV
GURNET	RED-EYE	SHRIMP
HALION	REMORA	SILURE
HAUTIN	RIGGLE	SNACOT
HILSAH	ROBALO	SOOSOO
INKBAG	ROCCUS	*SUCKER*
INKSAC	ROCHET	TAMBOR
IVIGAR	ROMERO	TARPON
KIPPER	RUFFIN	TARPUM
LAITHE	SABALO	TAUTOG
LAUNCE	SADINA	TINKER
LIMPET	SAITHE	TITLER
LOLIGO	*SALMON*	TOMCOD
MAHSIR	SALTIE	TOMPOT
MARGOT	SAMLET	TRITON
MATIES	SARDEL	TRYGON
MEAKER	SARGUS	TURBOT
MEDUSA	SARSIA	(TURTLE)
MENNAD	SAUGER	TWAITE
MILTER	SAUREL	URCHIN
MINNOW	SAURUS	(WALRUS)
MORGAY	SAYSAY	WAPPER
MULLET	SCARUS	WEEVER
MUSSEL	SEA-BAT	WINKLE
MYXINE	SEA-BUN	WRASSE

ZANDER
ZINGLE

7-letters
ACALEPH
ACTINIA
ALE-WIFE
ANCHOVY
ANEMONE
ANODONT
ASCIDIA
ASTERID
BARNAGH
BERGYLT
BIVALVE
BLOATER
BOCKING
BONETTA
BRASSIE
BRIABOT
CALAMAR
CAPELIN
CATFISH
(CETACEA)
CICHLID
CIDARIS
CODFISH
CODLING
CROAKER
CROWGER
CRUCIAN
CRUSIAN
(DOLPHIN)
ECHINUS
ETHERIA
FINBACK
FINFISH
FINNACK
FINNOCK

GARFISH
GARPIKE
GARVOCK
GIRROCK
GLADIUS
GALUCUS
GOSNICK
GOURAMI
GOURNET
(GRAMPUS)
GRUNDEL
GRUNTER
GUDGEON
GURNARD
GWINIAD
HADDOCK
HAGFISH
HALIBUT
HERLING
HERRING
KEELING
LAMPERN
LAMPREY
LOBSTER
MAHSEER
(MANATEE)
MEDUSA
MERLING
MOLLUSC
MONODON
MOONEYE
MORRHUA
MUDFISH
(NARWHAL)
NAUTILI
OARFISH
OCTOPUS
OPHIURA
PATELLA

PEGASUS
PELAMID
PENFISH
PETEREL
PIDDOCK
PILTOCK
PINCHER
PIN-FISH
POLLACK
POLLOCK
POLYPUS
POLYZOA
POMFRET
QUAHAUG
QUINNAT
RED-BASS
RED-DRUM
RED-FISH
RHYTINA
RIPSACK
RONCHIL
RONQUIL
(RORQUAL)
ROTCHET
SAND-DAB
SAND-EEL
SARDINE
SARGINA
SAWFISH
SCALLOP
SCHELLY
SCOLLOP
SCOMBER
SEA-BASS
SEA-COCK
SEA-DACE
SEA-FISH
SEA-LILY
SEA-LUCE

SEA-MINK	XIPHIAS	LUNGFISH
SEA-PERT	ZIPHIAS	MACKEREL
SEA-PIKE	ZYGAENA	MONKFISH
SEA-ROSE		NAUTILUS
SEA-RUFF	**8-letters**	PICKEREL
SEA-SLUG	ACALEPHA	PILCHARD
SEA-WIFE	ACEPHALA	(PORPOISE)
SEA-WOLF	ALBACORE	ROCKFISH
SELACHE	BILLFISH	SAIL-FISH
SERIOLA	BLUEFISH	SALMONET
SEVRUGA	BOARFISH	SANDFISH
SHADINE	BRISLING	SEA-ADDER
SHALLOW	BUMMALOE	SEA-BREAM
SILLAGO	(CACHALOT)	SEA-DEVIL
SILURUS	(CETACEAN)	SEA-PERCH
SKIPPER	COALFISH	SEA-ROBIN
SKULPIN	CRAYFISH	SEA-SHARK
SNAPPER	DRAGONET	SEA-SNAIL
SNEDDEN	EAR-SHELL	SEA-SQUID
SOCKEYE	ESCALLOP	SEA-TENCH
SPUR-DOG	(FIN-WHALE)	SEA-TROUT
STERLET	FLATFISH	SOLASTER
SUNFISH	*FLOUNDER*	SPARLING
TORPEDO	FORKTAIL	STARFISH
TREPANG	FROGFISH	STINGRAY
TUBFISH	GILT-HEAD	STURGEON
VENDACE	GOLDFISH	THRASHER
VESTLET	GRAYLING	UNIVALVE
WHIP-RAY	(HUMPBACK)	ZOANTHUS
WHITING	LUMPFISH	

3. *Constellation* (Pisces); (12th) sign of *Zodiac*.

FIT HALE, IN FORM, *SOUND, WELL*. SEIZURE, SPASM. CORRESPOND, FILL UP, MATCH, RIGHT SIZE. ADAPT, COMPETENT, PROPER, RIGHT, SUITED. EQUIP, MEASURE, TRY ON (clothes).

FIVE 1. See *number*. PENTAD, V. BLUE BALL (snooker). *FAMOUS* ~. [*Holmes* case]. 2. *Symbols* at your *door* (*song*); golden *rings* (*Christmas* song). **Pl** = GAME.

~ **CLASSIC ORDERS** COMPOSITE, CORINTHIAN, DORIC, IONIC, TUSCAN.

500 See *number*. D.

£500 DL, LD, MONKEY.

FIVE TOWNS BURSLEM, FENTON, HANLEY, LONGTON, STOKE (potteries).

FIX DILEMMA, QUANDARY. ARRANGE, *FIDDLE*, JOIN. BOLT, FASTEN, *NAIL*, *SCREW*, SECURE. *DRUG*, INJECTION, SHOT. ESTABLISH POSITION (naut); DETERMINE, SPECIFY.

FLAG BUNTING, ENSIGN, FLIER, PENNANT, STANDARD. PIN. *IRIS*, *PLANT*. DROOP, FADE, FAIL, FALTER. (PAVING) STONE. QUILL FEATHER.

FLAK AA. CRITICISM.

FLAPPER YOUNG THING. FIN, FLIPPER. BIRD. PANICKER.

FLAT APARTMENT, PENTHOUSE. EVEN, LEVEL, SMOOTH. RUN DOWN, UNCHARGED (elect). PUNCTURE (US).

FLATTER BUTTER UP, FAWN, PRAISE. BECOME, SUIT. MORE EVEN, SMOOTHER, IRONER, LAUNDRYMAID (crypt).

FLEET *FAST*, QUICK, RAPID. RN, SHIPS, USN, TASK FORCE. *GAOL*. ISLAND, *RIVER*. [~ Street].

FLIER *FLAG*. AVIATOR, PILOT. *BIRD*. *DAEDALUS*, *ICARUS*.

FLIGHT 1. STAIRS, *STEPS*. ARROW. ESCAPE, EVASION. FLYING, TRAJECTORY. FLOCK. VOLLEY. 2. *Assembly* (*ducks*).

FLOCK 1. WOOL, TUFT. CONGREGATION, *FOLD*. TROOP. 2. *Assembly* (*geese*, *sheep*).

FLORA 1. *FLOWERS*, *PLANTS* [fauna]. ~ MACDONALD [Bonnie Prince Charlie]. 2. Rom *goddess* of *FLOWERS* (Gk = CHLORIS). 3. A minor *PLANET*.

FLORENCE *NIGHTINGALE*. FIRENZE (old *capital* city of Italy in Tuscany).

FLOUNDERING *Anag.* WALLOWING. FISHING (crypt).

FLOW CIRCULATE, GLIDE, MOVE(MENT) [fluent, smoothly]. GUSH, *RUN*, SPRING, WELL UP. STREAM.

RISE (tide). UNDULATE (dress, figure). BELLY, CAMBER, DRAFT (sails).

FLOWER 1. CHOICE, CREAM, ESSENCE, PICK. CURRENT, *RIVER* (q.v.), SPRING, TIDE, WELL (all crypt). BLOOD (crypt). ICHOR (crypt). 2. ANNUAL, *BLOOMER*, PERENNIAL. **Pl** = BOUQUET, BUNCH, NOSEGAY, GARLAND, LEI, SPRAY; **goddess: Gk** = CHLORIS, **Rom** = FLORA; **saying;** *anniversary* (4th). [Ikebana (*Jap*)]. **Types:**

3-letters	PEONY	NERINE
LIS (herald)	PHLOX	NERIUM
MAY	POPPY	NUPHAR
	STOCK	ORCHID
4-letters	TULIP	ROSULA
ARUM	VINCA	SCILLA
DISA	YUCCA	SHASTA
FAAM	YULAN	SQUILL
FLAG		TAGETE
FLAX	6-letters	THRIFT
IRIS	*ADONIS*	VIOLET
LILY	AZALEA	YARROW
MUSK	BELLIS	ZINNIA
PINK	BIZARD	
ROSE	BOODLE	7-letters
	CALTHA	ACONITE
5-letters	CAMASS	ALTHAEA
ASPIC	CISTUS	ANEMONE
ASTER	CLOVER	BANKSIA
BRIAR	CROCUS	BEGONIA
CALLA	CYPHEL	CAMPION
DAISY	DAHLIA	CUP-ROSE
DILLY	FUNKIA	DOG-ROSE
GOWAN	JASMIN	FREESIA
LILAC	KERRIA	FUCHSIA
LOTUS	KOWHAI	GLADWYN
LUPIN	MARIET	GODETIA
OX-EYE	MIMOSA	HONESTY
OXLIP	MOUTAN	JASMINE
PANSY	MUGGET	JONQUIL

KINGCUP
LOBELIA
NELUMBO
NIGELLA
PETUNIA
PICOTEE
PRIMULA
RAMBLER
SERINGA
SHIRLEY
SYRINGA
TEA-ROSE
TRIPOLY
TRITOMA
VANILLA
VERBENA

8-letters
AGRIMONY
AMARANTH
ASPHODEL
AURICULA
BLUEBELL
BUDDLEIA
CAMELLIA
CLEMATIS
CYCLAMEN
DAFFODIL
DIANTHUS
DOG-BRIER

FOXGLOVE
GERANIUM
GILLENIA
GIRASOLE
GLOXINIA
GOLD-LILY
HAREBELL
HAWTHORN
HIBISCUS
HOTTONIA
HYACINTH
JAPONICA
LARKSPUR
LAVENDER
LENT-LILY
MAGNOLIA
MARIGOLD
MYOSOTIS
NOISETTE
PLUMBAGO
PRIMROSE
SNOWDROP
SWEET-PEA
TUBEROSE
TURNSOLE
WISTARIA
WOODBINE

9-letters
BUSY LIZZY

CAMPANULA
CANDYTUFT
CARNATION
DANDELION
GOLDENROD
HYDRANGEA
NARCISSUS
SPEEDWELL

10+ letters
ANTIRRHINUM
BUSY LIZZIE
CANTERBURY BELL
CHRYSANTHEMUM
CORNFLOWER
DELPHINIUM
FRANGIPANI
GUERNSEY LILY
GYPSOPHILA
LADY'S MANTLE
LOVE IN A MIST
FORGET ME NOT
MORNING GLORY
NASTURTIUM
RED HOT POKER
RHODODENDRON
SNAPDRAGON
STEPHANOTIS
SWEET WILLIAM
WALLFLOWER

FLUORINE F (*chem*) [halogen].

FLUSH BLUSH, *COLOUR*, REDDEN. POKER HAND;
SUITED (crypt). RICH, WELL OFF. PUT UP (game bird).
Assembly (mallards). *DOG* (celebrated).

FLUTER PHIL; INSTRUMENTALIST, WHISTLER. REBATE
PLANE.

FLY DESERT, FLEE, RUN AWAY, TURN TAIL. AVIATE,
PILOT; SCRAMBLE (code word). *INSECT*. AWARE,

KNOWING. *BOAT*. *CARRIAGE*.

FLYING BOMB BUZZBOMB, DOODLEBUG, DIVER (code name), *ROCKET*, VI.

FLYING FORTRESS *AIRCRAFT* (bomber), B17, BXVII, BOEING: CASTLE IN THE AIR (crypt).

FO FOLIO. FOREIGN OFFICE. BACK OF (crypt, e.g. **Back of Whitehall = FO**).

FOC ADMIRAL, FLAG OFFICER COMMANDING.

FOG BRUME, FRET, HAZE, MIST [FIDO]. CLOUD (photo). BEWILDER, OBFUSCATE, PERPLEX. AFTERMATH, LONG WINTER *GRASS*.

FOLD (s/l foaled). ENCLOSE, *PEN*, POUND. CHURCH, CONGREGATION, *FLOCK*. BEND, *CONCERTINA*, *DOUBLE*. CLASP, EMBRACE, ENVELOP, *WIND*.

FOLLOWER 1. *DISCIPLE*, FAN, SUPPORTER; ADHERENT. 2. Next letter in alphabet, e.g. **A follower = B**; **Paul's last follower = M**.

FOOD BOARD, COMMONS, EDIBLES, FARE, GRUB, KEEP, MEALS, MESS, NOURISHMENT, NUTRIMENT, PROVISIONS, RATIONS, SCOFF, *TABLE*, VICTUALS. **Saying.**

FOOL ASS, BUFFOON, CLOT, DUPE, GOOSE, IDIOT, TWIT (**saying; opp** = *expert*). CLOWN, *JESTER*. 0 (*tarot*). DECEIVE. PLAY, TINKER. FRUIT CRUSH, PUDDING, SWEET. TRINCULO (*Shak*).

FOOT 1. DISTANCE, *MEASURE*, 12 INCHES. *DANCE*, PACE, *STEP* (**saying**), TREAD. *BASE*, BOTTOM, PEDESTAL, ROOT. LIMB, MEMBER (*bone*). LEGEND (crypt). UNDERSTANDING (crypt). 2. Stress on syllable in metre of a verse: ANAPEST ($\cdot\cdot$—), CHORIAMB (—$\cdot\cdot$—), DACTYL (—$\cdot\cdot$), IAMBUS ($\cdot$—), MOLUSSUS (— — —), SPONDEE (— —), TRIBRACH ($\cdot\cdot\cdot$), TROCHEE (—$\cdot$).

FOOTBALL BALL GAME; AMERICAN ~, ASSOCIATION ~, RUGBY ~, RUGGER, SOCCER [FA, FIFA, UEFA, World Cup (Rimet Trophy); League, Rugby ~]. **Celebrated teams (US):**

Home	Name
Atlanta	FALCONS
Baltimore	*COLTS*

Buffalo	*BILLS*
Chicago	*BEARS*
Cincinnati	BENGALS
Cleveland	*BROWNS*
Dallas	*COWBOYS*
Denver	BRONCOS
Detroit	*LIONS*
Green Bay	PACKERS
Houston	*OILERS*
Kansas City	CHIEFS
Los Angeles	RAIDERS
Los Angeles	*RAMS*
Miami	DOLPHINS
Minnesota	VIKINGS
New England	PATRIOTS
New Orleans	*SAINTS*
New York	GIANTS
New York	JETS
Philadelphia	*EAGLES*
Pittsburgh	STEELERS
St Louis	CARDINALS
San Diego	CHARGERS
San Francisco	49-ERS
Seattle	SEAHAWKS
Washington	*REDSKINS*

competition: Superbowl; **venue:** Rose Bowl

Celebrated teams (UK)

Team	Nickname	Ground
Aberdeen	*Dons*	Pittodrie Park
Arsenal	*Gunners*	Highbury
Bournemouth	Cherries	Dean Court
Brighton	Seagulls	Goldstone
Bristol City	*Robins*	Ashton Gate
Cardiff City	Bluebirds	Ninian Park
Chelsea	*Pensioners*	Stamford Bridge
Coventry City	Sky Blues	Highfield Park
Crystal Palace	Glaziers	Selhurst Park
Derby County	*Rams*	Baseball Ground

England		Wembley
Everton	Toffees	Goodison Park
Glasgow Rangers	Light Blues	Ibrox Park
Huddersfield	*Terriers*	Leeds Road
Hull City	*Tigers*	Boothferry Park
Ireland		Lansdowne Road
Liverpool	*Reds*	Anfield
Manchester United	Red Devils	Old Trafford
Mansfield Town	*Stags*	Field Mill
Middlesbrough	Boro'	Ayresome Park
Northampton	*Cobblers*	County Ground
Norwich	Canaries	Carrow Road
Notts County	*Magpies*	Meadow Lane
Portsmouth	Pompey	Fratton Park
Scotland		Hampden Park
Sheffield Wednesday	*Owls*	Hillsborough
Southampton	*Saints*	The Dell
Torquay	*Gulls*	Plainmoor
Tottenham Hotspur	*Spurs*	White Hart Lane
Wales		Cardiff Arms Park
West Ham United	*Hammers*	Upton Park
Wolverhampton Wanderers	*Wolves*	Molineux

FOOTBALLER PLAYER; BACK, CENTRE-BACK, FORWARD, FULL-BACK, GOALIE, GOALKEEPER, HALF-BACK, INSIDE, KEEPER, OUTSIDE, STRIKER, SWEEPER, WINGER.

FOOTMAN BUTLER, *WAITER*. GI, INFANTRY, PBI (crypt). HIKER, PACER, RAMBLER, RUNNER, WALKER. TRIVET. *BUTTERFLY*.

FOOTWEAR BOOT, CLOG, GUMBOOT, GYMSHOE, MOCCASIN, MULE, PUMP, SABOT, SANDAL, SHOE, SLIPPER, SOCK, STOCKING, WELLINGTON BOOT.

FOR (s/l *fore, four*). FAVOURING, IN FAVOUR, PRO (**opp** = *con*). BECAUSE.

FORBIDDEN BANNED, BARRED, EXCLUDED,

PREVENTED. TABOO, TABU.

FORCE COERCE, CRAM, DRIVE, LEVER, PRISE, PROPEL,
PUSH, SHOVE. IMPOSE, *PRESS*. *POLICE*; TROOPS.
EFFORT, IMPETUS, POWER, STRENGTH, VIOLENCE;
DYNE, ERG (eng). COMPEL, RAVISH; CAPTURE,
OVERPOWER.

FORCED SEED HOTHOUSE PLANT. RAPE (crypt).

FORD WADE; CROSSING. *CAR*®, T. *GAOL*. *PRESIDENT*
(US).

FORE (s/l *for*, *four*). *BOW* (naut). FRONT. *CAVE*, (golf).

FOREGROUND FRONT, NEAR PLAN. *GOLF COURSE*
(crypt).

FOREIGN 1. ABROAD. STRANGE. 2. Translate, e.g. **He's
abroad** = IL (Fr), ER (Ger) etc.

~ **OFFICE** FO. BUREAU (crypt, Fr), AMT (crypt, Ger).

FOREST [Football team]. TREES, WOODLAND; TAIGA
(USSR) [**opp** = Savannah (tropics), Steppe (USSR), Tundra
(Arctic), *desert*, *plain*]; **celebrated (UK):**

2-letters	DREVA (Sc)	MINARD (Sc)
AE (Sc)	GAICK (Sc)	OGMORE (Wal)
	ORKEL (Sc)	*QUEENS* (Sc)
3-letters	SALEN (Sc)	RADNOR (Wal)
BIN (Sc)	STRUY (Sc)	RHEOLA (Wal)
MOY (Sc)		SALCEY (Eng)
NEW (Eng)	6-letters	
	ACHRAY (Sc)	7-letters
4-letters	ATHOLL (Sc)	ARDROSS (Sc)
AMAT (Sc)	ATTRIC (Sc)	ASHDOWN (Eng)
BERE (Eng)	BORGIE (Sc)	BENMORE (Sc)
DEAN (Eng)	CLUNES (Sc)	BOWLAND (Sc)
PLYM (Eng)	COULIN (Sc)	BOWMONT (Sc)
TOWY (Wal)	CULBIN (Sc)	CARRICK (Sc)
WARK (Eng)	EPPING (Eng)	CHANGUE (Sc)
WYRE (Eng)	FINDON (Sc)	CRYCHAN (Wal)
	LAGGAN (Sc)	CULACHY (Sc)
5-letters	LENNOX (Sc)	DEVILLA (Sc)
ARDEN (Eng)	LOSSIE (Sc)	EREDINE (Sc)
CRAIK (Sc)	MIDMAR (Sc)	FIUNARY (Sc)

GLENGAP (Sc)
GLEN LOY (Sc)
HARWOOD (Eng)
KIELDER (Eng)
LOCH ARD (Sc)
.LOCH ECK (Sc)
LYMINGE (Eng)
MAMLORN (Sc)
MILBURN (Eng)
NEWTYLE (Sc)
ROSARIE (Sc)
SKIDDAW (Eng)
TRAWDEN (Eng)
WAREHAM (Eng)
WINDSOR (Eng)

8-letters
ATTADALE (Sc)
BALMORAL (Sc)
BEINNEUN (Sc)
BEN DAMPH (Sc)
BOBLAINY (Sc)
BORROBOL (Sc)
BRAEMORE (Sc)
DUNLOINN (Sc)
CALLODEN (Sc)
CARDRONA (Sc)
DELAMERE (Eng)
DUNDEUGH (Sc)
ERCHLESS (Sc)
FEARNOCH (Sc)
GLENISLA (Sc)
HAREWOOD (Eng)
KERSHOPE (Eng)
KINFAUNS (Sc)
KNAPDALE (Sc)
LEITHOPE (Sc)
MORANGIE (Sc)
NEEDWOOD (Eng)

QUANTOCK (Eng)
RINGWOOD (Eng)
ROTHBURY (Eng)
ST GWYNNO (Wal)
SHERWOOD (Eng)
SHOTOVER (Eng)
TORRIDON (Sc)
TUNSTALL (Eng)
WAUCHOPE (Sc)
WYCHWOOD (Eng)
YAIR HILL (Sc)

9-letters
ABERNETHY (Sc)
ALICE HOLT (Eng)
BEDGEBURY (Eng)
BLAIRADAM (Sc)
CLOCAENOG (Wal)
CORLARACH (Sc)
EAST MONAR (Sc)
FASNAKYLE (Sc)
GLENCOICH (Sc)
GLENDEVON (Sc)
GLENDUROR (Sc)
GLENGARRY (Sc)
GLENLIVET (Sc)
GLENTRESS (Sc)
GLENTROOL (Sc)
GRISEDALE (Eng)
GUISACHAN (Sc)
INVERINEN (Sc)
INVERTAEL (Sc)
INVERWICK (Sc)
LAURISTON (Sc)
LEANACHAN (Sc)
LETTEREWE (Sc)
MONAUGHTY (Sc)
PARKHURST (IofW)
PITFICHIE (Sc)

PORTCLAIR (Sc)
REDESDALE (Eng)
SAVERNAKE (Eng)
SCOOTMORE (Sc)
SPEYMOUTH (Sc)
STRATHYRE (Sc)
TEINDLAND (Sc)
TENTSMUIR (Sc)

10+ letters
ACHAGLACHGACH (Sc)
APPLECROSS (Sc)
BALLOCHBUIE (Sc)
BARCALDINE (Sc)
BRIGHTSTONE (IofW)
CAIRN EDWARD (Sc)
CARRON VALLEY (Sc)
CAENNACROC (Sc)
CLASHINDARROCH (Sc)
COIGNAFEARN (Sc)
COIRRIEYAIRACK (Sc)
CORRIEHALLIE (Sc)
DAILNAMAIN (Sc)
DALBEATTIE (Sc)
DRUMTOCHTY (Sc)
DUNDREGGAN (Sc)

FETTERESSO (Sc)
FISHERFIELD (Sc)
GLAS FYNYDD (Wal)
GLENARTNEY (Sc)
GLENBRANTER (Sc)
GLENCARRON (Sc)
GLENFESHIE (Sc)
HAMSTERLEY (Eng)
INVERMONSTON (Sc)
KILDERMOIRE (Sc)
KILMICHAEL (Sc)
MICHELDEVER (Eng)
MONTREATHMONT (Sc)
PENNINGHAME (Sc)
RENDLESHAM (Eng)
RHIDORROCH (Sc)
ROCKINGHAM (Eng)
ROSSENDALE (Eng)
ROWARDENNAN (Sc)
ST LEONARDS (Eng)
STRATHCONON (Sc)
STRATHDEARN (Sc)
STRATHLACHLAN (Sc)
STRATHNAIRN (Sc)
TOLLOMUICK (Sc)
WHITEHAUGH (Sc)

FOR EXAMPLE 1. EG, (FOR) INSTANCE, SAY. 2. Shows word
starting IM (I am), e.g. **Bristol for example** (6) = IM*PORT.
3. Answer describes word indicated, e.g. **I, for example,
accumulated wealth** (7) = CAPITAL.
FORFEND AVERT, KEEP OFF.
FORGER COPIER, COUNTERFEITER, FABRICATOR,
INVENTOR; COMPEYSON (Great Expectations, *Dickens*).
BLACKSMITH, *SMITH* (crypt). ADVANCER,
PROGRESSER (crypt).
FORGET 1. NEGLECT, OMIT: DISREGARD, SLIGHT
(**saying**). 2. Omit letter(s) indicated, e.g. **Don't forget the duck** =
D*NT.

FOR INSTANCE 1. EG, FOR EXAMPLE, SAY. 2. Shows word starting IM (I am), e.g. **Rose, for instance** (7) = IM*PLANT.

FORM BENCH. CONDITION, *FIGURE*, SCHEDULE. *CLASS*. *CAST*, MOULD, *PATTERN*, *SHAPE*. TRACK RECORD. *Habitation* (hare).

FORMER 1. ERSTWHILE, *EX*, *LATE*, OLD. CASTER, MOULDER, POTTER (crypt). PUPIL, SCHOOLBOY/GIRL (crypt). 2. Indicates use of old-fashioned word(s), e.g. **The former** (2) = YE; **was formerly** (4) = WERT.

FORM OF *Anag*.

FORTE (s/l *forty*). F, LOUD. SWORD BLADE, STRONG POINT. RESTAURANT®, SERVICE STATION®.

FORTH (s/l fourth). INTO VIEW, OUT; FORWARD. *RIVER* (Sc).

FORTISSIMO FF, VERY LOUD; NOISY (**opp** = pianissimo, *piano*).

FORTUNE 1. CHANCE, DESTINY, LUCK [*tarot*]. PROSPERITY, RICHES, WEALTH. HAP, HAPPEN, OCCUR. 2. **Goddesses: Gk** = TYCHE, **Rom** = FORTUNA.

FORTY (s/l *forte*). See *number*. XL. *TOPS* (darts). L (crypt; life begins at ~).

FORWARD ADVANCED, AHEAD, ON. PERT, PRECOCIOUS. PROMOTE. CENTRE, INSIDE, OUTSIDE, STRIKER (*football*, hockey). **Pl** = SCRUM (rugby).

FOUL (s/l *fowl*). CONTRAVENTION, ERROR, FAULT, INFRINGEMENT. BAD, EVIL, LOATHSOME, STINKING.

FOUND DISCLOSED, DISCOVERED, REVEALED. ESTABLISH, ORIGINATE, SET UP. *CAST*, FUSE, MELT, MOULD.

FOUNDATION *AUC*, ESTABLISHMENT. BASE, GROUND, PRINCIPLE. [corset]. **Pl** = BASE, UNDERPINNING (archit).

FOUR (s/l *for*, fore). 1. See *number*. IV, QUARTET, TETRAD. BOUNDARY (*cricket*). BROWN BALL (snooker). TEAM (horses, card players). POMPEY (*rh sl*). **Pl** = RACE (rowing). GLOVES, SHOES (size). 2. *Gospel*-makers (*song*); calling birds (*Christmas* song). [*Holmes* case].

~ **POINT** IVE, IVS etc (crypt). NEWS (crypt). SQUARE.

FOURTH (s/l *forth*). QUARTER, QUARTUS. TOP (mech gear). F, HARMONIC, INTERVAL (mus).

INDEPENDENCE DAY (US).

~ **ESTATE** THE PRESS.

~ **MAN** SETH.

FOX DISSEMBLE, FOOL, OUTWIT. FUR. *AMERICAN INDIAN*. QUADRUPED; FENNEC, REYNARD, RUSSEL, VOLPONE (Ben Jonson); **assembly** = skulk; **habitation** = *earth*; **male** = dog; **female** = vixen; **offspring** = cub [cunning; uneatable (Wilde)]. **Celebrated:** BASIL BRUSH (TV), BRER ~ (Uncle Remus, Tar-baby; Harris), CHARLES JAMES ~ (polit), GEORGE ~ (*Quakers*).

FR FATHER. FRANCE, FRENCH [*patron saint*]. **Pl** = Fellow of the Royal Society; SAVANT.

FRANCISCAN *GREYFRIAR*; MENDICANT FRIAR. CAPUCHIN.

FRANK (s/l franc). 1. CANDID, *FREE*, OPEN, OVERT. CANCEL, STAMP. *BIRD*. *COIN*. 2. Free men of lower Rhine, who warred with the Romans and settled in Gaul under Clovis in A.D. 496.

FRATERNITY BROTHERHOOD, ASSOCIATION; **celebrated:** BUFFALOES (RAOB), FREEMASONS, ODDFELLOWS, ROUND TABLE.

FREE FOR NOTHING, GRATIS, UNCHARGED. ENLARGE, LIBERATE, RID; LIBERAL, LOOSE (**opp** = *limited*). *FRANK*, OPEN. UNOCCUPIED, VACANT (**opp** = *engaged*). 'FRANCIS'.

FRENCH 1. F, FR. DRINK, VERMOUTH. 2. Translate, e.g. **A (or the) French . . .** = UN/UNE or LA/LE/LES.

~ **MAN** M, MONS.

~ **ONE** UN, UNE.

~ **REVOLUTIONARY CALENDAR** Revised calendar of France, 1789. Months (with starting dates) were:

VENDEMIAIRE (22 Sept)	GERMINAL (21 Mar)
BRUMAIRE (22 Oct)	FLOREAL (20 Apr)
FRIMAIRE (21 Nov)	PRAIRIAL (20 May)
NIVOSE (21 Dec)	MESSIDOR (19 June)
PLUVIOSE (20 Jan)	THERMIDOR (19 Jul)
VENTOSE (19 Feb)	FRUCTIDOR (18 Aug)

FRESH *Anag.* *NEW*; *GREEN*, YOUNG (**opp** = old, stale).
CHEEKY, FORWARD, IMPERTINENT.

FRESHER NEWER, MORE FORWARD. COLLEGE
STUDENT (1st year), UNDERGRADUATE.

FRESH START CARTE BLANCHE, CLEAN SHEET. TARTS,
RATTS (crypt, *anag*).

FRET ADORN, CHEQUER, PATTERN (saw). CHAFE,
CONSUME, CORRODE, GNAW, RUST. ANNOY,
DISTRESS, IMPATIENCE, IRRITATE, RUFFLE, WORRY.
SEA-MIST. BAR, RIDGE (mus).

FREY(R) Nor *god* of fertility and sunshine; br of *Freya*; k when he
gave away his magic sword to win the love of Gerda.

FREYA Norse *goddess* of love. Second wife of *Odin* and sis of *Frey*;
travelled in chariot drawn by two cats. Received the souls of those
slain in battle. Her prized possession was the necklace
Brisingamen, guarded by Heimdal, *watchman* of the gods.

FRIAR (s/l fryer). *FATHER*, RC MENDICANT, *Chaucer*
character. AUGUSTINIAN (Austin Friar, *hermit*),
CARMELITE (White Friar), DOMINICAN (Blackfriar, Friars
Major), FRANCISCAN (Capuchin, *Greyfriar*, Friars Minor)
[Trinity/Red Friar and Crutched/Crossed Friar = Canons
Regular. Monks are not friars].

FRIDAY 1. F. MAN ~ (Robinson Crusoe). 2. Day of *Frigg*. ~'s
child = loving & giving. [Solomon *Grundy*].

FRIEND ALLY, *COMPANION*, MATE, OPPO (sl), PAL (**opp** =
foe); **saying**. *QUAKER*.

FRIEZE (s/l frees, freeze). RELIEF WORK (sculpture). CLOTH.

FRIGG(A) 1. Nor *goddess* of fertility; mar *Odin*, m of *Balder*
[*Friday*]. 2. A minor *PLANET*.

FRINGE BORDER, EDGE, SURROUND. *BANG*,
HAIRSTYLE.

FROG BUTTONING. SWORD STRAP. FASTENING (rly).
FRENCHMAN (sl). HORN (horse's foot). AMPHIBIAN,
ANGLER ~, ANOURA, PADDOCK (*offspring*). TOAD;
JUMPER (crypt). **Celebrated:** JEREMY FISHER (Beatrix
Potter), KERMIT (TV), MOWGLI (Jungle Book), TOAD (~ of
Toad Hall; *Grahame*).

FROM 1. EX, OUT OF. ORIGIN, STARTING POINT.
2. Hidden word, e.g. **Two from a group Air Show** (4) = P*AIR.

3. Indicates *anag*, e.g. **Queen is from army** (4) = MARY.

FROWN DISAPPROVE, FURROW, KNIT BROWS.
HEADLINES (crypt).

FRUIT 1. PRODUCT, REVENUE. *OFFSPRING* (bibl). **Pl** =
CONSEQUENCE, ISSUE, RESULT. 2. Edible seed; **types:**

3-letters	*LEMON*	MUSCAT
FIG	LOGAN	*ORANGE*
HAW	MANGO	PAPAYA
HIP	MELON	PAW-PAW
NUT	MOREL	PIPPIN
	MORUS	PISANG
4-letters	OLIVE	POMELO
CRAB	PAPAW	PUMELO
DATE	*PEACH*	PUNICA
DIKA	RHEIC	*QUINCE*
DOUM	RHEUM	RAISIN
EJOO	RIBES	RAMOON
GEAN	WHORT	RENNET
KAKI		RUDDOC
KIWI	**6-letters**	RUSSET
LIME	BANANA	SHARON
PEAR	BURREL	TAMPOE
PLUM	CHERRY	TOMATO
SKEG	CITRON	WAMPEE
SLOE	CITRUL	
TUNA	CODLIN	**7-letters**
UGLI	COLMAR	ACHAENE
	DAMSON	APRICOT
5-letters	DRUPEL	AVOCADO
ABHAL	DURIAN	BOUCHET
ACORN	DURION	BULLACE
ANANA	EGROIT	BURLACE
APPLE	GROSER	CANDOCK
BERRY	LITCHI	CODLING
GOBBO	LOQUAT	COSTARD
GRAPE	LUCAMA	CUMQUAT
GUAVA	LYCHEE	CURRANT
JUMBO	MAMMEE	DEUTZIA

ETAERIO	SOROSIS	MYOSOTIS
GENIPAP	SULTANA	PEARMAIN
GOLDING	SYRINGA	PLANTAIN
KARATAS	WINESAP	PRUNELLO
KUMQUAT		SHADDOCK
LEECHEE	**8-letters**	XYLOCARP
MORELLA	ABDALAVI	
MORELLO	BERGAMOT	**9+ letters**
PASSION	BILBERRY	BLACKBERRY
POMELOE	BLENHEIM	BLACKCURRANT
POMEROY	BROMELIA	GOOSEBERRY
POMPION	BURGAMOT	LOGANBERRY
POMPIRE	CADILLAC	NECTARINE
PUMPKIN	CLEMATIS	PINEAPPLE
(RHUBARB)	FAEBERRY	RASPBERRY
RIBSTON	FENBERRY	REDCURRANT
ROSE-HIP	JAPONICA	STRAWBERRY
RUDDOCK	MANDARIN	TANGERINE
SAFFRON	MARIGOLD	WHITECURRANT
SATSUMA	MULBERRY	
SHALLON	MUSCATEL	

FRY 1. QUAKER (*Fox*). *COOK*. *WRITER*. 2. *Offspring* of
FISH.

FUEL ALCOHOL, AVGAS, BUTANE, CALOR®,
CHARCOAL, COAL, DERV, DIESEL, GAS(OLINE),
KEROSENE, METHS, OIL, PARAFFIN, PETROL,
PROPANE, WOOD; [*Pluto*]. FEED FIRE, STOKE.

FULLER EARTH; CLOTH CLEANER. MORE REPLETE.
GROOVED TOOL.

FUNNY COMICAL, HUMOROUS [peculiar/ha-ha]. *BOAT*.

FURIAE *FURIES* (Rom).

FURY 1. ANGER, PASSION, RAGE. VIOLENCE (met). *DOG*
(*Alice*). 2. VIRAGO, *SHREW*. **Pl** = avenging minor *goddesses*
with snakes for hair, sent from Tartarus to punish crimes of
perjury, murder etc; hence any avenging spirit. **Gk** =
ERINYES/EUMENIDES (ALECTO, MEGAERA,
TISIPHONE); **Rom** = DIRAE/FURIAE.

FUSE AMALGAMATE, BLEND, MELD. DETONATE,

IGNITER (impact ~, magnetic ~, time ~, vibratory ~).
BLOW-OUT, SAFETY LINK; MELT, SHORT-CIRCUIT;
UNEARTH (crypt).
FUSTIAN *MATERIAL*. BOMBAST, TURGID SPEECH.

G GENERAL AUDIENCE (film *censorship*, US). *GERMAN(Y)*.
GIGA (*int unit*). GRAMS. *GRAND*. GRAVITY. GREAT.
GREEK. *KEY*; *NOTE*.
GAEA *GE*.
GALAHAD Kt of the *Round Table*, s of *Lancelot* and Elaine
[*Camelot*. Holy Grail. Purity, virtue].
GALATEA 1. Gk myth ivory statue, who came to life and was mar
by *Pygmalion*. [Hermione, W. Tale (*Shak*)]. 2. Gk myth sea
nymph, d of *Nereus* and *Doris*. 3. A minor *PLANET*.
GALL (s/l *Gaul*). ANNOY; NERVE. CLUBROOT,
HYPERTROPHY. *FLY*. LIVERBILE. HORSE-SORE.
GALLERY BALCONY, *GODS*. COLONNADE, PORTICO.
PLATFORM. CORRIDOR, PASSAGE. EXHIBITION;
TATE.
GALLEY SLAVE *PRISONER*, *ROWER*. CHEF, *COOK*,
PANTRY BOY, PROOFREADER, SCULLERY MAID (all
crypt).
GALLOPHILE *Lover* of French ways.
GALLOPHOBIA *Aversion* to French ways.
GALOFARO *CHARYBDIS*.
GAMBLE (s/l *gambol*). *BET*, SPEC(ULATE), WAGER.
GAMBOL (s/l *gamble*). FROLIC, PLAY [*lamb*].
GAME COURAGEOUS, PREPARED, READY, WILLING (**opp**
= reluctant). *CRIPPLED*. *MATCH*, PARTIE; **types:**
BASEBALL, *CARDS*, *CRICKET*, *FIVES*, *FOOTBALL*,
GOLF, HOCKEY, LACROSSE, LAX, LUDO, POLO,
RUGBY, SQUASH, *TENNIS* etc. WILDLIFE: *GROUSE*,
HARE, PARTRIDGE, PHEASANT etc.
G & S Gilbert and Sullivan. **Operas:**

Title	Alternative	Detail
The Gondoliers	The King of Barataria	Venice. Duke of Plaza Toro

The Grand Duke	The Statutory Duel	Grand Duchy of Pfennig Halbpfennig, Rudolph, Ernest Dummkopf, Ludwig
Iolanthe	The *Peer* and the *Peri*	*Parliament*, *Fairies*, Lord Chancellor
Mikado	The Town of Titipu	*Japan*. Nanki-Poo, Yum-Yum, Ko-Ko, Pooh-Bah, Pitti-Sing, Wandering *Minstrel*, Lord High Executioner
Patience	Bunthorne's Bride	Dragoons, Raffle, Capt Rees, Mantelpiece
HMS Pinafore	The Lass that Loved a *Sailor*	Dick Deadeye, Buttercup
Pirates of Penzance	The Slave of Duty	Cornwall. Frederic (*pirate*), *Ruth* (*maid*, *nurse*)
Princess Ida	Castle Adamant	King Hildebrand, Gama (*monster*), Hilarion, *women warriors*
Ruddigore	The Witch's Curse	*Cornwall*. *Ghosts*, Mad Margaret, Sir Ruthven Murgatroyd
Sorcerer	—	Country house. John Wellington Wells
Trial by Jury	—	Law courts. Angelina, Edwin

Utopia Limited	—	King Paramount I, Scaphio, Phantis, Tarara, Princess Zara
Yeoman of the Guard	The Merryman and his *Maid*	Tower of London. Wilfred Shadbolt (*gaoler*), Col Fairfax, Meryll, Jack Point (*jester*)

GANGSTER GODFATHER, GUNMAN, HOOD(LUM), MAFIA
BOSS, MOBSTER, VILLAIN; **notorious:** AL CAPONE,
BONNIE & CLYDE, PRETTY BOY FLOYD, LUCKY
LUCIANO, BUGSY MALONE, DUTCH SCHULTZ, BUGSY
SIEGEL.

GANYMEDE 1. Gk myth youth, abducted by *Zeus* as his cupbearer
on Mount *Olympus*. 2. A satellite of the *planet Jupiter*.

GAOL *BRIG* (naut), CAN, CELL, CHOKEY, CLINK, COOLER,
GLASSHOUSE (mil), INSIDE, JAIL (US), JUG, *NICK*,
PETER, PRISON, QUOD, SLAM(MER), STIR [porridge. Fry,
Howard; M for M (*Shak*)]; **celebrated:**

ALBANY	(Eng)	*FORD*	(Eng)
ALCATRAZ	(US, ex)	FRESNES	(Fr)
ARMLEY	(Eng)	HOLLOWAY	(Eng, fem)
BARLINNIE	(Sc)	HULL	(Eng)
BASTILLE	(Fr)	KINGSTON	(Eng)
BORSTAL	(Eng, jun)	LONG LARTIN	(Eng)
BOTANY BAY	(Aus, hist)	LEEDS	(Eng)
BRIDEWELL	(Eng, ex)	MARSHALSEA	(Eng, ex)
BRIXTON	(Eng)	THE MAZE	(Ire)
BROADMOOR	(Eng, med)	MILLBANK	(Eng, ex)
		THE *MOOR*	(Eng)
CAMP HILL	(Eng)	NEWGATE	(Eng, ex)
COOKHAM WOOD	(Eng)	NORFOLK IS	(Aus, ex)
DARTMOOR	(Eng)	NORTHEYE	(Eng)
DEVIL'S ISLAND	(Fr, ex)	OSSINING	(US)
DURHAM	(Eng)	PARKHURST	(Eng)
FLEET	(Eng, ex)	PENTONVILLE	(Eng)

PORTLAND	(Eng)	WAKEFIELD	(Eng)
RAMPTON	(Eng, med)	WALTON	(Eng)
RISLEY	(Eng)	WINSOM GREEN	(Eng)
THE SCRUBS	(Eng)	WINCHESTER	(Eng)
SING SING	(US, ex)	WORMWOOD	
STYAL	(Eng)	SCRUBS	(Eng)
VERNE	(Eng)		

Fictional: Chateau d'If (Dumas), Zenda (Hope).

GAOLER JAILER (US), KEY-HOLDER (crypt), KEY MAN (crypt), PRISON OFFICER, SCREW (sl), TURNKEY (arch), WARDER. WILLIAM SHADBOLT (*G & S*).

GARBLED *Anag.* MUDDLED, *SCRAMBLED*.

GARDEN CULTIVATION, *PLOT*. BABYLON, EDEN, KEW [Elizabeth].

GARDENER CULTIVATOR. *ADAM* (crypt). 'CAPABILITY' BROWN; ANDRE LENOTRE (Fr); ANDREW FAIRSERVICE (Rob Roy, Scott). ELIZABETH, INIGO JONES, MR MCGREGOR (*Potter*). **Pl** = SPADES (*Alice*).

GARLAND ADORN, BEDECK, *DECK*, LEI; FLOWERS. JUDY (films).

GARNET GEM (red). *Birthstone* (January).

GARTER *HERALD* [Black Rod]. KNIGHTHOOD [Honi soit qui mal y pense; stocking]. BAND, STRAP.

GATE (s/l gait). 1. ACCESS, BARRIER, CLOSURE, *ENTRANCE*, EXIT, *OPENING*, POSTERN, WICKET. SHUTTER (mech). ATTENDANCE, CROWD, SPECTATORS; TAKE, TAKINGS. MOUTH (sl). 2. ~s of **London:** ALDERSGATE, ALDGATE, BISHOPSGATE, BRIDESGATE, CRIPPLEGATE, DOWGATE, LUDGATE, MOORGATE, NEWGATE, POSTERN, PRAETORIAN WAY.

GATHERING *ASSEMBLY*, MEETING. COLLECTING, CULLING. BOIL, SWELLING, TUMOUR.

GAUGE *EM*, *TT*. *Z*. CAPACITY, EXTENT, *MEASURE*, SCOPE, STANDARD, WIDTH, *TRACK*. INSTRUMENT. ASSESS, CALCULATE, ESTIMATE.

GAUL (s/l *gall*). GALLIA, ROMAN FRANCE (cisalpine, trans-alpine).

GB GREAT BRITAIN (*car plate*).

GBA ALDERNEY (*car plate*).

GBG GUERNSEY (*car plate*).

GBJ JERSEY (*car plate*).

GBM ISLE OF MAN (*car plate*).

GE = GAEA. Gk *goddess* of the EARTH. Mother (by Uranus) of the *Titans* (**Rom** = TELLUS, TERRA).

GEAR *CLOTHES*, GOODS, KIT, RIG. APPARATUS, EQUIPMENT, FITTINGS, HARNESS, KIT, TACKLE. MESHING COGS (mech).

GEESE Pl of *Goose*.

GEHENNA HELL (bibl), PLACE OF BURNING.

GEM BEST/CHOICEST PART. JEWEL, PRECIOUS STONE, ENGRAVED SEMI-PRECIOUS STONE: *AGATE, AMETHYST, AQUAMARINE, BERYL, BLOODSTONE, CHALCEDONY, CHRYSOBERYL, CHRYSOLITE, CHRYSOPRASE, CORAL, CORNELIAN, DIAMOND, EMERALD, GARNET, JADE, LAPIS LAZULI, ONYX, OPAL, PEARL*, PERIDOT, PYROPE, *RUBY, SAPPHIRE, SARD*, SARDIUS (bibl), *SARDONYX, TURQUOISE, ZIRCON* [*anniversary, birthstone*].

GEMINI 1. *TWINS* (Castor and Pollux). 2. *Constellation*; (3rd) sign of *Zodiac*. 3. *SPACECRAFT*.

GEN *GENERAL* (mil). *INFORMATION*.

GENERAL G (film *censorship*, US). GEN, OFFICER: LEE, SMUTS, SLIM (and see *military leaders*). IMPARTIAL, MAIN, UNIVERSAL (**opp** = particular).

GENES (s/l jeans). CHROMOSOMES, *DNA* (heredity).

GENIE GOBLIN, IMP, *SPIRIT* [Aladdin's lamp].

GENIUS 1. ABILITY, BRILLIANCE; **saying**. 2. Rom myth *god* of fertility and marriage (**Gk** = *HYMEN*).

GENOPHILE *Lover* of people.

GENOPHOBIA *Aversion* to people.

GEORGE PATRON SAINT (Eng; Port; armourers) [dragon, order of garter, 23 April]; 'A RUSTIC'. *WRITER*. [*Three* Men in a Boat].

GERMAN 1. G. HEINIE, HEINZ, JERRY, FRITZ, KRAUT, *HUN*. D, DDR (*car plate*). 2. Translate, e.g. **The German** = DAS. DER. DIE; **German song** = LIED.

GERMANY DDR, *FDR*, REICH, FATHERLAND, WEIMAR.

GET ON *AGREE*. *BOARD*, EMBARK. *AGE*.

GET OUT EMERGE, FLEE, *LEAVE*. BOWL, CATCH, RUN OUT, STUMP (*cricket*).

GET UP STYLE (clothes). *DRESS*, MAKE TOILET, RISE. *MOUNT* (horse). Write upwards (dn). BECOME VIOLENT, WORK UP (sea, temper). ORGANIZE. TEG (dn; crypt).

GHOST DOUBLE IMAGE, OUTLINE, SEMBLANCE. (HACK) WRITER. APPARITION, MANES, *SHADE*, SOUL, SPECTRE, *SPIRIT*, POLTERGEIST; HAUNT, PROWL; **celebrated:** BANQUO (Macbeth), CANTERVILLE (Wilde), CLAUDIUS (Hamlet's father), ELVIRA (Blithe Spirit, Coward) [Christmas Carol (*Dickens*); Ruddigore (*G & S*); *lemur*].

GI SOLDIER, PFC, PRIVATE (US).

GIANT 1. LARGE, MONSTROUS, SUPERHUMAN, TITANIC (**opp** = *dwarf*). **Pl** = New York baseball team. 2. Myth *MONSTER*: *DACTYLS*, *GIGANTES*, GOG, MAGOG, ORGOGLIO (Faerie Queen, Spenser), GARGANTUA & PANTAGRUEL (Rabelais), GOLIATH (bibl), *PERIPHITES* (Gk myth).

GIBRALTAR ROCK. *STRAIT*. [pillars of *Hercules*].

GIGANTES Gk myth *monsters* (not to be confused with the *Titans*); ALCYONEUS, ENCELADUS, EPHIALTES, MIMAS, PALLAS, PHRYTOS, PORPHYRION, RHOETUS. They had wings, and snakes for feet.

GILL (s/l Jill). GIRL. *MEASURE*, ¼ PINT, hence, P, I, N or T. DEWLAP, WATTLE (poultry). *BREATHER* (*fish*). RAVINE. SAIL IDLY. YOUNG WOMAN. FERRET, POLECAT (fem).

GIN (s/l djinn, ginn). *DRINK*, GENEVA, HOLLANDS. *NET*, SNARE, TRAP. CRANE, WINDLASS. COTTON MAKER. *CARD GAME*.

GIRDLE BELT, CORD, CORSET. RING, SURROUND. GRILL. [labour of *Hercules*].

GIRL HER, SHE. DAMOSEL, DAMSEL, GAL, LASS, MISS, WENCH. ANN, DORA, ENID, SUE etc [~ **and boy** = pigeon pair].

GIVE AWAY DONATE. *BETRAY*, SHOP.

Gk Greece, Greek.

GLASS 1. BAROMETER. MIRROR. MAGNIFIER.
MICROSCOPE. GLAZING, WINDOW, TRANSPARENCY.
DRINKING VESSEL: BUMPER, COPITA, POKAL, PONY,
SCHOONER, TANKARD, TUMBLER; BRANDY ~,
LIQUEUR ~, PORT ~, SHERRY ~, WINE ~.
LORGNETTE, MONOCLE, QUIZZING ~. **Pl =**
BINOCULARS, BIN(N)S (sl), SPECTACLES. 2. Mixture of
sand and potash (*chem*), hence by *anag* (crypt) A SHOP STAND,
or PASS TO HAND etc.

GLEE PART-SONG. DELIGHT, MERRIMENT, MIRTH.

GO ANIMATION, DRIVE, *PEP*, VIGOUR, ZIP. DEPART,
FARE, OFF, PART, *REPAIR*, START. ATTEMPT, SHOT,
TRY, TURN. BOARD-GAME (Jap).

GOAT 1. SILLY FOOL. ATTACK, SHOT*AT, TRY*AT
(crypt). *ISLAND*. 2. Ruminant, genus CAPRA; BUTTER
(crypt). MURIEL (*Orwell*). **Breeds:** BAGOT, CHAMOIS,
IBEX, MARKHOR, TAHR (see also *antelope*, *deer*). **Assembly**
= *flock*, herd; **offspring** = *kid*; **male** = BILLY; **female** =
NANNY. 3. *Constellation* (Capricorn); (10th) sign of *Zodiac*.

GOBLIN BROWNIE, ELF, GENIE, IMP, *SPIRIT*, SPRITE.

GOBY *FISH*. PASS (crypt). TRAVEL*BY/IN (crypt).

GOC GENERAL OFFICER COMMANDING, OFFICER (mil).

GOD 1. ADORED/INFLUENTIAL MAN. DEITY, JAHBULON
(*Masonic*), JEHOVA, YAHVEH (Heb), OBJECT OF
WORSHIP: IDEA, IDOL, IMAGE, SUPERHUMAN (MALE)
BEING; **saying** [ambrosia, nectar, trinity]. EXCLAMATION:
GOLLY, GOSH. **Pl =** GALLERY (theat); **opp** = parterre,
stalls. 2. Gods and *goddesses* figured largely in the lives of the
ancient world. Most of the seasons, ideas and natural events such
as love, war, hunting and the harvest (with earth, sun and moon)
which influenced life were personified by early peoples such as the
Egyptians, Phoenicians, Indians and Norsemen; those of Greece
and Rome were particularly literate, so their deities are well
documented. In the lists which follow, the alert reader will note
that interesting qualities such as fertility rate no less than ten
Greek and Roman gods and goddesses (not to mention another
dozen Nordic and eastern equivalents), while dull old virginity has
only one deity from among all the nations (and even that one is
also the goddess of Nature, so there is hope for her yet). Greece

was responsible for much of the lore and mythology which grew up, and much of this was handed on to the Romans; in general terms, there were six principal Greek gods and six principal goddesses, who all lived on Mount *Olympus*: *APOLLO*, *ARES*, *HEPHAESTUS*, *HERMES*, *POSEIDON* and *ZEUS*; *Aphrodite*, *Artemis*, *Athene*, *Demeter*, *Hera* and *Hestia*. **Celebrated** gods and minor gods include (**Greek**):

AEOLUS	winds
AGATHODAEMON	prosperity
ALASTOR	fate
APELIOTES	east wind
APOLLO	beauty, healing, music, oracles, plagues, prophecy, sun
ARES	war
ASCLEPIUS	medicine
BOREAS	north wind
CRONOS	harvest
DIONYSUS	fertility, wine
ERIS	discord
EROS	love
EUROS	SE wind
GANYMEDE	cup-bearer
HADES	underworld
HELIOS	sun
HEPHAESTUS	fire
HERMES	dreams, messenger, *robbers*
HORUS	doorway
HYMEN	fertility, marriage
KAIKAS	NE wind
LIPS	SW wind
MOMOS	ridicule
NEREUS	sea
NOTOS	south wind
OCEANUS	river
PAN	herds, hunting, shepherds
PLUTUS	wealth
POSEIDON	sea

SKIRON	NW wind
THANATOS	death
URANUS	heaven
ZEPHYRUS	west wind
ZEUS	chief ~, king

Roman:

AESCULAPIUS	medicine
AFRICUS	SW wind
AMOR	love
APOLLO	beauty, healing, music, oracles, plagues, prophecy, sun
AQUILO	NE wind
ATLAS	world
AUSTER	south wind
BACCHUS	fertility, wine
CAURUS	NW wind
CUPID	love
DIS	underworld
DISCORDIA	discord
FAUNUS	herds
FAVONIUS	west wind
FULGURATOR	storms
FULMINATOR	lightning
GENIUS	fertility, marriage, prosperity
IACCHUS	= *BACCHUS*
INUUS	= *FAUNUS*
JANUS	doorway
JOVE	chief ~, king, thunder
JUPITER	chief ~, thunder
LAR(ES)	household
LIBER	= *BACCHUS*
LUPERCUS	= *FAUNUS*
MARS	husbandry, war
MERCURY	messenger
MORPHEUS	dreams
MORS	death

NEPTUNE	sea
ORCUS	underworld
PENATES	household
PHOEBUS	sun
PLUTO	underworld
PLUVIUS	rain
SATURNUS	harvest
SEPTENTRIO	north wind
SOL	sun
SUBSOLANUS	east wind
TERMINUS	boundaries
TONANS	thunder
VOLTURNUS	SE wind
VULCAN	fire

Equivalent gods include:

Agriculture: Gk *CRONOS*; **Roman** *SATURNUS*; **Other** SEB (Egy)

Beauty: Gk *APOLLO*; **Roman** *APOLLO*

Boundaries: Roman TERMINUS

Chief: Gk *ZEUS*; **Roman** *JOVE, JUPITER*; **Other** WODEN (A-Sax), ANU, BEL/BELUS (Bab), XANGTI (Ch), AMEN-RA, OSIRIS, TEMU (Egy), BRAHMA, SHIVA (Ind), ODIN (Nor), *BAAL* (Phoen), NQA, NQING, NQONG (Aus, *Kipling*)

Death: Gk THANATOS; **Roman** MORS; **Other** ANUBIS/*OSIRIS* (Egy), SHIVA, YAMA (Ind)

Discord: Gk *ERIS*; **Roman** DISCORDIA

Doorway: Gk *HORUS*; **Roman** *JANUS*; **Other** HOR (Egy)

Dreams: Gk *HERMES*; **Roman** *MORPHEUS*; **Other** SERAPIS (Egy)

Fate: Gk ALASTOR

Fertility: Gk *DIONYSUS, HYMEN*; **Roman** *BACCHUS, GENIUS*; **Other** *OSIRIS* (Egy), KRISHNA (Ind), *FREY* (Nor)

Fire: Gk *HEPHAESTUS*; **Roman** *VULCAN*; **Other** *LOKI* (Nor), AGNI (Ind)

Harvest: Gk CRONOS; **Roman** SATURNUS; **Other** SEB (Egy)

Healing: Gk *APOLLO*; **Roman** *APOLLO*; **Other** MARDUK (Bab), VISHNU (Ind)

Heaven: Gk *URANUS*; **Other** VALHALLA (Nor)

Herds: Gk *PAN*; **Roman** *FAUNUS*, INUUS, LUPERCUS

Household: Roman *LAR(ES)*, PENATES

Hunting: Gk *PAN*

Husbandry: Roman *MARS*

Lightning: Gk *ZEUS*; **Roman** FULMINATOR

Love: Gk *EROS*; **Roman** *AMOR*, *CUPID*; **Other** KAMA (Ind)

Marriage: Gk *HYMEN*; **Roman** *GENIUS*

Medicine: Gk *ASCLEPIUS*; **Roman** AESCULAPIUS

Messenger: Gk *HERMES*; **Roman** *MERCURY*

Night: Other *SET* (Egy)

Oracles: Gk *APOLLO*; **Roman** *APOLLO*

Plagues: Gk *APOLLO*; **Roman** *APOLLO*

Prophecy: Gk *APOLLO*; **Roman** *APOLLO*

Prosperity: Gk AGATHODAEMON; **Roman** *GENIUS*

Rain: Gk *ZEUS*; **Roman** *JUPITER*, *PLUVIUS*; **Other** *OSIRIS* (Egy), INDRA (Ind)

Ridicule: Gk MOMOS

River: Gk *OCEANUS*

Robbery: Gk *HERMES*

Sea: Gk *NEREUS*, *POSEIDON*; **Roman** *NEPTUNE*; **Other** AEGIR, NIORDHR (Nor)

Shepherds: Gk *PAN*

Storms: Gk *ZEUS*; **Roman** FULGURATOR

Sun: Gk *APOLLO, HELIOS*; **Roman** *PHOEBUS, SOL*;
    Other APIS, *HORUS*, PTAH (Egy), *FREY* (Nor),
    MITHRA (Pers), *BAAL* (Phoen)

Thunder: Gk *ZEUS*; **Roman** *JOVE, JUPITER, TONANS*;
    Other *THOR* (Nor)

Truth: Other MAAT (Egy)

Underworld: Gk *HADES*; **Roman** *DIS, ORCUS, PLUTO*;
    Other *OSIRIS*, SERAPIS (Egy)

War: Gk *ARES*; **Roman** *MARS*; **Other** TIW (Ger),
    MORRIGAN (Ire)

Watchman: Other HEIMDAL (Nor)

Wealth: Gk *PLUTUS*

Winds: Gk *AEOLUS* (see *winds*); **Rom** (see *winds*)

Wine: Gk *DIONYSUS*; **Roman** BACCHUS, LIBER

Wisdom: Other THOTH (Egy)

World: Roman *ATLAS*.

GODDESS 1. ADORED/INFLUENTIAL WOMAN. DEITY,
OBJECT OF WORSHIP: IDEA, IDOL, IMAGE, (FEMALE)
SUPERHUMAN BEING [ambrosia, nectar]. LOVED ONE. 2.
See *gods* for brief description of the deity ethos of ancient
peoples. The Greeks had six principal *gods* and goddesses, who
all lived on Mount *Olympus: Apollo, Ares, Hephaestus, Hermes,
Poseidon* and Zeus; *APHRODITE, ARTEMIS, ATHENE,
DEMETER, HERA* and *HESTIA*. **Celebrated** goddesses and
minor goddesses include, **Greek:**

AMPHITRITE	sea
APHRODITE	beauty, love
ARTEMIS	hunting, messenger, nature
ATE	infatuation, retribution

ATHENE	arts, war, wisdom
CHLORIS	flowers
CYBELE	fertility
DANAE	fertility
DEMETER	nature
EOS	dawn
ERINYES	*furies*
EUMENIDES	*furies*
GAEA/GE	earth
HEBE	cup-bearer, youth
HERA	childbirth, queen ~
HECATE	night, underworld, witchcraft
HESTIA	hearth
HYGIEA	health
IRENE	peace
IRIS	rainbow
MAIA	eldest of the *Pleiades*
MOIRAI	*fates*
NEMESIS	retribution
NIKE	victory
PALLAS	= *ATHENE*
PERSEPHONE	underworld
PLEIADES	rain
RHEA	fertility
SELENE	moon
TERPSICHORE	dance, song
TYCHE	fortune
UPIS	childbirth

Roman:

AURORA	dawn
CERES	earth, fertility, nature
DIANA	fertility, nature, hunting, moon
FAUNA	earth
FLORA	flowers
FORTUNA	fortune
FURIAE	*furies*
JUNO	queen ~, childbirth, moon
JUVENTAS	youth

LIBERA	= *PROSERPINE*
LUNA	moon
MAIA	oracles
MINERVA	arts, invention, war, lightning, wisdom
OPS	earth, nature
PARCAE	*fates*
PAX	peace
PROSERPINE	underworld
SALUS	health
TELLUS/TERRA	earth
VENUS	beauty, love
VESTA	hearth
VICTORIA	victory

Equivalent goddesses include:

Arts: **Gk** *ATHENE*; **Roman** *MINERVA*

Beauty: **Gk** *APHRODITE, ARTEMIS*; **Roman** *DIANA, VENUS*

Chief: **Gk** *HERA*; **Roman** *JUNO*; **Other** *ISIS, UPIS* (Egy), *DEVI* (Ind), BELIT/BELTIS (Bab)

Childbirth: **Gk** *HERA*; **Roman** *JUNO*

Cup-bearer: **Gk** *HEBE*; **Roman** *JUVENTAS*

Dance: **Gk** *TERPSICHORE*

Dawn: **Gk** *EOS*; **Roman** *AURORA*

Destruction: **Other** *KALI* (Egy), *HEL* (Nor)

Earth: **Gk** *GAEA/GE*; **Roman** *CERES, FAUNA, MAIA, TELLUS/TERRA*; **Other** LUA (It)

Fates: **Gk** *MOIRAI*; **Roman** *PARCAE*

Fertility: **Gk** *CYBELE, DANAE, RHEA*; **Roman** *CERES, DIANA, OPS*; **Other** *FRIGG* (Nor), BELIT, INNIN, ISHTAR (Bab), ATERGATIS (Syrian), EOSTRE (A-Sax [easter])

Flowers: Gk *CHLORIS*; **Roman** *FLORA*

Fortune: Gk TYCHE; **Roman** FORTUNA

Furies: Gk *ERINYES*, EUMENIDES; **Roman** *FURIAE*

Health: Gk *HYGIEA*; **Roman** SALUS

Hearth: Gk *HESTIA*; **Roman** *VESTA*

Hunting: Gk *ARTEMIS*; **Roman** *DIANA*

Infatuation: Gk *ATE*

Invention: Roman *MINERVA*

Lightning: Roman *MINERVA*

Love: Gk *APHRODITE*; **Roman** *VENUS*; **Other** *ISHTAR*
(Bab), *ISIS* (Egy), *FREYA* (Nor), *ASTARTE* (Phoen)

Messenger: Gk *ARTEMIS*

Moon: Gk *ARTEMIS*, *SELENE*; **Roman** *DIANA*, *JUNO*,
LUNA

Nature: Gk *ARTEMIS*, *DEMETER*; **Roman** *CERES*,
DIANA, *OPS*; **Other** *ISIS*, *UPIS* (Egy)

Night: Gk *HECATE*, *NYX*; **Other** *HEL* (Nor)

Oracles: Roman *MAIA*

Peace: Gk *IRENE*; **Roman** *PAX*

Rainbow: Gk *IRIS*

Retribution: Gk *ATE*, *NEMESIS*

Sea: Gk *AMPHITRITE*

Song: Gk *TERPSICHORE*

Truth: Other MA, MAAT (Egy)

Underworld: Gk *HECATE*, *PERSEPHONE*; **Roman**
LIBERA, *PROSERPINE*; **Other** *HEL* (Nor)

Victory: Gk *NIKE*; **Roman** *VICTORIA*

Virginity: Gk *ARTEMIS*

War: Gk *ATHENE*; **Roman** BELLONA, *MINERVA*; **Other**
   BRUNHILDA (Nor), SERIO (Sabine)

Wisdom: Gk *ATHENE*; **Roman** *MINERVA*

Witchcraft: Gk *HECATE*

Youth: Gk *HEBE*; **Roman** *JUVENTAS*

GOD'S BLOOD ICHOR.
GOD WILLING DG, DV.
GO IN(TO/SIDE) 1. ENTER, PENETRATE. 2. Hidden word, e.g.
   Miss Theresa Wayman goes in with a will (6, 1, 3) = THERE'S A
   WAY. 3. Word or letter goes into another, e.g. **To serve, I have to
   go into the water** (6) = WA*I*TER.
GOLD AU (*chem*). OR (*herald*). BULLSEYE (archery).
   OLYMPIC WINNER. YELLOW *COLOUR*. *Anniversary*
   (50th). [**fool's gold** = pyrites. *Company* (livery); *Danae*].
~ **DIGGER** FORTY-NINER, PANNER, PROSPECTOR.
   LEECH, TRAMP, VAMPIRE.
GOLDEN FLEECE Skin of fabled golden ram which rescued *Helle*
   and her br Phrixus. It was hung in the temple of Ares until
   brought back by *Jason* and the *Argonauts*.
GOLF CLUB BLASTER, BRASSIE, CLEEK, *DRIVER*, *IRON*,
   MASHIE, NIBLICK, *PUTTER*, SAND-WEDGE, *SPOON*,
   WEDGE, *WOOD*. PGA, R AND A, USGA. HOYLAKE,
   PORTLAND, ST ANDREWS.
GOLF COURSE LINKS; FOREGROUND (crypt). BIRKDALE,
   HOYLAKE, MUIRFIELD, PORTLAND, ST ANDREWS,
   SANDWICH, SUNNINGDALE, TROON. [par, bogey (evens),
   birdie (1 under), *eagle* (2 under), *albatross* (3 under)].
GOLLY DOLL. GOSH, MY.
GOOD ADEQUATE, EFFICIENT, GENUINE, RIGHT,
   SATISFACTORY, SOUND, VALID. AGREEABLE,
   BENEVOLENT, COMMENDABLE, EXCELLENT,
   FAVOURABLE, KIND, UNTAINTED, VIRTUOUS,
   WHOLESOME [Sabbath/Sunday's *child*]; (**opp** = evil).
   OBEDIENT, PROPER, WELL-BEHAVED/MANNERED (**opp**
   = *bad*). **Pl** = FREIGHT, LINE, MERCHANDISE, WARES.

THE REAL THING.

GOODFELLOW SOCIABLE PERSON. ROBIN; *FAIRY*.
SAINT, ST (crypt).

GOODMAN FATHER, HUSBAND. SAINT, ST (crypt).

GOON DOLT, FOOL. GUARD (mil sl). HEAVY, THUG.
CONTINUE, PROCEED (crypt go*on).

GOOSE 1. SILLY CREATURE, SIMPLETON. IRON (tailor's).
POKE. 2. *BIRD* of genus ANSER: BARNACLE, BEAN,
BRENT, CANADA, GREYLAG, PINKFOOTED, SOLAN
(gannet), WHITEFRONTED. **Assembly** = flock; **male** =
GANDER; **female** = GOOSE; **offspring** = gosling. Sixth day of
Christmas song.

GORGON Gk myth winged *monsters*, with snakes for hair:
EURYALE (the Leaper), *MEDUSA* (the Ruler), STHENO (the
Strong).

GOSPEL DOCTRINE, GLAD TIDINGS; CHRIST'S
BIOGRAPHY [Matthew, Mark, Luke, John]. Four
gospelmakers in *song*. BASIC TEACHING/TRUTH.

GOVERNOR BEY (Turk). HE. CONTROLLER (mech).
FATHER. WARREN HASTINGS (hist).

GO WRONG *Anag*. ERR, SIN. GET LOST. OG (crypt).

GP *DOCTOR*. *GROUP*.

GR GRAND, GREAT. GREECE. GRAIN. GRAM(ME).

GRACE 1. ADORN, *HONOUR*, *SET OFF*. CHARM,
ELEGANCE, REFINEMENT [Tuesday's *child*]. FAVOUR,
LIKING, BOON, CONCESSION, PRIVILEGE. CLEMENCY,
MERCY. PRAYERS, THANKSGIVING. ADDRESS (form
of, for Archbishop, Duchess, Duke). EXTRA NOTE (mus).
BATSMAN, CRICKETER, EM, GF, WG. *DARLING*.
'HANNAH'. 2. Gk *goddess* daughters of Zeus, bestowers of
beauty, charm and mirth: AGLAIA, EUPHROYSNE and
THALIA.

~ **ROAD** TEST GROUND (*cricket*).

GRADUATION MARKING, *MEASUREMENT*, SCALE;
VERNIER. ACADEMIC DEGREE, PASS,
QUALIFICATION.

GRAHAME KENNETH, *WRITER* (Wind in the Willows; Toad of
Toad Hall; *Badger*, *Mole*, Ratty, *Toad*).

GRAND G, GR. CHIEF, HIGHEST RANK. DISTINGUISHED,

FINE, GRANDIOSE, GREAT, MAGNIFICENT, SPLENDID. PIANO. RIVER (Can). WATERFALL. $1,000; £1,000; THOUSAND, hence M or K.

GRASS 1. *BETRAY*, NARK, SNEAK. *SNAKE. DRUG*, HERB, POT. FELL, KNOCK DOWN (sl). 2. *PLANT*. GRAZING, HERBAGE, PASTURE, SWARD, TURF; FODDER. ASPARAGUS (sl) [aftermath; hay, ted]. **Types:**

3-letters	CUTCH	TWITCH
ERS	DURRA	UNIOLA
FOG	HALFA	
RYE	HAULM	**7-letters**
	MELIC	ALFALFA
4-letters	ORYZA	CLIVERS
AIRA	*PANIC*	ESPARTO
ALFA	SEDGE	EULALIA
BENT	*SPEAR*	FESTUCA
BLUE	VETCH	FOGGAGE
COIX		FOXTAIL
DISS	**6-letters**	LUCERNE
DOUB	BAJREE	SORGHUM
DURA	BARCOO	SQUITCH
KANS	CACTUS	TIMOTHY
LYME	DARNEL	VETIVER
REED	FESCUE	WAGWANT
RUSA	FIORIN	ZIZANIA
TARE	LOLIUM	
TEFF	MARRAM	**8-letters**
TORE	MEDICK	CLEAVERS
	NARDUS	DOG-GRASS
5-letters	PAMPAS	DOG-WHEAT
ARROW	PHLEUM	ELEUSINE
BRIZA	QUITCH	GYNERIUM
BUNCH	REDTOP	PUSS-TAIL
COUCH	RUPPIA	

GRASSHOPPER CICADA, *CRICKET*, GRIG, KATYDID; *INSECT*; JUMPER (crypt).

GRATE (s/l *great*). FIREPLACE [Adam]. GRIND, IRRITATE,

RASP, RUB. GRATING, GRILLE. GRATITUDE (arch).

GRAVE TOMB, TRENCH. CARVE, ENGRAVE, ETCH, SCULPT. IMPORTANT, SERIOUS, WEIGHTY; DIGNIFIED, PLAIN, SOLEMN, SOMBRE. CLEAN, SCRAPE, SCRUB (naut). ACCENT (`). 'TRISTRAM'.

GRAVITY G. MASS, WEIGHT. SERIOUSNESS.

GRAYS INN LAW SOCIETY [benchers, call to the bar, griffin].

GREAT (s/l *grate*). ABLE, IMPORTANT, PRE-EMINENT; **saying**. G, BIG, LARGE. **Pl** = Final exam in classics/philosophy (O). [Alexander the ~ (Gk), Alfred the ~ (Eng), Catherine the ~ (Russ), Frederick the ~ (Prussia), Peter the ~ (Russ)].

GREAT LAKES Group of *lakes* in Canada and US; **in both:** ERIE, HURON, ONTARIO, SUPERIOR (biggest); **in US only:** MICHIGAN.

GREEK G, Gk. CUNNING PERSON, SHARPER. DOUBLE DUTCH, INCOMPREHENSIBLE.

~ **GOD** See *GOD*.

~ **GODDESS** See *GODDESS*.

GREEN *COLOUR*, VERT (*herald*). IN LEAF, VERDANT, VITAL. FRESH, UNRIPE. ISLAND. DEB, GULLIBLE, IMMATURE, INEXPERIENCED, MILD, *RAW*, TYRO, YOUNG, *VIRGIN* (**opp** = *experienced*). COMMON LAND. PUTTING AREA (golf). RIVER (US). **Pl** = VEGETABLES.

GREENBACK BUCK, DOLLAR (sl). NEERG (crypt).

GREEN RUSHES See *song*.

GREET ACCOST, HAIL, *SALUTE*; AVE, HI, WELCOME. CRY, WEEP (Sc).

GREETING AVE, HEY, HI, HO; *SALUTE*. HALLO, HELLO, HILLO, HOLLO, HULLO (**opp** = farewell). CRYING, WEEPING (Sc).

GREGORY APERIENT, POWDER. PECK (film). POPE.

GREY *COLOUR*. *WHIG*. DEPRESSING, DISMAL. RIVER (NZ). ANONYMOUS, INDETERMINATE, UNIDENTIFIABLE. ANCIENT, EXPERIENCED, IMMEMORIAL. BERYL ~ (theat). LADY JANE ~. **Pl** = 2nd DRAGOONS (mil).

GREYFRIAR FRANCISCAN, *FRIAR*. **Pl** = *SCHOOL* [*Bunter, Famous Five*].

GRIEF DOLE, DOLOUR, MISERY, REGRET, SORROW, TROUBLE. DISASTER.

GRILSE *FISH*. *Offspring* of *salmon*.

GRIP *BITE*, CLASP, NIP, *PINCH*, SQUEEZE. *BAGGAGE*. RAVEN (Barnaby Rudge, *Dickens*).

GROOM FIANCE, HUSBAND, MATE. OSTLER; BRUSH, CURRYCOMB, TIDY.

GROUND EARTH (elect). EDUCATE, TEACH, TRAIN. PREVENT FLYING, KEEP OUT OF THE AIR. HONED, POLISHED, POWDERED. BOTTOM, SEABED; SOLID. BASE, FOUNDATION, SUBSTRATUM; SURFACE. AREA, EARTH, LAND, TERRITORY; STREET-LEVEL. PLAYING FIELD (*cricket* ~, *football* ~, *golf course*, *racetrack*, *rugby* ~, *tennis court*). **Pl** = BELIEF, PRINCIPLE, REASONS. GRANULES, POWDER. PREMISES, PROPERTY.

GROUND RENT HIRE CHARGE, LEASE. CANYON, CREVASSE, FISSURE, RAVINE (crypt); EARTHQUAKE (crypt).

GROUNDS FOR 1. AUTHORITY, FOUNDATION, REASON TO BELIEVE. 2. See *cricket*, *football*, *golf*, *racetrack*, *rugby*, *tennis*.

GROUP GP. CLIQUE, CLUSTER, KNOT. *SET*. CLASSIFY.

GROUSE *BIRD*, GAMEBIRD, CAPERCAILLIE, MOOR FOWL, PTARMIGAN; RED ~ (**assembly** = pack; **male red** ~ = GORLOCK). COMPLAIN, GRUMBLE, *TICK*.

GRUB STREET THE *PRESS*. HACK WRITERS (now Milton Street).

GRUMPY BEARISH, ILL-TEMPERED, SURLY. *DWARF* (Snow White).

GRUNDY 1. Solomon ~ (b on Monday, christened on Tuesday, mar on Wednesday, took ill on Thursday, got worse on Friday, d on Saturday and was buried on Sunday). 2. Mrs ~; personification of prudery (*unseen* neighbour of Mrs Ashfield in Tom Morton's Speed the Plough).

GUARD PROTECT, SENTRY, *WATCH*, VIGIL; CAVEMAN (crypt) [~ **of honour** = *chaperone*]. *CONDUCTOR* (rly), RAILWAYMAN. **Pl** = COLDSTREAM, FOOT, GRENADIER, HORSE, IRISH, LIFE, SCOTS, WELSH; BLUES, ROYALS [*household* ~]. OLD ~, PRAETORIAN ~,

PRUSSIAN ~, YEOMAN, YOUNG ~.

GUERNSEY SWEATER, WOOLLY (jersey). *CATTLE.*
ISLAND (CI). GBG (*car plate*). *LILY.*

GUEVERA CHE.

GUIDE ASSIST, LEAD, SHOW; ADVISER, CICERONE,
SCOUT. *CONDUCTOR*, DRAGOMAN, INTERPRETER,
PILOT. INSTINCT. MANUAL. STANDARD. CHANNEL.
GUARD, *RAIL*, ROD (mech).

GUIDED MISSILE ARROW, DART. *WEAPON* (and see
MISSILE).

GUINEA *COUNTRY* (ex Fr W Af). GOLD *COIN*,
21 SHILLINGS. (PROFESSIONAL) FEE.

~ BISSAU *COUNTRY* (ex Port Guinea).

~ FOWL *BIRD.*

~ PIG PET, RODENT. TEST CASE. PI (crypt).

GUINEVERE The queen of *King Arthur*, her infidelity with
Lancelot led to the break-up of the *Round Table*. [*Camelot*,
Mordred].

GULES RED (*herald*).

GULF ABYSS, CHASM, DEPTH, GAP. LARGE INLET/BAY
(geog); **celebrated:**

ADEN (Af/Arab)
ALASKA (US)
ANTALYA (Turk)
AQABA (Isr)
BOTHNIA (Fin/Swe)
CALIFORNIA (Mex)
CAMBAY (Ind)
CARPENTARIA (Aus)
CHIHLI (Ch)
CORINTH (Gk)
FINLAND (~)
GAETA (It)
GASCONY (Fr)
GENOA (It)
GIZHIGA (USSR)
GUINEA (NW Af)
HONDURAS (~)

ISKENDERUN (Turk)
IZMIR (Turk)
KUTCH (Ind)
LAKONIA (Gk)
LIONS (Fr)
MARTABAN (Bur)
MESSINA (Gk)
MEXICO (~/US)
MOSQUITOS (Panama)
OB (USSR)
OMAN (Arab/Pers)
ORISTANO (It)
PANAMA (~)
PAPUA (New Guinea)
PATRAS (Gk)
PERSIAN (Arab/~)
RIGA (USSR)

ST LAWRENCE (Can)	SUEZ (Egy)
ST MALO (Fr)	TARANTO (It)
SALERNO (It)	TARTARY (USSR)
SAN JORGE (Arg; Sp)	TONA (USSR)
SAN MATIAS (Arg)	TONKING (Ch)
SIAM (~ etc)	VALENCIA (Sp)
SPENCER (Aus)	VENICE (It)

GULL DUPE, FOOL. SEABIRD; **breeds:** BLACK-BACKED ~,
COMMON ~, FULMAR, HERRING ~, KITTIWAKE,
MEW ~, TERN. **Pl** = TORQUAY (*football* team).

GUN ARM, FIREARM, GAT, ROD, ORDNANCE, *WEAPON*.
SHOOT. **Celebrated:** BIG BERTHA, THE KING'S
DAUGHTER (H.v.), THE LONDON (H.v.), THE
MESSENGER (H.v.), MONS MEG, ZAM-ZAMMAH (Kim,
Kipling). **Pl** = RA (battery).

GUNMAN GANGSTER, MOBSTER. RA (crypt). STARTER.

GUNNEL *BUTTERFISH*. GUNWALE (boat's side).

GUNNER *GUNMAN* (q.v.). RIFLEMAN. [*patron saint*]. RA.
Pl = ARSENAL (*football*).

GUTTER PRESS NEWSPAPER, RAG.

GUY CHAP, FELLOW. FAWKES [Robert Catesby, Thomas
Percy]. ROPE, STAY.

GYGES Gk myth *MONSTER* (Uranid), s of *Uranus* and *Ge*, with
100 arms and 50 heads.

GYM LESSONS PE, PT; EXERCISES.

GYNOPHOBIA *Aversion* to women.

H 1. HARD. HORRIFIC (film *censorship*). HOSPITAL. HOT.
HOTEL. HOUR. HUNGARY (*car plate*). HYDROGEN
(*chem*). 2. Dropping the letter H is indicated by an apostrophe in
the clue, e.g. **Little brother makes money with 'is loaf** (5) =
BR'EAD (**loaf** = head; **money** = bread).

h Husband of.

HA HORSE ARTILLERY. HALF-LAUGH (crypt).

HABIT *CUSTOM*, WONT. *DRESS*.

HABITATION ABODE, *HOME*, *HOUSE*, LIVING QUARTERS;
specifically:

Animal	Habitation
Badger	*EARTH*, SET(T)
Beaver	*LODGE*
Bee	HIVE
Bird	NEST
Cattle	MANGER, MIDDEN
Eagle	EYRIE
Fox	BURROW, *EARTH*
Hare	*FORM*
Heron	COLONY
Horse	*STABLE*
Insect eggs	NIDUS
Otter	*HOLT, LODGE*
Penguin	*ROOKERY*
Pig	*STY*
Rabbit	*BURROW*, WARREN
Rook	*ROOKERY*
Seal	*ROOKERY*
Sparrow	COLONY
Squirrel	*DRAY*, DREY
Swan	COLONY
Wild beast	*DEN*, LAIR

Habitation	Animal
Burrow	*FOX, RABBIT*
Colony	HERON, SPARROW, *SWAN*
Den	WILD ANIMAL
Dray, Drey	SQUIRREL
Earth	*BADGER, FOX*
Eyrie	*EAGLE*
Form	HARE
Hive	*Bee*
Holt	OTTER
Lair	WILD ANIMAL
Lodge	*BEAVER*, OTTER
Manger	*CATTLE*
Midden	*CATTLE*
Nest	*BIRD*
Nidus	INSECT EGGS

Rookery	PENGUIN, *ROOK*, SEAL
Set(t)	*BADGER*
Stable	*HORSE*
Sty	*PIG*
Warren	*RABBIT*

HADES Gk *god* of the *UNDERWORLD*, s of *Cronos* and *Rhea*, br
of *Poseidon* and *Zeus*, mar to *Persephone* (**Rom** = *DIS*, ORCUS,
PLUTO). By association, *HELL* itself; ABADDON (Heb),
EREBUS (Gk), GEHENNA (bibl), INFERNO (Dante),
SHEOL (Heb), TARTARUS (Gk myth), VALHALLA (Nor);
asphodel meadows [*Cerberus*, *Charon*, *Hecate*, *Styx*].
HAGGARD 1. DRAWN, WILD LOOKING. UNTAMED
HAWK. 2. (Sir Henry) RIDER ~ (writer; **books**: Ayesha,
Dawn, King Solomon's Mines, Jess, She; Allan Quartermain).
HAIL (s/l *hale*). ALOHA, AVE; SALUTE. FROZEN RAIN.
HAIR FILAMENT. CURL, LOCK, TRESS [Esau, Nisus, Samson;
hirsute]; BARNET (*rh sl*).
HAIRDRESSER BARBER, COIFFEUR, WAVER; **celebrated:**
MISS MOUCHER (David Copperfield, *Dickens*); MR
PARTRIDGE (Tom Jones, Fielding); PAUL SWEEDLEPIPE
(Martin Chuzzlewit, Dickens); FIGARO (Barber of Seville,
Rossini); SWEENEY TODD. BRUSH, COMB, CURLER,
GRIP, SLIDE (crypt).
HAL HENRY.
HALE (s/l *hail*). FIT, WELL. ORIGINATE. HAUL.
HALF 1. DEMI, SEMI; SPLIT. 2. Half of preceding or next word,
e.g. **Half bottle** = BOT or TLE. 3. As, **Not** ~, remove half of word,
e.g. **Mrs Mopp's charming, not half!** (4) = CHAR(ming).
~ **BACK** *FOOTBALLER*. IMED, IMES (crypt). BA or CK
(crypt).
~ **DAY** EARLY CLOSING. AM, PM (crypt).
~ **HEARTED** 1. LUKEWARM, UNENTHUSIASTIC. 2. Remove
one of two identical letters in middle of word indicated, e.g. **Half
hearted rabble** = RABLE.
~ **HUNTER** WATCH. HUN or TER (crypt).
~ **SOVEREIGN** TEN SHILLINGS, XS. WILLIAM or MARY
(crypt).
HALT STOP (**opp** = *go on*). CRIPPLED, LAME, LIMP.

HAM BUTTOCK, THIGH. SALT PIG. AMATEUR RADIO
OPERATOR, BREAKER (sl), CB ENTHUSIAST. ACT BADLY
(hence CAT – crypt), CABOTIN, POOR PERFORMER.

HAMBLEDON *CRICKET* GROUND.

HAMLET VILLAGE. GREAT DANE, PRINCE OF
DENMARK (*Shakespeare*). PIGLET, PORKER (crypt).

HAMMER NAILER, TOOL; BIRMINGHAM SPANNER (sl);
STRIKE. EDWARD (hist). PIGFARMER (crypt). **Pl =**
WEST HAM (*football team*).

~ **THROWER** THOR (Nor myth).

HAMPDEN PARK *FOOTBALL* GROUND (Sc).

HAMPER BASKET [Fortnums; picnic]. HINDER, LET (**opp =**
help).

HAND MITT, PALM, PAW (*bone*; **saying**). HELP; PASS.
HOLDING (cards). CREWMAN, SEAMAN (naut). BUNCH
(bananas). JOINT (pork). POINTER (clock). 4 INS (horse).

HANDLE FEEL, TOUCH. *GRIP*, HOLDER. MANAGE,
TREAT. DEAL IN. ADDRESS, TITLE (sl).

HANGMAN EXECUTIONER; TOPPER (crypt) [*tarot*]; **celebrated:**
PETIT ANDRE (Quentin Durward, Scott), DERRICK,
KETCH, PIERREPOINT. GALLERY DIRECTOR (crypt).

HAPPY CONTENTED; **saying**. *DWARF* (Snow White).

HARD H; DURABLE, TOUGH. RELENTLESS.

~ **LINES** TOUGH LUCK. BR, *RAILWAY* TRACK, RLY
(crypt).

HARNESS EQUIP(MENT), FASTEN(ING), LIGAMENT,
STRAP. HORSE TRAPPINGS: BIT, BRIDLE, BRIDOON,
CURB, HACKAMORE, HEADSTALL, MARTINGALE,
PELHAM, REINS, RESTRAINT, SNAFFLE, TRACE
[loriner]. HOOK UP, UTILIZE. DEFENSIVE ARMOUR.

HARP NAG. PLUCK; *INSTRUMENT* (mus), LYRE [*Aeolus*].

HARPY 1. HARRIDAN, *SHREW*, TERMAGENT. LYRICAL
(crypt). 2. Malignant monsters with woman's head and vulture's
body, capable of defiling all they touched: AELLO, CELAENO,
OCYPETE, PODARGE.

HARRIER *BIRD*, HAWK. HUNTING *DOG*. COUNTRY
RUNNER (hare and hounds). *AIRCRAFT*®: FIGHTER, JUMP
JET, VTO. HARASSER, MOLESTER.

HARRIS *MATERIAL*, TWEED. [*Three* Men in a Boat; *unseen* in

Martin Chuzzlewit (*Dickens*)].

HARROW BREAKER, DRAG (farm). LACERATE, WOUND. HARRY, ROB. WRACK. *PUBLIC SCHOOL.*

HARRY HAL, HENRY; 'HOME RULER'. TATE. HARASS, MOLEST, WORRY. (Old ~ = devil).

HARVARD UNIVERSITY (US) [Cantabrigian]. AIRCRAFT (trainer).

HARVEST 1. CROP, GATHER. PRODUCE, YIELD. REAP. HUSBAND, LAY UP. 2. **God: Gk** = CRONOS, **Rom** = SATURNUS.

HAT HEAD COVERING: BEARSKIN, BERET, BILLYCOCK, BONNET, BOWLER, BUSBY, CAP, COVER, DERBY (US), EASTER BONNET, FEDORA (US), FLAT ~, GIBUS, HOMBERG, KEPI, LID, MITRE, OPERA ~, PEAKED ~, PORKPIE, SHAKO, SOMBRERO, STETSON, STOVEPIPE ~, TEN-GALLON ~, TILE, TITFER (*rh sl*), TOP ~, TOPEE, TOP GEAR (crypt), TOPI, TOPPER, TRILBY, WIDEAWAKE.

HATRED 1. *AVERSION*, DISLIKE, ABHORRENCE (**opp** = *love*). MILITARY POLICE, MP (crypt). STAFF OFFICER (crypt). 2. Prefix miso- as misogamy (marriage), misogyny (women), misology (reason), misoneism (novelty).

HAWK BIRD OF PREY; **breeds:** BUZZARD, CARACARA, *EAGLE*, FALCON, GOSHAWK, GYRFALCON, HOBBY ~, KESTREL, LANNER, *MERLIN*, MUSKET, OSPREY, PEREGRINE, RAPTOR, SPARROW ~, VULTURE; **assembly** = *cast*, **offspring** = bowet [falconer; ostringer]. AIRCRAFT. COUGH, SPIT. PEDDLE. PLASTERER'S BOARD. WARMONGER (**opp** = dove).

HAWKER *AIRCRAFT*. FALCONER [hood, jess, lure]. *PEDLAR*.

HAY DRIED GRASS [*measure*; ted]. *CASTLE*. DANCE FIGURE.

HE HELIUM (*chem*). HIS EMINENCE. HIS EXCELLENCY; GOVERNOR. HIGH EXPLOSIVE. MAN, MALE.

HEAD 1. BEAN, LOAF (*rh sl*), NAPPER, NOD, NODDLE, *NOGGIN*, NOODLE, ONION, PATE, POLL, SWEDE; [*bone*]. CHIEF, MASTER, TOP. CAPE, NESS (geog). FACE, OBVERSE (coin; **opp** = reverse, tail). 2. Use first letter, e.g. **Spithead** = s.

HEADGEAR *HAT* [*Church dress*]. PIT WINDING.

HEADINGLEY TEST(ING) GROUND (*cricket*).

HEADLINE BANNER, LEADER, STREAMER. PROFILE, SILHOUETTE. **Pl** = FROWN (crypt).

HEAD OFF 1. EXECUTE, GUILLOTINE. INTERCEPT. 2. Drop first letter, e.g. **Head off Jack's partner, and she's not very well** (3) = (J)ILL.

HEAD OF MI.5 M; Q.

HEADQUARTERS CENTRAL OFFICE, HQ. H, E, A or D (crypt). Q (crypt).

HEAL (s/l *heel*). GET BETTER, MEND (**opp** = wound).

HEALING 1. MENDING, RECOVERING. 2. **God: Gk and Rom** = APOLLO; **Ind** = VISHNU.

HEALTH 1. FITNESS, SOUNDNESS, WELFARE, WELLBEING (**Unions** = COHSE, NUPE). TOAST (drink). 2. **Goddesses: Gk** = HYGIEA, **Rom** = SALUS.

HEAR (s/l *here*). 1. HARK, LIST(EN), PERCEIVE. 2. *Sounds like*, often given as 'we hear', e.g. **We hear you when the cuppa's downed** (5, 3) = AFTER TEA (after T in the alphabet, comes U).

HEARD (s/l *herd*). 1. HARKENED, LISTENED, PERCEIVED. 2. *Sounds like*, e.g. **Elk are heard in loving talk** = DEAR.

HEARER AUDITOR, LISTENER. EAR (crypt).

HEART (s/l hart). 1. CENTRE, CORE, MIDDLE. COURAGE, WILL; BREAST, LOVE, MIND, SOUL, INTELLECT (**saying**). ORGAN (med, *study*), PUMP (sl). BRAVE FELLOW. **Pl** = CARDS, SUIT (*Alice*). 2. Middle of word, e.g. **heartbreak** = E; **lighthearted** = G. 3. Put word in another, e.g. **A man little by little at heart in the New World** (8) = A*M*ERIC*AN.

HEARTH 1. FIREPLACE. 2. **Goddesses: Gk** = *HESTIA*, **Rom** = VESTA.

HEARTLESS 1. CRUEL, PITILESS, MERCILESS. 2. Omit middle letters, e.g. **Heartless maple** = MALE.

HEAT ANGER, INFLAME. HOT WEATHER, WARMTH (**opp** = cold). ELIMINATOR, SINGLE RACE.

HEATHER ERICA, LING. WARM HER (crypt).

HEAVEN 1. FIRMAMENT, SKY, VAULT; GOD'S ABODE. Eleven who went to ~ (in *song*). 2. **God: Gk** = URANUS [Elysium]; **Nor** = *VALHALLA* [Nirvana (Ind)]; **opp** = *hell*.

HEAVENLY 1. ATTRACTIVE, DIVINE, EXCELLENT. 2. Of

or in the sky, thus **Heavenly pub** (6) = SK*INN*Y.

~ **BODY** MOON, ORB, *PLANET*, STAR, SUN. BATHING
BEAUTY, MISS WORLD®.

HEBE 1. Gk *goddess* of YOUTH; cup-bearer to the gods; d of *Zeus*
and *Hera*; mar *Hercules*. DIA. **Rom** = JUVENTAS. 2. A
minor *PLANET*. 3. SHRUB (evergreen).

HECATE 1. Gk *goddess* of night, witchcraft and the *underworld*
[Libera, *Persephone*, Proserpine]. 2. A minor *PLANET*.

HECTOR *BULLY*, *HARROW*, HARRY, INTIMIDATE. 2. Gk
myth s of *Priam* and *Hecuba*; mar Andromache; k by *Achilles* at
Troy. One of the *Nine Worthies*. [T and C (*Shak*)].

HECUBA 1. Gk myth wife of *Priam* (king of *Troy*), m of *Cassandra*,
Hector and *Paris*. 2. A minor *PLANET*.

HEEL (s/l *heal*). BASE OF MAST. PART OF FOOT [*Achilles*;
bone]. CAD, SCAMP. LEAN, LIST, TILT.

HEL (s/l *hell*). Nor *goddess* who received those who died of misery
and darkness; d of *Loki* and Angurboda.

HELD 1. DETAINED, GRASPED, GRIPPED, KEPT,
RESTRICTED. OCCUPIED, OWNED, POSSESSED.
SUPPORTED. CELEBRATED, OBSERVED (*custom*).
CONTINUED. 2. Hidden word, or word in another, e.g.
Wolfishly upheld by a thread (6) = L*UP*INE.

~ **BACK** 1. RESTRAINED. HESITATED, IMPEDED,
REFRAINED. 2. Hidden word backwards, e.g. **Held back by
Sir, approaching the Capital** (5) = PA*RIS. 3. Word reversed in
another, e.g. **It's held back by row over a joint** (7) = BA*STI*NG.

HELEN 1. GIRL. 'FIREBRAND'. 2. Gk myth d of Leda and
Zeus, the *twin* of *Clytemnestra*; mar Menelaus, king of Sparta,
whence *Paris* carried her off, thus starting the war at *Troy*.
Renowned for her beauty [T and C (*Shak*)]. 3. A minor
PLANET.

HELENUS Gk myth s of *Priam*.

HELIOS Gk *god* of the SUN. Son of Hyperion and The(i)a; br of
Eos (**Rom** = Aurora) and *Selene* (**Rom** = Luna). **Rom** = SOL.

HELIUM HE (*chem*).

HELL (s/l Hel). *HADES,* HECK, INFERNO, PIT,
UNDERWORLD; **opp** = *heaven*. HE WILL (crypt).

HELLE Gk myth d of Athamas and Nephele. She and her br
Phrixus were rescued by Nephele from sacrifice by Ino; they flew

away on a golden ram (origin of the *golden fleece*), but Helle was
drowned when she fell into the sea, which was thereafter called
the *Hellespont*.

HELLESPONT DARDANELLES. Strait between Asias Major
and Minor, named after *Helle*. [*Hero, Leander*].

HELP AID, ASSIST, HAND (**opp** = *hamper*); REMEDY.
AVOID, ESCAPE. *CHAR*.

HELPLESS 1. LACKING ASSISTANCE. 2. Remove letters AID
or HELP from word indicated, e.g. **Helpless maid** = M or, more
cryptically, **Helpless first aid man** (4) = first*man = ADAM.

HEM BORDER, EDGE, TURN-UP. HESITATION. *COUGH,
HAWK*.

HEN-HOUSE BATTERY, COOP.

HENRY HAL, HARRY. MEASURE (elect). DR JEKYLL
[Edward *Hyde*].

~ VIII's WIVES in order: CATHERINE OF SPAIN (div), ANNE
BOLEYN or BULLEN (beheaded), JANE SEYMOUR (d),
ANNE OF CLEVES (div), CATHERINE HOWARD
(beheaded), CATHERINE PARR (survived).

HEPHAESTUS Gk *god* of *FIRE*, s of *Zeus* and *Hera*. **Rom** =
VULCAN.

HERA Queen of Gk *goddesses* (and of childbirth); sis of and mar to
Zeus; m of Ares (**Rom** = *Mars*), *Hebe* (**Rom** = Juventas) and
Hephaestus (**Rom** = *Vulcan*). **Rom** = JUNO.

HERACLES Gk myth s of Zeus and Alcmene (**Rom** = Hercules);
mar to Megara; an *Argonaut*. Maddened by *Hera*, he killed his
children, and the Delphic *oracle* made him perform twelve
labours, as follows:

(1) Fight with Nemean *lion*.

(2) Killing the *hydra* at Lerna.

(3) Capture of the Arcardian *stag*.

(4) Destruction of the Erymanthian *boar*.

(5) Destruction of the Stymphalian *birds*.

(6) Cleansing of the *stable* of Augeas.

(7) Capture of the Cretan *bull*.

(8) Capture of the *mares* of Diomedes.

(9) Seizure of *Hippolyte's girdle*.

(10) Capture of Geryone's *oxen* in Erythia.

(11) Fetching of the golden *apples* of the *Hesperides*.

(12) Bringing *Cerberus* from *Hades*.

HERALD FORESHADOW, FORETELL, *PROPHESY*.
MESSENGER, TRUMPETER, USHER (~ **of the gods** =
HERMES). COURT OFFICIAL, OFFICER OF STATE
(armorial bearings, pedigree, precedence): BATH,
CLARENC(I)EUX, *GARTER*, LORD LYON, NORROY,
ULSTER (all kings of arms); and *CHESTER*, LANCASTER,
RICHMOND, SOMERSET, WINDSOR, *YORK*. *MONTJOY*
(*Shak*). **Heraldic colours: black** = sable, **blue** = azure, **brown** =
tenne or tenny, **green** = vert, **gold** = or, **orange** = tenny, **purple**
= purpure, **red** = gules, **silver** = argent. **Heraldic terms:**
accosted (side by side), achievement (shield), addorsed (back to
back), cabossed (head cut at the neck), *canton* (a corner),
couchant (beast lying with head up), crined (bearing a mane),
dexter (right hand side), disclosed, displayed (wings spread),
dormant (beast lying with head down), embowed (bent), estoile
(star), fess (horizontal band), gardant (beast looking outward),
gorged (beast with crown round the neck), hauriant (fish with
head up), in pride (peacock with tail spread), jessed (with
thongs), lymphad (ship with oars), naiant (fish swimming),
passant (beast walking), rampant (beast upright on hind legs),
regardant (beast looking over its shoulder), sinister (left hand
side), *wyvern* (winged serpent).

HERB HERBERT (abbr). ANNUAL PLANT. *SIMPLE*.
[flavour; *spice*]; **types of** ~**s and spices** (includes carrots, parsnips,
turnips etc):

3-letters	5-letters	INULA
BAY	AGAVE	MOULI
RUE	AMENT	MUDAR
	AVENS	ORVAL
4-letters	BASIL	SPIKE
ALOE	*CAPER*	TANSY
DILL	CHILI	THYME
GEUM	CHIVE	
MACE	CLARY	6-letters
MINT	CLOVE	BENNET
RACE	CUMIN	BORAGE
SAGE	CURRY	CATNIP

	7-letters	8-letters
CHILLI	CARAWAY	ALLSPICE
CUMMIN	CAYENNE	BRASSOCK
ENDIVE	CHERVIL	CAPSICUM
FENNEL	CHICORY	CHARLOCK
FERULA	GINSENG	CINNAMON
GARLIC	HARMALA	COSTMARY
GINGER	KEDLACK	MARJORAM
HARMEL	MUSTARD	ROSEMARY
HERBAR	OREGANO	SAMPHIRE
HYSSOP	PAPRIKA	TARRAGON
LOVAGE	PARSLEY	TRUE-LOVE
NUTMEG	PIMENTA	TURMERIC
ORIGAN	PIMENTO	
PEPPER	RUE-WORT	9+ letters
RATTLE	SAFFRON	ARTEMISIA
SAVORY	SINAPIS	CORIANDER
SESAME	WITLOOF	GILLYFLOWER
		HOREHOUND

HERCULES 1. *CONSTELLATION. HORSE.* 2. Rom equivalent
of *HERACLES* (q.v.); [*pillars of* ~].

HERD (s/l *heard*). 1. Noun of *assembly* (buffalo, cattle, elephants
etc); [*shepherd*]. **God: Gk** = *PAN*, **Rom** = *FAUNUS*, INUUS,
LUPERCUS. 2. *Constellation*.

HERE (s/l *hear*). 1. HAS ARRIVED. IN THIS PLACE. 2.
Means 'in this answer', e.g. **Here I have shot at Shakespeare's
villain** (4) = I*A*GO.

HEREWARD THE WAKE. HITHER (crypt).

HERMES 1. Gk myth s of *Zeus*, *HERALD* and MESSENGER of
the *gods*; he is said to have invented the *lyre* by putting strings
across the shell of a tortoise. (**Rom** = MERCURY) [*robbers*].
2. A minor *PLANET*.

HERMIT ANCHORITE, ASCETIC, *CAVEMAN*, CELLIST,
C(O)ENOBITE, EREMITE, LONER, MONK, RECLUSE,
STYLITE; 9 (*tarot*); **celebrated:** TIMON OF ATHENS, SIMON
STYLITES. CRAB.

HERO 1. Gk myth priestess of *Aphrodite* at Seston on the
Hellespont. Her lover Leander used to swim across from Abydos

to see her, and was drowned when the lighthouse failed one night. 2. IDOL. CHIEF CHARACTER, MALE LEAD (theat). BRAVE SOLDIER, SUPERMAN (**opp** = *coward*); **celebrated (male):** *ACHILLES, ACTAEON, ADONIS, AENEAS, AGAMEMNON, AUTOLYCUS, BELLEREPHON, CASTOR, DAEDALUS, GANYMEDE, HECTOR, HERACLES, HERCULES, ICARUS, JASON, LAERTES, LEANDER,* LYSANDER, *ODYSSEUS, OEDIPUS,* ORESTES, ORION, ORPHEUS, PARIS, PERSEUS, POLLUX, *PRIAM, PYGMALION, NARCISSUS, SISYPHUS, TANTALUS, THESEUS, ULYSSES;* **celebrated (female):** *ANDROMEDA, ARACHNE, ATALANTA, CASSANDRA, CLYTEMNESTRA, DAPHNE, DIDO, DORIS, ELECTRA, ELISSA, EUROPA, EURYDICE, GALATEA,* IPHIGENIA, *HELEN, HELLE, HIPPOLYTE, JOCASTA, NIOBE, PANDORA, PENELOPE.*

HERRING *FISH:* ALLICE, BLOATER (dried), KIPPER (smoked), SHAD, TWAIT [~ bone, ~ gull, ~ pond].

HESITATION DELAY, ER, UM (**saying**). STAMMERING, STUTTERING.

HESPERIDES Gk myth maidens (AEGLE, ERYTHEIA and HESPERUS), who guarded the golden apples given to *Hera* when she mar *Zeus*. [*Heracles*].

HESPERUS 1. One of the *Hesperides*; Gk and Rom name for *VENUS* as the EVENING STAR; **opp** = *Lucifer* (Rom), *Phosphoros* (Gk). 2. SCHOONER (Longfellow).

HESTIA 1. Gk myth *goddess* of the *HEARTH*; d of Cronos and Rhea (**Rom** = VESTA). 2. A minor *PLANET.*

HE WILL *HELL.*

HE WOULD HED.

HG MERCURY (*chem*).

HIDDEN CACHED, CONCEALED, DOGGO, ESOTERIC, *SECRET.*

Hidden word There are not as many ways of conveying that the answer is hidden somewhere in the clue, as there are of implying that an anagram is intended. Nevertheless, words such as 'found in . . .', '. . . we see', 'from', 'part of . . .' 'reads', 'reveals', 'some of . . .' and 'taken from . . .', all suggest that the word lies somewhere written before your eyes (see HELD/*HOLD BACK* for a hidden word reading backwards). The answer may also be revealed if you take note and respond sensibly to undue awkwardness in phraseology (this sentence has been included not only to warn the puzzler to be on the look-out for stilted sentence construction, which may betray the fact that the puzzle setter has been trying to work the answer into the clue, but also as an example itself. It starts by telling us that 'the answer may be revealed'; it goes on to instruct that a note – A, B, C, D, E, F, G or H – should be taken away somewhere from what follows. Thus, if we remove the letter D from 'respond sensibly' we find that we are left with RESPON*SE(nsibly) – which is another word for 'answer'.) So the clue may have to be added to or shortened, or even read in reverse, to find the hidden word; but the instruction will be there somewhere, together with an indication of the meaning of the answer itself – in the example above, it was the phrase 'the answer may also be revealed'.

HIDE (s/l hied, *hyde*). 1. PELT, SKIN. CONCEAL(MENT). HARBOUR, *SCREEN* (**opp** = reveal, *unearth*).

HIDING CANING, THRASHING, WHIPPING. CONCEALMENT.

HIGHBALL DRINK. LOB (crypt).

HIGH CLASS AI. U. FLYING SCHOOL (crypt).

HIGHLY 1. EXTREMELY, VERY. 2. High in the body, building etc, e.g. **Highly painful** (8) = HEADACHE, MIGRAINE.

HIGH POST TOP JOB. AIR MAIL (crypt).

HIGH STANDING TALL; ON STILTS, hence STILTED (crypt).

HIGHWAYMAN ROAD MENDER (crypt). BANDOLERO, FOOTPAD, ROBBER OF THE ROAD; **celebrated:** PAUL CLIFFORD (Bulwer-Lytton), CLAUDE DUVAL, TOM FAGGUS (Lorna Doone, Blackmore), CAPT MACHEATH and JEREMY TWITCHER (Beggar's Opera, Gay), DICK TURPIN.

HIJKLMNO WATER (H to O, hence H_2O – crypt).

HILL *BANK*, BUTTE, *DOWN*, DUN, EMINENCE, HEAP, INCLINE, MOUND, MOUNT, SLOPE, TOR (**opp** = *vale*). SYDNEY *CRICKET* GROUND. [Roland ~; postage, *stamp*].

HINDER DETER, HAMPER, IMPEDE, *LET*, MAR, OBSTRUCT, PREVENT, *STOP* (**opp** = *abet*). REARMOST. DEERSTALKER (crypt).

HINGE JOINT, SWING. ANKLE, ELBOW, KNEE, KNUCKLE, SHOULDER.

HINNY STALLION/ASS *offspring*.

HINT INDICATION, *TIP*, WRINKLE.

HIPPOCRATES Celebrated Gk *doctor*, b Cos c 460 B.C., d Thessaly 357 B.C. [doctor's oath].

HIPPOLYTE Gk myth d of *Ares*; Queen of the Amazons. She wore a girdle, the object of one of *Hercules'* 12 labours.

HIPPOPHILE *Lover* of horses.

HIPPOPHOBIA *Aversion* to horses.

HISTORY 1. ANNALS, CAREER, RECORD, SAGA. AUTOBIOGRAPHY (crypt). 2. **Gk muse** = *CLIO*.

HIT *Anag.* CUFF, PUNCH, SLAP, STRIKE. SUCCESS (**opp** = *miss*).

HM ER, HER/HIS MAJESTY, KING, QUEEN. HARBOURMASTER.

HO HOME OFFICE. HOUSE. HALLO, HELLO, HILLO, HOLLO, HULLO.

HOAX CANARD, FALSE REPORT; JAPE, PRACTICAL JOKE. HOCUS.

HOIST JACK (UP). RAISE(D) (**opp** = *lower*). ELEVATOR, LIFT (mech). FLAG SIGNAL (naut). PULLEY, *WHIP* (naut).

HOLD CATCH, CLASP, GET, GRAB, GRASP, *GRIP*, KEEP. DETAIN, RESIST. CONTAIN, RESTRICT. OWN, POSSESS. THREAT. BELIEVE, CONSIDER, THINK. CARGO COMPARTMENT. **Pl** = Hidden word (see *HELD*), or word round another, e.g. **He holds order in the house** (4) = H*OM*E.

~ **BACK** 1. IMPEDE, RESTRICT, RESTRAIN. 2. Hidden word backwards, e.g. **The Royal Aero Club holds back the money – quite right, it's Spanish** = REA*L.

HOLDING FARM, TENURE. PORTFOLIO. FISTFUL, HANDFUL.

HOLD UP 1. DETAIN. PROP, SUPPORT. RAID, STICK UP. 2. Word backwards in another (dn) clue, e.g. **The subject is: he holds me up after the car goes over us both** (5) = T*H*EM*E.

HOLLAND NL, NETHERLANDS. LINEN, *MATERIAL*. **Pl** = DUTCH, GIN.

HOLMES (s/l *homes*). *DETECTIVE*, SHERLOCK. Created by Sir Arthur Conan Doyle and based on Dr Joseph *Bell*; lived first in Montague Street and then at 221B Baker Street, London.

Stamford introduced him to Dr John H. Watson, ex-Indian Army, wounded Afghanistan in the leg/shoulder (some confusion) and saved by Murray his orderly. Holmes played the *violin*, took *cocaine*, kept his tobacco in a Persian slipper, had a gasogene for soda water, used the door as a target for revolver practice, and wore a *deerstalker* hat; his br Mycroft was a Civil Servant and a member of the *Diogenes* Club; his housekeeper was Mrs Hudson, his pageboy Billy, his young helpers the Baker Street Irregulars (leader: Wiggins); Scotland Yard detectives were Gregson and Lestrade; principal adversaries were Irene Adler ('the' Woman), Col Sebastian Moran, and Professor James Moriarty ('the Napoleon of Crime') who was killed – supposedly with Holmes – at the Reichenbach Falls in Switzerland. **Celebrated cases:**

A Study in Scarlet
The Sign of Four
A Scandal in Bohemia
The Red-headed League
A Case of Identity
The Boscombe Valley Mystery
The Five Orange Pips
The Man with the Twisted Lip
The 'Gloria Scott'
The Musgrave Ritual
The Reigate Puzzle
The Crooked Man
The Resident Patient
The Greek Interpreter
The Naval Treaty
The Final Problem
The Hound of the Baskervilles
The Valley of Fear
His Last Bow
The Adventure of:
   ~ the Blue Carbuncle
   ~ the Speckled Band
   ~ the Engineer's Thumb
   ~ the Noble Bachelor
   ~ the Beryl Coronet

~ the Copper Beeches
~ the Empty House
~ the Norwood Builder
~ the Dancing Men
~ the Solitary Cyclist
~ the Priory School
~ Black Peter
~ Charles Augustus Milverton
~ the Six Napoleons
~ the Three Students
~ the Golden Pince-Nez
~ the Missing Three-Quarter
~ the Abbey Grange
~ the Second Stain
~ Wisteria Lodge
~ the Cardboard Box
~ the Red Circle
~ the Bruce-Partington Plans
~ the Dying Detective
~ the Devil's Foot
~ the Illustrious Client
~ the Blanched Soldier
~ the Mazarin Stone
~ the Three Gables
~ the Sussex Vampire
~ the Three Garridebs
~ the Creeping Man
~ the Lion's Mane
~ the Veiled Lodger
~ Shoscombe Old Place
~ the Retired Colourman.

HOLT COPSE, WOOD. *HABITATION*, LAIR (otter). *CASTLE*.

HOLY (s/l wholly). SAINTLY; GOOD. *ISLAND*. HOLED (crypt).

~ **GRAIL** CHRIST'S CUP [*Galahad*; *Round Table*].

HOME COUNTRY (**saying**), DWELLING (**saying**), LAND, REFUGE, VILLA. FIND, LOCATE (radio). OWN

GROUND (*cricket*, *football*, *rugby*); **opp** = away. *PRIME MINISTER*.

~ **COUNTIES** SE (geog, crypt).

~ **HELP** *CHAR*. DIY.

~ **OFFICE** HO.

HOMER POET (Gk), *WRITER*. *RUN* (baseball). *PIGEON* (crypt).

HONEY DARLING, DEAR, PET, SWEETHEART. NECTAR, SWEETNESS [mead].

HONOUR 1. CBE, CH, KBE, MBE, OBE, OM etc. AWARD, KNIGHTHOOD. GRACE, RECOGNIZE. VIRTUE [**guard of** ~ = *chaperone*]. ACE, KING, QUEEN, JACK/KNAVE (cards). 2. TITLE which goes with some high honours, e.g. **Man of honour** (3) or (6) = SIR or KNIGHT.

HONOURED 1. ACCEPTED, PAID. CBE, CH, KBE etc (see *HONOUR*). DIGNIFIED, ENRICHED. ENTITLED. 2. TITLE which often goes with an honour or ennoblement, e.g. **Honoured lady** (4) = DAME.

HOOCH *DRINK*. *AMERICAN INDIAN*.

HOOD BONNET, COWL; CANOPY, COVER. GANGSTER, GUNMAN, HOODLUM, THUG; MAFIA. ROBIN, RICHARD LOCKSLEY [Friar Tuck, Little *John*, *Maid* Marion, Nottingham Sheriff, Sherwood Forest, Will Scarlet].

HOOK CATCH, SNARE, TRAP. ANGLED WIRE, ATTACHMENT, CROOK. CURVED BLADE. BEND. *HEEL* (rugby). PULL, STROKE (*cricket*, golf). BLOW, HIT, PUNCH (boxing). *PIRATE*.

HOOKER FORWARD (rugby). PROSTITUTE (US sl). *BOAT* (sl), SHIP. ANGLER, FISHERMAN (crypt).

HOOKY TRUANCY (US). ANGULAR; ANGLING, FISHING (crypt).

HOPE ASPIRATION, DESIRE, EXPECT, WISH; **saying**. PROBABILITY, PROMISE. BOB ~ (theat); ANTHONY ~ (*writer*; Prisoner of Zenda).

HOPPER *BOUNDER*; CRICKET, FLEA, FROG, *KANGAROO*. CONTAINER. HOP-PICKER; OAST HOUSE.

HORRIFIC H (film *censorship*). FRIGHTFUL, SCANDALOUS, SHOCKING.

HORSE (s/l hoarse). CLOTHES DRIER. *DRUG*, HEROIN.

ISLAND. *LARK*, *PLAY*. MAINSHEET SPAN (naut).
OBSTRUCTION (mining). VAULTING BLOCK.
QUADRUPED of genus equus; DOBBIN, GG, NAG (all sl);
ROCKING; BAY, CHESTNUT, DAPPLED, GREY,
PIEBALD, ROAN, SKEWBALD; **saying:** PONY, STEED;
KELPIE (Sc myth); [Thelwell]; **types:** CARTHORSE, CIRCUS
~, *COB*, *RACEHORSE*, *SCREW*, SHOW ~,
(STEEPLE)CHASER, *THOROUGHBRED*, TROTTER;
breeds: ARABIAN, CASPIAN, CONNEMARA,
CLYDESDALE, DARTMOOR, HANOVARIAN,
LIPPIZANER, NEW FOREST, PALOMINO, QUARTER ~,
SHETLAND, SHIRE, TARPAN, WELSH. **Assembly** = *herd*;
habitation = stable; **male** = stallion (colt), stud ~; **female** = mare
(filly); **offspring** = foal (colt, filly) [*racetrack*; stalking ~, white ~s
(waves)]. **Celebrated:** ARION (*Hercules*, *Neptune*), ARKLE
(steeplechaser), BLACK BEAUTY (Anna Sewell), BLACK
BESS (Dick Turpin), BOXER (*Orwell*), BORAK (*Mohammed*),
BUCEPHALUS (*Alexander* the Great), CHAMPION (Wonder
~), CICERO (drum ~, mil), COPENHAGEN (*Wellington*),
GOLDEN MILLER (steeplechaser), GRANE (Brunhilda,
Wagner's Ring); *HERCULES* (Soapey Sponge. Steptoe & Son),
INCITATUS (Caligula's consul), LAMRI (King Arthur),
MARENGO (*Napoleon*), MARSALA (Garibaldi), *PEGASUS*
(winged ~ of *Bellerophon*; *constellation*), RED RUM® (Grand
National), REKSH (Rustam), ROSINANTE (Don Quixote),
SILVER (Lone Ranger), SLEIPNER (eight-legged of *Odin*),
SORREL (William III), TRIGGER (Roy Rogers), TUC ~
(*Low*), VELVET (Enid Bagnold), VOLONEL (Field Marshal
Earl Roberts VC), WHITE SURREY (Richard III), Wooden ~
of *Troy*; XANTHUS (*Achilles*) [*centaur*; ~ power; wild ~s].
[Prince Monolulu].

HORSEGUARDS BLUES, *ROYALS*. PARADE GROUND.

HORSEPOWER HP (550 ft/lb/sec).

HORUS Gk form of Egy *god* of the SUN; s of *Isis*. God of
doorways.

HOSPITAL H. *NURSERY* (crypt), SANATORIUM,
SICKROOM.

HOST ARMY, COMPANY (arch). GREAT NUMBER, LOTS.
INNKEEPER, *LANDLORD*, *Chaucer* character (Harry

Bailey). ENTERTAINER, PARTY-GIVER, WELCOMER; *AMPHITRYON* (Molière). RECEIVER, RECEPTACLE (of commensal, parasite, transplant). CONSECRATED BREAD (eccles). **Pl** = ANGELS, STARS.

HOT H; CLOSE, NEAR, OPPRESSIVE, SULTRY, SWELTERING, TORRID, WARM (**opp** = *cold*). STOLEN (sl).
~ SPOT TROPICS; SAHARA. OVEN. VOLCANO.

HOUND HARRY, PURSUE, WORRY. BOUNDER, CAD. *DOG* (**assembly** = pack, **male** = dog, **female** = bitch, **offspring** = puppy) [Baskervilles; hunting].

HOUR (s/l our). H, HR.

HOUSE HO. MPS, COMMONS, *LEGISLATIVE ASSEMBLY*, LORDS, WESTMINSTER. *COMPANY*. BINGO®, FULL CARD, LOTTO®. BUNGALOW, COTTAGE, *HOME*, PREMISES, SEMI. (*ROYAL*) FAMILY. AUDIENCE (theat).

HOUSEHOLD CAVALRY BLUES, ROYALS.

HOUSEHOLDER OWNER-OCCUPIER, HEAD OF HOUSE (hence H). FRANCHISEE (arch). *LAR* (crypt). POKER PLAYER (crypt). SNAIL, WHELK (crypt). **Pl** = *GUARDS*; BLUES, ROYALS (crypt). *LARES*, PENATES (Rom, crypt).

HOUSEHOLD GODS *LARES*, PENATES (Rom).

HOUSE OF COMMONS DEBATING CHAMBER, *LEGISLATIVE ASSEMBLY*, MPS.

HOUSE OF LORDS UPPER HOUSE, OTHER PLACE. STATELY HOME.

HOUSEPARTY BINGO®, LOTTO®.

HOY CALL, HAIL. *BOAT*. *ISLAND*.

HP HOUSE OF PARLIAMENT, MPS, WESTMINSTER. *HORSEPOWER*. SAUCE®.

HQ HEADQUARTERS, hence H, E, A or D (crypt).

HR HOUR.

HST HIGH SPEED TRAIN.

HUMANIST ERASMUS (NL).

HUN ATTILA. GERMAN, NOMAD, PRUSSIAN. HALF-HUNTER (crypt).

HUNCHBACK CROOKBACK, HUMPBACK [*camel*, *whale*]; **celebrated (fact):** Alexander Pope, Richard III; **(fiction):** ~ of Notre Dame, Quasimodo (Hugo), Punch, Rigoletto (*jester*,

Verdi), Rumpelstiltskin (Grimm).

HUNDRED See *number*. C, CENTURY, TON. 100 [~ days (*Napoleon*); ~ years war]. LAND AREA.

HUNDREDWEIGHT CWT, *MEASURE*.

Hung Hungary, ~ian.

HUNGRY (s/l Hungary). 1. AVID, KEEN, STARVING. 2. Word with O added in it, e.g. **Joan is no longer hungry, and is quite a different girl** (3) = J*AN.

HUNTER 1. *HORSE*, HUNTSMAN: JOHN PEEL, JORROCKS (HERCULES), UNSPEAKABLE (Wilde). CHASER, SEEKER, ESAU (bibl), NIMROD (bibl) [*patron saint*]. *AIRCRAFT*. (COVERED) WATCH. 2. **Myth:** *ACTAEON*, *ARTEMIS*, *DIANA*, HECATE, *ORION*, UPIS. 3. *Constellation* (Orion).

HUNTING 1. CHASING, SEEKING (fox); SHOOTING (big game). OSCILLATING, PULSATING, WAVERING. 2. **God:** Gk = *PAN*; **goddess: Gk** = *ARTEMIS*, **Rom** = *DIANA*.

HURRIED UP HASTENED (**saying**). DECAR, NAR (dn; crypt).

HUSBAND CONSORT, MAN, MATE, OLD MAN, PARTNER, POT AND PAN (*rh sl*) [Darby and Joan]. CONSERVE, GUARD.

HUSBANDRY 1. *FARMING*. ACCOUNTING, MANAGEMENT. MARRIAGE (crypt). 2. **Rom god** = MARS.

HUSSY *BAGGAGE*, HUZZY, JADE, MINX.

HYADES Gk myth maidens guarding *Dionysus*, now a group of *seven stars* (in Taurus, near *Pleiades*; rain).

HYBRID CROSSBRE(E)D. *MULE*. HINNY.

HYDE (s/l *hide*, hied). HEATH, PARK. EDWARD ~ [Dr Henry Jekyll; R.L. Stevenson].

HYDRA 1. Gk myth nine-headed *monster*, destroyed by *Hercules* at Lerna. 2. *Constellation*.

HYDROGEN H (*chem*).

HYDROPHOBIA *Aversion* to water [rabies].

HYENA TASMANIAN WOLF. QUADRUPED (order Hyaenidae) [laughing; *Anubis*; jackal].

HYGIEA 1. Gk myth *goddess* of HEALTH, d of *Asclepius*. 2. A minor *PLANET*.

HYMEN 1. MEMBRANE, VIRGINITY. 2. Gk myth *god* of

fruitfulness and marriage; s of *Dionysus* (**Rom** = *Bacchus*) and *Aphrodite* (**Rom** = *Venus*). Also marriage song.

HYMN 1. SONG OF PRAISE. 2. **Gk myth muse** = POLYHYMNIA/POLYMNIA.

HYPERION A *Titan*, s of *Uranus* and *Ge*, f of *Eos*, *Helios* and *Selene*.

HYPNOS Gk myth *goddess* of SLEEP, d of *Nyx* without benefit of father [*Morpheus*].

I ACE. IODINE (*chem*). ISLAND. ITALY (*car plate*). ME, NUMBER ONE, PERSONAL PRONOUN.

IACCHUS = *BACCHUS*.

IAMBUS *FOOT*.

IAPETUS 1. Gk myth *TITAN*. All men are reputed to be descended from him. 2. A satellite of the *planet* Saturn.

IB(ID) IN THE SAME PLACE (**opp** = *alibi*).

IBA INDEPENDENT *BROADCASTING* AUTHORITY, LOCAL RADIO, TV.

IC IN CHARGE.

ICARUS 1. Gk myth s of *Daedalus*, who flew too near the sun and fell, when the wax securing his wings was melted [mausoleum]. 2. A minor *PLANET*.

ICE HARD WATER. DIAMONDS. CHOC ~, CORNET, DAIRY CREAM ~, KNICKERBOCKER GLORY, SORBET, VANILLA, WHIP. GROWLER, ~BERG, PACK ~.

ICED CHILLED, FROZEN. RINK (crypt).

ICENI Tribe of Ancient Britons in East Anglia [*Boadicea*].

ID I WOULD. THE SAME. *CARP*, *FISH*. INSTINCT.

IDLE INEFFECTIVE, VAIN, WORTHLESS. TICK OVER. INDOLENT, LAZY, UNOCCUPIED, USELESS (**saying**).

IE ID EST, THAT IS.

IF SUPPOSING, AN (arch). WHENEVER. INTERMEDIATE FREQUENCY. POEM (*Kipling*). *GAOL* (Dumas).

IGNIS FATUUS JACK O' LANTERN, WILL O' THE WISP; MARSH GAS [*mirage*].

II ELEVEN; TWO. SIDE, TEAM.

IL THE ITALIAN. ISRAEL (*car plate*). ILLINOIS (US *state*).

ILL NOT WELL, SICK. I WILL (crypt). ILLUSTRATED. ILLINOIS (US *state*).

IM 1. INTRA MUSCULAR. I AM. HALF-TIME (crypt). 2. Used in a clue at the start of a word to describe the solution, e.g. **'Imperfect' he could have said** (7) = GALAHAD; or may be included in the answer with the same effect, e.g. **Said by reporter to cut a figure** (7) = IM*PRESS. As 'im in the clue, implies omission of H from clue or answer, e.g. **Speech from 'im who held the bridge to the north** (7) = (H)ORATIO*N; may also in the answer be written as 'him commonly', e.g. **Years to him commonly give appearance** (5) = (h)IM*AGE.

IMITATE *APE*, COPY.

IMP AFREET, AFRIT, *DEVIL*, *PERI*, EVIL *SPIRIT*. IMPERATOR; IMPERIAL. IMPORTANT.

IMPAIRED DAMAGED, WEAKENED. II (crypt); AYE-AYE (crypt). TWINNED (crypt).

IMPRESS CONSCRIBE, CONSCRIPT, ENFORCE, *PRESS GANG*, SEIZE, SHANGHAI. DENT, EMBOSS, SEAL, STAMP, STRIKE. CUT A FIGURE, INFLUENCE. [*im*].

IMPRESSIONIST 1. IMITATOR, MIMIC. *PRESS GANG* (crypt). CARVER, ETCHER (crypt). INFLUENTIAL (crypt). 2. School of modern painting; **celebrated:** BOUDIN, CEZANNE, DEGAS, MANET, MONET, PISSARO.

IN 1. AT HOME, INSIDE, NOT OUT. *BATTING*. ESOTERIC. *FASHIONABLE*. INDIANA (US *state*). 2. One word in another, e.g. **An intent to be a leaseholder** (6) = TEN*AN*T, or **Four indulge to reveal** (7) = D*IV*ULGE.

INCENSE ANGER, ENRAGE. HOLY SMOKE, SPICE. PRAISE.

INCH IN. *MEASURE*, PART OF FOOT. *CREEP*. *ISLAND*.

IN CHARGE 1. IC, OVER. 2. By inference, word in synonym for charge, e.g. **The cadets and I are in charge – nonsense** (7) = RU*BB*I*SH.

INCITATUS *Horse* which belonged to the mad Rom emperor Caligula (A.D. 12-41), whose reign was characterized by orgies of cruelty and debauchery; he made his horse a Consul.

INCLINED ANGLED, BIASED, LEANING [Pisa], SLOPED, SLOPING, TILTED; BENT. HALF A MIND (hence MI or ND – crypt). READY, TENDED, TENDING.

INCLUDE 1. COMPREHEND, COMPRISE, CONTAIN,

EMBRACE, ENCLOSE. 2. The clue contains a *hidden word* as answer, e.g. **The king is included in his will, I am quite sure** (7) = WILL*I*AM.

INCOMPLETE 1. EMBRYO, IMMATURE, PART MADE, UNFINISHED. 2. Part of sentence, as a hidden word, e.g. **Spread an incomplete topic, nicely prepared** (6) = PIC*NIC.

IN DEBT 1. IN THE RED, OVERDRAWN, OWING. 2. Place word indicated into DEBT, e.g. **First appearance of society in debt** (5) = DEB*U*T. 3. Similarly place word in RED, e.g. **Fish in debt was pulled in** (6) = R*EEL*ED. 4. May also have IOUS added, e.g. **Officer in debt takes exception** (8) = CAPT*IOUS.

INDEED 1. CERTAINLY, REALLY, YEA, YES. 2. Word placed in DEED, e.g. **Bit indeed would go against one** (7) = DE*BIT*ED.

INDIA Subcontinent in Asia. IND (*car plate*). *ANTELOPE*. HINDU (and see *Religion*). **Provinces:** Andhra Pradesh, Arunnchal Pradesh, Assam, Bengal, Bihar, Gujarat, Haryana, Mimachal Pradesh, Jamm, Kashmir, Karnatak, Kerala, Madhya Pradesh, Maharashtra, Manipur, Meghalaya, Nagaland, Orissa, Punjab, Rajasthan, Sikkim, Tamil Nadu, Tripura, Uttar Pradesh (UP), West Bengal [*American* ~n (Red ~n); ~n ink; ~ paper; ~ rubber; ~ tea].

INDIVIDUAL EGO, I, ONE, SELF. CHARACTERISTIC, PARTICULAR, *SINGLE*, SPECIAL.

INDRA Ind *god* of *RAIN*.

INDUCED 1. BROUGHT ABOUT/ON, CAUSED. INFERRED, PERSUADED, PREVAILED ON. 2. Letter or word put into another, e.g. **Politician, nothing induced to clean** (3) = M*O*P. 3. Word placed into letters DUCED, e.g. **King induced a wetting** (6) = DUC*K*ED.

INDUS *RIVER*. *CONSTELLATION*.

INDUSTRY BUSINESS, FACTORY, MANUFACTURING, WORKS; CBI. APPLICATION, HARD WORK.

IN ERROR *Anag.* 1. OUT, WRONG, MISTAKENLY (**opp** = *right*). 2. Word placed in synonym for error, e.g. **Draw off wine in error; it is salty** = B*RACK*ISH.

INEXPERIENCED DEB, *GREEN*, IMMATURE, TYRO, VIRGIN, *YOUNG* (**opp** = *expert*).

INFATUATION 1. CRUSH, LOVESICKNESS. 2. **Goddess** = ATE (Gk).

INFERIOR LESSER, LOWER, SUBORDINATE, UNDER.
NON-U.

INFORMATION DATE, *DOPE*, *GEN*, GRIFF, INFO,
INTELLIGENCE, KNOW-HOW, LOW-DOWN. TABLES,
TIDINGS. [COI]. FLIGHT, SQUADRON, VEE (all crypt).

INIGO 1. JONES; *ARCHITECT*. 2. Place letter I in word
indicated, e.g. **Inigo cons money from it** (5) = CO*I*NS.

INITIALLY 1. AT FIRST, STARTING. 2. Use the first letters of
words indicated, e.g. **He is trying initially to make a success** (3) =
H*I*T.

INLAY 1. EMBED, FILLING, INSERT; ORNAMENT; **types:**
BOULE, BUHL, FILIGREE, MARQUETRY, OYSTER
VENEER, PARQUETRY, PIQUE, POSE D'OR,
TUNBRIDGE WARE. 2. Letter(s) or word(s) placed in letters
LAY, e.g. **Final inlay is idle** (4) = LA*Z*Y.

INN *BAR*, PH (abbr), PUB, REFUGE, TAVERN.

INNER INTERIOR, INTERNAL. (Second) TARGET RING
[*bullseye*, *magpie*, *outer*]. BATSMAN (crypt).
PUBCRAWLER, *LANDLORD*, PUBLICAN (crypt).

INNER TEMPLE LAW SOCIETY, *INN OF COURT*.

INNS OF COURT GRAY'S INN, INNER TEMPLE, LINCOLN'S
INN, MIDDLE TEMPLE [benchers; call to the bar].

IN ORDER 1. ALL RIGHT, ALLOWED, OK, PERMITTED.
BY ROTA, ON ROSTER, SERIATIM. SERVICEABLE,
WORKING. **Pl** = *CHURCHMAN*, ORDAINED. 2. Word
placed in *decoration* or order, e.g. **Latin in order like earth** (6) =
OB*LAT*E.

IN RUINS *Anag.* 1. BROKEN, COLLAPSED. 2. Word in RUINS,
e.g. **Briefly equal in ruins for French sharks** (7) = R*EQ*UINS.

INSECT 1. CREATURE, INVERTEBRATE (genus insecta),
LEPIDOPTERA; SIX-FOOTER (crypt) [arachnid: mite,
scorpion, spider, tick]. **Celebrated:** *ALEXANDER* (*Milne*).
Types:

3-letters	4-letters	WASP
ANT	FLEA	
BEE	GNAT	**5-letters**
DOR	MITE	APHID
FLY	*MOTH*	APHIS

EMMET	SAWFLY	COCKROACH
LOUSE	SCARAB	DRAGONFLY
MIDGE		*GRASSHOPPER*
	7-letters	HORSEFLY
6-letters	*CRICKET*	HOUSEFLY
BEETLE	CREEPER	*LEPIDOPTERA*
CADDIS	DAMOSEL	POND SKATER
CICADA		ROVE BEETLE
EARWIG	**8+ letters**	WATER BOATMAN
HORNET	ALDERFLY	WATER SCORPION
LOCUST	BLUEBOTTLE	WHIRLIGIG BEETLE
MANTIS	*BUTTERFLY*	
MAYFLY	CADDIS FLY	

2. Put letter(s) or word(s) into SECT, e.g. **Reticent about insect** (6) = SEC*RE*T, or **The Spanish insect is choice** (6) = S*EL*ECT.

INSIDE 1. CONTAINED. *GAOL*. FOOTBALLER: FORWARD, STRIKER. 2. Word in another, hidden word, e.g. **It's all go, inside any pain** (5) = A*GO*NY.

INSPIRATION ANIMATION, INTUITION, *MUSE*, PROMPTING, THOUGHT; **celebrated:** BEATRICE (Dante); DARK LADY (sonnets, *Shak*); LAURA (Petrarch); SVENGALI (Trilby, Gerald du Maurier); WH (Onlie Begetter, sonnets, *Shak*) [Enigma Variations (Elgar); see also *companions, lovers*]. BREATHING, INHALATION (crypt).

INSTALL(ED) 1. PUT IN, FITTED; STABLED (crypt). 2. Word placed in another, e.g. **Bed with girl installed is forbidden** (6) = B*ANN*ED.

INSTEAD 1. ALTERNATIVE, IN LIEU, SUBSTITUTE. 2. Word placed in letters STEAD, e.g. **Cooked me instead** (7) = STEA*ME*D.

INSTITUTE ORIGINATE, START, *FOUND*. *ORGANIZATION*, SOCIETY (tech); MIT.

INSTRUMENT 1. IMPLEMENT, TOOL. DIAL, MEASURING DEVICE, POSITION FINDER (aero, naut). ARRANGER, CHANNEL, PERFORMER. FORMAL/LEGAL DOCUMENT. 2. MUSICAL DEVICE, SOUND PRODUCER; **types:**

(strings, blown): *AEOLIAN* HARP; **(strings, bowed):**
ARPEGGIONE, CELLO, CRWTH, DOUBLE BASS,
HURDY-GURDY, JAPANESE FIDDLE, REBEC, TROMBA
MARINA, VIOL, VIOLA, *VIOLIN*; **(strings, hammered):**
CLAVICHORD, CLAVIER/KLAVIER, DULCIMER,
PANTALEON, *PIANO*(FORTE), SCHLAGZITHER,
ZIMBALON; **(strings, plucked):** BALALAIKA, BANJO, BELL
HARP, CEMBALO, CITTERN, CLARSACH, DITAL HARP,
GUITAR, *HARP*, HARPSICHORD, LUTE, *LYRE*,
MANDOLIN, PSALTERY, UKULELE, VICTALELE,
VIHUELA, VINA (Ind), VIRGINAL, ZITHER; **(wind, brass):**
ALPHORN, BUCCINA (Rom), BUGELHORN (Ger),
BUGLE, CORNET, FLUGELHORN (Ger), FRENCH HORN,
OLIPHANT, POSTHORN, SAXHORN, *SERPENT*,
TROMBONE, TRUMPET, TUBA, VAMPHORN; **(wind, reed):**
ACCORDION, *BAGPIPES*, BASSOON, BOMBARD,
CHENG (Ch), CLARINET, COR ANGLAIS, HARMONICA,
HORNPIPE, *MOUTHORGAN*, OBOE, PIBCORN, PIBROCH
(Sc), *QUAIL*, REGAL, SAXOPHONE, SHAWM, STOCK
HORN; **(wind, tube):** BIN (Ind), FIFE, FLAGEOLET, *FLUTE*,
GALOUBET, *NIGHTINGALE*, *ORGAN*, PANPIPES, PENNY
WHISTLE, PIPE, *RECORDER*, TIN WHISTLE, WHIFFLE;
(percussion): *ANVIL*, *BELL*, *BONES*, CASTANET,
CELESTA, CHANG (Ch), CRESCENT, CYMBALS,
DEAGAN, *DRUM*, DULCIMER, DULCITONE,
GLOCKENSPIEL, GONG, JEWS HARP, KETTLEDRUM,
MARIMBA, MARROWBONES, RATTLE, SALT BOX,
SANTIR (Pers), SNARE DRUM, TABOR, TAMBOURINE,
TARBOUKA, TIMPANI, *TRAPS*, *TRIANGLE*, WOOD
BLOCKS, XYLOPHONE.

INTELLIGENCE BRAINS, NOUS, IQ (**opp** = *stupidity*). *GEN*,
CIA, MIV, SOE [espionage; *agent*].
INTENT 1. BENT. MEANING. 2. Word in the letters TENT, e.g.
An intent leases = TEN*AN*T.
INTER AMONG, BETWEEN. BURY, ENTOMB.
INTERMINABLE 1. ENDLESS, PERPETUAL [eternity]. 2. Omit
last letter(s), e.g. **Interminable hate on one's head** (3) = HAT*.
INTERNATIONAL UNITS PEACEKEEPING FORCE, UN

PATROLS. MEASUREMENT SYSTEM, SI; **prefixes (multiples):**

Factor	Prefix	Symbol
10^{12}	tera-	T
10^{9}	giga-	G
10^{6}	mega-	M
10^{3}	kilo-	k
10^{2}	hecto-	h
10	deca-	da
10^{-1}	deci-	d
10^{-2}	centi-	c
10^{-3}	milli-	m
10^{-6}	micro-	μ
10^{-9}	nano-	n
10^{-12}	pico-	p
10^{-15}	femto-	f
10^{-18}	atto-	a

INTERVAL INTERMISSION, HALF-TIME (hence TI or ME), PAUSE. OCTAVE; SECOND, SEVENTH etc (mus).
INTRIGUE FASCINATE. CABAL, *PLOT*.
INUUS Rom god of *herds*. **Gk** = *PAN*.
INVENTION 1. BRAINCHILD, *DISCOVERY*, IDEA [**saying**; patent]; **celebrated:**

GUNPOWDER	(1320 Schwarz)
TELESCOPE	(1607 Galileo)
PIANOFORTE	(1710 Cristofalli)
MERCURY THERMOMETER	(1721 Fahrenheit)
SPINNING JENNY	(1763 Hargreaves)
STEAM ENGINE	(1764 Watt)
HOT AIR BALLOON	(1783 Montgolfier)
MINER'S SAFETY LAMP	(1815 Davy)
SEWING MACHINE	(1841 Howe)
STEEL	(1856 Bessemer)
DYNAMITE	(1868 Nobel)

TORPEDO	(1868 Whitehead)
TELEPHONE	(1876 Bell)
PHONOGRAPH	(1877 Edison)
WIRELESS	(1898 Marconi)
TANK	(1899 Simms)
AEROPLANE	(1903 Wright)
RADAR	(1935 Watson-Watt)
JET ENGINE	(1939 Heinkel)
POLYESTER	(1941 Whinfield & Dixon)
ROCKET WEAPON	(1944 von Braun)
ATOMIC BOMB	(1945 USA team)

2. **Goddess** = *MINERVA* (Rom).

INVERSE CAPSIZE, INVERT, UPEND. OPPOSITE. POETIC, RHYMING (crypt).

INVEST 1. BESTOW, CLOTHE, ENDOW. BESIEGE. PLOY, PUT MONEY IN, SPEND. 2. Place synonym for money in word or letters indicated, e.g. **Invested in bed, and lost everything?** (4) = B*L*ED.

INVOLVED *Anag.* COMPLICATED, CONVOLUTED, ENTANGLED, INTRICATE (**opp** = *simple*). ENTAILED, IMPLICATED. CONCERNED, IN QUESTION.

IN WRITING 1. IN LONGHAND, WRITTEN [libel]. 2. Put MS round word or letters indicated, e.g. **Put a small amount of money in writing atlases** (4) = M*AP*S.

IO 1. Gk minor *goddess*, d of King of Argos. Turned by *Zeus* into a heifer; guarded by *Argus*. Escaped, and swam to Asia Minor (whence Bosphorus = Ox-ford), before reaching Egypt and human form again. 2. A satellite of the *planet* Jupiter.

IODINE I (*chem*) [antiseptic].

ION (s/l *iron*). 1. PARTICLE [atom]. 2. Gk myth s of *Apollo*, who founded the Ionian race.

IOU *DEBT*, MARKER (US), PROOF OF DEBT, OWING.

IQ INTELLIGENCE QUOTIENT.

IR IRAN (*car plate*). IRIDIUM (*chem*).

IRE *ANGER*. IRELAND (*car plate* = IRL).

IRELAND Ire. IRL (*car plate*). EIRE, ERIN; EMERALD ISLE; HIBERNIA [*patron saint*]. *COMPOSER*. (*Shak* forger).

IRENE Gk *goddess* of PEACE, d of Themis and *Zeus*. **Rom** =
PAX.

IRIDIUM IR (*chem*).

IRIS 1. *EYE. FLAG, FLOWER, LILY*, ORRIS. 2. Gk *goddess* of
rainbow, mar to *Zephyrus*. 3. A minor *PLANET*.

IRISH MICK, PADDY, PAT etc [*RM*]. *SEA*.
CONTRADICTORY.

IRON (s/l *ion*). FE (*chem*), FERROUS [blacksmith; *Dactyls*].
AGE. CLUB; **opp** = *driver* (*golf*). *PRESS, SMOOTH(ER)*;
DECREASE, EVENING (crypt). **Pl** = CUTLERY (mil sl);
CHAINS, HANDCUFFS.

IRRITATE *Anag.* ANNOY, BOTHER, IRK, VEX. EXCITE.
DEFEAT, NULLIFY.

IS EXISTS. *ISLAND*. ISLES OF SCILLY. ICELAND (*car
plate*).

~ DOUBLE *ISIS* (crypt).

ISHTAR *Goddess* of *LOVE* (Bab).

ISIS 1. THAMES (at Oxford). Reserve *eight* (O). IS DOUBLE
(crypt). 2. Egy *goddess* of *LOVE*, motherhood and Nature, m of
Horus. 3. A minor *PLANET*.

ISLAM PREACHER IMAM, MUEZZIN, MULLAH.

ISLAND REFUGE. I, IS, AIT, AYOT, EYOT, *INCH*, ISLE,
ISLET; **saying**. ~s **of Britain and Ireland** (* = non-island):

3-letters		ARAN	(Ire)
ELY*	(Eng)	*BEAR*	(Ire)
EVE	(Ire)	*BIRD*	(Ire)
EWE	(Sc)	BUTE	(Sc)
HOY	(Ork)	*CALF*	(IOM, Ire)
MAN	(Eng)	COLL	(Sc)
MEW	(Ire)	*DOGS**	(Eng)
NEB	(Eng, IOM)	EDAY	(Ork)
RAT	(Eng, Wal)	EIGG	(Sc)
RED	(Ire)	*FAIR*	(Sc)
ROA	(Eng)	*GOAT*	(Ire)
RUM	(Sc)	GUGH	(IS)
		HERM	(CI)
4-letters		*HOLY*	(Eng, Sc, Wal)
ADAM	(Ire)	JURA	(Sc)

LONG	(Eng, Ire)	*GREEN*	(Ire)
MUCK	(Ire, Sc)	HANDA	(Sc)
MULL	(Sc)	*HORSE*	(Ire)
NOSS	(Sc)	ISLAY	(Sc)
OMEY	(Ire)	KEDGE	(Ire)
OSEA	(Eng)	*LAMBS*	(Wal)
PIEL	(Eng)	LEWIS	(Sc, Wal)
RHUM	(Sc)	LUING	(Sc)
RONA	(Sc)	LUNDY	(Eng)
SALT	(Wal)	MAGEE	(Ire)
SARK	(CI)	*SHEEP*	(Eng, Wal)
SKYE	(Sc)	SHELL	(Wal)
SUNK	(Eng)	SHUNA	(Sc)
SWAN	(Ire)	SPIKE	(Ire)
TORY	(Eng)	STERT	(Eng)
UIST	(Sc)	SULLY	(Wal)
ULVA	(Sc)	TIREE	(Sc)
UNST	(Sh)	*WHALE**	(Eng)
YELL	(Sh)	*WHITE*	(IS)
		WIGHT	(Eng)

5-letters

ANNET	(IS)		
ARRAN	(Sc)	**6-letters**	
BARRA	(Sc)	ACHILL	(Ire)
BARRY	(Wal)	*BADGER*	(Ire)
BURGH	(Eng)	*BOTTLE*	(Sc)
BURNT	(Sc)	*BURROW*	(Eng)
CAPEL	(Ire)	CALDY	(Wal)
CARNA	(Sc)	CANVEY*	(Eng)
CLARE	(Ire)	COQUET	(Eng)
CLEAR	(Ire)	*DRAKES*	(Eng)
CONEY	(Ire)	DURSEY	(Ire)
DANNA	(Sc)	FETLAR	(Sh)
EAGLE	(Ire)	FLOTTA	(Ork)
EORSA	(Sc)	*JERSEY*	(CI)
FARNE	(Eng)	JETHOU	(CI)
FLEET	(Sc)	HARRIS	(Sc)
FOULA	(Sh)	HESTAN	(Sc)
GRAIN*	(Eng)	HILBRE	(Eng)
		HORSEA	(Eng)

LAMBAY	(Ire)	PURBECK*	(Eng)
MAIDEN	(Ire)	RATHLIN	(Ire)
MERSEA	(Eng)	ROCKALL	(Sc)
OLDANY	(Sc)	ST AGNES	(IS)
POTTON	(Eng)	ST MARYS	(IS, Sc)
PRIEST	(Sc)	SCARIFF	(Ire)
PUFFIN	(Wal)	SHEPPEY*	(Eng)
RAASAY	(Sc)	SHERKIN	(Ire)
RABBIT	(Ire)	THORNEY*	(Eng)
RAMSEY	(Wal)	WESTRAY	(Ork)
ROUSAY	(Ork)	WHALSAY	(Sh)
SAMSON	(IS)		
SANDAY	(Ork)	**8-letters**	
SCARBA	(Sc)	ALDERMAN	(Ire)
SKIDDY	(Ire)	ALDERNEY	(CI)
SKOMER	(Sc, Wal)	ANGLESEY	(Wal)
STAFFA	(Sc)	BIRNBECK	(Eng)
STROMA	(Ork)	BROWNSEA	(Eng)
THANET	(Eng)	CARDIGAN	(Wal)
TRESCO	(IS)	COLONSAY	(Sc)
UTOPIA	(fict)	COPELAND	(Ire)
WALNEY	(Eng)	FLAT HOLM	(Wal)
WHIDDY	(Ire)	FOULNESS	(Eng)
		GATEHOLM	(Wal)
7-letters		GRAEMSAY	(Ork)
BARDSEY	(Wal)	GRUINARD	(Sc)
BRESSAY	(Sc)	*GUERNSEY*	(CI)
CORKBEG	(Ire)	MAINLAND	(Ork, Sh)
CUMBRAE	(Sc)	MINGULAY	(Sc)
FOULNEY	(Eng)	PORTLAND*	(Eng)
GOMETRA	(Sc)	ST HELENS	(IS)
GORUMNA	(Ire)	ST TUDWAL	(Wal)
HAYLING	(Eng)	SHETLAND	(Sh)
ISLEHAM	(Eng)	SKOKHOLM	(Wal)
KEERAGH	(Ire)	STRONSAY	(Ork)
KERRERA	(Sc)	VALENCIA	(Ire)
LISMORE	(Sc)	VATERSAY	(Sc)
OWENBOY	(Sc)		
PORTSEA	(Eng)		

9+ letters

BALLYCOTTON	(Ire)	LLANDDWYN	(Wal)
BENBECULA	(Sc)	MIDDLE MOUSE	(Wal)
BURNTISLAND	(Sc)	MUCKLE ROE	(Sh)
CALF OF MAN	(IOM)	N RONALDSAY	(Ork)
EAST MOUSE	(Wal)	NORTH UIST	(Sc)
GREAT CUMBRAE	(Sc)	PAPA STOUR	(Sh)
ISLEABBOTTS	(Eng)	PAPA WESTRAY	(Ork)
ISLE OF BREWERS	(Eng)	RONALDSAY	(Ork)
ISLE OF LEWIS	(Sc)	ST MICHAELS	(IOM)
ISLE OF MAN	(Eng)	SHAPINSAY	(Ork)
ISLE OF WIGHT	(Eng)	S RONALDSAY	(Ork)
ISLEORNSAY	(Sc)	SOUTH UIST	(Sc)
ISLEWORTH*	(Eng)	STEEP HOLM	(Wal)
LITTLE CUMBRAE	(Sc)	WEST MOUSE	(Wal)
LITTLE ROSS	(Sc)	WHITEHORN	(Sc)

~ **AREAS** See *Divisions*.

~ **GIRL** MIRANDA (The Tempest, *Shakespeare*). FLORA.

~ **RACE** BRITONS, IRISH. (MANX) TT.

ISLE OF MAN IOM; GBM (*car plate*). MONAVIA INSULA
(Rom). MONA (also Anglesey). MANX.

ISLE OF WIGHT IOW. VECTIS INSULA (Rom).

ISRAEL JACOB. JEWISH STATE; **12 tribes:** ASHER,
BENJAMIN, DAN, EPHRAIM, GAD, ISSACHAR, JUDAH,
MANASSEH, NAPHTALI, REUBEN, SIMEON, ZEBULEN.

IS SORRY APOLOGIZES, CARES, REGRETS, RUES.

ISSUE CHILD, *OFFSPRING*, PROGENY. DISCHARGE,
EMIT, OUTFLOW, OUTLET. COME OUT, EMERGE.
OUTCOME, PROCEED, RESULT. POINT, TOPIC.
PUBLISH; *BOOK*, EDITION, *VOLUME*.

IT ITEM, THING. SA, CHARM, SEX APPEAL. ITALIAN,
VERMOUTH.

It Italy, ~ ian.

ITA *BROADCASTING*, COMMERCIAL TV.

ITALIAN 1. IT, VERMOUTH. 2. Trans, e.g. **With Italian** = CON.

ITALY I (*car plate*).

ITEM ARTICLE, ENTRY, THING, UNIT. ALSO, LIKEWISE.
TIME-OUT, TIME-WARP (crypt).

ITV *BROADCASTING*, COMMERCIAL TV.

IVORY *COLOUR* (white). TOOTH, TUSK; *anniversary* (14th).
Pl = KEYBOARD (piano).

~ GATE Myth gate of sleep, transmission of false hopes from the
lower world.

IVY LEAGUE BROWN, CORNELL, COLUMBIA,
DARTMOUTH, HARVARD, PENNSYLVANIA,
PRINCETON, YALE (American college *football*).

I WILL *ILL*.

I WOULD ID.

IXION Gk myth king, tied by *Zeus* to an evermoving *wheel*.

J *JACK*. JAPAN (*car plate*). JOULE. *JUDGE*. [*Three* Men in a
Boat].

JACK 1. AB, *SAILOR*, TAR. (COURT) *CARD*, KNAVE.
LIFT, HOIST (car). JOHN. TARGET BALL (bowls). *FISH*,
PIKE. *MONEY* (sl). *FLAG* (naut). TUNIC. INDIAN
FRUIT. [~ CADE. ~ O' LANTERN (*ignis fatuus*).
~ SPRAT]. 2. Male animal, e.g. ass.

JADE *MINX*. *GEM*. *COLOUR* (green). NAG, SCREW (*horse*).

JAILER US for *GAOLER*.

JANUARY (1st) MONTH, M, JAN (Rom **Janus**). **Birthstone** =
garnet.

JANUS Rom *god* of the doorway; facing front and rear. **Gk** =
HORUS, **Egy** = HOR.

JAPAN 1. LACQUER, PAINT, VARNISH. SEA. 2. J (*car
plate*). CIPANGU (country), Jap (abbr); **islands:** Honshu
(biggest), Hokkaido, Kyushu, Shikoku. **Words:** akido (self-
defence), bugeikan (karate), bushido (mil honour code), daimo
(noble), dan (judo), jujitsu (unarmed self-defence), hara-kiri
(ritual suicide), ikebana (flower arrangement), kami (overlord),
kami-kaze ('divine wind', mil suicide), karate (martial art), kung-
fu (Ch karate), obang (gold coin), obi (sash), origami (paper
folding), seppuku (mil suicide), shogun (hereditary mil ruler), te
(karate) [Mikado, *G and S*].

JAR JERK, JOG, NUDGE. *EWER*. GRATING SOUND,
SHOCK. DISAGREEMENT, QUARREL.

JASON Gk myth hero, mar to *Medea*. Sent (to get him out of the way) by his half br Pelias at the head of the *Argonauts* to get the *golden fleece*, where he was sure to be killed. He returned with it and killed Pelias.

JEANS (s/l genes). DENIM TROUSERS.

JEHU Bibl s of Nimshi, who brought about the death of Jehoram and Jezebel, and was cruel towards their relations. Renowned for furious chariot driving.

JENNY 1. LOCOMOTIVE CRANE. JANET; GIRL; LEE; LIND. SPINNER. 2. *Female* donkey or mule; asses (crypt).

JEROBOAM 1. LARGE BOTTLE (8-12 times normal). 2. Son of Nabat, king of Israel; set up golden calves at Dan and Bethel.

JERSEY PULLOVER, SWEATER [*cardigan*, Guernsey]; KNITWEAR. *CATTLE. ISLAND* (CI). GBJ (*car plate*).

JESTER CLOWN, COURT COMEDIAN, FOOL; **celebrated (fact):** AUGUSTE (Fr), COCO (circus), GRIMALDI (Joseph, 18th cent), WILL KEMP (Shakespeare's company); **celebrated (fiction):** COSTARD (LLL); 'SIR' DAGONET (Idylls); FESTE (12th Night); GOBBO (Merchant of Venice); JUPE (Hard Times, *Dickens*); LAUNCE (Two Gentlemen of Verona); LAVACHE (All's Well), JACK POINT (Yeoman of the Guard); POMPEY (M for M); PUCK (MND); SPEED (Two Gentlemen of Verona); TOUCHSTONE (As You Like It); TRINCULO (Tempest); WAMBA (Ivanhoe); YORICK (Hamlet) and, all MND: BOTTOM (weaver), FLUTE (bellowsmender), QUINCE (carpenter), SNOUT (tinker), SNUG (joiner), STARVELING (tailor) [bauble, motley]. 0 (*tarot*). PAGLIACCIO.

JETTY KEY, QUAY, MOLE, PIER, WHARF. BLACK.

JEW HEBREW; **celebrated:** FAGIN (*Dickens*), ISAAC OF YORK (Scott), NATHAN DE WEISE (Lessing), SHYLOCK (*Shakespeare*), SVENGALI (du Maurier) [Wandering ~].

JEWEL THIEF *MAGPIE*. CAPT BLOOD (crown jewels, Tower of London).

JM BARRIE (Admirable Crichton. Peter Pan).

JOAN 1. ~ OF ARC, LA PUCELLE, THE *MAID* (of Orleans); *Shak* character (H.vi). 2. Wife of John Darby (Darby and ~).

JOCASTA Mother and wife of *Oedipus*.

JOG *TROT*. REMIND. *JAR*, NUDGE.

JOHN BOY. DOE. PRESTER. LITTLE ~ (Robin *Hood*). LONG ~ SILVER (*Stevenson*). LOO.

JOINT FORK, HINGE, JUNCTION, SEAM, T(EE), TENON. BARON, LEG, SIDE (beef, lamb etc). DIVE, NIGHTCLUB. REEFER (*drug*). ANKLE, ELBOW, HIP, KNEE, SHOULDER. COMBINED.

JOKER WILD CARD. *JESTER*, WAG.

JOLLIFICATION *DO*, FIESTA, PARTY.

JOLLY HAPPY, LIVELY. MARINE, RM.

JOLT *Anag*. JERK, SHAKE, SHOCK, SURPRISE.

JONES *INIGO* (*archit*). PAUL (US Navy).

JONSON BEN (The Alchemist, Epicoene, Volpone).

Jor Jordan.

JOURNALIST *REPORTER* (**Union** = NUJ).

JOURNEY *TRIP*.

JOVE = *JUPITER*, Rom chief *god* (**Gk** = *Zeus*).

JOY DELIGHT, GLEE, PLEASURE; SATISFACTION (**opp** = *dolour*); **saying**. GIRL.

JP JUSTICE OF THE PEACE, MAGISTRATE.

JUDGE J. ARBITER, ASSESS, *LAW* OFFICER. CENSURE, CONSIDER, CRITICIZE, DECIDE, DECREE, SENTENCE, SUPPOSE, TRY. DANIEL.

JUDGEMENT MISFORTUNE, SENTENCE. ASSESSMENT, DISCERNMENT, ESTIMATE, OPINION. 20 (*tarot*).

JUG *GAOL. EWER. NIGHTINGALE* SONG.

JULY (7th) MONTH, M, JUL (Julius *Caesar*). **Birthstone** = *cornelian*.

JUMPER CARDIGAN, GUERNSEY, JERSEY, PULLOVER. **Animal** ~s: *ANTELOPE*, CICADA, *CRICKET*, FLEA, *FROG*, *GRASSHOPPER*, KANGAROO. (STEEPLE)CHASER. PARA(CHUTIST). BOUNDER, LEAPER [*Gorgon*] (**saying**).

JUNCTION *JOINT*.

JUNE 1. GIRL. 2. (6th) MONTH, M, JUN (Juno). **Birthstone** = *Agate*.

JUNK *DRUG. BOAT* (Ch), LORCHA. SALT MEAT (naut). RUBBISH.

JUNO 1. BEAUTIFUL/STATUESQUE WOMAN. 2. Rom myth Queen of the *gods* and of marriage; w of *Jupiter*. **Gk** = *HERA*.

JUPITER 1. Rom myth King of the *gods*; also JOVE, PLUVIUS (rain) or TONANS (thunder). Son of *Saturn* and Ops, he mar his sis *Juno*. **Gk** = *ZEUS*. 2. Largest of the sun's *planets*.

JUST DESERVED, EQUITABLE, FAIR, WELL-GROUNDED.
BARELY. EVEN, EXACTLY, PRECISELY, QUITE,
RECENTLY. Also = JOUST.

JUSTICE JP; SHALLOW, SILENCE (*Shak*). THE LAW. FAIR
TREATMENT. 8 (*tarot*). Fifth age (Shak's *seven ages*; AYLI).

JUST SO SIC. STORIES (*Kipling*).

JUVENTAS Rom *goddess* of YOUTH. **Gk** = *HEBE*.

K KELVIN. KILO(METRE). KING. KOCHEL (mus).
POTASSIUM (*chem*). 1,000 (hence M).

k Killed. *Int unit*.

KAIKAS Gk myth NE *WIND* (**Rom** = AQUILO).

KALI Ind *goddess* of destruction, to whom practising *Thugs* sacrifice
their victims; she is the consort of Shiva, and is depicted with
many arms.

KANGAROO 1. *MARSUPIAL*, Macropus genus: BRUSH ~,
GREAT GREY ~, POTOROO, RAT ~, ROCK ~, TREE ~
[*Kipling*, *Lear*, pouch]. HOPPER, *JUMPER* (crypt). 2. ~ **court**
= lynch mob, rough justice.

KC KILOCYCLE. KING'S COUNSEL.

KEEN *ACUTE*, SHARP, STRONG, VIVID. EAGER,
WILLING; DETERMINED, SET UPON. *CRY*, DIRGE,
FUNERAL SONG, WAIL (Sc).

KEEP OFF AVERT, FORFEND, WARD OFF. STAY CLEAR.

KELVIN K.

KENT *Division* of UK, SE, GARDEN (of Eng); UNIVERSITY.
CABINET-MAKER. CLARK ~ (SUPERMAN® [*Krypton*;
Lois Lane]). **Pl** = *BUFFS* (mil).

KERNEL (s/l *colonel*). NUT CENTRE (hence U) [shelling].

KETCH EXECUTIONER, HANGMAN. (SAIL)BOAT.

KEY (s/l *quay*). A, B, C, D, E, F or G (mus). CLEF, CLEVIS,
MAJOR, MINOR, NOTE; TONIC (mus). CLUE,
SOLUTION. HYPE. IMPORTANT, CENTRAL. TAP.
WARD; *LOCKER* (crypt). **Pl** = *LEGISLATIVE ASSEMBLY*.

KEYHOLDER *GAOLER*.

KG KNIGHT OF THE GARTER [Edward III, Countess of
Salisbury, Honi soit qui mal y pense].

KHAN CARAVANSERAI (Arab), INN, WAYPOST. RULER

(Ch, Mong, Turk); **celebrated:** AGA ~, BATU, GENGHIS ~, HULEGU, KUBLAI ~, MONGKE, OGEDEI.

KICK *PUNT*, HACK (with foot) [*Sciron*]. RESILIENCE, STIMULUS, THRILL. RECOIL. DENT IN BOTTLE.

KID DUPE, FOOL, HOAX, HUMBUG. TUB. LEATHER. CHILD, TOT. *Offspring* of goat.

KIDDED FOOLED, HOAXED. GAVE BIRTH, PARENTHOOD (crypt).

KILL CULL, DEADEN, DESTROY, DISPATCH, EXTERMINATE, FINISH, WASTE (sl). BAG (game).

KILO K (*int units*).

KIND OF *Anag.* KIDNEY, SORT, TYPE. AMIABLE OF, GENEROUS OF.

KINEMOPHILE *Lover* of the cinema.

KING K, HM, R, REX. (COURT) *CARD*. *CHESSPIECE*. *SNAKE*. *Male monarch*, sovereign: C, ED, G, GEO, W etc, and LEAR, ARTHUR etc [Malory, Tennyson]. **Bibl** ~s: Agag, *Ahab*, Ahaz, Amon, Asa, Baasha, Bera, *David*, Eglon, Elah, Hezekiah, Hiram, Jabin, Jehoram, *Jehu*, Jeroboam, Joram, Josiah, Jotham, Manasseh, Nabat, Nebuchadnezzar, *Og*, Omri, *Pharaoh, Rehoboam*, So, Solomon. **Pl** = RIVER (Ire).

~ **ARTHUR** King of Silures in Ancient Britain. Son of Uther Pendragon (br of Morgana), mar *Guinevere*. Wounded fighting Mordred (his nephew) at Camlan in Cornwall, and d Isle of Avalon [*Camelot, Round Table*].

~ **EDWARD** POTATO. ED, RED, REXED, RTED, KTED (crypt).

~ **OF ARMS** CHIEF HERALD: BATH, *GARTER*, LORD LYON, *ULSTER* (St Patrick), CLARENCIEUX (thistle), NORROY.

~'s **COUNSEL** KC. RICHELIEU.

~s **OF UK** See *MONARCHS* for list.

KINGSWAY REGALLY, ROYALLY (crypt).

KIPLING Rudyard, writer; b Bombay 1865, d 1936 [Nobel (lit)]. **Works:** Actions and Reactions; Barrack Room Ballads; A Book of Words; The City of Dreadful Night; The Day's Work; Debits and Credits; Departmental Ditties; A Diversity of Creatures; The Five Nations; Gunga Din (watercarrier); If; The Jungle Book (animals); The Just So Stories [The Alphabet; Armadilloes;

Butterfly; *Camel* (hump); The *Cat* that Walked by Himself; *Crab*; The Elephant's Child ('satiable curtiosity; trunk); The First Letter; The Kangaroo (Yellow-Dog Dingo); The Leopard (spots); The Rhinoceros (skin); The *Whale* (throat)]; Kim (Anglo-Indian orphan); The Light that Failed; The Phantom Rickshaw; Plain Tales from the Hills; Puck of Pook's Hill; Rewards and Fairies; Schoolboy Lyrics; The Seven Seas; Soldiers Three; Stalky & Co (schoolboys); The Story of the Gadsbys; Traffics and Discoveries; Under the Deodars; Wee Willie Winkie; The Years Between.

KIPPER SALMON, SMOKED HERRING. SLEEPER (sl).

KISS BUSS, OSCULATE, *SALUTE*, X. BRUSH, TOUCH. CANNON (billiards). [Blarney Stone].

KIT *BAGGAGE*, EQUIPMENT, GEAR, RIG. CHRISTOPHER. KITCHENETTE, SMALL KITCHEN (crypt).

KITCHENER C IN C, EARL, GENERAL. CHEF, COOK, GALLEY SLAVE (crypt).

KITTY FUND, POOL. *CAT*, PUSS(Y). GIRL.

KLEPTOMANIA *Obsession* with stealing.

KNAP (s/l *nap*). CHIP, WORK FLINT.

KNIGHT (s/l *night*). 1. BART, BT, CHEVALIER, KG, KT, SIR; PALADIN. *Chaucer* character. [Round Table]. *CHESSPIECE*. 2. **Orders of knighthood, with motto:**

THE GARTER (KG)	Honi soit qui mal y pense
THE THISTLE (KT)	Nemo me impune lacessit
ST PATRICK (KP)	Quis separabit?
THE BATH (KB)	Tria juncta in uno
THE STAR OF INDIA (ex)	Heavens light our guide
ST MICHAEL & ST GEORGE (KMG)	Auspicium melioris aevi
THE INDIAN EMPIRE (ex)	Imperatricis auspiciis
ROYAL VICTORIAN ORDER	Victoria
THE BRITISH EMPIRE	For God and the Empire

KNIT (s/l nit). ENTANGLE, *KNOT*. CROCHET, PEARL, PLAIN, STITCH [*jersey*].

KNOCK RAP, *STRIKE*. CRITICIZE. ASTONISH. INNINGS. *CASTLE*.

KNOCKOUT *Anag.* KO. EMPTY (pipe). KONCK, NOCKK etc (crypt).

KNOCK UP WAKEN. SLEEP WITH (US). PAR (dn, crypt).

KNOT (s/l *not*). KT, *MEASURE* (naut), NMPH, RATE, SPEED (naut). *BIRD*, DUNLIN. PROBLEM. CLUSTER, GROUP. BEND, HITCH, LOOP: BECKET, *BOW*, BOWLINE, CLOVE HITCH, FISHERMAN'S BEND, GRANNY, HALF HITCH, REEF ~, SHEEPSHANK, SHEET BEND, STOPPER ~, TIMBER HITCH. SPLICE: *CROWN*, MATTHEW WALKER, MONKEY'S FIST, TURK'S HEAD, WALL ~. TIE; KNIT.

KNOW (s/l *no*). BE AWARE, RECOGNIZE. SLEEP WITH (bibl). **Pl** = (s/l noes, *nose*); REALIZES, *UNDERSTANDS*.

KOCHEL K, SCORE (mus) [Mozart].

KOP (s/l *cop*). *FOOTBALL* GROUND (Anfield, Liverpool).

KR KRYPTON (*chem*).

KRAKEN Nor myth sea *monster*.

KRISHNA Ind *god* of *fertility*.

KRYPTON KR (*chem*). GASEOUS ELEMENT. PLANET (fict; Superman).

KT *KNIGHT* OF THE THISTLE [James II, St Andrew, Queen Anne, Nemo me impune lacessit]. *KNOT* (naut).

L *LAKE*. LARGE. LATIN. *LEARNER*. *LEFT*. *LIBERAL*. LIRA. LITTLE. *LOVE*. LUXEMBOURG (*car plate*). FIFTY. POUND.

£1,050 CLASSIC, ONE THOUSAND GUINEAS.

£2,100 CLASSIC, TWO THOUSAND GUINEAS.

LA *LAKE*. LOS ANGELES. LOUISIANA. NOTE (mus; also LAH).

LAB LABORATORY. LABOUR.

LABOUR LAB. CHILDBIRTH. ELABORATE. EXERTION, TRAVAIL, TOIL, WORK [*Heracles*]. JOB CENTRE.

LABYRINTH 1. Complicated irregular structure in Gk myth, designed by *Daedalus* to house the *Minotaur* at King *Minos'* palace in Cnossos, hence any MAZE. 2. INNER *EAR*.

LACE CORD, TIE. BEAT, DEFEAT, LASH, WHIP. FLAVOUR, SPIKE. FINE FABRIC, *MATERIAL*, ORRIS; *anniversary* (13th).

LACKING 1. WITHOUT, UN-. 2. Put letters NO or UN (or similar) in front of word indicated, e.g. **Corner lacking approval** (4) = NO*OK. 3. Delete **ing** from clue-word, e.g. **Ingrate lacking speed** (4) = ***RATE. Note that this clue could also imply that a synonym for **speed** should be dropped, i.e. omit **rate** = ING****.

LADDER STEPS; CLIMBING FRAME. PATH, ROUTE. RUN (*tights*).

LADY WOMAN. Title (dame; d of earl; w of lord etc).

LADYBIRD Coleopterous insect of genus coccinella. LADYBUG (US), LADYCOW, LADYFLY (Bishop Barnaby, Cushcow Lady). Also (crypt) any female bird, e.g. hen, pen, reeve (see *Male & Female*) ['~, ~ fly away home . . .' (trad)].

LADY OF THE LAKE 1. ELAINE (*Lancelot*). 2. VIVIEN (*Merlin*). 3. ELLEN DOUGLAS (~, Sir Walter Scott). 4. LADY WINDERMERE (crypt).

LAERTES 1. Father of *Ulysses* [*Penelope*]. 2. Son of Polonius (Hamlet, *Shak*).

LAID UP ABED, ILL, SICK. HAULED OUT, WINTERING (naut). DIAL (dn, crypt).

LAKE L, LA, LOCH, LOUGH, TARN. PIGMENT; *COLOUR* (red). INLAND WATER [*Great ~s*]; **world's principal large ~s:**

3-letters	6-letters
XAU (Af)	BAIKAL (USSR; deepest)
	GENEVA (Swi)
4-letters	LADOGA (USSR)
ARAL (salt) (USSR)	MALAWI (Mal)
CHAD (Nig)	RUDOLF (salt) (Ken)
ERIE (Can/US)	
EYRE (salt) (Aus)	**7-letters**
NESS (Sc)	AGASSIS (N Am, primeval)
TANA (Ethiopia)	CASPIAN (Pers/USSR; largest salt)
	KOKO-NOR (salt) (Ch)
5-letters	LUCERNE (Swi)
HURON (Can/US)	ONTARIO (Can/US)
LEMAN (Swi)	TORRENS (salt) (Aus)
ONEGA (USSR)	
POOPO (Bol)	**8-letters**
	BALKHASH (USSR)

CONISTON (Eng)
ISSYK-KUL (USSR)
MICHIGAN (US)
REINDEER (Can)
SUPERIOR (Can/US;
  largest fresh)
TITICACA (Peru/Bol)
VICTORIA (Ken/Tan/Ug)
WINNIPEG (Can)

9+ letters
ATHABASCA (Can)
GREAT BEAR (Can)
GREAT SLAVE (Can)
MARACAIBO (Venez)
NICARAGUA (Nic)
TANGANYIKA (Tan/Zam/Z)
WINDERMERE (Eng)

LAMB (s/l lam). *JOINT*, MEAT. *Offspring* of sheep. SKIPPER (crypt). YEAN. *ISLAND*. INNOCENT. ELIA, ESSAYIST, *WRITER*. 'AGNES'.

LAMBETH *PALACE* (eccles). *THAMES BRIDGE*.

LAME *CRIPPLED*, DISABLED, HALT. IMPERFECT, UNCONVINCING. GOLD/SILVER-THREADED *MATERIAL*, ORRIS.

LANCELOT Kt of the *Round Table*; mar Elaine (*Lady of the Lake*), f of *Galahad*. Seduced *Guinevere*. [*Camelot, King Arthur*].

LANCING CUTTING, PIERCING, PRICKING. DANCING (quadrille). *PUBLIC SCHOOL*.

LAND *COUNTRY*, EARTH; ACRES, SPACE [*measure*]. ALIGHT, COME DOWN, PITCH, SETTLE. SET DOWN. GET, OBTAIN (job).

LANDING ALIGHTING, PANCAKE (av sl), SETTLEMENT (crypt) [*Fido*]. PLATFORM, PONTOON. BETWEEN FLIGHTS (crypt).

LANDLADY Keeper of boarding-house, inn, lodgings; **celebrated:** MRS CRUPP (David Copperfield, *Dickens*), MRS MACSTINGER (Dombey and Son, *Dickens*), MRS PIPCHIN (Dombey and Son, *Dickens*), MISTRESS QUICKLY (Boar's Head, H.iv, H.v, *Shak*), MRS TODGERS (Martin Chuzzlewit, *Dickens*).

LANDLORD LESSER, LETTER. *HOST*, INN-KEEPER, PUBLICAN; **celebrated:** HARRY BAILEY (The Tabard, Canterbury Tales, *Chaucer*), BENDIT (La Bohème, Puccini), BONIFACE (Beaux' Stratagem, Farquhar), JOHN WILLET (The Maypole, Barnaby Rudge, *Dickens*).

LAND'S END D or S (crypt). Tip of Cornwall. SW.

LANSDOWNE ROAD *FOOTBALL/RUGBY* GROUND.

LAPIS LAZULI GEM (blue). *COLOUR* (blue).

LARES Rom HOUSEHOLD *gods*. GIBBON, *MONKEY*.

LARGE M, L. BIG, GRAND, GREAT. BROAD, FREE, SWEEPING.

LARK GAME, HORSEPLAY; HOAX, JAPE, JOKE. *BIRD*, **assembly** = bevy, exaltation [singing].

LASER (s/l *lazer*). RADIATION, RAY.

LASS GAL, *GIRL*, MISS.

LAST 1. OMEGA, Z, ZED, ZEE (US). ENDURE. END, FINAL, FINALLY, LATEST, LOWEST (**opp** = *first*). [*Holmes* case]. MATRIX, SHOE MOULD. *MEASURE* (wool). 2. Last letter of word(s) concerned, e.g. **Last will and testament** = LDT.

~ **MONTH** DECEMBER; ULT. H (crypt). Any abbreviation for the current previous month.

~ **VEHICLE** E (crypt). HEARSE (crypt).

~ **WORDS** EPITAPH, OBITUARY. AMEN. PS, YOURS (FAITHFULLY/SINCERELY/TRULY). COBBLER, SHOE, UPPER, WELT etc (crypt).

LAT LATIN. *LATITUDE* [navigation].

LATE D, DEAD, EX, FORMER. RECENT. BACKWARD, OVERDUE, TARDY. EVENING, SMALL HOURS.

~ **NEWS** EPITAPH, OBIT(UARY).

LATIN 1. L, LAT [school]. 2. Put word(s) indicated into Latin, e.g. **I am Latin in total** (3) = SUM.

LATITUDE MOVEMENT, *PLAY*, SCOPE. CLIME, REGION, TROPIC [parallel]. BREADTH, LEEWAY, ROOM.

LAUGH BE AMUSED, CHORTLE, CHUCKLE, GIGGLE, GRIN, SMILE (**saying**); HA-HA [*funny*, ludicrous, risible]. RIDICULE, SCORN. [donkey, hyena, jackass (~ penguin), Kookaburra, laughing jackass, mockingbird].

LAUNCHER ROCKET PAD, *WEAPON* FIRER. ORIGINATOR, STARTER. COXSWAIN (naut).

LAUREL 1. *TREE*; BAY. **Companion**: Hardy. 2. In Gk myth, *DAPHNE* was changed into a laurel to escape *Apollo*.

LAW REGULATION, RULE; INJUNCTION. JUDICIAL REMEDY, LITIGATION. LEGAL KNOWLEDGE/PROFESSION; **celebrated practitioners**: Aedile

(Rom); Sampson and Sally Brass (Old Curiosity Shop, *Dickens*);
Sgt Buzfuz (Pickwick Papers, *Dickens*); Dodson and Fogg
(Pickwick Papers, *Dickens*); Fang (magistrate, Oliver Twist,
Dickens); Fips (legal agent, Martin Chuzzlewit, *Dickens*);
Miss Flite (Bleak House, *Dickens*); Fury (dog, *Alice*); Jaggers
(advocate, Great Expectations, *Dickens*); Portia (M of V,
Shakespeare); Reeve (*Chaucer*); Serjeant of Law (*Chaucer*);
Justice Shallow (Henry IV and Merry Wives, *Shakespeare*);
Justice Silence (Henry IV, *Shakespeare*); Snagsby (Bleak House,
Dickens); Spenlow and Jorkins (proctors, David Copperfield,
Dickens); Tulkinghorn (lawyer, Bleak House, *Dickens*); George
Warrington (barrister, Pendennis, Thackeray); Mr Whymper
(Animal Farm, *Orwell*); Mr Wickfield (lawyer, David
Copperfield, *Dickens*).

LAWFUL APPOINTED, PERMITTED, QUALIFIED,
RECOGNIZED. LEGAL, LICIT.

LAX LOOSE, REMISS, SLACK. LACROSSE (sl).

LAY AMATEUR, NON-PROFESSIONAL. NON-CLERICAL,
NOT IN ORDERS (hence UNORDERED – crypt). DEPOSIT,
PLACE, PUT DOWN; ARRANGE, DISPOSE, PREPARE.
PRODUCE (egg). LIE, TWIST (rope). POEM, *SONG*.
COPULATE WITH, BED (US).

LAYER COATING, FILM; *COURSE*, STRATUM. *BIRD*, HEN
(crypt).

LAYMAN AMATEUR, NON-EXPERT, UNPROFESSIONAL.
NON-CLERICAL; UNORDERED (crypt).
EGG-PRODUCER, CHICKEN FARMER (crypt).
CROONER, SINGER (crypt).

LAZER (s/l *laser*). *LOAFER*, IDLER.

LB *MEASURE*, POUND WEIGHT.

LEAD PB (*chem*), BASE METAL. DEPTH SOUNDER (naut).
CHANNEL, CONDUCT, *DIRECT*, GUIDE; DIRECTION,
GUIDANCE. PASS, SPEND. OPEN; PLAY CARD.
STARRING ROLE. GO FIRST; VAN. WATERCOURSE.

LEADER (s/l *lieder*). 1. DUCE, FUHRER. CO. DIRECTOR,
GUIDE, TOP PERSON [*military* ~]. COVER STORY,
LEADING ARTICLE. 2. First letter of word(s) indicated, e.g.
Military leader = M.

LEAGUE ASSOCIATION, CLIQUE. THREE MILES (arch).

LEAN *BANK*, BEND, INCLINE, LIST, *TILT*. FAT-FREE, SLENDER, SLIM (**opp** = fat, obese) [diet. Jack Sprat].

LEANDER 1. Gk myth lover of *Hero*, drowned when the lighthouse failed as he was swimming the *Hellespont* from Abydos to visit her at Sestos. 2. Rowing club.

LEANING ASLANT, LISTING, OBLIQUE, *TILTED* (**opp** = *upright*). BENT, INCLINATION, WISH.

LEAR 1. *MAD KING* (3 d: Cordelia, Goneril, Regan [*Shak*]). 2. Edward ~, writer. **Books/rhymes:** The Book of Nonsense, More Nonsense Rhymes, Laughable Lyrics; The Dong with the Luminous Nose, The Duck and the Kangaroo, The Jumblies, The Owl and the Pussycat, The Pobble Who Has No Toes, The Quangle-Wangle's Hat, The Two Old Bachelors, The Akond of Swat, The Pelican Chorus, Mr & Mrs Discobbolos. 3. Aircraft company.

LEARNER L, PUPIL; APPRENTICE, BEGINNER. TIRO, TYRO (**opp** = expert).

LEARNING KNOWLEDGE, LORE. FINDING OUT. EDUCATION.

LEATHERNECK JOLLY, MARINE, RM.

LEAVE ABANDON, *DESERT*, GET OUT, PART, QUIT (**opp** = *enter*). MAKE *WILL*, TESTIFY. EXEAT, FURLOUGH, HOLIDAY [AWOL]. **Pl** = FOLIAGE. FF, FOLIOS, SHEETS.

LEAVING 1. Indicates word or letter(s) removed from clue, e.g. **Ship leaving Moscow** = MO; or **Animal doctors leaving Moscow** (3) = COW. 2. **Pl** = DREGS, LEES, ORT, REMAINS.

LECTURE *LESSON*, READING, TALK. TAKE TO TASK, TALKING TO.

LEE SHELTER (**opp** = *open*, windward). *MILITARY LEADER* (US). **Pl** = DREGS, *LEAVINGS*, ORT, REFUSE, REMAINS, SEDIMENT.

LEFT L, P; LARBOARD, PORT (naut), *RED*, *SINISTER*. NOT RIGHT. ABANDONED, OVER, REMAINING. DEPARTED, GONE, WENT. COMMUNIST, LABOUR.

LEG LIMB, MEMBER [*bone*]. PROP, SUPPORT; UNDERSTANDING (crypt). WALK. HOP, LENGTH, RUN, SECTION, SPAN, STAGE, TACK. ON (*cricket*).

LEGISLATIVE ASSEMBLY *BOARD*, *CABINET*, COUNCIL,

DEBATING CHAMBER, FORUM, *HOUSE*, SENATE, e.g.
BUNDESTAG (W Ger), CONGRESS (House of
Representatives, Senate, US), CORTES (Port, Sp), DAIL
(Seanad, Eire), DIET (Holy Roman Empire), DUMA (Russia),
FOLKETING (Denmark), FORUM (Senate, Rom), *HOUSES*
OF PARLIAMENT (*Commons*, *Lords*, UK), REICHSRAT (A-
Hung), REICHSTAG (Ger), RIKSDAG (Swe), STORMONT
CASTLE (N Ire), STORTHING (Nor), THING (ON),
TYN(E)WALD (House of Keys, IOM), WITANAGEMOT
(Sax). [Iolanthe (*G & S*)].

LEMON *FRUIT*. *TREE*. *COLOUR* (yellow). ANSWER (crypt).

LEMUR Nocturnal mammal; **types**: BABAKATO, BUSHBABY,
GALAGO, KINKAJOU, KUKANG, LORIS, MAKI,
MALMAG, POTTO, QUANACO, RACOON, SIFAKA,
SLOTH, TARSIER [Madagascar, *monkey*; *ghost*].

LENGTH *MEASURE*. ELL, PERCH, POLE, ROD. FOOT, FT,
IN, INCH, YARD, YD etc. LEAGUE, METRE, VERST.

LENT (s/l leant). ABSTAIN, FAST TIME [Easter].
ADVANCED, LOANED (**opp** = borrowed).

LEOTARD DOUBLET (hence TT, crypt), TIGHTS [ballet].

LEPIDOPTERA WINGED *INSECTS*; BUTTERFLIES, MOTHS,
BUGS; **breeds (butterflies):** Birdwing, Blue Crow, Brimstone,
Cabbage White, Comma, Common Blue, Common White,
Copper, Crow ~, Diadem, *Footman*, Fritillary, Green-veined
White, Hairstreak, Heliconid, Large Skipper, Large White, Leaf
~, Meadow Brown, *Monarch*, Orange Tip, Owl ~, Painted Lady,
Peacock, Pearl Bordered Fritillary, Red Admiral, Ringlet,
Skipper, Small Copper, Small Heath, *Tiger*, Tortoiseshell, Wall
Brown, Woodnymph, Yellow Brimstone; **breeds (moths):** Buff
Tip, Burnet, Cinnabar, Drinker, Eggar, Elephant Hawkmoth,
Emperor, Eyed Hawkmoth, Hawkmoth, Hummingbird
Hawkmoth, Kentish Glory, Lackey, *Magpie*, Pussmoth, Silver Y,
Six-spot Burnet, Tigermoth, Vapourer, White Ermine,
Yellowtail, Yellow Underwing.

LES LESLIE. THE FRENCH.

LESSEN (s/l *lesson*). 1. *DECREASE*, DIMINISH, REDUCE. 2.
Delete letters EN, e.g. **If you lessen Penates, on your heads be it**
(4) = P**ATES.

LESSER 1. MINOR, SMALLER. *LANDLORD*. 2. Delete letters

ER, e.g. **Lesser copper ice-wood** (7) = COPP**ICE.

LESSON (s/l *lessen*). 1. INSTRUCTION, TEACHING [*study*]. READING, SCRIPTURE. ADMONISH, EXAMPLE, OCCURRENCE, PUNISHMENT, REBUKE. 2. Delete ON from clue, e.g. **Mutton lesson is stupid** (4) = MUTT**.

LESS THAN 1. UNDER. NOT SO MUCH. 2. Drop one or two letters from word indicated, e.g. **Inside is less than an evening meal** (5) = *INNER.

LET LEASE, RENT. *ALLOW*, PERMIT (**opp** = *hinder*). *HINDER*, PREVENT (arch; **opp** = *allow*).

LETHE Gk myth personification of oblivion; the *underworld* river from which souls of the departed drank and thereby forgot everything of the upper world [*Styx*].

LETTER MAIL, MESSAGE, POST. CHARACTER: A, B, C etc. *LANDLORD*. HINDRANCE, PREVENTER (arch).

~ **OPENER** L (crypt). KNIFE. DEAR MADAM/SIR (crypt).

~ **SENDER** CORRESPONDENT, WRITER, POSTER. YOURS FAITHFULLY/SINCERELY/TRULY (crypt).

LEVEL *EVEN*, HORIZONTAL. DRAWN, EQUAL, TIED. STRAIGHT. HEIGHT.

LEVY *COLLECT*, EXTORT, IMPOSE, RAISE; DUTY, RATE, SCOT, TAX, TOLL. CONSCRIBE, *ENLIST*, ENROL; CONSCRIPT, PRESSED MAN.

LIAR (s/l *lyre*). FIBBER, STORY TELLER. ANANIAS.

LIB LIBERAL. LIBERATION.

LIBER = *BACCHUS*.

LIBERA = *PROSERPINE*.

LIBERAL L, LIB; POLITICIAN. ABUNDANT, AMPLE (**opp** = *mean*), CANDID, *FREE*, GENEROUS, OPENHANDED.

LICK TASTE [tongue]. *BEAT* (sl). *SPEED* (sl).

LID *HAT*. COVER.

LIED FIBBED, TOLD STORY. *SONG* (Ger).

LIEDER (s/l *leader*). *SONGS* (Ger).

LIFE PAYMENT RANSOM. PENSION. CAPITAL PUNISHMENT.

LIFT RAISE, TAKE UP (**opp** = *lower*) [hitch hike]. ELEVATOR [Otis, inventor]. CHARGE, EXHILARATION, KICK. *STEAL* [robber].

LIGHT NOT DARK, BLOND(E), PALE. NOT HEAVY,

UNLADEN; TRIVIAL. *BEAM*, FLOOD ~, *RAY*, SPOT ~,
LAMP; ILLUMINE. 'PHOEBE'. *FIRE,.MATCH*. GIDDY,
NIMBLE, *NIPPY*. CLUE, PRINCIPLE, TENET.
PORTHOLE, WINDOW (naut). EYE (poet). SHORT,
UNDERSUBSCRIBED. **Pl** = INNARDS, KIDNEYS, LIVER,
LUNGS, OFFAL.

LIGHTER MATCH, SPILL. PALER. LESS BURDENED.
BARGE. GLAZIER (crypt). LAMP, SUN (crypt).

LIGHTNING 1. DISCHARGE (met). SPEEDY. *AIRCRAFT*.
2. **God: Rom** = FULMINATOR; **goddess: Rom** = *MINERVA*.

LIKE *AS*, EQUAL, SIMILAR. CONSENT. FIND
AGREEABLE.

LIKING FANCY, FONDNESS, REGARD, TASTE (**opp** =
aversion). See also *Lover of*.

LILY *FLOWER* of genus LILIUM: ARUM, BELLADONNA,
CALLA, *GUERNSEY*, *IRIS*, LENT, MADONNA, RED-HOT
POKER, TORCH ~, TRITOMA, WATER ~, WHITE ~.
'SUSAN'. [~ Langtry (Jersey ~); ~ Marlene (song)]. **Pl** =
ROYAL ARMS (Fr Bourbon).

LIMIT *BOUNDARY*. CONTROL. END, TERMINUS.
MAXIMUM SPEED.

LIMITED LTD, PLC. RESTRICTED (**opp** = *free*).

~ **FRENCH** SA.

~ **GERMAN** AG, GMBH.

LINCOLN 1. ABE. *AIRCRAFT*. GREEN. *PIG*. *RACETRACK*
(horses). *UNIVERSITY COLLEGE*. 2. LINDUM (Rom). US
state capital.

LINCOLN'S INN *INN OF COURT*, LAW SOCIETY.

LINE FILE, *ROW*, TIER. LETTER. BOAST. RAILWAY.
FIGURE. **Pl** = BR, RLY, RY. ODE, POEM, POETRY,
VERSE. IMPOT (sl), PUNISHMENT.

LINER 1. *BOAT*, SHIP, *STEAMER*. PROTECTION, SLEEVE.
COTTON, LINEN, LINING, SILESIA. ARTIST,
CARTOONIST, DRAUGHTSMAN, DRAWER (all crypt).
ACTOR, PLAYWRIGHT (crypt). RULER (crypt). 2. Put
word inside another, e.g. **Bag with thin liner is popular in the sea**
(7) = BA*THIN*G.

LINESMAN FOOTBALL OFFICIAL, TOUCHJUDGE.
SOLDIER (crypt). CONDUCTOR, ENGINE DRIVER,

GUARD, RAILWAYMAN, TRAIN DRIVER (all crypt).
AUTHOR, POET, WRITER (all crypt).

LINE UP ALIGN, DRESS. PARADE. REPRESENTATIVES, TEAM. ENIL (dn, crypt).

LING *FISH*. *HEATHER*.

LINKS (s/l *lynx*). CONNECTIONS, TIES. CUFF BUTTONS. *GOLF COURSE*.

LION 1. BIG *CAT*, KING OF BEASTS, LEO; **assembly** = pride, **offspring** = cub, lioncel (*herald*). [*Holmes* case]. 2. BRAVE PERSON, HERO. CELEBRITY, STAR, VIP. **Pl** = *Football* team (US). *RUGBY PLAYERS*. 3. One of the labours of *Hercules*. 4. *Constellation*; (5th) sign of the *Zodiac* (Leo). 5. Character in *Alice* and in *The Wizard of Oz*.

LIONHEART COEUR DE LION, RICHARD [Blondel, Durnstein castle]. *IO* (crypt).

LIP CHEEK, IMPUDENCE, INSOLENCE. EDGE, RIM. **Pl** = 1. MOUTH; SPEAKERS. 2. Gk myth SW *wind* (**Rom** = AFRICUS).

LIQUEUR ALCOHOL, AFTER-DINNER DRINK; **types** (all ®): ABSINTHE (wormwood), BENEDICTINE (brandy), COINTREAU (orange), CREME DE MENTHE (mint), CURAÇAO (orange), DRAMBUIE (whisky), KIRSCH (cherry), KUMMEL (caraway), GRAND MARNIER (brandy/orange), MARASCHINO (cherry), NOYAU (fruit kernels), TIA MARIA (coffee).

LIRA L.

LIST *BOOK*, CATALOGUE, INDEX, ROLL, *TABLE*. *HEEL*, *LEAN*, *TILT*. BORDER, EDGE, HEM. ATTENTION, HARK, HEED, LISTEN. **Pl** = TILTING GROUND (jousting).

LISTENER AUDITOR, HEARER; *EAR* (crypt). **Pl** = AUDIENCE.

LIT ILLUMINATED, ILLUMINED, LIGHTED. DRUNK. STRUCK; SET FIRE TO.

LITTER BROOD [*offspring*]. RUSHES, STRAW. RUBBISH. BED, BIER, HURDLE, STRETCHER; PALANQUIN (Ind) [Sedan chair].

LITTLE 1. L; DIMINUTIVE, MINI, SMALL, WEE (**opp** = *big*). 2. Use abbreviated or shortened version, e.g. **Each little** = EA.

~ **BOY** 1. LAD, YOUNGSTER. 2. Use abbreviated or familiar

version of boy's name, e.g. **A little boy is a handsome youth** (6) =
A*DON*IS.

~ **BY** ~ ERIC. LL (crypt).

~ **GIRL** 1. LASS, YOUNGSTER. 2. Use short or familiar form
of girl's name, e.g. **Laughing little girl joins the monarch** (6) =
JO*KING.

~ **MAN** 1. *DWARF*, MIDGET. 2. Use abbreviated form of name,
e.g. **Little man joins little particle to make lots** (7) = BILL*ION.

~ **MONEY** C, D, P etc. CENT, PENNY. SMALL CHANGE.

~ **TIME** HR, MIN, MO, SEC, TICK, TIM (crypt).

~ **WOMAN** 1. *DWARF*, MIDGET. *WIFE*. 2. Use abbreviated
form of name, e.g. **The little woman puts on weight and becomes
huge** (7) = MEG*A*TON. 3. AMY, BETH, JO, MEG (Louisa May
Alcott).

LIVE EXIST (saying). DOSS, HANG OUT, INHABIT. QUICK
(**opp** = *dead*). INSTANT; SPONTANEOUS,
UNRECORDED. CHARGED, ON, SHOCKING (elect).
Pl = EXISTS, IS.

LIVER SURVIVOR. ORGAN, OFFAL [*Prometheus*].

LIVING ALIVE, EXISTING, QUICK (**opp** = *dead*).
EXISTENCE, LIVELIHOOD; CAREER. BENEFICE,
PARISH (eccles).

LIZARD REPTILE (*dinosaur*, lacertilia); AGAMA, ANOLIS,
BASILISK, BEADED MONSTER, BLIND WORM,
CHAMELEON, GECKO, GILA, GREEN ~, IGUANA,
MONITOR, OLM, SALAMANDER, SAND ~, SEPS, SKINK,
SWIFT ~, UTA, WORREL, ZONURE [loses tail; newt]. BILL
(*Alice*).

LLAMA (s/l lama). Domesticated ruminant 2-toed quadruped (S
Am); **breeds:** ALPACA, GUANACO, HUANACO, PACO,
VICU(G)NA [*camel*].

LLOYDS *BANK*®. INSURERS, MARINE UNDERWRITERS
[coffee house; Lutine bell]. SHIP SURVEYORS; REGISTER
[A1; yachts]. *REFERENCE WORK* (ships).

LO BEHOLD, LOOK, SEE.

LOAF IDLE, SLACK (**opp** = *beaver*). BREAD, *COB*,
COTTAGE. HEAD (*rh sl*).

LOAFER IDLER, *LAZER*, SLACKER. *BAKER* (crypt).

LOBSTER CRUSTACEAN (10-footed); CRAWFISH,

CRAYFISH [langouste, langoustine, prawn, shrimp; quadrille (*Alice*)]. UNDERARM BOWLER (*cricket*). BRITISH SOLDIER (arch).

LOCAL BELONGING TO, PECULIAR TO; NEAR BY, NEIGHBOURING, VICINITY. PARTLY, RESTRICTED. *PUB. TRAIN. ANAESTHETIC.*

LOCH L, LAKE, LOUGH (Ire); NESS.

LOCK BOLT, KEY, WARD. CURL, *HAIR*, TRESS.

LOCKER CUPBOARD. CHEST, COMPARTMENT (naut). *KEY*; *GAOLER*, TURNKEY, WARDER (crypt). BARBER, *HAIRDRESSER* (crypt).

LOCK-KEEPER CANAL GATE OPERATOR. COMB, HAIR-GRIP, HAIRPIN, SLIDE (all crypt). *HAIRDRESSER* (crypt).

LOCO-MEN RAILWAY MEN (**Unions** = ASLEF, NUR). CRANKS, IDIOTS, MADMEN, NUTTERS.

LODGE DEPOSIT, LAY DOWN. PUT UP, RESIDE, STAY. *Habitation* (*beaver*, otter). BRANCH MEMBERS. COTTAGE, DWELLING.

LOG ENTER, *RECORD*, REGISTER; *LIST*. LOGARITHM [Napier]. BILLET (wood).

LOGGER LUMBERJACK, SAWYER. DIARIST, RECORDER (crypt).

LOKI Nor *god* of FIRE; m Angurboda; f of Fenris (*wolf*), *Hel* and Midgard (*serpent*).

LONDON 1. CAPITAL, SMOKE [*Gates. Thames bridges*]. *BOXER. UNIVERSITY. WRITER.* 2. LONDINIUM (*Rom*).

LONDON DISTRICT EC, SW, WC etc; hence N*ONE, W*EIGHT (i.e. N1, W8 – crypt).

LONG ENDURING, LENGTHY (**opp** = *short*). CRAVE, LANGUISH, PANT, *PINE*, YEARN. LONGITUDE [meridian, navigation]. ISLAND (Eng, Ire, US).

LONGING CRAVING, YEARNING, YEN. BELONGING TO (arch).

LONG LIFE UHT. OCTOGENARIAN; METHUSELAH. [*cat*].

LONG PANTS SLACKS, TROUSERS, COMBS, ~ JOHNS. *LONGING* (crypt).

LOOK *CON*, GLANCE, LEER, LO, *PEER*, PRY, REGARD, SEE, STARE, SURVEY (**saying**); BUTCHERS (*rh sl*); DEKKO (sl). AIR, ASPECT, *BEARING*, MIEN.

~ **BACK** 1. REFLECT, REMINISCE. TURN HEAD, TURN
ROUND [*Eurydice*, *Lot*, *Orpheus*]. 2. Word reads backwards,
e.g. **Royal looks back for his beer** (5) = LAGER.

~ **FOR** SEARCH, SEEK; *FISH*.

~ **OUT** *CAVE* (hence CAVEMAN – crypt), FORE, TAKE
CARE, WARE. OBSERVER, *SENTRY*, *WATCHER* [crow's
nest].

LOON *BIRD*, DIVER, GREBE. IDLER, SCAMP. DOLT,
IMBECILE, LUNATIC.

LORD NOBLE, PEER. DOMINATE, DOMINEER. **Pl** =
LEGISLATIVE ASSEMBLY, ANOTHER PLACE.
PEERAGE. *CRICKET* GROUND; TEST(ING) GROUND
(crypt). 12th day of *Christmas* in song.

LOSE 1. GET RID OF, MISLAY, MISPLACE (**opp** = *discover*).
BE/GET DEFEATED (**opp** = *beat*); SURRENDER. BECOME
SLOW. IMMERSE. 2. Delete letter(s) indicated, e.g.
Encourage to lose no ace (4) = ****UR*GE.

~ **HEART** 1. DESPAIR. ADORE, FALL IN LOVE. 2. Omit
middle letter(s), e.g. **Peter loses heart, the noble fellow** = PE*ER.

LOSING ONE Omit letter I, e.g. **I'm a rat, losing one French
Revolutionist** (5) = *M*A*RAT.

LOST CITY ATLANTIS, EL DORADO, LYONESSE,
SHANGRI-LA. [Mu (Continent)].

LOT 1. HIGH NUMBER, LASHINGS, MANY hence C, D, M.
SALE ITEM. CHANCE, DRAW, FATE, SORT, STRAW.
PLOT. TAX DUE. DEPARTMENT (Fr). 2. Abraham's
nephew, s of Haran. His wife was turned into a pillar of salt, on
looking back as she fled from the destruction of Sodom and
Gomorrah.

LOUD F, FF; DIN, NOISE, *ROW* (**opp** = *quiet*).

LOUGH L, IRISH LAKE.

LOVE 1. L, O, DUCK, EGG, NIL, ZERO, ZILCH. ADORE
(**saying**), DEAR, HONEY; ALOHA. 'Charity'. [Friday's
child]. 2. **Gods: Gk** = EROS, **Rom** = AMOR, *CUPID*;
goddesses: Gk = *APHRODITE*, **Rom** = VENUS, **Bab** =
ISHTAR, **Egy** = *ISIS*, **Nor** = *FREYA*, **Phoen** = ASTARTE.

~ **APPLE** TOMATO.

LOVER 1. AMANT, AMOUR, GIRL/BOY FRIEND,
INAMORATA, SWEETHEART; [*companion*; *inspiration*;

patron saint; *seven ages* (*Shak*)]; **Pl** = 6 (*tarot*); **celebrated:**
CASANOVA (It); DON JUAN (~, Byron); LOCHINVAR
(Marmion, Scott); LOTHARIO (The Fair Penitent, Rowe);
TOM JONES (~, Fielding). **Pl** = ABELARD/HELOISE (Fr);
ANTONY/CLEOPATRA (Rom/Egy and *Shak*);
CELADON/AMELIA (The Seasons, Thomson);
CHOPIN/GEORGE SAND; DARBY/JOAN (trad ballad);
HENRY II/FAIR ROSAMOND (Talisman, Scott);
LEANDER/HERO (Gk myth); NAPOLEON/JOSEPHINE (Fr);
NELSON/EMMA (UK); PYRAMUS/THISBE (Bab myth and
MND *Shak*); ROMEO/JULIET (~, *Shak*). 2. One who is keen
on a subject (**opp** = one who has an *aversion* to a subject), e.g.

Books	BIBLIOPHILE
Cinema	KINEMOPHILE
Death	NECROPHILE
Dogs	CYNOPHILE
English ways	ANGLOPHILE
Feet	PODOPHILE
Foreigners	XENOPHILE
French ways	FRANCOPHILE
God	THEOPHILE
Horses	HIPPOPHILE
Learning	PHILOMATH
Pain	ALGOPHILE
People	GENOPHILE
Russian ways	RUSSOPHILE
Wine	OENOPHILE
Women	PHILOGYNIST

3. In dn clue, put L before (or 'over') word indicated, e.g. **Oaf-
lover sounds needed** (4) = L*OAF.
LOVE-SICK AMOROUS (**saying**); LOST HEART, hence (crypt)
omit middle letter(s) as in *LOSE HEART* above.
LOW ABJECT, *BASE*, DEJECTED, DISPIRITED, DOWN,
HUMBLE (**opp** = high). COARSE, DEGRADED, MEAN,
VULGAR (**opp** = U). QUIET. COL, CYCLONE,
DEPRESSION (met). BELLOW, MOO. CARTOONIST
(Blimp, TUC horse).

LOW CREATURE *BULL*, *COW*, OX (crypt). SNAKE. TUC HORSE (crypt).

LOWER DEBASE, DEGRADE, DIMINISH, DISGRACE; BENEATH, NETHER. DESCEND, LET DOWN, SINK (**opp** = *hoist*, *lift*). FROWN, LOUR. BOVINE, *COW*, *OX*, NEAT etc (crypt).

LOW-LYING DEPRESSED. IN HIDING (crypt).

LP RECORD.

LSD (OLD) MONEY. *DRUG*.

LUCIFER 1. *MATCH* (arch). *DEVIL*. 2. Rom name for *VENUS* as the MORNING STAR; **Gk** = PHOSPHOROS (**opp** = *Hesperus*).

LUG PULL. PAWL. EAR.

LUGGAGE *BAGGAGE*.

LUNA (s/l *lunar*). Rom myth *goddess* of the *MOON* (**Gk** = *SELENE*).

LUNAR (s/l *luna*). MONTHLY. *MOON*. MOONIE (crypt).

LUNATIC *FOOL*, IDIOT, MADMAN, *NUTCASE*.

LYDIA 1. GIRL. 2. Part of Asia Minor, MAEONIA (**King** = *Croesus*).

LYNX (s/l *links*). *CAT*. HELICOPTER.

LYON (s/l *lion*). *HERALD*. RIVER (Sc). TOWN (Fr). **Pl** = CAFE (*Nippy*).

LYRE (s/l *liar*). 1. *BIRD*. INSTRUMENT (mus) [*Hermes*, *Orpheus*]. 2. *Constellation* (Lyra).

M *MAIDEN*. MALTA (*car plate*). *MARK*. *MARRIED*. *MALE*, MASCULINE. MEDIUM. MEGA (*Int unit*). *MEMBER*. MERIDIEM, NOON. METRE. MILLION. MONDAY. MONSIEUR. *MOTHER*. Head of MI5. THOUSAND.

MA MASTER OF ARTS; DEGREE. *MOTHER*, MUM. MASSACHUSETTS (US *state*). MOROCCO (*car plate*). *Goddess* of Truth (Egy).

MACBETH THANE; THE SCOTTISH PLAY [damned spot; *Shak*].

MACE NUTMEG, *SPICE*. SPIKED CLUB, *WEAPON*. STAFF OF OFFICE [House of Commons; Speaker].

MACRON ACCENT (ā = long sound).

MAD *Anag.* BATS, CRAZY, IDIOTIC, LUNATIC, *NUTTY*;
  saying [Bertha *Mason* (Jane Eyre, *Brontë*); Caligula (*Incitatus*);
  Mr Dick (David Copperfield, *Dickens*); Giselle (*Adam*); Hamlet
  (*Shak*); ~ Hatter (*Alice*); Landseer (arch); Mignon (Goethe);
  Nijinski (ballet); Ophelia (Hamlet, *Shak*); Schumann (composer);
  and see *Mad King*]. ANGRY, ANNOYED, *CROSS*.

MADE (s/l *maid*). BUILT, CONSTRUCTED, CREATED,
  FASHIONED (**opp** = *broke*, destroyed). ARRIVED, REACHED.

MAD KING CHARLES VI (Fr), GEORGE III (Eng), LEAR
  (*Shak*), LUDWIG (Bavaria).

MADMAN IDIOT, LUNATIC, *NUTCASE*.

MAGELLAN *EXPLORER*. *STRAIT*.

MAGICIAN CONJUROR, WIZARD; SORCERER,
  WARLOCK. **Celebrated (fact):** HOUDINI, MASKELYNE
  AND DEVANT; **(fiction):** FAUST (Goethe; Marlowe),
  MANDRAKE (bot, legend), *MEDEA* (Gk myth),
  MEPHISTOPHELES (Goethe; Marlowe), MERLIN (*King
  Arthur*), PROSPERO (Tempest, *Shak*).

MAGISTRATE JP, *LAW PRACTITIONER*, STIPENDIARY.
  Celebrated: FANG (*Dickens*).

MAGNESIUM MG (*chem*).

MAGNUM *BOTTLE* (double size).

MAGPIE TARGET RING (penultimate). CHATTERER,
  GOSSIP. COLLECTOR, *KLEPTOMANIAC*.
  LEPIDOPTERA (moth). *BIRD* (pica pica or crow family); (1)
  sorrow, (2) joy, (3) girl, (4) boy, (5) letter, (6) something better,
  (7) greeting, (8) wish, (9) kiss, (10) meeting; [bad luck, stealing;
  Thieving ~ (mus)]. **Pl** = NOTTS COUNTY (*football* team).

MAIA 1. Gk myth d of *Atlas* and Pleione; eldest of the *Pleiades*;
  m by *Zeus* of *Hermes*. 2. Rom myth *goddess* of Earth; the first
  fruits were offered in *May*.

MAID (s/l *made*). DAMOSEL, DAMSEL, *GIRL*, LASS;
  SPINSTER, UNWED. SERVANT, SERVING GIRL,
  WENCH, TWEENY. **Celebrated:** ABIGAIL (The Scornful
  Lady, Beaumont and Fletcher), FAIR ~ (of Kent), *JOAN* (of
  Arc), KEZIA (Mill on the Floss), MARIA (12th Night), MISS
  MIGGS (Barnaby Rudge, *Dickens*), CLARA PEGGOTTY
  (David Copperfield), GUSTER (Bleak House, *Dickens*),
  ~ MARION (Robin Hood), NERISSA (Merchant of Venice),

RUTH (Pirates of Penzance, *G & S*), SUZUKI (Madam
Butterfly) [Yeoman of the Guard, Mikado (3 pretty ~s) *G & S*].

MAIDEN M, UNMATED, UNWED, VIRGIN; [~ over, *cricket*].
FIRST. GUILLOTINE (hist Sc). 'CORA'. *CASTLE*.

MAIL (s/l *male*). LETTERS, POST. ARMOUR.
NEWSPAPER®.

MAIN (s/l mane). CHIEF, PRINCIPAL. SUPPLY (drains,
electricity, gas, water). *SEA*.

MAIN COURSE SHIP'S HEADING. PRINCIPAL DISH
(*course*). SEAFOOD (crypt).

MAJOR MAJ; OFFICER. PRINCIPAL (**opp** = minor). PITCH,
SCALE (mus). PIG (*Orwell*).

MAKE *Anag.* BUILD, CONSTRUCT, FABRICATE,
FASHION. COMPEL, FORCE, IMPEL(L). SUCCEED.
BRAND, MARQUE, MODEL, TYPE.

MAKER *Anag.* GOD. FABRICATOR, MANUFACTURER.

MAKE UP *Anag.* IMAGINE, INVENT. CONCOCT,
COMPOSE. COMPENSATE; COMPLETE. RECONCILE,
SETTLE. CHARACTER, TEMPERAMENT. COSMETICS;
WAR-PAINT (sl). EKAM (dn, crypt).

MALE MASCULINE; STAG. INTERNAL FITTING (mech).

~ AND FEMALE There are many special words for denoting male
or female genders for various animals. These are sometimes used
misleadingly, to lure the solver into an incorrect train of thought,
e.g. **Pen, pot and pan is nutty** (3) = COB ('pot and pan' being
rhyming slang for 'old man', or husband; the husband of a pen
(swan) is a 'cob', which also means a nut). Therefore particular
note should be taken of those genders which offer a second
meaning or cryptic clue, such as **tup** (put back), **queen** (*monarch*),
drake (*military leader*), **doe** (**pl** = does), **ewe** (you sound . . .) and
so on. **Genders include:**

Genus	Male	Female
Ass	JACKASS	*JENNY*
Bird	COCK	HEN
Bovine	*BULL*	*COW*
Canine	*DOG*	BITCH
Cat	*TOM*	*QUEEN*
Cattle	*BULL*	*COW*

Male

Chicken	COCK	HEN
Child	BOY	GIRL
Crab	COCK	HEN
Deer	BUCK, HART, *STAG*	DOE, HIND
Donkey	*JACK*	*JENNY*
Duck	*DRAKE*	*DUCK*
Elephant	*BULL*	*COW*
Ferret	*BUCK*	*DOE*, GILL
Fox	*DOG*	VIXEN
Goat	BILLY	*NANNY*
Goose	GANDER	*GOOSE*
Hare	*BUCK*	*DOE*
Hawk	T(I)ERCEL	
Horse	STALLION	MARE
Human	MAN	WOMAN
Hunting dog	*HOUND*	BRACH
Lobster	COCK	HEN
Monarch	*KING*	*QUEEN*
Monastic recluse	ABBOT, *MONK*	ABBESS, NUN
Ox	*BULL*	*COW*
Pig	BOAR	SOW
Rabbit	*BUCK*	*DOE*
Rat	*BUCK*	*DOE*
Ruff	RUFF	REEVE
Salmon	COCK	HEN
Sandpiper	RUFF	REEVE
Sheep	RAM, TUP	*EWE*
Sovereign	*KING*	*QUEEN*
Swan	*COB*	PEN
Walrus	*BULL*	*COW*
Turkey	COCK, *STAG*	HEN

Male	**Genus**
Abbot	MONASTIC RECLUSE
Billy	*GOAT*
Boar	*PIG*
Boy	CHILD

Buck	CATTLE, *DEER*, *RABBIT*, RAT
Bull	BOVINE, CATTLE, ELEPHANT, OX, WALRUS
Cob	*SWAN*
Cock	*BIRD*, *CHICKEN*, CRAB, LOBSTER, SALMON, TURKEY
Dog	CANINE, *FOX*
Drake	*DUCK*
Gander	*GOOSE*
Hart	*DEER*
Hound	HUNTING DOG
Jack	*DONKEY*
Jackass	ASS
King	MONARCH, SOVEREIGN
Man	HUMAN
Monk	MONASTIC RECLUSE
Ram	*SHEEP*
Ruff	SANDPIPER (RUFF)
Stag	*DEER*, TURKEY
Stallion	*HORSE*
T(i)ercel	*HAWK*
Tom	*CAT*
Tup	*SHEEP*

Female	Genus
Abbess	CONVENT/MONASTIC RECLUSE
Bitch	CANINE
Brach	HUNTING DOG
Cow	BOVINE, CATTLE, ELEPHANT, *WALRUS*
Doe	*DEER*, FERRET, HARE, *RABBIT*, RAT
Duck	*DUCK*
Ewe	*SHEEP*
Gill	FERRET, POLECAT
Girl	CHILD
Goose	*GOOSE*
Hen	*BIRD*, *CHICKEN*, CRAB, LOBSTER, SALMON
Hind	*DEER*

Jenny	ASS, *DONKEY*
Mare	*HORSE*
Nanny	*GOAT*
Nun	CONVENT/MONASTIC RECLUSE
Pen	*SWAN*
Queen	*CAT*, *MONARCH*, SOVEREIGN
Reeve	RUFF (SANDPIPER)
Sow	*PIG*
Vixen	FOX
Woman	HUMAN

MALLARD *DUCK*; **assembly** = flock, flush.

MAMBA *DANCE. SNAKE.*

MAN HE, HOMO SAPIENS, HUMANITY [Heidelberg ~, Java ~, Peking ~, Piltdown ~]; ONE, PERSON. *MALE,* MASCULINE GENDER. HUSBAND. BOB, TOM, WILL etc. *CREW, SAILOR.* FILL, FURNISH. SOLDIER. *CHESS*/GAMES PIECE. IOM, *ISLAND.* MANITOBA (*Province*, Can).

MANAGE ORGANIZE, *RUN. HANDLE.*

MANAGING DIRECTOR MD (**Union** = ASTMS).

MANDARIN OFFICIAL (Ch). BUREAUCRAT, ESTABLISHMENT FIGURE, GURU, PARTY LEADER (hence P – crypt). CHINESE LANGUAGE. *DUCK.* CITRUS *FRUIT.*

MANGANESE MN (*chem*). HARD METAL.

MANIA CRAZE, EAGER PURSUIT, EXCESSIVE ENTHUSIASM, *OBSESSION.*

MANLY BUTCH, MASCULINE, VIRILE (crypt).

MANOEUVRE *Anag.* MANEUVER (US). EXERCISE, PLAN (mil). FIGURE, MOVEMENT. HANDLE, MOVE, STEER, TURN (aero; naut).

MAN WOULD HED.

MANX CAT *CAT* (breed); it has no tail, hence CA (crypt).

MANX RACE TT, BIKE RACE. DOUBLET (crypt).

MANY LOTS, hence C, D, M; **saying**.

MAR (s/l *ma*). DISFIGURE, *HINDER, IMPAIR, RUIN, SPOIL. MARRIED. MARCH.* **Pl** = Rom *god* of war.

MARBLE LIMESTONE, POLISHED STONE. **Pl** = BRAINS

(sl). GAME (ally, taw).

MARCH 1. MEASURED TREAD, PARADE, *STEP*, *TRAMP*, TRUDGE, WALK. DISTANCE, PROGRESS. BORDER, *BOUNDARY*, FRONTIER; TERRITORY. 2. (3rd) MONTH, M, MAR (*Mars*). **Birthstone** = *bloodstone*.

MARE *HORSE* (fem) [labour of *Hercules*]. SEA (Lat); CRATER (moon).

MARGIN BORDER, BRIM, EDGE. ROOM, SPACE. CLEARANCE. LEEWAY.

MARINE JOLLY, LEATHERNECK, RM. MARITIME, NAUTICAL, SEA.

MARK BLAZE, DENT, IMPRESS, SCRATCH, SOIL, SPOT, STAIN. BRAND, *CROSS*. PUNTER, SUCKER (sl). TARGET. *COIN*. *ANTONY*; TWAIN.

MARKER CHALKER, SCORER. PYLON, SIGNPOST. IOU (US sl).

MARKET DEMAND. BARTER, BUY, SELL. EXCHANGE, SALES/TRADE PLACE; **London** ~s: BILLINGSGATE (fish); COVENT GARDEN (fruit, vegetables, flowers); LEADENHALL (meat); NINE ELMS (fruit, vegetables, flowers); SMITHFIELD (cattle); PETTICOAT LANE (street ~); PORTOBELLO ROAD (antiques). FLEA ~ (Paris), SOUK (Arab).

MARRIAGE 1. MATRIMONY, WEDDING; SPLICING, *UNION* [Darby and *Joan*]. 2. **Gods: Gk** = *HYMEN*, **Rom** = GENIUS.
~ **LICENCE** MATE'S TICKET; UNION CARD (crypt).

MARRIED M, *MAR*. COUPLED, HITCHED, JOINED, MATED, PAIRED, SPLICED, *WED*(DED).

MARRY COUPLE, HITCH, JOIN, MATE, PAIR, SPLICE, TAKE THE PLUNGE, WED. CORRELATE, UNITE. GOLLY, GOSH, GRACIOUS (arch).

MARS 1. Rom *god* of WAR; mar *Rhea* and f of *Romulus* and Remus [*March*]. **Gk** = ARES. 2. RED *PLANET*. *SPACECRAFT*.

MARSUPIAL POUCHED MAMMAL: BANDICOOT, GLIDER, KANGAROO, KOALA, OPOSSUM, PHALANGER, TASMANIAN DEVIL, WALLABY, WOMBAT.

MARXIST COMMIE, RED. KARL [Highgate cemetery]. CHICO, HARPO, GROUCHO, GUMMO, ZEPPO (all crypt).

MASCOT *PET*, TOTEM.

MASCULINE M; BUTCH, MANLY, VIRILE (and see *male and female*).

MASON 1. STONEWORKER. 2. Member of fraternity of Free and Accepted ~s [Grand Master, lodge, ritual]. 3. Bertha ~, *mad* w of Mr Rochester (Jane Eyre, *Brontë*).

MASS CONVOCATION, LITURGY, (MUSICAL) *SERVICE*. AGGREGATION, AMOUNT, EXPANSE; MATTER. MASSACHUSETTS (*State* of US).

~ MEETING CONVOCATION, RALLY, SYMPOSIUM, TEACH-IN. CHURCH SERVICE (crypt).

MASTER MA. MFH. DOMINIE, MR CHIPS, MONITOR, *SCHOOLMASTER*, TEACHER, TUTOR (**Union** NUT). DOMINATE, DEFEAT, OVERCOME. CAPTAIN, *SKIPPER* (naut). EMPLOYER; SAHIB, TUAN. HEAD OF HOUSE. CRAFTSMAN, *PAINTER*. MATRIX.

MATCH CONGREVE, FUSEE, LUCIFER, STRIKER, VESTA®. COMPARE, COPY, EQUAL, MATE, PAIR, TALLY. CONTEST, FRIENDLY, GAME, *TEST*. ENGAGEMENT, MARRIAGE, UNION, WEDDING.

MATCHBOX CONTAINER; **coll** = phillumenist. BOTTOM DRAWER, WEDDING PRESENT (crypt).

MATCHED ENGAGED, MARRIED, *WED*. FITTED, TONED. CONTESTED, PLAYED. *FIRED*, LIT (crypt).

MATCHLESS INCOMPARABLE, PEERLESS. BACHELOR, SPINSTER, UNWED (crypt).

MATE HUSBAND, *MATCH*, PAIR, WIFE. JOIN. ALLY, *COMPANION*.

MATERIAL 1. CLOTH, COTTON, DRAB, FABRIC, FLAX, KNITWEAR, POLYESTER, STUFF, WEAVE, WOOL [*measure*]. **Types** (most ®): ACRILAN, BARATHEA, BAYADERE, BROCADE, BURLAP, CALICO, CHIFFON, CORDUROY, CORPORAL (eccles), DACRON, DAMASK, DIMITY, DRILL, FELT, GABARDINE, HARRIS, HESSIAN, JUTE, LAME, LAWN, LUSTRE, MOREEN, MUNGO, MUSLIN, NAINSOOK, NANKEEN, NET, NYLON, ORGANDIE, ORGANZA, ORGANZINE, ORRIS, PARRAMATTA, PLAID, REP, SAMITE, SATIN, SHODDY, SILK, TERYLENE, TULLE, TWEED, VELVET,

WORSTED. 2. ELEMENTS. CORPOREAL, IMPORTANT. JOKES, LINES (theat).

MAUSOLEUM TOMB, especially that one designed by *Daedalus* for Artemisia in memory of King Mausolus. One of the *Seven Wonders of the World*.

MAXWELL GAUSS, MAGNETIC FLUX.

MAY 1. IS ALLOWED, CAN, MIGHT, PERMITTED (**opp** = *cant*). HAWTHORN. *CASTLE*. **Pl** = EXAMS (C); BOAT RACES. 2. GIRL. 3. (5th) MONTH, M (Rom *Maia*); **birthstone** = *emerald*.

MAYBE *Anag.* 1. MYTHICAL, PERHAPS. 2. Sounds like, e.g. **Massage may be wanted** (5) = KNEAD.

MAYFAIR WEST END. WI.

MB BACHELOR OF MEDICINE, DOCTOR.

MBE *DECORATION*, MEDAL.

MC MASTER OF CEREMONIES. MILITARY CROSS; DECORATION, MEDAL. MONACO (*car plate*).

MD DOCTOR (OF MEDICINE). MANAGING DIRECTOR. MUSICAL DIRECTOR, *CONDUCTOR*. MARYLAND (US *state*). 1500.

ME I, NUMBER ONE, PERSONAL PRONOUN, SELF. MAINE (US *state*). MIDDLE EAST. MIDDLE ENGLISH. AIRCRAFT (Ger); MESSERSCHMITT. HALF TIME (crypt). NOTE (mus; also MI).

MEAL FEAST, PICNIC, REPAST, SPREAD: BREAKFAST, BRUNCH, *DINNER*, LUNCH, SUPPER, TEA. GRAIN, MAIZE, PULSE. **Pl** = *BOARD*, KEEP.

MEAN (s/l *mien*). INTEND, IMPLY. AVERAGE. NEAR, MISERLY, NIGGARDLY, PARSIMONIOUS, STINGY (**opp** = *liberal*). **Pl** = FACILITIES, WHEREWITHAL.

MEANING DRIFT, EXPLANATION, INTENTION, SIGNIFICANCE. EXPRESSIVE.

MEASURE 1. *DANCE*. ACTION, LAW, LEGISLATION. *COMPARE*, EVALUATE, ESTIMATE, *GAUGE*. *DEGREE*, EXTENT; *STANDARD*; TRAVERSE. *ROD*, TAPE. MARK OFF; QUANTITY, SIZE. CC, CM, FT, IN, LB, MM etc; CUBIT; DRAM, FIFTH, FINGER, SLUG, TOT. *FOOT*, METRE, RHYTHM. 2. In the following lists of types of measure, the figures in parentheses between different units of measurement represent the quantity of the first unit which is required to make up one of the second:

Area: SQ IN (144) SQ FT (9) SQ YD (30¼) SQ *ROD/POLE/PERCH* (40) ROOD (4) ACRE (640) SQ MILE [SQ CHAIN, HECTARE].

Capacity: GILL or *NOGGIN* (4) PINT (2) QUART (4) GALLON (2) *PECK* (4) BUSHEL (8) *QUARTER* (4½) CHALDRON.

Beer: GILL (4) PINT (2) QUART (4) GALLON (4½) PIN (2) FIRKIN (2) KILDERKIN (2) BARREL (1½) HOGSHEAD (2) BUTT or *PIPE* (2) TUN [PUNCHEON, TIERCE].

Fish: BARREL, QUINTAL, *BOX*, WARP.

Timber: LOAD, STACK, CORD.

Wine: SPLIT (2) PINT (2) *BOTTLE* (2) MAGNUM (2) JEROBOAM (1½) REHOBOAM (1⅓) METHUSELAH (1½) SALAMANAZAR (1⅓) BALTHAZAR (1¼) NEBUCHADNEZZAR (= 20 bots).

Weight:

    Avoirdupois: DRAM (16) OUNCE/OZ (16) POUND/LB (14) *STONE* (2) *QUARTER* (4) HUNDREDWEIGHT/CWT (20) TON [GRAINS (7,000 = 1 LB)].

    Apothecaries: GRAIN (20) SCRUPLE (3) DRACHM (8) OUNCE/OZ (12) POUND.

    Troy: GRAIN (24) PENNYWEIGHT/DWT (20) OUNCE/OZ (12) *POUND*/LB.

    Hay: LB (56) TRUSS (36) LOAD.

    Wool: LB (7) CLOVE (2) *STONE* (2) TOD (6½) WEY (2) SACK (12) *LAST*.

Length: NAIL (2¼) *INCH*/IN (12) *FOOT*/FT (3) YARD/YD (22) CHAIN (10) FURLONG (8) MILE.

    Cloth: *INCH*/IN (2¼) NAIL (4) QUARTER (5) *ELL*.

    Land: LINK (25) *ROD/POLE/PERCH* (4) CHAIN (80) MILE.

    Naut: *FOOT*/FT (6) FATHOM (100) CABLE (10) NAUTICAL MILE [degree; knot].

Paper size: FOLIO (F), QUARTO (4to), OCTAVO (8vo), DUODECIMO (12mo). CROWN, DEMY, ELEPHANT, FOOLSCAP, IMPERIAL, LARGE POST, MEDIUM, *POST*, *ROYAL*.

Paper qty: SHEET (24) QUIRE (20) REAM (2) BUNDLE (5)
  BALE.
Biblical: DIGIT (4) PALM (3) SPAN (2) CUBIT (4) FATHOM
  (2) ARABIAN POLE (10) MEASURING LINE (3)
  STADIUM (5) SABBATH JOURNEY (2) EASTERN MILE
  (24) DAY'S JOURNEY.
Foreign: PICUL (Ch weight); LI (Ch mile); VERST (Russ mile).
MED MEDICAL, MEDICINE. MEDITERRANEAN.
  MEDIUM.
MEDAL VC, DSO, DSC, MC, DFC, DSM, MM, DFM, TD etc.
  GONG (sl). **Coll** = numismatist.
MEDEA Gk myth magician who mar *Jason*. She killed their children
  when he remarried, and then also slew the new wife.
MEDIA See *MEDIUM*.
MEDICAL *MO*.
MEDICINE 1. DOCTORING, HEALING, MEDICAL ART.
  ELIXIR, NOSTRUM, PILL, POTION. CHARM, FETISH,
  INCANTATION, SPELL. 2. **Gods: Gk** = *ASCLEPIUS*; **Rom** =
  AESCULAPIUS.
MEDIUM M, MED, MIDDLE QUALITY. CONDITIONS,
  ENVIRONMENT. AGENCY, MEANS. SPIRITUALIST,
  MADAME ARCATI (Blithe Spirit, Coward). NEWS
  SYSTEM. **Pl** (media) = *PRESS*, *RADIO*, *TV*, *WIRELESS*.
  COUNTRY (Pers).
MEDUSA 1. 'The Ruler'. In Gk myth, one of the *Gorgons*, m of
  Chrysaor and *Pegasus* by *Poseidon*. Anyone who looked at her
  head, even after it was cut off by *Perseus*, was turned to stone.
  2. JELLYFISH (Port man o' war; sea nettle).
MEDWAY TOWNS CHATHAM, GILLINGHAM, *ROCHESTER*.
MEET (s/l *meat*, mete). ENCOUNTER. FITTING, PROPER,
  SUITABLE. HUNT, RACE DAY [*fox*, *hounds*].
MEGA M (*int units*).
MEGAERA *FURY* (myth).
MEGALOMANIA *Obsession* with grandiose ideas.
MELPOMENE Gk myth; one of the nine *Muses* (Tragedy).
MEMBER M, MEP, MBE, MP. ARM, FINGER, HAND, LEG.
MEMORY RECALL, RECOLLECTION, REMEMBRANCE
  (**saying**); REPUTATION [rosemary]. ACCUMULATOR,
  COMPUTER CELL, RETRIEVAL BANK, STORAGE.

MENDER *Anag.* REPAIRER, RESTORER.

MEPHISTOPHELES *DEVIL* (Goethe). SORCERER (Marlowe).

MERCILESS *IRON*, PITILESS, RUTHLESS, UNPITYING; **saying**.

MERCURY 1. HG (*chem*). LIQUID METAL, QUICKSILVER. 2. Rom *messenger* of the *gods*, s of *Jupiter* and *Maia*; he wore a winged cap (petasus) and winged sandals, and carried the caduceus. **Gk** = HERMES. 3. A *PLANET*. 4. *SPACECRAFT*.

MERCY COMPASSION, FORBEARANCE, PITY, QUARTER, RUTH [*sisters* of ~].

MERE *LAKE*. *SIMPLE*. MAORI WAR-CLUB, *WEAPON*.

MERIT DESERVE, EARN. OM.

MERLIN *BIRD*. AIRCRAFT ENGINE. *MAGICIAN* [*King Arthur*].

MESH *NET*, WEAVE. [gears].

MESOLITHIC *AGE*.

MESS *Anag.* MIX-UP, MUDDLE. POTTER. *FOOD*, *MEAL* [officers].

MESSAGE *CABLE*, *LETTER*, *NOTE*. MEANING, SIGNIFICANCE.

MESSENGER 1. FORERUNNER, *HERALD*: HAIGHA, HATTA (*Alice*). 2. **Gods: Gk** = HERMES; **Rom** = *MERCURY*. **Goddess: Gk** = ARTEMIS.

METRE DISTANCE, *MEASURE*. *BEAT*. *FOOT*.

METRIC PREFIX See *International Units*.

METROPOLITAN *CAPITAL*, CENTRAL; HOME COUNTRY. *CHURCHMAN* (Gk).

Mex MEXICO.

MG MAGNESIUM (*chem*). *CAR*, MORRIS GARAGE.

MID 1. AMID; CENTRAL, MIDDLE. 2. Use middle letter(s), e.g. **Mid Sussex** = SS.

MIDAS 1. Gk myth king of Phrygia. All he touched turned to *gold*, even his food. He gained relief by bathing in the river Pactolus [Croesus, Dives]. 2. *SPACECRAFT*.

MIDDAY 1. NOON. TWELVE. A (crypt). 2. Put letter or word into synonym for day, e.g. **Airs nitrogen midday** (5) = TU*N*ES.

MIDDLE COURT *INN OF COURT*, LAW SOCIETY. U (crypt).

MIDNIGHT 0000. TWELVE. DARKNESS. G (crypt).

MIDSHIPMAN P (crypt). BRASS-BOUNDER (merchant navy),

ENSIGN (US), SNOTTY (sl); EASY (Marryat),
   MIDSHIPMITE (Nancy Bell, *G & S*).
MIEN   (s/l *mean*). APPEARANCE, *BEARING*, *LOOK*.
MIGHT COULD, MAY. *MAIN*, POWER, STRENGTH.
MILANION Gk myth m of *Atalanta* [*apples*].
MILITARY CROSS *DECORATION*, MC, MEDAL.
MILITARY LEADERS Celebrated soldiers, sailors and airmen, e.g.

Air
BADER, G/C Sir D.
BALBO, Gen (It)
BALL, Capt Albert VC
BISHOP, Col VC
CHESHIRE, G/C VC
DOOLITTLE, Gen J.
DOWDING, A/M Lord
GALLAND, Gen Adolf
GIBSON, W/C Guy VC
GOERING, F/M Hermann
MANNOCK, Major VC
RICHTOFEN, Baron von
RICKENBACKER, Capt
SPAATZ, Gen Carl
TEDDER, MRAF Lord
TRENCHARD, MRAF Lord
Land
ALEXANDER, q.v.
ANTIPATER, Macedon
CAESAR, Julius
CUSTER, Gen George
EISENHOWER, Gen
GENGHIS KHAN
HANNIBAL
JACKSON, Gen

KESSELRING, F/M
LEE, Gen Robert E.
MACARTHUR, Gen
MONTGOMERY, F/M Lord
NAPOLEON
PATTON, Gen George
ROMMEL, F/M Erwin
SLIM, F/M Lord
WELLINGTON, Duke of
Sea
BLIGH, Capt Wm.
DOENITZ, Gd Adm Karl
DRAKE, Sir Francis
HALSEY, Adm William
HAWKINS, Sir John
JONES, Capt John Paul
MOUNTBATTEN, Adm Lord
NELSON, Adm Lord
NIMITZ, Adm Chester
POUND, Adm Sir Dudley
RALEIGH, Sir Walter
RAEDER, Gd Adm
RODNEY, Adm Lord
SHOVEL, Adm Sir C.
SPRUANCE, Adm
YAMAMOTO, Adm

MILITARY POLICE MP, SP, REDCAP (hence R, crypt).
MILK NOURISHMENT, PAP. EXTRACT. *COLOUR* (white).
   RIVER (US).
MILLION M.

MILNE A.A., *WRITER* (*Alexander* Beetle, Edward Bear, Christopher *Robin*, Eeyore, Heffalump, Kanga, Piglet, Pooh, Roo, *Rabbit*, Rabbit's Friends and Relations, Winnie the Pooh, Wol, Tigger).

MINCE (s/l *mints*). MINCED MEAT; SWEETMEAT (~ pie). CUT SMALL; RESTRAIN. WAGGLE, WALK AFFECTEDLY. **Pl** = EYES (*rh sl*).

MIND (s/l *mined*). ATTENTION, FEELING, THINKING. NURSE, TAKE CARE. BRAIN, INTELLECT, SOUL [*study*]. OPINION; CONCERN, TAKE NOTE. MEMORY, REMEMBRANCE. FUSS, OBJECT, WORRY.

MINE EXCAVATION, PIT, SAP; *BURROW*, DIG, UNDERMINE. POSSESSIVE (**opp** = theirs, yours). *BANGER*, EXPLOSIVE, *WEAPON*.

MINER (s/l *minor*). COLLIER (**Union** = NUM), *PITMAN* (crypt). *WORKER*. *DIGGER*, FORTYNINER, PROSPECTOR.

MINERVA 1. Rom myth *goddess* of Invention, Wisdom and the Arts (**Gk** = PALLAS *ATHENE*), and later of War. 2. A minor *PLANET*.

MINI *LITTLE*, SMALL (**opp** = mega). SKIRT. *CAR*.

~ STATES Celebrated: ANDORRA, LIECHTENSTEIN, LUXEMBOURG, MONACO, MONTENEGRO (ex), SAN MARINO, TONGA.

MINOR (s/l *miner*). 1. *CHARGE*, INFANT, JUNIOR, *WARD*; UNDER 18/21. THE YOUNGER. PITCH, *SCALE* (mus). INFERIOR, LESSER (**opp** = *major*). 2. Use diminutive, abbreviation, e.g. **Minor operation** = OP.

MINOS Gk myth king of Crete. Son of *Zeus* and *Europa*, he mar Pasiphae. His palace at Cnossos contained the *labyrinth*, where the *Minotaur* was kept until killed by *Theseus*.

MINOTAUR Gk myth Cretan *monster* (half man, half bull) of *Minos*. Kept in the *labyrinth*, which was designed by *Daedalus*, it was fed on human flesh in the form of seven youths and seven maidens sent yearly as tribute from Athens, until *Theseus* volunteered to be included and he killed it.

MINSTREL ENTERTAINER, MUSICIAN, SINGER; LAYMAN (crypt) [Blondel (*Lionheart*). Mikado (*G & S*)]. **Pl** = NEGRO SINGERS.

MINT AROMATIC HERB. CANDY, SWEET. COIN, MAKE

MONEY, UTTER. LOT OF MONEY.

MINX *BAGGAGE*, HUSSY, JADE.

MIRAGE ILLUSION, REFLECTION, REFRACTION;
celebrated: BROCKEN (Harz Mt, Ger); DELIBAB (Hung);
FATA MORGANA (Messina, It) [*ignis fatuus*. Desert, water].
AIRCRAFT (Fr).

MIRROR NEWSPAPER®. 1. LOOKING GLASS, POLISHED
SURFACE; REFLECT, REVERSE IMAGE, hence read
backwards, or sometimes form a palindrome, e.g. **Midday mirror**
(4) = NOON. 2. Used by *Perseus* so as not to look directly at
Medusa when he slew her.

MIS- Added as prefix to mean 'amiss', 'badly' or 'wrongly'. In
crosswords, is often used to mean *anag.*, e.g. **Mistake** = KATE or
TEAK. It can also be included into the answer, e.g. **Lure** =
MISRULE.

MISER *BORE* (tech). HOARDER; NIGGARD, STINGY
PERSON; **celebrated:** GRANDET (Balzac), HARPAGON
(Molière), SCROOGE (*Dickens*), SHYLOCK (M of V, *Shak*).

MISO- *HATRED* OF –

MISS (s/l *mis*-). *GIRL*, MAIDEN. [**near** ~ = *chaperone (crypt)*].
SCHOOLMISTRESS. Any girl's name. AVOID, DODGE,
FAIL (**opp** = *hit*) [mile]. MISSISSIPPI (US *state*).

~ FRENCH MLLE.

MISSILE *ARROW*, BULLET, DART, FLECHETTE, ROCKET,
SLINGSHOT; WEAPON. **Celebrated:** CRUISE, ICBM,
PERSHING, POLARIS, MX, SAM, SS 10, SS 20, *V1*.

MIST (s/l missed). FRET, HAZE, VAPOUR. DIM, FILM, FOG.

MISTAKEN 1. *Anag.* IN ERROR, AT FAULT; GAFFED (crypt).
ROB, STEAL, THIEVE (crypt). 2. Take 'mis' as indicated, e.g.
remove the letters 'mis', as in: **Lock the mistaken courtesan** (5) =
***TRESS.

MISUSE *Anag.* ABUSE, ILL-TREAT. SUE (crypt).

MITHRA *God* of the SUN (Pers).

MIX *Anag.* COMBINE, JOIN, MINGLE, SCRAMBLE. FIX.
1009 (crypt, Lat).

MIXER *Anag.* BITTER LEMON, SODA, TONIC; *DRINK*.
BEATER, FOOD PROCESSOR, WHISK.

MIXTURE *Anag.* MEDICINE. AMALGAMATION,
COMBINATION.

MIX-UP *Anag*. CONFUSION, INVOLVEMENT. XIM (dn, crypt).

MLLE MADEMOISELLE; MISS FRENCH; FRENCH GIRL.

MM FRENCHMEN, MESSIEURS. MILITARY MEDAL. MILLIMETRE. 2,000.

MME MADAME; MRS FRENCH.

MNEMOSYNE 1. Mother by *Zeus* of the nine Gk *Muses* [memory]. 2. A minor *PLANET*.

MO MEDICAL OFFICER. MODUS OPERANDI. MOLYBDENUM (*chem*). MOMENT. *DOCTOR*. MISSOURI (US *state*).

MOA *BIRD* (ex; flightless; NZ) [cassowary, dinornis (NZ, ex), emu, nandoo, ostrich].

MOB GANG, RABBLE. ATTACK, MOLEST. CAP, *HAT*.

MOBY DICK *WHALE* [Ahab, Herman Melville. Vessel: *Pequod*].

MODEL FIGURE, PUPPET, REPRESENTATION. CARVE, FASHION, *FORM*, SHAPE. MANNEQUIN, POSER. *DESIGN*, MARK, MARQUE, MATRIX, PATTERN, STYLE, TEMPLET, TYPE. NORM, *PAR*, *STANDARD*.

MODEST *BASHFUL*, COY, DIFFIDENT, HUMBLE, RETIRING, SELF-EFFACING (**opp** = *bragging*). CHASTE, DECOROUS (**opp** = *arch*). RESTRICTED, SMALL.

MOHAMMED MOHAMET, MUHAMID, MUHAMMED etc. Founder of Islam, mar Ayesha; 1 d Fatima. Qur'an (Koran) tells of Allah, Adam, Abraham, Gabriel, Isaac, Jesus, Moses, Noah. **Priests:** Ayatollah, Muezzin, Mufti; **caliphs:** Abu Bekr, Omar, Ali; **sects:** Shiite, Sunni. Pilgrimage (haj) to Mecca; holy war (jehad); heretics, Druses (**opp** = Moronites). Leader Aga (Khan); M (crypt). **Companion:** mountain.

MOIRAI Gk *goddesses* of the three *FATES*. **Rom** = PARCAE.

MOLE BREAKWATER, JETTY, QUAY. *AGENT*, SPY. BURROWING RODENT [*Grahame*]. BLEMISH, *SPOT*.

MOLYBDENUM MO (*chem*).

MOMENT MO. INSTANT, MINUTE. IMPORTANT.

MONACO MC (*car plate*). *RACETRACK* (cars).

MONARCH 1. BUTTERFLY (*lepidoptera*). 2. EMPEROR, EMPRESS, KING, RULER, QUEEN, SOVEREIGN; **saying**.
~s **of England and Britain:**

England

Saxons and Danes

Egbert	827- 839
Ethelwulf	839- 858
Ethelbald	858- 860
Ethelbert	860- 865
Ethelred	865- 871
Alfred the Great	871- 899
Edward the Elder	899- 924
Athelstan	924- 939
Edmund	939- 946
Edred	946- 955
Edwig	955- 959
Edgar	959- 975
Edward the Martyr	975- 978
Ethelred the Unready	978-1016
Edmund Ironside	1016-1016
Canute (Knut)	1017-1035
Harold I	1035-1040
Hardicanute	1040-1042
Edward the Confessor	1042-1066
Harold II	1066-1066

Normans

William I	1066-1087
William II	1087-1100
Henry I	1100-1135
Stephen	1135-1154

Plantagenets

Henry II	1154-1189
Richard I	1189-1199
John	1199-1216
Henry III	1216-1272
Edward I	1272-1307
Edward II	1307-1327 (deposed)
Edward III	1327-1377
Richard II	1377-1399 (deposed)

Henry IV		1399-1413
Henry V	**Lancaster**	1413-1422
Henry VI		1422-1461 (deposed)
Edward IV		1461-1483
Edward V	**York**	1483-1483
Richard III		1483-1485

Tudors

Henry VII	1485-1509
Henry VIII	1509-1547
Edward VI	1547-1553
Jane (9 days)	1553-1553
Mary	1553-1558
Elizabeth I	1558-1603

Britain
Stuarts

James I (VI of Scotland)	1603-1625
Charles I	1625-1649 (beheaded)

Commonwealth

Oliver Cromwell	1649-1658
Richard Cromwell	1658-1659

Stuarts

Charles II	1660-1685
James II (VII of Scotland)	1685-1688 (deposed)
William and Mary	1689-1702
Anne	1702-1714

Hanovers

George I	1714-1727
George II	1727-1760
George III	1760-1820
George IV	1820-1830
William IV	1830-1837
Victoria	1837-1901

Windsors

Edward VII	1901-1910
George V	1910-1936
Edward VIII	1936-1936 (abdicated)
George VI	1936-1952
Elizabeth II	1952-

Celebrated monarchies: Bhutan, Cook Is, Denmark, Liechtenstein (Principality), Luxembourg (Grand Duchy), Nepal, Norway, Monaco (Principality), Spain, Sweden, Tonga, United Kingdom. **Recently extinct:** Afghanistan, Albania, Bulgaria, Egypt, Ethiopia, Germany, Greece, Hungary, Iraq, Italy, Iran, Romania, Russia, Siam (Thailand) and various Indian States.

MONDAY MON. DAY OF THE MOON. ~s child = fair of face. [Solomon *Grundy*].

MONEY C, D, L, P, S; CENTS, DOLLARS, POUNDS, SHILLINGS. BRASS, CASH, *COIN*, LOOT, PELF, READY, RHINO, TIN. RESOURCES, SHINERS, MINT. BEES AND (*rh sl*). [~ *spider*].

MONGREL *Anag.* CROSSBREED, IMPURE, MIXED [heinz].

MONITOR LIZARD. PREFECT. GUNSHIP, WARSHIP, *WEAPON*. *CONTROL*, EAVESDROP, TAP.

MONK MONASTIC RECLUSE (male), HERMIT; *Chaucer* character. CELLIST (crypt). BENEDICTINE, BUDDHIST, CARTHUSIAN, CISTERCIAN, ESSENE, TRAPPIST (silence); [*friar* (mendicant)]. Monks are not *friars*.

MONKEY 1. FIDDLE, INTERFERE, PLAY. £500. MACHINE HAMMER. WATER VESSEL. APE, MIMIC, MOCK. 2. MAMMAL, *PRIMATE*; APE; **breeds:** BABOON (Af, Arab), BARBARY (Gibraltar), BOONDER (Rhesus), BUSHBABY (Af), CAPUCHIN (Af), CEBUS (S Am), CHACMA (Af), CHIMPANZEE (Af), COAITA (S Am), COLOBUS (Af), DRILL (Af), ENTELLUS (Ind), GALAGO (Af), GIBBON (Asia), GORILLA (Af), GRIVET (Ethiopia), GUENON (Af), HANUMAN (Ind), HOWLER (S Am), LANGUR (Asia), *LAR(ES)* (Asia), *LEMUR* (Madagascar), MACAQUE (Asia), MACQUES (Af), MAGOT (Af), MANDRILL (Af), MARMOSET (Am), MURIQUI (Braz), ORAN(G)-OUTAN(G) (SE Asia), *OWL* ~ (S Am), PONGO

(Af), PROBOSCIS ~ (S Am), SAI (Braz), SAKI (S Am), SAGOIN(-UIN) (S Am), SAPAJOU (Am), SIAMANG (Malay), SIMPAI (Sumatra), *SPHINX* ~ (Af), SPIDER ~ (S Am), SQUIRREL ~ (S Am), TAMARIN (S Am), TEE-TEE, TITI (S Am), VARI (Madagascar), VERVET (Af), WEEPER; **celebrated:** BANDERLOG (*Kipling*), CHETA (*Tarzan*), KING KONG (Edgar Wallace) [PG Tips].

MONOMANIA *Obsession* with one idea.

MONSIEUR M; MR FRENCH (crypt).

MONSTER 1. ENORMOUS, HUGE. CRUEL, WICKED. ABORTION, MIS-SHAPEN. 2. IMAGINARY ANIMAL (incongruous, deformed or large);

celebrated monsters:

ABOMINABLE SNOWMAN/YETI	(Himalayas)
ARGUS	(100 eyes)
BIGFOOT/SASQUATCH	(N American Yeti)
BUNYIP	(Aus)
CENTAUR	(head human, body horse)
CHIMAERA	(head lion, body goat, legs dragon)
CRATAEIS	(12 feet, 6 heads; barked)
CYCLOPES	(one eye)
DRACULA	(Bram Stoker)
DRAGON	(fire-breathing)
FRANKENSTEIN'S CREATION	(manufactured humanoid)
GAMA	(Princess Ida, *G & S*)
GIGANTES	(winged; legs ending in snakes)
GOG & MAGOG	(British giants)
GOLIATH	(bibl)
GORGONS	(winged; snakes for hair)
GRIFFIN/GRYPHON	(winged; head eagle, body lion)
HARPY	(head woman, body vulture)
HYDRA	(nine heads)
IDRIS	(Welsh mountain giant)
KRAKEN	(Nor sea monster)
MAGOG	(See GOG above)

MINOTAUR	(Head bull, body man)
NESSIE	(Loch Ness, Sc)
ODIN	(Nor; one eye)
PAN	(head and body man, legs goat)
POLYPHEMUS	(one eye)
PYTHON	(serpent)
SASQUATCH/BIGFOOT	(N American Yeti)
SCYLLA & CHARYBDIS	(six-headed sea monsters)
SPHINX	(head human, body lion)
TYPHON	(100 heads; fire-breathing)
URANIDS	(100 arms, 50 heads)
WODEN	(A-Sax; one eye)
WYVERN	(*herald*)
YAMINSKAY	(S Andes Yeti)
YETI/ABOMINABLE SNOWMAN	(Himalayas)
YMIR	(frost, Nor)

MONTH *Calendar* ~: JAN, FEB, MAR etc; *lunar* ~: 4 WEEKS, 28 DAYS; *TIME*. LIKING, INCLINATION (arch).

MONUMENT COMMEMORATION, MEMORIAL, (TOMB)STONE; **celebrated:** ALBERT MEMORIAL (Prince Albert), ARC DE TRIOMPHE (French Army), BRANDENBURG GATE (Berlin), CENOTAPH (World Wars dead; Lutyens), CLEOPATRA'S NEEDLE (Embankment; Heliopolis), INVALIDES (Napoleon), MENIN GATE (Ypres), THE MONUMENT (Great Fire, London), PYRAMIDS (Gizeh; sacred rites), NELSON'S COLUMN (Trafalgar), QUEEN VICTORIA (The Mall, Brock), RUNNYMEDE (Commonwealth Air Forces), SOMME (Lutyens), UNKNOWN WARRIOR (Westminster Abbey/UK; Arc de Triomphe/Fr; Santa Maria degli Angeli/It; Arlington Cemetery/USA).

MOON 1. *MOPE*. EARTH SATELLITE, LUNAR BODY. 18 (*tarot*). [Monday]. 2. **Goddesses: Gk** = *ARTEMIS*, *PHOSPHOROS*, SELENE; **Rom** = *DIANA*, JUNO, LUNA.

MOOR FEN, HEATHLAND, OPEN LAND; MARSH. MAKE FAST, TIE UP (naut). *GAOL*. BACKROOM (crypt). BLACK MAN; **celebrated:** AARON (Titus Andronicus), OTHELLO (*Shak*), LAILA (Southey).

MOPED WAS BORED, DEPRESSED, LISTLESS, MOONED. (MOTOR) SCOOTER.

MORE WORK UTOPIA (crypt).

MORNING (s/l mourning). 1. AM, FORENOON. 2. ~ star = *Lucifer* (Rom), Phosphoros (Gk); **opp** = *Hesperus*.

MORPHEUS Rom myth s of Sleep and *god* of Dreams.

MORSE *WALRUS*. CLASP. ALPHABET CODE, SIGNAL (dot, dash).

MOSES Heb law-giver, s of Amram and Jochebed, br of Aaron and Miriam; mar Zipporah.

MOSQUITO ANOPHELES, CULEX. GNAT, *INSECT*; BLOODSUCKER. *AIRCRAFT*. **Pl** = GULF.

MOSTLY 1. MAINLY, PRINCIPALLY. 2. Nearly an anagram, e.g. **Material which is mostly a masked product** (6) = DAMASK (the E is omitted from **a masked**).

MOTH *INSECT*, *LEPIDOPTERA*. **Coll** = lepidopterist. RIVER (NZ).

MOTHER ABBESS. MA, MATER, MATERNAL PARENT, MUM **(saying)**; OLD LADY (sl); BEARER (crypt); **celebrated:** ~ Goose, ~ Hubbard, ~ Riley, ~ Shipton. *ISIS*. VINEGAR PRODUCT. HYSTERIA. BUG HUNTER, LEPIDOPTERIST (crypt).

MOTOR RACE GRAND PRIX. CAR*NATION (crypt). For ~ **tracks**, see *Racetrack*.

MOTORWAY MI, MIV, MV etc.

MOULD DECAY, MILDEW, ROT. *CAST*, *FORM*, MATRIX, PATTERN, SHAPE, TEMPLET.

MOUNT ASCEND, CLIMB. EMINENCE, HILL, MOUND, TOR. GET ON; SADDLE. STEED. CARD, MARGIN; DISPLAY, SET OFF. STAMP HINGE. ARRANGE, PRODUCE, STAGE (theat).

MOUNTAIN HEAP, PILE. ELEVATION, HILL, *MOUNT*; **pl** = range of hills; **celebrated:** ALASKA RANGE (US), ANDES (S Am), ALPS (Eur), APENNINES (It), APPALACHIANS (US), ATLAS (N Af), BLUE RIDGE (US), BROOKS RANGE (US), ETHIOPIAN HIGHLANDS (E Af), FLINDERS RANGE (Aus), GREAT DIVIDING RANGE (Aus), HAMMERSLEY RANGE (Aus), HINDU KUSH (Asia), HIMALAYAS (Asia), KUN LUN SHAN (Ch), LOMONDSOV RIDGE (Arctica),

MACDONNEL RANGE (Aus), PAROPAMISUS (Asia),
ROCKY ~s (Can/US), SIERRA MADRE (Mex), SIERRA
NEVADA (N Am), TIBESTI (N Af), TIEN SHAN (Asia),
TRANSANTARCTIC ~s (Antarctica), URALS (USSR),
VINSON PLATEAU (Antarctica).

MOUNTED ASCENDED, CLIMBED. ASTRIDE, HORSED,
RIDING, SADDLED, UP. HILLY (crypt). CARDED,
DISPLAYED, SET OFF. PRODUCED, STAGED (theat).

MOUNT OLYMPUS DIVINE ABODE, HEAVEN. See
OLYMPUS.

MOUTH FACE, GOB, KISSER, LIPS, TRAP (sl). CHATTER;
CHEEK, IMPUDENCE. OPENING. RANT, RAVE, SPEAK,
UTTER. GRIMACE.

MOUTHORGAN HARMONICA, *INSTRUMENT* (mus).
TONGUE (crypt).

MOVING *Anag*. EMOTIONAL, TENDER. AFOOT, AGATE,
MOBILE (**opp** = *still*). SHIFTING; CHANGING HOUSES.

MP MEMBER OF PARLIAMENT, REPRESENTATIVE.
MILITARY POLICE, REDCAP.

MR 1. MISTER. 2. *Male* of species named, e.g. **Mr Swan** = COB.

MRS 1. MISTRESS, MISSUS, WIFE. 2. *Female* of species named,
e.g. **Mrs Fox** = VIXEN.

~ FRENCH MADAME, MME.

MUFTI CHURCHMAN (Mos). CIVILIAN CLOTHES, CIVVIES
(*mil*; **opp** = *uniform*).

MUG BEAT UP (hence TAEB, dn crypt), COSH [GBH]. CUP,
TROPHY. *FACE, MOUTH*. FOOL. CRAM, SWOT.

MULE HYBRID; *offspring* of donkey and horse, hence DON or
KEY (crypt); **celebrated:** MUFFIN. OBSTINATE. DOLT,
FOOL. MACHINE, SPINNER. *SHOE*, SLIPPER.

MULL CONSIDER, PONDER, THINK. HUMUS. MESS,
MUDDLE. *MATERIAL*, MUSLIN. *ISLAND*. MAKE
PUNCH, DRINK. PROMONTORY (Sc). SNUFFBOX.

MURMURATION *Assembly* of starlings.

MURPHY POTATO, SPUD, TUBER.

MURRAYFIELD *RUGBY* GROUND.

MUSE (s/l mews). 1. PONDER, THINK. POET. 2. Gk myth
nine *goddesses* of song, who presided over the arts, sciences and
poetry. They were d's of *Zeus* and *Mnemosyne*, and lived on

Parnassus, being the companions of *Apollo*: CALLIOPE (epic poetry), CLIO (history), ERATO (love songs), EUTERPE (lyric poetry), MELPOMENE (tragedy), POLYHYMNIA/POLYMNIA (singing), TERPSICHORE (choral dance), THALIA (comedy) and URANIA (astronomy).

MUSEUM BM.

MUSIC 1. SONG. NOTES, SHEETS, SCORE [*instrument*; *tempo*]; **saying**. 2. **Gk god** = *Apollo* [*Muses*].

MUSICIAN B MUS. *APOLLO. TERPANDER* [*instrument, Muses*].

MUST HAVE TO. NEW WINE. MOULD. FRENZY.

MUSTANG *AIRCRAFT. HORSE.*

MUSTER GATHERING (mil). LIST, ROLL (mil). ENROL. SUMMON. *ASSEMBLY* (peacocks).

MYTH Mythology, especially the legends which grew up in Greece and Rome, played a large part in the lives of the ancients. Various poets and writers wove stories to account for natural phenomena such as volcanoes, whirlpools, cloud-capped mountains etc; they also sought to explain the Creation itself and some of the everyday events of life such as love, childbirth and the harvest, through personification in the form of *gods and goddesses* (q.v.). Most ancient civilizations and peoples developed their own folklore and mythology.

N NAME(D). NAPOLEON. NEUTER. NITROGEN (*chem*). NOON. NORWAY (*car plate*). NORTH; POINT. NOUN. BRIDGE PLAYER.

NA *SODIUM* (*chem*).

NAG *HORSE*, PONY, SCREW. HARP, SCOLD.

NAIAD *NYMPH.*

NAIL FINGER-TIP, TOE-TIP; HORN; CLAW, TALON [fingerplate]. FASTENING, SPIKE: BRAD, HOB, OVAL. CATCH, ENGAGE, FASTEN, FIX, SECURE. *MEASURE* (cloth).

NAKED *NUDE.*

NAME N. CALL, CHRISTEN. REPUTATION, REPUTE; **saying**. N*OR*M (catechism – crypt).

NANDOO BIRD (S American) [cassowary, dinornis (NZ, ex), emu, moa (ex), ostrich].

NANNY GOVERNESS, NURSE; **celebrated:** MARY POPPINS, NANA. GRANNY (sl). *Female goat.*

NAP (s/l *knap*). NAPOLEON; BONEY. DOZE, KIP, *SLEEP.* PILE. *CARD GAME.* CERT, SURE THING.

NAPOLEON N, NAP, BONEY. GOLD PIECE (Fr). PIG (Animal Farm, Orwell). [*Bellerophon*, First Consul. *Chesterton.* Moriarty (*Holmes*)].

NARCISSUS 1. *FLOWER.* 2. Gk myth youth, for whom *Echo* bore unrequited love, so that she pined away. He fell in love with his own reflection and also pined away, so that he turned into the flower which bears his name. [self-admiration].

NATIVE ABORIGINE; BORN, INDIGENOUS. BIVALVE, *OYSTER.* DOMESTIC. WILD MAN, SAVAGE. ~ **of Australia** = ABORIGINE, *EMU*; ~ **of Britain** = CELT; ~ **of Ireland** = PICT, CELT; ~ **of N Britain** = PICT, CELT; ~ **of NZ** = KIWI, MAORI; ~ **of USA** = *REDSKIN*; ~ **of Wales** = CELT.

NATURE 1. CHARACTER, INCLINATION. MOTHER EARTH. 2. **Goddesses: Gk** = *ARTEMIS, DEMETER*; **Rom** = *CERES, DIANA*, OPS; **Egy** = *ISIS*, UPIS. [*Pleiades*].

NAUT NAUTICAL, NAVAL, MARITIME. [*measure*].

NAVIGATE CON, *SAIL, STEER.*

NAVY *FLEET*, MARINE, NAUTICAL, RN, TARS, USN. *COLOUR* (blue).

NAY (s/l *neigh*). CONTRADICTION, DENIAL, NO, REFUSAL. AND MORE, EVEN, MOREOVER, RATHER, WELL, WHY.

NB NORTH BRITAIN. NOTA BENE, TAKE NOTE. NEW BRUNSWICK (*Province*, Can).

NCO CPL, RSM, SGT.

ND NO DATE, UNDATED.

NE *NEON* (*chem*). NEAR EAST.

NEAR BY; *CLOSE.* MEAN, *STINGY.*

NEARLY 1. ALMOST, NIGH. 2. Word less one or two letters, e.g. **The cricketer is nearly done** (3) = DON (Bradman).

NEAR MISS CLOSE THING, NARROW SHAVE. CHAPERONE, DUENNA, HONOUR GUARD (crypt).

NEAT UNDILUTED. ORDERED, TIDY; *CHIC*, DEFT,

ELEGANT, SMART. *CATTLE*, OX(EN); LOWER (crypt).

NEB NATIONAL ENTERPRISE BOARD. *BEAK* (Sc). HILL-CLIMB (dn, crypt).

NEBUCHADNEZZAR 1. LARGE *BOTTLE*. 2. King of Babylon who carried the Jews to Chaldea.

NECESSITY COMPULSION, CONSTRAINT, INDISPENSABILITY, NEED (**saying**).

NEEDLE IRRITATE, PROVOKE. KNIT, *SEW*. **Pl** = ROCKS (geog, IOW).

NEEDLER IRRITANT. ANAESTHETIST, ACUPUNCTURIST; NUMBER (crypt). SEAMSTRESS, *SEWER* (crypt). TATTOOIST.

NEEDLEWORK IRRITATION, PROVOCATION. ACUPUNCTURE; ANAESTHETICS, DEADENING, NUMBING (crypt). *TATTOO. KNITTING, SEWING.*

NEGLIGE NIGHTIE, PEIGNOIR, UNDRESS.

NEIGH (s/l *nay*). WHINNY (*horse*).

NEMESIS 1. Gk *goddess* of retribution (similar to *Ate*); d of *Nyx*. 2. A minor *PLANET*.

NEOLITHIC *AGE*.

NEON NE (*chem*).

NEPTUNE Rom *god* of the SEA (**Gk** = POSEIDON). On the overthrow of *Saturn*, his realm was divided: the heavens to *Jupiter*, the underworld to *Pluto* and the seas to Neptune.

NEREID 1. Gk myth sea-nymph (as opposed to fresh water nymphs), d's of *Nereus* and *Doris*. Propitious to sailors (especially to the *Argonauts*), one of them was Thetis, m of *Achilles* [*Andromeda*]. 2. A satellite of the *planet Neptune*.

NEREUS Gk myth *god* of the sea, s of Pontus and *Ge*, he had 50 d's by *Doris*, who were the *Nereids*. Also *POSEIDON*. **Rom** = *NEPTUNE*.

NESS CAPE, *HEAD*, POINT. LOCH [*monster*].

NET *GIN*, MESH, SNARE, *TRAP*, WEB. CLEAN, CLEAR. *BARRIER*, DIVIDER (*tennis*). PRACTICE AREA (*cricket*).

NETHERLANDS NL (*car plate*).

NETTLE ANNOY, *BOTHER*, IRK, IRRITATE, WORRY. *WILD PLANT, STING*. **Saying**.

NEUTER 1. N. ASEXUAL, NO SEX, CASTRATE. 2. Remove letters 'sex' from clue, e.g. **Neuter Middlesex** = MIDDLE.

NEVER-ENDING 1. CONTINUOUS, ENDLESS. CIRCLE, RING. 2. Word with last letter(s) removed, e.g. **Disapproval of the never-ending book** (3) = boo(k).

NEVER NEVER EASY TERMS, HIRE PURCHASE. PAN COUNTRY (*Barrie*; crypt).

NEVERTHELESS DESPITE THAT, *NOTWITHSTANDING*. EVERMORE (crypt).

NEW (s/l knew). *Anag.* CHANGED, DIFFERENT, FRESH, FURTHER, NOVEL, RECENT (**opp** = *old*). *DISCOVERED*, *INVENTED*. *FOREST*. **Pl** = INFORMATION, TIDINGS [*media*]. ALL POINTS, ALL QUARTERS, FOUR QUARTERS (crypt).

NEWSPAPER *DAILY*, JOURNAL, *PRESS*, RAG, SHEET, TABLOID, WEEKLY [Fleet Street].

NEW TESTAMENT NT (**opp** = OT).

NEXT MONTH PROX, PROXIMO; name of the current next month.

NI NICKEL (*chem*). NORTHERN IRELAND.

NICK *GAOL*. ARREST, DETAIN. *STEAL*. NOTCH, *SCORE*. THE *DEVIL*.

NICKEL NI (*chem*). *COIN* (US).

NICKNAME 1. *PRISON* (crypt). 2. Abbreviated or familiar name given to anyone, often associated with their surname or occupation, e.g.

American	= YANK
Arab	= WOG
Australian	= DIGGER
Englishman	= BRIT, GRINGO (S Am), LIMEY (US), POM (Aus), WHITEY
Frenchman	= FROG
German	= FRITZ, HUN, KRAUT
Irishman	= PADDY
Italian	= WOP
Scot	= JOCK
Welshman	= TAFFY
Bell	= DINGER
Clark	= NOBBY
Dean	= DIXIE

Grey	= DOLLY
Lane	= SHADY
Miller	= DUSTY
Smith	= SMUDGER
White	= CHALKY
Wilson	= TUG

NIGHT (s/l *knight*). 1. Darkness (**opp** = *day*). 2. **Gk goddess** = *HECATE*.

NIGHTCLUB CLIPJOINT, DIVE, SPEAKEASY. COSH, TRUNCHEON (crypt).

NIGHTFLIER BAT, MOTH, OWL.

NIGHTINGALE *BIRD*; SINGER [Hans *Andersen*; jug]. JENNY LIND (Swe). INSTRUMENT (mus). FLORENCE ~, LADY OF THE LAMP, *NURSE*, SANTA FILOMENA (Longfellow).

NIKE Gk *goddess* of VICTORY (**Rom** = VICTORIA); d of *Pallas* and *Styx*.

NIL O, *DUCK*, *LOVE*, ZERO.

NINE See *number*. IX; ONE OVER THE EIGHT. *MUSES*. DAYS WONDER. ~ GODS (Lars Porsena, Macaulay). ~ LIVES (*cat*). ~ Drummers drumming in *Christmas* song; ~ Bright Shiners in *song*. ~ of diamonds = curse of Scotland. **Saying. Pl** = ELABORATELY, TO PERFECTION (dress).

~ **ANGELIC ORDERS** *ANGELS*, ARCHANGELS, CHERUBIM, DOMINATIONS, *POWERS*, PRINCIPALITIES, SERAPHIM, THRONES, VIRTUES.

~ **WORTHIES** MEDIAEVAL HEROES: JOSHUA, DAVID, JUDAS MACCABAEUS, *HECTOR*, *ALEXANDER* THE GREAT, JULIUS *CAESAR*, *KING ARTHUR*, CHARLEMAGNE, GEOFFREY OF BOUILLON.

NIOBE 1. Gk myth d of Tantalus, w of the King of Thebes. She turned to stone at the death of her children and shed incessant *tears*. 2. A minor *PLANET*.

NIPPY BITING, COLD, CHILLY, PARKY. AGILE. WAITRESS (Lyons).

NITROGEN N (*chem*).

NL NETHERLANDS, HOLLAND (and *car plate*).

NO (s/l *know*). 1. NAY, NEGATIVE; REFUSAL; O, LOVE, NIL. NUMBER, NUMERO. NEIN (Ger), NIET (USSR),

NON (Fr); **opp** = *yes*. 2. Omit letter or word indicated, e.g. **No right turn for VAT** (3) = TU*N. 3. Opposite of word indicated, e.g. **No matter** (4) = MIND.

~ **BETTER** NOT WORSE, STATIC, THE SAME. *WINNER* (crypt). ANTI-GAMBLING (crypt).

~ **CHARGE** *FREE*, GRATIS. *FLAT*, RUN DOWN (elect). DEFENDING, NO ATTACK.

NODDY SIMPLETON. SEA-BIRD. [Toyland].

NOGGIN *HEAD*. *DRINK*. *MEASURE*: GILL, ¼ PINT hence P, I, N or T.

NO GOOD 1. *BAD*, DUFF, DUD. NE'ER-DO-WELL, RAKE. 2. Delete any reference to 'good' or its synonym from the clue, e.g. **No-good racecourse** (4) = ****WOOD.

NOISELESS QUIET, SILENT, SOUNDLESS. *ODIN* (crypt).

NOISY F, FF. ROWDY [DB] (**opp** = *quiet*).

NO LONGER EX, LATE, WAS. SHORTER.

NONCONFORMIST *Anag*. DISSENTING, FREE CHURCH.

NONPLUS AMAZE, ASTOUND. MINUS (crypt).

NON-U 1. *COMMON*. 2. Delete letter 'U' from clue, e.g. **Non-U guy** = G*Y.

NOON 1. N; MERIDIEM, MIDDAY, M. 2. Delete letters 'ON', e.g. **Noon Monday** = M**DAY.

NO-ONE 1. NOBODY. NOI (crypt). 2. Delete letter 'I' from clue, e.g. **Landlords no-one hoists** (5) = HO*STS.

NO QUARTER 1. *MERCILESS*, PITILESS. 2. Delete letters E, N, S and W from clue, e.g. **No quarter for Wales man in battle** (4) = *AL**MA*.

Nor Norse, Norway.

NO RIGHT 1. NO ENTITLEMENT. *LEFT*. NOR (crypt). 2. Delete letters 'R' or 'RT' from clue, e.g. **Reward no right party** (3) = PA**Y.

NORM ACCEPTED STANDARD, *PAR*; AVERAGE. NORMAN, NAME (catechism, crypt).

NORMAN BOY, MAN. INVADER, NORTH FRENCH (hence NORD, crypt). [*stone*].

NORTH 1. N; POINT; *BRIDGE PLAYER*. POLE. *SEA*. 2. Reads upwards (dn).

~ **AND SOUTH** NS, NANDS. MOUTH (*rh sl*). BRIDGING TEAM (crypt).

~ WIND Gk = BOREAS, **Rom** = SEPTENTRIO.

NORVIC *Episcopal sig* of NORWICH.

NORWAY N (*car plate*). *WRITER*; NEVIL SHUTE.

NORWICH Episcopal sig = NORVIC.

NOSE (s/l *knows*, noes). FEATURE; BREATHER, HOOTER, SCHNOZZLE (sl). *AIRPORT*, AIRWAY (crypt). AROMA, BOUQUET; SENSE OF SMELL.

NOT (s/l *knot*). 1. NEGATIVE. 2. Omit word referred to, e.g. **Hire character is not billed** (7) = CHAR**TER.

NOTABLE WELL KNOWN. EMINENT, REMARKABLE, STRIKING. BUSTLING, CAPABLE, HOUSEWIFELY (arch). INCAPABLE (crypt). MUSICAL (crypt).

NOTE *NOTICE*. *CASH*, MONEY [*currencies*]: *BUCK*, FIVER, ONCER, *QUID*, TENNER. *KEY*, PITCH, SOUND, TONE, *TONIC*: FLAT, NATURAL, SHARP; A, B, C, D, E, F, G; DO/DOH, RAY/RE, ME/MI, FA/FAH, SO/SOH, LA/LAH, TE/TI; BREVE = 2 SEMI-BREVES = 4 MINIMS = 8 CROTCHETS = 16 QUAVERS. COMPOSE (crypt, e.g. **He noted** = name of any composer).

NOTED 1. FELT, NOTICED, REGISTERED, REMARKED, SEEN. KEYBOARD; MUSICAL; SCORE (crypt). 2. Remove letters ED or TED from clue, e.g. **Noted Te Deum** = T**EUM or ***EUM. 3. Add any note to word indicated, e.g. **Is hesitantly noted before** = ER*E, or **Anger is noted for giving illusion** = MI*RAGE. 4. COMPOSER (crypt: 'he noted').

NOT EVEN NOT ONLY. *ODD*.

NOTHING *LOVE*, O, NIL, ZERO, e.g. **Is nothing to me** = IS*O*ME.

~ LESS 1. AT LEAST, IN TRUTH. 2. Omit synonym for nothing from clue, e.g. **Shocking Olive, nothing less** (4) = *LIVE.

NOTICE *AD*, POSTER, PROCLAMATION. REMARK, *SEE*, *SPOT*. MELTED, WARM (crypt).

NOTOS Gk myth SOUTH WIND (**Rom** = AUSTER).

NOT OUT AT HOME, *IN*. BATTING (*cricket*). BLACKLEG.

NOT RIGHT INCORRECT. LEFT. WRONG.

NOTWITHSTANDING ALL THE SAME, ALTHOUGH, NEVERTHELESS. SEATED, SITTING, LYING (crypt). GIVING WAY, YIELDING (crypt).

NOUN N.

NOVEMBER (11th) MONTH, M, NOV (Rom ninth month until *Caesar* reorganized the calendar). **Birthstone** = *topaz*.

NOWADAYS AT PRESENT. AD.

NT NEW TESTAMENT (**opp** = OT); BIBLE.

NUDE 1. NAKED (**opp** = *dressed*). [Hans *Andersen*]. 2. Remove synonym for clothes from clue, e.g. *Nude lawsuit* = LAW or, more cryptically, **Nude Ursula** = AN(dress).

NUMBER AGGREGATE, *NO*, QUANTITY, SUM; *COUNT*, RECKON, TELL. *ANAESTHETIC*, DEADENING, *DRUG*, NEEDLE (all crypt). V = 5, X = 10, L = 50, C = 100, D = 500, M = 1,000. **Pl** = BOOK (bibl, OT). **Specific ~s:**

0 = CYPHER, DUCK, EGG, LOVE, NIL, NIX, NOTHING, ROUND, ZERO, ZILCH; A- [calm (Beaufort scale), fool (*tarot*)].

1 = A, I; *FIRST*, MONAD, ONCE(-R), *ONE*, ONLY, SELF, *SINGLE*, SOLO, UNITY; EIN (Ger), UN, -E (Fr); MONO- [paper (*anniversary*), sorrow (*magpie*), red ball (*snooker*), all alone (*song*), partridge (*song*), juggler (*tarot*), First Letter (*Kipling*)].

2 = II; BIS (Fr), DEUCE, DUET, DUO, DYAD, ENCORE, SECOND, *TWICE*, *TWO*; DEUX (Fr), ZWEI (Ger); BI- [cotton (*anniversary*), cannon (*billiards*), joy (*magpies*), conversion (*rugby*), yellow ball (*snooker*), lilywhite boys (*song*), turtledoves (*song*), female pope (*tarot*), ~ bits].

3 = III; TER, *THIRD*, *THREE*, THRICE, TRIAD, TRIO; DREI (Ger), TROIS (Fr); TRI- [feather (*anniversary*), red ball (*billiards*), gableś (*Holmes*), Garridebs (*Holmes*), ~ quarters (*Holmes*), students (*Holmes*), Soldiers ~ (*Kipling*), girl (*magpie*), try (*rugby*), green ball (*snooker*), French hens (*song*), rivals (*song*), empress (*tarot*), ~ estates]. **Quotes:** 'There are ~ kinds of lies: lies, damned lies and statistics' (Disraeli); '~ little *maids* from school' (Mikado, *G & S*); 'Come the ~ corners of the world in arms, and we shall shock them' (John, *Shak*); '~ ravens sat on a tree' (ballad).

4 = IV; *FOUR(TH)*, QUARTET, TETRAD; VIER (Ger); QUAD(R)- [flower (*anniversary*), boundary (*cricket*), Sign of ~ (*Holmes*), boy (*magpie*), brown ball (*snooker*), calling birds (*song*), gospel makers (*song*), emperor (*tarot*); bissextile (leap year)]. **Quotes:** '~ essential human freedoms . . . speech . . .

worship . . . from want . . . from fear' *FDR* Jan 41).

5 = V; *FIFTH*, *FIVE*, PENTA, PENTAD, QUINQUE, QUINTET; **Pl** = ballgame [wood (*anniversary*), orange pips (*Holmes*), Nations (*Kipling*), letter (*magpie*), lustrum, quinquennium (period), ~ *towns* (potteries), golden rings (*song*), symbols (*song*), pope (*tarot*), ~ *classic orders*. **Quote:** 'Full fathom ~ thy father lies' (Temp, *Shak*).

6 = VI; HEXAD, SEXTET, SICE, *SIX*(TH); SEX- [~ *nations* (*American Indians*), candy (*anniversary*), boundary (*cricket*), ~ Napoleons (*Holmes*), ~ honest serving men (*Kipling*), something better (*magpie*), pink ball (*snooker*), geese a-laying (*song*), proud walkers (*song*), lovers (*tarot*)]. **Quote:** '~ days shalt thou labour' (Exodus).

7 = VII; HEPTAD, SEPTAD, *SEVEN*(TH); SEPTO-; **Pl** = rugby [copper or wool (*anniversary*), near gale (Beaufort scale), ~ Seas (*Kipling*), greeting (*magpie*), septenary (period), ~ hills (Rom), black ball (*snooker*), stars in the sky (*song*), swans a-swimming (*song*), chariot (*tarot*), ~ *ages* (*Shak*), ~ *deadly sins*, ~ *hills*, ~ *sages*, ~ *sisters*, ~ *wonders of the world*]. **Quotes:** 'If ~ maids with ~ mops swept for half a year' (*Alice* thro' the Looking Glass); 'His acts being ~ ages' (AYLI, *Shak*).

8 = VIII; EIGHT(H), OCTAD, OCTET; OCTO-; ROWING CREW, BLUE, GOLDIE (C reserve ~), ISIS (O reserve ~) [bronze (*anniversary*), gale (Beaufort scale), wish (*magpie*), maids a-milking (*song*), bold rangers (*song*), justice (*tarot*)]. **Quote:** 'Pieces of ~' (parrot, *Stevenson*).

9 = IX; *NINE*, NINTH, NONAD, NONET; NONA-, NOV-. **Pl** = ELABORATELY, TO PERFECTION (dress) [pottery (*anniversary*), kiss (*magpie*), bright shiners (*song*), drummers drumming (*song*), ~ of diamonds (curse of Scotland), hermit (*tarot*), ~ *Muses*, ~ points of the law, ~ *angelic orders*]. **Quote:** '~ bean rows will I have there' (Innisfree, Yeats).

10 = X; DECIMAL, TEN(TH); DECA- [tin (*anniversary*), storm (Beaufort scale), decade (period), *commandments* (*song*), green bottles (*song*), pipers piping (*song*), wheel of *fortune* (*tarot*)].

11 = II, XI; ELEVEN(TH); HENDECA-; IMPAIRED (crypt); **Pl** = SNACK [steel (*anniversary*), side/team (cricket, rugby etc), ladies dancing (*song*), ~ who went to Heaven (*song*), strength (*tarot*)].

12 = XII; DOZEN, DUODECIMAL, TWELFTH, TWELVE; DODECA- [silk (*anniversary*), hurricane (Beaufort scale), *apostles* (*song*), lords a-leaping (*song*), *hanged* man (*tarot*), glorious ~th (grouse shooting), ~th Night (*Shak*)].

13 = XIII; BAKER'S DOZEN, THIRTEEN(TH), UNLUCKY [lace (*anniversary*), side/team (rugby league), *death* (*tarot*)].

14 = XIV; FOURTEEN(TH) [ivory (*anniversary*), temperance (*tarot*)].

15 = XV; FIFTEEN(TH) [crystal (*anniversary*), side/team (rugby union), *devil* (*tarot*), rebellion (Old Pretender)].

16 = XVI; SIXTEEN [*tower* (*tarot*)].

17 = XVII; seventeen [*star* (*tarot*)].

18 = XVIII; eighteen [*moon* (*tarot*)].

19 = XIX; nineteen [*sun* (*tarot*)].

20 = XX; JACKSON (sl), *SCORE*, TWENTY [china (*anniversary*), TOPS (darts), day of *judgement* (*tarot*)]. **Quote:** '~ love-sick maidens we' (Patience, *G & S*).

21 = XXI; MAJORITY, VINGT-ET-UN (Fr) [world (*tarot*)].

25 = XXV; PONY (sl), QUARTER CENTURY [*silver* (*anniversary*)].

30 = XXX; THIRTY; 2nd XV (rugby) [*pearl* (*anniversary*), ~ Years' War]. **Quote:** 'And they covenanted with him for ~ pieces of silver' (St Matthew).

35 = XXXV [*coral* (*anniversary*)].

40 = XL; FORTY [ruby (*anniversary*), roaring ~s (*winds*), ~ winks (sleep)].

45 = XLV [sapphire (*anniversary*), rebellion (Young Pretender)].

50 = L; HALF CENTURY, HALF TON (sl) [gold (*anniversary*), bullseye (darts)].

52 = LII; PACK (cards).

55 = LV [*emerald* (*anniversary*)].

60 = LX [*diamond* (*anniversary*), ~ glorious years]. **Quote:** 'If you can fill the unforgiving minute with ~ seconds worth of distance run' (If, *Kipling*).

70 = LXX [*platinum* (*anniversary*)].

75 = LXXV [diamond (*anniversary*)].

78 = TAROC, *TAROT* (pack).

100 = C; CENTURY, *HUNDRED*, TON (sl); HECTO- [Old ~th (All people that on earth do dwell; psalm 100); Chiltern ~s (stewardship, MP's resignation)].

180 = MAXIMUM (darts).

200 = CC; DOUBLE CENTURY, TWO TON (sl).

500 = D; *MONKEY* (sl).

600 = DC [Balaclava, Cardigan, Light Brigade]. **Quote:** 'Into the valley of death rode the ~' (Charge of the Light Brigade, Tennyson).

1,000 = K, M; *GRAND* (sl), MIL (meas); KILO- [chiliad, millennium (period), ~ Guineas (*classic* horserace)].

1,009 = M*IX, AD*M*IX (crypt).

1,500 = *MD*.

1,760 = MILE (yards).

1,976 = ASCOT MILE (yards).

2,000 = KK, MM (~ Guineas (*classic* horserace)].

6,100 = VI*C (crypt).

6,350 = VI*TRIO*L (crypt).

~ **OF PLAYERS** DUET, OCTET, QUARTET etc. ELEVEN, FIFTEEN, *SIDE*, TEAM.

~ **ONE** *ME*, I, SELF; NO*I.

NUN (s/l none). *CHURCHWOMAN*; CONVENT GIRL, *SISTER*; *Chaucer* character. BIRD: BLUE TIT, *PIGEON*, SMEW.

NURSE DEVELOP, FOSTER, HARBOUR. WORKER (insect). *FISH*, *SHARK*. CARE, COSSET, LOOK AFTER, TEND; SUCKLE. AMAH (Asia), AYAH (Ind), NANNY, *SISTER*, SRN (**Union** = COHSE); **celebrated** (fiction): SARAH GAMP (Martin Chuzzlewit, *Dickens*); MARCHIONESS (Old Curiosity Shop, *Dickens*); MRS POOLE (Jane Eyre, *C. Brontë*); BETSY PRIG (Martin Chuzzlewit, *Dickens*); MISS PROSS (Tale of Two Cities, *Dickens*); RUTH (Pirates of Penzance, *G & S*); TILLY SLOWBOY (Cricket on the Hearth, *Dickens*); **celebrated** (fact): EDITH CAVELL, FLORENCE *NIGHTINGALE*.

NURSERY HOTHOUSE, PROPAGATION PLOT. HOSPITAL, WARD (crypt). CHILD'S BEDROOM; ROCKERY (crypt).

NURSERYMAN MARKET GARDENER. BOY BLUE, JACK

HORNER, SIMPLE SIMON etc (crypt, from ~ rhymes).
NUT FASTENING [bolt]. ENTHUSIAST, FAN; FOOL. HEAD
(sl). COAL LUMP. FRUIT (shell) [kernel]) **types:** ACORN,
ALMOND, BRAZIL, CASHEW, FILBERT, GROUNDNUT,
HAZEL, PEANUT, PECAN, PISTACHIO, WALNUT.
TEACHERS (*union*).
NUT-CASE LUNATIC, MADMAN. *SHELL* (crypt).
NYM CORPORAL, SOLDIER (*Shak*).
NYMPH 1. *INSECT* (immature), PUPA: DAMSELFLY,
DRAGONFLY. GIRL, HOURI (Mos). YOUNG WOMAN.
2. Gk myth Naiad, one of the fresh water maidens (as opp to the
salt water *Nereids*, or the Oceanides of the great oceans). Nymphs
are distinct from *goddesses*, in that they belong to one particular
spot, as opp to the goddesses' overall domain. **Mountain
nymphs** = OREADS; **tree nymphs** = DRYADS and
HAMADRYADS; **nymphs of the groves and glens** =
NAPAEAE.
NYMPHOMANIA Obsession (in women) with sex.
NYX Gk *goddess* of NIGHT (**Rom** = NOX); d of *Chaos* and m,
without benefit of husband, of many *gods* and *goddesses*,
including the *HESPERIDES*, *HYPNOS* and *NEMESIS*, also by
Erebus of *Charon*.
NZ NEW ZEALAND (and *car plate*).

O OHIO. OXFORD. OXYGEN (*chem*). DUCK, LOVE, NIL,
ROUND, ZERO.
OAK *TREE*. **Pl** = *CLASSIC*.
OAR (s/l *or*, ore). GALLEY SLAVE, *ROWER*. PADDLE.
OARSMAN *ROWER*: *BOW*, *STROKE*. *CHARON*.
OAST HOUSE DRIER, HOP DRIER, *HOPPER*.
OATH APPEAL, ASSERT, PROMISE, SWEAR [*Hippocrates*,
Witness]. CURSE, PROFANITY: BLAST, BLOW, BOTHER,
DAMN, DASH, DRAT etc.
OB *DIED*, OBIT. ALUMNUS, OLD BOY [Tom Brown's
Schooldays, T. Hughes' pseudonym]. OUTSIDE BROADCAST.
OBJECT 1. *AIM*, *END*, *POINT*. THING. *BAR*, COMPLAIN,
DISAPPROVE. 2. Accusative case, e.g. **I object** = ME.
OBSERVE *NOTE*, *SEE*, *WATCH*.

OBSESSION EAGER PURSUIT, EXCESSIVE ENTHUSIASM,
MANIA:

ANGLOMANIA	= **English customs**
BIBLIOMANIA	= **books**
EROTOMANIA	= **sexual passion**
KLEPTOMANIA	= **stealing**
MEGALOMANIA	= **grand ideas**
MONOMANIA	= **one idea**
NECROMANIA	= **death**
NYMPHOMANIA	= **sexual desire (in women)**
PYROMANIA	= **fire-raising**

OBTAINABLE *Anag.* e.g. **Camp follower obtainable from Ulster**
(6) = SUTLER. ACQUIRABLE; AVAILABLE,
ESTABLISHED, PREVALENT.

OBVERSE FACE, FRONT; HEAD (*coin*; **opp** = reverse).
COUNTERPART.

OC ONLY CHILD. OFFICER COMMANDING.

OCCIDENT(AL) W, WESTERN (**opp** = oriental).

OCEAN One of the main areas of sea water: ARCTIC,
ANTARCTIC, ATLANTIC, INDIAN, PACIFIC [*Pluto*
(acronym); seven seas].

OCEANIDES Gk myth *NYMPHS* of the great oceans.

OCEANUS Gk myth river flowing round the (supposedly circular
flat) earth, and also the associated *god*, mar to Tethys; later came
to mean the Atlantic (i.e. the water beyond the known
Mediterranean sea).

OCTOBER 1. BEER. 2. (10th) MONTH, M; OCT (8th Rom
month, before *Caesar* reorganized the calendar). **Birthstone** =
opal.

ODD *Anag.* e.g. **How odd** = WHO. 1. UNEVEN. CASTING,
EXTRA, OVER. REMAINING, ADDITIONAL, CASUAL,
UNCONNECTED. *ECCENTRIC*, EXTRAORDINARY,
QUEER, REMARKABLE, SINGULAR, STRANGE. 2. **Pl** =
ADVANTAGE, BALANCE, CHANCES, HANDICAP,
PROBABILITIES, SP (betting). REMNANTS.
DIFFERENCE, INEQUALITIES, STRIFE, VARIANCE.

ODIN 1. Nor myth chief warrior *god*, who mar (1) *Frigg* (s =
Balder) and (2) *Freya*. One-eyed, he lived in Valhalla; his horse

Sleipner had eight legs (**Gk** = *ZEUS*, **Rom** = *Jupiter*, **A Sax** = WODEN/WOTAN). 2. NOISELESS, QUIET (crypt).

ODYSSEUS = *ULYSSES*.

OEDIPUS Gk myth s of King Laius and Queen Jocasta of Thebes. Banished as a baby because an oracle prophesied that Laius would be killed by his own son, who would then marry his mother. Returning, Oedipus fulfilled the prophecy by slaying his unrecognized father on the way. He then relieved the Thebans by solving the riddle of the *Sphinx*, so that he was made king and mar his own mother. When the facts were revealed, Jocasta killed herself and Oedipus blinded himself. [~ complex; **opp** = *Electra*].

OF OLD FRENCH. FROM.

~ **COURSE** NATURALLY, OBVIOUSLY. [crypt = *golfing*; *meals*; *racing*].

OFF *Anag.* 1. APART, AWAY. NOT ON. *GO*, START. LOOSE, SEPARATE. CANCELLED. *BAD*, MOULDY. 2. Delete word or letters indicated, e.g. **Hit it off** = H(it).

OFFHAND CASUAL, INFORMAL. DIGITAL (crypt).

OFFICE BUREAU, QUARTERS. APPOINTMENT, DUTY, JOB, POSITION, POST, TASK. ATTENTION, KINDNESS, *SERVICE*. WORSHIP.

OFFICER FUNCTIONARY, MINISTER, SERVANT: BAILIFF, CHAIRMAN, CONSTABLE, HERALD, PRESIDENT, SECRETARY, TREASURER. Commissioned rank in mil services: CAPT, CDR, *CO*, *COL*, LT, PO etc; ENSIGN, *GENERAL*, SUBALTERN etc.

OFFING DISTANCE. TOPPLING, UNSEATING, UPSETTING (crypt).

OFFSPRING DIVE (crypt). BROOD, CHILD(REN), DESCENDANT, PROGENY, LITTER, YOUNG, **specifically:**

Adult	**Young**
Ass/mare	MULE
Bear	*CUB*
Bird	CHICK
Camel	*COLT*
Cat	KITTEN
Cow	*CALF*

Deer	FAWN
Dog	PUP
Duck	DUCKLING
Eagle	EAGLET
Eel	ELVER
Elephant	*CALF*
Fish	*FRY*
Fox	*CUB*
Frog	TADPOLE
Goat	*KID*
Goose	GOSLING
Hare	LEVERET
Hawk	BOWET, EYAS, NYAS
Hen	CHICK
Heron	CHICK
Horse	COLT (m), FILLY (f), FOAL
Human	BABY, CHILD
Lion	*CUB*
Pig	PIGLET, SHOAT
Salmon	PEAL, GRILSE, SMOLT
Sheep	*LAMB*
Stallion/Ass	HINNY
Swan	CYGNET
Tiger	*CUB*
Turkey	POULT
Walrus	*CALF*
Whale	*CALF*
Wild boar	GRICE
Wolf	*CUB*
Yak/Cow	DZHO, DZO

Young	Adult
Baby	HUMAN
Bowet	*HAWK*
Calf	*COW, ELEPHANT, WALRUS, WHALE*
Chick	*BIRD*, HEN, HERON
Child	HUMAN
Colt	*CAMEL, HORSE* (m)
Cub	*BEAR, FOX, LION, TIGER, WOLF*

Cygnet	*SWAN*
Duckling	*DUCK*
Dzho, dzo	YAK/COW
Elver	*EEL*
Eaglet	*EAGLE*
Fawn	*DEER*
Filly	*HORSE* (f)
Foal	*HORSE*
Fry	*FISH*
Gosling	*GOOSE*
Grice	WILD BOAR
Grilse	*SALMON*
Hinny	STALLION/*ASS*
Kid	*GOAT*
Kitten	*CAT*
Lamb	*SHEEP*
Leveret	HARE
Mule	*ASS*/MARE
Peal	*SALMON*
Piglet	*PIG*
Poult	TURKEY
Pup	*DOG*
Shoat	*PIG*
Smolt	*SALMON*
Tadpole	*FROG*

OG OLD GERMAN. GO BACK (crypt). KING (bibl).

OH CALL, *CRY*. OHIO (US *state*).

OILER GREASER, MECHANIC. BRIBER. **Pl** = TEAM (US *football*). OPEC (crypt).

OLD 1. ANCIENT, EX, FORMER, ONCE (**opp** = *new*). AGED, GREY [*study*]. 2. Use old form of word indicated, e.g. **Old enough** = ENOW; **the old** = YE. 3. Use Roman name, e.g. **Old Exeter** = ISCA.

~ **BOY** ALUMNUS, *OB*.

~ **FASHIONED** *DATED*, OUT OF DATE, SQUARE (**opp** = *in*). COCKTAIL, *DRINK*.

~ **FLAME** EX, PAST LOVE. ASH, EMBER (crypt).

~ **FRENCH** OF. VIEUX (trans).

~ **GERMAN** OG. ALT (trans).

~ **LADY** *MOTHER*. CRONE.

~ **MAN** *HUSBAND*; POT AND PAN (*rh sl*). GAFFER.

~ **RAILWAY** GWR, LMS, LNER, SR etc.

~ **STYLE** *OS*.

~ **TESTAMENT** OT.

~ **TRAFFORD** *CRICKET GROUND*, TESTING GROUND.

~ **WOMAN** *WIFE*.

OLIVER NOLL. CROMWELL. [Roland; more].

OLYMPIC 1. GAMES. MAGNIFICENT, SUPERIOR. 2. Of *Olympus*, hence relating to Gk myth *gods* and *goddesses*.

OLYMPUS Thessalian mountain, dwelling place of *Zeus* and the principal Gk *gods* and *goddesses*. [*Seven Wonders*].

OM ORDER OF MERIT.

OMAR KHAYYAM, TENT MAKER [astronomy, maths, poetry].

OMIT 1. *CUT*, FAIL, LEAVE OUT, NEGLECT. 2. Omit letter(s) or word(s) from clue as indicated, e.g. **Lord Peter omits tea apparently** (4) = PE*ER.

ON *BET*, WAGERED. AHEAD. POSSIBLE. *CONNECTED*.

~ **BOARD** 1. EMBARKED, LOADED, SHIPPED; NAUTICAL. FOOD, ON THE TABLE. SURFER (crypt). 2. Put letter(s) or word(s) into synonym for boat or ship (often into letters S...S), e.g. **Pool on board rolls** (6) = S*POOL*S. 3. Any object which is normally used on a board, e.g. **Food on board** = CHEESE; **piece on board** = CASTLE, PAWN, ROOK etc, and (crypt) DRAUGHTSMAN; also any boardgame: **game on board** = CHESS, LUDO, MONOPOLY etc.

ONCE ARCHAIC, EX. ONE TIME.

ONE 1. See *number*. A, ACE, I, MONAD, UNIT. RED BALL (snooker). 2. All *alone* in *song*; *partridge* in a peartree (*Christmas song*).

~ **BY ONE** IN ORDER, SERIATIM, SINGLY. ELEVEN, II (crypt).

~ **CARD** *ACE*.

~ **EYED** INEFFICIENT. *CYCLOPES*, ODIN, PHILIP (of Macedon, f of *Alexander*), NELSON, POLYPHEMUS, POPEYE, LONG JOHN *SILVER*, SQUEERS (Dickens), WODEN [*monster*].

~ **THOUSAND GUINEAS** CLASSIC.

ON SHOW 1. DEMONSTRATED, EXHIBITED, EXPOSED. 2.

Hidden word, e.g. **Fit for a king on show at the picture gallery** (5) = RE*GAL.

ONWARD FORWARD, FURTHER ON, PROGRESSING. IN HOSPITAL (crypt).

ONYX *GEM*, SEMI-PRECIOUS STONE; *CHALCEDONY*; *AGATE*.

OO EXCLAMATION, OH. BIRD (Hawaiian). *DUCKS*, EGGS, *LOVES*, OVA (all crypt).

OOH EXCLAMATION, OH. BACKWATER (H_2O backwards, crypt – but *chem* inaccurate).

OP OBSERVATION POST. MINOR OPERATION, OPERATION. OPUS, WORK. OPPOSITE PROMPT (theat). ORDER OF PREACHERS (DOMINICANS). OUT OF PRINT. OPTICAL. **Pl** = Rom *goddess* of *NATURE*.

OPAL *GEM*, PRECIOUS STONE. *Birthstone* (October). SILICA QUARTZ.

OPEN OVERT. WINDWARD, WINDY (**opp** = *lee*). CRACK, UNDO, UNWRAP. TAKE STRIKE (*cricket*). *UNIVERSITY*. GOLF CHAMPIONSHIP, TOURNAMENT; PRO-AM (crypt).

~ **AIR** AL FRESCO, OUTSIDE. CANDOUR.

OPENER 1. DOOR, GATE. *KEY*. (FIRST) BAT (*cricket*). TIN OPENER. **Pl** = QUALIFYING HOLDING (cards). 2. First letter, e.g. **Letter opener** = L.

OPENING 1. CRACK, FISSURE, GAP, HOLE [Sesame]. OVERTURE. GAMBIT. 2. First letter, e.g. **Clever opening** = C.

OPERATING THEATRE SURGERY. WORK ROOM. WORKSHOP.

OPERATION MANIPULATION, WORKING. OP. SURGERY. *BATTLE*; ACTION, ENGAGEMENT (mil).

OPERATOR MANIPULATOR, WORKER. SURGEON (crypt).

OPPORTUNITY CHANCE. PAT, TIMELY.

OPPOSITE ANTONYM. CONTRAST; FACING. [~ **sides** = EW, HC, LR (crypt)]. **Pl** = BACK/FRONT, CHALK/CHEESE, IN/OUT, ON/OFF.

OPS 1. WORKS. 2. Rom *goddess* of *NATURE*.

OPTION CHOICE; REFUSAL.

OR (s/l *oar*, ore). *GOLD* (*herald*). BEFORE, ERE (arch). EITHER (arch). ALTERNATIVE.

ORACLE 1. ADVISER, AUTHORITY, DIVINE INSPIRATION, JUDGEMENT. 2. Sacred place of divine response, given by a priest or priestess to enquiry by a votary. Often with a carefully worded double meaning. Two celebrated oracles were at Delphi (*Apollo*) and Dodona (*Zeus*); others were at Branchidae and Patara [*Sibyl*]. 3. **God: Gk/Rom** = *APOLLO*; **goddess: Rom** = *MAIA*.

ORAL (s/l *aural*). EXAM(INATION), VIVA VOCE. SAID, SPOKEN, VERBAL. BY MOUTH.

ORANGE *COLOUR*. FRUIT, *TREE* [*Holmes* case]. *RIVER* (SA). TOWN (Fr). ROYAL FAMILY (NL).

ORCUS Rom equivalent of *HADES*.

ORDER ASSOCIATION, *CLUB*, FRATERNITY, MOVEMENT. CLASS, KIND, RANK, SORT. DECREE, EDICT; BULL (papal), UKASE (Russ). ADJUST, ARRANGE, TIDY; ARRANGEMENT, *ROW*, SEQUENCE, SUCCESSION. DECORUM (**opp** = *chaos*) [*Speaker*]. NEATNESS, *SERIES*. COMMISSION, INDENT, SEND FOR. COMMAND, DO, INSTRUCT. AWARD, DECORATION, HONOUR: CBE, DSO, KBE, MBE, OBE, OM etc. **Pl** = CLERICAL STATUS, ORDINATION. [*five* classical ~s; *nine* angelic ~s].

ORDERED *Anag*. ARRANGED, TIDIED. SENT FOR. COMMANDED, INSTRUCTED. *CHURCHMAN* (crypt). Also CBE, DSO etc as *ORDER* (crypt).

ORDER OF MERIT OM. MITRE, TIMER etc (crypt).

ORDNANCE MOUNTED CANNON/GUNS, *WEAPONS*; **types:** BASILISK, BASSE, CANNON DOUBLE, CANNON ROYAL, CARRONADE, CULVERIN, DEMI-CANNON, DEMI-CULVERIN, DEMI-SLING, FALCON, FIELD-GUN, HOWITZER, MINION, MORTAR, SAKER, SLING, STERN-CHASER. *WEAPON*.

OREAD *NYMPH* (mountain).

ORESTES Gk myth s of *Agamemnon* and *Clytemnestra*. With his sis *Electra*, he killed his adulterous mother. [**Companion:** Pylades].

ORGAN 1. PART OF BODY (hence B, O, D or Y – crypt), e.g. APPENDIX, COLON, also *mouthorgan* = TONGUE (crypt). MAGAZINE, MEDIUM, MOUTHPIECE, NEWSPAPER. 2. HARMONIUM, MUSICAL INSTRUMENT; **parts:** backfall, bellows, diapason, feeder, keyboard, pallet, pipe, slider, sticker, stop, swell-box, tracker, wind-chest; **stops:** bourdon, diapason, flue, gamba, mixture, musette, mutation, reed, string-toned, tremulant.

ORGANIZATION *Anag.* ASSOCIATION, CLUB, FRATERNITY, MANAGEMENT, MOVEMENT, SCHEME, SET-UP.

ORIENT(AL) E, *EAST*, EASTERN (**opp** = occidental).

ORIGINAL 1. EARLIEST, FUNDAMENTAL, INITIAL, INNATE, PRIMITIVE, PRIMORDIAL. MATRIX, PATTERN. CREATIVE, INVENTIVE. 2. First letter, e.g. **Original sin** = s.

ORION Gk myth *HUNTER*. When killed in Crete with *Artemis*, he became a *constellation* [belt; sword; *dog*; Sirius].

Ork Orkneys.

ORPHEUS Gk myth poet, who charmed all Nature with his *lyre*; he accompanied the *Argonauts* [*siren*]. He mar *Eurydice* and, when she died, followed her to *Hades* and won her back with his music; but when he *looked back* to see if she was following, she was taken back again. His grief angered the Thracian women, who tore him to pieces, and his lyre was placed among the stars as a *constellation* (Lyra).

ORT LEAVING, *REFUSE*, *SCRAP*.

ORWELL 1. RIVER (Eng). 2. GEORGE (Eric Blair), writer. Animal Farm **characters**: dogs = Bluebell, Jessie, *Pitcher*; donkey = Benjamin; farmer = Mr Jones; goat = Muriel; horses = *Boxer*, Clover, Mollie; pigs = *Major*, Minimus, *Napoleon*, Snowball, *Squealer*; raven = Moses; solicitor = Mr Whymper. 1984 **words:** Big Brother, Double Think, Ministry of Truth, Newspeak, Thought Police, Unperson.

OS OLD STYLE. BIG, LARGE, OUTSIZE.

OSCAR *AWARD*® (US film; the original statuette reminded a secretary 'of her uncle Oscar').

OSIRIS Gk form of Egy *god* of death and eternal life. Mar *Isis*, br of *Set*.

OSP OBIIT SINE PROLAE (d without issue).

OSTRICH BIRD genus RATITAE STRUTHIO (Af; flightless; head in sand) [aepyornis (ex), cassowary, dinornis (NZ ex), emu, moa, mooruk, nandoo, rhea].

OT OLD TESTAMENT (**opp** = NT); BIBLE.

OTHELLO MOOR (*Shak*).

OTHERS ET AL, REST.

OUNCE *CAT. MEASURE*, OZ.

OUR TIME AD, NOWADAYS.

OUT *Anag*; e.g. **Eats out** = TEAS, or **outpost** = STOP. 1. NOT AT HOME, NOT IN. READY (e.g. **pan out** = READY TO COOK). AT FAULT, IN ERROR. BLOOMING, FLOWERING. B, CT, LBW (*cricket*). EMERGED, HATCHED, e.g. **Chickened out?** (7) = HATCHED. 2. Word outside another, e.g. **Directed me to help out** (5) = AI*ME*D. 3. Letter or word omitted, e.g. **Criminal, caught out, fleeced** (6) = (C)ROOKED.

OUTDOORS AL FRESCO. EXITS (crypt).

OUTER EXTERNAL. OBJECTIVE. BOWLER (crypt). *CRICKET GROUND* (Melbourne). TARGET RING [*bullseye*, *inner*, *magpie*].

OUTING EXPEDITION, TRIP. BOWLING, WICKET TAKING (*cricket*, crypt). BLOOMING, FLOWERING (crypt).

OUTLANDISH ODD. ABROAD, FOREIGN (crypt). Trans (crypt).

OUTLAW DISQUALIFY, FORBID, PROHIBIT. BADDIE, BADMAN, LAW-BREAKER (crypt **opp** = in-law); **celebrated:** BILLY THE KID, THE CISCO KID, THE CLANCEYS, THE DALTONS, DOC HOLLIDAY, THE DOONES, JESSE JAMES [*cowboy*, *highwayman*, *robber*]. (JUST) WILLIAM (BROWN), DOUGLAS, GINGER, HENRY [Violet Elizabeth]; Richmal Crompton.

OUT OF 1. EX. FOALED BY (mare). 2. Hidden word, e.g. **Horses out of form are stabled** (5) = M*ARE*S. 3. One word or letter placed outside another, e.g. **He is out of work with optimism** (4) = H*OP*E.

OUTPOST *SETTLEMENT*.

OUTRIGHT 1. ALTOGETHER, ENTIRELY, OPENLY. DIRECT, DOWNRIGHT, THOROUGH. 2. Remove letters RIGHT, RT or R from word, e.g. **Print outright for a drink** (4) = P*INT.

OUTSIDE 1. EXTERIOR, FIELDER (*cricket*, crypt). WINGER (*football*). 2. Word placed round another, e.g. **When in, he is outside the order** (4) = H*OM*E.

~ **BROADCAST** OB.

OUTSIDER 1. *BOUNDER*, *CAD*. FIELDER (*cricket*, crypt). 2.
Pl = first and last letters, e.g. **Complete outsiders** = C*E.

OUTSIZE BIG, OS.

OUTSTANDING CONSPICUOUS, EMINENT, REMARKABLE,
SIGNAL. *OVERDUE*, UNPAID, UNSETTLED. GROYNE,
JETTY, PIER (crypt). *CAMEO*, FRIEZE, TRIGLYPH (crypt).

OUTWARDLY 1. APPARENTLY, EXTERNALLY, VISIBLY. 2.
One word round another, e.g. **He is outwardly feline, the deceiver**
(5) = C*HE*AT.

OVA (s/l *over*). EGG, O.

OVAL EGG-SHAPED, ELLIPTICAL. *CRICKET GROUND*,
TESTING GROUND. *NAIL*.

OVER (s/l *ova*). 1. ABOVE. ENDED; LEFT, REMAINING.
CONCERNING. REVERSED. SIX BALLS/DELIVERIES
(*cricket*). 2. In down clue, word preceding another, e.g.
Residuum form of rise overdue (7) = RESI*DUE.

OVERDRAWN OD, IN THE RED, hence word in RED, e.g.
Overdrawn State stayed behind (8) = RE*MAINE*D.

OVERDRESS FLAMBOYANCY [Beau Brummel]. APRON,
PINAFORE (crypt).

OVERDUE LATE. *OUTSTANDING*, UNPAID, UNSETTLED.

OVERHAUL OVERTAKE, *PASS*. EXAMINE, PATCH,
REPAIR, *SERVICE*.

OVERHEAD FIXED COST, STANDING CHARGE. HAT
(crypt); ROOF (crypt); UMBRELLA (crypt). **Opp** = under
foot, understanding (crypt).

OVERLOOK FORGET, TAKE NO NOTICE. OVERSEE,
SUPERINTEND. GIVE ONTO, HIGHER THAN.
BEWITCH.

OVERMAN *BOSS*, FOREMAN, MANAGER,
SUPERINTENDENT. BOWLER (crypt).

OVERSIGHT OMISSION. EYEBROW, EYELASH,
FOREHEAD (crypt).

OVERTURE 1. OPENING (mus). FEELER, PROPOSAL.
2. First letter, e.g. **Handel's overture** = H.

OVERWEIGHT 1. FAT, OBESE. 2. In down clue, word
preceding, or over, synonym for weight, e.g. **Foolish Herb is**
overweight (9) = SIMPLE*TON.

OWE (s/l O, *Oh*). DEBT, DUE, *OVERDRAW*.

OWL BIRD; NIGHT-FLYER; **breeds:** BARN ~, BUBO, EAGLE ~, (GREAT) GREY ~, HAWK ~, LONG-EARED ~, MOPOKE, MOREPORK (Aus, NZ), SAWWHET (Arcadia), SHORT-EARED ~, SNOWY ~, TAWNY ~ [eyesight, wisdom]. **Celebrated:** *BUNTER*, OLD BROWN ~, (*Potter*), ~ and Pussycat (*Lear*), WOL (*Milne*). BUTTERFLY (lepidoptera). **Pl** = football team.

OWN POSSESS. *ADMIT*, CONFESS. ALONE, INDEPENDENT, PERSONALLY, UNRIVALLED; TOD SLOAN (*rh sl*).

OX BOVINE ANIMAL (genus Bos): AUROCHS (ex, and = URUS), BISON, BUFFALO, GAYAL (Ind), KOUPREY (SE Asia), MITHAN (Ind), MUSK-OX, WISENT, YAK, ZEBU.

OXFORD Episcopal sig = OXON. *UNIVERSITY*. *CASTLE*. *COLOUR* (dark blue). *BOSPHORUS*.

OXON *Episcopal sig* of OXFORD. *UNIVERSITY*.

OXYGEN O (*chem*).

OYSTER BIVALVE, *NATIVE* [*Colchester*, Whitstable]; *SHELL* (*close*, *silent*). *Alice* character.

OZ *OUNCE* [*measure*]. *WIZARD*.

P PAGE. PARK(ING). PENNY. PHOSPHORUS (*chem*). PIANO, QUIET, SUBDUED. PORT. PORTUGAL (*car plate*). *PRESIDENT*. **Pl** = PP, PS.

PA (s/l *par*). *FATHER*. PANAMA (*car plate*). PENNSYLVANIA (US *state*).

PACK 1. BUNDLE, KNAPSACK, *MEASURE*, PACKET, RUCKSACK; LOT, SET (cards). BAG, BOX, *COVER*, WRAP. CROWD, CRUSH, FILL. CARRY (gun). STACK (jury). *ICE*. CAKE (cosmetics, *medicine*). 2. *Assembly* of *brownies*, *cards*, *cubs*, *grouse*, *hounds*, *hyenas*, Rugby forwards, submarines, wolves.

PACKMAN PEDLAR (arch); BOB JAKIN (Mill on the Floss, Eliot). JACK, KING, KNAVE; DEALER (cards, crypt).

PAGE ATTENDANT, BUTTONS, BELL-BOY, BELL-HOP; (*Chaucer*). CALL, SUMMON. P, FOLIO, LEAF; BOOKMAKER (crypt). **Pl** = FF, PP.

PAIN (s/l *pane*). AGONY, HURT; STITCH. **Aversion to** ~ =
ALGOPHOBIA; **lover of** = ALGOPHILE. FRENCH BREAD
(trans, crypt).

PAINTED *MADE UP*. *COATED*, COLOURED, PIGMENTED;
PINXIT. [La Creevy, *Dickens*].

PAINTER RA; ARTIST, *MASTER*; CANVASSER (crypt).
[*Company* (livery)]. MOORING ROPE (naut).
COSMETICIAN (crypt). DECORATOR.

PAIR (s/l *pear, pare*). PR. BRACE, COUPLE, TWO (**pigeon** ~
= one of each sex]. AFFIANCE, *ENGAGE*, MARRY,
MATE, *WED*.

Pak Pakistan.

PALACE BISHOP'S/PRESIDENT'S/SOVEREIGN'S
RESIDENCE. Any grand building, theatre etc, **such as:**

ALEXANDRA (Eng)	NONSUCH (Eng)
BUCKINGHAM (Eng)	PINK (Arg)
CAESAR'S (US)	ST JAMES'S (Eng)
CRYSTAL (Eng)	ST STEPHEN'S (Eng)
DOGE'S (It)	TOWER OF LONDON (Eng)
ELYSEE (Fr)	VERSAILLES (Fr)
HAMPTON COURT (Eng)	*VICTORIA* (Eng)
HATFIELD (Eng)	*WESTMINSTER* (Eng)
HOLYROOD (Sc)	WHITEHALL (Eng)
KENSINGTON (Eng)	WINDSOR (Eng)
LAMBETH (Eng)	

PALAEOLITHIC *AGE*.

PALATIAL GRAND, SPLENDID; like a *palace*.

PALLADIUM PD (*chem*). THEATRE.

PALLAS 1. = *ATHENE*. 2. A *TITAN*, s of Orius and Eurybia,
mar *Styx* and f of *Nike*. 3. A minor *PLANET*.

PALM 1. *HAND*. CONCEAL. LAUREL, VICTORY
GARLAND. 2. TREE; **types:** ARECA, ARENG, BACTRIS,
BAMBOO ~, CALUMNUS, CARNAUBA, COCO(A)NUT,
COHUNE, COKERNUT, CURYPHA, DATE ~, DOUM,
EJOO, ELAEIS, FAN ~, GOMUTI, -O, JUPATI, KITOOL,
-TUL, MORICHE, NARGIL, NIPA, OIL ~, PALMETTO,
PALMYRA, PAXIUBA, *PHOENIX*, PIASSABA, -VA,

RAPHIA ~, RATTAN ~, RHAPSIS, SAGO ~, TALIPAT, -ET, -OT, -UT, TUCUM, WAX ~, WINE, ZALACCA, ZAMIA [frond, raffia].

~ OIL FAT, GREASE (candles, soap). BRIBE (crypt).

PAN 1. DISH, POT. BERATE, CRITICIZE. WASH *GOLD* [*digger*]. SWING (photo). PETER [*Barrie*; Never Never *Land*]. 2. Gk *god* of *shepherds*; chief *satyr*. 3. With hyphen = all-embracing, universal, e.g. pan-American.

PANDORA 1. STRINGED INSTRUMENT. 2. Gk myth first woman on earth. She opened the box containing all human ills, and only Hope remained inside. 3. A minor *PLANET*.

PANE (s/l *pain*). *SHEET*. HAMMERHEAD (hence H), PEEN.

PANIC ALARM, *FEAR*, FRIGHT, TERROR. *GRASS*.

PAPER PRESS, RAG **names** (all ®): HERALD, MIRROR, STAR, SUN, TELEGRAPH, TIMES, TRIBUNE etc. DECORATE. BUMF, DOCUMENT, RECORD. WRAPPER. PAPYRUS [*measure*]; *anniversary* (1st).

PAPERWORK ADMINISTRATION, ARCHIVES, BUMF (sl), RECORDS, RED TAPE, ORIGAMI (Jap, crypt).

PAR (s/l *pa*). *EQUAL*, *EVEN*, LEVEL. BOGEY, NORM, STANDARD (*golf*).

PARADISE EDEN, ELYSIUM, *HEAVEN*, UTOPIA, *VALHALLA* [Asphodel meadows].

PARASITE Animal or plant living on another [host, commensal], e.g. **bot:** DODDER, EPIPHYTE, FUNGUS, GALL-NUT, MISTLETOE, SAPROPHYTE, YEAST; **zool:** ACARNO, BACTERIUM, FLEA, GUINEA-WORM, ICHNEUMON FLY, LEECH, LOUSE, TAPE-WORM, TRICHINA; hence HANGER-ON, TOADY. DROPPING-ZONE (mil, crypt).

PARCAE Rom *goddesses* of the three *FATES*. **Gk** = MOIRAI.

PARE (s/l *pair*, *pear*). *CUT*, *PEEL*, SHAVE, *TRIM*, WHITTLE.

PARENTAL GUIDANCE A, *CENSORSHIP* (film).

PARIS 1. *Capital* of France, hence (crypt) F. PLASTER. 2. Gk myth s of *Priam*. He judged *Aphrodite* the fairest against *Athene* and *Hera* for a coveted golden apple. Loved Oenone before he ran off with *Helen*, who was mar to Menelaus, and thus started the way of *Troy*. He killed Achilles by shooting him in the heel. 3. *Shak* character(s).

PARKING P. [Mansfield Park, *Austen* (crypt)].

PARLIAMENT COUNCIL, DEBATING CHAMBER, *LEGISLATIVE ASSEMBLY* [Commons, Lords, the House).

PARNASSUS Gk myth mountain home of the *Muses*.

PARROT COPY, MIMIC, REPEAT. RIVER. *BIRD* (Psittaciformes). **Types:** BUDGERIGAR, BUDGIE, COCKATIEL, COCKATOO, CONURE, CORELLA, KAKA (NZ), KAKAPO (NZ), KEA (NZ), LORIKEET, LORY, MACAW, NESTOR, PAR(R)AKEET, PAROQUET, ROSELLA, ZATI. **Celebrated:** Capt Flint (*Stevenson*), Sea ~ = puffin.

PARSON *CHURCHMAN*, RECTOR, VICAR; *Chaucer* character. *BIRD*, TUI. [~'s nose].

PART 1. *Anag. GO*, *LEAVE*, QUIT. ROLE. PIECE, SOME (**opp** = *all*). COMPONENT, SPARE. SPLIT HAIRS (crypt). 2. Hidden word, e.g. **Love is part of Much Ado re Nothing** (5) = ADO*RE. 3. **Pl** = word split, e.g. **Romantic in parts about Talia** (7) = I*TALIA*N.

PARTNER ASSOCIATE, *COMPANION*, FELLOW, OPPO. WIFE/HUSBAND. **Pl** = EW, NS, HC, RL. MAST GATE (naut). DARBY & JOAN, NOW & THEN, PROP & COP etc.

PARTRIDGE GAME BIRD; **assembly** = covey. [1st day of Christmas].

PARTY AT HOME, BALL, *DANCE*, *DO*, FUNCTION, RECEPTION, SHINDIG. SIDE (leg). **Politics:** ALLIANCE, CON, DEM, L, LAB, LIB, REP, SDP, TORY, WHIG.

PASS *HAND*. OVERHAUL, OVERTAKE. ACCEPT, APPROVE, LET GO BY. *COL*, DEFILE. GRADUATE, SUCCEED; NO HONOURS (crypt). AMOROUS ADVANCE.

PASSENGER FARE. (FELLOW) TRAVELLER. BURDEN, LIABILITY.

PAST (s/l passed). 1. ANTIQUE, BYGONE, *EX*, FORMER, GONE BY. 2. Use past tense, e.g. **Past art** = WERT.

PASTE CONFECTION, MIXTURE. GLUE, STICK. IMITATION *DIAMOND/GEM*.

PATIENCE ENDURANCE, PERSEVERANCE (**saying**). CARD GAME. PLANT.

PATRICK *PATRON SAINT* (Ire). [Bishop, Pope Celestine, 17 March].

PATRON SAINT TUTELARY PROTECTOR; **celebrated (with**

feast day): AGATHA (bellfounders; 5 Feb), ANDREW (Scotland, 30 Nov), ANNE (Brittany; 26 Jul), ANTONY (lost property; poor; 13 Jun), BARBARA (*firemen*; *gunners*; 4 Dec), BLAISE (woolcombers; 3 Feb), BRIDGET (*Ireland*; 1 Feb), CATHERINE (attorneys; *scholars*; wheelwrights; 25 Nov), CECILIA (church music; 22 Nov), CHRISTOPHER (wayfarers; 25 Jul), CRISPIN(IAN) (leatherworkers; 23 Oct), *DAVID* (Wales; 1 Mar), DENYS (*France*; 9 Oct), ELMO/ERASMUS (*sailors*; 2 Jun), EUSTACE (*hunters*; Madrid; 20 Sep), FRANCIS OF ASSISI (animals; 4 Oct), *GEORGE* (England; *Portugal*; armourers; 23 Apr), GILES (*beggars*; blacksmiths; *cripples*; 1 Sep), HUBERT (*huntsmen*; 3 Nov), JOAN OF ARC (*France*; 30 May), JOHN OF GOD (*booksellers*; printers; 8 Mar), JOSEPH (*workers*; 1 May), JUDE (afflicted; 28 Oct), LEONARD (*prisoners*; 6 Nov), LUKE (physicians; 18 Oct), MARGARET (women in travail; 20 Jul), MAURUS (charcoal burners; 15 Jan), MENAS (merchants; 11 Nov), MONICA (Christian mothers; 27 Aug), NICHOLAS (*children*; *sailors*; 6 Dec), PANTALEON (physicians; 27 Jul), *PATRICK* (*Ireland*; 17 Mar), SABAS (Serbia; 14 Jan), TERESA (foreign missions; 3 Oct), URSULA (*schools*; 21 Oct), VALENTINE (lovers; 14 Feb), VITUS (*sickness*; 15 Jun), WENCESLAS (Bohemia; 28 Sep).

PATTERN (s/l patten). EXAMPLE. DESIGN, MATRIX, *MODEL*, MOULD, TEMPLATE, TEMPLET.

PAUL'S LETTERS COLOSSIANS, CORINTHIANS, EPHESIANS, GALATIANS, PHILEMON, PHILLIPIANS, *ROMANS*, THESSALONIANS, TIMOTHY, TITUS. P, A, U and L (crypt).

PAUSE (s/l paws). BREVE, *REST* (mus). BREAK, HESITATION, INACTION, *INTERVAL*. LINGER, TARRY (**opp** = go*on).

PAWNBROKER POP, UNCLE [pledge]. *PAWNEE* (crypt).

PAWNEE *AMERICAN INDIAN*. *PAWNBROKER* (crypt).

PAX 1. PEACE. TRUCE! 2. Rom *goddess* of PEACE: **Gk** = IRENE.

PAY PAYMENT, *SALARY*, *SCREW*, WAGES. DISCHARGE, RECOMPENSE, RETURN, REWARD, *SETTLE*. CAULK, STOP (naut).

PAYER PAYMASTER; *SETTLER* (crypt).

PB *LEAD* (*chem*). PAPERBACK.

PC PARISH COUNCIL. PER CENT. POLICE CONSTABLE.
POST CARD. PRIVY COUNCILLOR.

PD PALLADIUM (*chem*). POLICE DEPARTMENT.

PE PHYSICAL EXERCISE; GYMNASTICS, PT. PERU (*car
plate*).

PEACE (s/l *piece*). 1. ORDER, QUIET, TRANQUILLITY (**opp**
= *war*); RIVER (Can); **saying**. 2. **Goddess: Gk** = IRENE, **Rom**
= PAX.

PEACH *FRUIT*; *TREE*. *BETRAY*. DOLLY-BIRD, SMASHER.

PEAK (s/l pique). *HEAD*; HOLD; TILT (naut). BRIM, APEX,
SUMMIT. PINE, WASTE AWAY.

PEAL (s/l *peel*). *RING*. CLAP, LOUD NOISE (thunder).
GRILSE.

PEAR (s/l *pair, pare*). FRUIT/TREE (genus Pyrus communis)
[**beverage:** perry]; **types:** BERGAMOT, COMMICE,
CONFERENCE, FERTILITY, JOSEPHINE DE MALINES,
LOUISE BONNE, WILLIAMS BON CHRETIEN, WINTER
NELIS; ALLIGATOR, AVOCADO; ANCHOVY; PRICKLY.

PEARL *GEM* [oyster]; *anniversary* (30th); 'MARGARET'.
PRECIOUS THING. COLOUR (white). BEAD, DROP.
PICOT (lace). *BUCK* (films). RIVER (US).

PECK KISS; STAB WITH BEAK/BILL. *MEASURE*.
GREGORY (films).

PECULIAR *Anag*. PARTICULAR, SPECIAL. ODD,
STRANGE. EXEMPT. PRIVILEGED (eccles).

PEEL (s/l *peal*). PARE, *SKIN*. *JOHN* (huntsman). *RIVER*
(*Can*). *ROBERT* (*police*). SHOVEL. TOWER.

PEELED (s/l pealed). 1. PARED, SKINNED. 2. Remove first and
last letters, e.g. **Called peeled orange** (4) = *RANG*.

PEELER SKINNER (crypt). *POLICEMAN*.

PEER (s/l *pier*). NOBLEMAN: *BARON*, DUKE, EARL, *LORD*,
MARQUIS, VISCOUNT. EQUAL, *FELLOW*. APPEAR;
LOOK, PEEP, PRY. ~ GYNT (mus, Grieg). [Iolanthe (*G &
S*)].

PEERESS FEMALE OF PEER. LADY LOOKER (crypt).

PEGASUS 1. Gk myth winged *horse* of *Bellerophon*.
2. *Constellation*. 3. Badge of the Airborne Forces.

PELT *SHY*, THROW. *SKIN*.

PEN BALLPOINT, BIRO, QUILL, STYLO, WRITE(R); **saying**; SCRIBBLE. CAGE, CORRAL, ENCLOSURE, *FOLD*, STY. SWAN (*fem*).

PENELOPE 1. Gk myth wife of *Ulysses* and m of Telemachus who, to deter suitors in her husband's absence, said she could not answer them until she had finished making a robe for Laertes, her f-in-law; each night she undid the previous day's work. 2. A minor *PLANET*. BIRD.

PENNILESS 1. BROKE; BORACIC LINT (*rh sl*). 2. Remove letters D or P from word, e.g. **Encourage to clean out – penniless (4)** = (p)URGE.

PENNY D, P. *COIN, COPPER*; (**saying**).

PENNYWEIGHT DWT, *MEASURE*.

PENSION LIFE PAYMENT, RETIREMENT PAY. BOARDING HOUSE. [*football* team].

PENULTIMATE LAST BUT ONE, hence Y (crypt).

PEP *GO*, VIGOUR, ZIP. ENCOURAGE, GINGER.

PEPYS (s/l peeps). DIARIST, NAVY SECRETARY, SAM(UEL), *WRITER* [Evelyn].

PERCH LENGTH, *MEASURE, POLE, ROD* (5½ yds). BASS, FISH. BALANCE; BAR, RAIL, ROOST. ALIGHT, *REST, SETTLE*.

PERFORM ACT, PLAY, *SING*. CARRY OUT, *DO, EXECUTE*.

PERFORMING ACTING, ON STAGE; *TURNING* (crypt). DOING.

PERI FAIRY, GOBLIN (Pers myth), IMP, SPRITE [Iolanthe, *G & S*].

PERIOD CLASS, TUITION. FULL STOP (US). PORTION OF TIME (hence TIM, ME etc, crypt), e.g. YEAR, LUSTRUM (5 yrs), QUINQUENNIUM (5 yrs), SEPTENARY (7 yrs), DECADE (10 yrs), CENTURY (100 yrs), MILLENNIUM (1,000 yrs).

PERIODICAL RECURRING, REGULAR. MAGAZINE, WEEKLY. [astronomy; chemistry].

PERIPHITES Gk myth *giant*, too large for his own legs to carry, who beat travellers to death with a massive *club*; he was finally killed by *Theseus*.

PERMANENT LASTING, INDEFINITE. MARCEL, *WAVE*.

~ WAY *RAILWAY*; IRON WAY, *TRACK*.

Pers Persian.

PERSEPHONE Also CORA. Gk myth Queen of the *Underworld*;
d of *Zeus* and *Demeter*, she was carried off by *Pluto*. Hermes
finally got her back, but she had eaten (a pomegranate seed) in
the lower world, so she was permitted to spend only 8 months
each year in the upper world – in order that Demeter would allow
it to produce its fruits. **Rom** = PROSERPINE.

PERSEUS 1. Gk myth hero, who slew *Medusa*, helped by *Athene*,
the helmet of *Hades*, winged sandals, a magic bag and a mirror
(he looked at Medusa only in the mirror, put her severed head in
the bag, and escaped on winged heels, wearing the helmet which
made him invisible). Mar to *Andromeda*, he eventually fulfilled a
prophecy by (accidentally) killing Acrisius, his own grandfather.
2. *Constellation.*

PERSIAN IRANIAN [Xerxes, Darius, Satrap]. *CAT*, CATTY,
FELINE; MIAOW.

PERT *ARCH*, JAUNTY, SAUCY (**opp** = *retiring*).

PET CARESS, PAT; *DARLING*, FAVOURITE, MASCOT.
FONDLE, TAME (animal). TANTRUM, TIFF;
ILL-HUMOURED, OFFENCE.

PETER CORDITE, DYNAMITE, EXPLOSIVE, TNT. *PRISON*
CELL. SAFE. FADE, GIVE OUT. *PAN (Barrie)*. BLUE ~
(flag). 'A ROCK'.

PETERBOROUGH **Episcopal sig** = PETRIBURG.

PETRIBURG *Episcopal sig* of PETERBOROUGH.

PG PARENTAL GUIDANCE (film *censorship*). LODGER,
PAYING GUEST. [*monkey*].

PH ACIDITY, ALKALINITY (Sorensen).

PHAETON 1. CARRIAGE. BIRD. 2. Gk myth s of *Helios* and
Clymene. He drove his f's *chariot* so dangerously that *Zeus* struck
him down with a thunderbolt.

-PHAGY Eating of . . ., e.g. **hippophagy** = horses, **ichthyophagy** =
fishes.

PHALANX INFANTRY, LINE, *SOLDIERS* (Gk; hoplite).
BONE. STAMENS (bot).

PHANTOM GHOST, SPECTRE. *AIRCRAFT*.

PHARAOH (s/l faro). KING OF EGYPT (= GREAT HOUSE)
[*Ptolemy*].

PHIL (s/l fill). PHILADELPHIA. PHILHARMONIC (mus).

PHILOSOPHY. PHILIPPIANS. FLUTER.

PHILOGYNIST *Lover* of women.

PHILOSOPHER WISDOM SEEKER; MORALIZER, THEORIZER; **celebrated:** ANAXAGORAS (Gk), THOMAS AQUINAS (It), ARISTOTLE (Gk), DESCARTES (Fr), DIDEROT (Fr), *DIOGENES* (Gk), EPICTETUS (Gk), EPICURUS (Gk), ERASMUS (NL), EURIPIDES (Gk), HEGEL (Ger), KANT (Ger), MONTAIGNE (Fr), NEWTON (Eng), NIETZSCHE (Ger), PASCAL (Fr), RUSSELL (Eng), SANTAYANA (Sp), SCHWEGLER (Ger), SCHWEIZER (Swi), SENECA (Rom), SOCRATES (Gk), SPINOZA (NL), VOLTAIRE (Fr), ZENO (Gk). **Saying.** [~'s stone, alchemy; metaphysical ~, moral ~, natural ~].

PHLEGETHON PYRIPHLEGETHON.

PHOBIA *AVERSION*.

PHOEBUS 1. Rom *god* of the *SUN*, also SOL. **Gk** = *APOLLO*, HELIOS; **Egy** = HORUS, RA; **Nor** = FREY; **Pers** = MITHRA; **Phoen** = BAAL. 2. A satellite of the *planet* Saturn.

Phoen Phoenicia, ~n.

PHOENIX 1. Fabulous bird which, every 500 years, built a pyre and burned itself to death; it was then reborn from the ashes. 2. A *constellation*. 3. DATE *PALM*. 4. US *State* capital.

PI (s/l *pie*). 1. DEVOUT, OVER-RELIGIOUS, PIOUS. 2. Gk letter; in maths, the ratio of the circumference of a circle to its diameter.

PIANO P, *QUIET*. INSTRUMENT (mus). *TEMPO*.

PIE (s/l *pi*). Anag. PIZZA, SHEPHERD'S, TART. *BIRD*, MAGPIE. *DOG*, MONGREL. CHAOS.

PIECE (s/l *peace*). 1. *BIT*, MORSEL. 2. Hidden word, e.g. **Piece of Spanish amateur pretence** (4) = SH*AM. 3. Constituent part of object indicated, e.g. **Dollar piece** = CENT.

PIER (s/l *peer*). *JETTY*. BRIDGE SUPPORT.

PIG POLICEMAN (sl). BILLET, LUMP (iron). Quadruped (genus Suidae), SWINE; **assembly** = herd; **male** = BOAR; **female** = SOW; **offspring** = PIGLET, SHOAT. **Celebrated:** MAJOR, MINIMUS, *NAPOLEON*, SNOWBALL, *SQUEALER* (Animal Farm, *Orwell*); BLAND, ROBINSON (*Potter*); BLANDINGS, Empress of (*Wodehouse*). **Breeds:**

BABIRUSSA
BERKSHIRE
BUSH
ESSEX
LANDRACE
LARGE BLACK
LARGE WHITE

LINCOLN
SADDLEBACK
TAMWORTH
WARTHOG
WESSEX
WILD BOAR

PIGEON BIRD; HOMER (crypt); NUN ~, POUTER ~, TURBIT; **assembly** = flock. MARK, SUCKER. [~ **pair** = one of each (boy and girl)].

PIGS EAR BEER (*rh sl*).

PIKE *FISH*, JACK. HILLTOP. ROAD, TOLL, TOLL-BAR. BILL, HALBERD, *WEAPON*. DIVE (swim).

PILE CASTLE, HEAP, STATELY HOME. *POST*, STAKE. *NAP*. NUCLEAR FURNACE. **Pl** = HAEMORRHOIDS.

PILE-UP ACCIDENT, COLLISION, SMASH. CARPET (crypt). ELIP (dn, crypt).

PILGRIM 1. HOLY VOYAGER, TRAVELLER, VOYAGER [Haj (Mos); Islam; Mecca. Canterbury Tales (*Chaucer*); scollop/scallop]. MAYFLOWER SETTLER [~ Fathers (Plymouth, Mass, 1620)]. 2. From Bunyan's Pilgrim's Progress (from City of Destruction to Celestial City): CHRISTIAN, FAITHFUL, HOPEFUL [Apollyon (angel), Greatheart (guide to Christiana), Giant Despair (lord of Doubting Castle), Slough of Despond].

PILLAGE LOOT, PLUNDER, *SACK*. DISPENSARY (crypt).

PILLARS OF HERCULES Old name for ABYLA (CEUTA) and CALPE (GIBRALTAR).

PILOT AVIATOR, FLIER (**Union** = BALPA). *DOG* (Brontë). GUIDE, NAVIGATOR, *STEERSMAN*. TEST PRODUCT. *FISH*.

PINAFORE FROCK, PINNY; OVERDRESS (crypt). LIGHT OPERA (*G & S*).

PINCH *STEAL* [*robber*]. GRIP, NIP, SQUEEZE. SMALL QUANTITY. EMERGENCY. ARREST. DRUDGE (Martin Chuzzlewit, *Dickens*); *SCHOOLMASTER* (C of Errors, *Shak*).

PINE LANGUISH, LONG, YEARN; PEAK, WASTE. *TREE*; DEAL, TIMBER.

PINK *FLOWER*, CARNATION; COLOUR, PALE RED, *ROSE*.

SNOOKER BALL (score 6). RED HUNTING COAT.
PERFECT. PRICK, WOUND. KNOCK, PRE-IGNITION.
BOAT (sailing).

PINKERTON Lieutenant US Navy (Mme *Butterfly*, Puccini).
DETECTIVES (US).

PIOUS *PI*, RELIGIOUS.

PIPE BRIAR, CHURCHWARDEN, CLAY, MEERSCHAUM
[*Holmes*]. TUBE [*Pluto*]. DRESS, TRIM. *MEASURE* (beer,
port). REED (mus). CONDUIT, *SEWER*.

PIPER BAGPIPE PLAYER, MUSICIAN [10th day of *Christmas* in
song]. BOATSWAIN (crypt). HANDKERCHIEF (crypt).
SMOKER, SHERLOCK *HOLMES* (crypt). PAN (crypt).

PIRATE COPY, PLUNDER, STEAL. BUCCANEER,
CORSAIR, FREEBOOTER, PRIVATEER, ROVER [*cat. G &
S*]; **notorious:**

JOHN AVERY (LONG BEN)
JEAN *BART*
BLACKBEARD (EDWARD TEACH)
BONITO (BENNETT GRAHAM)
ANNE BONNY (m Rackham)
CALICO JACK (JOHN RACKHAM)
LORD CONRAD (Byron)
WILLIAM DAMPIER
JOHN ESQUEMELING
FLINT (Treasure Island)
FRANCIS *DRAKE*
FREDERIC (*G & S*)
HENRY EVERY
DIRK HATTERAICK
HOOK (Peter Pan)
PAUL JONES
WILLIAM KIDD
LAFITTE
SIR HENRY MORGAN
JOHN RACKHAM (CALICO JACK)
MARY *READ*
BASIL RINGROSE
BLACK BART ROBERTS

LONG BEN AVERY
LONG JOHN *SILVER*
BARTHOLOMEW SHARP
SMEE (Peter Pan)
SWAN
EDWARD TEACH (or THATCH)
EDWARD THATCH (or TEACH)
CAPT THOMPSON
LIONEL WAFER
WILLIAM WALKER
Pl = *Football* team (US). ~s of Penzance (*G & S*).

PISTOL (s/l pistil, pistole). DERRINGER, FIREARM, HANDGUN, *WEAPON*. *Shak* character (Merry Wives, H.iv, H.v; mar Ms *Quickly*).

PITCH GROUND, PLAYING FIELD (*cricket*, *football* etc). *CAST*, THROW. ASPHALT, BITUMEN, *TAR*. BLACK (*colour*).

PITCHER *EWER*, URN. DELIVERER, BASEBALL PLAYER. UNSTEADY ONE. ROADMAN, ROAD WORKER (crypt). STALLHOLDER (crypt). DOG (*Orwell*).

PITCHFORK HAYFORK. *CAST*, THRUST. TUNING FORK (mus, crypt).

PITMAN *MINER* (**pl** and **union** = NUM). SHORTHANDED (crypt).

PITY COMPASSION, MERCY; RUTH (arch). *ALAS*; REGRET, SORROW, SORRY.

PL PLURAL. POLAND (*car plate*).

PLACE (s/l *plaice*). PUT, *SET*. SPOT. COUNTRY HOUSE, *SEAT*, *STATELY HOME*.

PLACED PUT, SET. SEATED. LANDED GENTRY (crypt).

PLAGUE AFFLICTION, PESTILENCE, PUNISHMENT. *ANNOY*, BOTHER, NUISANCE, *TROUBLE*. **Gk** and **Rom** god = *APOLLO*. **Bibl** ~s: water into blood; frogs; lice; flies; murrain; boils; hail; locusts; darkness; death of firstborn.

PLAICE (s/l *place*). FLAT *FISH*.

PLAIN (s/l *plane*). CLEAR, EVIDENT, SIMPLE. STITCH (knitting; **opp** = purl). MOURN. LEVEL/OPEN TRACT: LLANO (S Am), PAMPA (S Am), PUSZTA (Hung),

SAVANNAH (tropics), SERENGETI (Tanz), STEPPES (USSR), TUNDRA (Arctic).

PLAN *Anag. CHART*, DESIGN, DIAGRAM, DRAWING, LAYOUT, MAP. ARRANGE, PLOT, METHOD, SCHEME. TIMETABLE.

PLANE (s/l *plain*). *TREE.* SCRAPER, SMOOTHER, TOOL. LEVEL, SURFACE. *AIRCRAFT*; GLIDE.

PLANET 1. CHASUBLE, VESTMENT (eccles). 2. Heavenly body, revolving round a star, as a satellite. **Major planets** of our own Sun (in order of increasing distance and with their own satellites or moons): *MERCURY, VENUS, EARTH* (Luna/Moon), *MARS* (Deimos, Phobos), *JUPITER* (Callisto, *Europa, Ganymede, Io*), *SATURN* (Dione, Euceladus, Hyperion, *Iapetus*, Janus, Mimas, *Phoebus, Rhea*, Tethys, Themis, *Titan*), *URANUS* (Ariel, Oberon, Titania, Umbriel), *NEPTUNE* (Triton, *Nereid*), *PLUTO*. There are also thousands of smaller bodies orbiting the Sun, mainly between Mars and Jupiter, and most of them lumps of rock. Some 2,000 are large enough to be identified and named as asteroids or **minor planets**, including: *CERES* (the largest; dia 800 km), *VESTA* (dia 530 km), *PALLAS* (dia 500 km) and *JUNO* (dia 240 km), plus *CHIRON*, HERMES, *HYGIEA, ICARUS, IRIS, ISIS*, KRYPTON (fict), *MINERVA, MINOS, MNEMOSYNE, NEMESIS, NIOBE, PENELOPE, TROJANS*.

PLANT 1. FACTORY, MILL, WORKS; MACHINERY, TOOLS. CONCEAL. HOAX. EMBED, FIX, SET. 2. *FLOWER* (q.v.), *FRUIT* (q.v.), *HERB* (q.v.), REED, SHRUB, *SPICE, TREE* (q.v.), *VEGETABLE* (q.v.), *WEED, WILD FLOWER/PLANT* (q.v.); **parts:** carpel (ovary, ovule, stigma, style), nectary, petal, pistil, root, sepal, stalk, stamen (anther, filament, pollen sac), stem (bud, leaf, shoot), tendril, torus; **types:**

3-letters	4-letters	
BOX	AIRA	COCA
ERS	ALFA	COIX
FOG	ANIL	DISS
HOP	BENE	DOCK
IVY	BENT	DOOB
RYE	*BLUE*	DURA
		FERN

FLAG
GILL
HEMP
HERB
IRID
KANS
KAVA
LING
LYME
MOSS
REED
RHEA
RUSA
RUSH
SEGO
SUNN
TARE
TEFF
TORE
TUTU
VINE
WEED
WELD
WHIN
WOAD
WORT
YARR

5-letters
ABACA
ANISE
AROLD
BHANG
BOHEA
BRIER
BRIZA
BROOM
BUGLE
BUNCH

CAPER
CAREX
COUCH
CUTCH
DURRA
DWALE
ERICA
FURZE
GORSE
GRASS
GUACO
HALFA
HAULM
KEMPS
LIANA
MELIC
ORYZA
PANAX
PANIC
RHYNE
SEDGE
SISAL
SPEAR
SUMAC
THORN
VETCH
VIOLA

6-letters
ALSIKE
ARNICA
ARRACH
ARUNDO
BAJREE
BARLEY
BEDDER
BEJUCO
BETONY
BIBLUS

BLINKS
BOCAGE
BORAGE
BRIONY
BRYONY
BURNET
CACTUS
CASSIA
CEREUS
CICELY
CICUTA
CISSUS
CITRUS
COCKLE
COFFEE
COMFRY
CONIUM
COTTON
COWAGE
CROTON
CUMMIN
DARNEL
DESMID
DODDER
FESCUE
FILAGO
FIMBLE
FIORIN
FRUTEX
FUNGUS
GARLIC
GERVAO
GERVAS
GNETUM
GROMEL
HEDERA
HYPNUM
IBERIS
JASMIN

KALMIA
KNAWEL
KOUSSO
LOLIUM
LUPINE
MADDER
MALLOW
MARRAM
MATICO
MEDICK
MYRTLE
NARDUS
NETTLE
ORACHE
ORCHIL
ORPINE
OX-HEEL
PAIGLE
PAMPAS
PHLEUM
PRIVET
PROTEA
PTERIS
QUITCH
RADISH
RAMSON
REDTOP
RICCIA
RUPPIA
SABINE
SESAME
SESBAN
SESELI
SMILAX
SPURGE
SUMACH
TWITCH
UNIOLA
URTICA

VISCUM

7-letters
ACANTHA
ACONITE
ALE-HOOP
ALFALFA
ALL-GOOD
ALLSEED
ALYSSUM
AMELLUS
ASH-WORT
ATROPIN
AWL-WORT
BLAWORT
BOG-BEAN
BOG-RUSH
BRACKEN
BRAMBLE
BUGLOSS
BUG-WORT
BURDOCK
CALUMBA
CAMPION
CARAWAY
CARLUUS
CASSAVE
CATMINT
CLIVERS
COMFREY
CONEINE
COWBANE
COWSLIP
CUDWEED
DIONAEA
DITTANY
DOGWOOD
ELF-WORT
ESPARTO

EULALIA
FESTUCA
FOGGAGE
FOXTAIL
GENISTA
HOGWEED
HEATHER
HEDEOMA
HEMLOCK
HENBANE
LUCERNE
MALACCA
MILFOIL
NAVETTE
OSMUNDA
POP-WEED
RAGWORT
SORGHUM
SQUITCH
THISTLE
TIMOTHY
VETIVER
WAGWANT
WHANGEE
ZIZANIA

8-letters
ACANTHUS
AGRIMONY
ANGELICA
BANEWORT
BEDSTRAW
BERBERRY
BINDWEED
BULLRUSH
CAMOMILE
CANWABIS
CLEAVERS
COWBERRY

DEMERARA	FLEA-WORT	PUSS-TAIL
DOG-GRASS	GYNERIUM	STAR-WORT
DOG-WHEAT	MANDRAKE	VALERIAN
ELEUSINE	PLANTAIN	VERONICA
FLAX-WORT	PONDWEED	VIRGINIA
FLEABANE	PUFFBALL	XANTHIUM

PLATE COVER, ENCASE, PROTECTION, VENEER.
ENGRAVING (print). FILM (photo). RAILROAD.
CUTLERY, EPNS, SHEFFIELD. GOLD/SILVER TROPHY.
DISH, PLATTER. FALSE TEETH. *RIVER* (Braz). **Pl** =
FEET (*rh sl*).

PLATINUM PT (*chem*); WHITE METAL; *anniversary* (70th).
BLONDE.

PLAY ACT, DO, DRAMA, *PERFORM*, PIECE, REP, SHOW,
STAGE. BUSK, STRUM. GAMBOL, HAVE FUN.
LATITUDE, MOVEMENT, SLAP. BOWL, *PITCH*, SERVE
(games).

PLAYERS ACTORS, *CAST*, THESPIANS; [**saying**, *Shak*
characters]. BAND, MUSICIANS (**saying**), OCTET,
ORCHESTRA, QUARTET, SEXTET. SIDE, TEAM.

PLAYFUL *ARCH.* FROLICSOME, HUMOROUS, SPORTIVE.

PLAYGROUND COURSE, COURT, DIAMOND, FIELD,
LINKS, *PITCH*, RINK, WICKET (all crypt). STAGE (crypt).
NURSERY (crypt). SCHOOL COURTYARD,
QUADRANGLE. And see *cricket*, *football*, *rugby* etc.

PLAYGROUP KINDERGARTEN, NURSERY SCHOOL. *CAST*
(crypt). *BAND*, ORCHESTRA, *PLAYERS* (crypt). *SIDE*,
TEAM, XI, XV (crypt).

PLAYTIME CURTAIN-UP (crypt). RHYTHM, TEMPO (crypt).
BULLY-OFF, FIRST BALL, KICK-OFF, START, WHISTLE
(crypt).

PLAY VIOLIN *BOW*, *FIDDLE*.

PLEASE (s/l pleas). BEGUILE, *CHARM*, GIVE PLEASURE
(**opp** = *annoy*). THINK FIT. BE GOOD ENOUGH, KINDLY.

PLEDGE PROMISE. HOCK, *PAWN*, *POP*.

PLEIADES Seven d of *Atlas*, placed among the stars and associated
with *rain* and *nature*; **names:** ALCYONE, CELAENO,
ELECTRA, *MAIA* (the eldest), STEROPE and TAYGETE,

with one who was invisible, MEROPE.

PLIERS PINCERS. CABDRIVERS, TAXIS (crypt).

PLOT CABAL, CONSPIRACY; CONSPIRE, INTRIGUE, *PLAN*. *CHART*, NAVIGATE. ALLOTMENT, BED, GARDEN, GREEN, LAWN, PATCH, YARD (US).

PLOVER WADING *BIRD*; **types:** AVOCET, CURLEW, DOTTEREL, KILLDEER, LAPWING, OYSTERCATCHER, PE(E)WIT, SNIPE, STILT, TURNSTONE, WHAUP, WHIMBREL.

PLUM (s/l plumb). BEST, GOOD. *COLOUR*, FRUIT TREE genus Prunus: **types:** CATALONIA, GREENGAGE, MIRABELLE, VICTORIA.

PLUTO 1. *DOG* (Disney). Pipe-line under the ocean (acronym); FUEL SUPPLY. 2. Rom *god* of the UNDERWORLD (**Gk** = HADES), br of *Jupiter* and *Neptune*, he carried off Proserpine (**Gk** = *Persephone*). Synonymous with AIDONEUS and DIS. 3. A *PLANET*.

PLUTUS Gk *god* of WEALTH.

PLUVIUS Rom *god* of *RAIN*. **Gk** = *JUPITER*.

PM AFTERNOON, POST MERIDIEM. PRIME MINISTER. POST MORTEM. PROVOST MARSHAL.

POET BARD, *WRITER*; LINESMAN (crypt). PHILAMON (*Argonaut*); Swan of Avon.

POETRY 1. LINES, ODE, *VERSE* (**opp** = prose). 2. **Gk myth Muse** = *CALLIOPE*, *ERATO*, EUTERPE.

POINT AIM, GIST, OBJECT. INDICATE, SHOW. HEADLINE, *NESS*, PT. APEX, *TIP*, TOE. NEEDLE, PIN. *CRICKETER*, FIELDER. E, N, S OR W, EAST, NORTH, SOUTH or WEST. PUNCTUATE. REFACE (bricks and mortar). SWITCH (rly).

POINTER *ARROW*, *DIRECTOR*, INDICATION. *DOG*.

POINTLESS 1. MEANINGLESS. NO SCORE. BLUNT. 2. Remove letters indicating cardinal points from word(s) indicated, e.g. **Type of communication that's read is now pointless** (5) = R*ADI**O*.

Pol Poland (*car plate* = PL). Political.

POLE (s/l *poll*). N, S, NORTH, SOUTH. *MEASURE* (length): *PERCH*, ROD. EAST EUROPEAN, SLAV. PILLAR, *POST*, MAST. QUANT.

POLICE CAR BLACK MARIA, PANDA-CAR, SQUAD-CAR, Z-CAR.

POLICEMAN BOBBY (Sir Robert Peel), BOW STREET RUNNER (Henry Fielding), COP, DICK, PEELER (Sir Robert Peel), *PIG*, ROZZER (all sl). *MP*, PC, SP. **Pl** = CID, FBI, FEDS, PD, FORCE, FUZZ, GESTAPO [*detective*]. **Celebrated:** DAY (*Kipling*), DIXON (TV).

POLISH *BUFF*, CLEAN, RUB; SHEEN, VENEER. OF POLAND.

Polit Political.

POLL (s/l *pole*). HEAD. VOTE. *PARROT*. SAMPLE. CUT OFF, LOP.

POLLUX 1. Gk myth *twin* of *Castor*. Skilful boxer and patron of seamen. 2. One of the *Argonauts*.

POLY(HY)MNIA 1. Gk myth; one of the nine *Muses* (hymns). 2. A minor *PLANET*.

POMPEY 1. PORTSMOUTH (sl). WHORE (*rh sl*). 2. Roman leader and general (B.C. 106-48). Maintained an uneasy alliance with *Caesar* (with Crassus, they formed the first triumvirate in B.C. 60); a great warrior. Mar Julia (d of Caesar). Political ambition finally brought him into open conflict with Caesar, and civil war followed. After being defeated at Pharsalus in B.C. 48, he fled to Egypt, where he was ass by Septimus on the orders of Ptolemy's ministers as he was being rowed ashore. 3. *Shak* character (A and C).

PONY *HORSE*, NAG. GLASS. £25 (sl).

POOL KIT BALLS, CUE, CHALK, REST, TABLE. DIVING BOARD, FILTER.

POP *FATHER*. BANG [weasel]. MUSIC. PAWN, PLEDGE. *DRINK*. SOCIETY (*Eton* prefects).

PORCELAIN *CERAMICS*.

PORPOISE 1. UNDULATE. *CETACEAN* MAMMAL; WHALE (genus Phocaena). **Assembly** = school. 2. Character in *Alice*.

PORT P, LARBOARD (arch), *LEFT*. WINE. *GATE*(WAY), HARBOUR. *BEARING*, CARRIAGE. LIGHT, OPENING, WINDOW.

Port Portugal (*car plate* = P). [*patron saint*].

PORTER BEER, *DRINK*. DOOR-KEEPER, GATE-KEEPER. BAGGAGE CARRIER. *WRITER*.

PORTUGAL P (*car plate*). [patron saint = St George].

POSEIDON Gk god of the sea (**Rom** = *NEPTUNE*), allied to Nereus (**Rom** = Oceanus). Son of Chronos (**Rom** = *Saturn*) and *Rhea*; mar *Amphitrite*; br to *Zeus*.

POSER PROBLEM. *MODEL*, SITTER.

POSSESSIVE 1. GRASPING, *MISERLY*, RAPACIOUS. *OWNING*. 2. Put into the possessive case, e.g. **He is possessive** = HIS.

POST *PILE*, *POLE*, STAKE. *DELIVERY*, MAIL; SEND. APPOINTMENT, JOB, *SITUATION*. *MEASURE* (paper size).

POSTER *AD*, *BILL*, HOARDING, NOTICE, PLACARD. LETTER SENDER (crypt).

POSTHOLDER INCUMBENT. ENVELOPE, LETTERBOX, MAILBAG, MAILBOX, PILLARBOX (all crypt).

POST HOLE LETTER/PILLAR BOX (crypt).

POST SCRIPT AFTERTHOUGHT, PS.

POT COOKPOT, PAN. *DRUG*. POCKET, SINK (billiards, pool, snooker).

POTASSIUM K (*chem*).

POTATO EARTH-APPLE (arch); MURPHY, SPUD, YAM; KING EDWARD (hence R*ED or R*TED [eyes]).

POTENTIALLY *Anag*. CAN BE, MAYBE; CAPABLE, POSSIBLY. CHARGED (elect).

POTTER 1. DAWDLE, LOITER, WANDER. WORK (desultorily). BILLIARD/POOL/SNOOKER PLAYER (crypt). CLAY WORKER, hence any maker of *ceramics* (q.v.), BOWLER, THROWER (crypt). 2. Stephen ~, WRITER (humorist; Lifemanship; One-upmanship). 3. Beatrix ~, WRITER (children's); **books:** Appley Dapply's Nursery Rhymes; Benjamin Bunny; Cecily Parsley's Nursery Rhymes; A Fierce Bad Rabbit; The Flopsy Bunnies; Ginger and Pickles; Jemima Puddle-Duck; Johnny Town-Mouse; Little Pig Robinson; Miss Moppet; Mr Jeremy Fisher; Mr Tod; Mrs Tiggy-Winkle; Mrs Tittlemouse; Peter Rabbit; The Pie and the Patty Pan; Pigling Bland; Samuel Whiskers; Squirrel Nutkin; The Tailor of Gloucester; Timmy Tiptoes; Tom Kitten; Two Bad Mice; **characters:** Babbity Bumble (bee); Cousin Ribby, Mittens, Moppet, Simkin, Tabitha Twitchit, Tom Kitten (*cats*); Chippy Hackee (chipmunk); John Joiner, Kep (*dogs*); *Drake*, Jemima & Rebecca Puddle-Duck (*ducks*); Mr

Jackson, Jeremy Fisher (*frogs*); Mrs Tiggy-Winkle (hedgehog); Farmer *Potatoes*, Mr & Mrs McGregor, Tailor of Gloucester (humans); Johnny Town-Mouse, Thomasina, Mrs Tittlemouse (mice); Old Brown (*owl*); Bland, Robinson (*pigs*); Benjamin, Flopsy, Mopsy, Cotton-Tail & Peter (*rabbits*); Aunt Maria, Samuel Whiskers (rats); Nutkin, Silvertail, Timmy & Goody Tiptoes, Twinkleberry (squirrels).

POTTERY *CERAMICS* [*five towns*]; *anniversary* (9th). BILLIARD/POOL/SNOOKER HALL or TABLE (crypt).

POUCHED BAGGED, CAUGHT, POSSESSED. *MARSUPIAL*.

POUND L, LB, *MEASURE* (weight). COIN, CURRENCY; QUID, SOVEREIGN (**saying**). PULSATE, THROB; *BEAT*, HAMMER, PUMMEL. ENCLOSURE, PEN. *MILITARY LEADER*. *WRITER*.

POUT *FISH*, WHITING. PROTRUDE, SULKY. [pigeon].

PP *PAGES*. PER PRO, PROXY. PAST PARTICIPLE.

PR PUBLIC RELATIONS, ADVERTISING.

PRECIOUS STONE *GEM*, JEWEL.

PRECIS *SUMMARY*.

PREFIX HANDLE, TITLE. ADD, QUALIFY; INTRODUCE. [metric ~, see *International units*].

PREMISE INFERENCE, INTRODUCE [logic]. AFORESAID, FOREGOING. **Pl** = *BUILDING*, HOUSE, OFFICES.

PREPARED *Anag.* COMPOSED, FIT, READY. MIXED (*chem*). ALREADY PEELED (crypt).

PRESENT NOW; EXISTING, OCCURRING. READY (arch). AT HAND, ON SITE, THERE. DONATION, GIFT; EXHIBIT, OFFER. APPEAR, INTRODUCE, RECOMMEND. AIM, SALUTE (mil). *PUT UP* (petition). **Pl** = DOCUMENT (leg).

~ **DAY** NOW, *AD. ANNIVERSARY*, BIRTHDAY, *CHRISTMAS* etc (crypt).

PRESIDENT P. MANAGING DIRECTOR (US). GOVERNOR (arch), HEAD (of Board, State, Country); ~s **of the USA since independence:**

*GEORGE WASHINGTON	Fed	1789-97
JOHN ADAMS	Fed	1797-1801
*THOMAS JEFFERSON	Rep	1801-09

JAMES MADISON	Rep	1809-17
JAMES MONROE	Rep	1817-25
JOHN QUINCEY ADAMS	Rep	1825-29
ANDREW JACKSON	Dem	1829-37
MARTIN VAN BUREN	Dem	1837-41
WILLIAM H. HARRISON	Whig	1841 (d in office)
JOHN TYLER	Whig	1841-45
JAMES K. POLK	Dem	1845-49
ZACHARY TAYLOR	Whig	1849-50 (d in office)
MILLARD FILLMORE	Whig	1850-53
FRANKLIN PIERCE	Dem	1853-57
JAMES BUCHANAN	Dem	1857-61
*ABRAHAM LINCOLN	Rep	1861-65 (ass)
ANDREW JOHNSON	Rep	1865-69
ULYSSES S. GRANT	Rep	1869-77
RUTHERFORD B. HAYES	Rep	1877-81
JAMES A. GARFIELD	Rep	1881 (ass)
CHESTER A. ARTHUR	Rep	1881-85
GROVER CLEVELAND	Dem	1885-89
BENJAMIN HARRISON	Rep	1889-93
GROVER CLEVELAND	Dem	1893-97
WILLIAM McKINLEY	Rep	1897-1901 (ass)
*THEODORE ROOSEVELT	Rep	1901-09
WILLIAM HOWARD TAFT	Rep	1909-13
WOODROW WILSON	Dem	1913-21
WARREN G. HARDING	Rep	1921-23 (d in office)
CALVIN COOLIDGE	Rep	1923-29
HERBERT C. HOOVER	Rep	1929-33
FRANKLIN D. ROOSEVELT	Dem	1933-45 (d in office)
HARRY S. TRUMAN	Dem	1945-53
DWIGHT D. EISENHOWER	Rep	1953-61
JOHN F. KENNEDY	Dem	1961-63 (ass)
LYNDON B. JOHNSON	Dem	1963-69
RICHARD M. NIXON	Rep	1969-74 (resigned)
GERALD R. FORD	Rep	1974-76 (nominated)

JIMMY CARTER   Dem   1976-80
RONALD REAGAN   Rep   1980-
  * = Head is carved at Mt Rushmore.

PRESS FOURTH *ESTATE*, NEWSPAPERS, *PAPERS*,
  MEDIUM. PRINTING MACHINE. API, BUP, GRUB
  STREET, REUTER, TASS, UPI, XINHUA. *IRON*; SQUASH,
  SQUEEZE. CONSCRIBE, SHANGHAI (naut arch). *URGE*.
~ **CHIEF** ED, PRO.
~ **GANG** RECRUITING PARTY [conscription, draft, national
  service, **opp** = *volunteer*]. EDITORS, NUJ, PRINTERS,
  REPORTERS (crypt).
~ **MAN** ED(ITOR), REPORTER. IRONER, LAUNDRYMAN
  (crypt).
PRETENDER CLAIMANT, OLD ~, YOUNG ~, (s, grandson of
  James II). ACTOR (crypt).
PRIAM Gk myth king of *Troy*; mar Hecuba, and f of *Cassandra*,
  Hector and *Paris*. [T and C (*Shak*)].
PRICKLY SPINY, THORNY. HEDGEHOG, PORCUPINE,
  URCHIN (crypt). TINGLING, UP-TIGHT.
PRIDE 1. AMOUR-PROPRE, ARROGANCE. BEST, PICK.
  [~ and Prejudice (*Austen*); fall]. 2. *Assembly* of lions.
PRIEST CANON, *CHURCHMAN*, MINISTER; *Chaucer*
  character. ELI, ELIJAH, ELISHA, EZEKIEL. *ISLAND*.
PRIMARY COLOURS GREEN, RED, VIOLET (in painting:
  BLUE, RED, YELLOW).
PRIMATE SENIOR *CHURCHMAN*. APE, HIGH MAMMAL,
  MAN, *MONKEY*.
PRIME MINISTER PRINCIPAL MINISTER OF STATE, PM;
  CABINET MAKER (crypt). **British ~s since 1900:**

MARQUIS OF SALISBURY	Cons	1895-1902
A.J. BALFOUR	Cons	1902-05
SIR H. CAMPBELL-BANNERMAN	Lib	1905-08
H.H. ASQUITH	Lib	1908-15
H.H. ASQUITH	Coaln	1915-16
D. LLOYD GEORGE	Coaln	1916-22
A. BONAR LAW	Cons	1922-23
STANLEY BALDWIN	Cons	1923-24

J. RAMSAY MACDONALD	Lab	1924
STANLEY BALDWIN	Cons	1924-29
J. RAMSAY MACDONALD	Lab	1929-31
J. RAMSAY MACDONALD	Nat	1931-35
STANLEY BALDWIN	Nat	1935-37
NEVILLE CHAMBERLAIN	Nat	1937-39
NEVILLE CHAMBERLAIN	War Cab	1939-40
WINSTON S. CHURCHILL	War Cab	1940-45
CLEMENT ATTLEE	Lab	1945-51
SIR WINSTON CHURCHILL	Cons	1951-55
SIR ANTHONY EDEN	Cons	1955-57
HAROLD MACMILLAN	Cons	1957-63
SIR ALEC DOUGLAS-HOME	Cons	1963-64
HAROLD WILSON	Lab	1964-70
EDWARD HEATH	Cons	1970-74
HAROLD WILSON	Lab	1974-76
JAMES CALLAGHAN	Lab	1976-79
MARGARET THATCHER	Cons	1979-

PRIMUS ELDEST, FIRST. BISHOP (Sc).

PRINCE(SSE)S ROYALS.

PRINCIPAL (s/l *principle*). CHIEF, *HEAD*, MAIN. *CAPITAL*.

PRINCIPLE (s/l *principal*). *LIGHT*, STANDARD, TENET.

PRISE (s/l *prize*). *FORCE*, LEVER, PURCHASE. Also = *PRIZE*.

PRISON *GAOL* [M for M (*Shak*)].

PRISONER GAOLBIRD, LAG, CONVICT; [*patron saint*];
CELLIST (crypt); **celebrated:** COL ALTAMONT (Pendennis,
Thackeray); SAMUEL BURTON (Kingsley); COUNT OF
MONTE CRISTO (Dumas); *LIONHEART* (Eng king);
MAGWITCH (Great Expectations, *Dickens*); M. MANETTE
(shoemaker, 105 North Tower, Tale of Two Cities, *Dickens*);
MAN IN THE IRON MASK (Dumas); JEAN VALJEAN (Les
Misérables, Victor Hugo); ~ OF ZENDA (Elphburg, Hope).

PRIVATE PERSONAL, RESTRICTED, RETIRED,
SECLUDED, SECRET; ARCANE, ESOTERIC (**opp** =
public). GI, PFC (US), RANKER, SOLDIER, TOMMY
(ATKINS).

PRIZE (s/l *prise*). CUP, *REWARD*, TROPHY. CAPTIVE. Also
= *PRISE* (arch).

PRO PUBLIC RELATIONS OFFICER, ADMAN.
PROFESSIONAL (**opp** = amateur). FOR (**opp** = *anti*, con).
PUBLIC RECORD OFFICE.

PROCEED GO, GO ON, MAKE WAY. *ACT*, SUE. *ISSUE*,
ORIGINATE. **Pl** = *Anag.* MONEY, RECEIPTS.

PROCESSED *Anag. TREATED.* PROGRESSED,
TRAVELLED.

PROCRUSTES Gk myth *robber*, who tailored his victims to his *bed*
(by amputation or stretching, as appropriate); killed by *Theseus*.

PRODUCT *Anag.*, e.g. **Nuclear product** = UNCLEAR. GOODS,
LINE, OUTPUT, RESULT. MULTIPLIED.

PROFIT (s/l *prophet*). ADVANTAGE, BENEFIT, GAIN,
RETURN.

PROMETHEUS Gk myth *TITAN*, who stole fire from Mt *Olympus*
to give to mankind. Chained by *Vulcan* to a rock, where a vulture
fed daily on his liver, only for it to grow again each night.
Rescued by *Hercules*.

PRONOUNCED DECIDED, MARKED. DELIVERED,
SOUNDED, UTTERED. See *Pronunciation* below.

PRONUNCIATION Many words sound like others which are spelled
differently, and this can affect the meaning of a clue, or otherwise
lead to the correct answer. 'Court' and 'caught' can introduce an
obvious play on courtship and being caught in matrimony;
sometimes there are three different interpretations, such as
'cruise', 'crews' and 'cruse'. Such words are often hinted at by use
of phrases like '. . . we listen to . . .', '. . . it sounds as though
. . .', '. . . a pronounced . . .', or some such in the clue. Thus: **We
hear of a sea voyage – unending for widows** (5) means that, when
read aloud, the answer sounds like a sea voyage, or cruise;
unending for widows reveals that it should be the widow's CRUSE
which, in biblical times, never emptied.

But don't necessarily think that all is as straightforward even as
this. If the puzzle setter can turn a word to his advantage, he will
do so. An obvious example is 'flower' which, besides meaning a
plant, can mean something which flows, i.e. a river. Even if you
are prepared for this kind of deviousness, you may allow your
mind to be programmed to accept the wrong pronunciation. The
clue **Rows of beans cultivated by our forefathers?** (6, 4) may lead
to the following train of thought: 'Rows could be tiers, ranks,

lines or files; beans could be haricot, runner or broad.' But the popular phrase 'a row of beans' has been deliberately suggested in order to mislead, for rows can also mean 'dins, noises, battles, fights, or shindies'. This clue requires the answer FRENCH WARS.

The moral is to examine clues for words or phrasing which might imply alternative spelling to produce a similar sound, or alternative sound to produce a different meaning. Where an entry in this Companion sounds like another word, its explanation starts (s/l . . .). Those words capable of unusual interpretation, not always through different pronunciation but frequently, are too many to list separately but they have been noted in their individual entries, usually by the addition of the word (crypt) to show that a cryptic interpretation is necessary. Besides **flower** = plant and river, and **row** = tier or din mentioned above (or paddle), examples include **banker** = financier or river (between two banks), **sewer** = drain or seamstress, **number** = digit or anaesthetic (makes one numb), **fast time** = high speed or lent/ramadan, **crew** = ship's complement or the past tense of crow (like a cockerel). There are many, and the puzzle setter will usually be one jump ahead of you, so be alert. See also *punctuation*.

PROOF OF DEBT BILL, INVOICE, IOU, MARKER.

PROPERTY ATTRIBUTE, CHARACTERISTIC, *QUALITY*. BELONGINGS, CHATTELS, POSSESSIONS; OWNING; REAL ESTATE. COSTUME, FURNITURE (theat).

PROPHECY FORETELLING. **Gk god** = *APOLLO* [Cassandra; Macbeth (*Shak*), A and C (*Shak*); *Oedipus*; *Perseus*].

PROPHET (s/l *profit*). FORECASTER, DIVINER, *SEER*, SOOTHSAYER, VISIONARY. **Gk myth** AMPHIARUS (*argonaut*), *CASSANDRA* (fem), MOPSUS (*Argonaut*), MOTHER SHIPTON (fem), TIRESIAS. [Old Moore. *Sibyl*].
Biblical:

AMOS	EZEKIEL
DANIEL	HABBAKKUK
DEBORAH (fem)	HAGGAI
ELI	HOSEA
ELIJAH (*ELIAS*)	ISAIAH
ELISHA	JEREMIAH

JOEL	NAHUM
JONAH	OBADIAH
MALACHI	ZACHARIAH
MICAH	ZEPHANIAH

PROSERPINE 1. Rom eq of *PERSEPHONE*. 2. A minor *PLANET*.

PROSPERITY God: Gk = AGATHODAEMON. **Rom** = GENIUS.

PROVERB ADAGE, APHORISM, BYWORD, MAXIM, SAW, *SAYING*. **Pl** = BOOK (bibl). GAME.

PROVINCE 1. AREA, BRANCH, BUSINESS, DEPARTMENT, FIELD, SPHERE. 2. DISTRICT (eccles), ADMINISTRATIVE DIVISION, TERRITORY. 3. **Specifically of Canada:**

ALBERTA	AL
BRITISH COLUMBIA	BC
MANITOBA	MAN
NEW BRUNSWICK	NB
NEWFOUNDLAND	NF
N W TERRITORIES	NWT
NOVA SCOTIA	NS
PRINCE EDWARD ISLAND	PEI
ONTARIO	ONT
QUEBEC	Q
SASKATCHEWAN	SAS
THE YUKON	YUK

PS POST SCRIPT, AFTERTHOUGHT. POLICE SERGEANT. PRIVATE SECRETARY. PROMPT SIDE. PSALM.

PSYCHE 1. Gk myth immortal lover of *Cupid*. 2. A minor *PLANET*.

PT PHYSICAL TRAINING; PE, GYMNASTICS. PLATINUM (*chem*). *POINT*.

PTOLEMY KING OF EGYPT. Successive kings (I-IX) reigned from B.C. 323-81, notable chiefly for their cruelty, incest (they regularly married their sisters or mothers, who were as regularly called *Cleopatra* and as cruel as their husbands), and the loss of territory. Particularly notable were ~ V (Epiphanes; B.C. 205-181) who is the subject of the *Rosetta Stone*; ~ X (Alexander II; B.C. 81) who married his cousin Cleopatra Berenice and immediately had her assassinated, whereupon rioters did the same for him; ~ XI (Auletes; B.C. 80-51) who was expelled to Rome, where he bribed *Pompey* to reinstate him in B.C. 55 (he murdered his own daughter Berenice); ~ XII (son of ~ XI; B.C. 51-47) who reigned jointly with his sis Cleopatra (the well-known one) with whom he quarrelled and, when *Caesar* took her side, he was drowned escaping; ~ XIII (br of ~ XII; B.C. 47-43) who was appointed by Caesar to marry his sis Cleopatra and rule jointly, but she had him assassinated during the Alexandrine war.

PUB *BAR*, BISTRO(T), INN, *LOCAL*, PH (abbr), *TAVERN*. *PUBLIC*. PUBLISHED.

PUBLICAN *HOST*, INNKEEPER, *LANDLORD*. TAX-GATHERER (bibl).

PUBLICATION *ISSUE*. BOOK, MAGAZINE, PAPER, WEEKLY.

PUBLIC SCHOOL BOARDING-, ENDOWED-, PRIVATE-SCHOOL; **celebrated:**

ALLEYN'S		founded 1619
ALLHALLOWS		16th century
AMPLEFORTH	(Fr 1608)	1802
ARDINGLY		1858
BEDALES		1893
BLOXHAM		1860
BLUECOAT		1553
BLUNDELLS		1604
BRYANSTON		1928
CANFORD		1923
CHARTERHOUSE		1611
CHRIST'S HOSPITAL		1553
CHURCHER'S		1722
CLIFTON		1862
CRANLEIGH		1863
DAUNTSEY'S		1543
DOUAI	(Fr 1615)	1903
DOWNSIDE	(Fr 1606)	1789
EPSOM		1853

ETON	founded 1440
FELSTED	1564
GORDONSTOUN	1934
GRESHAM'S	1555
HABERDASHERS'	1690
HAILEYBURY	1862
HARROW	1571
HURSTPIERPOINT	1849
LANCING	1848
THE LEYS	1875
LORETTO	1862
MALVERN	1862
MARLBOROUGH	1843
MERCHANT TAYLOR'S	1561
MONKTON COMBE	1868
OSWESTRY	1407
OUNDLE	1556
RADLEY	1847
REPTON	1557
ROSSALL	1844
RUGBY	1567
SAINT PAULS	1509
SEDBURGH	1525
SHERBORNE	1550
STONYHURST	1593
STOWE	1923
TONBRIDGE	1553
UPPINGHAM	1584
WELLINGTON	1841
WESTMINSTER	1560
WHITGIFT	1596
WINCHESTER	1382
WORKSOP	1890
WREKIN	1880
WYCLIFFE	1882

PUCK 1. *SPRITE* (MND, *Shak*); IMP. 2. Ice hockey disc.

PUDDING *Anag.* AFTERS, *COURSE*, SWEET; types: APPLE ~,
BLACK ~, FRUIT ~, HASTY ~, MILK ~, PLUM ~,

SPONGE ~, STEAMED ~, YORKSHIRE ~, ROLY POLY, SPOTTED DICK. FAT PERSON. PAD, PROTECT (naut).

PULLER DRAWER, EXTRACTOR; DENTIST (crypt). TOWER, TUG.

PUMP BALE, DISCHARGE, EMPTY. *SHOE*. INTERROGATE, QUESTION.

PUNCH *DRINK*, NEGUS. BLOW, HOOK, JAB, KNOCK, SWING, UPPERCUT. [~ and Judy].

PUNCTUATION Commas and even full stops are ruthlessly used by the puzzle setter to mislead. The object, as with use of words with different *pronunciation*, is to brainwash the reader into putting a certain interpretation on a word, particularly one which may have two or more meanings. Note how the clue **Offers more doubt, is uncertain** (7) points to lack of sureness or confidence, but moving the comma (and this has to be done mentally, because the puzzle setter won't do it for you) from after the word 'doubt' to before it, changes the complexion of things: 'Offers more, doubt is uncertain' gives a word which must mean 'offers more' and must be an 'uncertain' rendering (thus an anagram) of 'doubt is'; the answer = OUTBIDS. See also *Question mark*.

PUNT *BET*, WAGER. *BOAT*; QUANT. COUNTRY (pre-bibl [Queen Hatshepsut]). KICK.

PUP PUPPY; *offspring* of dog. DUD. *AIRCRAFT*.

PUPIL L, STUDENT, SCHOLAR [*class, form*]. IRIS, EYE CENTRE (hence Y, crypt); *SEER* (crypt).

PURPLE *COLOUR*; *PURPURE* (*herald*).

PURPURE *COLOUR*; *PURPLE* (*herald*).

PUSSYFOOT LURK, PROWL, SNEAK. OVERCAUTION. *TT*, PROHIBITIONIST [W.E. Johnson]. CATSPAW (crypt).

PUT *PLACE, SET*.

~ **BACK** DEMOTE. REPLACE. DEFER. TES, TUP (crypt).

PUTTER *CLUB*; *GOLFER*. PLACER, SETTER.

PUTTING *GOLF*, HOLING. PLACING, SETTING.

PUT UP BUILD, CONSTRUCT, ERECT. TOLERATE. EMPLOY (jockey). *FLUSH* (game bird). *LODGE* (guest). OFFER (fight, prayer). *PRESENT* (petition). PROPOSE (candidate). *RAISE* (price). SHEATHE (sword). TUP (dn).

PYGMALION Gk myth king of Cyprus, who fell in love with the ivory statue he had sculpted. He persuaded *Aphrodite* to give it life, and mar her as *Galatea*. [G. B. Shaw].

PYRIPHLEGETHON Gk myth underworld river; literally: flaming with fire.

PYROMANIA *Obsession* with fire-raising.

PYROPHOBIA *Aversion* to fire.

Q QUEBEC (*Province*, Can). QUEEN. QUESTION. HEAD OF MI5.

QC QUEEN'S COUNSEL, SILK.

QT ON THE QUIET, QUIET(LY).

QUAIL FLINCH. GAME *BIRD*; **assembly** = bevy. *INSTRUMENT* (mus).

QUAKER FRIEND, FRY; **pl** = FRIENDLY SOCIETY [Fox]. EARTHQUAKE, TREMBLER (crypt) [Richter]. GUNPORT.

QUALITY ACCOMPLISHMENT, APTITUDE, ATTRIBUTE, *CHARACTERISTIC*, FACULTY, *PROPERTY*, SKILL, TIMBRE. DEGREE, EXCELLENCE. GENTRY, *RANK*, STANDING.

QUARTER E, N, S, W, NE, SE, *NORTH*, *EAST* etc. *MERCY*, PITY. TRAVERSE. FOURTH PART, *MEASURE*. COIN (US). AREA, NEIGHBOURHOOD. **Pl** = BILLET, LODGING.

~ **DAYS** D, A, Y or S (crypt). **England/Ireland:** LADY DAY (25 Mar), MIDSUMMER (24 Jun), MICHAELMAS (29 Sep), CHRISTMAS (25 Dec); **Scotland:** CANDLEMAS (2 Feb), WHITSUN (15 May), LAMMAS (1 Aug), MARTINMAS (11 Nov).

~ **HOUR** H, O, U or R (crypt).

~ **PINT** P, I, N or T (crypt). GILL, *MEASURE*.

QUAY (s/l *key*). BUND, *DOCK*, *JETTY*, *MOLE*, PIER, WHARF.

QUEEN 1. CARD (*Alice*). *CAT* (fem). CHESSPIECE. 2. King's wife, *MONARCH* (fem; q.v.), REGINA, SOVEREIGN (fem); EII, ER, HM, Q, R; **celebrated:** AETHELFLED (Mercia), ANNE (Eng), BESS (Eng), BILKIS (Sheba), *BOADICEA*, CANDACE (bibl), CATHERINE (Eng, Fr, Russ), *CLEOPATRA*, *CLYTEMNESTRA*, *CORA*, ELEANOR (Eng [Charing Cross, Waltham Cross, etc]), ELIZABETH (Eng),

ESTHER (bibl), GERTRUDE (*Shak*), *GUINEVERE*,
HATSHEPSUT (Egy [Punt]), *HECUBA*, *HELEN*, *HERA*,
HEPHZIBAH (bibl), HERMIONE (*Shak*), *HIPPOLYTE*,
ISABELLA (Sp), JEZEBEL (bibl), *JOCASTA*, *JUNO*, LEDA
(*Helen*), MARIA THERESA (A), MARIE ANTOINETTE (Fr),
MICHAL (bibl), NEFERTITI (Egy), *NIOBE*, PASIPHAE
(*Minos*), *PERSEPHONE*, *PROSERPINE*, TITANIA (*Shak*),
VASHT (bibl), *VICTORIA*.

QUEENS OF ENGLAND *See* Monarchs.

QUEER *Anag.* *ODD*, PECULIAR [*Chesterton*]. *FAIRY*, GAY.

~ STREET BANKRUPTCY, INSOLVENCY; CAREY STREET.
DEAD END (crypt). Anag. of 'street', e.g. TESTER.

QUESTION Q; PROBLEM (**opp** = answer). INTERROGATE,
GRILL, *PUMP*.

~ MARK A question mark is used when the puzzle setter is feeling
benevolent and wishes to draw attention to a double meaning. In
effect, it warns that the answer, while relating well to one half of
the clue, only responds to the other half in a punning or cryptic
way. One of the shortest examples is **Regal liner?** (5) = RULER
(where the answer = 'regal' because it means a king, but it =
'liner' because it may be said to help in ruling lines); another
instance is **Bulls-eye at the mortuary?** (4, 6) = DEAD CENTRE
(where the answer = 'bulls-eye' happily enough, but must be
looked at cryptically to arrive at a centre for dead people, or
'mortuary').

It can also be used to indicate that a different meaning should
be put on a word by giving it a different spelling, e.g. **Purchaser
for the old cow shed?** (4) = BYRE (where the answer is an old-
fashioned word for 'cowshed', but it has to be turned into BUYER
before it can mean 'purchaser'). See also *punctuation*.

QUEUER (s/l *cuer*). ONE WHO QUEUES/WAITS IN LINE;
WAITER.

QUICK *ALIVE*. RAPID, *SMART*. SUBCUTANEOUS
TENDERNESS.

QUICKLY RAPIDLY, *SMARTLY*, SPEEDILY. *ALIVE* (crypt).
Shak character.

QUID *NOTE*, *POUND*. TOBACCO WAD.

QUIET P, PP, SH; LOW, PIANO, SILENT, WHIST (**opp** = *loud*).

QUIETLY P, PP, QT, SH.

QUINCE *FRUIT* (tree). CARPENTER (MND, *Shak*).

QUIT DEPART, *GO*, LEAVE, PART. SHOT.

QUIXOTIC IDEALISTIC, LOFTY, VISIONARY [Cervantes; Rosinante (horse)].

QUOD *GAOL*. WHICH (Lat).

QV QUOD VIDE, WHICH SEE.

Q without U ABU QIR (Egy), AL QAFA (Egy), AL QATIF (Arab), AL QATRUN (Libya), AL QAYARA (Iraq), AQABA (Jor), AQIQ (Sudan), AQRABA (Jor), ASH QELON (Isr), DAQM (Oman), IQBAL, IRAQI, LUQA (Malta), NQA, NQING, NQONG (little, med, big, Aus gods, Just So Stories, *Kipling*), PETAL TIQWA (Isr), Q-BOAT, QED, QAFAR (Arab), QAIYA (Arab), QALA (Afghan), QALA MASHIZ (Iran), QALAT (Yemen), QAMA BAY (Arab), QARA (Egy), QARA QUM (USSR), QARDAHA (Syria), QARTABA (Lebanon), QASIM (Arab), QASR (Iraq), QA'TABA (Yemen), QATANA (Syria), QATAR (Isr), QATIF (Arab), QATTARA (Egy), QAYEN (Iran), QAZRAN (Iran), QAZVIN (Iran), QESHM (Isr, Iran), QEYS (Isr, Iran), QISHM (Iran), QISHN (Arab), QISHRAN (Isr, Arab), QIZAN (Arab), QIZIL UZUN (Iran), QOM (Iran), QOTUR (Iran), QOZ BAL AIR (Arab), SAWQIRAH BAY (Oman), SHAQA (Arab), SHUQRA (Yemen), TAQAH (Oman).

R *RAILWAY*. RAND. REAMUR. RECTO. REGIMENT. *REGINA*. *RESTRICTED* (film *censorship*). REVEREND. REX. RIGHT. *RIVER*. *ROYAL*. RUMANIA (*car plate*). RUNS. KING (= EDWARD, GEORGE, HENRY etc).

RA RADIUM (*chem*). ROYAL ACADEMICIAN (painter, Burlington House). ROYAL AND ANCIENT (golf). ROYAL ARTILLERY. SUN *GOD* (Egy). **Pl** = Abyssinian King.

RABBIT (s/l rabbet, rarebit, rebate). CHATTER. DUFFER, POOR PLAYER. BOTHER, CONFOUND, DRAT. *ISLAND*. BURROWING RODENT, HARE; BUNNY, CONEY; **breeds:** ANGORA, LOP-EARED; **celebrated:** BENJAMIN BUNNY (Beatrix *Potter*); BRER RABBIT (Uncle Remus; Joel Chandler Harris; Brer Fox, Tar-Baby); BUGS BUNNY® (cartoon); FIVER; HAZEL (Watership Down);

FLOPSY, MOPSY, COTTONTAIL, PETER (Beatrix *Potter* [Mr McGregor]); HARVEY (invisible, Mary Chase); RABBIT (*Milne* [Friends and Relations]); MARCH HARE, WHITE RABBIT (*Alice* in Wonderland); THUMPER® (Bambi®) [*habitation*; myxomatosis; playboy].

RAC ROYAL ARMOURED CORPS. ROYAL AUTOMOBILE CLUB [AA, cars].

RACE *BREED*, ETHNIC GROUP. *TIDE-RIP*. GINGER ROOT, *SPICE*. *CLASSIC*, COMPETITION, EGG AND SPOON, EVENT, GRAND PRIX, INDY, MARATHON, OBSTACLE, RELAY, *TT*, SACK ~. [*Atalanta*].

~ OF MAN HOMO SAPIENS. *TT* (crypt).

RACETRACKS 1. **Celebrated (horses):**

AINTREE (Eng)	HAYDOCK PARK (Eng)
ASCOT (Eng)	HEREFORD (Eng)
AUTEUIL (Fr)	KEMPTON (Eng)
AYR (Sc)	LEICESTER (Eng)
BANGOR ON DEE (Wal)	*LINCOLN* (Eng)
BATH (Eng)	LONGCHAMPS (Fr)
BEVERLEY (Eng)	LUDLOW (Eng)
BRIGHTON (Eng)	MAISONS-LAFFITTE (Fr)
CARTMEL (Eng)	MARKET RASEN (Eng)
CAMPTOWN (US)	NAAS (Ire)
CATTERICK (Eng)	NEWBURY (Eng)
CHANTILLY (Fr)	NEWMARKET (Eng)
CHEPSTOW (Wal)	NEWTON ABBOT (Eng)
CHESTER (Eng)	PERTH (Sc)
CHURCHILL DOWNS (US)	RIPON (Eng)
CRAVEN (Ire)	SAINT-CLOUD (Fr)
CURRAGH (Ire)	SANDOWN PARK (Eng)
DEVON & EXETER (Eng)	STRATFORD (Eng)
EDINBURGH (Sc)	UTTOXETER (Eng)
EPSOM (Eng)	WARWICK (Eng)
FOLKESTONE (Eng)	WINDSOR (Eng)
FONTWELL PARK (Eng)	WOLVERHAMPTON (Eng)
GOODWOOD (Eng)	YARMOUTH (Eng)
HAMILTON (Sc)	*YORK* (Eng)

2. **Celebrated (motor cars):**

BRANDS HATCH (Eng)   MONZA (It)
BROOKLANDS (ex Eng)   NURBURGRING (Ger)
DAYTONA BEACH (US)   RICHMOND (US)
GOODWOOD (Eng)   SILVERSTONE (Eng)
LE MANS (Fr)   *SPA* (Belg)
MONACO (Fr)   THRUXTON (Eng)
MONTLHERY (Fr)   ZANDVOORT (NL)

RACKET DIN, NOISE, UPROAR. *DODGE*, SCHEME. ORDEAL. *BAT*; **Pl** = *GAME*.

RADIO *BROADCAST*, WIRELESS; *MEDIUM*.

RADIUM RA (*chem*).

RAFFIA PALM FIBRE, *PALM* [bass].

RAF TYPE AC, AIRMAN, FO, *PILOT* etc.

RAG CHAFF, RIB, *TEASE*. FROLIC, GAMBOL. CLOTH, SCRAP. BAD PRESS, GUTTER PRESS. SLATE; STONE. CLUB (sl: Army & Navy).

RAIL(WAY) BR, RLY, RY; IRON WAY; HARD LINES (crypt). LOCOS, ROLLING STOCK. *BIRD*. GUIDE, PERCH, ROD. [Bluebell, Severn Valley, Volks (elect), Watercress. *cat*].
~ **GUIDE** ABC®, BRADSHAW®.

RAILWAYMEN LOCOMEN; TRAINERS (crypt); **Unions** = ASLEF, NUR. TOBY VECK (The Chimes, *Dickens*).

RAIN (s/l *reign, rein*). 1. PRECIPITATION, DELUGE, *SHOWER*; DRENCH [piano wires, stair-rods]. 2. Put RA in word indicated, e.g. **Rainbox for crystalline salt** (5) = BO*RA*X. 3. **God: Gk** = JUPITER, *ZEUS*; **Rom** = PLUVIUS; **Egy** = OSIRIS; **Ind** = INDRA. [*Pleiades*].

RAINBOW 1. ARCH [REFRACTION] (**colours in order:** red, orange, yellow, green, blue, indigo, violet). 2. **Goddess: Gk** = IRIS.

RAISE (s/l *raze*). 1. ELEVATE, ERECT, HOIST, *PUT UP* (**opp** = *lower*). 2. Word in dn clue, written up, e.g. **Raise Cain** = NIAC.

RALLY BANTER, *CHAFF*. REASSEMBLE, RECOVER, REVIVE. *RACE*. DEMONSTRATION, PARADE.

RAM SHEEP (male), TUP; sign of *Zodiac* (1st, ARIES). BEAK, PROD (battering, mil). PISTON, PLUNGER (mech). BEAT DOWN, CRAM, DASH, DRIVE, PACK, PUSH, SHOVE, STRIKE, STUFF, TAMP. ROYAL ACADEMY OF MUSIC. **Pl** = *Football* team (UK/US).

RANGER GIRL GUIDE. FORESTER, PARK WARDEN. COMMANDO (US). COWBOY (crypt). **Pl** = CAVALRY. 8 in *song*.

RANK *CLASS*, GRADE, QUALITY, STANDING; **mil** = CAPT, COL, LT etc. LINE, QUEUE, *ROW*, *TIER* (**opp** = file); ARRAY, ORDER. COARSE, CORRUPT, FOUL, GROSS, INDECENT, LOATHSOME, OFFENSIVE. LUXURIANT.

RAPT (s/l rapped, wrapped). ABSORBED, CARRIED AWAY, *ENGROSSED*, ENRAPTURED, INTENT.

RASH HASTY, IMPETUOUS, OVERBOLD, RECKLESS (**saying**). ERUPTION, *GATHERING*, *SPOTS*.

RASPBERRY BRAMBLE, SOFT *FRUIT*. BIRD, DERISION, DISAPPROVAL.

RATE *LEVY*, LOCAL TAX. MPH, SPEED. COST, VALUE; CONSIDER, ESTIMATE, *RANK*, REGARD. CLASS; MAN OF WAR (arch naut). DRESS DOWN, *REPRIMAND*, SCOLD, SLANG.

RATING AB, JACK, *SAILOR*, TAR. ABC, TAM, GALLUP®. HANDICAP (naut). (HOUSE) TAX.

RAW UNRIPE. UNCOOKED (**opp** = *done*). *GREEN*, UNTRAINED. PART-MADE (hence MAD). BITING, CHILLY. SKINNED, SENSITIVE, SORE.

RAY *BEAM*, *LIGHT*, SHAFT [hope]. *FISH*: MANTA, *SKATE*, STING. NOTE (mus; also RE).

RC RED CROSS. ROMAN CATHOLIC. **Pl** = Royal College of Surgeons.

RD BOUNCE, DUD CHEQUE [refer to drawer]. RURAL DEAN. ROAD. RNR DECORATION.

RE *ABOUT*, CONCERNING, DESCRIBING. AGAIN. ROYAL ENGINEERS, SAPPERS. NOTE (mus; also RAY).

READ (s/l reed, *red*). 1. INTERPRET, STUDY, UNDERSTAND [books]. *PIRATE*. 2. Word reads differently if split (or read differently), e.g. **A measure of justice, we read** (8, 5) = FREEZING POINT (just*ice).

READY APT, FACILE, INCLINED, PREPARED, PROMPT, QUICK, WILLING. *CASH*. OUT (e.g. **Happen to be ready to cook** (3, 3) = PAN OUT).

RECEDING 1. DECLINING, SHRINKING, WITHDRAWING. 2. Answer reads backwards, or partly backwards, e.g. **The Hittite's top hair is receding** (5) = U*RIAH.

RECEIVER BANKRUPTCY OFFICIAL. RADIO, HEADPHONES, TV SET. FENCE. HOST. ACCEPTER, TAKER (**opp** = giver, donor).

RECKONING AC, *ACCOUNT*, *BILL*, *NOTE*, SUM, TOTAL.

RECLUSE *HERMIT*, INTROVERT. MISS HAVISHAM (*Dickens*).

RECORD DISC, EP, LP. ANNAL, ARCHIVE, *CHART*, DIARY, *ENTER*, ENTRY, LIST, *LOG*, *NOTE*, REGISTER, ROLL, TAPE, WRITE. BEST PERFORMANCE, CHAMPIONSHIP. TIE AGAIN (crypt).

RECORDER TAPE. DIARIST. LOGGER. CHAMPION, *WINNER*. FLUTE. *INSTRUMENT* (mus). JUDGE.

RED (s/l *read*). BILLIARD/SNOOKER BALL (score 3/1). BOLSHEVIK, COMMIE, COMMUNIST, LEFTIE, REVOLUTIONARY, RUSSIAN; MARX(IST), STALIN, *TROT*(SKY); IVAN. *SEA*. ERIC. *COLOUR*; GULES (*herald*) [*blush*]. *CASTLE*. OVERDRAWN. RIVER (Can; US; Viet). **Pl** = (*football* team).

REDCAP MILITARY POLICEMAN, MP, SP. *BIRD*.

REDCOAT HUNTING PINK. SOLDIER (arch); **pl** = BRITISH ARMY, LOBSTERS (arch). HOLIDAY CAMP GUIDE (Butlins).

REDHEAD COPPERNOB. COMMUNIST LEADER (crypt); hence C. R (crypt).

REDSKIN *AMERICAN INDIAN*. **Pl** = *football* team (US).

REEFER JOINT (*drug*). *SAILOR* (crypt). JACKET.

REEL *Anag*. DANCE, LURCH, STAGGER, SWAY. COIL, SPOOL: *WIND*.

RE-ENACTED *Anag*. REPEATED, REPLAYED, RE-RUN.

REEVE MAGISTRATE, SHERIFF. THREAD (naut). *FEMALE* RUFF (*bird*). *Chaucer* character.

REFERENCE MARK Direction sign referring reader to note, e.g. ASTERISK (*), DAGGER/OBELISK (†), DOUBLE OBELISK

(‡), PARAGRAPH (¶), PARALLEL (‖), SECTION (§).

REFERENCE WORK BOOK, CONSULTATION DOCUMENT, FILE; *DEVILRY* (crypt); **celebrated** (®): ABC (rly), ALMANACH DE GOTHA (genealogy and statistics), BAEDEKER (countries and travel), MRS BEETON (cook), BLUE BOOK (US aristocracy), BRADSHAW (rly), BRITANNICA (encyclopaedia), BURKE'S (aristocracy), CHAMBERS (dictionary), COLLINS (dictionary), CROCKFORDS (*churchmen*), DEBRETT'S (aristocracy), *LLOYDS* (shipping, yachts), MEDICAL REGISTER (doctors), NAUTICAL ALMANAC (naut tables and ephemera), OED (dictionary), OLD MOORE (statistics, prophecy), REEDS (naut ephemera), ROGET (thesaurus), STUD BOOK (racehorses), WHITAKER'S ALMANAC (statistics), WHO'S WHO (people).

REFLECTION 1. CENSURE. RECONSIDERATION. (MIRROR) IMAGE. *ECHO*. 2. Word reads backwards, or is a palindrome, e.g. **On reflection, I lead to a certain amount of evil-smelling** (7) = NO*I*SOME.

REFRAIN ABSTAIN, CURB, DESIST, RESTRAIN. (RECURRING) PHRASE/*TUNE*.

REFORM *Anag.* ABOLISH, CORRECT, CURE. FORM AGAIN (hence FROM, crypt).

REFUSE *DECLINE*, DENY, REJECT, SAY NAY, SHUN, *SHY* (**opp** = *allow*). GARBAGE, LEAVINGS, ORT, RUBBISH, SCRAP, TRASH.

REGINA QUEEN, R.

REGIONS OF SCOTLAND See *Divisions*.

REGRET APOLOGIZE, GRIEVE, RUE; [Miss Otis].

REHOBOAM 1. Large *BOTTLE*, twice the size of a *Jeroboam*. 2. King of Judah, s of Solomon.

REIGN (s/l *rain*, *rein*). RULE, SOVEREIGNTY, SWAY; REALM, SPHERE. HOLD ROYAL OFFICE, BE KING/QUEEN/MONARCH/SOVEREIGN.

REIN 1. (s/l *rain*, *reign*). *CONTROL*, CURB, GOVERN, RESTRAIN. *HARNESS*. 2. Put RE in word indicated, e.g. **The little man's horserein** (4) = G*RE*G. 3. **Pl** = KIDNEYS, LOINS (arch).

REINDEER CARIBOU, SUBARCTIC DEER; **celebrated:** BLITZEN, *COMET*, *CUPID*, *DANCER*, DASHER,

DONDER, PRANCER, *VIXEN* (Moore); RUDOLF. *LAKE*.

REJECT 1. EVACUATE, VOMIT. *DECLINE, REFUSE*, TURN ASIDE. 2. Letter or word dropped, e.g. **Treaty rejecting the French fever** (4) = (le)AGUE.

RELATED AGNATE; ALLIED, KIN, KITH. NARRATED, TOLD.

RELATION CONNECTION, FAMILY, KIN, KITH. ACCOUNT, NARRATIVE, STORY, TALE.

RELIEF WORK AID TO POOR, OXFAM, UNICEF. CAMEO (**opp** = intaglio), ENGRAVING; BAS, FRIEZE. BRAILLE (crypt).

RELIGION DIVINE RECOGNITION, FAITH, PIETY, WORSHIP; MONASTIC LIFE [*church, friar, monk*]. **Celebrated vedantisms:** HINDUISM (**gods:** Shakti, Shiva, Vishnu; **goddesses:** Durga, Lakshmi; **priest:** brahmin); BUDDHISM (**versions:** Mahayana, Theravada, Ch'an (Ch), Zen (Jap); **founder:** Gautama; Nirvana (bliss); **priests:** monks); BABISM; BAHAISM; JAINISM (non-violence); LAMAISM (Tibet); PARSISM (**founder:** Zoroaster); SAKTIISM (Tantras); SIKHISM (**founder:** Guru Nanak); ZOROASTRIANISM. **Celebrated oriental:** CONFUCIANISM (**concepts:** chan-tza, hsaio, jen, li, shu, tao, t'ien); SHINTOISM (**concept:** kami); TAOISM (**concepts:** tao, te, we wei, yang, yin). **Celebrated Judaisms:** CHRISTIANITY (**founder:** Jesus); ISLAM (**founder:** *MOHAMMED*; **prophets:** Abraham, Adam, Jesus, Moses, *Mohammed*, Noah); ZIONISM (**founders:** Abraham, Isaac, Jacob [**Israel**]). **Celebrated paganisms/atheisms:** MARXISM (communism); SATANISM (black magic); VOODOO (ju-ju); WITCHCRAFT (magick, wicca).

RELIGIOUS HOLY, *PI*.

REMEDY *Anag. CURE*, NOSTRUM, PALLIATIVE.

REMOVE 1. ABSTRACT, TAKE AWAY/OFF. DISMISS. CHANGE, DEPARTURE, DISTANCE, DISTANT, REMOTE. DISH. DEGREE. PROMOTION (school); *CLASS*, FORM [*Bunter*]. 2. Take away letters indicated, e.g. **Remove the courtesan's curves in this joint** (5) = MI(s)TRE(ss).

REMOVED 1. APART. TAKEN AWAY. 2. Remove letter D from clue, e.g. **Dart removed skill** (3) = *ART. 3. Remove letters RE from clue, e.g. **Refuse removed igniter** (4) = **FUSE.

REMUS 1. Uncle ~ (book, Joel Chandler Harris; Brer *Fox*, Brer *Rabbit*, Brer Terrapin, Tar-baby). 2. Rom myth *twin* br of *Romulus*, s of *Mars* and *Rhea*. They were suckled by wolves, and Romulus later slew Remus.

RENT CLEAVE, RIP, TEAR; CLEFT, FAULT, FISSURE. LET; HIRE CHARGE, PAYMENT.

REP *MATERIAL*. REPERTORY. REPRESENTATIVE; CONGRESSMAN, MP. *CHAPMAN*, DRUMMER, SALESMAN, TRAVELLER. REPUBLICAN.

Rep Republican [donkey].

REPAIR *Anag.* MEND, OVERHAUL, PATCH, *SERVICE*. GO, HIE.

REPEAT 1. BIS, ENCORE. DO/SAY AGAIN, IMITATE, RECITE, REHEARSE, REPRODUCE. RECUR. BELCH, BURP. 2. Write word/letter again, e.g. **Flower is repeated** (4) = IS*IS.

REPEATER FIREARM, *WEAPON*. CLOCK, *WATCH*. DUPLICATE DIAL/SIGNAL; RELAY, RETRANSMITTER. ACTOR, RECITER, REPETITEUR, SOLILOQUIST (crypt).

REPEL 1. BEAT BACK, REPULSE, WARD OFF. DISPLEASE, BE DISTASTEFUL (**opp** = *attract*). 2. Word(s) read backwards, e.g. **Little Sarah is repellant to Eliot's weaver** (5) = SI*LAS (Marner).

REPORTER ACCOUNTANT, NARRATOR. ED, JOURNALIST. *BANGER*, BOMB, EXPLOSIVE, GUN, RIFLE (crypt).

REPRIMAND *CARPET*, DRESS DOWN, REPROVE, *ROCKET*, TELL OFF (**opp** = praise).

REPTILE Genus reptilia: CROCODILE, LIZARD, SNAKE, TORTOISE, TURTLE, **especially:** ALLIGATOR, CAYMAN, GECKO, IGUANA, MONITOR.

REPUBLICAN PRO-REPUBLIC. POLITICIAN [donkey]. SOCIAL.

RE-ROW REPECHAGE. RE-ARGUE.

RESERVE *BOOK*. POSTPONE, WITHHOLD. SERVE AGAIN [let; tennis]. COOLNESS, RETICENCE. **Pl** = REINFORCEMENTS; TERRITORIALS (mil).

RESOLVE *Anag.* ANALYSE, SOLVE, *SETTLE*; DISSIPATE, DISSOLVE. DECIDE, DETERMINE.

REST (s/l wrest). DREGS, LEES, REMAINS. HOLIDAY; BREAK, PAUSE. *BAR* (mus). BRIDGE, CUE-PROP, SPIDER (pool/snooker).

RESTRICTED CONFINED, LIMITED, NUMBERED. OFF-LIMITS. R (film *censorship*).

RESUME CARRY ON, CONTINUE. *SUMMARY*.

RETAIL NARRATE, RECOUNT, RELATE. SELL, TRADE.

RETIRED 1. *LEFT*, RECEDED, RETREATED, WITHDRAWN. PENSIONED. ABED, SLEEPING. 2. Word reads backwards, e.g. **Retired officer is sweet** (3) = JAM. 3. Word/letter is put into 'bed', e.g. **Retired woman is disbarred** (6) = B*ANN*ED.

RETIRING As *Retired* and: SHY, UNSOCIABLE, WITHDRAWN (**opp** = *pert*).

RETORT 1. CHEMICAL VESSEL, STILL; ALEMBIC (arch). REPARTEE, REPLY, RETALIATE. 2. Word reads backwards, e.g. **Mad retort stops the flow** = DAM.

RETRIBUTION 1. RECOMPENSE, REQUITAL, VENGEANCE. 2. **Goddess: Gk** = ATE, NEMESIS.

RETURN 1. COME/GO/SEND BACK (hence EMOC/OG/DNES, crypt); CONVEY/GIVE/PAY/PUT BACK (do). DIVIDEND, INTEREST, PAY, PROFIT. COME-AND-GO, DOUBLE JOURNEY. 2. Reads backwards, e.g. **Beat in return game** (4) = FLOG. 3. Turn letters RE = ER, e.g. **Go and return for a quick one** (4) = GO*ER.

REVEALS 1. BETRAYS, DISCLOSES, DIVULGES, MAKES KNOWN, *SHOWS*. 2. *Hidden word*.

REVERSE 1. DEFEAT, MISFORTUNE. CAPSIZE. VERSO, TAIL (coin); **opp** = obverse, head. CONTRARY. ANNUL, REVOKE. TRANSPOSE. 2. Reads backwards, e.g. **Gained some ground? Now reverse** (3) = WON.

REVISE *Anag.* AMEND, CORRECT, EDIT, IMPROVE. CHANGE, RECONSIDER. SECOND SIGHT (crypt).

REVOLUTIONARY *Anag.* AGITATOR, REBEL, RED; CHE. SPINNER, *TOP*, *WHEEL* (crypt).

REVOLVER COLT®, PISTOL, *WEAPON*, WEBLEY®. *TOP*, TURNSTILE, WHEEL, (WIND)MILL (all crypt).

REWRITE *Anag.* EDIT, REVISE, SUB-EDIT.

REX KING, R.

RHEA (s/l rear). 1. Gk *goddess* of FERTILITY; mar *Cronos*, m of
Hera, Hestia, *Poseidon*, Remus, *Romulus*, *Zeus*. Synonymous
with CYBELE, *DANAE*. **Rom** = *CERES*, *DIANA*, OPS. 2. A
satellite of the planet Saturn. 3. *BIRD* (*ostrich*).

RHINESTONE IMITATION *DIAMOND* [paste].

RHINO PACHYDERM, TOXODON (ex). *NOSE*. MONEY (sl).

RHYMING SLANG Form of cockney slang code, which involves
paired words, the second of which rhymes with the meaning (and
is often not spoken – this is indicated below by the use of
parentheses)

Slang	Meaning
Apples (and pears)	STAIRS
Ball of chalk	WALK
Bangers and mash	CASH
Barnet (Fair)	HAIR
Bees and (honey)	MONEY
Bird (lime)	TIME
Boat race	FACE
Boracic lint	SKINT
Bull and cow	ROW
Burnt cinder	WINDOW
Butcher's (hook)	LOOK
Cain and Abel	TABLE
Cherry (Ripe)	PIPE
Cobbler's (awls)	BALLS
Dicky (dirt)	SHIRT
Frog and toad	ROAD
Jam roll	DOLE
Lady Godiva	FIVER
Loaf (of bread)	HEAD
Mince (pie)s	EYES
Mutt and Jeff	DEAF
North and south	MOUTH
Pen and ink	STINK
Pig's ear	BEER
Plates (of meat)	FEET
Pompey (whore)	FOUR
Pot and pan	OLD MAN

Rosie (Lee)	TEA
Rub a dub (dub)	PUB
Sexton (Blake)	FAKE
Square (and round)	POUND
Tea leaf	THIEF
Titfer (tat)	HAT
Tod (Sloan)	OWN
Trouble (and strife)	WIFE
Whistle (and flute)	SUIT

Meaning	**Slang**
Balls	COBBLER'S (awls)
Beer	PIG'S EAR
Cash	BANGERS AND MASH
Deaf	MUTT AND JEFF
Dole	JAM ROLL
Eyes	MINCE (pie)S
Face	BOAT RACE
Fake	SEXTON (BLAKE)
Feet	PLATES (of meat)
Fiver	LADY GODIVA
Four	POMPEY (whore)
Hair	BARNET (fair)
Hat	TITFER (tat)
Head	LOAF (of bread)
Husband	POT AND PAN
Look	BUTCHER'S (hook)
Money	BEES AND (honey)
Mouth	NORTH AND SOUTH
Old Man	POT AND PAN
Own	TOD (Sloan)
Pipe	CHERRY RIPE
Pound	SQUARE (and round)
Pub	RUB A DUB (dub)
Road	FROG AND TOAD
Row	BULL AND COW
Shirt	DICKY (dirt)
Skint	BORACIC LINT
Stairs	APPLES (and pears)

Stink	PEN AND INK
Suit	WHISTLE (and flute)
Table	CAIN AND ABEL
Tea	ROSIE (Lee)
Thief	TEA LEAF
Time	BIRD (lime)
Walk	BALL OF CHALK
Wife	TROUBLE (and strife)
Window	BURNT CINDER

RHYTHM *BEAT*. SEQUENCE [scan verse for each *foot*].

RI RELIGIOUS INSTRUCTION. RHODE ISLAND. ROYAL INSTITUTION.

RIB BONE [*Eve*]. CHAFF, *TEASE*. RIVER (Eng).

RICH ABUNDANT, COSTLY, FATTY, SPLENDID, SUGARY. WEALTHY (**opp** = *broke*); VALUABLE [*Croesus*, *Midas*, Dives]. LAUGHABLE, LUDICROUS.

RIDER ABACK, BACKED (crypt), EQUESTRIAN, JOCKEY, *MOUNTED*. ADDITION, CODICIL, EXTRA, PS. *HAGGARD* (writer).

RIG *DRESS*, GEAR. PROVIDE. DODGE, FIX, MANIPULATE. *STAY*. BARK, BARQUE, BERMUDAN, BRIG, CUTTER, GAFF, KETCH, LATEEN, SCHOONER, SLOOP, SQUARE, YAWL.

RIGGING FIXING, MANIPULATION, TRICKERY. STAYS, WIRES: BACKSTAY, BRAIL, BUNTLINE, CLUELINE, FORESTAY, *GARNET*, *JUMPERS*, MARTNET, REEF, RUNNERS, SHROUD, TRIATIC.

RIGHT (s/l *rite*, write). R, RT, S; DEXTER, STARBOARD (**opp** = *left*, port, larboard, *sinister*). CORRECT (**opp** = *wrong*). UPTURN, LIEN. TORY. **Pl** = CHARTER.

~ **AWAY** 1. IMMEDIATELY, NOW. 2. Delete letter(s) R or RT e.g. **Smooth part right away** (3) = PA*T.

~ **ONE** *CASE*, CAUTION, WAG. R*ONE, R*I (crypt).

RING O (crypt). BUZZ, *CALL*, *DIAL*, PHONE, TOLL [STD]. ARENA, CIRCLE, CIRCUS. CARTEL, CLIQUE. *CASTLE*. ENGAGED SIGNAL (crypt). HOOP. [Wagner].

RINGED CIRCLED, MARKED. AFFIANCED, ENGAGED (crypt).

RINGER *BELL*; CAMPANOLOGIST. COPY, DOUBLE,
DUPLICATE. QUOIT. FIANCE (crypt).

RINGING 1. CALLING, PHONING. MARKING. TINNITUS.
2. Word round another, e.g. **Hot and bothered, Fred's ringing the
First Lady** (7) = F*EVE*RED.

RINGLEADER AGITATOR, INSTIGATOR. R (crypt).
DIALLING (crypt).

RINGMASTER CIRCUS MC. *BOXER*, CHAMPION, PRIZE
FIGHTER, PUGILIST (crypt). JEWELLER (crypt).

RITE (s/l *right*, write). CEREMONY, PROCEDURE, LORE.

RIVAL 1. COMPETITOR, COMPETE, VIE. COMPARABLE.
2. Three in *song*.

RIVER R; BECK, *BOURN*, BROOK, BURN, CREEK,
ESTUARY, RILL, RIVULET, STREAM, TRIBUTARY,
WATERCOURSE; **crypt:** *BANKER*, CURRENCY, *FLOWER*,
RUNNER; **myth:** *ACHERON*, COCYTUS, LETHE,
PYRIPHLEGETHON, *STYX*. [Cebren (god), *Cerberus*,
Charon]. **Celebrated:**

1-letter	DAL (Swe)
E (Sc)	DEE (Ire, Sc, Wal)
	DJA (Cam)
2-letters	*DON* (Eng, Sc, USSR)
AA (Fr, USSR)	DUA (Z)
II (Fin)	ELY (Eng)
OB (USSR)	*EMS* (Ger)
PO (It)	ESK (Eng)
	EXE (Eng)
3-letters	FAL (Eng)
AAR (Sw)	ILI (USSR)
AHI (Ger)	JIU (Rum)
ALN (Eng)	KUR (Iran)
ALT (Eng)	LEA (Eng)
AXE (Eng)	LEK (NL)
AYR (Sc)	LIM (Y)
BUG (Pol, USSR)	MOY (Ire)
CAM (Eng) [Granta]	NAR (Eng)
CAN (Eng)	OBI (USSR)
CHU (USSR)	ORD (Aus)

OKA (USSR)
PIC (Can)
PUR (USSR)
RED (Can, US, Viet)
RIB (Eng)
ROE (Ire)
RYE (Eng)
SIR (USSR)
TAF (Wal)
TAW (Eng)
TAY (Sc)
TYE (Eng)
USK (Wal)
VAR (Fr)
VER (Eng)
WEY (Eng)
WYE (Eng)
YEO (Eng)

4-letters
AARE (Swi)
ADUR (Eng)
AGRA (Sp)
AGRI (It)
ALPH (Gk)
ALTA (N)
AMOO (USSR)
AMUR (USSR)
ARNO (It)
ARUN (Eng)
AUBE (Fr)
AUDE (Fr)
AVON (Eng, Sc)
BACK (Can)
BANN (Ire)
BRUE (Eng)
BURE (Eng)
BUSH (Ire)
CARY (Eng)

CHER (Fr)
CHEW (Eng)
CHIR (USSR)
COLN (Eng)
CREE (Sc)
DART (Eng)
DOON (Sc)
DOVE (Eng)
EARN (Sc)
EBRO (Sp)
EDEN (Eng, Sc)
ELBE (Ger)
ELWY (Wal)
ERNE (Ire)
EURE (Fr)
FINN (Ire)
GILA (US)
GLAN (Ger)
GLEN (Eng)
GREY (NZ)
HASE (Ger)
HULL (Eng)
IRIN (A)
ISIS (Thames, Eng)
ISLA (Sc)
JUBA (Som)
KAMA (USSR)
LEAF (Can)
LECH (Ger)
LENA (USSR)
LIMA (Port)
LUNE (Eng)
LYON (Sc)
MAAS (NL)
MAIN (Ger)
MEON (Eng)
MILK (US)
MOLE (Eng)
MOTH (NZ)

NENE (Eng)
NILE (Egy)
ODER (Pol)
OHIO (US)
OISE (Fr)
ORNE (Fr)
OUSE (Eng)
OXUS (USSR)
PEEL (Can)
PLYM (Eng)
QENA (Egy)
RENO (It)
ROCK (US)
RUHR (Ger)
SAAR (Ger)
SEAL (Can)
SPEY (Sc)
STYX (myth)
SUIR (Ire)
TARA (USSR, Y)
TAWE (Wal)
TEES (Eng)
TEST (Eng)
TOWY (Wal)
TYNE (Eng, Sc)
TYWI (Wal)
UGIE (Sc)
URAL (USSR)
VAAL (SA)
VIRE (Fr)
WAAG (Cz)
WAAL (NL)
WEAR (Eng)
WICK (Sc)
WOLF (US)
WYRE (Eng)
YALN (Ch)
YARE (Eng)
YORK (US)

YSER (Belg)
ZORN (Fr)

5-letters
ADIGE (It)
ADOUR (Fr)
AERON (Wal)
AGANO (Jap)
AISNE (Fr)
ALDAN (USSR)
ANNAN (Sc)
AVOCA (Ire)
BOYNE (Ire)
BRORA (Sc)
BRIDE (Ire)
CAIRN (Sc)
CAMEL (Eng)
CEDAR (US)
CLARE (Ire)
CLWYD (Wal)
CLYDE (Sc)
COLNE (Eng)
CONGO (Zaire)
CONWY (Wal)
DEBEN (Eng)
DERRY (Ire)
DOURO (Port)
DOVEY (Wal)
DVINA (USSR)
ELLEN (Eng)
FLEET (Eng, Sc)
FLINT (US)
FORTH (Sc)
FOWEY (Eng)
FOYLE (Ire)
FROME (Eng)
GABON (Gab)
GARRY (Sc)
GRAND (Can)

GREEN (US)
HONDO (Mex)
INDRE (Fr)
INDUS (Pak)
ISERE (Fr)
ISHIM (USSR)
JUMNA (Ind)
KINGS (Ire)
LETHE (myth)
LIPPE (Ger)
LOIRE (Fr)
LOTTA (USSR)
MARNE (Fr)
MEUSE (Belg)
MIAMI (US)
MOSEL (Ger)
NAIRN (Sc)
NEATH (Wal)
NEGRO (Arg, Braz)
NIGER (Nig)
PAYNE (Can)
PEACE (Can)
PEARL (US)
PELLY (Can)
PIAVE (It)
PLATE (Braz)
PRUTH (Rum)
PURUS (Braz)
RHINE (Ger)
RHONE (Fr)
ROPER (Aus)
SARRE (Fr)
SEINE (Fr)
SIONT (Wal)
SLAVE (Can)
SNAKE (US)
SNOWY (Aus)
SOMME (Fr)
SPREE (Ger)

STOUR (Eng)
SWALE (Eng)
TAGUS (Port)
TAMAR (Eng)
TARIM (Ch)
TEIFI (Wal)
TEIGN (Eng)
THAME (Eng)
TIBER (It)
TRENT (Eng)
TWEED (Eng)
VITIM (USSR)
VOLGA (USSR)
WESER (Ger)
WHALE (Can)
WHION (Wal)
WHITE (US)
XINGU (Braz)
YANDA (Aus)
YARTY (Eng)
YONNE (Fr)
YTHAN (Sc)
YUKON (Can, US)
ZAIRE (Cong)

6-letters
ALBANY (Can)
AMAZON (Braz)
ANGARA (USSR)
ARAGON (Sp)
BARROW (Ire)
BOURNE (Eng)
BUCHAN (Sc)
CALDER (Eng)
CARRON (Sc)
CONWAY (Wal)
COQUET (Eng)
DANUBE (Aus)
ESCAUT (Belg, Fr)

FRASER (Can)
GAMBIA (Gam)
GANGES (Ind)
GRANDE (Mex)
GRANTA (Cam, Eng)
HUDSON (US)
HUELVA (Sp)
HUMBER (Eng)
HWAN-HO (Ch)
IRTYSH (USSR)
ITCHEN (Eng)
JORDAN (Jor)
KENNET (Eng)
KOLYMA (USSR)
LIDDEL (Sc)
LIFFEY (Ire)
MEDINA (Eng)
MEDWAY (Eng)
MEKONG (Viet)
MERSEY (Eng)
MOHAWK (US)
MOISIE (Can)
MOSKVA (USSR)
MURRAY (Aus)
NECKAR (Ger)
NEISSE (Ger, Pol)
NELSON (Can)
NOATAK (US)
ORANGE (SA)
OTTAWA (Can)
PARANA (Arg)
PARROT (Eng)
PRIPET (USSR)
QUOILE (Ire)
RIBBLE (Eng)
ROTHER (Eng)
RUPERT (Can)
SABINE (US)
SALMON (US)

SCHELD (Belg, Fr)
SEIONT (Wal)
SEVERN (Can, Eng)
TANANA (US)
TEVIOT (Sc)
THAMES (Eng) [Isis]
THURSO (Sc)
TIGRIS (Iraq)
TUGELA (SA)
TUMMEL (Sc)
TURKEY (US)
VIENNE (Fr)
VILYNY (USSR)
WABASH (US)
WEAVER (Eng)
WENSUM (Eng)
YAMUNA (Ind)
YARROW (Sc)
YELLOW (Ch)

7-letters
ACHERON (myth)
ALABAMA (US)
ANALONG (Ire)
BIG HORN (US)
CLEDDAU (Wal)
COCYTUS (myth)
DARLING (Aus)
DERWENT (Aus, Eng)
DEVERON (Sc)
DNIEPER (USSR)
DOUGLAS (Eng)
DURANCE (Fr)
ETTRICK (Sc)
GARONNE (Fr)
GIRONDE (Fr)
HOANG-HO (Ch)
LIMPOPO (Moz)
LA PLATA (Braz)

MADEIRA (Braz)
MEANDER (Turk)
MOSELLE (Fr)
OCEANUS (myth)
ORINOCO (Venez)
OWENBOY (Ire)
RED DEER (Can)
ROANOKE (US)
SCHELDE (Belg, Fr)
SELENGA (Mong)
SHANNON (Ire)
SUNDAYS (SA)
SUNGARI (USSR)
TRINITY (US)
WELLAND (Eng)
YANGTSE (Ch)
YENISEI (USSR)
YSTWYTH (Wal)
ZAMBESI (Zam)

HAMILTON (Can)
ILLINOIS (US)
MISSOURI (US)
MITCHELL (Aus)
PARAGUAY (Arg)
SAVANNAH (US)
STINCHOR (Sc)
SUWANNEE (US)
TORRIDGE (Eng)
TUNGUSKA (USSR)
WANSBECK (Eng)

9+ letters
BLACKWATER (Ire)
BRAMAPUTRA (Pak)
EUPHRATES (Iraq)
HACKENSACK (US)
HELMSDALE (Sc)
INDIGIRKA (USSR)
IRRAWADDY (Bur)
MACKENZIE (Can)
MISSISSIPPI (US)
QU'APPELLE (Can)
RICHELIEU (Can)
RIO GRANDE (Mex)
ST LAWRENCE (Can)
TENNESSEE (US)
YANGTSEKIANG (Ch)

8-letters
AMU-DARYA (USSR)
COLORADO (US)
COLUMBIA (US)
DELAWARE (US)
EVENLODE (Eng)
FINDHORN (Sc)
FLINDERS (Aus)

RIVERSIDE *BANK*; ON EDGE.

RLY *RAILWAY*.

RM ROYAL MARINES; JOLLIES. [Irish ~, Major Yeates].

ROACH *CARP*, *FISH*. CONVEX PART OF SAIL. COCKROACH.

ROAD (s/l rowed). AVE, RD, MI, MIV, ST. DRAG, HIGHWAY, PIKE, STREET. FROG AND TOAD (*rh sl*).

ROBBER BANDOLERO, BURGLAR, CRACKSMAN, PILFERER, SHOPLIFTER, *STEALER*, SWAGMAN, THIEF, YEGG; TEA LEAF (*rh sl*); [*cat*]. **Gk god** = *Hermes*; **celebrated:**

AUTOLYCUS (Gk myth); *BARABBAS* (bibl); *CACUS* (Rom myth); DANE, WILLIAM (Silas Marner, Eliot); DIDDLER, JEREMY (Raising of the Wind, Kenny); DODGER, ARTFUL (Oliver Twist, *Dickens*); DOONES (Lorna Doone, Blackmore); FAGIN (Oliver Twist, *Dickens*); FILCH (Beggars Opera, Gay); KAMAL (East and West, Kipling); MEG MERRILIES (Guy Mannering, Scott); *PROCRUSTES* (Gk myth); *SCIRON* (Gk myth); SINIS (Gk myth); SIKES, BILL (Oliver Twist, *Dickens*); *TOM* (Piper's son); *WILD*, JONATHAN (~, Defoe, Fielding).

ROBERTSON WILLIAM I (crypt).

ROBIN *BIRD*, REDBREAST, RUDDOCK. CHRISTOPHER (*Milne*). GOODFELLOW, PUCK. *HOOD*, *OUTLAW*. Pl = BRISTOL CITY, CHARLTON ATHLETIC (*football* teams).

ROCHESTER **Episcopal sig** = ROFFEN. *CASTLE*. *MEDWAY TOWN*. Character in Jane Eyre [*Mason*] (Brontë).

ROCKERY GARDEN (ROCK/STONE). QUARRY (crypt). CRADLE, NURSERY (crypt).

ROCKET BAZOOKA, BANGER, CONGREVE, FIREWORK, FLYING BOMB, FLARE, *SPACECRAFT*, *WEAPON*. *CARPET*, *REPRIMAND*. RAILWAY ENGINE [Stevenson].

ROCK SINGER ELVIS. LORELEI, SIREN (crypt). NANNY, NURSEMAID [Lullaby] (crypt).

ROD SYMBOL; BAR, CANE, *POLE*, SWITCH, WAND. SHAFT. GUN, PISTOL, REVOLVER (sl). EYEPIECE, RETINA. *PERCH*, *MEASURE*. [Black ~, *Garter*].

ROFFEN *Episcopal sig* of *ROCHESTER*.

ROLLING STONE NOMAD, WANDERER [no moss; *Sisyphus*]. **Pl** = POP GROUP.

Rom *Roman*; (and see *Roman Place Names*).

ROMAN 1. LATIN. UPRIGHT TYPE. OF ROME (**noblest** ~ = Brutus). 2. Put into Latin, e.g. **He is Roman** = EST.

~ **COIN** AS, DENARIUS, SOLIDUS, TALENT.

~ **GOD** LAR (and see *god*).

~ **GODDESS** See *goddess*.

~ **PLACE NAME** The following are some of the better known names of Roman towns in Britain, with their modern equivalents.

4-letters
DEVA *Chester*

ISCA Caerleon
~ (Dumnuniorum) *Exeter*

5-letters
BANNA Bewcastle
DANUM Doncaster
ITIIS (Ins) St Michael's
   Mount
NIDUM Neath
RATAE Leicester
SARUM *Salisbury*
VENTA Caistor
~ (Belgarum) *Winchester*
~ (Silurium) Caerwent

6-letters
ABONAE Sea Mills
ALABUM Landovery
ALAUNA Learchild
ARBEIA South Shields
BREMIA Llanio
DUBRIS Dover
GLEVUM Gloucester
LINDUM *Lincoln*
MAGNIS Kenchester
OTHONA Bradwell
SPINIS Speen
VECTIS (Ins) *Isle of
   Wight*

7-letters
BINOVIA Binchester
BURRIUM Usk
CALLEVA Silchester
CAONIUM Rivenhall
CICUTIO Y-Glaer
CONDATE Northwich
CUNETIO Mildenhall
ISURIUM Aldborough
LEMANIS Lympne
MONAVA (INS) *Isle of
   Man*

SALINAE Droitwich

8-letters
AD PONTEM East Stoke
ANDERITA Pevensey
BLESTIUM Monmouth
CANOVIUM Caerhun
CARINIUM Cirencester
EBORACUM *York*
LINDINIS Ilchester
MAMUCIUM Manchester
RUTUPIAE Richborough
SEGENTUM Caernarvon
VERLUCIO Sandy Lane

9-letters
ARDOTALIA Melandra
LAGENTIUM Tadcaster
LONDINIUM *London*
MORIDUNUM Carmarthen
REGULBIUM Reculver
URICONIUM Wroxeter
VAGNIACAE Springhead
VONDOMORA Ebchester

10-letters
AQUAE SULIS Bath
BRANODUNUM Brancaster
CLAUSENTUM Southampton
DORNOVARIA Dorchester
DURNOVARIA Chesterton
DUROBRIVAE *Rochester*
DUROLIPONS Cambridge
DUROVERNUM *Canterbury*
GORBANNIUM Abergavenny
LACTODORUM Towcester
LUGUVALIUM Carlisle
MEDIOLANUM Whitchurch

NOVIOMAGUS *Chichester*
~ Crayford
VERULAMIUM *St Albans*
VIROCONIUM Wroxeter

11+ letters
CAESAROMAGUS
Chelmsford
CAMULODUNUM
Colchester
CATARACTONIUM
Catterick

DUROCOBRIVAE
Dunstable
DUROVIGUTUM
Godmanchester
LONGOVICIUM
Lanchester
MAGIOVINIUM
Dropshort
SERVIODUNUM Old
Sarum
VINDOCLADIA Badbury

~ **ROADS** The following are some of the better known Roman roads in Britain:

AKEMAN'S ST
ASHWELL ST
DERE ST
DEVIL'S CAUSEWAY
ERMINE ST
FOSSE WAY
ICKNIELD WAY

PEDDAR'S WAY
PILGRIM'S WAY (path)
PORTWAY
RIDGE WAY
RYKNILD ST
STANE ST
WATLING ST

~ **SOLDIER** See *SOLDIER*.
~ **TRIBES** See *TRIBES*.
ROME (s/l roam). 1. ETERNAL CITY, SPQR [*Aeneas, AUC,* Seven Hills, *Romulus* and *Remus*; A and C, Cor, Titus (*Shak*)]. 2. Implies Latin, e.g. **They go out in Rome** (6) = EXUENT.
ROMULUS Rom myth *twin* br of *Remus*, s of *Mars* and *Rhea,* suckled by wolves, founded *Rome*. Slew his br.
ROOK *BIRD, CROW. CHEAT, ROB. CHESSPIECE* (*CASTLE*).
ROOKERY HABITATION (penguins, *rooks*, seals). BURGLARY, *ROBBERY* (crypt).
ROSE (s/l roes, *rows*). *FLOWER, TREE*; [St Dorothy] 'RHODA'. ASCENDED, *MOUNTED*, SOARED; GOT UP (hence TOG, dn crypt). REBELLED. SPRINKLER. *WORLD-GIRDLER. WRITER.*

~ BOWL FLOWER VASE. *FOOTBALL* GROUND/COMPETITION (US college).

ROSETTA STONE Memorial inscription to *Ptolemy* V (205-181 B.C.) in hieroglyph, demotic (coptic) and Greek languages on a slab of black basalt, discovered in 1799 by a French officer in the Nile delta. It proved the key to the meaning of hieroglyphics.

ROSE WATER SCENTED WATER, COMPLIMENT [gentle handling]. *SHOWER*, SPRAY (crypt).

ROSIE LEE *TEA* (*rh sl*).

ROSINANTE NAG, *HORSE*, SCREW (Don *Quixote*).

ROT DECAY, PUTREFACTION. BOSH, NONSENSE, RUBBISH. BANTER, CHAFF, *TEASE*.

ROUGH (s/l *ruff*). *Anag.* CRUDE. SHAGGY, UNEVEN. BOISTEROUS, RIOTOUS, SEVERE, VIOLENT.

ROUND 1. O (crypt). DRINKS, TURN, TREAT. SANDWICH. CONTINUOUS, ENTIRE, UNBROKEN. CANDID, GENUINE. CIRCULAR, REVOLVING, ROTUND, SPHERICAL. BULLET, SHELL. GAME (golf). **Pl** = INSPECTION ROUTE, VISITS (med). 2. Word round another, e.g. **He's round at the sports eliminators** (5) = HE*AT*S. 3. Letter A before any synonym for 'round', e.g. A*BOUT, A*CIRCLE, A*DISC, A*RING, A*WHEEL, A*NIL, A*ZERO (crypt).

ROUNDABOUT 1. C, CA, CIRCUMLOCUTION. ROAD JUNCTION. CONVOLUTED. MERRYGOROUND (fairground). 2. Word round synonym for 'about', e.g. **The roundabout between two and four** (5) = TH*RE*E. 3. Word or letter plus synonym for 'round' placed about word or letter indicated, e.g. **When roundabout fifty, too** (4) = A*L*S*O.

ROUNDHEAD 1. PARLIAMENTARIAN (**opp** = Cavalier). SKINHEAD. R (crypt). 2. Place letter o before synonym for 'head', e.g. OHEAD, OPATE, ONUT. 3. Place letter o before any word or letter indicated, e.g. **At Roundhead fodder** (3) = O*AT.

ROUNDSMAN *DELIVERY MAN*: MILKMAN, PAPERBOY, POSTMAN. GOLFER (crypt).

ROUND TABLE BUSINESS ASSOCIATION, ROTARY CLUB. ORDER OF CHIVALRY (hist) [*Camelot*, *King Arthur*; **knights:** Bedivere (Tennyson), Bors (Tennyson), Calidore (Spenser), *Galahad* (Tennyson), Gawain (Tennyson), Geraint (Tennyson), *Lancelot* (Tennyson), Launfal (Lowell), Mordred (Tennyson),

Pelleas (Tennyson), Percivale (Tennyson), Tristram (Malory);
Ladies: Elaine (loved Sir *Lancelot*), Enid (wife of Geraint),
Ettarre (loved Gawain, loved by Pelleas), Guinevere (wife of
King Arthur, loved *Lancelot*), Iseult (Tristram), *Lady of the Lake*
(Vivien), Lady of Shalott (*weaver*), Morgan le Fey (*sorceress*)].

ROUSE (s/l rows). AWAKEN, INFLAME, PROVOKE,
STARTLE, STIR (UP), WAKEN. BUMPER, DRAUGHT;
DRINKING BOUT, REVEL, TOAST. HAUL. CURE FISH.

ROW (s/l roe). OAR, PULL, SCULL. ALIGNMENT,
DRESSING, FILE, LINE, RANGE, RANK, TERRACE,
TIER. BATTLE, DISAGREEMENT, FIGHT, WAR. DIN,
NOISE, *RACKET*, SHINDY.

ROWER OARSMAN, SCULLER, *STROKE*, WET-BOB.
ARGUER, FIGHTER, SCOLD, SHREW (all crypt). DRILL
SERGEANT (crypt).

ROWING SCULLING, STROKING; PADDLING.
ALTERCATION, ARGUING, DISAGREEING, FIGHTING.
ALIGNING, DRILLING, LINING-UP (crypt).

ROYAL R; MAJESTIC, REGAL. *COLOUR* (blue).
ANTELOPE. SAIL. MEASURE (paper). **Pl** = ROYAL
FAMILY. HORSEGUARDS, HOUSEHOLD CAVALRY.

~ **AIR FORCE** RAF. *AIRMEN*.

~ **AND ANCIENT** RA. *GOLF CLUB*.

~ **ARMOURED CORPS** RAC. TANKERS (crypt).

~ **ARTILLERY** RA. *GUNMEN*, GUNNERS.

~ **AUTOMOBILE CLUB** RAC. CARMEN.

~ **ENGINEER** RE. SAPPER. EMINENCE GRISE (crypt;
Richelieu).

~ **FAMILY** *HOUSE*, RULING LINE [court cards]; **celebrated:**

Country	Family
Austria	HABSBURG/HAPSBURG
Belgium	COBURG
China	HWAN, MANCHU, MING, TANG
Denmark	OLDENBURG
France	BOURBON, CAPET, VALOIS
Franks	CHARLEMAGNE
Germany	HOHENZOLLERN
Greece	SCHLESWIG-HOLSTEIN

Holy Roman Empire	HABSBURG/HAPSBURG, HOHENSTAUFEN
Hungary	HABSBURG/HAPSBURG
India	GUPTA
Ireland	DESMOND, MCCARTHY, O'BRIEN, O'CONNOR, O'NEILL
Italy	*SAVOY*
Monaco	GRIMALDI
Netherlands	*ORANGE*
Poland	JAGELLON
Portugal	BRAGANZA
Prussia	HOHENZOLLERN
Romania	HOHENZOLLERN
Russia	ROMANOFF
Scotland	STUART
Spain	BOURBON, HAPSBURG
Sweden	BERNADOTTE, VASA
UK	HANOVER, PLANTAGENET, STUART, TUDOR, WINDSOR
Wales	GLYNDWR, LLEWELLYN, MORTIMER

~ **SOCIETY** RS. THE *COURT*, PALACE ENTOURAGE (crypt).

RR RIGHT REVEREND, hence *BISHOP*.

RRR BASIC EDUCATION, THREE R'S.

RT RIGHT. RADIO TELEPHONE.

RUBBISH BOSH, *ROT. REFUSE.*

RUBY *GEM*, PRECIOUS STONE; BALAS, CORUNDUM; *anniversary* (40th). *COLOUR* (red).

RUDE COARSE, IMPOLITE, INSOLENT, OFFENSIVE, UNCIVILIZED. CRUDE, PRIMITIVE, SIMPLE. ABRUPT, SUDDEN, VIOLENT. HEARTY, VIGOROUS.

RUFF (s/l *rough*). FRILL, NECK-PIECE. *BIRD*, PIGEON, SANDPIPER (**female** = reeve). *FISH*. TRUMP (cards) hence *TRUMPERY* (crypt).

RUGBY FOOTBALL. RUGGER [**Grounds:** Cardiff Arms Park (Wal), Lansdowne Road (Ire), Murrayfield (Sc), Twickenham (Eng)]. [2 for conversion; 3 for try]. *PUBLIC SCHOOL.*

SERVANT (to Dr Caius, Merry Wives, *Shak*).

~ MAN FOOTBALLER. SCHOOLBOY. TOM BROWN, FLASHMAN. W.W. ELLIS. **Pl** = ALL-BLACKS, LIONS, SPRINGBOKS, WALLABIES.

RUIN *Anag*. 1. DOWNFALL. REMAINS, RESIDUE. HAVOC, IMPAIR, MAR, SPOIL. BANKRUPT, BREAK, WRECK. 2. Put RU in word before or after, e.g. **Did ruin Welsh priest** (5) = D*RU*ID.

RULER AMEER, AMIR, KING, MONARCH, SOVEREIGN, SULTAN; CHIEF (**opp** = *subject*). *MEASURE*, STRAIGHT-EDGE; LINER (crypt). *GORGON*.

RUM *DRINK*, LIQUOR, SPIRIT; NELSON'S BLOOD, TOT. DANGEROUS, DIFFICULT. *ODD*, QUEER, STRANGE. *ISLAND*.

Rum Romania, ~n.

RUN DOUBLE, LOPE, SCAMPER, SPEED, STREAK (**saying**). COURSE, FLOW. MANAGE, ORGANIZE. SINGLE (*cricket*). CAGE, PEN. SMUGGLE. *LADDER*. CRESTA. **Pl** = SCORE (cricket).

RUNNER *FLOWER*, RIVER, R (crypt). SMUGGLER. ATHLETE. BEAN.

~ UP *SECOND*, SILVER MEDALLIST. DRESSMAKER. NAEB (dn, crypt).

RUN UP APPROACH, INTRODUCTION. (DRESS) MAKE. NUR (dn, crypt).

RURAL DEAN RD. *CHURCHMAN*.

RUSH ADVANCE PRINT, CLIP (film). MARSH PLANT, REED, STRAW. ASSAULT, DASH, DRAG, FORCE, IMPEL, SWARM. OVERCHARGE. FALL, FLOW, HURRY. **Pl** = see *song*.

Russ Russia, ~n (as opposed to USSR).

RUSSIAN RED. IVAN, SERGE.

RUSTLER CATTLE-THIEF, HORSE-THIEF; STEERSMAN (crypt). FORAGER. *SILK*, TAFFETA (crypt).

RUTH 1. COMPASSION, PITY. 'A FRIEND'. BABE (*baseball*). *G & S*. 2. Moabite who mar (1) Mahlon (2) Boaz [Naomi (Mara) mother-in-law. *Tears* amid the alien corn (Keats)].

RV REVISED VERSION, BIBLE. RENDEZ-VOUS, MEETING PLACE, TRYST.

RYE *DRINK*, WHISKY. CORN. *GRASS*. CINQUE PORT.
RIVER (Eng).

S *SAINT*. SAN, SANTA. SATURDAY. *SECOND*.
SINGULAR. SMALL. SOCIETY. SOLIDUS, SHILLING.
SON. *SOUTH*. ST. STARBOARD. SULPHUR (*chem*).
SUNDAY. SWEDEN (*car plate*). BRIDGE PLAYER.
DOLLAR.
SA SEX APPEAL; *CHARM*, IT. SOUTH AFRICA.
SABLE BLACK (*herald*). DREAD, DUSKY, GLOOMY.
MARTEN. PAINTBRUSH.
SABRE CUTLASS, SWORD, *WEAPON*. *AIRCRAFT*.
SACK *DISCHARGE*. PILLAGE, PLUNDER. *BAG*. *DRESS*.
FABRIC, *MATERIAL*. *MEASURE* (wool). SHERRY, *WINE*.
SADDLE *MOUNT*, RIDE. BURDEN. *COL*.
SADLY *Anag*. REGRETFULLY, RUEFULLY,
SORROWFULLY.
SAGE DISCREET, JUDICIOUS, WISE; MAGUS, SAVANT,
WISEACRE, WISEMAN [Nestor (*Argonaut*), Solomon, Solon].
HERB. *CHEESE*.
SAID 1. RECITED, SPOKEN, UTTERED; ORAL. PORT
(Egy). 2. *Sounds like* another word.
SAIL (s/l sale). CANVAS, PROPELLANT (naut), **types:**
BONNET, COURSE, DRABBLER, DRIVER, FLYING JIB,
FORESAIL, GENOA, JIB, GAFF, LATEEN, MAINSAIL,
MIZZEN, ROYAL, SKYSAIL, SPANKER, SPINNAKER,
SQUARESAIL, STAYSAIL, STUDDING SAIL,
TOPGALLANT, TOPSAIL, YANKEE.
COLLECTION/*ASSEMBLY* OF SHIPS, SHIP; JOURNEY,
NAVIGATE, VOYAGE (**opp** = *steam*). DORSAL FIN (fish).
BLADE (windmill [Don Quixote]). SOAR (aero).
SAILOR AB, CREW, DECKHAND, GOB (US), *HAND*, JACK,
OS, RATING, SALT, TAR; (**Union** = NUS), *REEFER* (crypt).
RN, USN. YACHTSMAN. **Celebrated:** CAPT AHAB (*Moby
Dick*), ANCIENT MARINER (Coleridge), TOM BOWLING
(Smollett), BILLY BUDD (Melville), CHUCKS (Marryat),
LONG TOM COFFIN (Fenimore Cooper), CAPT CUTTLE
(*Dickens*), DICK DEADEYE (HMS *Pinafore*, *G & S*),

MIDSHIPMAN EASY (Marryat), LEMUEL GULLIVER (Swift), RAPHAEL HYTHLODAY (More), DANIEL & HAM PEGGOTTY (*Dickens*), LT *PINKERTON* (Mme *Butterfly*, Puccini), SHIPMAN (*Chaucer*), SIN(D)BAD (Arabian Nights), DISCO TROOP (Kipling), SALVATION YEO (Kingsley); [*military leaders, world-girdlers, patron saint*].

SAINT S, ST. *ANGEL*. GOODMAN (crypt). [*patron* ~]. **Pl =** *Football* teams (UK & US).

ST ALBANS 1. **Episcopal sig** = ALBAN. 2. VERULAMIUM (*Rom*).

ST CATHERINE Virgin martyr of Alexandria (4th century). Tradition represents her as tied to a *wheel* [*firework*].

ST LEGER *CLASSIC* (horserace).

SALAMIS Site of a great sea *battle* near Athens in B.C. 480, in which 300 Gk ships under Themistocles defeated over five times their number of *Xerxes'* invading fleet.

SALARY EMOLUMENT, INCOME, PAY, *SCREW*, STIPEND, WAGE.

SALISBURY 1. **Episcopal sig** = SARUM. 2. HARARE (ex-*capital* of Rhodesia/Zimbabwe). SARUM (*Rom*).

SALLY BELL ROPE. COCONUT SHY. OUTBURST, WIT. SALVATION ARMY. SORTIE. STONE-FLY. WREN. SARAH. LUNN [tea-cake].

SALMON RIVER (US). *FISH* (genus salmonidae); **stages:** ALEVIN (fry), BAGGIT (after spawning), KELT (spent), SAMLET (young), SMOLT (1st sea migration), SPRAG (young), SPROD (2nd year); **types:** BARRAMUNDI (Aus, NZ), BLUE-BACK, BLUE-CAP, CAPLIN, FORKTAIL, GWINIAD (fresh water), KIPPER, PALLAN (Ire), PARR, QUINNAT (King ~), RED ~, SEWIN (Wal), SMELT, SOCKEYE, SPARLING; **male** = cock, **female** = hen, **offspring** = grilse, peal.

SALT SEASONING; BRINE, SODIUM CHLORIDE (NACL, *chem*) [*Lot*'s wife]. ARMS TALK. *ISLAND*. PUNGENCY, STING, WIT. *SAILOR*. ~ **meat** = *JUNK*.

SALUTE *BOW, GREET, HAIL, KISS*; ACCOST (Aloha, Ave, Hallo, Hi). HOMAGE; GUNFIRE.

SAM BROWNE (mil). SMALL (theat). MISSILE (*rocket*), *WEAPON*.

SAME DITTO, DO, IDEM. MONOTONOUS, UNIFORM, SIMILAR.

~ **PLACE** IB(ID).

SAMPHIRE *HERB*; CLIFFHANGER (crypt).

SAMSON STRONG MAN (bibl). MOORING POST (naut).

SANDHURST ACADEMY, RMA (mil).

SANDWICH PICNIC LUNCH, SNACK; SQUARE MEAL
(crypt); SARNIE (sl). LAYER CAKE. INSERT, SQUEEZE
IN. *CASTLE*. *CINQUE PORT*. *GOLF COURSE*.

SAN(TA) S. SPANISH SAINT. (FATHER CHRISTMAS).

SAPPER RE; ENGINEER. LEECH (crypt).

SAPPHIRE *GEM*, PRECIOUS STONE (blue), CORUNDUM;
anniversary (45th). *COLOUR* (blue).

SARAH *SAL(LY)*.

SARD *GEM*; SEMI-PRECIOUS STONE, CORNELIAN (orange).

SARDINE FISH, SARDELLE, YOUNG PILCHARD [herring].
GEM, SEMI-PRECIOUS STONE. **Pl** = *GAME* [tight-packed].

SARDONYX *GEM*, mix of *sard* and *onyx* (orange and white);
birthstone (August).

SARK CI, CHANNEL ISLAND. SHIRT. ROOFBOARDING.

SARUM SALISBURY (*Rom*). *Episcopal sig* of SALISBURY.

SAS SPECIAL AIR SERVICE. SCANDINAVIAN AIR
SERVICE (air line®).

SATAN *DEVIL*, IMP, LUCIFER, OLD NICK (lit = adversary).

SATELLITE 1. FOLLOWER, HANGER-ON, HENCHMAN.
DEPENDENT COUNTRY. 2. Moon or other body orbiting a
planet or star. 3. A *SPACECRAFT*.

SATIRIST CYNIC, LAMPOONIST [irony, ridicule, sarcasm];
celebrated: BUTLER (Eng), BYRON (Eng), DRYDEN (Eng),
HOGARTH (Eng), HORACE (Rom), JUVENAL (Rom), LA
BRUYERE (Fr), POPE (Eng), RABELAIS (Fr), *SWIFT* (Eng),
VOLTAIRE (Fr).

SATURDAY S, SA, SAT. Day of *Saturn*. ~s **child** = works hard
for its living. [Solomon *Grundy*].

SATURN 1. Rom *god* of agriculture, after whom Italy was called
Saturnia at one time; mar to Ops. **Gk** = CRONOS. [Saturday].
2. *PLANET*.

SATYR Gk myth woodland deities, half man half *goat*, with horned
head, pointed ears and a tail. Chief among them was *Pan*.
Representatives attended *Bacchus*, at the feasts staged by humans
to him. **Rom** = FAUN.

SAUCE (s/l *source*). CHEEK, IMPERTINENCE, IMPUDENCE.
RELISH, KETCHUP: HP®, PARSLEY, TOMATO,
WORCESTERSHIRE® etc. DRINK (US sl).
SAUCY *ARCH*, CHEEKY, IMPUDENT (**opp** = *retiring*, *shy*).
SEASONED (cook, crypt).
SAVE DELIVER, PRESERVE, PROTECT, RESCUE. BUT,
EXCEPT, UNLESS.
SAVOY CABBAGE. HOTEL. *ROYAL FAMILY* (It).
SAW NOTICED, SPOTTED. SERRATED/TOOTHED TOOL;
types: BAND ~, COPING ~, CROSS-CUT ~, CIRCULAR ~,
FRET ~, HACK ~, JIG ~, TENON ~; CUT, RIP. ADAGE,
MAXIM, PROVERB, *SAYING*.
Sax Saxon.
SAY EG, FOR INSTANCE. *Sounds like . . .*
SAYING ADAGE, APHORISM, BON MOT, BYWORD,
DEFINITION, MAXIM, MOTTO, PROVERB, QUOTATION,
SAW. **Examples:**

Divinity, God

God tempers the wind to the shorn lamb (Sentimental Journey,
Sterne).

There's a divinity that shapes our ends, rough hew them how
we will (Hamlet).

Man proposeth, God disposeth (Jacula Prudentum, Herbert).

Though the mills of God grind slowly, yet they grind exceeding
small (Retribution, Longfellow).

To err is human, to forgive divine (Essay on Criticism, Pope).

Whom the gods love, die young (Don Juan, Byron).

The year's at the Spring, the day's at the morn . . . God's in
His heaven, all's right with the world (Pippa Passes,
Browning).

Devil, evil, sinning

The Devil can cite Scriptures for his purpose (M of V).

Devil take the hindmost (Hudibras, Butler).

He must needs go that the Devil drives (All's Well).

He will give the Devil his due (H.iv).

The evil that men do lives after them; the good is oft interred with their bones (J. Caesar).

I am a man more sinned against than sinning (Lear).

The Devil makes work for idle hands (anon).

Life, living

All the world's a stage and all the men and women merely players (AYLI).

Variety's the spice of life that gives it all its flavour (The Task, Cowper).

One crowded hour of glorious life is worth an age without a name (Old Mortality, Scott).

A custom more honoured in the breach than in the observance (Hamlet).

Full many a flower is born to blush unseen, and waste its sweetness on the desert air (Elegy, Gray).

Do not look a gift horse in the mouth (Hudibras, Butler).

Hearth, home

Mid pleasures and palaces though we may roam, be it ever so humble there's no place like home (Home Sweet Home, Payne).

A man's house is his castle (Third Institute, Sir Edward Coke).

I am monarch of all I survey, my right there is none to dispute (Cowper).

Breathes there a man with soul so dead, who never to himself hath said, This is my own, my native land! (Lay of the Last Minstrel, Scott).

Death, dying

To live in hearts we leave behind is not to die (Hallowed Ground, Campbell).

Lives of great men all remind us we can make our lives sublime and, departing, leave behind us footsteps in the sands of time (A Psalm of Life, Longfellow).

All men think all men mortal but themselves (Night Thoughts, Young).

The most unkindest cut of all (J. Caesar).

Unwept, unhonoured and unsung (Lay of the Last Minstrel, Scott).

Women, men, marriage, beauty, love

Age cannot wither nor custom stale her infinite variety (A and C).

A thing of beauty is a joy for ever (Endymion, Keats).

I could not love thee dear so much, loved I not honour more (To Lucasta, Lovelace).

None but the brave deserves the fair (Alexander's Feast, Dryden).

How happy I could be with either, were t'other dear charmer away (Beggar's Opera, Gay).

Distance lends enchantment to the view (Pleasures of Hope, Campbell).

And out of mind as soon as out of sight (Sonnet 56, Brooke).

Faint heart ne'er won fair lady (Love Laughs at Locksmiths, Colman).

The course of true love never did run smooth (MND).

Of one that lov'd, not wisely but too well (Othello).

'Tis better to have loved and lost, than never to have loved at all (In Memoriam, Tennyson).

Whom the gods love, die young (Don Juan, Byron).

Thus grief still treads upon the heels of pleasure; married in haste, we may repent at leisure (The Old Bachelor, Congreve).

Men must work and women must weep (The Three Fishes, Kingsley).

Oh woman! in our hour of ease, uncertain, coy, and hard to please, . . . when pain and anguish wring the brow, a ministering angel thou (Marmion, Scott).

Wisdom, virtue

Defer not till tomorrow to be wise; tomorrow's sun to thee may never rise (Letter to Cobham, Congreve).

Genius is an infinite capacity for taking pains (Frederick the Great, Carlyle).

Virtue is its own reward (Imitations of Horace, Prior).

To maken a vertue of necessite (Knight's Tale, Chaucer).

Goodness, kindness, happiness
So shines a good deed in a naughty world (M of V).

Cruel only to be kind (Hamlet).

Kind hearts are more than coronets, and simple faith than Norman blood (Lady Clara Vere de Vere, Tennyson).

Blow blow thou winter wind, thou are not so unkind as man's ingratitude (AYLI).

Damn with faint praise, assent with civil leer (Pope).

Find tongues in trees, books in running brooks, sermons in stones, and good in everything (AYLI).

Madness

That way madness lies, let me shun that (Lear).

Though this be madness, yet there's method in't (Hamlet).

Character

Brevity is the soul of wit (Hamlet).

Manners makyth man (William of Wykeham).

The quality of mercy is not strained; it droppeth as the gentle rain from Heaven upon the place beneath; it is twice bless'd: it blesseth him that gives and him that takes (M of V).

The wish was father, Harry, to that thought (AYLI).

Uneasy lies the head that wears the crown (H.iv).

The fault, dear Brutus, is not in our stars but in ourselves that we are underlings (J. Caesar).

Hope

Hope springs eternal in the human breast (Essay on Man, Pope).

All hope abandon – ye who enter here (Inferno, Dante).

The best laid schemes of mice and men gang aft agley (To a Mouse, Burns).

Sorrow

When sorrows come, they come not single spies, but in battalions (Hamlet).

Misery acquaints a man with strange bedfellows (Tempest).

She sat like Patience on a monument, smiling at grief (12th N).

Nought shall make us rue, if England to itself do rest but true (John).

Friendship

The friends thou hast and their adoption tried, grapple them to thy soul with hoops of steel (Hamlet).

What's in a name? That which we call a rose, by any other name would smell as sweet (R and J).

Greatness

The path of duty was the way to glory (The Duke of Wellington, Tennyson).

Beneath the rule of men entirely great, the pen is mightier than the sword (Richelieu, Lytton).

Some are born great, some achieve greatness, and some have greatness thrust upon them (12th N).

'Tis not in mortals to command success, but we'll more, Sempronius, we'll deserve it (Cato, Addison).

This royal throne of kings, this scepter'd isle, this earth of majesty (R.ii).

Uneasy lies the head that wears the crown (H.iv).

Philosophy, learning, study

Where ignorance is bliss, 'tis folly to be wise (To Eton College, Gray).

Beneath the rule of men entirely great, the pen is mightier than the sword (Richelieu, Lytton).

There are more things in heaven and earth, Horatio, than are dreamt of in your philosophy (Hamlet).

A little learning is a dangerous thing; drink deep or taste not the Pierian spring (Pope).

With just enough learning to misquote (Byron).

Know then thyself, presume not God to scan; the proper study of mankind is man (Essay on Man, Pope).

O wad some power the giftie gie us, to see oursels as others see us (To a Louse, Burns).

Truth, deception

To thine own self be true and it must follow, as the night the day, thou canst not then be false to any man (Hamlet).

'Tis strange – but true; for truth is always strange! Stranger than fiction (Don Juan, Byron).

Tell the truth and shame the Devil (H.iv).

Oh what a tangled web we weave when first we practise to deceive (Marmion, Scott).

Nought shall make us rue, if England to itself do rest but true (John).

Dreams, sleep

To sleep, perchance to dream; ay, there's the rub (Hamlet).

Sleep that knits up the ravelled sleave of care (Macbeth).

Our birth is but a sleep and a forgetting (Intimations of Immortality, Wordsworth).

We are such stuff as dreams are made on, and our little life is rounded with a sleep (Tempest).

Food and drink

Bread is the staff of life (Tale of a Tub, Swift).

Wouldst thou both eat thy cake and have it? (The Size, Herbert).

What's one man's poison, signor, is another's meat and drink (Love's Cure, Fletcher).

The cups that cheer but not inebriate (The Task, Cowper).

Cowardice, valour, danger

Cowards die many times before their deaths; the valiant taste of death but once (J. Caesar).

Thus conscience doth make cowards of us all (Hamlet).

Out of this nettle danger, we pluck this flower safety (H.iv).

The better part of valour is discretion (H.iv).

Peace hath her victories no less renowned than war (To the Lord General Cromwell, Milton).

Seeking the bubble reputation even in the cannon's mouth (AYLI).

He who fights and runs away, lives to fight another day (trad).

Music

Music hath charms to sooth the savage breast, to soften rocks, or bend a knotted oak (The Mourning Bride, Congreve).

If music be the food of love, play on, give me excess of it (12th N).

It is the little rift within the lute, that by and by will make the music mute (Merlin and Vivien, Tennyson).

Weather

One swallow doesn't make a summer (trad).

Red sky at night shepherd's delight; red sky at morning shepherd's warning (trad).

Ne'er cast a clout 'fore May is out (trad).

Rain before seven, fine before eleven (trad).

Long foretold, long last; short notice, soon past (trad).

First rise after low, foretells a stronger blow (trad).

Work

The devil makes work for idle hands (trad).

Many hands make light work (trad).

Too many cooks spoil the broth (trad).

More haste less speed (trad).

A stitch in time saves nine (trad).

If at first you don't succeed, try, try, try again (Hickson).

Necessity, the mother of invention (The Twin Rivals, Kingsley).

Men must work and women must weep (The Three Fishes, Farquhar).

Sc Scotland, ~ish.

SCALE 1. CLIMB, *MOUNT*. CLASSIFICATION, GRADUATION [vernier]. PITCH ARRANGEMENT (chromatic, diatonic, *major*, *minor*, pantatonic; A-G). FLAKE, HUSK, PLATE, POD, SCAB. INCRUSTATION, RUST. BALANCE, WEIGHING INSTRUMENT. 2. A *constellation* (Libra); sign of the *Zodiac* (7th).

SCAMPER *DASH*, *RUN*.

SCAN EXAMINE, LOOK AT, OVERLOOK. RESOLVE. READ RHYTHMICALLY (test verse by examining each metric *foot*). SCANDINAVIA.

SCENE (s/l *seen*). STAGE. ACTION, INCIDENT. LANDSCAPE, LOCATION, PAINTING, PLACE, VIEW, VISTA. LIFESTYLE. QUARREL, *ROW*.

SCENT (s/l *cent*, sent). AROMA, FRAGRANCE, ODOUR, PERFUME, SMELL. SPOOR, TRACK, TRAIL. CLUE, DETECT, SNIFF, SUSPECT.

SCH *SCHOOL*.

SCHOLAR BA, MA, L; SCHOOLBOY/GIRL. SECOND AGE (AYLI, *Shak*). LEARNED PERSON, CHELA (Ind), DISCIPLE, SAVANT [*patron saint*]; *Chaucer* character, ERASMUS.

SCHOOL DISCIPLINE, TAME, TEACH, TRAIN. DISCIPLES, FOLLOWERS, IMITATORS. *Assembly* of cardplayers, fish, porpoises, whales. ALMA MATER, CLASS, PLACE OF EDUCATION, SCH [*patron saint*]; **celebrated (fiction):** BROOKFIELD (Goodbye Mr Chips, James Hilton), DOTHEBOYS HALL (Nicholas Nickleby, *Dickens*), GRANGE

HILL (TV), GREYFRIARS (*Famous Five*, Frank Richards),
LOWWOOD (Jane Eyre, C. *Brontë*), ST TRINIANS (Ronald
Searle), SALEM HOUSE (David Copperfield, *Dickens*);
celebrated (public): see *Public Schools*.

SCHOOLMASTER BEAK, DOMINIE (Sc), *MASTER*,
TEACHER, TUTOR; SIR (**opp** = *miss*); **celebrated:** DR
ARNOLD (*Rugby*); DR BLIMBER (Dombey and Son,
Dickens); BROCKLEHURST (Jane Eyre, C. *Brontë*);
CHIPPING (Goodbye Mr Chips, James Hilton); CREAKLE
(David Copperfield, *Dickens*); GRADGRIND (Hard Times,
Dickens); HOLOFERNES (LLL); PARTRIDGE (Tom Jones,
Fielding); PINCH (C of Errors); QUELCH (*Greyfriars*,
Richards); SQUEERS (Nicholas Nickleby, *Dickens*); DR
STRONG (David Copperfield, *Dickens*).

SCHOONER *BOAT*, (SAILING) VESSEL, SHIP. GLASS
(sherry).

SCIRON Gk myth *robber* who kicked all strangers over a cliff; slain
by *Theseus*.

SCOFF GIBE, MOCK, TAUNT. EAT, *WOLF*; FOOD, GRUB,
MEAL (sl).

SCOLD NAG, RAIL, REBUKE, *UPBRAID*; SHREW,
SPITFIRE, TERMAGANT, VIRAGO [Kate (*Shak*).
Xanthippe].

SCORE BLAZE, *MARK*, *NICK*, SCRATCH, SLASH.
TWENTY, XX. COMPOSE, *MUSIC*, *NOTED*. (MAKE)
RUNS, POINTS, POT, TOTAL.

SCOREBOARD DISPLAY, TALLYWAG. MUSIC STAND
(crypt).

SCORPION 1. ARACHNID (*insect*). BALLISTA (hist).
GIBRALTARIAN (Sl). TANK (mil). *WHIP* (bibl).
2. *Constellation* (Scorpio); sign of the *Zodiac* (8th).

SCOT NATIVE OF SCOTLAND; IAN, JOCK, MAC, MC,
MON. *TAX*.

SCOTCH SCOTS, SCOTTISH; GAELIC; CELTIC. DRINK,
WHISKY. BRAKE, WEDGE (mech). MARK, *SCORE*,
WOUND. END, FRUSTRATE.

SCOTT (s/l *scot*). 1. Sir Giles Gilbert ~; archit. 2. Capt Robert
Falcon ~; *explorer*. 3. Sir Walter ~; *writer*; **books:** Bride of
Lammermoor, Guy Mannering, Ivanhoe, Kenilworth, *Lady of the*

Lake, Lay of the Last Minstrel, Marmion, Rob Roy, Rokeby,
Talisman, Two Drovers. 4. Gloria ~ (*Holmes* case).

SCOUT SERVANT, VALET (Oxford [C = gyp]). REJECT,
RIDICULE. ADVANCE PARTY, FORAGER, RANGER,
RECCE, RECONNOITRE, TRAIL-BLAZER, VANGUARD
(mil). FIGHTER (*aircraft*). CHAP, FELLOW. CADET,
BOY. PATROLMAN. BIRD.

SCRAMBLE *Anag*. e.g. **Scrambled eggs** = GEGS, SEGG etc.
CLAMBER, CRAWL. *MIX, STIR. FLY*, TAKE OFF (av sl).

SCRAP *BATTLE*, CONTEST, DISPUTE, FIGHT, QUARREL,
ROW, SCRIMMAGE. *REFUSE*, WASTE. DISCARD.
FRAGMENT, ODDMENT, PIECE, *RAG*, REMNANT.

SCRATCH NOTCH, *SCORE*. ITCH, SCRAPE. PAR,
UNHANDICAPPED. ERASE, WITHDRAW. *DEVIL*.

SCREEN DISPLAY, PROJECT (films, radar). *BLIND*,
PARTITION, REREDOS, SHADE. GRID, MESH, SIEVE.
CHECK, *TEST*. *CONCEAL*, HIDE, PROTECT.

SCREW *GAOLER*. PAY, *MONEY*, SALARY, WAGES.
COUPLING, FASTENING. PROPELLER [Archimedes].
REVOLVE. CONTORT, DISTORT. SQUEEZE. NAG,
POOR *HORSE* [Rosinante].

SCRIBE AMANUENSIS, ARCHIVIST, CLERK, COPYIST,
SCRIVENER, WRITER. MARKER, STYLE. JURIST,
THEOLOGIAN (bibl, Jew) [Pharisee]; **celebrated:** EZRA.

SCULL (s/l *skull*). OAR; *ROW. BIRD*, SKUA.

SCULLERY KITCHEN, WASHROOM. ROWING [Henley]
(crypt).

SCYLLA 1. Six-headed sea monster on a rock which, with
Charybdis, formed a hazard for seafarers in the Straits of
Messina. 2. A minor *PLANET*.

SE SELENIUM (*chem*). SOUTH EAST; HOME COUNTIES,
KENT (crypt).

SEA (s/l *see*). 1. MAIN, SALT WATER. *COLOUR* (blue). **The
Seven Seas** = ANTARCTIC, ARCTIC, INDIAN,
N. ATLANTIC, S. ATLANTIC, N. PACIFIC, S. PACIFIC
OCEANS. 2. **Gods: Gk** = NEREUS, *POSEIDON*; **Rom** =
NEPTUNE; **Nor** = AEGIR. **Goddess: Gk** = *AMPHITRITE*.
Celebrated seas:

3-letters
RED

4-letters
ARAL
AZOV
DEAD
JAVA
KARA
SULU

5-letters
BANDA
BLACK
CERAM
CORAL
CRETE
IRISH
JAPAN
NORTH
TIMOR
WHITE

6-letters
AEGEAN
BALTIC
BERING
CELTIC
FLORES
IONIAN
LAPTEV
TASMAN
WADDEN

7-letters
ANDAMAN
ARABIAN
ARAFURA
BARENTS
CASPIAN
CELEBES
GALILEE
MARMARA
MOLUCCA
OKHOTSK
SOLOMON

8-letters
ADRIATIC
AMUNDSEN
BEAUFORT
BISMARCK
HEBRIDES
LIGURIAN
SARGASSO (weed)

9+ letters
CARIBBEAN
EAST CHINA
EAST SIBERIAN
HUDSON BAY
MEDITERRANEAN
NORWEGIAN
SOUTH CHINA
TRANQUILLITY (moon)
TYRRHENIAN

SEAFOOD Any fish or shellfish eaten at a meal: CLAMS, COCKLES, CRABS, *FISH*, LOBSTER, MUSSELS, OYSTERS, PRAWNS, SHRIMPS, SQUID, WINKLES. MAIN COURSE, MAIN MEAL, HARD TACK (crypt).
SEASON AUTUMN, *FALL*, *SPRING*, *SUMMER*, WINTER.

(PROPER) TIME; PERIOD. ACCLIMATIZE. ADD
PIQUANCY (jests, wit; pepper, salt etc).

SEASONAL SUITABLE, TIMELY. CONDIMENTS,
MUSTARD, PEPPER, *SALT* (crypt).

SEAT BENCH, CHAIR, STOOL, THRONE; BOTTOM,
BUTTOCKS. POSTURE. SIT. ABIDING PLACE,
COUNTRY HOUSE, PLACE, *STATELY HOME*.

SEATED ASTRIDE; *CHAIRED*, *MOUNTED* (crypt). SAT
(UPON). LANDED GENTRY (crypt).

SEAWEED ALGA(E); **types:** AGAR, BROWN, CARRAGEEN,
CEYLON MOSS, CLADOPHORA RUPESTRIS,
CORALLINE, CORAL WEED, DEVIL'S APRON, GRASS
KELP, IRISH MOSS, (PURPLE) LAVER, OARWEED,
OREWEED, SARGASSO, SEA LETTUCE, SUGAR KELP,
THONG WEED, BLADDER-, CHANNELLED-, FLAT-,
KNOTTED-, SERRATED-WRACK.

SEC SECANT. SECOND(ARY). SECRETARY. *DRY* (Fr).

SECOND 1. S, SEC, TIME. B; AFTER FIRST, NEXT BEST,
NUMBER TWO, RUNNER UP, SECUNDUS; SILVER
MEDALLIST. TRANSFER. ATTENDANT. D (mus).
BACK, *SUPPORT*. FAULTY GOODS, SUB-STANDARD. 2.
Second letter of previous or following word, e.g. **Second rate** = A.

~ **CLASS** B. E (*Lloyds*). L (crypt).

~ **HAND** USED, PART-WORN. MATE (naut, crypt). A (crypt).

SECRET ARCANE, CLOSE, DARK, ESOTERIC, *HIDDEN*,
MYSTERY, PRIVATE, PRIVY, RETICENT. RESTRICTED,
CONFIDENTIAL.

~ **AGENT** BOND, *MOLE*, SPY.

SECURE CLOSE, FORTIFY, LATCH, LOCK. CONFIDENT;
IMPREGNABLE, RELIABLE, SAFE. GET, OBTAIN.

SEE (s/l *sea*). 1. DESCRY, DISCERN, ESPY, LO, LOOK,
NOTE, NOTICE, OBSERVE, REFLECT, *SPOT*, *WATCH*.
REFER TO, VIDE. BISHOPRIC, DIOCESE, hence
CHESTER, ELY etc [*episcopal sig*]. 2. Means that the answer is
then visible, i.e. if you . . . you will see . . ., e.g. **Miss Chan is
outside to see the President** (8) = CHA*IRMA*N.

SEED GRAIN, MILT, PIP, SEMEN. DESCENDANTS,
OFFSPRING, PROGENY. BEGINNING, CAUSE, GERM,
ORIGINS. SCREENED COMPETITOR (tennis).

SEEDSMAN *SOWER*. MILLER (crypt). HANDICAPPER, SCREENER (crypt, tennis).

SEEN (s/l *scene*). *NOTED*, NOTICED, REMARKED, *SPOTTED*.

SEER (s/l sear, sere). *PROPHET*. FISH (Ind). *MEASURE* (Ind). EYE, PUPIL; SPECTATOR, VIEWER (crypt). SEE RIGHT (crypt).

SEE RIGHT ENSURE FAIRNESS. OBSERVE CORRECTLY. *SEER* (crypt).

SEETHE BOIL, COOK, SIMMER. FESTER. NOTE THE . . . (crypt).

SELECT CHOICE, ELITE, PICK. CHOOSE, ELECT.

SELENE Gk *goddess* of the *Moon* (**Rom** = LUNA); d of Hyperion and sis of *Helios* (Sun) and Eos (Dawn). Loved Endymion. Identical with *ARTEMIS*.

SELF 1. ME, NUMBER ONE. INDIVIDUALITY, PERSON. *UNIFORM*, SAME, ALL ONE (colour). **Pl** = FLOWERS (natural coloured).

~ **HELP** DIY. SELF-SERVICE. BURGLARY, *ROBBERY*, SHOP-LIFTING (crypt).

SENSE APPRECIATION, JUDGEMENT, MEANING, PERCEPTION, SENTIMENT, WISDOM. Any of the five senses: HEARING, SIGHT, SMELL, TASTE, TOUCH (**sixth** = INTUITION). SANITY, WIT. DIRECTION. [~ and Sensibility, *Austen*].

SENTENCE CONSIGN. GAOL TERM, STRETCH, *TIME*, PUNISHMENT. GRAMMATICAL CONSTRUCTION, QUOTATION; *SAYING*.

SENTRY *GUARD*, LOOK-OUT, SENTINEL, *WATCH*, WATCH-KEEPER. BOXED, *BOXER*, BOXMAN, CAVEMAN (crypt).

SEPTEMBER 9th month, M, SEPT (seventh Rom month, before *Caesar* reorganized the calendar). **Birthstone** = chrysolite.

SEPTENTRIO Rom myth N *WIND* (**Gk** = BOREAS).

SERGEANT NCO, RSM, SGT. **Celebrated:** BUZFUZ (*Dickens*), KITE (Farquhar), ~ AT LAW (*Chaucer*), TROY (Hardy).

SERIES (s/l *Ceres*). *ORDER*, *ROW*, SEQUENCE, *SET*, SUCCESSION [seriatim].

SERPENT REPTILE, *SNAKE*; URAEUS (Egy), WYVERN

(*herald*) [caduceus]. *Constellation*. Midgard (*Loki*). DEVIL. FIREWORK. *INSTRUMENT* (mus).

SERVANT *AGENT*, FACTOR. BUTLER, *COOK*, *DOMESTIC*, *FOOTMAN*, *GARDENER*, GOVERNESS, *MAID*, *NANNY*, TWEENY, VALET. *CONSTABLE*, FACTOTUM, MAJOR DOMO, (MAN) FRIDAY. [*Six*]. **Celebrated:** ADAM (AYLI); ADMIRABLE CRICHTON (Barrie); *AMPHITRYON* (Molière); CALEB BALDERSTONE (Scott); *BUNTER* (Dorothy Sayers); CROMWELL (H.viii); HUMPHREY CLINKER (Smollett); JOHN GRUEBY (*Dickens*); GUMBO (Thackeray); HUDSON (TV); JEEVES (*Wodehouse*); JOSEPH (E. *Brontë*); LITTIMER (*Dickens*); BETTY MUXWORTHY (Blackmore); SANCHO PANZA (Cervantes); PAROLLES (All's Well); PASSE-PARTOUT (Jules Verne); CLARA PEGGOTTY (*Dickens*); PETO (H.iv); RUGBY (Merry Wives); SIMPLE (Merry Wives); SCAPIN (Molière); SPEED (2 G of V); CPL TRIM (Sterne); JOB TROTTER (*Dickens*); SAM WELLER (*Dickens*); SIMPLE (Merry Wives).

SERVICE *ACE*, FAULT (tennis). DEAL. ARMED FORCE: AIR FORCE, ARMY, NAVY, RAF, RN, USAF, USN. CHURCH MASS, MASS-MEETING, WORSHIP. MAINTAIN, OVERHAUL, REPAIR. *CHINA*, DISHES, PLATES. TREE.

SERVICEMAN *AIRMAN*, *SAILOR*, *SOLDIER* (**opp** = civilian, civvy). PARSON, PRIEST, VICAR, *CHURCHMAN* (crypt).

SESAME *HERB*, PLANT. PASS-WORD [open].

SET 1. FIRM, GO OFF, RIGID. GAME. CABAL, CLIQUE, COTERIE, ESTABLISHMENT, GROUP, *SERIES*. *DANCE*. BATCH, CLUTCH. EQUIPMENT. PLACE, PUT. BOX, RADIO, TELLY, TV. SCENE, STUDIO (film, theat).
2. *Habitation* of badgers. 3. Egy *god* of DARKNESS.

SETH ADAMSON (crypt).

SET OFF *Anag*. BEGIN, *START*. *Anag*. of 'set', e.g. STE, TSE. COMPLEMENT, ENHANCE, FOIL, *GRACE*. CARDED, MOUNTED,ORNAMENT.

SET ON ENCOURAGE, SICK, *URGE*.

SET OUT *Anag*. BEGIN, *START*. *Anag*. of 'set', e.g. STE, TSE, EST etc.

SETTLEMENT *AC*, *BILL*; PAYMENT. *CAMP*, COLONY,

OUTPOST, HOMESTEAD. SUBSIDENCE.

SETTLER COLONIST, HOMESTEADER, IMMIGRANT.
ARBITER, COMPOSER, JUDGE, PEACEMAKER. *COIN*,
CHECK (US), CHEQUE, PAYER (crypt).

SEVEN See *number*. HEPTAD. BLACK BALL (snooker). *Stars*
in the sky (song). *Swans* a-swimming (*Christmas* song)
[~ maids with ~ mops (*Alice*; Walrus)].

~ **AGES** (AYLI, *Shak*): (1) INFANT (mewling and puking); (2)
SCHOOLBOY (whining; snail); (3) LOVER (sighing like
furnace); (4) SOLDIER (bubble reputation); (5) JUSTICE (full
of wise saws); (6) PANTALOON (lean and slipper'd); (7)
SECOND CHILDISHNESS (oblivion; sans teeth, sans eyes, sans
taste, sans everything).

~ **DEADLY SINS** ANGER, AVARICE, ENVY, GLUTTONY,
LUST, PRIDE, SLOTH.

~ **HILLS** (of Rome): AVENTINE, CAELIAN, CAPITOLINE,
ESQUILINE, PALATINE, QUIRINAL, VIMINAL.

~ **SAGES** BIAS (of Priene), CHILON (of Sparta), CHOBULUS
(of Lindus), PERIANDER (of Corinth), PITTAEUS (of
Mitylene), SOLON (of Athens), THALES (of Miletus).

~ **SEAS** ANTARCTIC, ARCTIC, N and S ATLANTIC, INDIAN,
N and S PACIFIC *OCEANS*.

~ **SISTERS** HILLS, WHITE CLIFFS (of Dover).

~ **WONDERS** COLOSSUS (of Rhodes), HANGING GARDENS
(of Babylon), *MAUSOLEUM* (at Helicarnassus), PHAROS (at
Alexandria), STATUE OF *JUPITER* (at *Olympus*), PYRAMIDS
(of Egypt), TEMPLE OF DIANA (at Ephesus).

SEWER CONDUIT, DRAIN. MACHINE, *SINGER* (*invention*);
NEEDLER, SEAMSTRESS; MIMI (Puccini – crypt); **saying**.
FOOD TASTER, PLACE SETTER, TABLE LAYER (arch).

~ **COVER** MANHOLE LID. THIMBLE (crypt).

SEWN STITCHED. *NEEDLED* (crypt); **saying**. COMPASS
POINTS (crypt).

SEX APPEAL CHARM, IT, OOMPH, *SA*.

SEXY ATTRACTIVE, PROVOCATIVE, SENSUOUS. X (film
censorship).

Sh Shetlands.

SHADE *COLOUR*, HUE. BLIND, *SCREEN*; UMBRAGE.
GHOST.

SHAKESPEARE THE BARD, DRAMATIST, SWAN OF AVON
(1564-1616), mar Ann Hathaway (2d; Susanna, Judith; 1s:
Hamnet). Fake play = VORTIGERN (W.H. IRELAND).
Characters:

3-letters

NYM	(*coward*; H.v, Merry Wives)
SLY	(tinker; Taming)

4-letters

ADAM	(*servant*; AYLI)
BONA	(sis to Fr queen; H.vi)
CADE	(rebel; H.vi)
DULL	(*constable*; LLL)
FANG	(*sheriff's* officer; H.iv) [*Dickens*]
FORD	(mistress; Merry Wives)
HERO	(Much Ado)
IAGO	(villain; Othello)
JAMY	(Sc *soldier*; H.v)
JOHN	(*king*; ~)
KATE	(*shrew*; Taming ~)
LEAR	(*mad king*; ~)
LION	(play character; MND)
MOTH	(*fairy*; MND. page; LLL)
PAGE	(mistress; Merry Wives)
PETO	(servant; H.iv)
PUCK	(*sprite*; MND)
SNUG	(joiner; MND)
WALL	(play character; MND)
WART	(recruit; H.iv)

5-letters

ARIEL	(*sprite*; Tempest)
BAGOT	(toady; R.ii)
BATES	(soldier; H.v)
BELCH	(Sir Toby; 12th N)
BLUNT	(Sir Walter; H.iv)
BUSHY	(toady; R.ii)
CAIUS	(*doctor*; Merry Wives)
CASCA	(*conspirator*; J. Caesar)
CINNA	(*conspirator*; J. Caesar)

COURT	(*soldier*; H.v)
DIANA	(All's Well)
ELBOW	(*constable*; M for M)
FESTE	(*jester*; 12th N)
FLUTE	(*bellowsmender*; MND)
GOBBO	(*clown*; M of V)
GOWER	(Eng soldier; H.v. Chorus; Pericles)
GREEN	(toady; R.ii)
HELEN	(beauty; T and C)
HENRY	(king; H.iv, v, vi, viii)
JULIA	(beloved of Proteus; 2 G of V)
MARIA	(*maid*; 12th N)
MOPSA	(shepherdess; W Tale)
PARIS	(nobleman; R and J; T and C)
PERCY	(Hotspur; H.iv)
PINCH	(*schoolmaster*; C of Errors)
POINS	(*servant*; H.iv)
PRIAM	(king of Troy; T and C)
REGAN	(graceless d; Lear)
ROBIN	(page; Merry Wives)
ROMEO	(Montague; R and J)
RUGBY	(*servant*; Merry Wives)
SNARE	(sheriff's officer; H.iv)
SNOUT	(tinker; MND)
SPEED	(*servant*; 2 G of V)
TIMON	(nobleman; ~ of A)
VIOLA	(impersonates man; 12th N)

6-letters

AENEAS	(commander; T and C)
ANTONY	(triumvir; J. Caesar, A and C)
BANQUO	(general and *ghost*; Macb)
BIANCA	(Kate's sis; T of S; courtesan; Othello)
BOTTOM	(*weaver*; MND)
BRUTUS	(*conspirator*; J. Caesar)
CAESAR	(general, orator; J ~)
CIMBER	(*conspirator*; J. Caesar)
COBWEB	(*fairy*; MND)
DORCAS	(shepherdess; W Tale)

DROMIO	(*twin servants*; C of Errors)
DUNCAN	(king of Sc; Macb)
FEEBLE	(recruit; H.iv)
HAMLET	(prince of Denmark; ~)
HECTOR	(nobleman; T and C)
IMOGEN	(princess, Cymb)
JAQUES	(cynic; AYLI)
JULIET	(Capulet; R and J. minor lady; M for M)
LAUNCE	(clownish *servant*; 2 G of V)
MOULDY	(recruit; H.iv)
NESTOR	(commander; T and C)
OBERON	(king of *fairies*; MND)
OLIVIA	(countess; 12th N)
ORSINO	(nobleman; 12th N)
PISTOL	(*coward*; Merry Wives, H.iv, v)
POMPEY	(clownish *servant*; M for M)
PORTIA	(impersonates man, *lawyer*; M of V. w of Brutus; J. Caesar)
QUINCE	(*carpenter*; MND)
SCROOP	(archbishop; H.iv. Lord; H.v, R.ii)
SHADOW	(recruit; H.iv)
SILVIA	(beloved of Valentine; 2 G of V)
SIMPLE	(*servant*; Merry Wives)
THISBE	(play character; MND)
VERGES	(*constable*; Much Ado)
YORICK	(*jester* and skull; Hamlet)

7-letters

ANTONIO	(merchant; M of V. Also minor parts Much Ado, Temp, 12th N, 2 G of V)
CALIBAN	(*monster*; Temp)
CASSIUS	(*conspirator*; J. Caesar)
COSTARD	(*jester*; LLL)
GONERIL	(graceless d; Lear)
HORATIO	(friend of Hamlet; ~)
HOTSPUR	(Percy; H.iv)
JESSICA	(Shylock's d; M of V)
LAERTES	(s of Polonius; Hamlet)
LAVACHE	(*jester*; All's Well)

MACBETH	(general; ~)
MALCOLM	(s of Duncan; Macb)
MIRANDA	(d of Prospero; Temp)
MONTJOY	(Fr *herald*; H.v)
NERISSA	(*maid*; M of V)
OPHELIA	(d to Polonius; Hamlet)
ORLANDO	(Rosalind's lover; AYLI)
OTHELLO	(*Moor*; ~)
PERDITA	(princess; W Tale)
PROTEUS	(one of the 2 G of V)
PYRAMUS	(play character; MND)
QUICKLY	(landlady; Merry Wives; H.iv, v)
SHALLOW	(*justice*; Merry Wives, H.iv)
SHYLOCK	(Jew; M of V)
SILENCE	(*justice*; H.iv)
SLENDER	(*clerk* to justice; Merry Wives)
SYCORAX	(*witch*; Temp)
TITANIA	(queen of *fairies*; MND)
TROILUS	(s of Priam; T and C) [*Chaucer*]
ULYSSES	(commander; T and C)

8-letters

ACHILLES	(commander; T and C)
BARDOLPH	(*coward*; Merry Wives, H.iv, v)
BASSANIO	(Antonio's friend; M of V)
BULLCALF	(recruit; H.iv)
CLAUDIUS	(king of Denmark and *ghost*; Hamlet)
CORDELIA	(dutiful d; Lear)
CRESSIDA	(d of Calchas; T and C) [*Chaucer*]
CROMWELL	(*servant*; H.viii)
DOGBERRY	(*constable*; Much Ado)
FALSTAFF	(drunken knight; Merry Wives, H.iv)
FLUELLEN	(Wal soldier; H.v)
GERTRUDE	(queen of Denmark; Hamlet)
HERMIONE	(queen of Sicilia; W Tale)
MALVOLIO	(*constable*; 12th N)
MERCUTIO	(prattler; R and J)
OVERDONE	(mistress, a bawd; M for M)
PAROLLES	(*servant*; All's Well)

POLONIUS	(pontificator; Hamlet)
PROSPERO	(noble *magician*; Temp)
ROSALIND	(impersonates man; AYLI)
TRINCULO	(*fool*; Temp)
WILLIAMS	(soldier; H.v)

9-letters

AGAMEMNON	(general; T and C)
AUTOLYCUS	(rogue; W Tale)
CASSANDRA	(prophetess; T and C)
CLEOPATRA	(Queen of Egy; A and C)
DESDEMONA	(w of Othello; ~)
DONALBAIN	(s of Duncan; Macb)
FERDINAND	(nobleman; Temp; king, LLL)
FREDERICK	(nobleman; AYLI)
KATHARINA	(shrew; Taming)
MACMORRIS	(Ire soldier; H.v)
MOONSHINE	(play character; MND)
PETRUCHIO	(tames Kate; Taming)
SEBASTIAN	(nobleman; Temp; 12th N)
TEARSHEET	(Doll, a bawd; H.iv)

10+ letters

FORTINBRAS	(prince of Norway; Hamlet)
HOLOFERNES	(*schoolmaster*; LLL)
MUSTARDSEED	(*fairy*; MND)
PEASBLOSSOM	(*fairy*; MND)
STARVELING	(tailor; MND)
TOUCHSTONE	(*jester*; AYLI)

Shakespeare's Plays:

ALL'S WELL THAT ENDS WELL (*abbr*: All's Well.
France, Tuscany; Florentine war).
ANTONY AND CLEOPATRA (*abbr*: A and C. *Rome*,
Egypt. *Asp*; *Pompey*).
AS YOU LIKE IT (*abbr*: AYLI. Forest of Arden. *Adam*,
Rosalind).
THE COMEDY OF ERRORS (*abbr*: C of Errors. Ephesus.
Twins).

CORIOLANUS (*abbr*: Cor. *Rome*).

CYMBELINE (*abbr*: Cymb. Britain, Italy).

HAMLET, PRINCE OF DENMARK (*abbr*: *Hamlet*. Elsinore. *Madness*. Horatio, Ophelia, Polonius. **Saying**).

JULIUS CAESAR (*abbr*: *Caesar*. Rome, Sardis. *Conspirators*: Brutus, Cinna etc).

KING HENRY THE FOURTH (*abbr*: H.iv. England. Two parts. Plot. Harry Hotspur, Owen Glendower, Mistress *Quickly*, Falstaff, Bardolph, *Pistol*).

KING HENRY THE FIFTH (*abbr*: H.v. England, France, Agincourt. Nym, Bardolph, *Pistol*, Mistress *Quickly*).

KING HENRY THE SIXTH (*abbr*: H.vi. England, France. Three parts. *Joan* of Arc).

KING HENRY THE EIGHTH (*abbr*: H.viii. London, Westminster. Anne Bullen, Queen Katherine, Cardinal Wolsey).

KING JOHN (*abbr*: John. England, France. Bastard).

KING LEAR (*abbr*: *Lear*. Britain. *Madness*, ingratitude. Goneril, Regan, Cordelia).

THE LIFE AND DEATH OF KING RICHARD II (*abbr*: R.ii. England, Wales. Bolingbroke, John of Gaunt).

THE LIFE AND DEATH OF KING RICHARD III (*abbr*: R.iii. England. Hunchback. Princes in the Tower. Richmond. Horse).

LOVE'S LABOUR'S LOST (*abbr*: LLL. Navarre. Court life, letters).

MACBETH (*abbr*: Macb. Scotland. Murder, *prophecies*. Three *witches*, *ghost*; damned spot).

MEASURE FOR MEASURE (*abbr*: M for M. Vienna. *Prison*. *Elbow*).

THE MERCHANT OF VENICE (*abbr*: M of V. Belmont. Shylock, pound of flesh; Portia, male impersonator, pleads. *Saying*).

MERRY WIVES OF WINDSOR (*abbr*: Merry Wives. Falstaff, Bardolph, Nym, *Pistol*, Mistress *Quickly*).

A MIDSUMMER NIGHT'S DREAM (*abbr*: MND. Athens, woods. *Fairies*, Oberon, Titania; Cobweb, Moth etc; *Puck*; Snug, Bottom etc. Pyramus, Thisbe).

MUCH ADO ABOUT NOTHING (*abbr*: Much Ado.

Messina, Padua. Dogberry, Verges).
OTHELLO, THE *MOOR* OF VENICE (*abbr*: Othello.
Cyprus. Desdemona, Iago).
PERICLES, PRINCE OF TYRE (*abbr*: Per. Antioch,
Pentapolis).
ROMEO AND JULIET (*abbr*: R and J. Verona, Mantua.
Lovers. Capulet, Montague).
THE TAMING OF THE SHREW (*abbr*: Taming. Katharina,
Petruchio, Bianca).
THE TEMPEST (*abbr*: Tempest. Island. *Ariel*, Caliban,
Miranda, Prospero).
TIMON OF ATHENS (*abbr*: Timon. *Athens*).
TITUS ANDRONICUS (*abbr*: Titus. *Rome*).
TROILUS AND CRESSIDA (*abbr*: T and C. *Troy*. War.
Priam, *Hector*, *Helen*, *Agamemnon*, Menelaus, *Cassandra*).
TWELFTH NIGHT; or, WHAT YOU WILL (*abbr*: 12th N.
Illyria. Olivia, Viola, Malvolio, cross-garters, Sir Toby Belch,
Sir Andrew Ague-Cheek. **Saying**).
TWO GENTLEMEN OF VERONA (*abbr*: Two G of V.
Milan. Julia, male impersonator; Proteus).
THE WINTER'S TALE (*abbr*: W Tale. Sicilia, Bohemia.
Perdita; *shepherd*/ess).

SHANGHAI CARRY OFF, IMPRESS, PRESS. CITY (Ch).
SHAPE *FASHION*, *FORM*, FIGURE. MAKE, MOULD
  (*saying*). HQ, HEADQUARTERS (mil).
SHARK 1. ADVENTURER, SWINDLER. 2. *FISH*; **breeds:**
  ANGEL ~, BASKING ~, *BLUE* ~, GREAT WHITE ~,
  GREY *NURSE*, HAMMERHEAD, HORN ~, MAKO, MAN-
  EATING ~, *NURSE*, PENNY-DOG, PORT JACKSON ~,
  SELACHE, SPUR-DOG, SUNFISH, TOPE, *WHALE* ~,
  WHITE ~, WHITE POINTER, ZYGAENA [pilot fish, remoru,
  shagreen, squaloid].
SHARPSHOOTER 1. MARKSMAN, SNIPER. *GUN*. 2. Crooked
  dicer, hence CIDER, RICED etc (crypt).
SHAW (s/l shore, sure). 1. THICKET, WOOD (arch). 2. George
  Bernard ~, Irish dramatist. **Plays:** Androcles and the Lion, The
  Apple Cart, Buoyant Billions, Caesar and Cleopatra, Candida,
  Doctor's Dilemma, Heartbreak House, Pygmalion, Saint Joan.

3. Aircraftsman ~ = Lawrence of Arabia = Ross.

SHE FEMALE SUBJECT, WOMAN. [~ who must be obeyed, *Haggard*].

SHED CAST, DOFF(ED), DROP(PED), HIVE(D) OFF, PART(ED) WITH, SPILL(ED). DIFFUSE(D), DISPERSE(D). REDUCE(D). HUT, SHELTER, STORE. *FOOTBALL GROUND* (Chelsea). SHE WOULD (crypt).

SHEEP 1. BASHFUL/DOCILE PERSON, NONENTITY. *ISLAND*. 2. Horned ruminant, genus ovis. HOGGET, RAM, TEG, TUP, WETHER. *Constellation*; sign of Zodiac (9th). **Breeds:** AOUDAD (N Af), ARGALI (Asia), BHARAL (Ind), BLACKFACE, BORDER, CARACUL, CHEVIOT, COTSWOLD, DORSET, HAMPSHIRE DOWN, HERDWICK, HIGHLAND, JACOB'S, LEICESTER, MERINO, MUFFLON (wild), ROMNEY MARSH, ROUGH FELL, SCOTTISH BLACKFACE, SOAY, SOUTHDOWN, SUFFOLK, SWALEDALE, ST KILDA, URIAL (Asia), WELSH MOUNTAIN, WENSLEYDALE (**assembly** = flock, herd; **male** = ram; **female** = ewe, theave; **offspring** = lamb).

SHEER (s/l shear). PERPENDICULAR, PLUMB, VERTICAL. HOIST, JURY CRANE. RISE OF DECKLINE. YAW (naut). MERE, OUT AND OUT, SIMPLE, UNDILUTED. BREAK, SNAP. DEPART, PART COMPANY. RAKE, WOMANIZER (crypt).

SHEET *LAYER*, STRATUM. ROPE (naut). PANE. *MEASURE* (paper); F, FOLIO, PAGE. COVERING. **Pl** = BED LINEN, COVERS.

SHELF LIFE STAY-FRESH PERIOD, STORAGE TIME. SPINSTERHOOD (crypt).

SHELL BOMBARD, FIRE AT, LAY BARRAGE, STONK. CARTRIDGE, PROJECTILE, *WEAPON*. PETROL; OIL COMPANY®. SHE WILL (crypt). *FORM*, SEMBLANCE, SHOW. CARAPACE, CASE, CRUST, HUSK, *NUTCASE* [*kernel*], POD; [crustacean, *study*]; **types (marine):** ABALONE, BARNACLE, COCKLE, CONCH, COWRIE, GAPER, LAVER, LIMPET, MUSSEL, ORMER, *OYSTER*, PERIWINKLE, RAZOR, SCALLOP (pilgrim), SEA EAR, SEA SNAIL, SNAIL, SPIRAL LAVER, SPIROBIS, WAMPUM, WHELK, WINKLE.

SHEPHERD 1. FARMER, *TENDER*; MARSHAL, TEND [Astrophel (Spenser); Lycidas (Milton); W Tale (*Shak*)]. *CHURCHMAN*, MINISTER, PARSON, VICAR. 2. **Gk god** = PAN. 3. *Constellation* (Bootes).

SHIELD PROTECT, *SCREEN*. *ARMOUR*, BUCKLER; AEGIS (*Athene*). BADGE, ESCUTCHEON [coat of arms (*herald*)].

SHIFT *Anag*. MOVE. GANG, SPELL, TURN, WATCH. DODGE, TRICK. CONTRIVE. CHEMISE, SARK, SHIRT.

SHINER BLACK EYE. *FISH* (US). Nine bright, in *song*. **Pl** = *MONEY*.

SHIP SS; *BOAT*, SQUARE RIGGER. *AIRCRAFT* (US). STOW, TAKE ABOARD. DELIVER, SEND. EMBARK.

SHIPMAN *Chaucer's* sea captain. *SAILOR*.

SHIPWRECK FOUNDERING, SINKING, STRANDING. Any anag of SHIP.

SHIRT CHEMISE, JERSEY, SARK, SHIFT.

SHIVA Chief Ind *god*; mar to Devi.

SHOCKER ELECTRICITY (crypt). *JAR*, JERK, JOLT. MURDER MYSTERY, THRILLER.

SHOCKING DISGUSTING, HORRIFYING, IMPROPER, SENSATIONAL. ELECTRIC, LIVE. STOOKING.

SHOE (s/l *shoo*). *BOOT*, CLOG, FOOTWEAR, *MULE*, *PUMP*, SABOT, SLIPPER, TOPBOOT, *WELLINGTON*, ZORI (Jap) [cobbler, heel, last, snob, sole, tongue, upper, vamp]. HORSE ~. FERRULE, SOCKET. KEEL-BAND, MAST-STEP (naut). IRON STRAP; SPRIG, WHEEL DRAG. **Pl** = SHOON (arch).

SHOOT (s/l chute). DISCHARGE, EMIT, *FIRE*, LOOSE OFF. KILL. BUD, SUCKER. *FILM*, PHOTOGRAPH, TURN. SCORE. SPEAK!

SHOP BUY, PURCHASE. EMPORIUM, SALEROOM, SUPERMARKET. BUSINESS. *BETRAY*. WOOLWICH (mil sl).

SHOPPER PURCHASER. *BETRAYER*.

SHORN (s/l Sean). 1. CLIPPED, CUT; DISTRESSED (crypt). 2. Remove synonym for hair from word, e.g. *German shorn huntress* (3) = HUN(tress).

SHORT 1. BRIEF, CONCISE, CURTAILED, CUT, RUNT, SMALL (**opp** = *long*, tall). CURT. OWING, SHY. BREAK

INSULATION, UNEARTH (elect). CRUMBLING, FRIABLE (cook). **Pl** = BERMUDAS. **Pl** = *DRINKS*, SPIRITS. 2. Use any abbr, short or diminutive word, e.g. **Short ton** = T; **Short test** = EXAM; **Short measure** = TOT.

SHORT TIME HR, MIN, MO, SEC (crypt). QUICKLY.

SHOT CUT, DRIVE, GLANCE, PULL, PUTT (games). *FIRED*, LOOSED OFF, POTSHOT; KILLED. FILMED, SNAPPED; VIEW (photo). *GO*, TURN.

SHOUT BAWL, CALL, *CRY*, HAIL (**opp** = whisper). TREAT, TURN.

SHOW *CONDUCT*, GUIDE. DEMONSTRATE, PROVE. DISCLOSE, DISPLAY, EXHIBIT, MANIFEST, OFFER. EXHIBITION, PAGEANT, PANTO, *PLAY*, RODEO, SPECTACLE. PROJECT, SCREEN.

SHOWER DOWNPOUR, HAIL, PEPPER, PRECIPITATION, RAIN; DOUCHE [*Danae*]. DEMONSTRATOR, EXHIBITOR (crypt); *CONDUCTOR*, DRAGOMAN (crypt).

SHOWPLACE CINEMA, THEATRE (crypt). SIGHT, TOURIST SPOT.

SHREW INSECTIVORE (~ mouse). GRIMALKIN, SCOLD, SPITFIRE, TERMAGANT, VIRAGO; **celebrated:** EPICOENE (Ben Jonson), KATE (Taming, *Shak*), *XANTHIPPE* (Gk).

SHUN AVOID, ESCHEW, EVADE. CUT, SNUB. ATTENTION (mil).

SHUT *BAR*, CLOSE, FASTEN. GAG, *SILENCE*.

SHUTTLE BOBBIN, WEFT-CARRIER. BIRD (badminton). BRANCH LINE, COMMUTE, FEEDER SERVICE, TRAVEL TO AND FRO. *SPACECRAFT* (Challenger, Columbia).

SHY *ARCH*, CHARY, COY, NEBBISH, RETIRING, TIMID. REAR UP. ELUSIVE, UNEASY. *CAST*, FLING, *PELT*, THROW; AUNT SALLY. OWING, *SHORT*.

SI SYSTEME INTERNATIONALE, *INTERNATIONAL UNITS*. SILICON (*chem*). STAR OF INDIA (*order*). **Pl** = *SISTER*.

SIB AKIN, RELATED; *BROTHER, SISTER* (hence SIBLING, one of two or more children with the same parent or parents).

SIBYL FORTUNE TELLER, PROPHETESS, ORACULAR MOUTHPIECE. HAG, *WITCH*. Girl's name.

SIC (s/l *sick*). SO, THUS.

SICK (s/l *sic*). AEG(ROTAT), *ILL*, INDISPOSED [*patron saint*].

VOMIT. ENCOURAGE, SET ON, *URGE*.

SIDE 1. ELEVEN, FIFTEEN, II, XI, XV; PLAYERS, TEAM. BOASTING, SWANK. 2. Use either or both sides (i.e. end) of word indicated, e.g. **Both sides of some Kentish area** = S**E; **This side of the moon** = MO**. 3. **Pl** = any common pair of items which may be on either side, e.g. ON and OFF, L and R, E and W.

~ LINE ALTERNATIVE, SECOND STRING [moonlighting]. *BAY*, SIDING; TOUCH, TRAMLINES (games).

SIDING SWITCH-LINE (rly). PARTISANSHIP.

Sig Signature.

SIGN (s/l sine). CROSS, MARK; GUARANTEE, PASSWORD, TOKEN. OMEN, PORTENT. SYMPTOM. PLUS, MINUS, MULTIPLY etc. ARROW, BOARD, POSTER. UNDERWRITE. [*Zodiac*].

SIGNAL *SIGN*, INDICATION. *ARROW, DIRECTOR*. MORSE, SEMAPHORE [*aldis, flag code*]. FLARE, PYROTECHNIC, ROCKET. OUTSTANDING, REMARKABLE.

SILENCE NOISELESS, PEACE, QUIET. P, PP, SH; HUSH, MUM, WHIST [*oyster, Shak character*].

SILICON SI (*chem*).

SILK 1. KC, QC: BARRISTER, COUNSEL. GOWN; RACING COLOURS. *MATERIAL*: BOMBAZINE, TAFFETA, TULLE; RUSTLER (crypt). 2. *Anniversary* (12th).

SILVER AG (*chem*). *ARGENT* (*herald*). *Anniversary* (25th). *COINS* (nickel). *HORSE*. *PIRATE* (Treasure Island, *Stevenson*).

SIMPLE ARTLESS, BASIC, EASY, PLAIN, UNCOMPLICATED (**opp** = *involved*). ABSOLUTE. *MERE*. FOOLISH. HUMBLE, LOWLY. HERBAL REMEDY, HERB. SERVANT (*Shak*).

SIN 1. DO WRONG, ERR, SLIP, TRANSGRESS; **saying**. 2. **Seven deadly, or mortal, sins:** ANGER, AVARICE, ENVY, GLUTTONY, LUST, PRIDE, SLOTH.

SINGER DIVA, CROONER, TROUBADOUR, VOCALIST; ALTO, BARITONE, BASS, CONTRALTO, SOPRANO, TENOR; **celebrated:** BLONDEL (minstrel), CARUSO, GIGLI, *JENNY* LIND, LORELEI, MELBA, ORPHEUS (*Argonaut*), *SIREN* (myth). *BETRAYER* (sl). BURNER, TOASTER (crypt). *SEWER* (crypt).

SINGLE 1. *ACE*, I, ONE, UNIT. BACHELOR, SPINSTER, UNMARRIED, UNWED. **Pl** = game of tennis. 2. Remove indication of marriage (i.e. letters 'm' or 'wed') from clue, e.g. **Secure single wedlock** (4) = ***LOCK.

SINGULAR S. ODD, PECULIAR, STRANGE. INDIVIDUAL, UNIQUE; ONE ONLY (**opp** = plural).

SINIS Gk myth *robber* who tied his victims to twin bent fir trees, and split them on release. Slain by *Theseus*.

SINISTER EVIL, MALIGNANT, VILLAINOUS. *LEFT* (**opp** = *dexter*); BASTARDY (*herald*).

SIRE *FATHER*, GOVERNOR (arch), PA, POP. BEGET. LORD, MASTER, MAJESTY.

SIREN 1. HOOTER, SIGNAL, WARNING [*police*]. SINGER, TEMPTRESS. 2. Sea nymphs whose sweet singing lured sailors to shipwreck. *Ulysses* filled his sailors' ears with wax and had himself tied to the mast. *Orpheus* surpassed them in singing, so they threw themselves into the sea and were turned into rocks. A siren also lured sailors at Lorelei on the Rhine.

sis Sister.

SISTER *CHURCHWOMAN*, NUN. *SIB* (**opp** = *brother*). *NURSE*. **Pl** = CONVENT, NUNNERY; ~ OF MERCY. **Celebrated:** ANDREWS, BEVERLEY, NOLAN.

SISYPHUS Gk myth king of Corinth, condemned to atone for his sins in the Underworld, by rolling a boulder uphill, at the top of which it always rolled down again. [*Autolycus*].

SITTER EASY, FACILE. *MODEL*, POSER. BABYMINDER.

SITUATION APPOINTMENT, JOB, POSITION, *POST*. LOCATION. PASS.

SIX See *number*. HEXAD, SICE, VI. BOUNDARY, UNBOUNCING (*cricket*). *PINK BALL* (*snooker*). *Proud walkers* (*song*). *Geese* a-laying (*Christmas song*). [*Holmes* case; ~ honest serving men: What, Why, When, How, Where, Who (*Kipling*)].

~ **FOOTER** ANT, *INSECT* (crypt).

~ **NATIONS** Iroquois confederation of *American Indian* tribes, west of New York (1770).

SKATE ICE ~, ROLLER ~. *FISH*, *RAY*.

SKIN FELL, FLEECE, *HIDE*, PELT. PARE, PEEL, RIND,

CICATRIZE, FLAY. PLANKING, PLATING (naut).

SKINNER FURRIER. *PEELER*. [~'s Horse (mil)].

SKINT BROKE; BORACIC LINT (*rh sl*); **opp** = *flush*.

SKIPPER *BOSS*, CAPT. *BUTTERFLY. DEER. FISH*. ABSCONDER, RUNAWAY (crypt). *LAMB* (crypt). [bowls, curling].

SKIRON Gk myth NW *WIND* (**Rom** = CAURUS).

SKULK 1. LURK, SHIRK DUTY. 2. *Assembly* of foxes.

sl Slang.

s/l *Sounds like* (and see *Pronunciation*).

SLACK IDLE, LAZE, LAZY. LATITUDE, MARGIN, PLAY. COAL DUST. **Pl** = TROUSERS.

SLAVE DEPENDENT UNIT (mech/tech). SUBORDINATE ANT. DRUDGE; VICTIM; BONDSMAN, HUMAN CHATTEL, UNPAID SERVANT; **celebrated:** AESOP (when young; fables), ANDROCLES (lion, thorn), CALIBAN (Tempest, *Shak*), GUMBO (Virginians, Thackeray), MORGIANA (Arabian Nights), SPARTACUS (Rom), TOPSY, UNCLE TOM ('I 'spects I growed', Uncle Tom's Cabin, H.B. *Stowe*). HELOT (Gk). RIVER (Can).

SLEEPER KIPPER, NAPPER (sl) [*Morpheus*; **saying**]. EARRING. RAILBED.

SLEEPY DOZY, DROWSY, SOMNOLENT. INATTENTIVE, INDOLENT, UNOBSERVANT. *DWARF* (Snow White).

SLIGHT LITTLE, SLIM, *SMALL*. INSULT.

SLING BALLISTA, CATAPULT [David and Goliath (bibl)]. *DRINK*. HOIST, SUPPORT, SUSPEND. BANDAGE, BELT, STRAP.

SLIP *FALL*, SLIDE. ESCAPE. ERROR, FAULT, GAFFE, MISTAKE. QUAY, LANDING, RAMP, WAY (naut). PETTICOAT, UNDERSKIRT. DROP. *CRICKETER*, FIELDER.

SLIPPER INDOOR *SHOE*, *MULE*. BEAT, CHASTISE, LEATHER, WALE. BRAKE, SKID (mech). CLAY. EEL, SKATE, SKI, SLEDGE, TOBOGGAN (all crypt).

SLOPING *INCLINED*, LEANING, LISTING, SLANTING. ITALIC.

SLOTH IDLENESS, INDOLENCE, LAZINESS. TREE MAMMAL; **2-toed:** CHOLEOPUS, UNAU; **3-toed:** AI,

BRADYPUS. ~ BEAR (Ind); ~ MONKEY (loris). [And see *lemur*].

SMACK BLOW, SLAP. *BOAT*. HEROIN, *DRUG*. TASTE; LICK (lips).

SMALLHOLDING ACRE, ALLOTMENT. MINORITY SHARE. BRIEFCASE, ETUI, RETICULE (crypt).

SMALL VOLUME CC, VOL (crypt). QUIET (crypt), HENCE P.

SMART A LA MODE, CHIC, DAPPER, FASHIONABLE, IN, MODISH, SWELL, TONISH. HURT, STING. CLEVER, EFFICIENT [Alec]. QUICK.

SMASHED BROKEN, SHATTERED. *DRUNK* (sl).

SMEE (s/l It's me). *DUCK*. *PIRATE* (*Barrie*).

SMELT FISH, *SALMON*. EXTRACT, MELT (tech). SNIFFED; STANK.

SMITH METAL WORKER; FORGER (crypt); *IRONER* (crypt); **celebrated:** JAMES BURTON (Kingsley); JOE GARGERY (Great Expectations, *Dickens*); THE VILLAGE BLACKSMITH (Longfellow); FE. SMUDGER (*nickname*).

SMOKER COMPARTMENT (rly). CIGARETTE, CIGAR, PIPE (crypt). CHIMNEY, FIREPLACE, FLUE, FUNNEL, LUM, STACK (all crypt).

SMUGGLE AVOID DUTY, RUN; CONCEAL, *HIDE*, STASH [contraband, Customs].

SN *TIN* (*chem*).

SNAFFLE *STEAL*. *BIT*, *HARNESS*.

SNAKE 1. SWAY, WIGGLE. EMF (European Monetary Fund). RIVER (US). 2. Limbless reptile, ASP; **breeds:** *ADDER*, ANACONDA, BOA, BOLOBI, COBRA, CORAL, CRIBO, DABOIA, *GRASS*, JIBOYA, KING, KRAIT, *MAMBA*, MOCCASIN, PYTHON, RATTLER, TAIPAN (Aus), VIPER. **Celebrated:** KAA (Kipling), A and C (*Shak*). 3. *Constellation* (Serpens).

SNAP *BREAK*. *CARD* GAME. PHOTO, PICTURE. QUICK, SPUR OF THE MOMENT.

SNEAK *BETRAY*. *CREEP*.

SNEEZY *DWARF* (Snow White).

SNIPE AMBUSH, ATTACK [*sharpshooter*]. GAMEBIRD; **assembly** = wisp.

SNOOKER POOL [*black, blue, brown, green, pink, red, yellow*

balls]; BLOCK, OBSTRUCT. DEFEAT, THWART.
GESTICULATOR (crypt).

SNOW ICE CRYSTALS. COCAINE, *DRUG. BOAT.*
SILVER/NICKEL *COINS.*

SNUB CUT, *SHUN.* PULL, TUG (naut).

SO SOUTH. STANDING ORDER. STATIONERY OFFICE.
ERGO, SIC, THUS; AS. NOTE (mus; also SOH). KING
(bibl). **Pl** = MAYDAY.

SOCIETY S. ASSOCIATION, *CLUB*, ORGANIZATION.

SOCRATES Gk philosopher, mar *Xanthippe* in self-penance.
Condemned to death, he chose to drink hemlock in front of his
friends.

SODIUM NA (*chem*).

SOFT P, PP, SH; HUSH, QUIET; DULCET. EASY, GIVING
(**opp** = *hard*).

SOILED DIRTY, UNWASHED. EARTHY; BEDDED, LAID
OUT, PLANTED (crypt).

SOL Rom *god* of the SUN; also PHOEBUS (**Gk** = APOLLO,
HELIOS).

SOLDIER 1. Any rank in the Army, usually abbreviated, e.g.
BRIG, CAPT, *COL*, CPL, *GEN*, LT, MAJ, RSM, SGT. 2.
POILU (Fr); HOPLITE (Gk); BERSERKER (ON); KERNE
(Ire); CENTURION, LEGIONARY, PRIMUS PILUS (Rom);
LOBSTER (arch), PBI, PONGO, REDCOAT (arch),
SWADDY, TOMMY ATKINS (UK); DOUGHBOY, GI, PFC
(US). **Celebrated:** ALEXANDER (the Great), BEN BATTLE
(Faithless Nelly Gray, Hood), *CLUBS* (*Alice*), FOURTH AGE
(The *Seven Ages* of Man, *Shak*), MONTY (Lord Montgomery),
OLD BILL (Bruce Bairnsfather), and, all from H.v (*Shak*):
BARDOLPH, BATES, COURT, FLUELLEN (Wal), GOWER
(Eng), JAMY (Sc), MACMORRIS (Ire), NYM, PISTOL and
WILLIAMS; [*military leaders*]. **Pl** = ARMY, INFANTRY,
MEN, TROOPS, ~s of the Queen. **Gk** = *PHALANX*, **Rom** =
LEGIONARY (100) CENTURY, MANIPLE (6) COHORT
[eagle, vexillum] (10) LEGION (commanded by a Legatus);
Irregulars = AUXILIA (Rom); FENCIBLES, HOME GUARD,
LDV, MILITIA, TA, TERRIERS, VIGILANTES.

SOLE EXCLUSIVE, ONLY. UNMARRIED (leg). *FISH*, FLAT-
FISH. BASE, BOTTOM, FOUNDATION; SHOE-TREAD.

SOLICITOR BEGGAR, IMPORTUNER, TOUT. LAWYER [Sampson and Sally Brass, *Dickens*]. See *law*.

SOLIDARITY COMMUNITY INTEREST, INTERDEPENDENCE. *UNION* (Pol).

SOLIDUS S. *COIN* (Rom) [£ s d]. OBLIQUE STROKE, VIRGULE.

SOLUTION ANSWER, *KEY*, RESOLUTION, SOLVING, DISSOLUTION, SEPARATION.

SOLVE ANSWER, PUZZLE OUT. DISSOLVE, LOOSEN, UNTIE.

Som Somalia.

SOME (s/l *sum*). 1. A FEW, APPROXIMATELY. A QUANTITY, AT LEAST. WONDERFUL. 2. Hidden word, as *part* (2). 3. Part of word following, e.g. **Some money for my Scots friend** (3) = MON**.

SON (s/l *sun*). 1. S; BOY, LAD. 2. Used after a name to indicate 'the son of', e.g. **Adamson** = CAIN or ABEL or SETH [*Ap*].

SONG 1. AIR, ARIA, *CATCH*, CHANSON, DITTY, *GLEE*, *LAY*, *LIED*, SHANTY, TUNE. CHEAP. 2. **Gk goddess** = *TERPSICHORE*. 3. **Celebrated**: Green grow the rushes-oh:

    (1) All *alone* and evermore shall be so;
    (2) Lilywhite *boys*;
    (3) *Rivals*;
    (4) *Gospel* makers;
    (5) *Symbols* at your *door*;
    (6) Proud *walkers*;
    (7) *Stars* in the sky;
    (8) Bold *rangers*;
    (9) Bright *shiners*;
    (10) *Commandments*;
    (11) Who went to *Heaven*;
    (12) *Apostles*.

    Twelve days of *Christmas*:
    (1) *Partridge* in a pear-tree;
    (2) Turtle *doves*;
    (3) French *hens*;
    (4) Calling *birds*;

(5) Golden *rings*;
(6) *Geese* a-laying;
(7) *Swans* a-swimming;
(8) *Maids* a-milking;
(9) *Drummers* drumming;
(10) *Pipers* piping;
(11) Ladies *dancing*;
(12) *Lords* a-leaping.

SONGSTER *BIRD*. CROONER, SINGER; POET; COMPOSER, LYRICIST.

SOON 1. *ANON*, PRESENTLY, SHORTLY. WILLINGLY. ETC (crypt). 2. Add 'so' to word, e.g. **Lace and so on brings comfort** (6) or **Lace soon brings comfort** (6) = SO*LACE.

SORCERER ENCHANTER, ~RESS, *WITCH*, *WIZARD*. LIGHT OPERA (*G & S*).

SORRY APOLOGIZE, CARE, DEJECTED, LAMENTATION, PENITENT, REGRETFUL, REPINING, RUEFUL, SELF-REPROACH, UNHAPPY; **saying**. PALTRY, SHABBY, WRETCHED.

SORT SIEVE, SIFT. *LOT*. KIND, TYPE. MANNER, WAY. **Pl** = HEALTH, SPIRITS, TEMPER.

SOUND 1. DIN, NOISE, *RACKET*, *ROW*, TONE. FIND DEPTH, PLUMB (naut). *FIRM*, *FIT*, HALE. 2. Implies that the sound invoked by the following word is required, e.g. **Sound asleep** = SNORE or ZZ.

SOUNDER MORE STABLE. FITTER. LEAD-LINE (naut). *Assembly* of swine.

SOUNDS LIKE Indicated in this Companion by use of the letters s/l at the appropriate entries, it means that other spellings may sound similar, e.g. BORN, BORNE, BOURN all have *pronunciation* (q.v.) which is similar. Can also require the sound made by . . . (onomatopoeic), e.g. **Sounds like a sheep** = BAA.

SOUP *Anag*. BOUILLON, BROTH, CONSOMME, STEW, STOCK; *COURSE*. NITRO-GLYCERINE (sl).

SOURCE (s/l *sauce*). *Anag*. EMITTER, ORIGIN. FOUNTAINHEAD, SPRING, *WELL*.

SOUTH S, SO; POINT, POLE. *BRIDGE PLAYER* (crypt).
~ WIND Gk = NOTOS, **Rom** = AUSTER.

SOVEREIGN GOLD *COIN*, POUND. *MONARCH.*

SP SERVICE POLICEMAN. STARTING PRICE: BETTING, ODDS.

Sp Spain, ~ish.

SPA (s/l *spar*). 1. HEALTH RESORT, SPRING, WATERING PLACE (town in Belgium). *RACETRACK* (cars). 2. **Celebrated resorts:** AIX LES BAINS, BADEN BADEN, BATH, BUXTON, CONTREXEVILLE, CHELTENHAM, DROITWICH, HARROGATE, OSTEND, TUNBRIDGE WELLS, VICHY, WIESBADEN.

SPACECRAFT *ROCKET, SPACE TRAVELLER*, SPACE VEHICLE [NASA]. SCIENCE OF SPACE. **Celebrated (US):** *APOLLO*, AQUARIUS, ARIEL, *ATLAS*, CHALLENGER, COLUMBIA, COURIER, *DISCOVERER, ECHO, EXPLORER, GEMINI*, MARINER, *MARS, MERCURY, MIDAS*, NIMBUS, PIONEER, RANGER, SAMOS, SHUTTLE, SKYLAB, SPACELAB, TELSTAR, VANGUARD, VIKING, VOYAGER. **Celebrated (USSR):** COSMOS, LUNA, LUNIK, SALYUT, SOYUS, SPUTNIK, TIROS, VOSHKOD, VOSTOK.

SPACE TRAVELLER ASTEROID, COMET, METEORITE, *MOON, PLANET*, SHOOTING STAR. *SPACECRAFT.* ASTRONAUT, COSMONAUT. **Celebrated (US):** ALDRIN (2nd on moon), ARMSTRONG (1st on moon), BORMAN, CARPENTER, CERNAN, COLLINS, CONRAD, COOPER, GLENN (1st US), GORDON, GRISSOM, LOVELL, MCDIVITT, SALLY RIDE (1st US fem), SCHIRRA, SCOTT, STAFFORD, *WHITE, YOUNG.* **Celebrated (USSR):** BELYAEV, BYKOVSKY, FEOKTISTOV, GAGARIN (1st man in space), LAIKA (*dog*; 1st space traveller), LEONOV (1st *EVA*), NIKOLAYEV, POPOVICH, TERESHKOVA (1st woman), TITOV, YEGOROV [Jules Verne; H. G. Wells].

SPAIN SP. E (*car plate*).

SPANIARD DON, SENOR, SR.

SPANNER TOOL, WRENCH. *ARCH, BRIDGE* (crypt).

SPAR (s/l *spa*). BOOM, GAFF, MAST, SPRIT, *YARD. BOX*, FIGHT. MINERAL. HOOP, STAPLE (thatching).

SPEAKER ORATOR (chairman; Commons). *LIP*, MOUTH, TONGUE (crypt).

SPEAR HALBERD, HARPOON, JAVELIN, PIKE, *WEAPON*. RUN THROUGH, SPIKE, SPIT. MALE (**opp** = distaff). EAR, SPRIG [asparagus (bot)]. *GRASS*.

SPECTACLE EXHIBITION, *SHOW*, SIGHT. **Pl** = BIN(N)S, GLASSES [*Company* (livery)].

SPECTATOR ONLOOKER, VIEWER, WATCHER. **Pl** = *CROWD*.

SPECULATOR *BEAR*, PUNTER, *STAG* (comm).

SPEECH *ADDRESS*, *DELIVERY*, LECTURE, TALK. LANGUAGE.

SPEED KNOT, KPH, LICK, MPH, *RATE*, *TEMPO* (**saying**). *DRUG*. SERVANT/JESTER (2 G of V, *Shak*).

SPELL ATTRACTION. CANTRIP, CHARM, INCANTATION. DUTY, PERIOD, TURN, *WATCH*. RELIEVE. INVOLVE, PRESAGE, RESULT. MAKE or FORM WORDS.

SPELLER *WITCH* (crypt).

SPENT *TIRED*. PASSED (time), STAYED. BLEW, BLUED, EXPENDED, SQUANDERED.

SPHINX 1. Egy male *monster* (head human, body lion; strangler) representing the god Horamkhu. Also Gk female counterpart who put a riddle to the Thebans and killed all who could not solve it. *Oedipus* solved it and the Sphinx committed suicide. The riddle was 'A being with 4 feet has 2 feet and 3 feet, and only one voice; but its feet vary, and when it has most it is weakest. Who or what is it?' Oedipus' answer was 'Man, who in infancy crawls on all fours, then stands up on two feet, and in old age supports himself with a stick.' 2. Monkey (strangler).

SPICE FLAVOUR, MALICE, ZEST: ARTEMISIA, CARAWAY, CAYENNE, CHILI, CHIVE, CINNAMON, CLOVE, CORIANDER, CURRY, GARLIC, GILLYFLOWER, GINGER, MACE, MOULI, MUSTARD, NUTMEG, OREGANO, PAPRIKA, PEPPER, PIMENTO, RACE, SAFFRON, TURMERIC [*herb*].

SPIDER ARANEIDA. 8-LEGGED ANTHROPOID: BLACK WIDOW, MONEY ~, SOLPUGA, TANT, TARANTULA; *SPINNER*, WEBSTER (crypt). [*Arachne*, Robert the Bruce]. CUE-REST. CRAB. CARD GAME. *MONKEY*.

~ GIRL *ARACHNE*. MISS MUFFET.

SPILL *Anag.* LIGHTER, TAPER. SHED, UPSET.

SPINNER FISHERMAN, TROLLER. TOP. DRIER. GYROSCOPE. *SPIDER*. SCHEHERAZADE (crypt). RUMPLESTILTSKIN (Grimm).

SPIRIT *DRINK*. *GHOST*, SHADE, SOUL. ELAN, GO, LIFE, MORALE, PEP, VERVE, VIM. AFREET, AFRIT, ANGEL, BANSHEE, BROWNIE, DEMON, DJINN, ELF, GENIE, GOBLIN, HOBGOBLIN, IMP, KELPIE, PIXY(IE), PUCK, SPRITE. ELIXIR, ETHOS.

SPITFIRE *SHREW*, TERMAGANT. *AIRCRAFT*.

SPLIT CLEAVE, DIVIDE. CLEFT, CRACK, FISSURE, RENT. BREACH, RUPTURE, SCHISM. *BETRAY*. *DRINK*, MIXER. *BOTTLE*. DISH. TOWN (Y).

SPOIL DAMAGE, *MAR*, *RUIN*. BOOTY, LOOT.

SPONDEE *FOOT*.

SPOON UTENSIL. SCOOP. BILL AND COO, CANOODLE, WOO. *GOLF-CLUB*.

SPORTING CLUB MCC, RFU, FA etc. BAT, *RACKET* (crypt).

~ **JUDGE** REFEREE, UMPIRE.

~ **SET** *SIDE*; TEAM.

SPOT 1. PLACE, LOCALITY. ACNE, PIMPLE. MARK, SOIL, STAIN. CIRCLE, PATCH. *DASH*, DROP, *LITTLE*. BEAM, FLOOD (light). DETECT, ESPY, LOCATE, SEE. 2. May indicate a location connected with the following word(s) in the clue, e.g. **Spot of gambling** (5, 5) = MONTE CARLO.

SPOTTED SEEN. DAPPLED, SPECKLED.

SPRING BOUND, JUMP, LEAP. COIL ~, LEAF ~. *SEASON*. FLOW, WELL [*spa*]. *Assembly* of teal.

SPRINGBOK *ANTELOPE*. *RUGBY* PLAYER.

SPRINGTIME SEASON; MARCH, APRIL, MAY.

SPRITE *SPIRIT*; PUCK (MND, *Shak*), ARIEL (Temp, *Shak*).

SPRUCE *TRIM*. *TREE*.

SPUR URGE. **Pl** = *FOOTBALL* TEAM.

SPY AGENT. SEE, SPOT. SNOOP.

SQUARE 1. *DATED*, OLD FASHIONED. PLACE, PIAZZA. RIGHTANGLED ['you broke a Br ~'; Fuzzy Wuzzy (*Kipling*)]. T-, SET-. 2. Any square number, 9, 100 etc, hence IX, C. [*measure*].

~ **MEAL** GOOD SPREAD. BISCUIT, SANDWICH (crypt).

SQUASH CORDIAL, *DRINK*. *VEGETABLE*. CRUSH,

SQUEEZE. *GAME.*

SQUEALER *BETRAYER*, *GRASS*, SNEAK, TELL-TALE. PIG (*Orwell*).

SS *SAINTS.* *SHIP.* GESTAPO, *SECRET* POLICE.

ST *SAINT*; GOODMAN (crypt). *STREET.* *STONE.*

STABLE 1. *FIRM*, SOUND, STEADY. RACEHORSE. STRING; *habitation* of horses. 2. Gk myth stable of *Augeus*, the subject of one of the labours of *Hercules*.

STAG 1. Male *DEER*, BROCKET (2nd year), CERVUS. MALE (party). BEETLE. SHARE BUYER, SPECULATOR. **Pl** = *Football team.* 2. Gk myth *ACTAEON*. 3. One of the labours of *Hercules*.

STAGE DAIS, PLATFORM, STEP, SCAFFOLD. ACTING PROFESSION, DRAMA, THEATRE; **saying**. ARRANGE, PRESENT, PRODUCE. BUS-STOP, LEG, PERIOD, POINT, STATION, STOP-OVER. *CARRIAGE*, COACH.

STAIRS FLIGHT, STEPS [ladder]. APPLES (*rh sl*).

STAKE (s/l steak). ANTE, *BET*, RISK, *WAGER*. POST, SPIT, STICK. *ANVIL.* FASTEN, *SECURE*.

STAMP FRANK, IMPRESS(ION), IMPRINT; (HALL)MARK. BANG, CLUMP, THUMP, TRAMPLE, TREAD, TRUDGE. POSTAGE ~: **coll**: philatelist. [Roland *Hill*].

STANDARD BANNER, EAGLE, ENSIGN, *FLAG*, FLIER (crypt), PENNANT. DEGREE, LEVEL, *MEASURE*, NORM, PAR, QUALITY, REGULAR, YARDSTICK.

STANDING ORDER SO. ATTENTION, GET UP (crypt).

STAR 1. ASTERISK, *MARK*; 17 (*tarot*). *CASTLE.* ACTOR, ACTRESS, CELEBRITY, *LION*, VIP; ACT, FEATURE, PLAY LEAD. MAIN, OUTSTANDING, PRINCIPAL. 2. NEBULA; CELESTIAL/HEAVENLY BODY, NOVA, SUN; SKYLIGHT (crypt): **saying** (binary-, day-, double-, evening-, falling-, morning-, multiple-, pole-, shooting- [black hole, *planet*, pulsar, quasar, white dwarf]). 'ESTHER'. 3. Seven ~s in the sky in *song*.

STARBOARD S; RIGHT (**opp** = *port*, larboard). PLAYBILL.

STARLING *BIRD* (*assembly*). YOUNG ACTOR (crypt).

START FRIGHT, JUMP. SCRATCH. BEGIN, FOUND, INITIATE (**opp** = *end*). OPENING. *GO*, OFF, *REPAIR*. EASE (naut).

STARTER 1. *BEGINNER*. APPETIZER, *COURSE*, ENTREE (cook). JUMPER (crypt). GUNMAN (sports, crypt). A, ALPHA (crypt). ADAM, EVE (crypt). 2. First letter of word concerned, e.g. *Race starter* = R; note that this could also be GUNMAN or ADAM/EVE.

STARTING 1. BEGINNING. JUMPING (crypt). 2. First letter, e.g. **Starting time** = T; but note **Failure starting with a cry** (7) = W*A*SHOUT, which is revealed by the secondary word **failure**.

STAR TURN MAIN ITEM, LEAD PART. Anag. 'star' as RATS, TSAR etc.

STATE ANNOUNCE, SAY. CONDITION. ANXIOUS, EXCITED, UNTIDY. DIGNITY, POMP, RANK. GOVERNMENT, COMMUNITY, NATION. **Pl** = *LEGISLATIVE BODY* (CI). DIVISION OF THE USA, **namely:**

State	Abbr	Abbr	Capital
ALABAMA	ALA	AL	Montgomery
ALASKA	ALAS	AK	Juneau
ARIZONA	ARIZ	AZ	Phoenix
ARKANSAS	ARK	AR	Little Rock
CALIFORNIA	CALIF	CA	Sacramento
COLORADO	COLO	CO	Denver
CONNECTICUT[13]	CONN	CT	Hartford
DELAWARE[13]	DEL	DE	Dover
DISTRICT OF COLUMBIA		DC	Washington
FLORIDA	FLA	FL	Tallahassee
GEORGIA[13]		GA	Atlanta
HAWAII		HI	Honolulu
IDAHO	IDA	ID	Boise
ILLINOIS	ILL	IL	Springfield
INDIANA	IND	IN	Indianapolis
IOWA		IA	Des Moines
KANSAS	KANS	KS	Topeka
KENTUCKY		KY	Frankfort
LOUISIANA		LA	Baton Rouge
MAINE		ME	Augusta
MARYLAND[13]		MD	Annapolis
MASSACHUSETTS[13]	MASS	MA	Boston

MICHIGAN	MICH	MI	Lansing
MINNESOTA	MINN	MN	St Paul
MISSISSIPPI	MISS	MS	Jackson
MISSOURI		MO	Jefferson City
MONTANA	MONT	MT	Helena
NEBRASKA	NEBR	NE	Lincoln
NEVADA	NEV	NV	Carson City
NEW HAMPSHIRE[13]		NH	Concord
NEW JERSEY[13]		NJ	Trenton
NEW MEXICO	N MEX	NM	Santa Fe
NEW YORK[13]		NY	Albany
NORTH CAROLINA[13]		NC	Raleigh
NORTH DAKOTA	N DAK	ND	Bismarck
OHIO	O	OH	Columbus
OKLAHOMA	OKLA	OK	Oklahoma City
OREGON	OREG	OR	Salem
PENNSYLVANIA[13]		PA	Harrisburg
RHODE ISLAND[13]		RI	Providence
SOUTH CAROLINA[13]		SC	Columbia
SOUTH DAKOTA	S DAK	SD	Pierre
TENNESSEE	TENN	TN	Nashville
TEXAS	TEX	TX	Austin
UTAH		UT	Salt Lake City
VERMONT		VT	Montpelier
VIRGINIA[13]		VA	Richmond
WASHINGTON	WASH	WA	Olympia
WEST VIRGINIA	W VA	WV	Charleston
WISCONSIN	WISC	WI	Madison
WYOMING	WYO	WY	Cheyenne

[13] = one of the original 13 states.

STATECRAFT DIPLOMACY. PRESIDENTIAL YACHT, ROYAL *BARGE* (crypt).
STATELY HOME COUNTRY HOUSE, PLACE, SEAT (dignified, grand, imposing; open to the public); **celebrated:**

APSLEY HOUSE

ARUNDEL CASTLE

BEAULIEU

BELVOIR CASTLE

BERKELEY CASTLE

BLAIR CASTLE

BLENHEIM PALACE	LEEDS CASTLE
BODIAM CASTLE	LONGLEAT
BROADLANDS	LUTON HOO
BURGHLEY HOUSE	PETWORTH HOUSE
CAWDOR CASTLE	POWDERHAM CASTLE
CHARTWELL	SCARISBRICK HALL
CHATSWORTH HOUSE	SCONE PALACE
COMPTON WYNYATES	STRATFIELD SAYE
GLAMIS CASTLE	SUDELEY CASTLE
HAMPTON COURT	WARWICK CASTLE
HAREWOOD HOUSE	WILTON HOUSE
HATFIELD HOUSE	WINDSOR CASTLE
HEVER CASTLE	WOBURN PLACE
HOLKHAM HALL	WOOLATON HALL
KNEBWORTH HOUSE	

STATESMAN POLITICIAN. AMERICAN (crypt).

STAUNCH FIRM, LOYAL, TRUSTWORTHY. CHECK, DAM, STEM, STOP. AIRTIGHT, WATERTIGHT.

STAY AVAST (naut); REMAIN, STOP (**opp** = *go, go on*). PREVENT. GUY (ROPE), PROP, RIG, *SUPPORT*. **Pl** = CORSET.

STEAL (s/l *steel*). *BONE* (sl), BURGLE, FILCH, NICK, PINCH, PURLOIN, *ROB*. SNAFFLE, THIEVE. CREEP, GLIDE (AWAY).

STEAMER *BOAT*, LINER, SS (**opp** = *sailing* craft). ENGINE, TRAIN. COOKER, COOKPOT.

STEEL (s/l *steal*). 1. METAL [Bessemer]. HONE, SHARPENER. BRACE, HARDEN, RESOLVE. 2. Alloy of carbon, iron and manganese, hence (crypt) letters CFEMN. 3. *Anniversary* (11th).

STEEP PRECIPICE, SHEER, VERTICAL. IMMERSE. DRENCH, SOAK. DEAR, EXPENSIVE.

STEEPLECHASER *HORSE*; JUMPER; FENCER (crypt).

STEER *CON*, CONDUCT, DIRECT, DRIVE, HELM. *COW*.

STEERSMAN HELMSMAN, PILOT, TILLER-MAN; CONMAN (crypt). *COWBOY* (crypt). GLAUCUS (*Argonaut*).

STELLA GIRL: 'STAR'. *AWARD* (Br film)®.

STEM CHECK, DAM, *STA(U)NCH*, *STOP*. *BOW*, FRONT

(naut). ADVANCE. LINE, ORIGIN, STALK.

STEP (s/l steppe). MARCH, PACE. DANCE. RISER, TREAD. **Pl** = FLIGHT, LADDER, STAIRS.

~ **DOWN** DECLINE, GIVE WAY, CEDE. DESCEND. RESIGN. DEMOTION.

STERLING L, POUND. HIGH QUALITY.

STEVENSON (s/l Stephenson). 1. Engineer (Sc), lighthouse builder (not steam engines – he was -ph-); Bell Rock. 2. Robert Louis, writer; **celebrated books:** The Black Arrow, Catriona (sequel to Kidnapped), Inland Voyage (his first), Kidnapped (sequel: Catriona), The Master of Ballantrae, The Strange Case of Dr Jekyll and Mr *Hyde*, Travels with a Donkey in the Cevennes, Treasure Island (ex The Sea Cook) [Ben Gunn (marooned), Billy Bones, Black Dog, Blind Pew, Capt Flint (*parrot*; *pirate*), Israel Hands (coxswain), Jim Hawkins, Dr Livesey, Long John *Silver* (one-legged *pirate*, cook 'Barbecue', *parrot*), Capt Smollett, Squire Trelawney; the black spot (death sentence), Hispaniola (ship), Admiral Benbow (inn), the Spyglass (inn)].

STEW *Anag.* BOIL, COOK, FERMENT, *SEETHE*. DISH. *STUDY*. ANGER, ANXIETY, BOTHER, FUSS, WORRY. BROTHEL (sl). FISH-POND.

STILL EVER, YET. DISTILLERY [moonshine (sl)]. CALM, MOTIONLESS (**opp** = *moving*). EVEN.

STILTED BOMBASTIC, POMPOUS. AWKWARD, GRALLATORIAL, HIGH-STANDING, TALL (crypt).

STING NETTLE, HURT, PROVOKE. OVERCHARGE. *FISH*, RAY.

STINGY MEAN, MISERLY, NEAR, TIGHT. HURTFUL, INSULTING, WOUNDING. BEE, WASP (crypt).

STIR *Anag.* AROUSE, INFLAME. *ADMIX*, *MIX*, WHIP. COMMOTION, EXCITEMENT, TO-DO. *GAOL* (sl).

STOAT ERMINE, *WEASEL*.

STOCK CREDIT, REPUTATION. PROVIDE, RESERVE, STORE. BREED, BLOOD, FAMILY, *STRAIN*; ANIMALS, *CATTLE*. BASE, BUTT, HANDLE, STUMP. *FLOWER*. SHIPYARD WAY/SLIP. CRAVAT, SCARF, TIE. BRICK. **Pl** = wooden punishment device.

STOCKTAKING COUNTING, REVIEW. RUSTLING (crypt).

STOIC 1. AUSTERE, COURAGEOUS, SELF-CONTROLLED.

2. *Philosopher* of Athens school founded by ZENO: BRUTUS, CATO, CLEANTHES, CICERO, EPICTETUS, MARCUS AURELIUS, SENECA.

STOLEN *ROBBED*; HOT [*steal*].

STONE COBBLE, GRANITE, PEBBLE, ROCK (Norman, Portland); **saying**. *AGATE, GEM. AGE. MEASURE* (weight), *ST*, XIVLB. [*Atlas, Medusa, Niobe*].

STONED DRUGGED, DRUNK. PELTED. SCULPTED (crypt).

STOOL PIGEON *BETRAYER*, GRASS, SNEAK, SHOPPER.

STOP 1. ARREST, BAR, CLOSE, CUT OFF, GAG, OBSTRUCT, PARRY, PREVENT, STAUNCH, STIFLE. CEASE, CHECK, DESIST, GIVE OVER, HALT, PAUSE. CALL AT, REMAIN, SOJOURN, *STAY*. HALT, STATION (rly). APERTURE, DIAPHRAGM, ORGAN CONTROL, VALVE. PUNCTUATE: COLON, COMMA etc. MAKE FAST. CAULK, PAY (naut). *CARD GAME*. 2. Word with last letter(s) removed, e.g. **Drink stops play** (4) = DRAM(a).

~ **TALKING** BUTTON UP, CLAM UP. GAG, SILENCE.

STOREY (s/l *story*). FLOOR, LEVEL.

STORM *Anag*. 1. ASSAULT. RAGE. SHOWER. GALE, HAILSTORM, HURRICANE, RAINSTORM, SNOWSTORM, TEMPEST, THUNDERSTORM, TORNADO. 2. **Rom god =** FULGURATOR.

STORY (s/l *storey*). ACCOUNT, NARRATION, NARRATIVE, *RELATION*. FIB, LIE, TALE.

STOUT *BRAVE*, DOUGHTY, RESOLUTE, STAUNCH, STUBBORN, STURDY [Cortes]. BULKY, CORPULENT, FAT, OBESE (**opp** = *thin*). *BEER*, GUINNESS®.

STOVE COOKER [oven]. BREACHED, BROKEN.

STOWE (s/l stow). 1. *PUBLIC SCHOOL*. TOWN. 2. Harriet Beecher ~, writer; **book:** Uncle Tom's Cabin (Legree, *bully*; Li'l Liza; Topsy [*slave*; I 'spects I growed]).

STRAIN AIR, MUSIC, SONG, TONE, TUNE. INJURE, OVERTASK, PULL, STRESS, STRETCH. FILTER. BREED, *STOCK*.

STRAIT (s/l straight). RIGOROUS, STRICT. CONFINE, LIMITED, NARROW. **Pl** = DISTRESS, NEED. PASSAGE OF WATER; **celebrated:**

4-letters
BASS
COOK
PALK

5-letters
BANKS
CABOT
DAVIS
DOVER
KERME
KOREA
LUZON
NARES
SUNDA

6-letters
BERING
HORMUZ
HUDSON
TORRES

7-letters
DENMARK
FLORIDA
FORMOSA
FOVEAUX
MALACCA
MESSINA
OTRANTO

8+ letters
BELLE ILE
BONIFACIO
BOSPHORUS
GIBRALTAR
LA PEROUSE
MAGELLAN
MAKASSAR
PENTLAND
SINGAPORE
SKAGERRAK

STRANGER ALIEN, FOREIGNER. TEA LEAF (fig). MORE PECULIAR, RUMMER.

STREAK BAND, LINE, STRIPE. ELEMENT, SERIES, SPELL, STRAIN. DASH, RUN; RUN NAKED.

STREET ST; DRAG, *ROAD*.

~ MARKET BRICK LANE, FLEA-MARKET, MARCHE DES PUCES (Fr), MIDDLESEX STREET, PETTICOAT LANE, PORTOBELLO ROAD; AGORA (Gk), SOUK (Mos), MONOPOLY® (crypt, game).

STRIKE BAT, HIT, INNINGS, *KNOCK*, RAM, SMACK, SWING. IMPRESS. DIVERGE. LEVEL. FIND (gold/oil). LOWER FLAG, SURRENDER. STOP WORK, TAKE (industrial) ACTION.

STRIKER BATTER, HITTER. FLINT, FUSEE, LUCIFER, MATCH (crypt). PROSPECTOR. YIELDER. NON-WORKER. LIGHTNING (crypt).

STRIKING BATTING, HITTING, INNINGS (*cricket*).

LIGHTING (match). YIELDING. IDLING, OUT. EYE-
CATCHING.

STRING CORD, PULL, TAG, TIE. *STABLE* (racehorses). **Pl** =
OBLIGATION.

STRIP DENUDE, DOFF, UNDRESS (**opp** = *dress*). SHEAR.

STROKE CARESS, FONDLE. OARSMAN, *ROWER*.
APPROACH, CHIP, DRIVE, HOOK, LOFT, PUTT, SLICE,
SWING (golf); BLOCK, CUT, DRIVE, HOOK, GLANCE,
LOFT, PULL, SLASH, SWING (*cricket*). BRAIN STORM.

STUCK UP SUPERCILIOUS, SUPERIOR. BILLED, POSTED
(crypt).

STUDENT L, LEARNER, *PUPIL* (**Union** = NUS).

STUDY DEN, SANCTUM. *CON*, EXAMINE, READ, *SCAN*,
SCRUTINISE; OVERLOOK (arch and crypt). Any subject thus
investigated, e.g.

animals	ZOOLOGY
antiquities	ARCHAEOLOGY
beetles	COLEOPTEROLOGY
birds	ORNITHOLOGY
blood (med)	H(A)EMATOLOGY
bones (med)	OSTEOLOGY
caves	SPEL(A)EOLOGY
character	ETHOLOGY
China (geog)	SINOLOGY
coins	NUMISMATOLOGY
culture	SOCIOLOGY
disease (body)	PATHOLOGY
~ (mental)	PSYCHOLOGY
~ (female)	GYNAECOLOGY
earth's crust	GEOLOGY
Egypt (ancient)	EGYPTOLOGY
ferns	PTERIDOLOGY
fossil life	PAL(A)EONTOLOGY
handwriting	GRAPHOLOGY
heart	CARDIOLOGY
insects	ENTOMOLOGY
languages	PHILOLOGY
life (fossil)	PAL(A)EONTOLOGY

mankind	ANTHROPOLOGY
medals	NUMISMATOLOGY
mind (med)	PSYCHOLOGY
minerals	MINERALOGY
mountains	OROLOGY
old age	GERONTOLOGY
religion	THEOLOGY
shells (zool)	CONCHOLOGY
sleep	HYPNOLOGY
soil management	AGRONOMY
teeth	ODONTOLOGY
tissue (med)	HISTOLOGY
weather	METEOROLOGY
weevils	COLEOPTEROLOGY
wine	OENOLOGY
words	ETYMOLOGY
writing	GRAPHOLOGY
~ (ancient)	PAL(A)EOGRAPHY

STUVW S*TO*W (crypt).

STY (s/l *stye*). ENCLOSURE, PEN; *habitation* (pigs).

STYE (s/l *sty*). *EYESORE*, IRITIS.

STYX Gk myth principal river of the Underworld, d of Oceanus and Tethys [*Acheron, Charon, Cocytus, Lethe, Pyriphlegethon*].

SU SUNDAY. SOVIET RUSSIA (*car plate*).

SUBJECT SUBDUE; VASSAL (**opp** = *ruler*). EXPOSE, INFLICT, TREAT. LIABLE TO. NOUN, NOMINATIVE (e.g. **My subject** = I). THEME. EGO, MIND. PHOTO, PIC, POSER, MODEL, STILL LIFE.

SUBMIT *BOW*, GIVE WAY, SURRENDER, YIELD. OFFER, PRESENT, RENDER.

SUBSCRIBE CONTRIBUTE, ENGAGE, RAISE (money). SIGN, UNDERWRITE (arch).

SUBSOLANUS Rom myth EAST *WIND* (**Gk** = APELIOTES).

SUBSTITUTE 1. DEPUTY, EXCHANGE, REPLACE(MENT), SURROGATE. 2. Exchange a letter, usually in anag, e.g. **I substitute a revision of pure ideas for a dramatist** (9) = EURIPIDES (anag of 'pure ideas' with 'a' substituted by 'I').

SUCCEED ENSUE, FOLLOW, INHERIT. ACCOMPLISH, GET

ON, PROSPER, WIN (*saying*).

SUCCESSOR One who succeeds, e.g. HEIR, FOLLOWER, WINNER.

SUCKER (s/l succour). BARNACLE, LEECH, LIMPET. BUD, SHOOT. GREENHORN, GULLIBLE FELLOW, MARK, PIGEON.

SUIT ADAPT, FIT, SATISFY; *BECOME*. SET (*armour*, clothes, sails). ACTION, CLAIM, COURT CASE, ISSUE, PETITION. CLUBS, DIAMONDS, HEARTS, SPADES. WHISTLE (*rh sl*).

SUITABLE 1. APPROPRIATE, FITTED, FITTING, MEET, PROPER. 2. In a *suit* [*bridge, cards*].

SUITED CLOTHED, DRESSED. COURTED, WOOED (crypt). ACCOMMODATED, SATISFIED. FLUSH (*cards*).

SULKY MOROSE PET(ULANT), POUTING, SULLENLY. *CARRIAGE*.

SULPHUR S (*chem*).

SULTRY *HOT*. PROVOCATIVE, PASSIONATE, SENSUAL.

SUM (s/l *some*). *ADD UP*, TOT, TOTAL. AMOUNT. SUBSTANCE, SUMMARY. I AM (Lat).

SUMMARY (s/l summery). ABSTRACT, DIGEST, PRECIS, RESUME, SUBSTANCE, SYNOPSIS.

SUMMER SEASON (**saying**). HORIZONTAL BEAM, JOIST, RAFTER. ADDER, CALCULATOR, COUNTER (crypt).

SUN (s/l son). 1. *SUNDAY*. STAR; SKYLIGHT (crypt); 19 (*tarot*); **saying**. NEWSPAPER®. YEAR (crypt). SUNBATHE, TAN. 2. **Gods: Gk** = APOLLO, HELIOS; **Rom** = PHOEBUS, SOL.

SUNDAY S, SU, *SUN*. Day of the *Sun*; day of rest. ISLAND. ~'s **child** = bonny & blithe, good & gay [Solomon *Grundy*]. **Pl** = RIVER (SA).

SUPERIOR ABOVE, HIGHER, UPPER. BETTER, MORE, U.

SUPERMAN IDEAL/SUPERIOR MAN. [Clark *Kent*].

SUPPLIED *Anag*. 1. FUNDED, FURNISHED, PER, PROVIDED (BY). 2. Hidden word, e.g. **Food is supplied by great ingenuity** (6) = (gr)EAT*ING(enuity).

SUPPORT 1. CARRY, CONFIRM, HOLD UP, *SECOND*. BRA, CORSET, TRUSS. BACK, BRACKET, GUY, LEG, PROP, SLING, STAY. 2. Directs attention to second half of dn answer, e.g. **Age supports us by custom** = US*AGE.

SUPPORTER BACK, FOOT, LEG, PROP, SLING, STAY.
BELT, BRA, BRACES, SUSPENDERS. FAN, FOLLOWER.

SWAGMAN AUSSIE, DIGGER. *ROBBER* (crypt).

SWALLOW 1. ABSORB, DOWN, EAT, ENGULF. GULLET,
WEASAND. REPRESS, SUPPRESS. *BIRD* [Sea ~ = tern]
(**saying**). 2. Word put into another, e.g. **We are swallowed by me,
a patron of the arts** (4) = M*US*E; the same answer is given more
cryptically by **A patron of the arts, I engulf** (or, **take in**) **America**.

SWAN 1. RUBBER-NECK, SIGHT-SEEING (RAF sl).
ISLAND. PIRATE. Constellation (Cygnus). 2. Waterbird of
genus CYGNUS; BEWICK ~, BLACK ~, MUTE ~; **assembly**
= wedge; **male** = COB; **female** = PEN; **offspring** = CYGNET.
[Ugly Duckling (Hans *Andersen*)]. 3. Seven ~s a-swimming in
Christmas song. ~ of Avon (*Shak*).

SWARM 1. CLUSTER, LARGE GROUP. CONGREGATE.
ABOUND, BE OVERRUN, CLAMBER, CLIMB,
SCRAMBLE. 2. *Assembly* of bees.

Swe Sweden, ~ish.

SWEDEN S (*car plate*). Swe (abbr).

SWEETHEART DONAH, FLAME, *LOVER*, POPSIE (RAF sl).
HARD/SOFT CENTRE (crypt). E (crypt).

SWELL *SMART*, TOFF. HEAVE, SCEND, SURGE, WAVES.
BULGE, CRESCENDO, DILATE, EXPAND, RISE [*organ*].

Swi Switzerland, Swiss.

SWIFT 1. FAST, PROMPT, QUICK, RAPID, SOON. FRAME
(winding yarn). *LIZARD. BIRD* [*swallow*, martin]; DEVIL'S
BIRD (arch). 2. Jonathan ~, Ire writer and *satirist*; ordained.
Books: Battle of the Books, The Drapier's Letters, Journal to
Stella, Gulliver's Travels (to Brobdingnag, to the Houyhnhnms,
to Laputa and to Lilliput), Meditation on a Broomstick, Tale of a
Tub.

SWIMMER *FISH* (crypt). BATHER [natation]; **celebrated:**
LEANDER (Gk), 7 swans (*Christmas* song), ESTHER
WILLIAMS (films), TARZAN (Edgar Rice Burroughs).

SWINDLE *Anag. CHEAT*, CON, COZEN, *DO, FIDDLE,
RACKET, RAMP*.

SWINE BEAST, BRUTE, CAD, GLUTTON, HEEL, LOUT,
SCOUNDREL. HOG, *PIG*; **assembly** = herd, sounder; **male** =

BOAR; **female** = SOW; **offspring** = PIGLET. [pearls before ~]. **Patron saint** = Anthony.

SWISS CANTON Division of Switzerland: AARGAU, APPENZELL, BASELAND, BERN, FRIBOURG, GRAUBUNDEN, GLARUS, LUCERN, NEUCHATEL, OBWALDEN, ST GALLEN, SCHWYZ, SOLOTHURN, THURGAU, TICINO, UNTERWALDEN, VALAIS, VAUD, ZURICH.

SWITCHED *Anag.* DEVIATED, EXCHANGED, SWAPPED (rly lines). TURNED OFF/ON (elect). BEATEN, CANED (rod).

SWITZERLAND CH (*car plate*). Swi (abbr).

SYMBOL (s/l cymbal). ANALOGY, ASSOCIATION. CHARACTER, LETTER, NOTATION, SIGN. CREED. 5 ~s at your door in *song*.

SYNOPSIS *SUMMARY*.

T TENANT. TERA (*Int unit*). TON. TUESDAY. TURN. JUNCTION, SQUARE. CAR, FORD.

TA (s/l *tar*). TERRITORIAL ARMY. THANKS.

TABARD *CLOAK* (knight), COAT (*herald*). INN (*Chaucer*).

TABLE DUMMY (*bridge*). FACET. COLUMN, LIST, SCHEDULE. FURNITURE, CAIN AND ABEL (*rh sl*); BOARD, FOOD, KEEP, MEALS.

TACK BOARD, COURSE (naut). BISCUIT, FOOD (naut). GEAR, *HARNESS*. FASTENING, PIN. STITCH.

TAIL BACKSIDE, BOTTOM, REAR. SCUT, WAGGER. FIN AND RUDDER (av). WAKE. DOG, SHADOW, TRACK. RAIL, TRAIN. REVERSE (coin **opp** = obverse). DOCK. **Pl** = EVENING DRESS (**opp** = heads).

TAILED FOLLOWED, TRACKED; hence *COMET* (crypt). FADED. EVENING DRESS, WHITE TIE (crypt). DOCKED; hence remove last letter e.g. **Pete is tailed, the dear boy** (3) = PET*.

TAIL ENDER SCUT; RABBIT. L (crypt). LAST MAN.

TAKE OVER BUY OUT, COMMANDEER, SEQUESTER. RELIEVE. *BOWL* (crypt).

TALENT ABILITY, APTITUDE, FACULTY, GIFT. *COIN*,

MONEY; WEIGHT (Gk, Rom).

TAN BRONZE, BROWN, SUNBURN, SUNTAN. *COLOUR* (brown). BEAT, CANE, THRASH, WHIP. BARK. CURE. TANGENT.

TANTALUS Gk myth s of *Zeus*. Stood to his neck in water, which receded when he tried to drink; food above his head wafted out of reach when he tried to take it. Father of *Niobe* and Pelops (tantalize).

TAP DRAW OFF, SIPHON. FAUCET (US). EAVESDROP, MONITOR. BROACH, PENETRATE. SOLICIT. CUT THREAD. KNOCK, RAP, STRIKE. **Pl** = LIGHTS OUT (US mil).

TAR (s/l *ta*). AB, JACK, GOB (US), *SAILOR*, SALT. ASPHALT, BITUMEN, PITCH.

TAROT TAROC; card game; fortune telling cards; 78 in pack, 22 trumps.

0 = *fool/jester*	11 = strength
1 = juggler	12 = *hanged* man
2 = female pope	13 = *death*
3 = empress	14 = temperance
4 = emperor	15 = *devil*
5 = pope	16 = *tower*
6 = *lovers*	17 = *star*
7 = *chariot*	18 = *moon*
8 = *justice*	19 = *sun*
9 = hermit	20 = day of *judgement*
10 = wheel of *fortune*	21 = *world*

TART ACID, BITING, CUTTING. PROSTITUTE. PASTRY, PIE, SWEET; **celebrated:** apple, Bakewell, cherry, custard, fruit, jam, mince, peach, walnut.

TARTAN PATTERN, PLAID (Sc); *MATERIAL*. *BOAT*.

TARZAN Jungle-dwelling character of Edgar Rice Burroughs, 'real' name Lord Greystoke [Jane. Cheta (monkey)].

TATTOO NEEDLEWORK (crypt). MARK, STAIN; DECORATE. DRUMMING, SIGNAL. PAGEANT.

TAUNT RAG, REPROACH, RIB, *TEASE*, UPBRAID.

TAVERN *BAR*, INN, PH (abbr), PUB; **celebrated:** Admiral

Benbow (Treasure Island, *Stevenson*); Boar's Head (H.iv, H,v, *Shak*); Garter (Merry Wives, *Shak*); Spyglass (Treasure Island, *Stevenson*); Tabard (Canterbury Tales, *Chaucer*). *CRICKET CROWD* (Lord's).

TAW LEATHER, *WHIP*. MARBLE (game). RIVER (Eng).

TAX (s/l *tacks*). DUTY, EXCISE, LEVY, PAYE, SCOT, TOLL, VAT [*customs*, *smuggle*]. ASSESS, DEMAND, DRAIN, *TEST*, TRY. [~ **gatherer** = PUBLICAN (bibl)].

TEA (s/l t, tee). *MEAL*. DRINK (genus camellia); CHA, CHAR, CUPPA, ROSIE LEE (*rh sl*); **types:** CEYLON, CHINA (BOHEA, EARL GREY, JASMINE, KEEMUN, LAPSANG, OOLONG, ORANGE PEKOE, SUCHONG); INDIAN (DARJEELING, KASHMIRI, NILGIR). [Jap ~ ceremony (Chanoyu, Koicha, Ususha)].

~ **GIRL** POLLY (nursery rhyme).

TEAM (s/l teem). 1. II, XI, XV, ELEVEN etc. GANG, PLAYERS, *SIDE*, SQUAD. YOKED OXEN. 2. *Assembly* of young ducks, oxen.

TEA-MAKER KETTLE, POT, SAMOVAR. POLLY. ATE, EAT (crypt).

TEA-PARTY AT-HOME, ENTERTAINMENT. FRACAS (sl). CHAR-LADY, POLLY (crypt) [Mad Hatter (*Alice*); Boston].

TEAR (s/l tare, *tier*). *DASH*, HURRY, *RUN*. PULL, REND, *RIP*. DRIP, DROP, LACHRYMA [*Niobe, Ruth*].

TEASE (s/l t's, *teas*, tees). *CHAFF*, CHIP, *RAG*, RIB, TAUNT, TWIT. PICK FIBRES. IRRITATE, VEX.

TEASING *ARCH*, COY. *CHAFF*, TAUNTING. PICKING, SEPARATING FIBRES.

TED EDWARD. TEDDY BOY. DRY/MAKE HAY. HEATH (Prime Minister).

TEETH CHAMPERS, MASHERS, MOLARS [*study*]; DENTURES (see *bone, tooth*). COGS (mech).

TEETOTAL AA, ABSTAINER, TT; RECHABITE. [Richard *Turner*].

TEG *SHEEP* (young). GET UP (dn). GET BACK.

TELEPHONE BELL (sl), CALL, DIAL, PHONE, RING [STD].

TELEVISION BOX, MEDIUM, SET, TV. [BBC, IBA, ITA, ITV; ABC, CBS, NBC (US)].

TELL RECOUNT, RELATE, NARRATE. *COUNT*. BOWMAN

(crypt), WILLIAM [Rossini].

~ **OFF** CARPET, *REPRIMAND*. COUNT, *NUMBER*.

~ **TALE** FIBBER, LIAR. *BETRAY*. INDICATOR, SIGNAL. RELATE, NARRATOR.

TELLUS Rom eq of *GE* (also TERRA).

TEMPER ANGER, IRE. HARDEN. MITIGATE, RESTRAIN; TUNE.

TEMPLE 1. Part of head/skull. STRETCHER (weaving). SHIRLEY ~ (film). 2. *INNS OF COURT* (Knights Templar). 3. FANE, PLACE OF WORSHIP (*oracle*); **celebrated:** ABU SIMBEL (Nile), *APOLLO* (Delphi; Palatine), *ARTEMIS* (Ephesus), *DELPHI* (*Apollo*), *DIANA* (Aricia), KARNAK, LUXOR, MICAH (Jewish), PARTHENON (Athens), PHILAE (Aswan Dam), SOLOMON'S ~ (Jerusalem), THE TEMPLE (Jerusalem, Solomon).

TEMPO RHYTHM, TIME (mus): ACCELERANDO, ADAGIO, ALLEGRETTO, ALLEGRO, ANDANTE, ANIMATO, CALANDO, CON BRIO, CRESCENDO, DIMINUENDO, LARGAMENTE, LARGO, LEGATO, LENTO, MAESTOSO, MORENDO, MOSSO, *PIANO*, PIANISSIMO, PRESTO, PRESTISSIMO, RALLENTANDO, RUBATO, SOSTENUTO, SOTTO VOCE, STACCATO, STRINGENDO, TREMOLO, VIBRATO. **Pl** = TEMPI.

TEMPTRESS ENCHANTRESS, HOURI, SEDUCTRESS, VAMP.

TEMU Egy *god* of gods, Creator. **Gk** = *ZEUS*; **Rom** = JOVE, JUPITER.

TEN See *number*. DECADE, IO, VV, X. TWE or NTY (crypt). [tithe]. *Commandments* in *song*; pipers piping, in Christmas *song*. ~ green bottles.

TENANT T. HOLDER, LESSEE, OCCUPANT. [*Brontë*].

TEN COMMANDMENTS Spoken by God to Moses: (1) Thou shalt have no other gods before me. (2) Thou shalt not make unto thee any·graven image. (3) Thou shalt not take the name of the Lord thy God in vain. (4) Remember the sabbath day, to keep it holy. (5) Honour thy father and thy mother. (6) Thou shalt not kill. (7) Thou shalt not commit adultery. (8) Thou shalt not steal. (9) Thou shalt not bear false witness against thy neighbour. (10) Thou shalt not covet thy neighbour's house, his wife . . . nor anything that is his.

TEND *APT*, CONDUCE, INCLINE, SERVE. CARE, *NURSE*, WAIT ON.

TENDER OFFER, PRESENT, PROFFER. SOFT, SORE. NEEDING CARE, TICKLISH. AFFECTIONATE, CONSIDERATE, FOND, LOVING, SOLICITOUS. ATTENDANT BOAT/WAGON, GUARDIAN. SHEPHERD (crypt). MATRON, NANNY, *NURSE*, SISTER (crypt).

TENNE/TENNY BROWN (*herald*).

TENNIS BALL GAME; **venues**: Forest Hills, Flushing Meadows, Queen's Club, Stade Roland Garros, Wimbledon. DECK ~, LAWN ~ [WCT], REAL ~ [dedans, grille, hazard side, penthouse, service side, tambour], RING ~, TABLE ~.

TENT CANOPY, (CANVAS) SHELTER. WOUND PLUG, WAD. (RED) WINE.

~ MAKER CANVAS WORKER. BREWER, VINTNER; OMAR (KHAYYAM). NETT (crypt, anag).

TERM BOUNDARY, LIMIT, PERIOD, *SENTENCE*, SPAN. CONDITION, FOOTING, RELATION, STIPULATION. CALL, DENOMINATE; LANGUAGE. HALF, SEMESTER: Easter (C), Hilary (O), Lent (C, O), Michaelmas (C, O) Trinity (O).

TERPANDER The first historical *musician*, who lived at Antissa in Lesbos B.C. 700-650.

TERPSICHORE Gk myth, one of the nine *Muses* (*dance* and *song*).

TERRA Also TELLUS. Rom eq of *GE*, *goddess* of EARTH.

TERRITORIAL ARMY TA, TERRIERS (hence *football team*). *RESERVES*.

TERRY BOY, MAN. TOWEL.

TEST EXERCISE, TAX, TRIAL, *TRY*; EXAMINE. ASSAY, REFINE. *MATCH* (games). *RIVER*.

TESTER ANALYST, ASSAYER, EXAMINER. (BED) CANOPY. *COIN* (Eng). CRICKETER (crypt).

TESTING GROUND LABORATORY, LAB, WIND TUNNEL, *CRICKET GROUND*.

TH *THORIUM* (*chem*). *THURSDAY*.

THALIA 1. Gk myth, one of the nine *Muses* (comedy and bucolic poetry). 2. A minor *PLANET*.

THAMES RIVER. *ISIS*. LONDON BANKER (crypt). CAPITAL CURRENCY (crypt). **Bridges of the** ~ (in order from the sea):

Barrier	Chelsea
Tower	Albert
London	Battersea
Cannon St (rly)	Battersea (rly)
Southwark	Wandsworth
Blackfriars (rly)	Putney (rly)
Blackfriars	Putney
Waterloo	Hammersmith
Hungerford (foot)	Barnes (rly)
Charing Cross (rly)	Chiswick
Westminster	Kew (rly)
Lambeth	Kew
Vauxhall	*Twickenham*
Grosvenor Rd (rly)	Richmond

THANKS *GRACE*, GRATITUDE, TA.

THANKSGIVING Expression of gratitude, usually to God; specifically 4th Thursday in Nov (US) and 2nd Mon in Oct (Can).

THAT YON.

~ **FRENCH** CA, CELA.

~ **IS** ID EST, IE.

~ **LATIN/ROMAN** ID, ILLE.

~ **ONE** HE, SHE.

THAT'S ID EST, IE.

~ **RIGHT** IER (crypt).

THEATRE ART, PLAYHOUSE, REP, SHOW-PLACE, STAGE [*cat*]. LECTURE HALL, OPERATING ROOM. FIELD, SCENE; ARENA, BATTLE ZONE.

~ **GOER** PLAY-WATCHER. PATIENT, SURGEON (crypt).

~ **WORK** ACTING, PLAYING. MEDICINE. OPERATION, SURGERY (crypt).

THE FRENCH LA, LE, LES.

~ **GERMAN** DAS, DER, DIE.

~ **ITALIAN** IL.

THERMOPYLAE Narrow defile in the mountains 100 miles north of Athens, where 300 Spartans under Leonidas withstood *Xerxes* and his army of about 1,000,000 men for three days. They only failed in the end because the treachery of Ephialtes revealed a secret path through the hills to their rear. The sole Gk survivor was received in Athens with reproaches for having fled.

THESE TIMES AD, NOW(ADAYS).

THESEUS Gk myth hero, to whom *Ariadne* (d of king *Minos*) gave a ball of string so he could find his way back out of the labyrinth after he had killed the *Minotaur*. He was one of the *Argonauts* and, on his successful return to *Attica*, he neglected to hoist the white sail which was the signal of his triumph; Aegeus, his father, thought him dead so he leaped into the sea and was drowned – thus jumping to a *conclusion*.

THE SPANISH EL.

THEY PEOPLE, PERSONS. AUTHORITY, THE ESTABLISHMENT. OPPONENTS (*bridge*).

THIEF *ROBBER*; TEA LEAF (*rh sl*). [Ali Baba].

THIN CULL, DILUTE. LEAN, SKINNY, SLENDER (**opp** = fat, *stout*). FINE, NARROW. BALDING. INSUBSTANTIAL, INSUFFICIENT. FLIMSY, SCANTY, SHALLOW, TRANSPARENT (**opp** = thick).

THING OBJECT; RES (Lat). CONVENTION. OBSESSION. LIFESTYLE. *LEGISLATIVE ASSEMBLY* (ON). **Pl** = BELONGINGS, PROPERTY.

THIRD Next to second, hence 'a second before'; BRONZE. E (mus). INTERVAL (mus). DIVISION, RIDING.

~ **CLASS** C. A (crypt).

~ **MAN** ABEL (crypt). *CRICKETER*. HARRY LIME. N (crypt).

~ **PERSON** CAIN (crypt). HE, SHE, THEM. R (crypt).

THIS 1. Indicates near at hand (**opp** = that). EXISTING, PRESENT. 2. Answer is added to preceding or following word, to make a further word as also indicated, e.g. **Play no to this remedy** (5) = (no)STRUM; or **Elevated this way for the main road** (4) = HIGH(way). 3. This side of . . . indicates the first part of the next word, e.g. **Musical instrument this side of violence** (4) = VIOL(ence).

~ **MONTH** INST. Current month, as JAN, FEB etc.

THOR (s/l thaw). 1. Nor *god* of THUNDER, s of *Odin*. He possessed a magic throwing hammer called Miolnir. **Rom** = TONANS. [Thursday]. 2. HEYERDAHL (Kon-Tiki).

THORIUM TH (*chem*).

THOROUGHBRED HIGH-SPIRITED, METTLESOME,

PURE-BRED (**opp** = mongrel) [**original horse studbook ancestors** = BYERLY TURK, DARLEY ARABIAN, GODOLPHIN BARB].

THOUSAND See *number*. K, KILO; M (Lat). CHILIAD.

~ **GUINEAS** *CLASSIC*; LML (crypt).

THREE See *number*. TRIAD. GREEN BALL (snooker). *Rivals* in *song*. French *hens* in *Christmas song*. [*Holmes* cases]. ~ Men in a Boat (George, Harris, J and the dog Montmorency) by Jerome K. Jerome.

~ **ESTATES** COMMONS, LORDS SPIRITUAL, LORDS TEMPORAL [**fourth estate** = *press*].

~ **FEET** YARD, *MEASURE*. TRIPOD.

~ **QUARTERS** BACKS, WINGS (*rugby*) [*Holmes* case]. 75%. Any 3 of E, N, S and W (crypt).

THRICE TER, THREEFOLD, THREE TIMES.

THRILL FRISSON, PULSATION, THROB, TREMOR; EXCITE, WOW.

THROUGHWAY BY-PASS, FLYOVER. ARCH, TUNNEL (crypt).

THROWER BALLISTA, CATAPULT, SLING, TREBUCKET. GARDENER; POTTER (crypt). *THOR*.

THUG 1. ROUGHNECK, RUFFIAN, TOUGH GUY. 2. Indian religious fanatic of 19th century, who garotted victims as sacrifice to *Kali*, Hindu *goddess* of Destruction.

THUNDER 1. CLAP, CRASH, LOUD NOISE. ADVANTAGE, CREDIT, THREATEN. 2. **Gods: Gk** = *ZEUS*; **Rom** = JOVE/*JUPITER*, *TONANS*; **Nor** = *THOR*.

THUNDERBOLT DESTRUCTION, LIGHTNING, SHAFT, THREAT. *AIRCRAFT*. [Jove, *Jupiter*, *Tonans*, *Zeus*].

THUNDERER *THOR*, *TONANS*. THE TIMES®.

THURSDAY TH, THURS; day of *Thor*. ~'s **child** = far to go [*Chesterton*, Solomon *Grundy*].

TI *TITANIUM* (*chem*). BACK IT (crypt). NOTE (mus, also TE). *TREE* (Polynesia, NZ).

TICK CR, CREDIT. CHECK OFF, MARK. CASE, COVER. BLOODSUCKER, *INSECT*, PARASITE. CLICK. INSTANT, MO, MOMENT, SEC. GROUSE, GRUMBLE (sl).

~ **OFF** 1. CHECK, MARK. BERATE, CHASTISE, REPRIMAND. STOPWATCH. 2. Delete any synonym for 'tick' from clue, e.g. **Tick off sector hill** = ***TOR.

~ **OVER** IDLE, RUN SLOWLY. STOPPED CLOCK (crypt).

TIER (s/l *tear*). LINE, RANGE, RANK, *ROW*. DRAWER,
EQUAL WINNER. BINDER, KNOTTER.

TIGER TANK, *WEAPON*. CHEER. *LEPIDOPTERA* (moth).
MANELESS FELINE; BIG CAT; SHERE KHAN (Kipling);
offspring = cub. **Pl** = *Football team*.

TIGHT CLOSE, FIRM. IMPERMEABLE (**opp** = porous).
NEAR, MEAN, MISERLY. STRETCHED, TAUT, TENSE,
TENSIONED. DRUNK. **Pl** = HOSE, UNDERWEAR.

TILBURY *DOCK*. *CARRIAGE*. *CASTLE*.

TILDE ACCENT (ñ = ng).

TILL UNTIL, UP TO. CASHBOX. CULTIVATE, FARM,
PLOUGH, TURN UP. CLAY.

TILLER SALESMAN/WOMAN (crypt). *FARMER* (crypt).
HELM. DANCING GIRL.

TILT AWNING. *CANT, LEAN*, LIST, SLOPE. JOUST.

TIM BOY. SPEAKING CLOCK. LITTLE TIME (crypt).

TIMBER (s/l timbre). *FOREST*, TREES, WOOD [*measure*].
FRAME, RIB (naut).

TIME *DATE*, HOUR, MOMENT, SECOND. EST, GMT etc.
ENEMY (sl). CLOCK, RECORD, REGISTER. PERIOD;
DAY, MONTH, SEASON, WEEK, YEAR; *AGE*, AEON,
EON, ERA. BIRD, GAOL TERM, PETER, *SENTENCE*,
STRETCH. *TEMPO*. **Pl** = PAPER®, THUNDERER. X,
MULTIPLY BY. [O tempora, O mores (Cicero)].

~ **OUT** BREAK, BREATHER, INTERVAL. EMIT, ITEM
(crypt, anag).

~ **WARP** FOURTH DIMENSION [Einstein]. EMIT, ITEM
(crypt, anag).

TIN 1. SN (*chem*); *anniversary* (10th). CAN. MONEY. 2. Put
letter 't' in word(s) following, e.g. **Tin spoon precisely** (4, 2) =
SPO*T*ON.

TINY 1. MINUTE, SMALL, WEE (**opp** = *giant*). 2. Use
diminutive or offspring of, e.g. **Tiny Tom** = KITTY or TH.

TIP 1. EDGE, END, POINT, RIM. CUE, HINT. WRINKLE.
CANT, TILT, TOPPLE. GRATUITY. 2. First or last letter of
word, e.g. **Asparagus tip** = A or S.

~ **OFF** 1. CUE, HINT, WRINKLE. 2. First or last letter removed, e.g. **Communist Fred's tip-off** (3) = *RED.

TIRE (s/l tyre). BORE, EXHAUST, FATIGUE, WEARY. US = TYRE (UK). ATTIRE, DRESS.

TISIPHONE One of the *Furies*.

TIT NIPPLE. CONTROL, KNOB (av). BIRD: bearded ~, blue ~, coal ~, crested ~, great ~, longtailed ~, marsh ~, willow ~.

TITAN (s/l tighten). 1. Gk myth children of *Uranus* and *Ge* (sometimes incorrectly confused with the *giants* or *monsters* called Gigantes): OCEANUS and TETHYS (sea), HYPERION and THEA (sun and moon), COCUS and PHOEBE (light), CREIOS and EURYBIA (strength), CRONOS and RHEA (heaven and earth), THEMIS and MNEMOSYNE (law and memory), IAPETUS (father of mankind). 2. A satellite of the *planet* SATURN.

TITANIUM TI (*chem*).

TITFER HAT (*rh sl*).

TITLE HANDLE, NAME. BARON, COUNT, DUKE, EARL, LORD, VISCOUNT etc. DEED, RIGHT.

TO (s/l too, two). 1. AS FAR AS. TOWARDS. COMPARED WITH. BY WAY OF, FOR. CONTAINED, INCLUDED, INVOLVED. 2. Letters or word put before word indicated, e.g. **As to this, it's in pieces below** = (as)UNDER.

TOAD (s/l toed, towed). CAD, SYCOPHANT. Amphibian of genus bufo: FROG [Grahame; Badger, Mole, Ratty, Wind in the Willows].

TOAST BROWN, COOK, HEAT, SCORCH, SINGE, WARM; COOKED BREAD. CHEERS, CHIN CHIN, SKOLL, PROSIT; ROUSE.

TOASTER COOKER; *SINGER* (crypt). HEALTH-DRINKER (crypt).

TOBACCO Plant genus Nicotiana: VIRGINIA, TURKISH. QUID, TWIST [chewing, snuff].

TOD *MEASURE* (wool). ALONE (*rh sl*).

TODAY MON, TUES, WED etc according to date.

TOM *CAT*. ~ *BROWN*; ~ DICK and HARRY; ~ THUMB. *BELL* (Oxford). DR or UM (half of tom-tom).

TOMMY LAD, SMALL BOY. BAR. GUN. TUCKER. ATKINS, SOLDIER.

TON (s/l *tun*). C, T. 100 (mph). CENTURY, HUNDRED. *FASHION*.

TONANS Rom *god* of THUNDER.

TONE PITCH, QUALITY, MODULATION; SOUND. FITNESS, CHARACTER. HARMONIZE. SHADE, TINT.

TONIC BRACING, INVIGORATING. TREATMENT. KEYNOTE, TONAL (mus). *DRINK*, MIXER.

TONY *AWARD* [Antoinette Perry] (theat)®. ANT(H)ONY.

TOOTH *BONE* (q.v.), CHAMPER, *FANG*, IVORY, MASHER, MOLAR [caries]. COG, SPROCKET.

TOP 1. ACE, ACME, APEX, *HEAD*, SUMMIT, UPPER, U. COVER, PIECRUST. BEST, OVERCOME. BEHEAD, EXECUTE. DIABOLO, SPINNING TOY. BEST, FIRST CLASS. 2. Omit first letter, e.g. **Top gear for listener** (3) = EAR. 3. **Pl** = DOUBLE TWENTY, hence FORTY, XL (darts).

TOPAZ *GEM* (blue, green, white, yellow). *Birthstone* (November). Sir ~ (*Chaucer* character).

TOPAZOLITE *GEM* (green, yellow); GARNET.

TOPE *DRINK*, TIPPLE. MANGO-GROVE. *SHARK*. SHRINE.

TOPLESS 1. BALD. BAREBREASTED. 2. Remove letters 'bra' from word, e.g. **Topless bravery is extreme** (4) = ***VERY. 3. No first letter in dn answer.

TOPPING AI, FIRST CLASS, FIRST RATE. HALO, *HAT*, ROOF, TIARA (crypt).

TORY C, POLITICIAN, RIGHT WING. *ISLAND* (Ire).

TOT CHILD. *DRINK*, MEASURE. SUM; *COUNT*, TELL. SCAVENGE.

TOUCH *SENSE*; BRUSH, CONTACT, FEEL. REACH. INJURE, MARK. AFFECTED, CRAZY. SYMPATHY. SIDE-LINE (games).

TOWED (s/l *toad*, toed). DRAWN, PULLED, TUGGED. HEMPEN.

TOWER TALL BUILDING, SKYSCRAPER. 16 (*tarot*). CITADEL, FORTRESS. SOAR. *DRAWER*, PULLER, TUG (crypt). *THAMES* BRIDGE.

TOXIPHOBIA *Aversion* to poisons.

TOYMAKER DR COPPELIUS (Coppelia, Delibes), CALEB PLUMMER (Cricket on the Hearth, *Dickens*), TACKLETON (Cricket on the Hearth, *Dickens*). OTY, YOT etc (crypt, anag).

TRACE *SIGN*, VESTIGE. DELINEATE, *MARK*, SKETCH,

WRITE; *COPY*, FOLLOW. ASCERTAIN, OBSERVE,
PURSUE, TRACK. *HARNESS*, STRAPS.

TRACK COURSE, FOOTPRINTS, PATH, SCENT.
RACECOURSE. DOG, FOLLOW, TAIL, TRACE.
GROOVE (disc, EP). TREAD (tank, tractor). GAUGE,
WIDTH (wheels, rails); BR, RLY, RY, IRON WAY: HARD
LINES (crypt).

TRACT GROUND, PLOT, STRETCH. HAND-OUT,
PAMPHLET.

TRADE TERMS DISCOUNT. GATT. CIF, EX WORKS, FAS,
FOB (crypt).

TRADING COMPANIES MUSCOVY ~ (1555), EASTLAND ~
(1579), LEVANT ~ (1581), AFRICA ~ (1588), EAST INDIA ~
(1600), HUDSON BAY ~ (1670).

TRAGEDY 1. CALAMITY, DRAMA. 2. Any celebrated play of
tragic nature, e.g. KING LEAR. 3. **Gk Muse** = MELPOMENE.

TRAIN KEEP FIT [PE, PT]. *COACH*, *DRILL*, INSTRUCT,
PREPARE. CORTEGE, RETINUE, SKIRT, STRING, TAIL.
APT, BR, HST, RLY, RY, ENGINE, *LOCAL* [commuting].
EXPLOSIVE CHARGE, *FUSE*.

TRAINEE APPRENTICE, LEARNER. COMMUTER,
PASSENGER, RAILMAN, TRAINER (all crypt).

TRAINER *COACH*, TEACHER. COMMUTER (crypt). **Pl** =
RAILMEN (**Unions** = ASLEF, NUR).

TRAINING COACHING, LEARNING, TEACHING.
EXERCISING, KEEPING FIT, REGIME. COMMUTING
(crypt).

TRAITOR DESERTER, RAT, RENEGADE, TURNCOAT. SIR
MORDRED (Knight of the *Round Table*, Tennyson).
[Quisling].

TRAMP BAGLADY (US sl), BUM, HOBO, SUNDOWNER.
BOAT, CARGO SHIP. FOOTSLOG, *MARCH*, STAMP,
TRAMPLE, TREAD, TRUDGE, WALK, YOMP.
GOLDDIGGER.

Trans Translate.

TRANSFER *Anag*. CONVEY, HANDOVER, REMOVE.
CHANGE, MOVE, SWITCH. WATERCOLOUR.

TRANSLATION *Anag*. 1. *TRANSFER*, TRANSFORM.
INTERPRET. 2. Put into foreign language, e.g. **My French**

translation at the beginning of the week (3) = MON. 3. Reverse the syllables, **Translate the German stable** (6) = MAN*GER.

TRANSPORT EMOTION, RAPTURE. CONVEY, MOVE; BR, CAB, CAR, *CARRIAGE*, BUS, LORRY, RLY, *TRAIN*, TRAM, VAN (**Union** = TGW).

TRAP CATCH, *GIN*, SNARE. *CARRIAGE*. **Pl** = *BAGGAGE*, CASES, GRIPS, LUGGAGE. DRUMS, *INSTRUMENTS* (mus).

TRAPPIST BENEDICTINE, CISTERCIAN MONK [silence]. HUNTER (crypt). DRUMMER (crypt).

TREAT *Anag*. MANIPULATE, MINISTER, NEGOTIATE, PROCESS. REGALE, ROUND, SHOUT, STAND. EXCURSION; PLEASURE.

TREBLE ALTO; CLEF. *BET*.

TREE 1. ANCESTORS, GENEALOGY. FRAME-WORK. BOOT-BLOCK. Celebrated actor. 2. PERENNIAL PLANT; **types:**

3-letters	DALI	SAGO
ASH	*DATE*	SAUL
ASP	DHAK	SHEA
BAY	DOUM	SORB
BEN	EJOO	TEAK
BOX	GEAN	TEIL
ELM	HOLM	TOON
FIG	ILEX	*UPAS*
FIR	JALA	
GUM	KOLA	**5-letters**
JAK	LANA	ABELE
KOA	LIME	ABIES
OAK	MORA	ALDER
SAL	NIPA	*APPLE*
YEW	*PALM*	ARECA
	PEAR	ARENG
	PINE	ASPEN
4-letters	*PLUM*	BALSA
ACER	POON	BEECH
AKEE	RATA	BIRCH
BAEL	*ROSE*	BODHI (sacred)
COCO		

BUNYA
CACAO
CAROB
CEDAR
EBONY
ELDER
HAZEL
HOLLY
IROKO
JAMBU
JUDAS
LARCH
LEMON
LILAC
MAPLE
OLIVE
OSIER
PAPAW
PEACH
PLANE
ROHAN
ROWAN
SALIX
TAXUS
TIKUL
TILIA
TINGI
TUCUM
WITHY
YACCA
ZAMIA
ZANTE

6-letters
ACACIA
ACAJOU
ALMOND
ANTIAR
BAMBOO

BANANA
BANIAN
BANYAN
BAOBAB
BOG-OAK
BOMBAX
CARAPA
CARICA
CASHEW
CERRIS
CHERRY
COHUNE
CONKER
COWDIE
DEODAR (sacred)
ELAEIS
FUSTIC
GINGKO (*sic*)
GINKGO
GOMUTI
GOMUTO
GOPHER
JARRAH
JUPATI
KITOOL
KITTUL
LAUREL
LINDEN
LOCUST
LONGAN
MABOLA
MACACO
MALLEE
MASTEL
MIMOSA
NARGIL
OBECHE
ORANGE
PEEPUL (sacred)

PLATAN
POPLAR
PRUNUS
RATTAN
RED-BUD
RED-GUM
RED-OAK
RHAPIS
SAPELE
SAPIUM
SISSOO
SORBIN
SORBUS
SPRUCE
TUPELO
WALNUT
WATTLE
WILLOW
YARRAH

7-letters
AILANTO (sacred)
ARBUTUS
BACTRIS
BAY-TREE
BAYWOOD
BEBEERU
BEE-TREE
BURR-OAK
CAJEPUT
CALAMUS
CAMPHOR
CANELLA
CARYOTA
CEDRELLA
CHAMPAC
COCONUT
COG-WOOD

CONIFER
COQUITO
CORYPHA
CYPRESS
DURMAST
ELK-WOOD
EMBLICA
FAN-PALM
FILBERT
QUIACUM
HICKORY
HOLM-OAK
JUGLANS
JUNIPER
MORICHE
MORINGA
OIL-PALM
PALMYRA
PAXIUBA
PHOENIX
PLATANE
QUERCUS
REDWOOD
ROBINIA
SAPLING
SEQUOIA
SERVICE
SHITTAH
SUNDARI

TALIPAT
TALIPET
TALIPOT
TALIPUT
TANGHIN
WALLABA
WAX-PALM
WYCH-ELM
YEWTREE
ZALACCA

8-letters
AGUE-TREE
ALGAROBA
BEDEWEEN
BLACK-GUM
BOURTREE
CARNAUBA
CASTANEA
CHESTNUT
COCOANUT
COKERNUT
CORKWOOD
CRABWOOD
DATE-PALM
HAWTHORN
HEMP-PALM
HORNBEAM
JACKWOOD

KINGWOOD
LABURNUM
MAGNOLIA
MAHOGANY
MANGROVE
MULBERRY
PALMETTO
PIASSABA
PIASSAVA
PINASTER
ROSEWOOD
SAGO-PALM
SCRUB-OAK
SYCAMORE
WITCH-ELM
ZIZYPHUS

9+ letters
BLACKTHORN
CLUSTER-PINE
COPPER BEECH
FLAME OF THE
  FOREST
FRANGIPANI
MONKEY PUZZLE
SILVER BIRCH
SPINDLETREE
TURKISH OAK
WELLINGTON

TREMBLER VIBRATOR (elect). *BIRD* (W Ind).
  EARTHQUAKE (crypt).
TRENT BRIDGE *CRICKET GROUND.*
TRIANGLE FIGURE (geom); **types:** EQUILATERAL ~,
  ISOSCELES ~, SCALENE ~, OBTUSE/ACUTE ANGLED ~,
  [Bermuda; eternal]. INSTRUMENT (mus).
TRIBE GROUP (zool). FAMILY, NUMBER, SET. CLAN,
  DIVISION [*African*; *American Indian*; *Israel*; and see
  TRIBESMAN]. **Roman Britain:** ATREBATES, BELGAE,

BRIGANTES, CANTII, CARVETII, CATUVELLAUNI,
CORITANI, CORNOVII, DECEANGLI, DEMETAE,
DOBUNNI, DUMNONII, DUROTRIGES, ICENI,
ORDOVICES, PARISI, REGENSES/REGNI, SILURES,
TRINOVANTES; **chiefs:** *Boudicca*, Cartimandua (f); Caratacus,
Cunobelinus, Epilus, Togodumnus, Verica (m).

TRIBESMAN BARBARIAN, NOMAD, SAVAGE; YAHOO
(Gulliver's Travels, Swift). CLANSMAN, NATIVE; **celebrated:**
ANGLE (Eur), ARAB (Af), ASHANTI (Af), BANTU (S Af),
BERBER (NW Af), BELGA (Eur), COSSACK (Russ),
DORIAN (Gk), FRANK (Eur), GAUL (Fr), GOTH (Ger),
HITTITE (bibl), HOTTENTOT (Af), HUN (Asia), HYKSOS
(Egy), JUTE (Eur), KIKUYU (Af), MAGYAR (Eur), MASAI
(Af), MEDE (bibl), MONGOL (Asia), MOOR (NW Af
[Othello]), OSTROGOTH (Ger), PARTHIAN (Asia),
PHOENICIAN (bibl), PYGMY (Af), SAXON (Eur),
SPARTAN (Gk), TARTAR (Russ), TAUREG (Af), VANDAL
(Ger), VISIGOTH (Ger), ZOUAVE (Af), ZULU (Af)
[*American Indian*; impi; *Israel*; and see *TRIBE*].

TRICKY ADROIT, CRAFTY, DECEITFUL, DELICATE,
TICKLISH. RESOURCEFUL. *CARD GAME* (bridge, solo,
whist etc; crypt).

TRIFLE BAGATELLE, CIPHER, MODICUM [*Autolycus*].
NEGLECT, PLAY/TOY WITH, SKIMP. CONFECTION,
PUDDING, SWEET. PEWTER.

TRILBY *HAT*. BOOK, CHARACTER (Gerald du Maurier,
inspiration).

TRIM NEAT, SMART, *SPRUCE*, TIDY. ADORNMENT,
DECORATION, PIPING. BALANCE, BALLAST; *TUNE*.
CUT, PARE, PRUNE, WHITTLE. FIT, GOOD SHAPE.
SERVANT (Sterne).

TRIP EXPEDITION, JOURNEY, OUTING, TOUR, VOYAGE.
FALL, STUMBLE. RELEASE, TRIGGER.
HALLUCINATION (drugs).

TRIPOD STAND, STOOL, TABLE (3 feet; hence YARD, crypt).
ALTAR (*Delphi*).

TRIPPER GROCKLE, HOLIDAYMAKER, RUBBERNECK,
TOURIST. DANCER (crypt). TRIGGER (crypt).
PROJECTION, SNAG (crypt). DRUG TAKER.

TROCHEE *FOOT* (—˘).

TROJAN 1. FIGHTER. CITIZEN OF TROY. 2. **Pl** = minor *planets*.

TROT GAIT, RUN. PRODUCE. COMMIE, *RED*, REVOLUTIONARY. DAVID COPPERFIELD (*Dickens*).

TROUBLE *Anag.* ADO, BOTHER, DO, FUSS, RIOT, TO-DO. AIL, FIX. WIFE (*rh sl*).

TROUSERS BAGS, DUCKS, PANTS (US), SHORTS, SLACKS.

TROY 1. System of weight *measure* (precious metals). 2. HISSARLAK, also ILIUM. According to *Homer*'s Iliad, a city of Asia Minor, scene of 10 years' war (*c*. B.C. 1250), when Gks under *Agamemnon* beat the Trojans under King Priam's s Paris (whose abduction of *Helen*, w of Menelaus, started it all), by means of hiding soldiers (as suggested by *Ulysses*) in a wooden horse, which was taken into the city by the unsuspecting defenders. 3. Scene of T and C (*Shak*).

TRUE ACCURATE, GENUINE, REAL; STRAIGHT. CONSTANT, HONEST, LOYAL (**opp** = *false*). 'VERA'.

TRUMPERY BRIC-A-BRAC, NONSENSE, RUBBISH. DELUSIVE, SHALLOW, WORTHLESS. BRIDGE, WHIST (crypt); RUFFING (crypt).

TRUMPETER BUGLER, MUSICIAN. AGAMI, *BIRD*, CRANE, ELEPHANT, *FISH*, HERON, HOOPOE, PIGEON, SWAN.

TRURO Episcopal sig = TRURON.

TRURON *Episcopal sig* of TRURO.

TRUTH 1. ACCURACY, HONESTY, LOYALTY (**saying**). 2. **Egy god** = MAAT.

TRY THREE POINTS (hence any 3 of E, N, S and W, crypt); SCORE, TOUCHDOWN. ATTEMPT, EXPERIMENT, ESSAY, GO, TEST (**saying**). INVESTIGATE. ARRAIGN, JUDGE.

TRYING ATTEMPTING. IRRITATING. *RUGBY* (crypt). IN COURT, JUDGING (crypt).

TT ABSTAINER, DRY, *PUSSYFOOT*, TEETOTAL [Richard *Turner*; W.E. Johnson]. BIKE RACE, MANX RACE. GAUGE (model rly). MILK. DOUBLET (crypt).

TUB FATSO, FATTY. BATH. BARREL, VAT [*Diogenes*].

TUC TRADE UNION CONGRESS, WORKERS. Dn = CUT

UP, hence CHOPSTICKS (crypt). CUT BACK (crypt).

TUESDAY TUES. Day of Tiw, Ger *god* of war. ~s child = full of grace. [Shrove ~; Solomon *Grundy*].

TUN (s/l *ton*). *MEASURE* (beer, wine).

TUNA *FISH*, TUNNY. EEL (NZ). PRICKLY PEAR.

TUNE AIR, CATCH, LILT, REFRAIN, *SONG*, STRAIN. ADJUST, BREATHE ON, *TRIM*, TWEAK (mech).

TUP *SHEEP* (male, RAM. PUT UP (dn, crypt).

TUPPENCE DD, PP (crypt).

Turk Turkey, ~ish (abbr); (**car plate** = TR).

TURKISH OFFICIAL AGHA, BEG, BEY, DEY, EGA, EMIR, PASHA, SATRAP, WALI [*Eastern official*].

TURN (s/l tern). 1. T, TN. U ~. ADAPT, CONVERT, DIVERT, INVERT, REVERSE, REVOLVE, TWIST, *WHEEL*. BEND, CORNER, DEFLECTION. CHANGE, CURDLE, NAUSEATE, SHOCK. SPASM, STATE. CHARACTER, DISPOSITION, TENDENCY. DRIVE, RIDE, STROLL, WALK. ACT, PERFORMANCE. *GO*, OCCASION, OPPORTUNITY, PRIVILEGE, PURPOSE, SPELL, *TIME*, TRICK [Buggins' ~]. COIL, WRITHE. 2. Word reads backwards, e.g. **Gratuities for the turnspit** (4) = TIPS; or, in conjunction with another word, e.g. **It turns colour when sleepy** (5) = TI*RED.

TURNER 1. ACROBAT, ARTISTE, GYMNAST, PERFORMER, TUMBLER. PAINTER, CARPENTER, WOODWORKER [*Company* (livery)]. AXLE, LATHE, ROTOR, SPINNER, TOP, WHEEL (crypt). BIRD. 2. Reverse, or turn, word, e.g. **Jolly Mr Turner** = RM. 3. Richard ~, who coined the word *teetotal*, because he stammered when describing t-total abstinence.

TURNING CORNER, JUNCTION; T. MACHINING, WOODWORKING. ACTING, PERFORMING (crypt). **Pl** = SHAVINGS (mech).

TURNKEY *GAOLER*. YEK (crypt).

TURN-OUT APPEAR. PRODUCE. DRESS, GEAR, KIT, OUTFIT, RIG. TOU, UTO (anag, crypt); RUNT, TRUN (anag, crypt).

TURNOVER *Anag*. ROLL, UPSET. BUSINESS, THROUGHPUT. PIE, TART. REVO, ROVE, VORE etc (crypt).

TURN UP APPEAR, ARRIVE. [Micawber, *Dickens*]. PLOUGH, PLOW (US), TILL. CUFF (clothes). PU (crypt). NRUT (dn, crypt).

TURQUOISE *GEM*, PRECIOUS STONE (blue/green). *Birthstone* (December). *COLOUR* (blue/green).

TV BOX, BROADCASTING, IDIOT'S LANTERN, MEDIUM, SET, TELEVISION, TELLY. BBC, IBA, ITA, ITV.

TWELVE See *number*. DODECA, DOZEN, XII. *Apostles* in song. *Lords* a-leaping in *Christmas song*.

TWENTY See *number*. SCORE, XX. JACKSON (sl).

TWENTY-FIVE See *number*. £~ (PONY). XXV.

TWICE 1. BIS, ENCORE. TWO TIMES, DOUBLY. 2. Letter or word repeated, e.g. **The priest is twice a small boy** = A*A*RON; but beware **Is twice the river**, which is not THE*THE, but = IS*IS.

TWICKENHAM *RUGBY GROUND*; TRYING PLACE (crypt). *THAMES BRIDGE*.

TWIN 1. DUPLICATE, EXACT *COPY*, FACSIMILE, MIRROR IMAGE, REPLICA. TWO-ENGINED (Av). COUPLE, PAIR. 'THOMAS'. 2. Two children born at the same time; **celebrated:** AMOREL/BELPHOEBE (Faerie Queen, Spenser), ANTIPHOLUS bros (C of Errors, *Shak*), *APOLLO/ARTEMIS* (myth), *CASTOR/POLLUX* (myth), CHEERYBLES (Nicholas Nickleby, *Dickens*), DROMIO bros (C of Errors), ESAU/JACOB (bibl), *GEMINI* (stars), *HELEN/CLYTEMNESTRA* (myth), *ROMULUS/REMUS* (myth), TWEEDLEDUM/TWEEDLEDEE (*Alice* in Wonderland, Lewis Carroll), VALENTINE/ORSON (Legends of Charlemagne). 3. *Constellation* (*Gemini*); sign of the *Zodiac* (3rd).

TWIST *Anag*. CHANGE, DISTORT, WARP. CURL. INTERWEAVE, SPIRAL. ROPE, TWINE. *DANCE*. SWINDLE. TOBACCO. OLIVER ~ [ask for more; *Dickens*].

TWO See *number*. BIS, DUO, TWAIN. YELLOW BALL (snooker). Lilywhite *boys* in *song*. Turtle *doves* in *Christmas song*.

~ BITS 25 cents (US), from two bits, or pinches, of gold dust as payment in a bar during the gold rush.

~ HUNDRED CC, TWO TON.

~ PENCE DD, PP.

TWO THOUSAND See *number*. MM. KK (crypt).

~ GUINEAS *CLASSIC*; LMMC.

TYNESIDE NE (crypt).

TYPE CHARACTERISTIC, EXAMPLE, GENUS, KIND, *SORT*. TAP, WORD-PROCESS. GOTHIC, ITALIC, PICA, ROMAN.

TYPHON **Gk myth** *monster*; embodiment of earthquakes and volcanoes, breathing fire and hurricane winds. Father of *Chimaera* and the inclement *winds*.

TYPICAL CHARACTERISTIC, SYMBOLIC. PRINTING, TYPESETTING (crypt).

TYRANT *BULLY*, OPPRESSOR, THUG. *ATTILA, CERCYON,* NERO.

TYRE (s/l *tire*). CROSSPLY, RADIAL, SOLID. *BIBLICAL TOWN*, PORT (Phoen) [Sidon].

U (s/l *ewe*, you). URANIUM (*chem*). UNIVERSAL (film *censorship*). UPPER CLASS; ACCEPTABLE, DONE, SUPERIOR, TOP (**opp** = *low*). BEND, *TURN*.

UD UT DICTUM; AS DIRECTED.

UGLY *Anag*. DISCREDITABLE, UNPLEASANT, VILE; THREATENING, UNPROMISING. REPULSIVE, UNPLEASING (**opp** = *attractive*). BONNET, SHADE.

UHT ULTRA HEAT TREATED (milk).

UK UNITED KINGDOM.

ULSTER *HERALD*. KING OF ARMS. COAT. NI, N IRELAND. *UNIVERSITY*.

ULT ULTIMO. LAST MONTH.

ULTIMATE FINAL, LAST, OMEGA, Z. MAXIMUM. FUNDAMENTAL, PRIMARY.

ULYSSES (Gk = ODYSSEUS). 1. Rom myth s of Laertes, mar to *Penelope*. In the Odyssey, Homer describes his return from the Trojan war, how he blinded Polyphemus, one of the *Cyclopes*, then navigated between the *monsters* on the rocks *Scylla* and *Charybdis*, and was tempted by the *sirens*. Only he could bend the black bow of Eurytus. 2. T and C character (*Shak*).

UMBRAGE INJURY, OFFENCE, SLIGHT. SHADE.

UMLAUT ACCENT (¨).

UN 1. UNITED NATIONS, A FRENCH (crypt). 2. As prefix indicates 'lacking'. 3. Often implies anag when used as a prefix, e.g. 'undone', 'uneven' or 'unwrapped'. 4. Remove synonym for word indicated, e.g. **Uncertain gratification** (4) = PLEA(sure). or **Uncatalogued medallist** (5) = MEDAL****.

UNCIVIL ILL-MANNERED, IMPOLITE, RUDE. MILITARY (crypt).

UNCLE RELATION [*Remus*; Sam]. PAWNBROKER; POPIST, POPPER (crypt) [pledge, three balls]. BOB (catchphrase).

UNDER 1. BELOW, BENEATH, LESS THAN, LOWER. 2. Word under another in dn clue, e.g. **Little man has under 100** (4) = C*HAS. 3. Indicates what goes under, or beneath, the word indicated, e.g. **Underclothes** (4) = BODY or SKIN; or **Underrider** (6) = SADDLE.

~ **CANVAS** CAMPING. SAILING. INTENT (crypt), hence TE . . . NT.

UNDERCURRENT 1. INFLUENCE. HIDDEN ACTIVITY. 2. **Any of the rivers of the Underworld** = *ACHERON, COCYTUS, LETHE, PYRIPHLEGETHON, STYX.*

UNDERSTANDING 1. COMPREHENSION, *GRIP*, INTELLIGENCE. AGREEMENT, CONVENTION, HARMONY. 2. Anything beneath the legs (crypt), e.g. DAIS, FEET, *FOOT*, PAWS, PLATFORM, SHOES, SOLES, *STAGE*.

UNDERTAKER BURIAL/FUNERAL DIRECTOR; **celebrated:** WILLIAM BANTING (dietician), MOULD (Martin Chuzzlewit, *Dickens*), OMER (David Copperfield, *Dickens*). DOER, GUARANTOR (crypt). PROCUROR (arch).

UNDERWEAR UNDERCLOTHES. PANTS, SHOES, SKIRT, SOCKS, TROUSERS or any garment worn on nether part of the body (crypt).

UNDERWORLD ABODE OF THE DEAD, *HELL*, NETHER REGIONS, **specifically:** ABADDON (Hebr), ABYSM, ABYSS (Heb), EBLIS (Asia), EREBUS (Gk myth), GEHENNA (bibl), *HADES* (Gk myth), INFERNO (Dante), ORCUS (Rom myth), TARTARUS (Gk myth) [asphodel]. **Gods: Gk** = *HADES*; **Rom** = *DIS*, ORCUS, *PLUTO*; **Egy** = OSIRIS, SERAPIS; **goddesses: Gk** = *HECATE, PERSEPHONE*; **Rom** = PROSERPINE; **judges** = AEACUS, MINOS, RHADAMANTHYS. **Hebr** = BOR, SHAHAT, SHEOL; **Nor** = HEL; ANTIPODES. ATLAS (crypt). GANGLAND, ORGANIZED CRIME.

UNDERWRITE ACCEPT LIABILITY. SIGN (crypt).

UNEARTH DISCLOSE, DISCOVER, FIND (**opp** = *hide*). DIG UP. FUSE, SHORT CIRCUIT (crypt).

UNEATABLE BAD, INEDIBLE. *FOX* [*unspeakable* (Wilde)].

UNFAIR BIASED, CHEATING. ROUGH, UNEVEN. *UGLY.* BRUNETTE, DARK, REDHEAD (crypt).

UNIFORM CONSTANT, SAME, UNVARYING. CONFORMING. MILITARY/SCHOOL DRESS (**opp** = mufti, civvies). *SELF.*

UNION COALITION, JUNCTION. *MARRIAGE,* MATRIMONY, WEDDING, WEDLOCK. ENGLAND/SCOTLAND; GB/IRELAND. AGREEMENT, CONCORD. PIPE JOINT. WORKERS' ASSOCIATION; **celebrated:** APEX (professional and executive), ASLEF (locomotive *engineers* and *firemen*), ASTMS (scientific technical and *managerial*), AUEW (*engineering* workers), BALPA (air line *pilots*), COHSE (health service), ETU (*electricians*), GMBU (boilermakers), ISTC (iron and steelworkers), NALGO (local government officers), NATSOPA (operative printers), NFU (farmers), NGA (printers), NUJ (*journalists*), NUM (*miners*), NUPE (public employees), NUR (*railwaymen*), NUS (seamen, students), NUT (teachers), POEU (Post Office Engineers), SLADE (graphical and allied trades), SOLIDARITY (Polish workers), TGW (*transport* and general workers), TUC (Trades Union Congress).

~ **CARD** MARRIAGE LICENCE (crypt).

~ **MAN** TRADE UNIONIST, WORKER. (BRIDE) GROOM, BEST MAN, USHER (crypt).

UNIT I, INDIVIDUAL, ONE. FACTORY. And see *International units.*

UNIVERSAL *U* (film *censorship*). GENERAL, WIDESPREAD. PAN-.

UNIVERSITY FURTHER EDUCATION ESTABLISHMENT. BAs. **Celebrated:**

3-letters	4-letters
CUA (US)	BATH (Eng)
MIT (US)	CCNY (US)
USC (US)	HULL (Eng)

IOWA (US)
KENT (Eng)
OPEN (Eng)
OXON (Eng)
UCLA (US)
YALE (US)
YORK (Can, Eng)

5-letters
ASTON (Eng)
ESSEX (Eng)
KEELE (Eng)
LAVAL (Can)
LEEDS (Eng)
PADUA (It)
POONA (Ind)
WALES (Wal)

6-letters
ACADIA (Can)
BOMBAY (Ind)
BRUNEL (Eng)
DUBLIN (Ire)
DUNDEE (Sc)
DURHAM (Eng)
EXETER (Eng)
LONDON (Eng)
MCGILL (Can)
OTTAWA (Can)
OXFORD (Eng)
PRAGUE (Cz)
QUEBEC (Can)
QUEEN'S (Can, Ire)
SURREY (Eng)
SUSSEX (Eng)
ULSTER (Ire)
VASSAR (US)

7-letters
ALBERTA (Can)
BELFAST (Ire)
BOLOGNA (It)
BRISTOL (Eng)
CALGARY (Can)
CARDIFF (Wal)
CHICAGO (US)
CORNELL (US)
FLORIDA (US)
GLASGOW (Sc)
HARVARD (US)
LEIPZIG (Ger)
LOUVAIN (Belg)
LUCKNOW (Ind)
MONCTON (Can)
NEW YORK (US)
READING (Eng)
SALERNO (It)
SALFORD (Eng)
TORONTO (Can)
WARWICK (Eng)

8-letters
ABERDEEN (Sc)
ADELAIDE (Aus)
AUCKLAND (NZ)
BRADFORD (Eng)
CALCUTTA (Ind)
CAPE TOWN (SA)
CARLETON (Can)
CARNEGIE (US)
COLUMBIA (US)
FLINDERS (SA)
FREIBURG (Ger)
ILLINOIS (US)
MANITOBA (Can)
MICHIGAN (US)
MONTREAL (Can)

SORBONNE (Fr)
STAMFORD (Eng)
STIRLING (Sc)
SYRACUSE (US)
TASMANIA (Aus)
VICTORIA (Aus)

9-letters
CAMBRIDGE (Eng)
DALHOUSIE (Can)
EDINBURGH (Sc)
FRANKFURT (Ger)
GOTTINGEN (Ger)
JAMES COOK (Aus)
LANCASTER (Eng)
LEICESTER (Eng)
LIVERPOOL (Eng)
MELBOURNE (Aus)
MINNESOTA (US)
NEWCASTLE (Eng)
NOTRE DAME (Can)
PRINCETON (US)
ROCHESTER (Eng)
SHEFFIELD (Eng)
SINGAPORE (S'pore)
ST ANDREWS (Sc)
WISCONSIN (US)

10+ letters
BIRMINGHAM (Eng)
CALIFORNIA (US)
CANTERBURY (NZ)
CINCINNATI (US)
CITY COLLEGE (US)
CONNECTICUT (US)
EAST ANGLIA (Eng)
GOETTINGEN (Ger)
HEIDELBERG (Ger)
HERIOT-WATT (Sc)
LETHBRIDGE (Can)
LOUGHBOROUGH (Eng)
MANCHESTER (Eng)
MASSACHUSETTS (US)
MILTON KEYNES (Eng)
MOUNT ALLISON (Can)
NEW BRUNSWICK (Can)
NEW ENGLAND (Aus)
NOTTINGHAM (Eng)
PENNSYLVANIA (US)
PITTSBURGH (US)
SASKATCHEWAN (Can)
SHERBROOKE (Can)
SIMON FRASER (Can)
SOUTHAMPTON (Eng)
S CALIFORNIA (US)
STRATHCLYDE (Sc)
WASHINGTON (US)

~ **COLLEGE** Colleges of Cambridge (C) and Oxford (O):

3-letters
NEW (O)

KINGS (C)
ORIEL (O)

5-letters
CAIUS (C)
CLARE (C)
JESUS (C, O)
KEBLE (O)

6-letters
DARWIN (C)
EXETER (O)
GIRTON (C)
MERTON (O)

QUEENS' (O)
QUEEN'S (C)
SELWYN (C)
WADHAM (O)

MAGDALEN (O)
PEMBROKE (C, O)
ROBINSON (C)
ST HILDA'S (O)

7-letters
BALLIOL (O)
CHRIST'S (C)
DOWNING (C)
LINCOLN (O)
NEWNHAM (C)
ST ANNE'S (O)
ST HUGH'S (O)
ST JOHN'S (C)
TRINITY (C, O)

9-letters
BRASENOSE (O)
CHURCHILL (C)
MAGDALENE (C)
WORCESTER (O)

10+ letters
CHRISTCHURCH (O)
CORPUS CHRISTI (C, O)
FITZWILLIAM (C)
LADY MARGARET HALL (O)
PETERHOUSE (C)
SIDNEY SUSSEX (C)
SOMERVILLE (O)
ST CATHARINE'S (C)
TRINITY HALL (C)
UNIVERSITY (O)

8-letters
ALL SOULS (O)
EMMANUEL (C)
GONVILLE (C)
HERTFORD (O)
HOMERTON (C)

~ **GRANT** BURSARY, EXHIBITION, SCHOLARSHIP. DEGREE (crypt).

UNKNOWN STRANGE, UNFAMILIAR. X, Y (maths).

UNLIMITED 1. GREAT, UNRESTRICTED, VAST. 2. Delete both end letters, e.g. **Old money is unlimited cash** = *AS*.

UNLOCKED OPENED, UNBOLTED, UNFASTENED. *CUT*. DISTRESSED, SCALPED, SHORN (crypt).

UNMARRIED 1. BACHELOR, SINGLE, SPINSTER. 2. Delete **m** or **wed** from clue, e.g. **Unmarried man** = *AN.

UNORDERED HIGGLEDY-PIGGLEDY, RANDOM, SCATTERED, UNTIDY. SPONTANEOUS, VOLUNTARY. LAY, NON-CLERICAL (crypt).

UNQUALIFIED 1. UNRESTRICTED. INCOMPETENT. UNTRAINED. COMPLETE, PERFECT, UTTER. 2. Remove any letters implying technical or educational qualification (BA,

FCA, MB etc). e.g. **Early South African unqualified bomber** (4)
= BO**ER.

UNQUIET 1. UNEASY. NOISY, F. 2. Delete any indication of
quiet from clue (e.g. **p, sh** etc). e.g. **Unquiet tipper leads to row**
(4) = TI**ER.

UNREADY UNPREPARED. LACKING ADVICE, RASH:
ETHELRED.

UNSAINTLY 1. UNHOLY. 2. Delete letters **st** from word, e.g.
Ernest is unsaintly bird (4) = ERNE**.

UNSEEN 1. INVISIBLE, NOT NOTICED, NOT READ [*eminence
grise*]. 2. ~ characters in literature: BUGGINS (~ turn):
BUNBURY (*The Importance of Being Ernest*, Wilde): MRS
GRUNDY (Thos Morton); MRS HARRIS (Martin Chuzzlewit,
Dickens): HARVEY (*rabbit*, Mary Chase): INVISIBLE MAN
(H. G. Wells): LT KIJE (Troika, Prokofiev): MACAVITY (*cat*,
T. S. Eliot); MRS PARTINGTON (Sydney Smith).

UNSPEAKABLE OBJECTIONABLE, REPULSIVE. HUNT,
HUNTERS, HUNTSMEN [*uneatable* (Wilde)].

UNSUPPORTED 1. SECONDARY, SOLO, UNAIDED,
UNSUBSTANTIATED. DESTITUTE. CANTILEVER.
2. Remove synonym for 'support' (bra, guy, prop, stay), e.g.
Prohibit unsupported staybar (3) = ****BAR.

UNWATERED 1. DRY, PARCHED: DESERT, NOT
IRRIGATED. NEAT, UNDILUTED. 2. Delete synonym for
water from clue (hoo, sea etc), e.g. **Volume of unwatered
choochoo** = C**C**.

UNWILLING RELUCTANT. INTESTATE (crypt).

UP 1. ON HIGH, TO HIGHER PLACE (**opp** = *down*). AT
UNIVERSITY. FINISHED. RISEN. MOUNTED, RIDING,
SADDLED. 2. Dn answer reads backwards, or upwards, e.g.
Dickens lived up (5) = DEVIL.

UPAS *TREE*. EVIL INFLUENCE, MALEVOLENCE. SA (dn,
crypt).

UPBRAID CHIDE, SCOLD. PUT UP HAIR [bun] (crypt).

UPHOLD 1. CONFIRM, MAINTAIN, SUPPORT. 2. In dn
answer, word holds another inside, and one or both reads
backwards, e.g. **Every account he upholds** (4) = E*AC*H.

UPIS 1. Egy chief *goddess*, and of *NATURE*. 2. *SI* (dn, crypt).

UP-MARKET SOPHISTICATED. TRAM (dn, crypt).

UPPER HIGHER, TOP. SHOE TOP, VAMP. REP (dn, crypt).

~ CLASS U; ARISTOCRACY, GENTRY. FIRST FORM, SIXTH FORM, SENIOR.

UPRIGHT CORRECT, RIGHTEOUS. VERTICAL (**opp** = *leaning*). PIANO. ROMAN TYPE. TR (dn, crypt).

UPSET *Anag.* 1. CAPSIZE, DISTURB, OVERTURN, SPILL. ANXIOUS, WORRIED. TES (dn, crypt). 2. Answer reads up (dn).

UPSTART NOUVEAU RICHE. U (crypt).

URANIA 1. Gk myth, one of the 9 *Muses* (astronomy). 2. A minor *PLANET*.

URANIDS Gk myth sons of *Uranus* and *Gaea*, identified with the *GIGANTES*, who conquered the *Titans* when the latter made war on the gods; they were *monsters* with 100 arms and 50 heads: AEGAEON or BRIAEREUS, COTTUS and GYGES or GYES.

URANIUM U (*chem*).

URANUS Gk *god* of HEAVEN, f (by Ge) of the *Titans* and the *Uranids*. When he was killed, *Aphrodite* sprang from the sea foam where his limbs were thrown.

URGE ABET, ADVOCATE, EGG, ENCOURAGE, ENTREAT, EXHORT, IMPEL, SET ON, SICK, SPUR, STIMULATE. DRIVE, DESIRE, WISH, YEARNING.

URIAH HEEP (David Copperfield, *Dickens* ['umble]). HITTITE.

US WE. UNITED STATES OF AMERICA.

USA UNITED STATES OF AMERICA (*car plate*).

USS US SHIP, *BOAT*.

USSR SOVIET RUSSIA (as opposed to **Russ** = Russia).

UTHERSON *KING ARTHUR* (son of Uther Pendragon) [*Guinevere, Lancelot, Round Table*].

UTTER EXPRESS, SAY, SPEAK. CIRCULATE, ISSUE (money). COMPLETE, *UNQUALIFIED*, TOTAL.

UTTERLY COMPLETELY, TOTALLY. Sounds like . . ., *pronounced* like . . . (crypt).

V VANADIUM (*chem*). VATICAN CITY (*car plate*). VERSUS, VS; AGAINST. VICTORY SIGN. SEE, VIDE. VOL(UME). VOLTS. *FIVE*.

VALE CHANNEL, VALLEY (**opp** = *hill*). FAREWELL.

VALHALLA Nor myth; *Odin's* great hall, the house of warriors slain in battle [*Valkyries*].

VALKYRIES Nor myth; *Odin's* handmaidens, who selected those to be slain in battle and thus go to *Valhalla*.

VAMP ADVENTURESS, FLIRT. ALLURE, EXPLOIT, SEDUCE. UPPER (shoe). FURBISH, REPAIR. IMPROVISE, STRUM (mus).

VANADIUM V (*chem*).

VARIETY *Anag.* DIVERSITY, CHANGE; **saying.** SPECIMEN, TYPE. SHOWBIZ, VAUDEVILLE. [spice of life].

VAT CISTERN, CONTAINER, TANK, TUB, VESSEL. TAX.

VAULT JUMP, LEAP, *SPRING. ARCH*, CELLAR, CRYPT, FIRMAMENT.

VEGETABLE 1. MONOTONOUS, UNEVENTFUL. APATHETIC, CATALEPTIC, INCAPACITATED. 2. PLANTLIFE (not animal, mineral or abstract). **Pl** = GREENS.
Types:

3-letters	OKRA	6-letters
COS	*PEAR*	BATATA
DAL	RAPE	CARROT
OCA	SOYA	CELERY
PEA	SPUD	CYNARA
SOY		DAUCUS
UDO	5-letters	ENDIVE
YAM	APIUM	LENTIL
ZEA	CHARD	LOMENT
	CHICH	MARROW
4-letters	CRESS	PHASEL
BEAN	MAIZE	PORRET
BEET	NAVEW	*POTATO*
COLE	ONION	PYROLA
CORN	ORACH	RADISH
DOHL	PEASE	RUNNER
EDDO	PULSE	SPROUT
FABA	SWEDE	*SQUASH*
KALE	TUBER	TOMATO
KOHL		TURNIP
LEEK		

7-letters
CABBAGE
CHICORY
GHERKIN
LETTUCE
PARSNIP
PUMPKIN
SALSIFY
SEAKALE
SEAWEED
SHALLOT
SPINACH
TRUFFLE

8-letters
BEETRAVE
BEETROOT
BORECOLE
BRASSICA
CELERIAC
CHICK-PEA

CHOW-CHOW
COLERAPE
COLEWORT
CUCUMBER
EGG-PLANT

9+ letters
ARTICHOKE
ASPARAGUS
AUBERGINE
BROAD BEAN
BRUSSELS SPROUT
CAULIFLOWER
COLOGASSI
COURGETTE
FRENCH BEAN
JERUSALEM ARTICHOKE
MANGE-TOUT
RUNNER BEAN
SWEET CORN

VEHICLE AUTO, CAB, CAR, *CARRIAGE*, LORRY. BUS, CHARABANC, MINI-BUS, MINI-CAB. TRUCK, VAN. AIRBUS, AIRCRAFT, PLANE. *BOAT*.

VENETIAN OF VENICE; MARCO (POLO). BLIND.

Venez Venezuela.

VENUE RENDEZVOUS. GAME PARK, MATCH SITE; AWAY, HOME. GROUND (*cricket, football, rugby, tennis*).

VENUS 1. Rom *goddess* of *LOVE*; m of *Aeneas* by Anchises and of *Cupid* by Jupiter. **Gk** = *APHRODITE*, HESPER (US); **Phoen** = ASTARTE; **Nor** = *FREYA*; **Bab** = ISHTAR; **Egy** = *ISIS*. 2. *PLANET*.

VERSE POEM, POETRY, STANZA. FURROW. VERSICLE (bibl).

VERSED EDUCATED, SCHOOLED, *TRAINED*. POETIC, IN POETRY (crypt).

VERSION *Anag.* ACCOUNT. BOOK. VARIANT. TURNING (crypt).

VERSUS V, VS; AGAINST.

VERT VERTICAL. GREEN (*herald*).

VERY BIG OS.

VERY LOUD FF.

VESSEL *BOAT*; HMS, SS, USS. **Celebrated:** ARK (Noah), BEAGLE (Darwin), *BELLEROPHON* (Napoleon), BOUNTY (Bligh), *CINQUE PORTS* (*Crusoe*), *DISCOVERY* (Cook, Scott), ENDEAVOUR (Cook), FRAM (Nansen), GOLDEN HIND (ex Pelican, *Drake*), HISPANIOLA (Treasure Island), MARY ROSE (Henry VIII), MAUD (Amundsen), NINA (Columbus), PELICAN (later Golden Hind, *Drake*), PEQUOD (*Ahab*), PINTA (Columbus), RESOLUTION (Cook), REVENGE (Grenville), *VICTORY* (Nelson). *BOWL*, CROCK, CRUSE, CUP, DISH, *EWER*, GLASS, LAVER, PAN, POT, STOUP, URN.

VESTA 1. MATCH®, LUCIFER. 2. Rom *goddess* of the HEARTH; **Gk** = *HESTIA*. 3. A minor *PLANET*.

VESTMENT *CHURCH DRESS*, GARMENT, ROBE. BLOCKADE, SIEGE (mil; arch).

VETO BAN, BAR. WRONG VOTE (crypt).

VI SIX. VIOLET. BUZZBOMB, DOODLEBUG, FLYING BOMB, *ROCKET*, *WEAPON*.

VICTOR CONQUEROR, WINNER. *AIRCRAFT*, BOMBER.

VICTORIA 1. *QUEEN*; REGINA. RLY STATION. *CARRIAGE. LAKE. UNIVERSITY.* 2. Rom *goddess*, eq of *NIKE*. 3. A minor *PLANET*.

VICTORY 1. TRIUMPH, WIN. WARSHIP [Nelson]. 2. **Goddesses: Gk** = *NIKE*; **Rom** = VICTORIA.

~ **SIGN** LAUREL, MEDAL, PALM, GARLAND; V.

Viet Vietnam.

VIGORN *Episcopal sig* of WORCESTER.

VINTNER WINE-MERCHANT. NABOTH (bibl) [f of *Chaucer*].

VIOLIN *FIDDLE*, *INSTRUMENT*, ROCTA (mus) [viol, viola]; **parts:** back, bass bar, belly, block, bout, bridge, button, fingerboard, fret, head, neck, nut, peg-box, rib, scroll, sound-hole, string, tail-piece, waist. [Strad(ivarius)].

VIOLINIST FIDDLER; *BOWER*, BOWMAN, SCRAPER (crypt). *HOLMES*. [Amati, Strad(ivarius)].

VIP VERY IMPORTANT PERSON; CELEBRITY, LION,

NOTABLE, *STAR*.

VIPER *ADDER*.

VIRGINITY 1. INNOCENCE. FLORIMEL (Faerie Queen, Spenser). 2. **Goddess: Gk** = ARTEMIS. 3. *Constellation* (Virgo); sign of the *Zodiac* (6th).

VIRGO *Constellation* (Virgin); sign of the *Zodiac* (6th).

VISIT CALL, GO TO SEE, STAY. ATTACK; PUNISH (bibl). BLESS, COMFORT (arch).

VIXEN FOX (*female*). SCOLD, TERMAGANT. *REINDEER*.

VO/VOL VOLUME. BOOKLET, SHORT BOOK (crypt).

VOLCANO ERUPTING MOUNTAIN; HOT SPOT (crypt). [active, dormant, extinct; magma; lava; crater]. **Celebrated:** ETNA, FUJIYAMA, MT ST HELENS, KRAKATOA, MAUNA LOA, PARICUTIN, MT PELEE, STROMBOLI, SURTSEY, SUSWA, TANGSHAN, VESUVIUS.

VOLTS V; SHOCKING (crypt).

VOLTURNUS Rom myth SE *WIND*; **Gk** = EUROS.

VOLUME BOOK, TOME, VOL. CAPACITY, CC, CL, GAL, *MEASURE*, *PECK*.

VOLUNTEER OFFER, UNDERTAKE; ENLIST, JOIN UP (**opp** = conscribe, conscript, *press gang*). Type of snooker. **Pl** = DAD'S ARMY, HOME GUARD, LDV, TA, TERRIERS [*soldiers*].

VOTE BALLOT, CROSS, POLL, X; CHOOSE, ELECT, SUGGEST, VOICE.

VOWEL A, E, I, O, U (Y). Open sound of speech capable of forming a syllable. Word with all ~s in correct order: FACETIOUS; word with five ~s consecutively: QUEUEING; 6-letter word with no ~s: RHYTHM; 9-letter word with only one ~: STRENGTHS. **Opp** = consonant.

VS V; AGAINST, VERSUS. FIVES (crypt).

VULCAN 1. *AIRCRAFT*, BOMBER. 2. Rom *god* of *FIRE*; **Gk** = HEPHAESTUS.

VULGAR 1. COARSE, COMMON, LOW, PLEBEIAN (**opp** = U). FREQUENT, PREVALENT, POPULAR. 2. Use slang or abbreviation, e.g. **Quiet! Isn't Edward vulgar made up like that** (7) = P*AINT*ED.

W WATTS. WED, WEDNESDAY. WEST. WHITE. WICKET. WIDE. WIFE. WITH. WOLFRAM (*chem*). WOMEN'S (size). *BRIDGE PLAYER*.

WAGE CARRY ON, CONDUCT. REQUITAL. PAY, *SCREW* [salary].

WAGER COMBATANT (crypt). *BET*. PAID WORKER (crypt).

WAIF ABANDONED CHILD, MITE, SCRAP. TINY TIM.

WAIT (s/l *weight*). ATTEND, AWAIT, REMAIN, *STAY*. CAROL SINGER. AMBUSH.

WAITER ATTENDANT, COMMIS, GARCON, MAITRE D'HOTEL. RUNNER (Stock Exchange). CAROL SINGER (crypt). QUEUER (crypt).

Wal Wales, Welsh. Cambria, ~n. [*patron saint*].

WALK BALL OF CHALK (*rh sl*), FOOTPATH, PERAMBULATE, PROMENADE, PATH; CONSTITUTIONAL, OUTING; AMBLE, TRAIPSE.

WALKER PEDESTRIAN, PERAMBULATOR; 6 proud ~s in *song*. WALKING AID.

WALRUS SEA-MAMMAL, MORSE; **male** = *bull*; **female** = *cow*; **offspring** = *calf* [seal, sealion]. *Alice* character.

WANDERING *Anag*. ERRING, MEANDERING, WINDING [*Jew*].

WAR BELLIGERENCE, CONTENTION, FIGHT, HOSTILITIES, STRIFE, STRUGGLE (**opp** = *peace*). **Gods: Gk** = *ARES*, **Rom** = MARS, **Ger** = TIW; **goddesses: Gk** = *ATHENE*, PALLAS, **Rom** = *MINERVA*, **Nor** = *BRUNHILDA*.

WARD (s/l *warred*). CONFINEMENT, CUSTODY. CHARGE, MINOR. LOCK FLANGE. DEPARTMENT, DISTRICT, DIVISION; ROOM; NURSERY (crypt). DEFENCE; BAILEY. AVERT, PARRY. DRAWBACK (crypt).

WARDER *GAOLER*. DOCTOR, HOUSEMAN, INTERN (US), *NURSE*, PATIENT (all crypt).

WAR OFFICE WO; OPS ROOM, BUNKER, COMMAND POST.

WASP *INSECT*; STINGER (crypt). WOMEN'S AIR FORCE (US).

WATCH ATTENTION, GUARD, LOOK-OUT, OBSERVATION, VIGILANCE; CAVE-MAN (crypt). CARE FOR, OBSERVE. DUTY SPELL. STREET PATROL. VIGILANTE [posse]. CLOCK, (HALF) HUNTER,

REPEATER, TIMEPIECE. *Assembly* of nightingales.

~ **CASE** SENTRY BOX (crypt).

WATCHMAN 1. GUARD(IAN), SENTINEL, SENTRY [cave, curfew]. PEEPING TOM, VOYEUR (crypt). SAILOR. HOROLOGIST, JEWELLER (crypt). SPECTATOR (crypt). 2. ~ **of the gods** = HEIMDAL (Nor) [*Cerberus*].

WATER LAKE, RAIN, *RIVER*, SEA, SPRING, STREAM, WELL **(saying)**; ADAM'S ALE: HOO (crypt). DRIBBLE, SALIVATE. DILUTE.

~ **CARRIER** 1. AQUEDUCT, GOURD, MAINS, PIPE [Gunga Din (Kipling)]. 2. *Constellation* (Aquarius); sign of the *Zodiac* (11th).

WATERFALL CASCADE, CATARACT, FALLS [Minnehaha]; **celebrated falls:** *ANGEL* (S Am), ANGRABIES (S Af), BOYOMA (W Af), CEDAR (USA), CHURCHILL (Can), *GRAND* (Can), IGUACA (S Am), IROQUOIS (Can), KABALEGA (Af), NIAGARA (Can/USA), NGONEYE (Af), OWEN (Af), PARK (USA), REICHENBACH (Swi, *Holmes*), SIOUX (USA), SMITHS (Can), VICTORIA (Af). RAIN(DROP) (crypt). TEARS (crypt).

WATERLOO *BATTLE*; FINISH, UNDOING. STATION (rly); ~ and City Line = THE DRAIN. THAMES BRIDGE.

WATER TOWER MAIN SUPPLY, TANK. TUG (crypt).

WATTS W.

WAVE BREAKER, BRINY, COMBER, FOAM, RIPPLE, ROLLER, SEA, SURF, WHITE HORSE; BORE, EAGRE. CURL, HAIR, LOCK, MARCEL [permanent]. BRANDISH, FLUTTER, VIBRATE; CURVE, UNDULATE.

WAVING OSCILLATION, SIGNALLING. HAIRDRESSING (crypt). SURFING, SWIMMING (crypt).

WAX (s/l whacks). BEESWAX, RESIN [*Daedalus*, Icarus]. POLISH. GROW, INCREASE. FIT OF ANGER, TEMPER.

WAY (s/l weigh]. AVENUE, CUL-DE-SAC, LANE, PASSAGE, PATH, RAIL, ROAD, ROUTE, STREET, TRACK [Appian, Fosse, Icknield, Pilgrim's (*Roman roads*); Milky]. MANNER, METHOD, SYSTEM. MOMENTUM [kinetic energy]. SLIPWAY, STOCK. N, E, S, W.

WEALTH 1. ABUNDANCE, OPULENCE, PROFUSION, RICHES [*Croesus*, Dives, *Midas*]. 2. **God: Gk** = PLUTUS.

WEAPON INSTRUMENT; WAR MATERIAL:

Clubs
COSH
CUDGEL
MACE
MERE

Blades
BATTLEAXE
CUTLASS
DAGGER
EPEE
FOIL
JAVELIN
KNIFE
LANCE
RAPIER
SABRE
SPEAR
STILETTO
SWORD

Launchers
ARQUEBUS
AUTOMATIC
BAZOOKA
BIG BERTHA
BOW
BREN
BROWNING
CANNON
CARBINE
CATAPULT
COLT
CROSSBOW
DERRINGER
FLAMETHROWER
FOWLING PIECE

GAT
GATLING
GUN
HOWITZER
LUGER
MONS MEG
MUSKET
PIAT
PISTOL
REPEATER
REVOLVER
RIFLE
SHOTGUN
SLING
STEN
WALTHER
WEBLEY
WINCHESTER

Missiles
ARROW
BOMB
BULLET
GRENADE
GUIDED *MISSILE*
ICBM
MILLS BOMB
MINE
MISSILE
ROCKET
SAM
SHELL
SLINGSHOT
TORPEDO
V1

Vehicles (manned)	FRIGATE
AIRCRAFT	*MONITOR*
ARMOURED CAR	MTB
BATTLESHIP	Q-BOAT
BOMBER	SHUTTLE
CARRIER	SUBMARINE
CRUISER	TANK
DESTROYER	WARSHIP
FIGHTER	

WEASEL EQUIVOCATE, QUIBBLE. TRACKED VEHICLE (mil). QUADRUPED: *FERRET*, GLUTTON, MARTEN, MEERKAT, MONGOOSE, POLECAT (fitch; US skunk), STOAT (ermine), SURICATE, WOLVERINE.

WEATHER (s/l whether). CURE, DRY, EXPOSE, SEASON; DISCOLOUR. OVERCOME, PASS; WINDWARD (naut). ATMOSPHERE, CONDITIONS, METEOROLOGY; **forecast areas:** Bailey, Biscay, Cromarty, Dogger, Dover, Faeroes, Fair Isle, Finisterre, Fisher, Forth, Forties, German Bight, Hebrides, Humber, Irish Sea, Lundy, Malin, Minches, Plymouth, Portland, Rockall, SE Iceland, Shannon, Sole, Thames, Tyne, Viking, Wight.

WEAVER CLOTH/TAPESTRY MAKER; [*company* (livery); Aubusson]; **celebrated:** *ARACHNE*, BOTTOM (MND, *Shak*), *Chaucer* character, LADY OF SHALOTT (Tennyson), SILAS MARNER (G. Eliot/Marian Evans). PLOTTER, SCHEMER. AMADAVAT, TAHA, *BIRD*. RIVER (Eng). *SNAKE* (crypt). *SPIDER* (crypt).

WEBSTER DICTIONARY®. *SPIDER* (crypt).

WED WEDNESDAY. HITCHED, JOINED, MARRIED, MATCHED, MATED, PAIRED, SPLICED, WEDDED [*union*, matrimony]. WE WOULD.

WEDDING *MARRIAGE*, MATRIMONIAL, *UNION*.

~ **PRESENT** DOT, DOWRY. GIFT.

WEDGE V-SHAPE. JAM, PACK, SQUEEZE IN. *GOLFCLUB*. *Assembly* of swans.

WEDNESDAY W, WED. Day of *Odin*, *Woden*. ~**'s child** = full of woe. [Ash ~; Solomon *Grundy*].

WEED (s/l we'd). WILD HERB, *WILD PLANT*. LANKY,

WEAK PERSON. *DRUG*, MARIJUANA; TOBACCO. **Pl =** mourning clothes.

WEEK (s/l weak). SEVEN *DAYS*, SENNIGHT. MON-FRI. PERIOD, *TIME*.

WEEP CRY, GREET (Sc), KEEN, (**saying**). DRIP, EXUDE, SWEAT. DROOP.

WEIGHT (s/l *wait*). 1. EFFECT, IMPORTANCE. HEAVINESS, MASS, *MEASURE*: CWT, DWT, KG, KILO, LB, *OUNCE*, OZ, *POUND*, TON, *TROY*. LONDON DISTRICT (W8, hence WVIII). 2. **Boxing ~s:** FLY ~, BANTAM ~, FEATHER ~, JUNIOR LIGHT ~, LIGHT ~, JUNIOR WELTER ~, WELTER ~, JUNIOR MIDDLE ~, MIDDLE ~, LIGHT HEAVY ~, HEAVY ~.

WELL ARTESIAN, FOUNTAIN, GUSHER, SOURCE, *SPA*, SPRING. INKPOT. FIT, HALE, NOT ILL, SOUND. CAREFULLY, EASILY, PROBABLY, SATISFACTORILY, THOROUGHLY, WISELY (**opp** = *badly*). WE WILL (crypt).

WELLINGTON *BOOT*. IRON DUKE, NOSEY, *MILITARY LEADER* [Wellesley]. *PUBLIC SCHOOL*. *CAPITAL* (NZ). WIMPY (aircraft nickname).

WELSH (s/l welch). CELTIC, CYMRIC [leek, Taffy]. ABSCOND, DECAMP, FLIT.

WELT SHOE LEATHER; RIBBING, TRIM. BLOW, CUFF, SMACK. WORLD (Ger).

WEMBLEY *FOOTBALL GROUND*, STADIUM.

WENDY DARLING [Peter Pan]. CURVY, SINUOUS (crypt).

WEST 1. W, OCCIDENT. MAE. *WRITER*. *BRIDGE PLAYER*. 2. Reads from right to left, e.g. **Childish seat of learning looks west** = SKOOL.

~ END LONDON, MAYFAIR, WI.

WESTERN W, OCCIDENTAL. COWBOY FILM, B MOVIE [*outlaw*].

WESTMINSTER *LEGISLATIVE ASSEMBLY*, PARLIAMENT. *PUBLIC SCHOOL*. *THAMES BRIDGE*.

WH ONLIE BEGETTER (*Shak*).

WHALE (s/l wail). BEAT, THRASH, WHACK. HUGE, LARGE. *ISLAND*. RIVER (Can). CETACEAN MAMMAL: BALEIN, BELUGA, BLUE ~, BOOPS, CACHALOT, FIN ~, GRAMPUS, GREY ~, HUMP-BACKED ~, KILLER ~,

NARWHAL, ORC, ORCA, PILOT ~, POTHEAD, RIGHT ~,
RORQUAL, SEI, SINGING ~, SPERM ~; **assembly** = school,
offspring = *calf* [Ahab, Moby Dick].

WHALER (s/l wailer). WHALE HUNTER; AHAB [Moby Dick,
Herman Melville]. BOAT, CUTTER, GIG.

WHEEL (s/l weal). BALANCE, CATHERINE, COG, FLY,
MILL, PADDLE, POTTER'S, SPINNING, STEERING
[*Company* (livery); *Ixion*. *St Catherine*, *tarot*). PIVOT, *TURN*
(mil). REVOLVER (crypt).

WHIG (s/l *wig*). PARLIAMENTARIAN, LIBERAL [BURKE,
FOX, *GREY*: *Prime Minister*].

WHIP DART, *DASH*, JERK, NIP, SNATCH. BIND, SEIZE,
SERVE (naut). BURTON, HANDY-BILLY, *HOIST*,
PULLEY, PURCHASE (naut). BEAT, FLOG, LASH,
LEATHER, *URGE*; CANE, *CAT* (O'Nine-Tails), QUIRT,
ROD, ROMAL, *SCORPION*, SCOURGE, STRAP, *TAW*
[bolas, lariat, lasso]. COACHMAN, HUNTSMAN.
DISCIPLINE, ORDER (polit).

WHISKER BEARD, BEAVER, BRISTLE, HAIR. SHORT
DISTANCE. EGG-BEATER (crypt).

WHISKEY *DRINK*, USQUEBAUGH (Ire); POTEEN.

WHISKY *DRINK*, SCOTCH. *CARRIAGE*. MOUSSE, SNOW
(cook, crypt). WHIPPY (crypt).

WHIST *CARD GAME*; TRUMPERY (crypt). P, PP, SH; HUSH,
QUIET, SILENCE.

WHISTLE SHRILL. THROAT (sl). *SUIT* (*rh sl*).

WHITE *COLOUR*. BILLIARD/SNOOKER BALL.
CAUCASIAN. *ISLAND*. RIVER (US). *SEA*. SPACE
TRAVELLER. *WRITER*. 'BLANCHE'. **Pl** = CRICKET
TROUSERS, CREAMS.

WHITEFRIARS CARMELITES.

WHITSTABLE NATIVE, *OYSTER* [Colchester].

WHO DOCTOR, DR. WORLD HEALTH ORGANIZATION.
[*six*].

WI LONDON, MAYFAIR, WEST END. WEST INDIES.
WOMEN'S INSTITUTE. WILLIAM THE
CONQUEROR.

WICKED EVIL, MISCHIEVOUS, SINFUL, SPITEFUL.
CANDLE, OIL LAMP (crypt).

WIDELY BROADLY. ABROAD, FOREIGN, TRANSLATED (crypt).

WIDOW SHORT LINE (print). BEREAVED WIFE, surviving fem spouse; **celebrated:** BRADY (Garrick); CLIQUOT (Veuve, champagne); TWANKY (theat) [cruse; grass ~; ~'s peak; ~'s weeds].

WIFE CONSORT, MATE, PARTNER; BETTER HALF, DUTCH, MRS, OLD WOMAN, *RIB*; TROUBLE (*rh sl*).

WIG (s/l *whig*). TOUPEE; RUG (sl).

WILD *Anag.* ANGRY, BARBAROUS, DESOLATE, DISORDERLY, EAGER, IRREGULAR, RASH, UNTAMED, WAYWARD. [joker]. *ROBBER*.

~ **CAT** HOT TEMPERED, IMPROMPTU, RECKLESS, SNAP, VIOLENT. UNOFFICIAL. *AIRCRAFT*. And see *CAT*.

~ **FLOWER** WILD PLANT. CASCADE, WATERFALL, WHITE WATER (crypt).

~ **PLANT** UNCULTIVATED FLOWER, WEED (and see *plant*). **Breeds:**

4-letters
FLAG
LING
REED
RUSH
WELD
WORT

5-letters
AVENS
DAISY

6-letters
BALSAM
BURNET
CLOVER
MEDICK
NETTLE
SORREL
SPURGE

SUNDEW
TEASEL
YARROW

7-letters
BISTORT
BOG-BEAN
BUGLOSS
CAMPION
COMFREY
EELWORT
FROGBIT
HEATHER
LUCERNE
MAYWEED
RAGWORT
RAMSONS
SPURREY
VERVAIN

8-letters
ASPHODEL
BILBERRY
BINDWEED
CHARLOCK
COW-WHEAT
CROW-FOOT
FLEABANE
HAREBELL
HAWKWEED
KNAPWEED
MARJORAM
MILKWORT
PLANTAIN
SCABIOUS
SCULL-CAP
SELFHEAL
SOAPWORT
TOADFLAX
VALERIAN

9-letters
BUCKTHORN
BUTTERCUP
CHICKWEED
COLTSFOOT
DANDELION
EYEBRIGHT
GIPSYWORT
GOLDEN ROD

GROUNDSEL
LOUSEWORT
MARESTAIL
PIMPERNEL
SPEARWORT
SPEEDWELL
STONECROP
TORMENTIL
WOUNDWORT

10+ letters
BUTTERWORT
CINQUEFOIL
CRANESBILL
CUCKOOFLOWER
DEADLY NIGHTSHADE
DEADNETTLE
GOATS BEARD
HERB ROBERT
LOOSESTRIFE
MEADOWSWEET
RAGGED ROBIN
RESTHARROW
SILVERWEED
SNEEZEWORT
SOWTHISTLE
STITCHWORT
STORKSBILL
WATERCRESS
YELLOW RATTLE

WILL IMPULSE, INTENTION, VOLITION. TESTAMENT [legacy]. BILL, WILLIAM. [*ignis fatuus*].

WILLIAM BILL, WILL, WM; 'A DEFENDER'. KING. CONQUEROR. ORANGE; TELL; WILBERFORCE. Old Father ~ (*Alice*).

WILLING CONSENTING, GAME, *KEEN*, READY. DEVISING, LEAVING, TESTATOR (crypt). [Barkis is willin' (*Dickens*)].

WIMBLEDON *TENNIS VENUE. COURTED* (crypt). [Wombles].

WINCE FLINCH, START. ROLLER. CWE (crypt).

WINCHESTER 1. RIFLE, WEAPON. VENTA BULGARUM (*Rom*). *CASTLE. PUBLIC SCHOOL.* 2. **Episcopal sig** = WINTON.

WIND 1. COIL, CRANK, REEL, TURN, TWIST; MEANDER [serpent, *snake*]. EMBRACE, ENTWINE. AIR, BREATH, FLATULENCE. BREEZE, BLOW, CYCLONE, GALE, GUST, HURRICANE, PUFF, STORM, TEMPEST, TORNADO, TYPHOON, ZEPHYR (**opp** = calm, doldrums, horse latitudes); **saying. Celebrated:** ANTANE (Toulouse), BERG (S Af), BISE (Alps), BORA (Adriatic), BUSTER (Aus), CHINOOK (Rocky Mts), ETESIAN (Mediterranean), FOHN (Alps), FREMANTLE DOCTOR (Aus; cricket); GHIBLI (Libya), GRIGALE (Malta), HARMATTAN (W Af), HELM (Lake District), KAMIKAZE (Jap), KHAMSIN (Egy), KUBAN (Java), LEVANTER (E Med), MELTEMI (Aegean), MISTRAL (Fr), MONSOON (Ind Ocean), PAMPERO (Andes), PASSAT (N Atlantic), PUNA (Peru), ROARING FORTIES (Antarctic), ROGER (E Anglia), SAMIEL (Turk), SANTA ANNA (Nevada), SIMOON (Arab), S(C)IROCCO (Libya), SOLANO (Sp), SUMATRA (Sing), SURES (Chile), TRADE ~ (Cancer/Capricorn), TRAMONTANA (Adriatic), TWISTER (Aus), ZONDA (Arg). 2. **Gk myth god/king** = AEOLUS, m = Aurora. [Mt Haemus. Typhoeus. Sleipnir (Nor *horse*)]. **Individual winds: N** = BOREAS (Gk), SEPTENTRIO (Rom); **NE** = KAIKAS (Gk), AQUILO (Rom), ARGESTES; **E** = APELIOTES (Gk), SUBSOLANUS (Rom); **SE** = EUROS (Gk), VOLTURNUS (Rom); **S** = NOTOS (Gk), AUSTER (Rom); **SW** = LIPS (Gk), AFRICUS (Rom); **W** = ZEPHYRUS (Gk), FAVONIUS (Rom); **NW** = SKIRON (Gk), CAURUS (Rom).

WINE (s/l whine). 1. *COLOUR* (dark red). FERMENTED DRINK, GRAPE JUICE [*study*]; TENT (arch); **celebrated** (all ®): ASTI SPUMANTI, BARSAC, BEAUJOLAIS, BEAUNE, BORDEAUX, BORDELAIS, BURGUNDY, CHABLIS, CHAMPAGNE, CHATEAUNEUF DU PAPE, CHATEAU YQUEM, CHIANTI, CLARET, COTE DU RHONE, COTE

Wing

D'OR, GRAVES, HOCK, LIEBFRAUMILCH, MACON,
MALAGA, MARSALA, MEDOC, MOSELLE, MUSCADET,
NUITS ST GEORGES, POMAGNE, PORT, POUILLY FUISSE,
POUILLY FUME, REISLING, RETSINA, RIESLING, RIOJA,
OUSO, SAKE, ST EMILION, SANCERRE, SAUTERNES,
SHERRY, TOKAY, VOUVRAY. **Lover of** ~ = oenophile.
Gods: Gk = DIONYSUS [Ganymede], **Rom** = *BACCHUS*,
IACCHUS [*Hebe*].

WING 1. PINION [bird; *Daedalus*, Icarus]. PROJECTING ARM
(arch). FORWARD, STRIKER (football). Group of fighter
aircraft. **Pl** = PILOT'S BADGE. 2. Myth endows *Hermes* (Gk)
and *Mercury* (Rom) with winged sandals as messengers of the
gods, *Pegasus* with winged hooves, and *Hades* with a winged
helmet (borrowed by *Perseus*); the caduceus was a winged wand
or staff (*Asclepius*).

WINGER *FOOTBALLER*. *BIRD* (crypt).

WINTON *Episcopal sig* of WINCHESTER. TOWN (crypt: W in
TO( )N).

WIRELESS 1. *BROADCAST*, MEDIUM, RADIO; SET. 2. Word
with letters 'wire' or synonym removed, e.g. **Wireless sage is in
command** (4) = (wi)SEAC(re).

WISDOM 1. EXPERIENCE, KNOWLEDGE, PRUDENCE,
SAGACITY [Nestor, Solomon]; **saying**; *TOOTH*. 2. **Goddesses:
Gk** = *ATHENE*, **Rom** = MINERVA.

WISEMAN MAGUS (**pl** = magi), SAGE [Solomon, Nestor].

WISP BUNDLE, TWIST. SMOKE. *Assembly* of snipe.

WITCH (s/l which). GRIMALKIN, HAG, SIBYL, SORCERESS;
SPELLER (crypt); **male** = warlock; **assembly** = coven;
celebrated: ~ OF ENDOR (Saul), MORGAN LE FEY (Malory),
SYCORAX (Temp), VIVIEN (Tennyson), 3 in Macbeth (*Shak*)
[*HECATE*, Walpurgis night].

WITCHCRAFT 1. CHARM, SORCERY; SPELLING (crypt).
BROOMSTICK (crypt). 2. **Goddess: Gk** = *HECATE*
[Macbeth. Walpurgis night. Hallowe'en].

WITH 1. AMONG, BESIDE, IN COMPANY. AGREEABLY,
HARMONIOUS. CARRYING, CUM, HAVING,
POSSESSING, IN CARE OF, BY MEANS (**opp** = sine).
CONCERNING. AGAINST, DESPITE,
NOTWITHSTANDING. 2. Two words to form one, e.g.

Victoria, for example, with 'er provider of newspapers (9) = STATION*ER.

WITHIN Hidden word. INSIDE, INTERNALLY.

WITHOUT 1. LESS; SINE (**opp** = cum). OUTSIDE. 2. Word outside another, e.g. **Hen without trouble colliding** (4, 2) = HE*AD O*N. 3. Delete word or letter(s) indicated, e.g. **No railway is without trouble in this country** (6) = NOR***WAY. 4. Start answer with letters 'no', e.g. **Seen without Edward** (5) = NO*TED.

WIZARD SUPER. *MAGICIAN*, SORCERER: MAGUS, MERLIN, OZ (cowardly lion, tin man, Frank Baum). *COMIC*.

WODEHOUSE Pelham Grenville, writer; broadcast for enemy in World War II. **Books:** Big Money, Blandings Castle, The Code of the Woosters, The Inimitable Jeeves, Leave it to Psmith, Money in the Bank, Quick Service, Spring Fever. **Characters:** Aunt Agatha, Bertie Wooster, Lord Emsworth, Jeeves, Psmith.

WODEN A-Sax chief *god*. One-eyed, he looked after warriors. **Gk** = *ZEUS*, **Rom** = *JUPITER*, **Nor** = *ODIN* [wednesday].

WOLF GOBBLE, SCOFF. FLOW BACK (crypt, hence EBB). *COMPOSER*. RIVER (US). CANIS LUPUS; **offspring** = cub [Isengrim (Reinecke Fuchs); Little Red Riding Hood; cry ~]. *Constellation*. Fenris (*Loki*). **Pl** = *Football team*.

WOLFRAM W (*chem*); TUNGSTEN.

WOMAN EVE, HER, SHE [**Little women** = AMY, BETH, JO, MEG (Louisa May Alcott) or, more generally, any abbreviated *girl's name*]. **Saying**.

WOMANIZER LECHER; SHEER (crypt). CASANOVA (It); DON JUAN (Byron); LOTHARIO (The Fair Penitent, Rowe).

WOMAN WARRIOR AMAZON, *BOUDICCA*, BRITOMART (Spenser), *BRUNHILDA*, HIPPOLYTE, JOAN OF ARC, THE MAID, PHILOSTRATE (MND, *Shak*), VALKYR **pl** = ~IES (Nor). **Goddess of War** = ATHENE (Gk), BELLONA, MINERVA (Rom).

WOMEN'S ORGANIZATION ATS, RWI, WAAF, WASP (US), WAVE (US), WI, WRAC, WRAF, WRNS, WRVS.

WONDER MIRACLE. PONDER, THINK. [*Seven* ~s].

WOOD DRIVER, *GOLFCLUB* (**opp** = iron). BIASED BALL (bowls). *FOREST*, GROVE; *anniversary* (5th). TIMBER.

WOODEN CLUMSY, EXPRESSIONLESS, STIFF, STILTED. SILVAN, TIMBER. *XOANON*; *anniversary* (5th).

WOODPECKER BIRD, genus picidae; **breeds:** AWLBIRD, GREATER SPOTTED ~, GREEN ~, HICKWAY, LESSER SPOTTED ~, NICKER, PICUS, SASIA, WOODPIE, WOODWALL, WRYNECK, YAFFIL, YAFFLE, YUCKER.

WOOL ALPACA, ANGORA, LAMBS, MOHAIR, MERINO, WORSTED [measure]; *MATERIAL*; *anniversary* (7th).

WORCESTER **Episcopal sig** = VIGORN. CATHEDRAL. *CERAMICS. UNIVERSITY COLLEGE.*

WORK 1. LABOUR, EFFORT (**saying**). BOOK, PLAY, MUSIC, OP, OPUS. 2. When associated with author's name, requires the title, e.g. **More work** (6) = UTOPIA. 3. **Pl** = FACTORY, MILL. FUNCTIONS, GOES, RUNS.

WORKER ARTISAN, HAND, LABOURER [*patron saint*]; ANT, BEE. **Pl** = TUC.

WORKSHOP ATELIER, STUDIO. DISCUSSION GROUP. FIRM'S DANCE (crypt).

WORLD 1. *EARTH*, GLOBE, ORB; 21 (*tarot*). 2. **God: Rom** = ATLAS (see also *earth*).

~ **GIRDLER** EQUATOR, LATITUDE, LONGITUDE. MOON, SATELLITE. **Celebrated:** ARIEL (Temp), CHICHESTER (Gypsy Moth), COOK (Endeavour), DRAKE (Golden Hind), PHINEAS FOGG (80 days, Verne), MAGELLAN (Trinidad, Vittoria), PUCK (MND), *ROSE* (Lively Lady), SLOCUM (Spray).

WORST BAD, BADLY, POOREST (**opp** = *best*). BEST, BEAT, DEFEAT, OUTDO, OVERCOME. SCUM, YEAST.

WORSTED BUNTING, *MATERIAL*, WOOLLEN YARN. DEFEATED, OUTDONE.

WRECK *Anag.* DESTRUCTION, RUIN. REMAINS. REMNANT.

WRESTLER FIGHTER. **Celebrated:** *CERCYON* (Gk myth), CHARLES (AYLI), SAMSON AGONISTES (Milton); *Chaucer* character (the Miller).

WRITER BALLPOINT, BIRO, PEN, PENCIL, QUILL, STYLO. AMANUENSIS, AUTHOR, GHOST, SECRETARY, STENOGRAPHER. **Celebrated:**

1-letter

Q   (Sir Arthur Quiller-Couch), Eng

2-letters

AA	(Milne), Eng
YY	(Robert Lynd), Ire

3-letters

BOZ	(Charles *Dickens*), Eng
FRY	Christopher, Eng
POE	Edgar Allan (Bostonian), US

4-letters

BELL	Acton (Anne Brontë), Eng
BELL	Currer (Charlotte Brontë), Eng
BELL	Ellis (Emily Brontë), Eng
BIRD	Cyril Kenneth (Fougasse), Eng
BUCK	Pearl Sydenstricker, US
CARY	Joyce, Ire
ELIA	(Charles Lamb), Eng
GIDE	Andre, Fr
GRAY	Thomas, Eng
HOPE	Anthony (A. Hope Hawkins), Eng
HOWE	Edgar Watson, US
HUGO	Victor Marie, Fr
KERR	Jean, US
KNOX	John, Sc
LAMB	Charles (Elia), Eng
LAMB	Mary Ann, Eng
LIVY	(Titus Livius), Rom
LYLY	John, Eng
LYND	Robert (YY), Ire
MANN	Thomas, Ger
MARX	Karl, USSR
NASH	Ogden, US
OVID	(Publius Ovidus Naso), Rom
PHIZ	Hablot K. Browne
POPE	Alexander, Eng
QUIZ	(Charles *Dickens*), Eng
ROSE	Alexander, US
ROSS	(T.E. Lawrence), Eng
SADE	Marquis de, Fr

SAKI	(H.H. Munro), Sc
SAND	George (Amandine Dupin, Baronne Dudevant), Fr
SHAW	(T.E. Lawrence), Eng
SHAW	George Bernard, Ire
WEST	Rebecca (Cicely Maxwell Andrews), Eng
ZOLA	Emile (Fr)

5-letters

ADAMS	Franklin, US
ADAMS	Henry, US
AESOP	Gk
AGATE	James Evershed, Eng
AUDEN	Wystan Hugh, US
BACON	Francis, Eng
BEHAN	Brendan, Ire
BEYLE	Marie Henri (Stendhal), Fr
BLAIR	Eric Arthur (George Orwell), Eng
BLAKE	Nicholas (C. Day Lewis), Eng
BLAKE	William, Eng
BREDE	Baron de la (Montesquieu), Fr
BURKE	Edmund, Eng
BURNS	Robert, Sc
BYRON	Lord George Gordon, Eng
CAMUS	Albert, Fr
CHASE	James Hadley (Rene Raymond), US
COOKE	Alistair, Eng/US
DANTE	Alighieri, It
DEFOE	Daniel, Eng
DONNE	John, Eng
DOYLE	Sir Arthur Conan, Eng
DUMAS	Alexandre (fils), Fr
DUMAS	Alexandre (pere), Fr
DUPIN	(George Sand), Fr
ELIOT	George (Mary Ann Evans), Eng
ELIOT	Thomas Stearns, US/Eng
EVANS	Mary Ann (George Eliot), Eng
GORKY	Maxim (Alexei Peshkov), USSR
HARDY	Thomas, Eng

HENRY	O (William Sydney Porter), US
HOMER	Gk
HOYLE	Edmond, Eng
IBSEN	Henrik Johan, Nor
JAMES	Henry, US
JOYCE	James, Ire
KEATS	John, Eng
LEWIS	Cecil Day (Nicholas Blake), Eng
LUCAN	(Marcus Annaeus Lucanus), Rom
MASON	William, Eng
MILNE	Alan Alexander, Eng
MUNRO	Hector Hugh (Saki), Sc
O'HARA	John, US
PAINE	Thomas, Eng
PEPYS	Samuel, Eng
PLATO	Gk
PLINY	(Caius Plinius) Rom
POUND	Ezra Loomis, US
SAGAN	Francoise (Quoirez), Fr
SCOTT	Sir Walter, Sc
SHUTE	Nevil (Norway), Aus
SMITH	Dodie (C.L. Anthony), Eng
SMITH	Sydney, Eng
SOLON	Gk
STAEL	Anne Louise (Necker), Swi/Fr
STEIN	Gertrude, US
STOWE	Harriet Elizabeth Beecher, US
SWIFT	Jonathan, Eng
TWAIN	Mark (Samuel Langhorn Clemens), US
VERNE	Jules, Fr
VIDAL	Gore, US
WAUGH	Evelyn Arthur St John, Eng
WELLS	Herbert George, Eng
WHITE	Gilbert, Eng
WILDE	Oscar Fingal O'Flahertie Wills, Ire/Eng
WOOLF	Virginia, Eng
YATES	Dornford (Cecil William Mercer) Eng
YEATS	William Butler, Ire
ZWEIG	Arnold, Ger

ZWEIG   Stefan, A

6-letters
ANSELM   Saint, Eng
ARNOLD   Matthew, Eng
AROUET   Francois Marie (Voltaire), Fr
ASCHAM   Roger, Eng
AUSTEN   Jane, Eng
BALZAC   Honore de, Fr
BARRIE   Sir James Matthew (Gavin Ogilvie),
                  Eng
BELLOC   Hilaire, Eng
BRECHT   Bertolt, Ger
BRONTË   Anne (Acton Bell), Eng
BRONTË   Charlotte (Currer Bell), Eng
BRONTË   Emily Jane (Ellis Bell), Eng
BUNYAN   John, Eng
BURNEY   Fanny Frances (Mme D'Arblay), Eng
BURTON   Sir Richard Francis, Eng
BUTLER   Samuel, Eng
CAESAR   Gaius Julius, Rom
CICERO   Marcus Tullius, Rom
COFFIN   Joshua (H.W. Longfellow), Eng
COLTON   Charles Caleb, Eng
CONRAD   Joseph (Teodor Konrad Korzeniowski),
                  Pol
COWARD   Sir Noel, Eng
COWPER   William, Eng
DARWIN   Charles Robert, Eng
DRYDEN   John, Eng
EVELYN   John, Eng
FRANCE   Anatole (Jacques Anatole François
                  Thibault), Fr
FULLER   Thomas, Eng
GEORGE   Henry, US
GIBBON   Edward, Eng
GOETHE   Johann Wolfgang von, Ger
GRAVES   Robert, Eng
GREENE   Graham, Eng

HARRIS	Joel Chandler (Uncle Remus), US
HERZOG	Emile (Andre Maurois), Fr
HOLMES	Oliver Wendell, US
HORACE	(Quintus Horatius Flaccus), Rom
HUXLEY	Aldous Leonard, Eng
IRVING	Washington, US
JEROME	Jerome Klapka, Eng
JONSON	Ben, Eng
KELLER	Helen Adams, US
KRUTCH	Joseph Wood, US
LANDOR	Walter Savage, Eng
LAOTSE	(Laotzu or Latze), Ch
LONDON	Jack (John Griffiths), US
LOWELL	James Russel, US
LUCIAN	Gk
MAILER	Norman, US
MALORY	Sir Thomas, Eng
MERCER	Cecil William (Dornford Yates), Eng
MILLER	(Agatha Christie), Eng
MILLER	Arthur, US
MILLER	Henry, US
MILTON	John, Eng
NATHAN	George Jean, US
NEWTON	Sir Isaac, Eng
NORWAY	Nevil Shute, Aus
O'NEILL	Eugene Gladstone, US
ORWELL	George (Eric Arthur Blair), Eng
PARKER	Dorothy Rothschild, US
PASCAL	Blaise, Fr
PINDAR	Gk
PINERO	Sir Arthur Wing, Eng
PIOZZI	Hester Lynch (Mrs Thrale), Eng
PORTER	William Sydney (O. Henry), US
POTTER	Stephen, Eng
PROUST	Marcel, Fr
RACINE	Jean Baptiste, Fr
RUSKIN	John, Eng
SARTRE	Jean-Paul, Fr
SENECA	Lucius Annaeus, Rom

SEWELL	Elizabeth M., Eng
SONTAG	Susan, US
STEELE	Richard, Ire/Eng
STERNE	Laurence, Eng/Ire
THOMAS	Dylan Marlais, Wal
THRALE	Hester Lynch (Piozzi), Eng
VIRGIL	(Publius Virgilius Maro), Rom
WALTON	Isaak, Eng
WARNER	Charles Dudley, US
WILCOX	Ella Wheeler, US
WILDER	Thornton Niven, US

7-letters

ADDISON	Joseph, Eng
ANDREWS	Cicely (Rebecca), Eng
ANOUILH	Jean, Fr
ANTHONY	C.L. (Dodie Smith), Eng
AQUINAS	St Thomas, It
BALDWIN	James, US
BARNETT	Lincoln, US
BECKETT	Samuel, Ire
BEECHER	Henry Ward, US
BENTLEY	Edmund Clerihew, Eng
BOSWELL	James, Sc
BRIDGES	Robert, Eng
CARLYLE	Thomas, Sc
CARROLL	Lewis (Dodgson), Eng
CHAPMAN	George, Eng
CHAUCER	Geoffrey, Eng
CLEMENS	Samuel Langhorn (Mark Twain), US
COLLINS	William Wilkie, Eng
COCTEAU	Jean, Fr
COLETTE	Sidonie Gabrielle, Fr
D'ARBLAY	Mme (Frances Burney), Eng
DA VINCI	Leonardo, It
DICKENS	Charles John Huffam (Boz, Quiz), Eng
DIDEROT	Denis, Fr
DODGSON	Rev Charles Lutwidge (Lewis Carroll), Eng

DOUGLAS	Lord Alfred, Eng
DUHAMEL	Georges, Fr
DURRELL	Lawrence, Eng/Ire
EMERSON	Ralph Waldo, US
GALLICO	Paul William, US
GILBERT	Sir William Schwenck, Eng
GLASGOW	Ellen, US
GRAHAME	Kenneth, Eng
HAGGARD	Sir Henry Rider, Eng
HAKLUYT	Richard, Eng
HAWKINS	A.H. (Anthony Hope), Eng
HAZLITT	William, Eng
HERBERT	Sir Alan Patrick, Eng
HERRICK	Robert, Eng
HOPKINS	Gerard Manley, Eng
HOUSMAN	Alfred Edward, Eng
HOWELLS	William Dean, US
HUBBARD	Albert Green, US
JOHNSON	Dr Samuel, Eng
JUVENAL	(Decimus Junius Juvenalis), Rom
KIPLING	Rudyard, Eng
MARLOWE	Christopher, Eng
MAUGHAM	William Somerset, Eng
MAURIAC	François, Fr
MAUROIS	André (Emile Herzog), Fr
MENCIUS	Gk
MENCKEN	Henry Louis, US
MOLIERE	(Jean Baptiste Poquelin), Fr
OGILVIE	Gavin (J.M. Barrie), Eng
PEACOCK	Thomas Love, Eng
PESHKOV	(Maxim Gorky), USSR
PUBLIUS	Syrus, Rom
QUOIREX	(Françoise Sagan), Fr
RAYMOND	Rene (James Hadley Chase), US
ROLLAND	Romain, Fr
RUSSELL	Earl Arthur William, Eng
SALLUST	(Gaius Valerius Sallustius Crispus), Rom
SHELLEY	Mary, Eng

SHELLEY	Percy Bysshe, Eng
SIMENON	Georges, Belg/Fr
SOUTHEY	Robert, Eng
SPENSER	Edmund, Eng
TACITUS	Cornelius, Rom
THOREAU	Henry David, US
THURBER	James Grover, US
TOLKIEN	John Ronald Renel, Eng
TOLSTOI(Y)	Count Leo, Russ
VACHELL	Horace Annesley, Eng
WALLACE	Edgar, Eng
WALPOLE	Earl Horace, Eng
WHITMAN	Walter, US

8-letters

BEERBOHM	Sir Max, Eng
BROWNING	Lady (Daphne Du Maurier), Eng
BROWNING	Elizabeth Barrett, Eng
BROWNING	Robert, Eng
CALDWELL	Erskine Preston, US
CATULLUS	Gaius Valerius, Rom
CHILDERS	Erskine, Ire
CHRISTIE	Agatha (Miller), Eng
CLERIHEW	(Edmund Clerihew Bentley), Eng
CONGREVE	William, Eng
CYNEWULF	A-Sax
DAY-LEWIS	Cecil, Ire
DISRAELI	Benjamin (Earl of Beaconsfield), Eng
DUDEVANT	Baronne (George Sand), Fr
FAULKNER	William, US
FIELDING	Henry, Eng
FLAUBERT	Gustave, Fr
FOUGASSE	(Cyril Kenneth Bird), Eng
FRANKLIN	Benjamin, US
GINSBERG	Allen, US
GINSBERG	Louis, US
GONCOURT	Edmond, Fr
GONCOURT	Jules, Fr
GRIFFITH	(Jack London), US

KINGSLEY	Rev Charles, Eng
LAWRENCE	David Herbert, Eng
LAWRENCE	Thomas Edward (Ross, Shaw), Eng
LIPPMANN	Walter, US
LOVELACE	Richard, Eng
MACAULAY	Lord Thomas Babington, Eng
MCCARTHY	Mary, US
MARQUAND	John Phillips, US
MELVILLE	Herman, US
MENANDER	Gk
MEREDITH	George, Eng
PHAEDRUS	Rom
PLUTARCH	Gk
RABELAIS	François, Fr
RATTIGAN	Sir Terence Mervyn, Eng
ROSSETTI	Dante Gabriel, Eng
ROUSSEAU	Jean-Jacques, Swi/Fr
SANDBURG	Carl, US
SCHILLER	Johann Christoph Friedrich von, Ger
SHERIDAN	Richard Brinsley, Ire/Eng
SOCRATES	Gk
STENDHAL	(Marie Henri Beyle), Fr
STOPPARD	Tom, Eng
TEASDALE	Sara, Eng
TENNYSON	Lord Alfred, Eng
THIBAULT	(Anatole France), Fr
TROLLOPE	Anthony, Eng
VOLTAIRE	(François Marie Arouet), Fr
WESTCOTT	Edward Noyes, US
WILLIAMS	Tennessee (Thomas Lanier Williams), US
XENOPHON	Gk

9+ letters

AESCHYLUS	Gk
ARISTOPHANES	Gk
ARISTOTLE	Gk
BAUDELAIRE	Charles, Fr
BEACONSFIELD	Earl of (Disraeli), Eng

BURROUGHS	John, Eng
CERVANTES	Miguel de, Sp
CHATEAUBRIAND	Viscomte de, Fr
CHESTERFIELD	Lord, Eng
CHESTERTON	Gilbert Keith, Eng
CHURCHILL	Sir Winston Leonard Spencer, Eng
CLAUSEWITZ	Karl von, Ger
COLERIDGE	Samuel Taylor, Eng
CONFUCIUS	Ch
CORNEILLE	Pierre, Fr
DICKINSON	Emily Elizabeth, US
DOSTOEVSKY	Fyodor Mikhailovich, USSR
DU MAURIER	Daphne (Lady Browning), Eng
EHRENBURG	Ilya, USSR
EURIPIDES	Gk
FITZGERALD	Francis Scott Key, US
GALBRAITH	Paul William, Can
GALSWORTHY	John, Eng
GOLDSMITH	Oliver, Ire/Eng
LONGFELLOW	Henry Wadsworth, Eng
LUCRETIUS	(Titus Lucretius Carus), Rom
MACMILLAN	Sir Maurice Harold, Eng
MONTAIGNE	Michel Eyquem, Fr
MONTESQUIEU	Charles de Secondat (Baron de la Brede), Fr
NIETZSCHE	Friedrich Wilhelm, Ger
OMAR KHAYYAM	Pers
PARKINSON	Cecil Northcote, US
PASTERNAK	Boris Leonidovich, USSR
PETRONIUS	Gaius, Rom
PRIESTLEY	John Boynton, Eng
SHAKESPEARE	William, Eng
SOLZHENITSYN	Alexander Isayevich, USSR
SOPHOCLES	Gk
STEINBECK	John Ernst, US
STEVENSON	Robert Louis Balfour, Eng
STRINDBERG	John August, Swe
SWINBURNE	Algernon Charles, Eng
TARKINGTON	Newton Booth, US

THACKERAY	William Makepeace, Eng
THEOCRITUS	Gk
THUCYDIDES	Gk
WODEHOUSE	Pelham Grenville, Eng
WORDSWORTH	William, Eng

WRITE-UP 1. CRIT, *NOTICE*, PUFF, REVIEW. 2. A dn answer written upwards, e.g. **Press's bad write-up** (3) = DAB.

WRITING MS. PS. TS. (*study*).

~ OFF 1. CANCELLING, STRIKING OFF. 2. Delete letters meaning 'writing' (MS, PS, TS) from the clue, e.g. **Writing-off terms, in triplicate?** (3) = TER(ms).

WRONG *Anag.* INCORRECT, IN ERROR, OUT OF ORDER; NOT RIGHT (hence delete letters 'r' or 'rt' from clue, e.g. **Divert wrong plunge** (4) = DIVE(rt).

WRY *Anag.* ASKEW, DISTORTED, SKEW. DISAPPOINTED. *BIRD*.

WYVERN WINGED *DRAGON* (myth). WINGED SERPENT [*Asclepius*, caduceus, *herald*, viper].

X (s/l ex). 10, TEN. ANTEPENULTIMATE. CHRIST. EXTRA LARGE. KISS. OVER 18 (film *censorship*). UNKNOWN QUANTITY; graph co-ordinate. ABSCISSA (**opp** = y or ordinate). VOTE. WRONG.

XANGTI Ch chief *god*.

XANTHIC *COLOUR* (*yellow*).

XANTHIPPE 1. Wife of *Socrates*, notorious for her peevish and nagging nature. It is said that Socrates mar her as a penance. 2. SCOLD, SHREW, SPITFIRE, TERMAGANT.

XAU LAKE (Af).

XE *XENON* (*chem*).

XEBEC *BOAT*.

XENOPHILE Lover of foreigners/strangers.

XENOPHOBIA Aversion to foreigners/strangers.

XER- Prefix for DRY, e.g. **xeransis** = desiccated; **xerophilous** = adapted to dry climate.

XERES SPANISH SHERRY, WINE.

XERXES King of Persia B.C. 485-465. Conquered Egypt and then invaded Greece (B.C. 480) by crossing the *Hellespont* on a bridge of boats. Checked by the Spartans at *Thermopylae*, he was finally forced to withdraw after his fleet was beaten by the Greeks at *Salamis*. He was ass in B.C. 465.

XHOSA BANTU, TRIBE (SA).

XINGU RIVER (Braz).

XINHUA Newsagency (Ch).

XIPHOID SWORD-SHAPED.

XOANON Gk myth wooden god, supposedly fallen from Heaven.

X-RAYS RONTGEN RAYS.

XX TWENTY.

XYLONITE CELLULOID.

XYLOPHONE *INSTRUMENT* (mus), MARIMBA.

XYSTUS EXERCISE AREA (Gk). TERRACE, WALK (Rom).

Y (s/l why). PENULTIMATE. UNKNOWN QUANTITY; graph co-ordinate, ORDINATE (**opp** = x or abscissa). YTTRIUM (*chem*). YUGOSLAVIA.

YAMA Ind *god* of Dead.

YANKEE AMERICAN (**opp** = Confederate). *BET*. JIB, *SAIL*. **Pl** = *BASEBALL TEAM*.

YARD AREA; GARDEN (US). *MEASURE*, THREE FEET; hence TRIPOD (crypt). SPAR (naut).

YARN THREAD. STORY, TALE.

~ SPINNER BOBBIN, SPOOL. NARRATOR, STORY TELLER.

YEAN *KID*, LAMB.

YEAR AD, BC. Either of these added to Rom numerals to make a word, e.g. **year 1009** (5) = ADMIX.

YEARN HANKER, LONG, PANT FOR.

YEGG *ROBBER*.

YELLOW *COLOUR*. *SNOOKER* BALL (score 2). AFRAID, *COWARDLY*. RIVER (Ch). *SEA*. CRY OUT, SHOUT 'OW' (crypt).

YES AY, AYE, CERT, SURE; NOD; AGREE. DA (USSR); JA (Ger); OUI (Fr); SI (It, Sp).

YIELD CEDE, GIVE WAY, SUBMIT. AMOUNT, OUTPUT,

PRODUCE. CONSENT.

YMIR Frost giant (Nor).

YOKE (s/l yolk). BAR, CROSS-BAR, *HARNESS*, LINK; WAIST; TEAM. BOND, DOMINION, SWAY.

YOLK (s/l *yoke*). YELK. SECRETION, WOOL OIL. EGG CENTRE (hence G, crypt).

YORK 1. HAM. BOWL OUT (*cricket*). 2. EBORACUM (*Rom*). **Episcopal sig** = EBOR. *CASTLE. UNIVERSITY RACETRACK* (horses). RIVER (US). [white rose]. 3. *HERALD*.

YOU HEAR . . . The answer is *pronounced*, but not spelled, like the word indicated, e.g. **Shaggy bird you hear** (5) = ROUGH, whereas **You hear shaggy bird** (4) = RUFF; place a semi-colon mentally between 'shaggy' and 'bird' in each case, and the principle will be clear.

YOUNG 1. BABY, YOUTHFUL; *OFFSPRING. SPACE TRAVELLER*. 2. Put name in diminutive, e.g. **Young David** = DAVE.

YOU SEE Hidden word, e.g. **You see gold in Gothic origins** (5) = IN*GOT(hic).

YOUTH 1. ADOLESCENCE. INEXPERIENCE (**opp** = *age*). [Picture of Dorian Gray (Wilde)]. 2. **Goddesses: Gk** = *HEBE*, **Rom** = JUVENTAS.

YTTRIUM Y (*chem*).

YU YUGOSLAVIA (*car plate*).

YUX HICCOUGH.

Z Zanzibar. GAUGE (model rly). FINAL, LAST (crypt).

ZA SOUTH AFRICA (*car plate*).

Z-CAR *POLICE CAR*.

ZEBRA STRIPED ANIMAL (genus equus), QUAGGA (S Af). BELISHA/PELICAN CROSSING; CROSS-PATCH (crypt).

ZECHIN *COIN*.

ZENITH HIGH POINT, OVERHEAD, TOP (**opp** = nadir).

ZENO *STOIC*.

ZEPHYRUS Gk myth WEST *WIND*; **Rom** = FAVONIUS.

ZERO O, DUCK, EGG, LOVE, NIL, NOTHING, ZILCH.

ZEST GUSTO, KEENNESS, RELISH. LEMON PEEL.

ZEUS Gk chief *god*; s of *Cronos* and *Rhea*, mar to his sis *Hera* as his chief among many wives; br of *Demeter*, *Hades*, Hera, *Hestia* and *Poseidon*. On dividing the world with his two brs, Hades got the underworld and Poseidon the seas; Zeus obtained the heavens and upper regions, and lived on *Mt Olympus*; his shield was called *Aegis*. He had many children by his various wives, but his marriage to Hera remains the archetype. **Rom** = JOVE, *JUPITER*.

ZILCH ZERO (sl).

ZINC ZN (*chem*).

ZINNIA *FLOWER*.

ZIRCON *GEM*; HYACINTH, JARGON.

ZIRCONIUM ZR (*chem*).

ZLOTY *CURRENCY* (Pol).

ZN *ZINC* (*chem*).

ZODIAC 1. FULL CYCLE. 2. HEAVENLY BELT (*constellations*), TRIGON. **Signs:** ARIES (the *Ram*), TAURUS (the *Bull*), GEMINI (the *Twins*), CANCER (the *Crab*), LEO (the *Lion*), VIRGO (the *Virgin*), LIBRA (the *Scales*), SCORPIO (the *Scorpion*), SAGITTARIUS (the *Archer*), CAPRICORNUS (the *Goat*), AQUARIUS (the *Watercarrier*), PISCES (the *Fishes*).

ZONDA *WIND* (Arg prevailing northerly).

ZR ZIRCONIUM (*chem*). ZAIRE (*car plate*).

ZULU TRIBE (Bantu, SA). **Pl** = IMPI.